CASE STUDIES in
BILINGUAL
EDUCATION

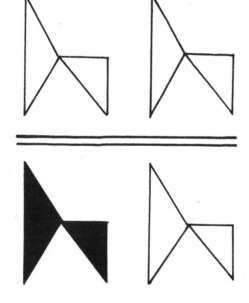

Bernard Spolsky
University of New Mexico

Robert L. Cooper
The Hebrew University of Jerusalem

Editors

NEWBURY HOUSE PUBLISHERS / ROWLEY / MASSACHUSETTS

Library of Congress Cataloging in Publication Data
Main entry under title.

Case studies in bilingual education.

1. Education, Bilingual--Case studies. 2. Bilingual-
ism--Case studies. I. Spolsky, Bernard. II. Cooper,
Robert Leon, 1931-
LC3719.C37   371.9'7   78-1461
ISBN 0-88377-092-X

NEWBURY HOUSE PUBLISHERS, INC.

Language Science
Language Teaching
Language Learning

ROWLEY, MASSACHUSETTS 01969

Cover design by Gail Robinson.

Printed in the U.S.A.   First printing: April 1978
                                          5   4   3   2

CONTRIBUTORS

I   Hugo Bustamente, Maurits Van Overbeke, and Albert Verdoodt, University of Louvain

II   Merrill Swain and Henri C. Barik, The Ontario Institute for Studies in Education

III   Beverly Hong Fincher, Dartmouth College

IV   Lachman M. Khubchandani, Regional English Language Centre, Singapore

V   Richard A. Benton, New Zealand Council for Educational Research

VI   E.G. Malherbe, Natal

VII   E. Glyn Lewis, Wales

VIII   E. Glyn Lewis, Wales

IX   J.L. Dillard, University of Puerto Rico

X   Sandra Parker, Northeastern University

XI   Bernard Spolsky, The University of New Mexico

XII   Robert L. Cheng, University of Hawaii, Honolulu, Hawaii

XIII   Dennis R. Craig, University of the West Indies, Jamaica

XIV   Ali A. Mazrui, Department of Political Science, The University of Michigan, Ann Arbor, and Pio Zirimu, Department of Literature, Makerere University, Kampala

XV   George M. Blanco, The University of Texas at Austin

TABLE OF CONTENTS

ACKNOWLEDGMENTS

The original impetus for this volume and its companion, *Frontiers of Bilingual Education,* was an invitation from Professor Thomas A. Sebeok to suggest topics for inclusion in a series of books he was planning to survey current trends in the language sciences. Bilingual education seemed both current and a trend, and so we invited a number of international scholars to contribute to a collection on this topic. Most of the papers had been written and submitted when the original publishers found themselves unable to continue with the planned series. After a search, we found a publisher prepared to handle an undertaking of this size. The editors and contributors are grateful to Mr. Rupert Ingram of Newbury House Publishers for his willingness to accept the challenge.

Other thanks are due. The editors wish to express their appreciation to the contributors for the patience with which they have borne the uncertainties of delay. We would like to thank Judy Benedetti and Maia Cramer for the clerical assistance they gave during the somewhat prolonged process of preparing the volume, and also a number of University of New Mexico graduate students, among them especially John Read, for editorial advice and help.

Part I

NATIONAL PERSPECTIVES

I

Bilingual Education

in Belgium

Hugo Bustamante, Maurits Van Overbeke
and Albert Verdoodt

The current bibliography concerning bilingual education in Belgium is either pedagogical (Bong 1972; Bustamante 1973; Decroly 1926; Decoster and Derume 1962; Decoster, Leclercq and Vande Velde 1968; Emma 1968; Hogenraad 1969; Hogenraad and Mertens 1970; Lebrun and Hasquin 1970; Leconte 1971; Mussafia 1965, 1967; Nuttin 1969; Ripoche 1966; Toussaint 1935; Vanderick 1972; Vanhuysse s.d.; Verheyen 1928) or linguistic (Baetens Beardsmore 1971a, 1971b, Boileau 1946, 1969; Brecht 1966; Bruneau 1952; Cohen 1954; Debrock and Jouret 1971a, 1971b; De Rooij and Berns 1972; De Vriendt and Wambach 1966; Florquin 1968; Galle 1967; Geerts 1969a, 1969b; Goossens 1968; Grootaers 1953; Hanse 1964, 1965; Leys 1962; Nelde 1974; Nieuwborg 1969; Pauwels 1948, 1954, 1956, 1965, 1967; Renson 1972; Skalmowski and Van Overbeke 1969; Van Overbeke 1968, 1971a, 1971b, 1974; Van Loey 1954, 1958; Van Nierop 1962; Weisshaupt 1970; Wind 1947, 1960). An avowed sociology of bilingual education—let alone of bilingualism—is still in its infancy (Anon. 1967; Decoster et al. 1971; Geerts, Van Den Broeck, and Verdoodt in press; Kirfel 1967; Pietkin 1904; Querinjean 1954; Verdoodt 1968, 1971, 1972, 1973, in press a, b). Moreover, each of these three disciplines (pedagogy, linguistics, and sociology) has conducted its work in isolation from the others. This chapter is the first attempt

3

to bring together a representative of each of these different disciplines in order to arrive at a coherent review of the major efforts in the study of bilingual education in Belgium.

MORE THAN ONE LANGUAGE OF INSTRUCTION

If we define bilingual education as the use of two or more languages of instruction in a subject matter other than language instruction per se, we can safely state that only a small minority of students in Belgium receives this type of education. This particular minority attends the schools in the German-language region, which includes only 62,100 inhabitants and represents 0.64% of the total national population.[1] Instruction in these schools is initiated either in German or in French alone, but soon after (depending on the direction of the school) the other language is used in the presentation of some courses. This practice is intensified throughout the years of secondary and technical study in the region (Verdoodt 1968:42-45).

In the European schools in Brussels and in Mol, the courses are taught in different languages (plurilingual instruction), at least in the last years of secondary (high school) education (Ripoche 1966).

The remainder of the country was divided into three zones under the law of July 14, 1932. In the first, Dutch is the sole language of instruction. In 1970, this zone included 5,432,000 inhabitants and represented 56.06% of the total national population. French is the sole language of instruction in the second zone, which included 3,124,000 inhabitants and represented 32.25% of the national population. In the zone of "Brussels capital" (1,071,200 inhabitants, or 11.05% of the population), the parents were obliged to enroll their children in a French-speaking or Dutch-speaking school depending on the mother tongue or else the language usually spoken by the child. However, since September 1, 1970, the choice of the language of instruction in "Brussels capital" is no longer dictated by the law (Verdoodt 1973:148-149).

We should bring out here that a new law of July 30, 1963, did not fundamentally modify the law of 1932 except in one instance: the law of 1963 eliminated the transition classes which were authorized by the earlier law. A transition class consisted of a brief period in the early part of schooling where the language of instruction was gradually changed from the language usually spoken by the child at home to the language of the region. But in fact in 1963 there were barely more than a hundred of these classes. All were in the Flemish region.[2]

In Flanders a bilingual (French-Dutch) secondary school level instruction existed in which a minimum of two courses had to be given in Dutch. This was in the period beginning with the law of June 15, 1883, until 1932. Before 1883, French was the sole language of instruction at the secondary level in the entire country, and until 1930 it remained as such at the university level. At that time courses taught in Dutch were gradually created at the University of Louvain and the language of instruction at the University of Ghent was converted from uniquely French to uniquely Dutch.[3] Later at the University of Brussels a Dutch section was created; however, this required a long period of transition (1945-1970) of bilingual instruction. Finally at the European College for Post University Study at Bruges, the courses are taught in either English or French.

Having been confronted with the official opinion that a monolingual program of instruction is the most effective, we should inquire as to the opinion of the general public. A 1966 study made by an independent polling association obtained the following answers to the question: "If you had the opportunity of having your children follow one or two courses at school in the other national language, would you use this option?"

	Total	Dutch Region	French Region	Brussels Capital
Yes	65.8%	64.5%	66.6%	69%
No	33.6%	34.8%	32.6%	30%
No opinion	0.6%	0.7%	0.8%	1%

The results are quite conclusive as well as exceptionally homogeneous (Anon. 1967:24-25, 69-70).

A LANGUAGE OF INSTRUCTION OTHER THAN THE MOTHER TONGUE

If we understand by bilingual education the use of a language of instruction other than the mother tongue, we can safely say that the vast majority of the people in this country receives this type of education. To arrive at this conclusion, we should consider three factors:

1. The large number of dialect speakers.

2. The children educated in an official linguistic zone or in a school not corresponding to their mother tongue.

3. The children of migrant workers.

With regard to the dialect speakers, we can divide the country up into four parts which correspond approximatively to the official linguistic regions. In fact since the high Middle Ages three groups of dialects have been spoken in the north of actual Belgium: Flemish, Brabantine, and Limburger (grouped for the sake of simplicity under the term Flemish), three groups of dialects in the South: Walloon, Picard, and Lorraine (grouped for the sake of simplicity under the term Walloon), one group of German dialects in the East, and finally in Brussels a hybrid language which is a mixture of French and Dutch (Baetens Beardsmore 1971a:45-56).

To the objection that contradicts our assumption that the above dialects are indeed languages, we answer with the words of Fishman (1971:1):

> The distinction between dialects and languages is considered to be basically a within-community functionally-evaluative distinction rather than one that can be made primarily on the basis of objective external criteria. Certainly a diachronic view amply supports this approach (revealing any number of once

"mere" dialects that were subsequently functionally, evaluatively and structurally "elevated" to the position of languages, as well as many cases of reverse progression); however much a synchronic view may reveal objective differences between co-existing languages and dialects with respect to such matters as extent of elaboration and codification.

In fact the existence of profound differences between the dialects and the related official languages in Belgium has to be admitted simply because in many cases they are not intercomprehensible (Pauwels 1965:33).

But more important is the question of how many inhabitants really speak these dialects and if they are used in everyday life (for example, in the home and to their children). It is quite unfortunate that no published studies concern this. Based on certain unpublished documents, however, we can draw up the following observations: that the use of dialects is more common in the countryside than in urban areas, that dialects are more common in the Flemish and the German regions than in Wallonie, and that they are accepted more by men than by women.[4]

In addition, until recently the authorities concerned with the issues of linguistic education agreed with one another throughout the country that no place should be given to dialects in the schools. But today a reverse current is being felt in Wallonie, and it is meeting up with relative success (Hanse 1964). The dialect is being viewed not as a threat, but rather as an avenue for attaining a target, that being French. In the rest of the country the monolingual exclusionism described above is true more in principle than in fact. Education in the countryside of Flanders would be impossible if this exclusionism were observed. It is known, moreover, that children learn to express themselves as much in conversation between themselves in their habitual language as in class in the official language. A final element to consider is the fact that many primary schools rely on municipal governments, which prefer to nominate a teacher who comes from the region and consequently is able to express himself in the local dialect.

In looking at children educated in an official linguistic zone or in a school not corresponding to that of their mother tongue and at children of migrant workers, we discover individual cases more germane to a pedagogical or psychological study.

We should first point out that the teaching of the other national language as an individual and separate course is compulsory neither in elementary nor in secondary schools with the exception of Brussels capital, 40 municipalities (mostly very small) near the language borders, and the German-language region. In the rest of the country, the teaching of the other national language(s) is not even allowed before the fifth grade in the elementary schools. This rule applies equally to courses outside of the regular timetable, i.e., private classes held in state-supported schools.[5] As a result, parents who move from one linguistic region to another are obliged to send their children to schools with a completely new language of instruction. Children may attend boarding schools in their region of origin, but this is quite an expensive operation, reserved in fact for privileged families.

BILINGUALISM, KNOWLEDGE OF
MOTHER TONGUE, AND SCHOOL ACHIEVEMENT

One of the more common objections to a bilingual schooling is that bilinguals often fail to master either language or at the very least are behind monolinguals in the mastery of their mother tongue. Such detrimental effects were studied for the first time in Belgium by Verheyen in 1928. The purpose of his research was to determine the influence of bilingual education on the performance of a student in his mother tongue. The group tested included 217 bilinguals from Brussels schools whose mother tongue was Dutch and whose language of instruction in school was French. A control group consisted of Dutch-speaking monolingual children from Antwerp. Both groups were invited to fill in the blanks of a series of phrases and images. The results that were obtained may be summarized as follows:

Monolingual children: 66% correct answers.

Bilingual children: 21.2% correct answers.

The author attributed the inferior performance of bilinguals in their mother tongue to the influence of the second language (French). We should note that the attention of the investigator was directed exclusively to vocabulary. Indeed, the group of children having the more complete bilingual education (the use of French and Dutch at home, at school, and with peers) were the weakest (15% of correct answers) in tests of their mother-tongue vocabulary.

More recently, N. Leconte in her undergraduate dissertation (1971) focused attention on the differences existing between bilinguals and monolinguals in the oral and written performances in the mother tongue. She chose a sample of thirty-one fifth grade bilingual children from Antwerp and the same number of French-speaking monolinguals from Brussels. After administration of the California Reading Test she obtained the following results: similar scores in syntax and vocabulary in the two groups, but a greater variety of errors among bilinguals.

A further study dealing with the influence of the second language on the mother tongue was conducted in 1971-1972 by Bustamente. He designed his investigation to compare the linguistic performances of French-Dutch bilinguals and monolinguals in both these languages. The bilinguals in this study were individuals who were educated in a language different from their mother tongue. All the tests were written and were intended to cover four important features of language competence: sentence construction, applied grammar, reading comprehension, and vocabulary. The sample group was composed of 500 schoolboys and girls, attending schools in different towns, with ages varying from 7 to 17. In an attempt to isolate the bilingual variable, the author used several techniques to control other concomitant variables such as home linguistic background, parental attitude toward the second language, the linguistic history of the subjects, the sociocultural status, the age at which second-language training began, and the IQ of the students. Bilingual students were divided into two groups according to their degree of bilingualism and according to their average score obtained in tests of word association, word detection, and word completion. All the students took the linguistic achievement tests according to their age. The following conclusions were noted:

1. There was no evidence of a mother-tongue handicap due to the knowledge of the second language, although bilinguals did obtain lower average scores.

2. The group comprising the more balanced bilinguals (i.e., with a good knowledge of both languages) performed better in both languages than did the other bilinguals.

3. The performance in the school language of instruction did not differ significantly between the bilingual groups and the monolinguals.

4. The average results of the group of more balanced bilinguals were higher than those of the monolingual group.

Such findings led the author to state that individuals being schooled in a language different from their mother tongue show a trend to perform as undertrained in their mother tongue. But he indicated that they should not be considered as linguistically handicapped because their results in the school language of instruction were definitely not inferior to those of monolinguals. A complementary training in their mother tongue could have given them a good level of proficiency in both languages. In fact, this last suggestion agrees with the successful results of the experiment that was undertaken in Brussels by Decoster (1968), who arranged for extracurricular training in the mother tongue for students of foreign families.

The presence in Belgium of no less than 800,000 foreigners originating from many different Mediterranean countries and speaking a variety of languages creates a sort of "melting pot." This is particularly true in industrial and mining regions where the immigrant workers and families have settled. In order to demonstrate this linguistic variety, Decoster (1968), quoting from the official statistics for the academic year 1966-1967 of inscriptions in the Brussels nursery, elementary, technical, and professional schools, indicated that 25 nationalities were represented among the boys and 24 among the girls. The evening courses in the commerce schools had students representing 31 different nationalities. An extreme case of a disproportioned ratio between native Belgian and foreign students was noted in an elementary school located in the vicinity of the North Railway Station in Brussels where 211 children out of 396 were foreigners. It is not unlikely that an avoidance of such schools by Belgian parents contributes to the increase in the proportion of foreigners. In fact, although no formal study has ever been conducted, it is a common belief among teachers that there is an inferior level of achievement in those classes where there is an important proportion of foreign pupils.

The research carried out by Decoster and Derume (1962) was an attempt to clarify this point. The authors were concerned with the inferior results in school achievement of children of immigrant families attending schools where French was the medium of instruction. Schools were chosen in the mining center of Borinage. Attention was directed to school achievement among foreigners where French was the school language of instruction, regardless of the degree of proficiency in either French or the language of the country of origin. Examination of the data reveals that the average score of Belgium pupils was always higher than the average score of the best of the groups of foreign students. In addition, it seems that the more recently the foreign student settled in Belgium, the lower his score was. The groups of Belgian students scored higher in intelligence tests as well. And the gap between the average scores of Belgian and foreign children was more marked in the French-language tests.

The attention paid by the author to other variables such as the socioeconomic and the cultural situations explains his conclusion that the underachievement of the immigrant children is due not only to a poor mastery of the French language, but also to the particularly unsatisfactory social conditions which prevail in most cases.

BILINGUALISM AND INTELLIGENCE

In addition to a study by Decroly (1926) in which some attention was directed to the intellectual level of bilinguals through the application of the Ballard test, a more recent investigation carried out at Mouscron by Vanhuysse deals more particularly with the influence of bilingualism on the verbal and the nonverbal aspects of intelligence. Mouscron is a small industrial city near the French national border and close to the Dutch linguistic frontier. A sample of 320 boys with ages varying between 10 and 16 was chosen for this study. An experimental group of 173 bilinguals and a control group of 147 monolinguals (French or Dutch) were considered. Four subgroups were created according to the different degrees of language dominance among the bilinguals:

DF: Dutch is dominant with a very good knowledge of French.
Df: Dutch is dominant with a not as good knowledge of French.
FD: French is dominant with a very good knowledge of Dutch.
Fd: French is dominant with a not as good knowledge of Dutch.

The application of Coetsier's verbal test of intelligence and of the Raven 48 nonverbal test led the author to the following conclusions:

1. In the verbal tests, the monolinguals scored significantly higher than those bilingual groups in which Dutch was dominant, but not so with those groups where French was dominant.

2. No significant difference was observed between bilinguals and monolinguals in the nonverbal intelligence test.

Thus the results obtained in this research would not support the hypotheses that there is a negative relationship between bilingualism and intellectual development.

BILINGUALISM AND SPEECH DISORDERS

The multilingual setting prevailing in the Brussels European School has tempted more than one researcher to explore the effects of bilingual or multilingual training on speech normalcy. Are some speech disorders dependent on bilingualism in some consistent way?

Emma (1968) reports that 34% of the 142 pupils sent to him with school problems were multilingual, and that 47% of the students who had followed a treatment for language disorders (in written or in oral language) were multilingual. Emma had the impression that even if multilingualism was not the only explanation for these difficulties, it certainly did play an important role. His analysis of nine students from the European School who were suffering from language disorders led him to emphasize the importance of having one's own vernacular language as the medium of instruction. But his assertion does not mean that bilingualism or multilingualism is responsible for these evils. Lebrun and Hasquin (1970) in their critical review of three different studies concerning the relation between bilingualism and speech disorders found Emma's cases inconsistent with regard to the causal relationships between speech disorders and bi- or multilingualism. In fact, a close examination of Emma's nine cases reveals that the problem here was not bi- or multilingualism, but rather inadequate exposure to a multilingual environment along with negative social and family situations.

Another study on this issue was conducted by Mussafia (1967), who was interested in examining language disorders in oral and written forms occurring in multilingual settings, while taking into account the emotional components (attitudes of acceptance or refusal, shyness, fear, etc.) of these settings. In an attempt to achieve this, one questionnaire was addressed to the schoolteachers and another to the pupils themselves. Her findings support the idea that language setting. In fact, in the sample considered by Mussafia, it was the social environment, both at home and at school, that was multilingual, and the school language of instruction was either French or Dutch—which were unknown to the parents of the children. Linguistic defects such as dyslalia, stuttering, and misspelling reflect a situation of linguistic inadaptation from which affective troubles arise.

An inquiry (Decoster 1968) carried out among 1874 children of immigrant families showed that pupils having a good IQ and having a certain knowledge of the school language were well adapted to the school situation, whereas other foreign students demonstrated signs of shyness and anxiety. An examination of the questionnaire answers of students and the appreciation reports of teachers showed 21% of foreign pupils were afraid of speaking, and 23% thought that the native speakers made fun of them at school (this feeling was more prevalent among the girls). With regard to the attitude toward the host language, 1.5% were opposed to learning it, and 7% completely lacked the motivation to learn it. It was the author's belief that these difficulties tended to disappear after the initial frustrations with the new language.

From an inquiry (Ripoche 1966) concerned with the reactions of pupils to multilingualism again at the European School (where the choice of first, second, and third languages is made from a selection of five), we see that 86% of the elementary school children show a tendency to associate with those who speak the same mother tongue. The choice of a friend of a different mother tongue increases markedly after the third grade (eight or nine years old). During the "European hours" at the school in which all the different linguistic sections participate, 85% of the pupils of the Dutch, Italian, and German sections speak a foreign language as opposed to 33% of the pupils of the French section. On the secondary level, the author observed an astonishing lack of motivation on the part of the pupils in the French section with regard to the study of school matters in a language other than French. However, as the pupils became more proficient in a second language, they did show a greater interest in the cultural expressions of this language. According to the author, this interest is rather late in showing itself, since it is noticeable only in the last two years of high school. Finally, it was among the pupils of the Italian section that the author found the greatest interest in profiting from the multilingual facilities of the school; and this in spite of the fact that only 14% have a bilingual setting at home as opposed to the students in the other sections (25% in the Dutch section, 36% in the German section, and 42% in the French section).

BILINGUALISM AND PERSONALITY PROBLEMS

Except for a single study by Vanderick carried out in 1972 as an undergraduate dissertation, this point has not received an experimental treatment in Belgium. And even that particular research dealt only with a comparison between coordinate and compound bilinguals. The author concluded that personality problems occur more frequently among coordinate than among compound bilinguals.

BILINGUALISM AND COMMUNICATION

Hogenraad and Mertens (1970) designed a study to explore the question of the differences in perception due to the language usually spoken (Dutch or French) in the interaction of bilingual individuals. One year management training was evaluated along a before-after design, in which association and semantic differential procedures were used. It was shown that differences in languages (and culture) led to eventual differences in the perception of the training content by the two linguistic (and cultural) subgroups involved, that is, differences in the way human experiences were structured.

ATTITUDE TOWARD THE OTHER LINGUISTIC COMMUNITY

The presence of two major linguistic national groups at the University of Louvain suggested to Nuttin (1969) a research on the relationship and attitudes between students of the two communities. The interaction processes were studied in homogeneous and in mixed groups by means of the problem-solving and free-discussion-group techniques. Attitude measurements among Flemish students confirm the general thesis that members of one cultural group having many personal contacts with the other cultural group usually have a more favorable attitude toward that group than do members who have no personal contacts with it. A further follow-up study showed that a real-life contact made the anti-Walloon students less unfavorable, and the pro-Walloon students a bit less favorable. Finally it was found that the influence of this personal contact on attitude change varies as a function of the attitude that was held before the contact was made (i.e., favorable or unfavorable).

LINGUISTIC ASPECTS

Bilingual education has, apart from its psychological and social aspects, also purely linguistic facets, which determine the success or failure of this specific pedagogic task. Anyone who is interested only in the presumably universal interferential mechanism between two concurring languages may, as Weinreich (1953:3) once suggested, entirely ignore the question as to how much these two structures are different or to which branch of the genealogical and typological tree of languages they can be traced back. To the pedagogue, these questions are extremely important because they determine the choice of specific strategies of acquisition. Extreme linguistic difference, as in Chinese-English bilingualism (Yoshioka 1929), and strong affinity, as in bilingualism based on the knowledge of a language and a related dialect (Österberg 1961, Nuijtens 1962, Renson 1972), are the causes of specific inhibitions and resistance which can hardly be reduced to the same denominator. Even up till now, there have been no uniform research results showing that partial resemblance or relationship would promote or facilitate a so-called (Lambert 1955, Boileau 1969) "balanced bilingualism." See Vildomec's objections (1963:164) to Weinreich.

As in Belgium officially three cultural languages are spoken (viz., French, Dutch, and German), in principle three kinds of bilingualism should be considered, viz., French-Dutch, Dutch-German, and German-French. From the foregoing it should be clear that the second kind (Dutch-German), based on the knowledge of two Germanic languages, cannot be considered, from a pedagogic and didactic point of view, on the same basis as the other two kinds, in which a Romance language (French) is confronted with a Germanic language (respectively, Dutch and German). In this linguistic analysis we will restrict ourselves to the kind of bilingualism which is most widespread in Belgium, i.e., Dutch-French. In order to avoid all misapprehension, it may be useful to indicate that by this kind of bilingualism we mean the individual's skill to establish efficient communication by means of these two languages. This evidently implies a minimal command of both languages, but it does not include a perfect mastery nor could it be used to make a conclusive distinction between real or perfect bilingual speakers and others.

THE FRENCH-DUTCH RELATIONSHIP

The two languages which are most widespread in Belgium, viz., French (F) and Dutch (D), are both of Indo-Germanic origin. As such they have a number of profound correspondences which cannot be found outside this group. But of more importance is the fact that for centuries they have existed next to each other, as components of, respectively, the Romance and the Germanic language groups—a neighborhood resulting in permanent mutual influences which have considerably reduced the grammatical and lexical distance. Historically these influences can be regarded primarily as a "one-way traffic." Yet, a distinction should be made between (1) the mutual influence of these two *standardized languages* as far as they are associated with two political entities, viz., France and the Netherlands, and (2) the mutual influence of these languages as far as they are regional or local representations of their respective standard forms.

With respect to (1), little or no structural influence can be found in the direction D → F. Also the official French vocabulary, as ascertained by the "Académie," does not show any intense lexical influence from the Dutch (Valkhoff 1931). A small number of direct or indirect borrowings (*affaler* < *afhalen* "to fetch," *babord* < *bakboord* "port," *beaupré* < *boegspiet* "bowsprit," *colza* < *koolzaad* "colza," etc.) can be mentioned, but their usage is limited to a few cultural areas such as navigation and commerce, in which import and export of goods and techniques are often accompanied by adoption of lexical material. The inverse influence F → D, on the other hand, can more or less be compared with the sweeping word inflation the English language experienced after 1066 (Van Loey 1954). Quite remarkable is the adoption in Dutch of a considerable number of terms for which an original Germanic word was already available. In this way, the Dutch vocabulary has developed a whole series of doubles, particularly in the terminology of the human sciences. They resemble the modern English doubles of the type *sheep/mutton, game/play*, although it cannot be said that the semantic differentiations which such forms always entail are as much advanced in Dutch as they are in English. Take, for instance, forms such as *analyse/ontleding* ("analysis"), *situatie/toestand* ("situation"), *conclusie/besluit* ("conclusion"), *traditie/overlevering* ("tradition"), *cultuur/beschaving* ("culture"), *principe/beginsel* ("principle"), *compleet/volledig* ("complete"), etc. This condition puts the lexical competence of a F-D bilingual speaker in another light. With respect to bilingual education, two consequences should be noted. First, it appears that the F-D bilingual speaker, on the basis of a spontaneous economizing tendency (Van Overbeke 1974), in many cases will resort to an "intermediate lexical item" (ILI) enabling him to manage in both languages. Overrating this device, which in the following example is used grammatically under (1), often results in ungrammatical transpositions as under (2). Purely formal imitation of the French model sometimes results in wrong semantic representation, as under (3), in which the original expression refers to a public which is fond of sports, while the Dutch imitation suggests that it is a public which also is good at sports or even "a good sport" (fair).

(1)   *un vase antique* ——— *een antieke vaas*
      "an antique vase"

(2)   *une capsule spatiale* ——— *een spatiale capsule*
      "a space craft"

(3)   *le public sportif* ——— *het sportief publiek*
      "the sports fans"   "the fair public"

Second, as a consequence of this abundant borrowing of French words, the acquisition method of the French speaker (FS) learning Dutch is different from that of a Dutch speaker (DS) learning French. In the first case, the learner experiences an uneasiness because he does not know how far he can go in applying the ILI; in the second case he runs another risk, i.e., that of slavishly retranslating what he considers French borrowings. For example, on the basis of the sentence *"De dirigent leest de partituur,"* a DS may be inclined for conscience's sake to translate *"Le dirigeant lit la partiture"* (correct: *Le chef d'orchestre lit la partition*; "The conductor reads the score"). These two tendencies give an idea of the ambiguous role which linguistic resemblances in general, and the ILI in particular, can play in the bilingual's competence.

With respect to the influence mentioned under (2), it is generally felt in Belgium that the relatively high number of persons frequently using both cultural languages corrupts, contaminates, or at least impoverishes speech itself (Bourgeois 1963; Hanse 1964, 1965; Geerts 1969a). The sources defending this opinion are so numerous that the objective observer perforce wonders whether he is being confronted with a scientifically obtained image of reality or a personal projection of a few specialists which has been distributed on a large scale. The related facts (defective pronunciation, abundant use of borrowing in places where original language forms do exist, slavish adoption of idioms or "calques," clumsy wording of ideas as soon as they transcend everyday reality) always confirm the usually unspoken thesis that it is impossible to command two languages, i.e., two phonological, grammatical, and lexical systems, as excellently, i.e., in an equally "correct," "pure," and "rich" manner, as one single language.

So far this remains a prescientific statement for the simple reason that from the comparison of two conditions, of which one has only an incomplete and presumably inaccurate knowledge, no valid conclusions can be deduced. How rich or how poor is an average Frenchman's French? How pure or how contaminated is a unilingual Dutchman's Dutch? The answer to these questions is a *conditio sine qua non* for any evaluation of the state of contamination of Belgian speech (cf. Boileau 1969). Anyway, it can a priori be denied that the presumed contamination and impoverishment would be due exclusively to the presence of a neighboring language and the alternative use of the native and neighbor languages by a considerable part of the population. Many noncorrespondences of Belgian French with the standard French of the "Ile de France" type are based to a large extent on an old-established dialectical substructure noticeable in local pronunciation, vocabulary, and idioms (Boileau 1946). The same is true for the Belgian Dutch. It has not been proved that its regional particularities can be explained by the vicinity of the French language and an age-old tradition of bilingualism. Indeed, long before the unification and standardization of the official Dutch language, there existed in the southern Netherlands indigenous Germanic (Low Franconian; later on Flemish, Barbantine, and Limburger) words and idioms, which never have penetrated in the standard language, but up to the present still live on in Belgian Dutch (Pauwels 1948, 1954; Goossens 1968; De Rooij and Berns 1972). The propensity to overlook this often results, as in other bilingual regions, in contradictory tendencies. On the one hand, the "country of origin" is often considered a linguistic paradise in which the (obviously unilingual) speech is regarded as perfect and homogeneous, but on the other hand, it cannot be denied that the regional linguistic reservation—even when, as in Belgium, it is situated outside the territory of the "country of origin"—has its own idiomatic arsenal able to enrich the cultural language in many respects. These tendencies will be discussed later.

ZONES OF INTERFERENCE BETWEEN FRENCH AND DUTCH

The attempts at an analysis of the two concurring languages on the basis of a contrastive model—either a traditional structural model such as that of Stockwell (1968) or a transformational model as suggested by Di Pietro (1968)—have primarily a pedagogic and didactic aim. In this, two complementary principles should be adhered to. Acquisition of the second language and correct usage of both languages will be considerably facilitated by the implication in the language acquisition model of strategies, (1) optimally exploiting the *tertium commune* or the intersection of the two structures and (2) delimiting, and hence avoiding, as carefully as possible the zones of interference. However, it is well known that, according to the Whorf hypothesis, the application of the first principle is practically impossible because the two groups of native speakers have developed their own irreducible world on the basis of their native language. This is undoubtedly an important point of view with respect to a kind of bilingualism which is associated with a strong biculturalism. But this is not the case in Belgium. With a few exceptions it may well be said that the structuralization of human experience among FS is essentially the same as that of DS. It should also be taken into account that, as Mounin indicates (1963:236), age-long association as well as the exchange of goods, information, and customs can gradually reduce a widely diverging world picture to a modus vivendi which can no longer be called hybrid since the persons involved no longer experience it as such. It really is not sufficient that FS call traffic lights "feux" ("fires") while DS indicate the same as "lichten" ("lights"), or that DS have no specific word to indicate the French "agrumes" (a subset of fruit consisting of oranges, lemons, melons, etc.), to indicate widely diverging world pictures.[6] This, of course, does not mean that there would be no difference in the wording of experience and hence no danger of interference. The contrary is true, but this is an internal linguistic problem for which the expert, for methodological reasons, may safely ignore anthropological and social factors.

The zones of interference between French and Dutch can best be described by means of the traditional levels which even in the most up-to-date linguistic models are still valid, viz., the phonological, grammatical, and lexical levels. On the phonological level it is generally felt that the Dutch system is much more dangerous to the FS than the French system to the DS (Valkhoff 1950). This may appear somewhat strange if one considers that the French system contains a number of phonemes which are totally alien to the DS (e.g., the nasal sounds /œ̃, õ, ɛ̃, ɑ̃/, the explosive sounds /g/). However, short circuits in the French communication of a DS due to phonological problems are very rare. To the FS, on the other hand, they are real obstacles (Boileau 1946; Devriendt-Wambach 1966). If also orthophonic aspects are considered a part of the field of phonological interferences, the ratio is more or less balanced: Dutch speech habits strongly penetrate in a DS's (or even a bilingual's) French (Grootaers 1953, Baetens-Beardsmore 1971b and bibliography) to about the same extent as French speech habits penetrate in a FS's Dutch (Debrock and Jouret 1971a, Van Overbeke 1968). Few bilinguals manage to achieve a "perfect agreement" in this matter: it always is a heavy task to unify the articulation of The Hague and Paris on one single speaker, with respect to not only phonemes but also word stress and prosodic features. The study of the reduction process of phonological differences, as it spontaneously develops in bilingual regions, has aroused little interest in Belgium except among dialectologists and onomasts (Leys 1962). Yet this process constitutes one of the strongest external forces behind linguistic evolution and therefore would deserve more attention.

As far as the zones of grammatical interference are concerned, a distinction should be made between syntactic and morphological interference. A survey of descriptions which are usually very detailed but often theoretically insufficiently grounded (Wind 1947, Cohen 1954, Bruneau 1952, Van Loey 1954, Brecht 1966, and others) suggests that the zones of morphological interference between Dutch and French would almost completely correspond with what can be deduced from a contrastive study of Germanic and Romance languages. As far as formation and extension of words are concerned, these languages contrast with each other as respectively synthetic and analytical languages. Thus French often possesses a word the composition or derivation of which can no longer be accounted for (e.g., *hebdomadaire*, "weekly"), while the Dutch equivalent is a motivated compound (e.g., *weekblad*) which, on the basis of well-known substitution processes, can frequently be used for lexical extension (e.g., *dagblad*, "newspaper"; *maandblad*, "monthly review"; *sluikblad*, "underground paper"; *lijfblad*, "favorite paper"). Psycholinguistic tests (Van Overbeke 1971a) show that these processes are significant for the various ways in which the two vocabularies are stocked in the bilingual's lexical memory, and for the various economizing tendencies which subconsciously affect bilingual performance (Skalmowski and Van Overbeke 1969).

Further danger of morphological interference lurks in the use of the genders, as under (4); in the use of the possessive pronoun which, with respect to gender, is subject-directed in the Germanic languages and object-directed in the Romance languages, as under (5); and in the use of auxiliaries, as under (6). This quotes only a few of the most frequent instances discovered in a large number of inquiries:

(4) F. *l'âne*   *la vache*   *le cheval*   *une cheval* *
     D. *de ezel*   *de koe*   *het paard*   *de paard* *
         ("the jackass") ("the cow")   ("the horse")

(5) F. *son chapeau*   *son chapeau*   *sa tête*   *sa tête*
     D. *zijn hoed*   *haar hoed*   *zijn hoofd*   *haar hoofd*
         ("his hat")   ("her hat")   ("his head")   ("her head")
         **son tête*
         **haar hoofd* (speaking about the head of a male person)

(6) F. *il a été*   *il s'est rasé*   *il s'a rasé* *
     D. *hij is geweest*   *hij heeft zich geschoren* *hij heeft geweest* *
         ("he has been")   ("he has shaved")

Contrastive syntactic analysis F-D has so far been investigated only very sporadically (Fourquet 1959). In Belgium, the meritorious work of Pauwels (1967) has been applied for many years with the purpose of cautioning the FS through the use of obvious examples against cases of Dutch word order and expressions which do not correspond with those of French. More recent investigations attempt to delimit and predict the general syntactic zones of syntactic interference on the basis of statistically processed corpuses (Nieuwborg 1969, Weisshaupt 1970). Here too, it appears that the most frequent deviations in word order can finally be traced back to the distinction between Germanic and Romance languages, even though this cannot be said for the English language, which in this respect occupies an intermediate position.

The fields of lexical interference have already been given some attention above. Concerning the large-scale adoption of French words in the Dutch language (terms which can hence be considered integrated interferences), it should be noted that in the target language they are not on a par with their equivalents of Germanic origin if one attempts to enter them in a rank-frequency relation (Van Overbeke 1974). This indicates that they cannot function as each other's equivalents in everyday usage. Usually the terms of Romance origin appear in a scientific context, and that even with slightly metaphorical shades of meaning. A one-to-one translation by means of the ILI is usually impossible for the bilingual speaker. Thus, for example, for the French *général* ("general") there are two

Dutch terms *generaal* and *algemeen*; for the French *société* ("society") there are two Dutch terms *sociëteit* and *maatschappij*. Translation by means of ILI processes would result in (7) and (8):

(7)   *de generale regel** (correct: *de algemene regel*, "the general rule")
(8)   *de consummatiesociëteit** (correct: *de consumptiemaatschappij*, "the consumers' society")

These three kinds of interference which we have just discussed become clearly outlined only if they are projected against the background of a standard norm. Such a norm, however, raises a number of problems which are not absent in a bilingual context.

LANGUAGE USAGE AND LINGUISTIC NORM

Even linguists who reproach the newest linguistic trends with their normative character (Martinet 1972) take the view that one can speak of interference only if an explicit description of the two language systems is available. One is needed in order to determine the origin of the interference, the other to indicate to what rule of the target language the interference is a violation. Yet, as we briefly suggested above, the linguistic norm is an abstraction which could be realized completely only if there were a homogeneous linguistic community whose members speak a language which would not be marked by age differences (in a normal community three generations exist next to each other), social stratification, territorial diffusion, political or religious diversification, or ethnic origin. What is already difficult to determine in one single-language community coinciding with one political or national territory is even more obscure when one is dealing with bilingual countries obliged to get their linguistic norm from their respective "countries of origin." Thus, in Belgium there exist at least two regionally affected realizations of language systems which find their final norm abroad. As to the German system, see Nelde's contribution (1974). The ambiguity of this situation leads in both main parts of the country to a phenomenon which could be called the "purist syndrome." There are innumerable (often very pugnacious) newspaper and magazine articles and radio and television programs pointing out how FS and DS Belgians should speak their native language (Florquin, Galle). They usually apply the somewhat simplistic rule: "Do not say this, but say that." This creates among the common people the sure impression that the language which they have learned as children and use spontaneously every day is not the *real* language and must be replaced by a pure language imposed from outside. In this way we come to the startling discovery that, while the citizens of Marseille pay no attention whatsoever to Parisian French, feeling that Parisians "parlent pointu," FS Belgians do their utmost to come as close as possible to the "Ile de France" French. The same is apparently true of the Flemish, who in recent years have been flooded with attempts to convince them that the sole future of their language lies in a standardization between Holland

and Flanders, to be realized as soon as possible (Van Nierop 1962, Paardekooper s.d.). The immediate result of this tendency is that linguistic integration is pursued in virtue not only of the appeal of the "native country" but also of the repulsion of the concurring language in the abandoned province. When the regional forms of the respective standard languages are found reprehensible, this is mostly on account of the corrupting influence which is imputed to the second language: in Belgian French especially "dutchisms" are crossed out, in Belgian Dutch "gallicisms."

A well-known side effect of the purist syndrome is hypercorrection. In Flanders, French words and expressions which have been considered normal Dutch in Holland are reexamined and denounced (Pauwels 1954). It is not our intention to evaluate these often contradictory endeavors which, for that matter, are still in evolution. Yet the matter is important because the educational development depends on the question whether FS Belgians should learn a kind of Dutch the norm of which is dictated in The Hague (and with which they will have little or no contact) or should acquire the Belgian type of Dutch from which there is very little escape (cf. Du Ry 1965). The same question can be put with respect to the kind of French that should be taught to Flemish children. If the purist tendency and linguistic integration are supported, as a consequence, the existing bilingualism must necessarily be put in an unfavorable light. In this way, bilingual persons are unvoluntarily considered "impure elements," "living incarnations of linguistic corruption," or according to the most tolerant version "victims of an historical derailment which has imposed the coexistence of two languages as a temporary solution" (Heeroma 1964).

LEXICAL AND CULTURAL STRUCTURE

Even when the view is held that two political systems such as Holland and Belgium, or France and Belgium, speak or should speak one single language, it remains difficult to carry a complete integration, since the political, judicial, and social structures of the two countries are different, which is reflected in their respective terminologies. These differences undoubtedly exist in the relationships both between France and Belgium and between Holland and Belgium. Under (9) a clear example of this is given from the administrative field.

(9)	French French	Belgian French	Belgian Dutch	Dutch Dutch
"mayor"	*maire*	*bourgmestre maïeur*	*burgemeester*	*burgemeester*
"alderman"	*adjoint au maire*	*échevin*	*schepen*	*wethouder*

A similar difference also appears in the forms of address of judicial, administrative, or educational authorities. The genesis of the Belgian statute book explains to a large extent why the Dutch version cannot entirely put aside the original French text. The structure of the Belgian state itself, modeled after the French example, does not fit the Dutch system so that it would have been rather difficult, if not impossible, for the translation of the French terms to draw on the Dutch political, judicial, and administrative vocabulary. Thus, for example, for "teachers' training school" the term *pedagogische academie* is used in Holland, the Belgian term of which is *normaalschool.* Although this is an adoption of the French *école normale,* its use can in no way be considered a gallicism. It is the sole correct Belgian Dutch term. The same is true for the terms *académique* and *universitaire,* which in France indicate notions which differ from the Belgian notions, precisely because in Belgium there is no entirely parallel educational structure for the French system.

In general bilingualism is nowadays viewed as an unfortunate burden by Belgian linguists who certainly do not consider it as a blessing which should be pursued beginning at an early age. And what has been achieved by educationists in an attempt to understand the implications of bilingualism, although of an undeniable psychological interest, has in fact been minimal from the point of view of consistency and reliability.

In short, Belgian pedagogues and linguists either condemn bilingual education (in the sense of more than one language of instruction) or recognize it only as a palliative for the small minority of the population who are obliged to live in a bilingual situation (e.g., in the German region and in the European schools).

It is our hope that there will be more scientific studies on bilingualism and that the long history of popular compromise between language groups in Belgium will finally triumph over the negative official opinions of today in order that some less simplistic views will be permitted to surface and evolve.

NOTES

1. Official statistics of 1970.

2. It is important to note that the schools not funded by the state have always been authorized to hold classes in a language other than that of the region. One such example is a school in Antwerp in which the instruction is uniquely in French. Others include the few schools which exist for foreigners (English- or Italian-speaking). In addition, the government subsidizes three primary schools for the dependents of military personnel where the mother tongue of the child is taught in the region of the other national language, as well as one primary and secondary school of French instruction for the children of the personnel of the French University of Louvain.

3. For a more complete sociohistorical background, see Verdoodt in press b.

4. A group of statisticians who in 1866 wanted to include dialects in the linguistic census were told that such a question would satisfy the curious but would be of no practical use ("question plus curieuse qu'utile"). However, the "Report of the Commission of the Linguistic Census" of 1960 included this proposition, but without any success. And most recently the linguistic census has been eliminated (Verdoodt 1973:120-123), the last having taken place in 1947.

5. This policy of regional linguistic homogeneity is the main reason for the actual transfer of the French University of Louvain from the official Dutch to the official French part of the country.

6. In fact, even in certain dictionaries, one may find the compound "citrusvruchten."

II

Bilingual Education

in Canada: French and English

Merrill Swain and Henri Barik

Canada has two official languages: English and French. The present legal basis of these linguistic rights has existed from the time of Confederation with the passing of the British North America Act in 1867. One hundred years later, through the Official Languages Act, Canada declared formally and precisely that the English and French languages are to be considered the official languages of Canada. They "possess and enjoy equality of status and equal rights" in Parliament and in the Government of Canada. The official status of French and English in Canada has meant that bilingual education has mainly involved the use of French and English as languages of instruction, and it is on these programs that we focus in this chapter.

For the purposes of this chapter we have chosen to use Stern's (1972) definition of bilingual education: "schooling provided fully or partly in a second language with the object of making students proficient in the second language while, at the same time, maintaining and developing their proficiency in the first language and fully guaranteeing their educational development" (p. 1).

The British North America Act made education in Canada the responsibility of the provincial governments with the exception that the education of Indians, Eskimos, and children of those in the Armed Forces and of those living in the Northwest Territories is to be the responsibility of the federal government. Each province legislates its own regulations for all matters pertaining to education.

Consequently the history of bilingual education and its present state differ from province to province.

Today Canada's population consists of about 60% English mother tongue speakers and 27% French mother tongue speakers, the remainder coming from other linguistic groups (Canada 1971 Census, Special Bulletin, Table 1). French as the language of the "official" minority has often struggled to obtain equality in education. The history of bilingual education in Canada is, in large measure, the history of the Francophone struggle to have French language schools. Legislation was imposed on minority Francophone populations in many provinces making it compulsory to use English as the language of instruction. This legislation was rarely followed in practice but rather was circumvented by the Francophones in an attempt to maintain their mother tongue. The resulting bilingual programs varied from school to school within each province, and were either ignored or mildly tolerated by the Departments of Education. This situation makes it difficult and in many cases impossible to detail accurately and thoroughly the historical development of bilingual education in Canada. However, general trends can be given, and specific bilingual programs which are somewhat typical of various regions can be described. This we do in the next section.

In preparation for this chapter, since little up-to-date material is published on bilingual education in Canada, a letter requesting information about historical developments, existing programs, and research findings was sent to school boards and Ministries of Education across Canada. Much of the information received has been incorporated into the first section of this chapter.[2] In our survey we found that very few of the bilingual education programs had undergone any thorough, long-term evaluation with the exception of the experimental French "immersion" programs for English-speaking children. The importance of a systematic investigation of the effectiveness of bilingual education programs cannot be underestimated; and it is for this reason that we have chosen to focus our attention in the second section of this chapter on French "immersion" classes.

HISTORICAL PERSPECTIVE

The majority of schools in Canada at the time of Confederation in 1867 were English language schools. However, there also existed a number of French language schools as well as some ethnic schools such as German language schools. To offer education in these languages was considered normal because it provided children with the opportunity of being instructed in their native language. There was a change from these liberal policies at the turn of the century: in many provinces English was imposed by law as the language of instruction; but as we have already noted, this was not necessarily followed in practice. Many of the bilingual education programs that exist today have their origin in the determination of the Francophones to ensure that their children have the legal right to be instructed at least partially in their mother tongue. In some cases the

Francophone populations have been completely successful, thus turning bilingual education programs into unilingual ones.

While the trend in recent years among the French-speaking population has been toward mother tongue education, among pockets of English-speaking populations it has been toward second language education. This has led to the initiation of a number of experimental programs in which English-speaking students are taught in French for all or some portion of the day. These two major trends have led to the currently existing bilingual (French and English) education programs in Canada, and they are considered below in the context of particular regions and provinces.

Quebec

Of all the Canadian provinces Quebec is unique: the majority population has always been French-speaking, the minority population has always been English-speaking. The principle of providing education in the mother tongue even where numbers were small has been quite strictly followed except perhaps in the rural areas where numbers of one of the two language groups were truly insufficient.

In the 1960s the political rumblings of possible separation of Quebec from the rest of Canada, and the strong movement toward establishing French as the working language of Quebec acted as stimuli to a group of English-speaking parents in St. Lambert (a suburb of Montreal) concerned about the possible fate of their children in Quebec if they were not skilled in the French language (Melikoff 1972). Their children were being taught French-as-a-second-language for short daily periods using traditional methods. However, the results of the programs were disappointing: students did not graduate as fluent bilinguals. What was needed, they believed, was a radical change. They proposed that their children be permitted to attend a kindergarten class in which instruction was provided entirely in French. They were convinced that if French was used as a medium of communication—as a means to an end rather than as an end in itself—language learning would be enhanced. The idea was radical, and it took the parents a great deal of time to persuade their school board to try it out even on an experimental basis. But they finally succeeded, and in 1965 a kindergarten class attended only by English-speaking children and taught completely in French by a native French speaker was initiated. The following year, again after strong parental pressure was exercised on the school board, these same children entered a grade one class which was taught entirely in French by a native speaker of French. French reading and writing were introduced at this grade level, and it was not until grade two, when approximately 60 minutes a day was devoted to instruction in English of an English Language Arts program, that English reading and writing were introduced. With each successive year greater proportions of the curriculum were taught in English, until an approximate 50-50 ratio was reached.

At the end of each year the students in the experimental class were given a battery of tests and their results were compared with those of English-speaking students attending a regular English program and with those of French-speaking students attending a regular French program. The results are described in the next section of the paper. Suffice it to say here that the success of the program was such as to encourage the establishment of similar programs which have come to be known as French "immersion" or "home-school language switch" programs. Currently some 20% of English-speaking children in the Montreal area enter French immersion kindergarten classes.

Ontario

In about 1890, the Ontario Provincial Government instructed the so-called French, German, and other language bilingual schools to follow the English Public School Program. English was declared the official language of instruction (Committee on French Language Schools in Ontario 1968).

In 1912, Regulation 17 was issued, formally imposing English as the language of instruction and permitting French to be the language of instruction until the end of grade 3, thus allowing a transition period for Francophone pupils from instruction in French to instruction in English. Beyond grade 3 only one hour of instruction per day in French reading, grammar, and composition was allowed and then only as an extra subject.

Needless to say, there was much bad feeling and numerous grievances by the Francophones of Ontario against this ruling. Gradually, the law was tempered so that local requests for permission to instruct in French beyond grade 3 could be made to the Chief Inspector, who would set the amount of time allowed for teaching in French in any individual school. This resulted in complete diversity from school to school with respect to the amount of instruction given through the two languages.

In 1950, the Royal Commission of Education in Ontario reported that at that time, although illegal, French was the basic language of instruction in many Francophone schools from kindergarten through grade 8. The Commission pointed out that a statute governing fully the use of French as a language of instruction was needed. This was not done at the elementary level until 1968 when, chiefly because of the recommendations of the Canadian Royal Commission on Bilingualism and Biculturalism (hereafter referred to as the B & B Commission), the School Administration Amendment Act was passed. It recognized the use of French as a language of instruction for Francophones. It gave Francophones the right to establish French elementary schools or to establish classes taught in French within otherwise English language elementary schools where desired and where the number of students was sufficient (Dufour 1973).

At the high school level, the Ontario Department of Education in 1961 granted Ontario Secondary Schools permission to teach Latin in French, and in 1966 granted them permission to teach History and Geography in French (B & B Commission 1968). And in 1968, again mainly because of the recommendations of the B & B Commission, the Secondary Schools and Board of Education Amendment Act gave Francophones the right to have French language high schools or to have classes taught in French within otherwise English language high schools where the number of students was sufficient.

In effect, the 1968 legislation legitimized or created the potentiality for French unilingual education, as well as for a multitude of organizational patterns of bilingual education. For example, in the Frontenac County Board of Education since about 1963, Francophone students from grades 1 to 6 have received about 50% of their instruction in English and about 50% in French. The English portion of the program focuses on Mathematics and English Language Arts; the French portion on Social Studies, Science, and French Language Arts (Murphy 1973). At Lakeway Collegiate in Sault Ste. Marie, History, Geography, and French have been offered in French to the Francophone students in the school since 1970 (Currie 1973). In Welland at Ecole Secondaire Confédération, which is a French language high school, almost all subjects are offered in the French language. However, a number of courses known as "cours bilingues" are offered in both English and French. And a few subjects, for example, several commercial mathematics courses, are given only in English (Giroux, Desjardins, and Babin 1974).

Today there exist approximately 330 elementary and 25 secondary French language schools in Ontario (Stewart 1973). In addition, approximately 40 high schools offer instruction in English and French. Organizationally, in some instances this involves placing English- and French-speaking students together in the same classes, taking courses both in English and French; in other instances, it involves placing French-speaking students together in classes housed within a basically English language high school, attending courses (in French, and perhaps some in English) separate from the English-speaking stream, or for purposes of the English portion of their program they may be combined with the English-speaking students.

Recently many English-speaking students have been refused admittance to French language schools. The reasons behind this policy are twofold. First, because the English-speaking students rarely had an adequate command of French, they slowed down the progress of the Francophone students. And second, because for the most part the Francophone students spoke both English and French, the presence of even a small percentage of English-speaking students tended to result in English becoming the language of the classroom and the playground.

For those Anglophone parents in Ontario who wanted their children to become bilingual and who had in the past sent their children to French language schools, the French language schools' policy of refusing admittance to English-speaking students forced the parents to consider alternative solutions. Other English-speaking parents who saw the potential advantages in English-French bilingualism in Canada but who were unwilling to send their children to French language schools, and who were dissatisfied with the results of

French-as-a-second-language programs, were also seeking alternative solutions. About this time, details concerning the St. Lambert French immersion program and its success were being made available. The combination of these factors, plus a major push by the federal government toward a policy of bilingualism and biculturalism in Canada, led several boards of education to establish French immersion classes on an experimental and optional basis. The Ottawa Roman Catholic Separate School Board began a number of French immersion kindergarten classes in 1969. The Ottawa Board of Education and the Carleton Board of Education initiated French immersion kindergarten classes in 1970. Also in 1970, the Elgin County Board of Education initiated a partial French immersion grade 1 class, and in 1971, the Peel County Board of Education initiated two partial French immersion classes at the grade 8 level. These programs have been carefully evaluated, and the findings are reported in the next section.

The demand for French immersion programs is increasing. But the search for other viable alternatives to the attainment of English-French bilingual skills is continuing. For example, a large grant from the federal government to the four Boards of Education in the National Capital Region (Ottawa) has made possible not only the expansion of French immersion programs at the primary level, but the possibility of experimenting with other options such as a grade 6 French immersion class, a bilingual high school, an expansion of the traditional 20 minutes a day French-as-a-second-language program to an enriched 40, 60, or 90 minutes a day program, and the teaching of one subject in French in addition to the traditional French class at various grade levels. Each of these alternatives is being evaluated by researchers who will also be looking at the cost of some of these programs. Although not expected until 1975, the results of these studies will contribute considerably to our knowledge and understanding of viable forms of bilingual education.

MANITOBA

Bilingual education in Manitoba developed along lines similar to those in Ontario. For much of the period between 1890 and the present, only English had legal status as the language of instruction; however, in 1910, for example, there were in Manitoba 126 French bilingual schools, 61 German bilingual schools, and a number of Polish, Ukrainian, and other ethnic group bilingual schools (Sissons 1964). This inconsistency between legislation and actual practice, as we have already seen, was rather typical.

It was not until 1967 that the Manitoba government recognized French as an official language of instruction for up to 50% of the school day (Article 240 of the Public School Act of 1954, amended in 1967). Later, in 1970, French was allowed as the language of instruction for entire school days in elementary and secondary schooling if desired (Dufour 1973). Although bilingual education is thus available by law for Francophones in Manitoba today, lack of appropriate texts and teacher training programs presently seems to be hampering its progress (B & B Commission). This is also a problem in other provinces.

An example of the development of a bilingual education program in Manitoba can be seen at St. Boniface, where the majority of families are French. In 1965, the St. Boniface School Board decided to start an elementary school which would enroll only French-speaking pupils. The plan was to adhere to the legislation that English be the language of instruction but to encourage the use of French in all noninstructional activities (B & B Commission). With the change in legislation in 1967, plans to offer a program of instruction half in French and half in English were initiated (Coleman 1973). Other bilingual education programs have been established in Manitoba, but precise information about them is not available.

Demand on the part of the English-speaking population for instruction in French appears to be quite limited. However, it is interesting to note that in the Winnipeg School Division No. 1 there is an elementary school in which instruction is largely in French, even though less than 10% of the students are of French background (Roy 1973).

The Western Provinces

Saskatchewan

The Saskatchewan School Act (section 203) of 1931 effectively limited bilingual education within Saskatchewan schools. The controversial section of the School Act which denied extended instruction in French in the schools reads as follows:

1. English shall be the sole language of instruction in all the schools, and no language of instruction other than English shall be taught during school hours.
2. When the board of any district passes a resolution to that effect the French language may be taught as a subject for a period not exceeding one hour each day as part of the school curriculum, and such teaching shall consist of French reading, French grammar and French composition.
3. Where the French language is being taught under the provisions of subsection (2), any pupils in the schools who do not desire to receive such instruction shall be profitably employed in other school work while such instruction is being given.

In 1967, the School Act was amended to allow French or any other language other than English to be used as the language of instruction for one hour per day at the discretion of the local school board (B & B Commission). More recently, the Department of Education of Saskatchewan has established "designated schools" where the language of instruction can be French and this according to a certain scale which begins from 100% in grade 1 and reduces to 40% in high school (Papen 1973).

In 1972-1973, there were 12 elementary schools and one high school designated as French language schools with a total of 990 students enrolled. Each of the schools offers a program of bilingual education, the typical format being approximately 50 to 75% instruction in French in grades 1, 2, and 3, 40 to 60% instruction in French in grades 4, 5, and 6, and less than 40% thereafter. Some of these schools, for example, the Saskatoon French School, are attended by English-speaking as well as French-speaking children. When the Saskatoon French School began, approximately 70% of the students were native speakers of English.

Alberta

Alberta is one of the few provinces that has allowed bilingual schooling prior to the last decade. In 1950, modifications to the School Act permitted instruction in French in the early primary grades. The 1952 Annual Report of the Alberta Department of Education described the standard program for instruction in the French language as follows:

> Grade 1—almost all instruction in French in the first part of the year; decrease in amount of instruction in French toward the end of the year.
> Grade 2—50% instruction in French; 50% instruction in English.
> Grades 3 and 4—1 hour of instruction in French.
> In subsequent years—little taught in French.

Changes enacted in the School Act in 1968 and 1970 permitted school authorities in Alberta to offer instruction in French in grades 1 through 12.

In the 1971-1972 school year instruction in French in various subjects was offered to approximately 4250 students in roughly 30 schools in Alberta. Of these students, approximately two-thirds ordinarily used French at home while one-third of the students either had no previous acquaintance with the French language or used the language with difficulty because they were either learning it as a second language or had forgotten it as a mother tongue (Alberta Department of Education 1973).

Bilingual education programs in Alberta presently exist which are basically intended for classes in which the majority of pupils speak French as a first language (e.g., in High Prairie School Division No. 48), classes in which the majority of pupils speak English as a first language (St. Charles Bilingual Elementary School), and classes in which some students speak French as a first language while others speak English as a first language (Grandin Separate School).

In the bilingual schools in High Prairie School Division No. 48, instruction time in French at the elementary level is approximately 40 to 50% of the total time. Subjects taught using French as the language of instruction are Social Sciences, Physical Education, Fine Arts, Religious Education, and the study of the French language. At Grandin School approximately 70% of the students are native-English speakers. In grades 1 and 2 the children receive up to 80% of their instruction in French while in grades 3 to 6 it is reduced to a minimum of 50%. The development pattern of the curriculum at St. Charles Bilingual Elementary School is one of transfer from English as a medium of instruction to French as a medium of instruction, although English continues to be used to a greater extent than French for instructional purposes (Alberta Department of Education 1973).

British Columbia

In British Columbia the Francophones are few in number and the demand for French language schools has not been as great as elsewhere in Canada. Neither has there been much emphasis on the teaching of French as a second language. Official recognition of French as a language of instruction was given without conflict in 1967: classes in which the language of instruction is French are allowed where the demand is sufficient.

Maillardville, within the Coquitlam Board of Education, is the largest French-speaking community in British Columbia. In 1967, the French-Canadian Federation of British Columbia requested the Coquitlam Board of Education to establish a bilingual program to serve the needs of the French-speaking community and any interested English-speaking families. The resulting program included instruction in French for 80% of the time in kindergarten, 30% in grade 1, 40% in grade 2, 50% in grade 3, 65% in grades 4 and 5. Interestingly, of the children enrolling in the first year the program was offered, none had French as the dominant language and two-thirds came from completely English-speaking homes (Wilton 1974).

In 1973, the Coquitlam Board of Education modified their program by making kindergarten and grade 1 100% French on the recommendation of district personnel who had visited the French immersion programs in St. Lambert and Montreal. Further, in 1973, two other schools in the area began French immersion kindergarten classes where the children are all English-speaking, as did several schools in Victoria and Vancouver. Interest in becoming bilingual appears to be growing in British Columbia.

The Atlantic Provinces

New Brunswick

In spite of the fact that approximately 34% of New Brunswick's population is French-speaking (Canada 1971 Census, Special Bulletin, Table 1), French was not recognized officially as a language of instruction in the schools until recently (Dufour 1973). Until the 1950s French instruction was allowed in the early grades if approved by the local school boards. Not until the late 1960s, however, was a law passed which guaranteed French-speaking elementary students the right to education in their mother tongue. The emerging pattern in New Brunswick, at least at the elementary level, appears to be one leading to two separate but parallel systems of education: one for French-speaking students and one for English-speaking students (B & B Commission). The degree of bilingual education actually existing in the French system is not known. In the English system several schools in Fredericton and Moncton have begun French immersion classes in which grades 1 to 4 are taught exclusively in French except for a daily period of English Language Arts introduced at the grade 3 or 4 levels.

At the secondary level, instruction was provided only in English until roughly 20 years ago. A measure of bilingual education was achieved by first allowing History (in 1959) and secondly Mathematics and Science (in 1965) to be taught in French where the local school board approved (B & B Commission). The tendency in recent years has been for French-speaking high school students and educators to argue for ever-increasing portions of instruction in French.

Nova Scotia

Until recently in Nova Scotia, French-speaking and English-speaking pupils were educated in the same programs. In Francophone communities, although the texts and exams were in English, the teachers, many being bilingual, often conducted classes through the medium of French in the lower elementary grades. Over the elementary years English gradually replaced French as the medium of instruction, with French being used only to explain new or difficult concepts. At the high school level all instruction was in English.

In the last six years as a result of the B & B Commission, changes have taken place. For example, in the Inverness County Municipal School Board where 78% of the students are from English-speaking homes and 22% are from French-speaking homes, all subject matter in grades 1 to 4 can be taught through the medium of French if desired. In grade 5 Science is introduced in English. From 6 to grade 8 English is the main language of instruction but History continues to be taught in French. The aim is eventually to offer a 50% English, 50% French program in high school (AuCoin 1973).

It is not known how widespread this form of bilingual education is in Nova Scotia. But it does appear that the province is presently involved in educational reform that will provide the opportunity for increased bilingual education.

Prince Edward Island

In Prince Edward Island, English is the only recognized language of instruction. There are no bilingual schools by law, but in practice it would appear that they exist. For example, teachers in schools where French-speaking children attend may resort to explanation in French when teaching (B & B Commission). It is interesting to note that plans for the initiation of a French immersion grade 1 class are currently being considered for the 1974-1975 academic year in Prince Edward Island.

Newfoundland

Newfoundland does not offer bilingual schooling on the island, but there are two elementary schools which offer instruction in both French and English on the mainland in Labrador City. It is unclear whether these programs are bilingual or simply two parallel programs, one in English and one in French, within the same school (B & B Commission). It is to be noted, however, that plans to begin an early immersion class in 1974-1975 in the Port au Port area have been approved.

One basic observation about the state of bilingual education in Canada can be made in concluding this section: decisions about the bilingual programs that exist have to a large extent been made in a political context, rather than on the basis of research. Evaluations of existing programs using a common set of testing instruments would be invaluable in aiding educators to make decisions about what kind of bilingual education program would be most effective given the particular sociolinguistic characteristics of their own setting. A start in this direction has been made in the studies investigating French immersion programs for English-speaking children in a variety of community settings. (See Swain, 1974, for a review of these findings.) Some of these studies are reviewed in the next section, several in considerable detail, as the results have not yet appeared in published form. The same type of systematic longitudinal evaluations are needed for bilingual education programs for French-speaking students as well as those in which English- and French-speaking students attend classes together.

RESEARCH FINDINGS: FRENCH IMMERSION PROGRAMS

The St. Lambert project is the most thoroughly examined experiment in bilingual education in Canada. The program, which began in 1965, was designed to develop high-level English-French bilingual competence in English-speaking children. This was to be achieved by having the students attend classes where French was the major medium of instruction. In the early grades French was in fact the only medium of instruction. Not until grade 2 were the children introduced to the English Language Arts program, and that for approximately an hour a day. With each successive year, larger proportions of class time were taught in English. For example, in the fifth grade approximately 35% of the curriculum (English Language Arts, Music, and Physical Education) was taught in English. In the sixth grade, the proportion of the curriculum taught in English (English Language Arts, Creative Arts, Music, Physical Education, and Science) increased to over 50%.

At each grade level the program of study in French followed closely the curricula of the French-Canadian school system of Montreal and that of France. The materials used were designed for children who spoke French as a native language. Similarly, the English portion of the program was comparable to that followed by the regular English-language classes in Quebec.

The progress of the students in the St. Lambert program has been carefully watched over the last six years by a team of researchers at McGill University (Lambert and Macnamara 1969; Lambert and Tucker 1972; Lambert, Tucker, and d'Anglejan 1973; Bruck, Lambert, and Tucker 1974; Bruck, Lambert, and Tucker in press). The progress of pupils in the initial year of the program, as well as that of pupils who entered the program in its second year of existence, has been compared each year to the progress of English-speaking pupils following a conventional English-language program and to the progress of French-speaking pupils following a conventional French-language program, both groups being equated with the experimental group in terms of their measured intelligence and socioeconomic level.

We will not discuss year-by-year findings here, but rather will summarize the results obtained from the evaluation of the grade 6 children who had been in the experimental bilingual program since it began. The evaluation covered seven separate domains:

1. English Language Arts.
2. French Language Arts.
3. French- and English-speaking skills.
4. French phonology.
5. Achievement in content subjects.
6. Intelligence.
7. Attitudes toward French Canadians, English Canadians, European French, and self.

In the area of English Language Arts (as measured by the Metropolitan Achievement Tests and the Peabody Vocabulary Test), the students in the experimental class performed as well as their English peers who had been educated in their native language.

In the area of French Language Arts, the bilingual students when compared with native French-speaking students are somewhat behind in vocabulary knowledge; write compositions in French which, although they contain no more grammatical errors, are less rich in content; and score at approximately the 60th percentile on a test of French achievement.

When asked to tell in English about a film they had been shown, the bilingual students performed similarly to their English instructed counterparts on all measures taken which included the number of episodes, details, and inferences recounted, as well as the number of false starts, grammatical self-corrections, and content self-corrections made. When asked to tell in French about the film, the bilingual students made more grammatical and content self-corrections than native French students, but otherwise performed similarly to them.

A number of phonological traits not characteristic of French native speakers were noted in the speech of many of the bilingual children. They included the diphthongization of the mid-vowels, the aspiration of voiceless stops, and inappropriate placing of stress on the first syllable.

The experimental and English instructed students were given standardized tests (in English) in Mathematics, Science, and Social Studies. The results obtained from the two groups were similar, suggesting that the progress of the bilingual children in subject content has not been impeded by participation in the experimental program.

In addition, on the Raven Progressive Matrices Test and the nonverbal battery of the Lorge Thorndike Test, the performance of the experimental and English educated students was equivalent. These results suggest that the bilingual students have not suffered in their intellectual development as a result of receiving a major portion of their education via a second language.

The attitudes profiles of the experimental and English educated students toward French Canadians, English Canadians, European French, and self were essentially similar and positive, indicating an open and friendly attitude not only to their own ethnic group but to French Canadians and European French people as well. In contrast, the French Canadian students tended to rate themselves and their own ethnic group higher than they rated English Canadians or European French.

Owing to the effectiveness of the St. Lambert program, a number of programs modeled after it have been established in various cities across Canada (e.g., Victoria, Vancouver, Coquitlam, Winnipeg, Cochrane, Toronto, Ottawa, Montreal, Fredericton, and Moncton). A few of these programs have been evaluated. In Ottawa and Toronto, the French immersion classes have been evaluated by a team of researchers associated with the Bilingual Education Project at the Ontario Institute for Studies in Education. These studies are described in detail below.

In the Ottawa Roman Catholic Separate School Board, a bilingual education program has been established which differs from the St. Lambert model in four important ways. First, children who attend a French kindergarten also attend the other half of the day an English kindergarten. Second, a period of time each day at each grade level is devoted to teaching French as a second language. Third, English Language Arts is not introduced until grade 3, and fourth, at each grade level Religious Studies is taught in English. This program has been evaluated by Edwards and Casserly (1971, 1972, 1973).

In addition to investigating the academic achievement, language skills, and general cognitive development of students in the experimental and regular English classes, Edwards and Casserly also obtained measures of behavior considered to be closely associated with dyslexia or learning disabilities (Pupil Rating Scale) and social maturity (The Vineland Social Maturity Scale), as well as measures on 13 personality traits (The Early School Personality Questionnaire).

With respect to the achievement measures, the same general trends as reported in St. Lambert and in the Bilingual Education Project studies were found, except that the grade 2 children (who had not yet been introduced to English Language Arts) were somewhat behind their comparison group in English reading, word discrimination, word knowledge, and spelling. However, by midway through the grade 3 year, the experimental students, having been given formal instruction in English Language Arts had caught up with their English instructed counterparts. Furthermore, on the Illinois Tests of Psycholinguistic Abilities, the grade 3 immersion students were rated higher than the comparison group of students on auditory reception, auditory association, visual association, verbal expression, visual and auditory closure, and visual sequential memory. There were no differences on visual reception, manual expression, grammatic closure, auditory sequential memory, or sound blending. Edwards and Casserly (1973) suggest that "such differences indicate that exposure to a French immersion program, far from resulting in a psycholinguistic lag, may, in fact, enhance the development of psycholinguistic skills" (p. 75).

Results obtained from the Pupil Rating Scale suggested that exposure during the first several years of elementary school to a French immersion program did not result in a measurable increase in the incidence of learning disabilities. A number of personality differences between the groups were observed, such as the tendency of the immersion group to be more assertive, independent, and less sociable. Edwards and Casserly (1973) suggest that these differences are probably "due less to the program than to preselection factors affecting the parents' choice of a second language option for their children" (p. 58). Ratings of social maturity at the grade 2 level yielded significant differences in favor of the immersion group.

There are two other important studies which relate to the early immersion model of bilingual education that are of considerable importance. The first is a study on the suitability of French immersion classes for working-class children (Bruck, Jakimik, and Tucker 1973; Tucker, Lambert, and d'Anglejan 1973). The second is a study of the effects of French immersion programs on children with language disabilities (Bruck and Rabinovitch 1974).

The results presented above have dealt mainly with children from middle to upper middle class families. However, little is known about the effectiveness of French immersion classes for children from lower socioeconomic levels. The language of the working-class child may be deficient relative to the demands of the school (Bereiter and Englemann 1966), and as Bruck et al. (1971:312) point out, "it is feared [by some] that if placed in an immersion class he will fall even further behind his middle-class peers than if instructed in his native language. In addition, it is thought that learning to read and write in a second language places an additional and unnecessary burden on the working-class-child who often has difficulty in mastering the elementary-school curriculum even in his native language." In contrast, however, Bruck et al. (1971) argue that there may be benefits for the working-class child in an immersion program. Bruck and Tucker (1974) have shown that the language of the working-class and middle-class child is similar in terms of grammatical and vocabulary abilities at the end of kindergarten, but that there are differences in terms of how effectively they use language for communication. Middle-class children make their messages more clear and explicit than do working-class children. Bruck et al. (1971) suggest that "Immersion education should not necessarily broaden this gap. In fact, one might argue that in learning via a second language the child may become more aware of the necessity of making communications clear, which might in turn favorably affect his ability to communicate effectively in his native language" (p. 313).

Bruck et al. (1971) administered a battery of tests to working-class immersion grade 1 and 2 students and to comparable groups of native English-speaking students and native French-speaking students. The tests were designed to measure the native and second language development, achievement in mathematics, and overall cognitive development. The investigators conclude that the pattern of results [with respect to English language skills] "conforms with that found for middle-class groups in the St. Lambert study," that the experimental working-class groups are able to use their native language as effectively for oral communication as are their comparison groups, that they are acquiring a sound passive knowledge of French in terms of vocabulary, reading, grammar, and comprehension although they are not at par with native

French-speaking children, that they "seem no less able than the middle-class groups to handle the challenge of learning a content subject [mathematics] via French," and that they "are not being adversely affected by their participation in this program." In summary, they tentatively suggest "that this educational program is as appropriate for working-class children as it has been found to be for middle-class children and that it is providing the children with the French language skills so necessary for education and occupational success in Quebec—at no apparent cost to their general cognitive and linguistic development" (p. 341).

A great deal of concern has been expressed about the feasibility of permitting children with language disabilities to enter a French immersion program. Bruck and Rabinovitch (1974) reported on a study they have begun of English-speaking children with diagnosed language difficulties who are enrolled in French immersion kindergarten and grade 1 classes. They are comparing the progress of these children with children who also have diagnosed language difficulties but who are enrolled in the regular English program, with children who are normal in their language development and are enrolled in the French immersion program, and with children who are normal in their language development and who are enrolled in the regular English program. Their progress is assessed in native language development, cognitive development, school achievement, and second language skills.

The children were identified as having language-learning disabilities according to their performance on a screening test battery which consists of an object manipulation test, a story retelling test, a sentence imitation test, and an echolalia test.

The results are based on a small number of students and must therefore be viewed as preliminary and tentative in nature. However, the general trend is worth noting: the children with language learning disabilities enrolled in a French immersion class do not fall differentially behind their counterparts enrolled in the English program. In those instances where they do not score as high as their counterparts in the English program, neither do the children with normal language development in the French immersion program relative to their counterparts in the English program.

The early immersion model is the most widespread program of bilingual education operating in Caanada. However, another model, referred to as "late immersion" (Tucker 1974), has been initiated in the Montreal area (Protestant School Board of Greater Montreal 1973; Swain 1974). Students entering a late immersion program have typically had one or more years of daily instruction in French-as-a-second-language. During the immersion year, most or all of the curriculum is taught in French. As a follow-up to this year, students have the option of taking certain subjects in French, for example, History or Geography. In the 1973-1974 academic year, over 30% of the English-speaking students in the Protestant School Board of Greater Montreal (PSBGM) enrolled in a grade 7 French immersion program.

The initial two years of operation of the grade 7 immersion program in Montreal were marked by stringent admission standards. However, in the third year (1971-1972), admission standards were lowered. The results of the 1971-1972 year are reported below, as they provide a greater fund of information for the overall effects of the late immersion course at various ability levels.

Two sections of the Stanford Achievement Test were given to the grade 7 immersion students and to grade 7 students in the regular English program to measure achievement in English: paragraph meaning and language usage. The results show that although performance on both sections was related to IQ, at each IQ level (high 116-130, medium 96-115, low 80-95) students in the immersion program obtained scores equivalent to those of students in a regular English grade 7 program (PSBGM 1973).

The evaluation of the grade 7 immersion students included a standardized written test of French achievement developed by the Commission des Ecoles Catholiques de Montréal (CECM) for native speakers of French at the grade 7 level, and a test of listening comprehension and speaking. The students' responses in the speaking test were rated according to their grammatical correctness, enunciation, rhythm, and intonation, vocabulary, and fluency.

Generally speaking, the results show that the grade 7 immersion students, although not at a par with the grade 7 native French-speaking students, showed significant gains over the year. In relation to their French-speaking skills, they scored highest in the areas of enunciation, rhythm, and intonation and lowest in the area of grammatical correctness, although all ratings placed them above average on the rating scales. Results on the written French achievement test placed the grade 7 immersion students in the bottom quartile of the CECM norms. Neither IQ nor sex affected the rate and level of achievement on oral skills. On the other hand, there was a striking and consistent relationship between IQ and performance on the written test of French achievement (PSBGM 1973).

We now turn to a detailed consideration of three studies which have been carried out by the Bilingual Education Project of the Ontario Institute for Studies in Education.[3] The studies are examined through the first two years of evaluation.

1. The Toronto Study involves a total French immersion program, and relates to one school (Allenby Public School, under the jurisdiction of the Toronto Board of Education). The program, patterned after the one in St. Lambert (Lambert and Tucker 1972) and Ottawa[4] was started in September 1971 at the kindergarten level and extended to the following grade level each succeeding year. In this program, classroom instruction is completely in French throughout the (half-day) kindergarten year and grade 1. During kindergarten and at the start of grade 1, the pupils are permitted to address the teacher in English (who, however, replies only in French), but they are increasingly encouraged to use French. By about the fourth month of the grade 1 year, the teacher begins to insist on the use of French by the pupils either when addressing her or among themselves, and French becomes almost exclusively the language of communication in the classroom. Immersion teachers to date have been native speakers of French, whether of Canadian or European origin.

Reading and writing are thus initially taught in French. In the second half of grade 2, instruction in English Language Arts is introduced for short (25-minute) daily periods.[4] As the program is presently envisaged, this amount of English instruction is to be increased in subsequent grades, so that in the upper years of elementary school the program is to be 50% French, 50% English.

Data are presented for two successive cohorts or groups of pupils in the Toronto study: those pupils who entered kindergarten in September 1971 (Cohort I), for whom kindergarten and grade 1 data are presented, and those who began in September 1972 (Cohort II), for whom data are presented for kindergarten only.

2. The Elgin study relates to a partial (50%) French immersion or bilingual program initiated in September 1970 by the Elgin County Board of Education in one school (Wellington Street Public School) in St. Thomas, Ontario. Following English (half-day) kindergarten, pupils enter a grade 1 program which involves instruction through the medium of French for half the day and through the medium of English for the other half. Subjects taught in French throughout grades 1 to 4 are French Language Arts (with French reading and French composition introduced in grade 2), Mathematics and Music. Subjects taught in English are English Language Arts, Science, Social Studies, Art, Physical Education, Health and Religion. Thus, in contrast to the total immersion program, reading and writing are initially taught in English in grade 1, with reading in French introduced in grade 2.

A point to note is that at each grade level in the evaluation considered here, the same teacher has conducted both French and English components of the program. The teachers involved have been native English speakers who are fluently bilingual.[5]

The first stream of pupils who entered the Elgin program in September 1970 (Cohort I) were not included in the evaluation carried out by the Bilingual Education Project during the first two years, so that data for them are presented for grade 3 only. The second stream of pupils (Cohort II) started in September 1971. Detailed data, however, are presented only for grade 2, as discussed subsequently. The third stream (Cohort III) started in September 1972, and is discussed in relation to grade 1 only.

3. The Peel study relates to a partial French immersion program starting in grade 8 which the Peel County Board of Education initiated in September 1971 in Brampton, Ontario, at William G. Davis Senior Public School, and subsequently expanded to higher grade levels at Brampton Centennial Secondary School. Like Toronto and St. Thomas, Brampton is a predominantly English-speaking community.

Pupils enter the grade 8 program with one year of prior studies in French-as-a-second-language taught in grade 7 for 20 minutes per day except for the last two months of the year during which pupils selected for the grade 8 program receive additional instruction in French for a total of one hour per day.

In grade 8 (last year before high school) the Peel program involves the use of French as the medium of instruction in the classroom for the following subjects: French, Mathematics, History, Geography, Science, and Art; while English, Physical Education, Home Economics/Industrial Arts, and Music are taught in

English. The proportion of French to English instruction is approximately 70 to 30%.

At the grade 9 level (first year high school) the subjects taught via French are French, History, and Geography, while English, Mathematics, Science, and other options are taught via English. Here the proportion is approximately 40% instruction in French, 60% in English. A similar program is to be followed in subsequent grades, although variation may be introduced in the subjects taught in French. To date, the teachers responsible for the French component of the grade 8 and grade 9 programs have been native speakers of French.

Two cohorts of the Peel study are discussed: Cohort I, which entered the grade 8 program in September 1971 and for whom data are presented for both grades 8 and 9, and Cohort II, which entered the program in September 1972, and for whom only grade 8 data are available.

With respect to the student population involved in the three studies discussed above, it may be said that in general they have tended to come from unilingual English-speaking middle class backgrounds. In the case of the Elgin and Peel studies, an informal criterion of mental ability (higher than average IQ) has been employed to date in the selection of pupils for the program.

In the evaluations carried out by the Bilingual Education Project the procedure has been to administer a battery of tests in the spring of each year, and in some instances, in the fall also, to pupils in the immersion or partial immersion programs and to comparison groups from the regular English programs. The comparison groups have been selected from the same schools as the immersion samples where possible and appropriate, or from matched populations. The design of the analysis has been to compare the experimental group with its comparison group, taking into account possible age and IQ differences through analysis of covariance.

We now consider each study separately.

Toronto Study

Toronto Cohort I

Cohort I represents the initial stream of pupils who entered the kindergarten French immersion program at Allenby Public School in September 1971. Enrollment consisted of 49 pupils in two kindergarten classes. These pupils together with pupils from two regular kindergarten classes (47 pupils) in the same school were evaluated in the spring of 1972.

Tests. The test battery administered to both groups at the end of kindergarten consisted of the following (references to all tests employed in the study are given in the Appendix at the end of this chapter):

1. Otis-Lennon Mental Ability Test (Primary I level), an intelligence or scholastic aptitude test which measures the pupil's facility in reasoning and in dealing abstractly with verbal, symbolic, and figural materials, and samples a broad range of cognitive abilities. The items in the test are pictorial in form and

do not require any reading. The test, like all other tests in the battery except the French Comprehension Test, was given in English.

2. Metropolitan Readiness Tests (1958), which measure the child's readiness for beginning school work. The test (MRT) consists of six sections: *word meaning*, a picture-vocabulary test; *listening*, a test of phrase and sentence comprehension; *matching*, a test of visual perception involving the recognition of similarities; *alphabet*, a test of ability to recognize lowercase letters of the alphabet; *numbers*, a test of number knowledge; and *copying*, a test of visual perception and motor control.

3. Stanford Early School Achievement Test (Level 1), which is designed to provide a measure of the child's cognitive abilities. The test (SESAT) consists of four parts. The first section, *the environment*, measures the degree of information the child has about his natural and social environments. The second section, *mathematics*, aims at measuring the development of numerical concepts learned from general experience rather than from direct intervention through teaching. The third section, *letters and sounds*, measures both the ability to recognize upper- and lowercase letters and the auditory perception of beginning sounds in English. The fourth section, *aural comprehension*, measures the child's ability to pay attention to, interpret, infer, and retain what has been heard.

4. French Comprehension Test (1972 edition). In order to evaluate the proficiency of the children in French, one of the priorities of the Bilingual Education Project at its inception was to develop a test of French comprehension, since none existed which could apply to the population under consideration. The test version administered in 1972 was experimental and has since been revised.[6] The test consisted of 91 items involving five different types: *words*, requiring the child to identify the picture referred to by a spoken French word; *phrases*, requiring the child to identify the picture referred to be a short phrase or sentence; *commands*, requiring the child to identify the picture referred to by an instruction or command frequently encountered in the classroom situation; *questions*, involving the selection of the pictorial answer to a question in French; and *stories*, requiring the child to choose the correct pictures in answer to questions based on short stories presented orally in French. Instructions were given orally in English, while the test items themselves were in French. Pupils in the comparison group were not administered the French Comprehension Test, since French is not taught in early grade levels in Toronto.

In order to check on the conceptual adequacy of the items, an English translation of the test was administered to pupils attending a regular English kindergarten in another locality (Ottawa; see Barik and Swain 1975a). The score of 86.0 out of 91 obtained by these pupils indicated that the test did not present any significant conceptual difficulties and thus that the score obtained by immersion pupils on the French version of the test could be taken as a measure of proficiency in French comprehension, independent of conceptual difficulty. A more direct method of checking on the conceptual adequacy of the test would have been to administer the French version to a group of native French-speaking pupils, but this was not administratively feasible.

Results. The data are shown in Table 1 (Cohort I, kindergarten). As seen, there is no significant difference between the French immersion and comparison (regular English kindergarten) groups in the age of the pupils. On the IQ measure, however, the immersion pupils score significantly higher than their regular program counterparts $(p < .01)$. The question arises whether this represents an initial difference between the two groups or whether it may be attributable to the effect of the program. Since no beginning-of-year scores were available, the issue could not be resolved. However, it was considered and discounted the following year on the basis of data collected from Cohort II, to be discussed subsequently. It may thus be assumed that the Cohort I end-of-kindergarten-year IQ difference between the two groups represents an initial difference in the composition of the two groups with respect to this factor. It might be that in the initial year of the program a more select group of children were enrolled in it, though no selection as such on the basis of mental ability was carried out by the school. On the basis of American norms for the IQ test, the immersion group's score of 110.7 falls at approximately the 75th percentile and the comparison group's score of 102.8 at the 57th percentile.

Since age and IQ are two factors which can have a bearing on performance in other areas of achievement, their effect is systematically taken into consideration in relation to other data, through the use of analysis of covariance.

As seen from Table 1, when unadjusted scores are considered, the immersion group scores significantly higher $(p < .05)$ than the comparison group on both the (total) readiness (MRT) and achievement (SESAT) tests, and in relation to some of the subtests.[7] When scores are adjusted for age and IQ, however, the differences disappear. Thus the immersion group is seen to perform equivalently to pupils in the regular English program with respect to school readiness and achievement in kindergarten. In terms of (American) norms for the test based on unadjusted scores, the immersion group scores at the 77th percentile on the MRT and at the 66th percentile on the SESAT while for the comparison group the corresponding figures are the 67th and 52nd percentiles.

As for French comprehension, the immersion group's performance cannot be compared with that of the comparison group, which did not take the test. Comparisons can be made, however, with the performance of pupils in another locality (Ottawa), where both immersion pupils and regular program pupils who begin instruction in French-as-a-second-language in kindergarten for periods of 20 to 30 minutes per day were given the test (based on data reported by Barik and Swain 1975a; see note 3). The Toronto group's score of 70.5 out of 91 on the French Comprehension Test is slightly lower than that of 74.4 obtained by kindergarten immersion pupils in Ottawa (which offers a more bilingual milieu than Toronto), but much higher than that of pupils in the regular program in Ottawa. That comparison is done on the basis of 82 items, since the Ottawa regular program pupils were not administered one section of the test (stories), which was judged too difficult for them. The Toronto kindergarten immersion pupils obtain a score of 64.3 out of 82, versus one of 37.9 for regular program kindergarten pupils and 45.9 for regular program grade 1 pupils.

Table 1.   Toronto Study: Data for Cohorts I and II

| | COHORT I | | | | COHORT II | | | |
| | Unadj. $\bar{X}$ | | Level of significance | | Unadj. $\bar{X}$ | | Level of significance | |
	Immersion Group	Comparison Group	Unadj. $\bar{X}$	Adj. $\bar{X}^a$	Immersion Group	Comparison Group	Unadj. $\bar{X}$	Adj. $\bar{X}^a$
KINDERGARTEN								
Age (mos., end of year)	70.71	71.74	n.s.		70.00	70.68	n.s.	n.s.
Otis-Lennon deviation IQ, start yr.	110.70	102.78	.01		108.63	105.22	n.s.	n.s.
Otis-Lennon deviation IQ, end yr.					114.50	107.83	n.s.	n.s.
Metropolitan Readiness Tests								
Total (mx = 102)	68.36[b]	63.35	.05	n.s.	63.88[b]	53.24	.01	n.s.
a. Word Meaning (16)	11.04	11.14	n.s.	n.s.	10.84	9.71	n.s.	n.s.
b. Listening (16)	9.45	9.51	n.s.	n.s.	10.20	10.75	n.s.	n.s.
c. Matching (14)	8.72	8.37	n.s.	n.s.	9.08	5.61	.001	.01
d. Alphabet (16)	13.74	11.90	.01	n.s.	13.28	11.35	n.s.	n.s.
e. Numbers (26)	15.04	13.00	.05	n.s.	13.76	10.86	.01	n.s.
f. Copying (14)	9.80	9.02	n.s.	n.s.	6.04	5.59	n.s.	n.s.
SESAT Total (mx = 126)	100.07[b]	93.16	.05	n.s.	97.28[b]	94.80	n.s.	n.s.
a. Environment (42)	35.24	33.32	n.s.	n.s.	35.27	34.43	n.s.	n.s.
b. Mathematics (28)	21.85	20.05	.05	n.s.	20.59	18.62	n.s.	n.s.
c. Letters and Sounds (28)	21.72	19.81	n.s.	n.s.	20.42	18.96	n.s.	n.s.
d. Aural Comprehension (28)	20.70	20.11	n.s.	n.s.	21.19	20.08	n.s.	n.s.
French Comprehension Test								
1972 ed. (mx = 91)	70.48							
1973 ed. K form (mx = 65)					39.58			

Table 1 (continued)

	COHORT I Unadj. $\bar{X}$		COHORT I Level of significance		COHORT II Unadj. $\bar{X}$		COHORT II Level of significance	
	Immersion Group	Comparison Group	Unadj. $\bar{X}$	Adj. $\bar{X}^a$	Immersion Group	Comparison Group	Unadj. $\bar{X}$	Adj. $\bar{X}^a$
GRADE 1								
Otis-Lennon Deviation IQ	116.27	109.47	n.s.					
Metropolitian Achievement Tests (standard scores)c								
a. Word knowledge (22-65)	50.74	55.00	.05	.01				
b. Word discrimination (21-68)	49.06	56.24	.01	.001				
c. Reading (20-70)	46.23	50.47	n.s.	.01				
d. Arithmetic concepts and skills (18-68)	51.69	51.00	n.s.	n.s.				
French Comprehension Test (1973 ed.) Grade 1 form (mx = 65)	50.47							
Test de Rendement en Français (mx = 30)	15.87							
Test de REndement en Mathématiques (mx = 33)	19.87							

[a] Adjusted for age and end-of-year IQ.

[b] See note 7 of text.

[c] Range of standard score scale for each section is given in parentheses.

Toronto Cohort I, Grade 1

In 1972-1973, 47 pupils were enrolled in two grade 1 French immersion classes at Allenby Public School. Rather than test all pupils in the program, in 1973 random samples of 15 pupils were selected from each immersion and each regular program class. The class male-female ratio was retained in the sample. Randomly selected replacements took the place of students in the sample who were absent for any one test.

Tests. The following tests were administered at the end of grade 1:

1. Otis-Lennon Mental Ability Test (Elementary I level), the appropriate form for grade 1 of the intelligence test given in kindergarten.

2. Metropolitan Achievement Tests (Primary I Battery, 1958). This test is concerned with reading and arithmetic skills taught in grade 1. It consists of four sections: *word knowledge,* a test of the child's word recognition ability in English; *word discrimination,* a test of auditory and visual discrimination; *reading,* a test of ability to read silently and comprehend sentences and paragraphs in English; and *arithmetic concepts and skills,* a test of mastery of basic numerical and quantitative concepts, ability to solve verbal problems, and ability to add and subtract.

3. French Comprehension Test (Kindergarten and Grade 1 levels, 1973 edition). On the basis of the earlier version of the test and some new items, the Bilingual Education Project developed two forms of the French Comprehension Test in 1973, one intended primarily for use in kindergarten and the other primarily for use in grade 1. Each form consists of 65 items of the types *words, phrases, questions,* and *stories* described earlier. The grade 1 immersion pupils were given the grade 1 level test (and the kindergarten pupils of Cohort II, to be discussed subsequently, were given the less advanced test). One of the two regular program classes was administered an English translation of the test to check on the conceptual adequacy of the items. (The test again proved to be conceptually adequate, as was the case with the kindergarten level.)

4. Test de Rendement en Français (Grade 1), a test of achievement in French developed for native French-speaking grade 1 pupils in Montreal by the Commission des Ecoles Catholiques de Montréal, and involving the identification of phonetic sounds, word definitions, vocabulary, spelling, and sentence comprehension in French. The test was administered to pupils in the French immersion program in order to obtain some measure of comparison with native French speakers.

5. Test de Rendement en Mathématiques (Grade 1), the corresponding test of achievement in mathematics developed by the Commission des Ecoles Catholiques de Montréal for native French-speaking grade 1 pupils in Montreal. The test consists of items which involve elementary set theory, addition and subtraction equations, and oral presentation of short problems in French. The test was again given only to the immersion pupils.[8]

Results. At the end of grade 1, as shown in Table 1, the immersion group still obtains a higher IQ score than the comparison group, but the difference between the two groups is no longer quite statistically significant ($p = .08$). This decrease in the significance of the IQ difference relative to kindergarten may be attributable in part to differences in the composition of the samples at the two periods of testing. In terms of population norms, the mean score of the immersion group falls at the 84th percentile and that of the regular group at the 72nd percentile, with both groups showing a slight increase in IQ over their kindergarten performance.

On the Metropolitan Achievement Test, the immersion pupils score significantly lower ($p < .01$) than the comparison pupils on all three subtests involving English language skills (word knowledge, word discrimination, reading) on the basis of scores adjusted for age and IQ. This is to be expected, since immersion pupils do not receive any formal instruction in English reading skills in grade 1. In terms of norms for the test, their scores on the three sections fall at the 58th, 50th, and 40th percentile, respectively. This suggests that there is a considerable amount of transfer of reading skills acquired in French to English.[9] The regular program pupils, in comparison, score at the 75th, 78th, and 60th percentile on the three sections, respectively. There is no significant difference between the two groups on the arithmetic section of the test, the scores of both groups falling between the 65th and 70th percentile. Thus, in grade 1, immersion pupils continue to acquire mathematical concepts as well via French as pupils in the regular program do via English, and can apply this knowledge in one language context or the other.

In terms of French performance, the Toronto French immersion group obtains a score of 50.5 out of 65 on the French Comprehension Test (Grade 1 level). This score is almost identical to that of 50.8 obtained by pupils in an immersion program in Ottawa (Barik and Swain 1975a) and substantially higher than that of 24.5 recorded for pupils in the regular grade 1 program, in that locality, who receive daily periods of instruction in French-as-a-second-language. On the Test de Rendement en Français, the Toronto group's score of 15.9 out of 30 is slightly higher than that of 14.5 obtained by their Ottawa counterparts, and on the Test de Rendement en Mathématiques the Toronto score of 19.9 is equivalent to that of 19.4 obtained by Ottawa grade 1 immersion pupils. In relation to norms for the two tests, the Toronto pupils score in the stanine 4 range in each instance, indicating that they do as well as from 23 to 39% of the French-speaking grade 1 pupils in Montreal, for whom the tests were developed. However, it must be pointed out that the tests are administered in late March by the Commission des Ecoles Catholiques de Montréal, whereas the immersion pupils were tested in June, so that they benefit from a 2½-month delay in administration in comparison with the norm population.

The end of grade 1 results are thus again rather favorable to immersion, indicating that pupils in the immersion program are not being harmed in terms of cognitive development, are progressing equivalently to pupils in the regular program in mathematical skills, and in French are much ahead of pupils in a regular program who receive daily periods of instruction in French, even performing reasonably well in comparison with native French speakers. Where immersion pupils are behind, quite understandably, is in English reading skills. But even in English reading there is evidence of a substantial transfer of reading skills from French to English, suggesting that the lag of immersion pupils vis-à-vis pupils in the regular program in English reading skills is only temporary, and may disappear once formal instruction in English is introduced into the immersion curriculum.

Toronto Cohort II, Kindergarten

The second French immersion cohort entered kindergarten at Allenby Public School in September 1972. It consisted of 37 pupils in two immersion classes. In spring 1973 random samples of 12 pupils from each class together with equivalent numbers from each of the two sections of the regular English kindergarten class were administered the same battery of tests as had been given to cohort I in kindergarten, except that the Cohort II pupils were administered the revised (1973) kindergarten level of the French Comprehension Test. Replacements were again employed if pupils were absent for any of the tests. In addition, to determine whether the previous year's (Cohort I, Kindergarten) end-of-year IQ difference reflected an initial difference in the samples on that dimension or a possible beneficial effect of the immersion program in the kindergarten year on cognitive development, the Otis-Lennon Mental Ability Test (Primary I level) was also administered early in the first half of the year (late November)[10] to all Cohort II pupils. Thus beginning- and end-of-year scores were available on this test.

Results. The data are presented in Table 1. As seen, there is no reliable difference between the two groups in age and either beginning-of-year or end-of-year IQ, and in the latter case this holds also when the beginning-of-year score is taken as a covariate. The conclusion can thus be reached that the type of program (immersion versus regular) does not appear to have a significant differential effect on cognitive development in the course of the kindergarten year, and thus the IQ difference noted at the end of kindergarten with Cohort I may be taken to have reflected an initial difference in the composition of the two groups at the time with respect to mental ability. With respect to American norms, the end-of-year IQ score of 114.5 for the Cohort II immersion group falls at the 82nd percentile and that of 107.8 for the comparison group at the 69th percentile.

On the basis of unadjusted scores the immersion group scores significantly higher ($p < .01$) than the comparison group on the Metropolitan Readiness Tests, but the difference disappears when scores are adjusted for age and IQ except with respect to the matching subtest. No reliable differences are observed on the achievement test (SESAT). These findings thus generally parallel those obtained with Cohort I and with the Ottawa kindergarten groups. In terms of norms, the immersion group scores at the 69th and 60th percentile on the MRT and SESAT, respectively, while the comparison group scores at the 46th and 56th percentile.

These sets of figures, notably the one for the comparison group's performance on the MRT, are generally lower than those recorded for Cohort I kindergarten pupils.

As for performance on the French Comprehension Test (kindergarten level), the Toronto immersion group's score (39.6) is somewhat lower than that of 43.0 obtained by comparable pupils in Ottawa, but considerably higher than that of regular program pupils in Ottawa who receive 20 to 30 minutes instruction of French-as-a-second-language per day. Kindergarten pupils in that program obtain a score of 24.1 while grade 1 pupils obtain a score of 30.3 and grade 2 pupils one of 33.2 on the same test (from data reported in Barik and Swain 1975a).

Summary of Total French Immersion Program,
Kindergarten and Grade 1

On the basis of the data reviewed above in relation to the Toronto early total immersion program which involves total French instruction in kindergarten and grade 1, the following points may be made:

1. The pupils at the end of the kindergarten year of a total French immersion program: (a) have learned more French than kindergarten, grade 1, and grade 2 pupils receiving 20 to 40 minutes a day of instruction in French as a second language; (b) are equally ready to enter an English grade 1 as are pupils who have attended an English kindergarten as far as numerical and English prereading skills and early school achievement are concerned; (c) have not suffered any setback in general mental and cognitive development relative to their peers in a regular English program.

2. The pupils at the end of grade 1 in a French immersion program: (a) although not at par with native French-speaking peers, have achieved a level of proficiency in French superior to that of their English-speaking peers who receive 20 to 40 minutes per day of French as a second language; (b) are somewhat behind their English-speaking peers attending the regular English program in such basic English language skills as word knowledge, word discrimination, and reading. However, their performance indicates a substantial transfer of reading skills from French to English, even without formal instruction in English, suggesting that this lag should disappear once formal instruction in English Language Arts is introduced in grade 2; (c) have mastered as much mathematical knowledge via French as the pupils attending a regular English program have via English, and can transfer this knowledge from French to English; (d) have not suffered any setback in general mental and cognitive development relative to their peers in a regular English program.

Elgin Study

The partial (50%) French immersion program starting at grade 1 in operation at Wellington Street School in St. Thomas, Ontario was initiated by the Elgin

County Board of Education in September 1970 with one class of 20 pupils. The pupils were informally selected on the basis of general mental ability.

In the evaluation of the program the performance of the partial immersion group has been compared with that of an equivalent group following the regular English program at Locke Street Public School in St. Thomas, which is comparable to Wellington Street School in terms of socioeconomic level and other demographic factors.

The first cohort was not followed by the Bilingual Education Project during the first two years (grades 1 and 2), so that only data relating to grade 3 are available. As for Cohort II, the evaluation carried out at the end of grade 1 in spring 1972 was fragmentary, owing to administrative problems, and measures of French performance could not be obtained in the spring but had to be postponed until the start of grade 2. Consequently, only the results of the spring 1973 evaluation will be presented below. The order of presentation is in terms of grade levels.

Elgin Grade 1 (Cohort III)

In 1972-1973, 28 pupils (constituting one class) were enrolled in the grade 1 partial (50%) French immersion program at Wellington Street Public School. These pupils were evaluated by the Bilingual Education Project, together with a comparison group consisting of one class of 23 pupils in the regular program at Locke Street Public School.

Tests. To obtain some beginning-of-year measures, the two groups were administered the Otis-Lennon Mental Ability Test (Primary I level), the Metropolitan Readiness Tests, and the Stanford Early School Achievement Test (level 1) in early fall 1972.

At the end of the school year, the two groups were administered the Otis-Lennon Mental Ability Test (Elementary level) and the Metropolitan Achievement Tests (Primary I battery, 1958). In addition, the partial immersion group was administered both the kindergarten and grade 1 levels of the French Comprehension Test (1973), described under Toronto Cohort I, grade 1. No measure of French was obtained with pupils in the regular program, who do not start French until grade 6.

Results. The data are shown in Table 2. As seen, there were no reliable differences between the two groups at the start of the year. The same applies with respect to all subtests of the MRT and of the SESAT, which are not shown in the table. The two groups obtain quite high IQ scores which fall at approximately the 90th percentile. On the readiness test, the scores of both groups also fall in the vicinity of the 90th percentile, while on the achievement test the partial immersion group scores at the 88th percentile and the comparison group at the 82nd.

At the end of grade 1, there is again no difference between the two groups on IQ or on achievement in English and arithmetic skills. The IQ scores for both

Table 2.   Elgin Study: Data for Grades 1, 2, and 3

	Unadjusted $\bar{X}$		Level of significance	
	Partial immersion group	Comparison group	Unadj. $\bar{X}$	Adj. $\bar{X}$[a]
GRADE I (COHORT III)				
Age (mos., end of year)	83.18	83.22	n.s.	
Otis-Lennon DIQ, start yr.	122.07	119.57	n.s.	
Metropolitan Readiness Tests (start yr.)				
Total (mx = 102)	75.32	76.70	n.s.	n.s.
SESAT (start yr.) Total (mx = 126)	115.04	113.22	n.s.	n.s.
Otis-Lennon DIQ end yr.	119.32	116.32	n.s.	n.s.
Metropolitan Achievement Tests (standard scores)[b]				
a. Word knowledge (22-65)	53.11	51.26	n.s.	n.s.
b. Word discrimination (21-68)	51.11	51.89	n.s.	n.s.
c. Reading (20-70)	48.22	47.10	n.s.	n.s.
d. Arithmetic concepts and skills (18-68)	54.37	55.10	n.s.	n.s.
French Comprehension Test (1973 ed.) (mx = 65)				
a. Kindergarten form	40.25			
b. Grade 1 form	24.85			
GRADE 2 (COHORT II)				
Age (mos., end of year)	96.21	94.40	n.s.	
Otis-Lennon Deviation IQ (end yr.)	112.39	114.56	n.s.	
Metropolitan Achievement Tests (standard scores)[b]				
a. Word knowledge (18-71)	50.58	52.52	n.s.	n.s.
b. Word discrimination (18-66)	48.44	56.54	.001	.01
c. Reading (18-68)	47.44	54.33	.01	.01
d. Spelling (28-67)	51.06	58.29	.01	.01
e. Arithmetic total (18-74)	57.61	56.48	n.s.	n.s.
Concepts and problem solving (15-71)	56.17	55.17	n.s.	n.s.
Computation (23-71)	57.56	54.91	n.s.	n.s.
French Comprehension Test (1973 ed.)				
Grade 1 form (mx = 65)	31.95			
IEA French Listening Test (mx = 35)	19.58			
Test de Rendement en Français				
Grade 1 level (mx = 30)	9.74			
GRADE 3 (COHORT I)				
Age (mos., end of year)	108.43	108.38	n.s.	
Otis-Lennon Deviation IQ (end of yr.)	115.60	111.04	n.s.	
Metropolitan Achievement Tests (standard scores)[b]				
a. Word knowledge (20-75)	51.71	57.13	.01	.001
b. Word discrimination (19-72)	53.71	56.50	n.s.	n.s.
c. Reading (19-75)	51.00	49.63	n.s.	n.s.

Table 2 (continued)

| | Unadjusted $\overline{X}$ | | Level of significance | |
	Partial immersion group	Comparison group	Unadj. $\overline{X}$	Adj. $\overline{X}^a$
Metropolitan Achievement Tests (continued)				
d. Spelling (29-71)	53.90	62.63	.001	.001
e. Language: usage (24-80)	49.30	54.04	n.s.	.05
f. Language: punctuation and capitalization (25-77)	44.45	51.67	.001	.001
g. Language: Total (20-85)	46.45	53.46	.001	.001
h. Arithmetic: computation (21-81)	46.43	49.22	n.s.	n.s.
i. Arithmetic: problem solving and concepts (20-80)	51.05	51.43	n.s.	n.s.
j. Arithmetic: total raw score (mx = 82)	43.95	46.09	n.s.	n.s.
French Comprehension Test (1973 ed.) Grade 1 form (mx = 65)	48.00			
IEA French Listening Test (mx = 35)	29.71			

[a] Adjusted for age and end-of-year IQ (start-of-year IQ in case of Grade 1 MRT and SESAT).
[b] Range of standard score scale for each section is given in parentheses.

groups are substantially the same as at the start of the year. The two groups score in the 60th to 70th percentile range on the word knowledge and word discrimination sections of the achievement test, but in the 45th to 50th percentile range on the reading section. Their score on the arithmetic section falls near the 80th percentile.

The Elgin grade 1 partial immersion group thus is seen to be performing at par with the regular group on all aspects of English and mathematical skills measured even though their contact with English in the classroom is necessarily reduced and their mathematics is acquired entirely via the medium of French, which means that mathematical concepts are not only acquired to the same degree in French as in English, but also can be transferred by the children from a French to an English setting.

On the French Comprehension Test, the partial immersion pupils obtain a score of 40.2 out of 65 on the Kindergarten level test and of 24.9 on the Grade 1 level test. By the end of grade 1, the amount of exposure to French in the 50% French immersion corresponds to one half-year of total French instruction, and thus to the amount encountered in the Kindergarten total French immersion program in Toronto. It is seen that the score of 40.2 for the Elgin grade 1 group is in fact quite similar to that of 39.6 for the Toronto (Cohort II) immersion kindergarten group given the same test. As for the results on the grade 1 level test, the Elgin partial immersion's score of 24.9 is considerably lower than that for the corresponding Toronto (Cohort I) immersion grade 1 group, which obtains a score of 50.5. However, the 50% partial immersion group has had only one-third the amount of exposure to French that the Toronto group had by the end of grade 1. Still, its performance on the grade 1 level test appears rather low, since it is equivalent to the score of 24.5 reported earlier for regular program pupils in Ottawa, who have received instruction in French-as-a-second-language for 20 to 30 minutes per day in kindergarten and 20 to 40 minutes per day in grade 1, and have thus had substantially less total time exposure to French than the Elgin group (approximately one-third the amount). There is no immediate explanation for this somewhat disconcerting finding.

Elgin Grade 2 (Cohort II)

The partial immersion class in grade 2 consisted of 20 pupils, while the comparison group consisted of a class of 24 pupils in the regular program at Locke Street Public School.

Tests. In the spring 1973 evaluation, the two groups were administered the Otis-Lennon Mental Ability Test (Elementary level) and the Metropolitan Achievement Tests (Primary II Battery, 1958). In addition, the partial immersion group was administered the Grade 1 level of the French Comprehension Test (1973) and of the Test de Rendement en Français described under Toronto Cohort I, grade 1, as well as a second test of French listening comprehension, the IEA Listening Test of French as a Foreign Language (Population I level). This test was designed by the International Association for the Evaluation of Educational Achievement (IEA) for 10-year-old students currently studying French who have had a year or two of minimal exposure to simple French vocabulary and grammatical structure (see Carroll 1975). The items are of a multiple-choice pictorial nature. Test instructions are given in English and the item stimuli, consisting of short sentences, are in French. The test was also administered in the same year to grade 2 immersion pupils in Ottawa (Barik and Swain 1975a), permitting comparisons to be made between the two programs.

Results. As seen in Table 2, there are no differences between the two groups in age and IQ. Both groups score in the vicinity of the 80th percentile on the mental ability test.

On the Metropolitan Achievement Tests, unlike in grade 1 (Cohort III), there is a significant difference ($p < .01$) between the ttwo groups on all English language skills sections except word knowledge, with the comparison group scoring higher than the partial immersion group. The scores of the immersion group range from the 53rd (reading) to the 68th (word knowledge) percentile, while those of the comparison group range from the 74th (word knowledge) to the 90th (spelling) percentile. On the arithmetic subtest there is again no reliable difference between the two groups who score in the vicinity of the 90th percentile.

By the end of grade 2, the Elgin partial immersion group has had the time equivalent of one year of total immersion in French; thus they have been instructed in French for two-thirds the amount of time associated with the Toronto total immersion grade 1 pupils (who had a half-day French program in kindergarten). Consequently, as is to be expected, the Elgin grade 2 partial immersion group scores lower (31.9) on the grade 1 level of the French Comprehension Test than the Toronto total immersion group (50.5). The Elgin group does, however, score higher than pupils in grade 1 or grade 2 regular programs in Ottawa who obtain scores of 2.54 and 22.4, respectively, on the test (Barik and Swain 1975a). Similarly, on the IEA French Listening Test, the Elgin grade partial immersion group scores considerably lower (19.6) than the corresponding Ottawa grade 2 total immersion pupils who have had the equivalent of 1.5 more years of exposure to French and who obtain a score of 31.0 out of 35. (An Ottawa grade 1 immersion class of 18 pupils administered the test scored.[11]) Likewise, on the Test de Rendement en Français, the Elgin partial immersion group scores lower on the grade 1 form of the test than the Toronto total immersion grade 1 group given the same test (9.7 vs. 15.9). The Elgin group's score corresponds to a stanine of 2, indicating a level of performance equivalent to that of from 4 to 10% of native French speakers.

Thus the grade 2 results for the 50% partial French immersion program show lower performance in French relative to the full immersion program.

Elgin Grade 3 (Cohort I)

In 1972-1973, the grade 3 partial French immersion class at Wellington Street Public School consisted of 21 pupils, while the comparison class in the regular grade 3 program at Locke Street Public School consisted of 24 pupils.

Tests. In spring 1973 these two classes were administered the Otis-Lennon Mental Ability Test (Elementary level) and the appropriate level of the Metropolitan Achievement Tests (Elementary Battery, 1958), which in addition to *word knowledge, word discrimination, reading,* and *spelling,* also has a *language* section which tests language *usage* (in which the pupil determines whether underlined words in a sentence are correct or incorrect) and *punctuation and capitalization.* The partial immersion group was also administered the Grade 1 level of the French Comprehension Test (1973) and the IEA French Listening Test (Population I level).

Results. As seen in Table 2, as in the case of the grade 1 and grade 2 samples, there is no reliable difference between the two grade 3 groups in age and IQ. On the mental ability test, the partial immersion group scores at the 83rd percentile and the comparison group at the 75th percentile.

On the achievement test, as with the grade 2 results, the partial immersion group scores lower than the comparison group on most English skills sections. The differences are significant with respect to word knowledge, spelling, punctuation and capitalization, and total language score, and also with respect to language usage when scores are adjusted for age and IQ. The percentile ranks associated with the scores range from 47 (language total) to 75 (spelling) in the case of the partial immersion group, and from 58 (reading) to 93 (spelling) in the case of the comparison group. The partial immersion group, it may be noted, scores as well as the comparison group on the reading subtest. With respect to arithmetic achievement, once again, no reliable differences are found between the two groups. Thus arithmetical concepts continue to be learned as efficiently via French as via English, and can be transferred from one language to the other. It is to be noted that the problem solving and concepts section of the arithmetic subtest requires the reading of verbal problems in English. The two groups rank at about the 65th percentile on that section of the test, while on computation the partial immersion group ranks at the 57th percentile and the comparison group at the 66th.

By the end of grade 3, thus, partial French immersion pupils still lag behind their peers in the regular program with respect to most tasks involving English skills, though, encouragingly, not with respect to reading. However, the partial immersion group continues to perform as well as the regular group on mathematics which is taught to them in French only.

By the end of grade 3, the Elgin partial immersion group has had the equivalent in terms of instruction time in French of 1.5 years of total immersion, thus corresponding to the amount of time associated with the Toronto grade 1 total immersion group. The Elgin grade 3 partial immersion pupils do in fact score relatively the same on the grade 1 form of the French Comprehension Test as the Toronto grade 1 immersion pupils (48.0 vs. 50.5). It would therefore appear on the basis of the test that by the end of grade 3, the partial immersion program is yielding results comparable with total immersion on the basis of a similar degree of exposure to French. Similarly, on the IEA French Listening Test the grade 3 partial immersion group's score of 29.7 out of 35 compares adequately with that of 31.0 obtained by total immersion grade 1 pupils in Ottawa given the same test (Barik and Swain 1975a). One factor contributing to the satisfactory performance of the grade 3 partial immersion group relative to grade 1 immersion pupils may also be the greater maturity of the grade 3 pupils; conceptually, the tests and the tasks may be easier for them than for grade 1 pupils.

Summary of Elgin Study

The results of the evaluation carried out on the 50% partial French immersion program are thus somewhat equivocal. At the end of grade 1, pupils in the partial immersion program, who receive English Language Arts instruction in grade 1, perform similarly to pupils in the regular program with respect to English language skills and also to arithmetic, which they acquire via French. With respect to French, they perform equivalently to kindergarten pupils in the full immersion program who have had the same amount of exposure to French. However, on a test developed for grade 1, they score similarly to pupils in a regular English grade 1 program in Ottawa who have had 20 to 40 minutes per day of instruction in French-as-a-second-language through two years of schooling. In grade 2, with the introduction of French Language Arts into the curriculum, performance in English language skills lags behind that of pupils in the regular program. Performance in arithmetic continues to be on a par with that of pupils in the regular program. In French, unlike in grade 1, grade 2 partial immersion pupils score considerably higher than their peers in a regular grade 2 program involving daily periods of instruction in French-as-a-second-language since kindergarten, but they also score substantially lower than pupils in a grade 1 full immersion program, who have had an additional half-year of exposure to French. By the end of grade 3, the lag of the partial immersion pupils in English language skills relative to pupils in the regular program continues to be evidenced, although reading is at a par with the regular program pupils. Performance in French is also now commensurate with the amount of exposure to the language when compared with pupils in a full immersion program. Mathematical achievement in the partial immersion program continues to be equivalent to that in the regular program.

There thus appears to be both a positive and a negative component to the results with respect to each grade level. The grade 3 results, however, are reasonably encouraging, indicating that the gap in English language skills may be narrowing at least with respect to reading, and that the "French" part of the program is beginning to bear fruit. It may thus be that results in the following grades will be more positive.

Peel Study

The Peel grade 8 partial French immersion program was started in September 1971 at William G. Davis Senior Public School in Brampton, Ontario, with two classes consisting of 55 students who had had one year of prior instruction in French-as-a-second-language in grade 7 (20 minutes per day, increased to 60 minutes per day during the last two months). The curriculum, as described earlier, was 70% in French (French, Mathematics, History, Geography, Science, and Art) and 30% in English. In September 1972, the students entered a grade 9 40% French program (French, History, Geography) and aa new grade 8 cohort entered the program.

Peel Cohort I, Grade 8

The pupils in the grade 8 partial immersion program were informally selected by the school authorities on the basis of above average IQ and general academic ability. To act as a comparison group, pupils with similar characteristics were selected from the regular grade 8 population at Centennial Senior Public School in the same locality. Students in the two groups were matched as closely as possible with respect to age, sex, IQ, and academic achievement. The comparison group consisted of 54 pupils from 5 grade 8 classes, who were combined into two classes for testing purposes. The comparison pupils had had 20 minutes of French per day in grade 7 and continued with this program in grade 8.

Tests. The following tests were administered to the two groups, both at the start (September) and at the end (May-June) of the grade 8 program, providing pre- and postprogram measures, and permitting end-of-year scores to be adjusted for beginning-of-year differences with respect to the same tests through analysis of covariance.

1. IEA Listening Test of French as a Foreign Language, Population I, as described under Elgin Cohort II (grade 2) and which, as stated, is intended characteristically for 10-year-old pupils who have received one or two years of instruction in French as a second language.

2. IEA Reading Test of French as a Foreign Language, Population I, the corresponding reading test, which consists of short sentences illustrated pictorially.

3. IEA Speaking Test of French as a Foreign Language, Population I. This test, forming part of the same battery as the two preceding tests and based on the same considerations, is a speaking test of French which is administered on an individual basis. All recording is on tape. The test contains three sections: *pronunciation, structural control,* and *fluency.* In the *pronunciation* section, the pupil is required to listen to and repeat a number of brief but complete and meaningful sentences. In the *structural control* section, the pupil must answer a series of questions, each question relating to a simple drawing. In the *fluency* section, the pupil is required to describe a single picture in some detail from a choice of two pictures presented to him. A global fluency rating ranging from 0 to 4 is assigned on the basis of the pupil's utterance. There was a procedural difference in the two administrations of the test, students being tested one at a time at the start of the year but in small groups at the end through the facilities of a language laboratory.

4. IEA Science Test, Population I (Booklet I). This test, developed by the IEA in the context of its International Educational Achievement Study, is a general test of Science which deals with different aspects of the subject. Most of the knowledge and understanding tested is not likely to be the result of specific Science teaching but of receptivity to opportunities provided by the environment in general elementary learning situations (see Comber and Keeves 1973). The Population I level test is aimed typically at 10- to 11-year-old students. Lacking access to a more advanced level of the test at the time of testing, that form was used with the Grade 8 samples.

5. IEA Literature Test, Population II (Booklet 8, Forms Y and Z). This is another test in the IEA battery, which is intended for English-speaking pupils of approximately 14 years of age (see Purves 1973). The booklet contains a short story of 85 to 100 lines, followed by a set of multiple-choice questions based on the story and involving not only factual information but also deductive and inferential reasoning. Two forms of the test were administered to both immersion and comparison pupils at the start of grade 8. At the end of grade 8, immersion pupils were again administered both forms, while each comparison class received only one form.

In addition to the above, the following test was administered at the end of grade 8 only:

6. Local High School Diagnostic Test in Mathematics. At the end of grade 8

pupils from all feeder schools to Brampton Centennial Secondary School, to which both immersion and comparison pupils would be going, were administered a multiple-choice mathematics test developed by the High School's Mathematics Department and covering concepts taught in the elementary school Mathematics curriculum. The test is based on a pool of items from several sources and involves computation, problem solving and set theory.

Results. The results are shown in Table 3. As seen, there is no reliable difference between the two groups in age and IQ measure (obtained by the school authorities at the start of grade 7 on the basis of the Canadian Lorge-Thorndike Test of Intelligence).

With respect to all three French tests (listening, reading, and speaking), the partial immersion group scores significantly higher ($p < .001$) than the comparison group on all measures both at the start and at the end of grade 8, with the exception of the beginning-of-year speaking global fluency rating, which shows no significant difference.[12] The beginning-of-year differences may be attributed to the extra training in French which the immersion pupils received during the last two months of grade 7, and also to the fact that pupils choosing to go into the immersion program may be pupils who were "better" in French to begin with; the composition of the immersion group.[13] On both reading and listening tests, the immersion groups obtains near maximum scores at the end of grade 8. On the French Speaking test, it is noted that both groups obtain lower pronunciation scores at the end of the year than at the beginning. The same finding also occurs with the comparison group with respect to global fluency rating. These anomalous results are difficult to explain. The possibility exists that they may be due in part to the procedural differences in the two administrations; the language laboratory setting employed at the end of the year may have permitted some pupils not to take the task as seriously as they did at the start of the year when tested individually under close supervision.

On the IEA Science Test there is no reliable difference between the two groups at the start of the year; however, the comparison group scores significantly higher than the partial immersion group at the end of the year even when scores are adjusted for age, IQ, and beginning-of-year performance on the test ($p = .05$). This finding may indicate that the immersion group suffers a little in comparison with pupils in the regular program with respect to the acquisition of general science concepts which are taught to them in French in grade 8.

Likewise on the IEA Literature Test there is no difference between the two groups at the start of the year; however, at the end of the year, the comparison group scores significantly higher than the partial immersion group on one of the two forms administered (Form Z) on the basis of either unadjusted ($p = .05$) or adjusted ($p < .01$) scores. This last finding may fortuitously result from the fact that the partial immersion group, administered the two forms of the test (in the order Form Y, Form Z) at the end of the year in contrast to the comparison group, each class of which was administered only one form, may have been less motivated for the second form (Z) than the corresponding comparison class.

As for the local Mathematics test, there is no reliable difference between the two groups at the end of the year. Thus being taught Mathematics in French in grade 8 does not have any negative effect on the performance of the immersion pupils relative to that of pupils taught in English.

Summary. To summarize the grade 8 data for Peel Cohort I, then, it is apparent that the partial immersion group is considerably more proficient in all aspects of French achievement at the end of the year than pupils in the regular program receiving instruction in French-as-a-second-language on a regular one period a day basis. The partial immersion group is already more proficient in French than the regular group at the start of the immersion year, presumably because of the additional exposure to French which they received at the end of grade 7 and to a probable self-selection factor, but end-of-year (grade 8) performance is better for the partial immersion group even when scores are adjusted for these beginning-of-year differences. With respect to other academic subjects, the data may be interpreted to reveal a slight negative effect of the partial immersion program on general science concepts attainment and on English literature comprehension skills, though the effect is not very pronounced. Performance in Mathematics, however, is equivalent to that of pupils in the regular program.

Peel Cohort I, Grade 9

In September 1972, the Cohort I samples started grade 9 (first year of high school) at Brampton Centennial Secondary School. Of the previous year's 55 partial immersion pupils, 39 elected to continue with the bilingual program (40% French) in grade 9, which was initiated that year by the Peel County Board of Education. They constituted two grade 9 classes. Of the 54 pupils in the previous year's comparison group, 35 elected to take French as an option in the regular grade 9 program. The evaluation in grade 9 was consequently carried out on the basis of these reduced samples.

Tests. The following tests were administered at the start of grade 9:

1. Pimsleur Language Aptitude Battery. This is a test intended primarily to predict student success in foreign language learning and also to diagnose language learning difficulties. The test consists of six parts, the first two of which are based on the student's grade point average in academic areas other than foreign languages and on his interest in learning a foreign language. The four remaining parts relate to vocabulary and language analysis, which together yield a *verbal ability* score and to sound discrimination and sound-symbol association, which yield an *auditory ability* score.[14]

2. Gates-MacGinitie Reading Tests (Survey E). The purpose of administering this test at the start of grade 9 was to determine whether the English reading skills of the pupils in the bilingual program had been affected by the previous year of partial French immersion. The test consists of three parts: *vocabulary, comprehension,* and *speed and accuracy.*

3. Comprehensive Tests of Basic Skills (Level 4). This battery of tests

measures skills in the areas of Reading, Language, Arithmetic, and Study Skills. Only two of the ten sections in the test battery were administered for purposes of evaluation: the *vocabulary* section, which overlaps with that in test (2) above, and the *study skills* section based on the use of graphic materials, which involves the understanding and use of symbols and legends, perceiving relationships, drawing conclusions, and extending interpretations beyond given data. Different forms of the test were employed at the start and at the end of the year.

4. IEA Listening Test of French as a Foreign Language, Population II. This is a more advanced level of the corresponding Population I level test, and is typically intended for 14-year-old pupils who have had two or three years of regular French instruction. The pupil is presented with a spoken taped text and then asked to answer multiple-choice questions in French based on these texts. Answers at this level are in both picture and printed form. This test was administered at the start of grade 9 to pupils in the bilingual program only.

5. IEA Reading Test of French as a Foreign Language, Population II, which is a more advanced level of the Population I French reading test discussed for grade 8. The items on the test involve sentence completion and questions based on short texts. This test also was administered only to pupils in the bilingual program at the start of grade 9.

At the end of grade 9, tests (3), (4), and (5) above were again administered, this time to both partial immersion and comparison pupils. In addition, two other instruments were given:

6. Test of Useful French Vocabulary. This test, developed in a study affiliated with the Bilingual Education Project, consists of multiple-choice items with a linguistically mixed format (a short French phrase containing the word to be tested, followed by answer choices given in English), thus focusing on key lexical items and eliminating other nonrelevant difficulties. The test contains sample of "useful" French words based on previously published material (Savard and Richards 1970). In addition to the usual frequency criterion, the list uses three other criteria (range, coverage, availability)[15] to get a more representative sample of French vocabulary.

7. Foreign Language Attitude Questionnaire. This instrument was likewise developed in conjunction with the Bilingual Education Project in order to obtain some measure of the students' attitudes to French, French culture, and French-speaking people. The questionnaire presents 60 statements covering a broad range of topics from interest in learning French to ethnocentrism, with which the student is asked to indicate his degree of agreement or disagreement on the basis of a five-point scale (strongly agree—agree—uncertain—disagree—strongly disagree). The questionnaire was based in part on the work of Gardner and Lambert (1972; see also Jakobovits 1970).

Both the Test of Useful French Vocabulary and the Foreign Language Attitude Questionnaire were pilot-tested prior to final use and were found to be reliable instruments.[16]

8. In addition to the above, scores on *local school examinations* were also obtained. Brampton Centennial Secondary School administers local objective-type

examinations in November, March, and June to all students of any one grade level. Scores for grade 9 bilingual program and comparison pupils were thus available in the following subjects: English, Mathematics, Science, History, and Geography. In History and Geography, however, the examinations administered to the two groups were different, the tests for the bilingual program pupils, who took these two subjects in French, being developed specifically for them.

Results. With respect to language aptitude, as can be seen from Table 3, there is no reliable difference between the two groups on total score or on verbal ability score. Interestingly, however, on auditory ability the comparison group scores significantly higher ($p < .05$) than the partial immersion group when scores are adjusted for age and IQ. In terms of population norms, the two groups score at approximately the 65th percentile on total test score. With respect to verbal ability, the groups score in the 45th to 50th percentile range, while on auditory ability they score in the 70th to 75th percentile range.

There is no reliable difference between the two groups on any of the beginning-of-year reading and vocabulary test measures (Gates-MacGinitie Tests and Comprehensive Tests of Basic Skills). Thus the previous year's (grade 8) immersion experience has not prevented pupils in the partial immersion program from keeping up with their peers in English reading ability and performance. In terms of population norms the two groups score approximately in the 70th to 75th percentile range on the vocabulary section of the Gates-MacGinitie Test and in the 75th to 80th percentile range on both the comprehension and the speed and accuracy sections. On the vocabulary section of the CTBS the partial immersion group at the beginning of the year scores at approximately the 75th percentile and the comparison group at the 67th percentile. Likewise there is no end-of-year difference with respect to the English vocabulary measure (variable 11a, Table 3). Thus the grade 9 bilingual program experience does not have any adverse effect on the students' English vocabulary skills. At the end of the year, the immersion group scores at the 80th percentile and the comparison group at the 77th.

The one significant difference between the two groups both at the start and at the end of the year on a measure not related to French is with respect to the study skills section (use of graphic materials) of the CTBS. As seen (variable 11b), the bilingual group scores consistently higher than the comparison group ($p < .01$ at the start of the year, $p < .001$ at the end, with percentile ranks of 75 and 90 for the bilingual group at the start and at the end of grade 9, respectively, and of 55 for the comparison group on both occasions). There is no obvious factor which accounts for the beginning-of-year difference between the two groups on study skills. Anticipating the results for Cohort II, however, it is worth pointing out that there also, the partial immersion group scores significantly higher on the test than the comparison group at the end of grade 8 (equivalent to beginning of grade 9). Some aspects of the partial immersion program in grade 8 may thus contribute to this finding.

On performance in French, the bilingual group, as might be expected, scores significantly higher ($p < .001$) than the comparison group on all three tests administered at the end of the year (variables 12 to 14). The bilingual group in fact scores substantially higher on the two IEA tests at the start of the year than the comparison group does at the end. As for attitudes toward French and French people and culture (variable 15), there is no reliable difference between the two groups, both groups showing a mildly positive attitude, with an average score per statement of 3.6 to 3.7 on a 5-point scale indicating a degree of (positive) attitude falling between "uncertain" (=3) and "agree" (=4).

Finally, with respect to the local school examinations, and considering the average of the students over the three sets of exams given during the year (variable 16), there is no reliable difference between the two groups on any of the exams common to both groups: English, Mathematics, and Science. Similar findings were obtained in relation to each set of exams separately. For the other two subject matters, Geography and History, the sets of exams for the two groups were different, so that the comparison is not valid. However, as seen from the scores, the two groups perform adequately on their respective examinations. The results relating to the local school examinations thus indicate that the grade 9 bilingual program is not harming the students in any way with respect to academic achievement.

Summary. To summarize the findings for Peel Cohort I by the end of grade 9, the pupils in the partial immersion program:

1. Are obviously much ahead of their peers in the regular program with respect to French achievement.

2. Do as well as their peers in the regular program in other areas, and this throughout grade 9. (The slight negative effects noted in grade 8 relative to performance in Science and English literature thus do not seem to persist through grade 9.)

3. Are in every way as competent with respect to English reading skills involving reading vocabulary, comprehension, and speed and accuracy.

4. Show a greater facility in study skills involving the use of graphic materials.

5. Do not differ significantly from their peers in the regular program with respect to degree of positive attitude shown toward French and French culture and people.

Peel Cohort II, Grade 8

Peel Cohort II started grade 8 in September 1972. The partial immersion group at William G. Davis Senior Public School consisted of 54 pupils, constituting two classes, while the comparison group consisted of 60 pupils from 5 classes in the regular grade 8 program at Centennial Senior Public School. Once again, the comparison pupils were combined into two classes for testing purposes. As with Cohort I, an attempt was made by the Peel Board research unit to match pupils in the two groups with respect to age, sex, IQ, and academic ability. (The difference in number between the two groups is due to the fact that some students initially registering for the partial immersion program did not take that option, but the comparison students with whom they had been matched were retained in the testing program.)

Tests. The following tests were administered to the two groups at the start of grade 8:

1. Pimsleur Language Aptitude Battery, as described for Cohort I, grade 9.

2. Comprehensive Tests of Basic Skills (Level 4), already discussed. Only the *vocabulary* section was administered at the start of the year.

3. Canadian Tests of Basic Skills. This test is similar in nature to the preceding test, and was administered by the Peel Board authorities in their own regular testing program. Only the *vocabulary, reading comprehension,* and *mathematics* sections were administered to the two groups.

4. IEA French Reading and French Listening Tests, Population I, as discussed previously.

At the end of grade 8, the two groups were administered the following tests:

1. Comprehensive Tests of Basic Skills. This time both the *vocabulary* test and the *study skills* (use of graphic materials) test were given. A different form was used at the end of the year than at the beginning.

2. Gates-MacGinitie Reading Tests, as discussed under Cohort I, grade 9. Only the *vocabulary* and *comprehension* sections were given. This test was used as an end-of-year replacement for the corresponding sections of the Canadian Tests of Basic Skills.

3. Cooperative Mathematics Test, Arithmetic. This test measures achievement in arithmetic and stresses understanding and application of mathematical principles embodied in arithmetic. The test was administered to the grade 8 pupils at the end of grade 8, in the place of the *mathematics skills* section of the Canadian Tests of Basic Skills.

4. IEA French Reading and French Listening Tests, Population I, as at the start of the year. In addition, the partial immersion group was also administered the Population II level of these tests.

5. Test of Useful French Vocabulary, as discussed under Cohort I, grade 9.

6. Foreign Language Attitude Questionnaire, as discussed previously.[17]

Results. The results are shown in Table 3. Unlike with Cohort I, there is a slight but significant difference ($p < .05$) between the two groups with respect to both age and IQ, with the partial immersion group being slightly younger and having a slightly higher IQ than the comparison group. It would appear that the matching of comparison pupils with partial immersion pupils on the basis of such factors as age and IQ was not quite as consistent with Cohort II as with Cohort I. Both groups again show higher than average IQ scores, reflecting the measure of selection employed by the school authorities in choosing pupils for the partial immersion program (and the matching associated with the comparison group).

The two groups also differ with respect to total language aptitude score, the partial immersion group scoring significantly higher ($p < .01$) than the comparison group. Interestingly, however, there is no difference between the two groups on the verbal ability and auditory ability sections of the test. This means,

Table 3.   Peel Study: Data for Cohorts I and II

	START OF YEAR				END OF YEAR			
	Unadj. $\bar{X}$		Level of significance		Unadj. $\bar{X}$		Level of significance	
	Partial immersion group	Comparison group	Unadj. $\bar{X}$	Adj. $\bar{X}^a$	Immersion group	Comparison group	Unadj. $\bar{X}$	Adj. $\bar{X}^a$
COHORT I, GRADE 8								
1. Age (yrs.)	13.06	13.03	n.s.					
2. IQ (start gr. 7)	118.55	117.90	n.s.					
3. IEA Fr. List. I (mx = 35)	23.00	16.96	.001	.001	31.13	20.06	.001	.001
4. IEA Fr. Read. I (mx = 35)	26.38	22.02	.001	.001	31.64	25.19	.001	.001
5. IEA Fr. Speak. I								
a. Pronun. (mx = 29)	10.26	8.10	.001	.001	9.38	5.69	.001	.001
b. Struct. Con. (mx = 40)	16.92	5.58	.001	.001	27.74	9.94	.001	.001
c. Glob. Fluency (mx = 4)	1.04	1.10	n.s.	n.s.	2.26	0.78	.001	.001
6. IEA Science (mx = 40)	29.87	30.13	n.s.	n.s.	30.88	32.30	.05	.05
7. IEA Lit. Y - Z (mx = 37)	25.80	24.31	n.s.	n.s.	26.09			
b. Form Y (mx = 18)	13.02	12.25	n.s.	n.s.	13.77	14.24	n.s.	n.s.
c. Form Z (mx = 19)	12.78	12.06	n.s.	n.s.	12.32	13.04	.05	.01
8. H.S. Math Test (mx = 62)					35.96	35.32	n.s.	n.s.
COHORT I, GRADE 9								
9. Pimsleur Lang. Apt.								
a. Total (mx = 117)	74.38	73.69	n.s.	n.s.				
b. Verb. Abil. (mx = 39)	19.13	18.74	n.s.	n.s.				
c. Audit. Abil. (mx = 54)	35.72	37.94	n.s.	.05				
10. Gates-McGinitie Read.								
a. Vocab. (mx = 50)	31.03	31.51	n.s.	n.s.				
b. Comprehension (mx = 52)	46.34	45.66	n.s.	n.s.				
c. Speed & Accur. (mx = 36)	21.34	20.17	n.s.	n.s.				

Table 3 (continued)

| | START OF YEAR | | | | END OF YEAR | | | |
| | Unadj. $\bar{X}$ | | Level of significance | | Unadj. $\bar{X}$ | | Level of significance | |
	Partial immersion group	Comparison group	Unadj. $\bar{X}$	Adj. $\bar{X}^a$	Immersion group	Comparison group	Unadj. $\bar{X}$	Adj. $\bar{X}^a$
COHORT I, GRADE 9 (continued)								
11. Comp. Test Basic Skills								
a. Vocab. (mx = 40)	29.87	27.85	n.s.	n.s.	32.95	32.06	n.s.	n.s.
b. Study Sk. (graphs) (mx = 30)	21.08	18.09	.01	.01	24.87	18.85	.001	.001
12. IEA Fr. List. II (mx = 40)	30.86				35.32	19.64	.001	.001
13. IEA Fr. Read. II (mx = 35)	25.49				30.03	14.82	.001	.001
14. Useful Fr. Vocab. (mx = 57)					45.68	31.68	.001	.001
15. For. Lang. Att. Quest. (mx = 5)					3.70	3.63	n.s.	n.s.
16. H.S. Exams (avg of 3) (%)								
a. English					74.49	74.09	n.s.	n.s.
b. Maths					73.92	69.31	n.s.	n.s.
c. Science					70.49	68.66	n.s.	n.s.
d. Geography					(78.97)	(76.49)		
e. History					(79.90)	(70.90)		
COHORT II, GRADE 8								
17. Age (yrs.)	13.05	13.21	.05					
18. IQ (start gr. 7)	115.94	112.12	.05					
19. Pimsleur Lang. Apt.								
a. Total (mx = 117)	75.46	69.00	.001	.01				
b. Verb. Abil. (mx = 39)	17.30	16.42	n.s.	n.s.				
c. Audit. Abil. (mx = 54)	37.06	36.80	n.s.	n.s.				

Table 3 (continued)

| | START OF YEAR | | | | END OF YEAR | | | |
| | Unadj. $\bar{X}$ | | Level of significance | | Unadj. $\bar{X}$ | | Level of significance | |
	Partial immersion group	Comparison group	Unadj. $\bar{X}$	Adj. $\bar{X}^a$	Immersion group	Comparison group	Unadj. $\bar{X}$	Adj. $\bar{X}^a$
COHORT II, GRADE 8 (continued)								
20. Can. Test Basic Skills								
a. Vocab. (mx = 48)	32.10	30.27	n.s.	n.s.				
b. Comprehension (mx = 80)	53.69	48.42	.01	.05				
c. Maths (mx = 41)	19.61	18.14	n.s.	n.s.				
21. Comp. Test Basic Skills								
a. Vocab. (mx = 40)	26.38	25.66	n.s.	n.s.	30.38	29.19	n.s.	n.s.
b. Study Sk. (graphs) (mx = 30)					20.83	16.00	.001	.001
22. Gates-McGinitie Read.								
a. Vocab. (mx = 50)					31.02	40.94	n.s.	n.s.
b. Comprehension (mx = 52)					44.60	29.69	.01	n.s.
23. Coop. Arith. (mx = 50)					34.94	19.89	.001	.001
24. IEA Fr. List I (mx = 35)	22.68	15.95	.001	.001	32.78	22.20	.001	.001
25. IEA Fr. Read I (mx = 35)	26.28	19.81	.001	.001	32.64	21.51	.001	.001
26. Useful Fr. Vocab. (mx = 57)					42.68		.001	.001
27. For. Lang. Att. Quest. (mx = 5)					3.62	3.51	n.s.	n.s.
28. IEA Fr. List II (mx = 40)					30.49			
29. IEA Fr. Read II (mx = 35)					25.00			

[a] Adjusted for age and IQ (and total language aptitude score for Cohort II French measures).

[b] Adjusted for age, IQ, and start-of-year score (or equivalent measure) where applicable (and total language aptitude score for Cohort II French measures).

[c] Different exams for the two groups.

consequently, that the overall difference on the test is due primarily to either one or both of the other two components of the total test score which relate to the grade point average of the pupils in academic areas other than foreign languages and to their expressed interest in learning a foreign language, which in effect are not direct measures of language aptitude as such. Separate scores for these two components are not available. However, since the groups do seem to differ slightly intellectually, this should be reflected in the grade point averages. It may also be anticipated that given the very nature of the partial immersion program, pupils in the partial immersion group would express a greater interest in learning a foreign language than pupils in the comparison group. These factors would affect the total Pimsleur score of the pupils, resulting in the findings observed.

In terms of population norms the partial immersion group scores at the 87th percentile rank on total score and the comparison group at the 76th percentile. On verbal ability, the figures are 56th and 50th percentile for partial immersion group and comparison groups, respectively, while on auditory ability both groups score in the 70th to 75th percentile range. On total score, Cohort II thus scores reasonably higher than Cohort I, which was situated at approximately the 65th percentile in the case of both groups (at the beginning of grade 9).

With respect to English skills, there is no reliable difference between the two groups on any of the vocabulary measures obtained either at the start or at the end of the year (variables 20a to 22a). The groups score in the 65th to 75th percentile range at the start of the year and in the 75th to 80th percentile range at the end, with slight variations depending upon the test. In reading comprehension, however, the partial immersion group scores significantly higher than the comparison group at the start of the year (variable 20b) and again at the end (variable 22b), though not, in the latter case, when scores are adjusted for age, IQ, and beginning-of-year score. In terms of norms, the partial immersion group scores in the 70th to 75th percentile range on both occasions, and the comparison group in the vicinity of the 60th percentile.

In Mathematics there is no reliable difference between the two groups at the start of the year (variable 20c) but on the end-of-year test (variable 23) the partial immersion group scores significantly higher ($p < .001$) than the comparison group, even on the basis of adjusted scores ($p = .001$). Thus being taught Mathematics in French in grade 8 has obviously not negatively affected the level of achievement of partial immersion pupils in that subject. In terms of norms, the partial immersion group scores at the 60th percentile and the comparison group at the 50th percentile at the start of the year on the basis of Canadian norms, while at the end of the year the corresponding figures are in the vicinity of the 75th and 59th percentile, respectively, on the basis of American norms.

The partial immersion group also scores significantly higher ($p < .001$) than the comparison group on the study skills test (use of graphic materials) administered at the end of the year (variable 21b). The partial immersion group scores at the 75th percentile and the comparison group at about the 50th, figures which are comparable to those for Cohort I at the start of grade 9.

As for performance in French, as might be expected, the partial immersion group scores significantly higher ($p < .001$) than the comparison group on all measures, at both the start and the end of the year (variables 24 to 26) even when scores are adjusted for age, IQ, language, aptitude, and beginning-of-year score where applicable. As in the case of Cohort I, the beginning-of-year scores of the partial immersion group are in fact superior to the end-of-year scores of the comparison group, emphasizing the initial difference in the two groups with respect to this factor.

It is interesting to note that on the Test of Useful French Vocabulary the Cohort II partial immersion group's score at the end of grade 8 (42.7) is almost equal to that of Cohort I partial immersion group's score at the end of grade 9 (45.7), indicating that much of the "useful" vocabulary is acquired in the course of the first year of the partial immersion program. With the comparison groups, however, the score of Cohort II at the end of grade 8 (21.5) is quite a bit lower than that of Cohort I at the end of grade 9 (31.7), implying that in the regular program of French instruction the acquisition of "useful" vocabulary is more progressive.

On the IEA Population II level tests (variables 28, 29) the Cohort II partial immersion group at the end of grade 8 obtains scores which are quite similar to those of the corresponding Cohort I group at the beginning of grade 9 (variables 12, 13) and considerably higher than those of Cohort I's comparison group at the end of grade 9.

Finally, with respect to the attitudinal measure obtained at the end of grade 8 (variable 27), as in the case of Cohort I, there is no reliable difference between the two groups in degree of (positive) attitude toward French and French culture and people. The average score per attitudinal statement of 3.5 to 3.6 exhibited by the two groups is similar to that obtained with the Cohort I groups, and shows a mild degree of positive attitude.

Summary. To summarize the data for Cohort II in grade 8, it is evident that by the end of the year the pupils in the partial immersion program are more proficient in French than pupils in the regular program, even when adjustment is made for initial differences between the two groups in French achievement and in other determining factors such as IQ and language aptitude. There is no difference between the two groups in English vocabulary skills either at the start or at the end of the year. Over the year, the partial immersion group maintains its superiority over the comparison group with respect to English reading comprehension (though the two groups do not differ in end-of-year performance if scores are adjusted for age, IQ, and beginning-of-year score), and performs significantly better in mathematics at the end of the year even though the subject is taught to them in French during the year. The partial immersion group also shows a greater facility in study skills relating to the use of graphic materials. Both groups reveal the same degree of moderately positive attitude toward French and French culture and people.

The findings reviewed above for Cohorts I (grades 8 and 9) and II (grade 8) thus show a generally positive picture with respect to the partial immersion program being followed by the Peel County Board of Education. Two basic questions were asked of the evaluation by the Board: (1) Do students in a French (partial) immersion program become markedly more proficient in French language skills than similar students not participating in such a program? (2) Are students who are receiving a large portion of their school instruction in French able to keep up in major academic subject areas (other than French) with their fellow students who are not in an immersion program? The answer would appear to be an unequivocal "Yes" in both instances.[18]

CONCLUDING COMMENT

All three types of programs considered by the Bilingual Education Project and reviewed above—the early grade programs involving either full immersion (Toronto study) or partial immersion (Elgin study), or the later grade partial immersion program (Peel study) thus present generally favorable results, with respect to both French achievement and performance in other subject areas. The one yielding the more equivocal results to date would seem to be the partial immersion program followed by the Elgin Board of Education, but a more prolonged evaluation of the program is necessary to assess its strengths and weaknesses adequately. It is clear, however, that all three programs reviewed above, as is the case with similar programs elsewhere, offer a viable approach to bilingual education in Canada.[19]

NOTES

1. The order of the authors was determined by the toss of a coin.

2. We wish to thank all those who took the time to respond to our search for information. We also wish to thank Grace Lake, who spent a great deal of time reading and organizing the incoming information, and without whose help this paper might never have been written.

3. The three studies reported in detail here (Toronto Study, Elgin Study, and Peel Study) have been supported in part by two Grants in Aid of Educational Research from the Ministry of Education of the Province of Ontario.

A large-scale French immersion program similar to the one in Toronto and one grade level ahead of it is also operating in a number of public schools in Ottawa. That program is being evaluated by the Bilingual Education Project but is not discussed here, since it has been reported elsewhere (Barik and Swain 1975a, Swain and Barik 1976a).

4. The formula has since been revised and English instruction is now delayed until grade 3, where it is given for one hour per day.

A few other schools in the Toronto area have since started early total French immersion classes, but they are not being evaluated by the Bilingual Education Project.

5. These conditions were dictated by administrative considerations. Since September 1973, the French portion of the program at grades 3 and 4 levels is being taught by a native French speaker.

6. Two levels of the test are now available commercially, one intended for pupils in a kindergarten immersion program (Barik 1976) and one for grade 1 pupils (Barik 1975).

7. Mean scores on any one test or subtest have been calculated on the basis of all available

data. Since some pupils missed some sections of the tests, there is a slight difference between the total MRT and SESAT scores in Table 3 and the sum of respective subtests. The same applies in relation to other sets of data discussed subsequently.

8. The Bilingual Education Project is indebted to the Commission des Ecoles Catholiques de Montréal (Bureau de l'Evaluation) and the Ministère de l'Education du Québec for permission to use their tests. Thanks are also expressed to the International Association for the Evaluation of Educational Achievement (IEA), whose tests were employed in the Elgin and Peel studies.

9. It is of course quite possible—and probable—that some informal instruction in English reading occurs at home in the case of some pupils enrolled in the immersion program, although this is discouraged by the school.

10. It would not have been practical to administer a group test to kindergarten pupils at an earlier date. It may be assumed that the influence of the program on test performance will have been minimal at the time of testing.

   If the immersion program were to have an effect on IQ, the use of the end-of-year IQ measure as a covariate, as is done in the analyses reported, might be questioned, though arguments can nevertheless be made for using it in this fashion under such circumstances. However, as discussed below, there is no evidence of such an effect.

11. The relatively slight difference between the Ottawa grade 1 and grade 2 scores is no doubt due in part to a "ceiling effect," since both groups obtain near maximum scores.

12. The end-of-year results in Table 2 are based on scores adjusted for age, IQ, and corresponding beginning-of-year score. The results do not change when only beginning-of-year score is taken as a covariate.

   Similarly, with respect to measures of French performance, adding the language aptitude score obtained at the start of grade 9 (see below) as a covariate does not affect the grade 8 or grade 9 results of Cohort I.

13. The initial difference in the two groups on French performance is underlined by the fact that on all French measures, the partial immersion group obtains a higher score at the start of grade 8 than does the comparison group at the end of grade 8 (though, in one instance, with respect to speaking global fluency measure, the comparison group's beginning-of-year score is in fact equivalent to the partial immersion group's score). Similar findings are noted in grade 9 and also with Cohort II.

14. The test should preferably have been given at the start of the immersion program in grade 8 rather than at the start of grade 9 so as to provide a measure of language aptitude before the immersion program. The test was given at the start of grade 8 to Cohort II.

15. *Range* is defined as the number of different texts where the word is found. *Availability* is the frequency of a word within a given semantic field. *Coverage* is the power of a word to replace or define other words.

16. The two instruments were developed primarily by T. Tuong.

17. For administrative reasons, the IEA French Speaking Test and IEA Literature and Science tests, administered to Cohort I in grade 8, were not included in the testing program for Cohort II. This decision, taken prior to the detailed analysis of the Cohort I data, was unfortunate, since, as was seen, these tests were of some significance in the Cohort I grade 8 results.

18. One factor to keep in mind in the evaluation of the Peel immersion program is that to date the students in the program have constituted a highly selective group with respect to IQ,

general academic ability, and motivation. There is evidence from similar programs, however, that this restriction can be relaxed somewhat (Protestant School Board of Greater Montreal 1973). An analysis of the Peel Cohort I data in relation to students scoring in the top third and bottom third with respect to IQ (average IQ: 127.6 vs. 109.8) fails to reveal any critical program (partial immersion vs. regular) by IQ (high vs. low) interaction effects.

19. Since the writing of this report further evaluations of the studies discussed have been carried out. For more details of the above findings and more recent research, see for Toronto study: Barik and Swain 1975b, 1976a, 1976b; for Elgin study: Barik and Swain 1974, 1976c; for Peel study: Barik and Swain 1976d; Barik, Swain, and Gaudino 1976; for Ottawa study mentioned above (note 3): Barik and Swain 1975a, 1977; Swain 1975; Swain and Barik 1976b, 1976c.

APPENDIX: LIST OF TESTS EMPLOYED IN
BILINGUAL EDUCATION PROJECT EVALUATION

Canadian Tests of Basic Skills, Form 2. Toronto: Thomas Nelson & Sons (Canada) Ltd., 1968.

Canadian Lorge-Thorndike Intelligence Tests. Form I (Lorge, I., R. L. Thorndike, and E. Haten) Toronto: Thomas Nelson & Sons (Canada) Ltd., 1967.

Clymer-Barrett Prereading Battery, Form A (Clymer, T., and T. C. Barrett). Princeton, N.J.: Personnel Press Inc., 1967.

Comprehensive Tests of Basic Skills, Level 4 (Forms Q and R). Monterey, Calif.: CTB/McGraw-Hill, 1968.

Cooperative Mathematics Test, Arithmetic, Form A. Princeton, N.J.: Educational Testing Service, 1962.

Foreign Language Attitude Questionnaire. Toronto: Bilingual Education Project, The Ontario Institute for Studies in Education, 1973.

French Comprehension Test (Experimental edition). Toronto: Bilingual Education Project, The Ontario Institute for Studies in Education, 1971, 1972, 1973 (Kindergarten Level, Grade 1 Level).

Gates-MacGinitie Reading Tests, Survey E, Form 3. (Gates, A. I., and W. H. MacGinitie). New York: Teachers College Press, Columbia University, 1964.

IEA French Tests. In *French as a Foreign Language, Phase II, Stage 3*. Stockholm: International Association for the Evaluation of Educational Achievement, 1970.
    a. French Listening Test, Populations I and II.
    b. French Reading Test, Populations I and II.
    c. French Speaking Test, Population I.

IEA Literature Test, Population II (Booklet 8, Forms Y and Z). International Educational Achievement Study. New York: The Psychological Corporation, 1969.

IEA Science Test, Population I (Booklet 1). International Educational Achievement Study. New York: The Psychological Corporation, 1969.

Metropolitan Achievement Tests (Durost, W. N., H. H. Bixler, G. H. Hildreth, K. W. Lund, and J. W. Wrightstone). New York: Harcourt, Brace & World, Inc., 1958.
    a. Primary I Battery, Form A (Grade 1).
    b. Primary II Battery, Form A (Grade 2).
    c. Elementary Battery, Form A (Grade 3).

Metropolitan Achievement Tests, Primer, Form F (Durost, W. N., H. H. Bixler, J. W. Wrightstone, G. A. Prescott, and I. H. Barlow). New York: Harcourt, Brace, Jovanovich, Inc., 1971.

Metropolitan Readiness Tests, Form A (Hildreth, G. H., N. L. Griffiths, and M. E. McGauvran). New York: Harcourt, Brace & World, Inc., 1964.

Otis-Lennon Mental Ability Tests (Otis, A. S., and R. T. Lennon). New York: Harcourt, Brace & World, Inc., 1967.
    a. Primary I Level, Form J (Kindergarten).
    b. Elementary I Level, Form J (Grades 1, 2, 3).

Pimsleur Language Aptitude Battery, Form S (Pimsleur, P.). New York: Harcourt, Brace & World, Inc., 1966.

Stanford Early School Achievement Test, Level I (Madden, R., and E. F. Gardner). New York: Harcourt, Brace, Jovanovich, Inc., 1969.

Test de Rendement en Français. Montreal: La Commission des Ecoles Catholiques de Montréal.
    a. Grade 1 test—1971-72 edition.
    b. Grade 2 test—1972-73 edition.

Test de Rendement en Mathématiques. Montreal: La Commission des Ecoles Catholiques de Montréal.
    a. Grade 1 test–1971-72 edition.
    b. Grade 2 test–1972-73 edition.
Test of Useful French Vocabulary. Toronto: Bilingual Education Project, The Ontario Institute for Studies in Education, 1973.

III

Bilingualism

in Contemporary China:

The Coexistence of Oral Diversity

and Written Uniformity

Beverly Hong Fincher

INTRODUCTION

Particularly since the intense 1966-1968 phase of the Cultural Revolution, the People's Republic of China has approached education as, like revolution, an "unending" process. The provision of classrooms for all school age children has diminished neither the emphasis on preschool and postgraduate study nor preoccupation with the relevance of school curricula to everyday life and to larger social and political issues. In a sense, the Chinese programs of a sort Americans usually call "continuing education" (i.e., on-the-job or after-hours study) set the tone for all educational programs.

While enormous self-consciousness about the school's social context pervades the educational system, bilingualism is accepted as an integral part of that social context. History has left bilingualism[1] a central feature of Chinese life. Such policy debate as the issue provokes in China turns (in contrast, for example, to the United States) to the means for promoting knowledge of the common national language (putong hua) and related reforms of the writing system instrumental to the increase in bilingualism that is taken for granted by all. Bilingualism (including, of course, multilingualism generally) has been for centuries an accepted part of the life of a huge part of China's many hundred million population. Nor has bilingualism (in contrast to most of the West) carried with it either any particular social stigma or social cachet. The patterns of migration among speakers of Chinese have been too complex and combined for too long with continuous and self-conscious cultural and political unity for too much of the population for the phenomenon to be more than peripherally associated with social status. The unilingualism of even the elite Manchu conquerors and rulers of China in the last dynasty (1644-1911) began to give way to the bilingualism characteristic of Manchus later in the dynasty with the existing proficiency of some early Manchu emperors in Chinese. The massive expansion southward and westward within and beyond China's border of Chinese speakers during the 19th Century led—as in other earlier centuries—to the kind of mixing of the population which facilitated bilingualism. The expansion of modern communications throughout the 20th Century has steadily increased bilingualism in China despite long periods of political fragmentation during the first half of the century. With the establishment of political unity under the People's Republic in 1949, certain social policies have further increased the opportunities for and necessity of bilingualism.[2]

Of the approximately 800 million population of the People's Republic of China, perhaps 500 million speak Mandarin Chinese as a first language. By now a clear majority of the remaining 300 million Han speak Mandarin as a second language. They do so in response to national language policies as well as to historical forces which also protect their native dialects. All signs suggest that China will in the foreseeable future have very few unilinguals among the 300 million who do not speak Mandarin as a first language. Though the other 500 million who speak Mandarin (or, more precisely, a dialect of Mandarin) as a first language are likely to remain unilingual, large numbers of them are being required by their work situations as well as policy to learn other dialects. Programs beginning in the early sixties and greatly expanded since 1968 have required millions of young people from urban areas to resettle in the countryside, often at great distances. Premier Chou told visitors that Chairman Mao's directive requiring all cadres to learn Mandarin (puton hua) had been complemented by the study of different dialects in their area of assignment by cadres from Mandarin speaking areas.

Considering both the linguistic diversity of China and (see below) the procedures for promoting knowledge of Mandarin, it becomes conceivable that an absolute majority of China's huge population may eventually be bilingual. There are two varieties of bilingualism. Distinct ethnic "minorities" comprise only some 6% or 50 million of China's population. Their languages, native primarily to the northwest and certain southwest border districts, differ structurally[3] from those of the overwhelming "Han majority" to a degree sufficient to win common acceptance in the literature as independent languages. The Han Chinese of the area within the Great Wall and in the northeast speak five varieties[4] of Chinese usually designated in the literature as "dialects." Mandarin, as noted before, is the majority variety, spoken by some 500 million of the inhabitants of north and central China. Among the south and southeastern Chinese we find: the Yüe dialects, with Cantonese the best known example, spoken primarily in Kwangtun province; the Wu dialects, of which Shanghaiese is the most prominent example, concentrated in the lower Yangtse valley; the Min or Fukien dialects, including Southern Min characteristic of the area from Amoy south and of the great majority of Taiwan's inhabitants; Kan-Hakka dialects, the former spoken in parts of Hunan and Kiangsi, the latter by communities (usually immigrants to these areas who arrived some centuries later from the north than did the rest of their populations) scattered primarily in Kiangsi, Kwangtung, and Taiwan; the Hsiang group of Hunan, in central China.

The Han dialects have greatest varieties in pronunciation and less important differences in daily vocabulary.[5] Grammar or syntactic structure tends to be the same throughout. In this article we have deliberately rejected use of the term "bidialectism." In the first place, each of the major Han languages—including Mandarin—are themselves composed of many distinct dialects. More importantly, *debate about whether the major varieties of Han Chinese might best be called "languages" or "dialects" has diverted scholars to unnecessarily formal criteria and has interested them in mechanical laboratory tests rather than the social context of language and the learning situations central to the interest of those who work on the phenomenon of bilingualism,[6] a situation we will return to below.* First, however, it is necessary to explore more elaborately the sociolinguistic environment in which Chinese bilingualism appears, noting the diversity of oral forms of the Chinese language behind the uniformity characteristic of written Chinese. As we shall see, language policy—including acceptance of bilingualism—in China is by and large subsumed by a broader sociopolitical policy aimed at increasing the general population's facility first in oral and secondly (but still very importantly) in written self-expression.

ON FLUENCY: NOURISHING AN ARTICULATE POPULACE IN THE NEW ORAL TRADITION

International politics and American policies changed in the early 1970s in a manner that allowed, rather suddenly, an extraordinary increase in the number of outside visitors to the People's Republic of China by contrast to all but a few years of the 1950s. Sometimes even among foreign visitors who know little or no Chinese, and commonly among returning or first-time visitors who are speakers of one or more Chinese dialects, a strong impression has developed: the existence of what seems to outsiders a very high percentage of extraordinarily fluent[7, 8] or articulate speakers and talkers from all walks of life in the People's Republic. The phenomenon (like that of lexical changes) is no doubt more striking because of the absolute and fully two-decades-long isolation of Taiwan or Overseas Chinese Communities from the 800 million members of the Chinese speech community who live in the People's Republic.

Typical examples of fluency observed during a 1971 visit are the leader of a commune in Shun-te County in Kwangtun Province, a man in his middle thirties. Though without more than a primary school education, he drew naturally and rapidly, in Mandarin, from a stock of data about his operation in a way reminiscent of well-briefed American cabinet officers appearing before Congressional committees as well as of the earthy peasant which he in fact still was. Another is a teenage girl, with two years of junior high school though several years of job experience, working as a chemist in a Fu Shan silicon factory whose mastery of her complex tasks was matched only by her ability to talk fluently and lucidly about them as well as about her personal background.

Since it was first raised in articles published soon after the autumn 1971 start of visits by, in particular, Chinese-Americans, the observation has been widely and easily confirmed.[9]

The poise and articulateness of elementary or nursery school children who perform for or talk with visitors to their schools has been positively unnerving for some foreign educators.[10] Such gifts—not at all unusual among Chinese children—have been the making of a handful of child stars of TV talk shows or commercials—like Mason Reece—in North America, where they are regarded as very rare. Indeed sociolinguists and social psychologists have been so concerned with ordinary inarticulateness of urban children and youth in America as to speculate both about the contrasting gifts for story telling among young but rural southern blacks and about the possibility deliberately overstated, but seriously argued, that some urban ghetto children have "no language" at all.[11]

The phenomenon has even been confirmed and discussed in the anticommunist official Kuo Min Tang (Nationalistic Party) newspaper in Taiwan, the *Central Daily News*. Students of the College of Sciences of the National Taiwan University in the spring of 1974 invited T'ang Chu-kuo, a sometime resident of the People's Republic who left the People's Republic for Taiwan, to speak about "why people who come out of the Mainland are such fluent speakers." Recounting his talk in the column he has written for the *Central Daily News*, T'ang agreed that such fluency was common and attributed it to training and experience at speaking deliberately emphasized in the People's Republic. Indeed, he argued that a phenomenon of "talk well and become an official"[12] (Shuo er iu ze shi) had replaced the Confucian injunction to "learn well and become an official" (Xue er iu ze shi).

T'ang, if not necessarily his audience, thought it self-evident that verbal "showing off" (chu fengtou) was distasteful to those nurtured in Confucian traditions (now under such vocal attack in the People's Republic), applauding a subdued or passive manner among the populace. In hundreds of Chinese and Asian-American solidarity organizations which have become increasingly vocal in North America and Hong Kong in recent years, such fluency is cultivated as well as honored, a change inspired partly by the new international situation of the People's Republic combined with the influence of Black Power and other ethnic movements in the United States.

To a large degree, such organizations fueled the demands which, after the case was brought from San Francisco, recently won requirement by the United States Supreme Court of instruction in Chinese for Chinese-American students.

In fact, the ideal of subdued silence was but one ideal (although a dominant one) of an elite literary tradition. It was somewhat inconsistent even with elite oral tradition, not to mention the popular oral tradition.[13] To a degree, the promotion of fluency in the New China can be regarded as the successor to the oral if not a dominant Confucian literary tradition of the Old China.

DIVERSITY WITHIN THE ORAL TRADITION

Bilingual education in China—primarily in Mandarin as a second, albeit national, language—is closely intertwined with education for fluency in the first language or dialect. Within the family itself, increasing opportunities for intermarriage of parents from different dialect groups has led to a corresponding rise in bilingualism among children as well as parents. Beyond the family, the same socializing institutions and practices which facilitate frequent and intense veral interaction in the first language also open avenues to bilingualism—at least to the extent that bilingualism is consistent with the society's prior value of fluency. These institutions sustain in the People's Republic a much higher degree of social solidarity than could be comprehended in previous visions of national unity. They multiply the situations in which people are encouraged to "speak up" or "speak out" to each other, making use of the fact that language is the primary mode of, if not synonymous with, social communication. Fluency—with allowances for personality differences—becomes a measure of the quality of as well[14] as means of participation by the individual in community life.

China's traditional cultural unity was associated much more with uniformity of written than with the diffusion of a single spoken language. Reformulation of the conviction of cultural unity into the goal of national unity inevitably led, with the rise of nationalism in the 20th Century, to promotion of a national language. This campaign has been continued since 1949 with a new emphasis on the social depth of the commitment to national unity, an emphasis that is on national solidarity.

The gradual combination of the goals of national unity and social solidarity can be traced in part in the terms used for the national language. The dialect of the Peking area which provides the original national norms has now become "common language" (Putong Hua) rather than national language (Guo Yu). This represents change in the social as well as geographic reach of Peking speech, which in imperial times (until the turn of the century) was called Official Speech (Guan Hua). The common English designation, Mandarin, translates literally this earlier term, though at the cost frequently of a mistaken impression that only officials used it; in fact, of course, it was used by commoners in the Peking area and much of the north—though not without pronounced local dialect variations. In early modern or premodern China, if there was an elite official social dialect it was, rather, Manchu, the language of ruler-conquerors of the last dynasty.

The strongest evidence for the nationalization of speech noted on recent trips is the lessening of "typical" accents among, for example, older Cantonese, Fukienese, or Shanghai speakers of Mandarin (or "common speech"), and the near elimination of such "typical" accents among those under about 25 years of age. Mandarin speakers have always laughed, often with more than a hint of arrogance, at the accents of speakers from other areas. There are still, of course, great regional variations in accents, but the Mandarin spoken outside the north is now much further away from home dialects.

Radio broadcasts on a centralized network system no doubt have made the largest contribution to this change in China as to similar developments in most other countries of the world. This is not to say that there has been any special effort to make out of these broadcasts a carefully modeled example for Mandarin speakers. To take an extreme example of a natural evolution of national speech through greater communication rather than deliberate policy, Taipei radio's Mandarin, apart from the question of usages, differs from Peking radio's Mandarin more in rhythm than in pronunciation.

Also important are professional theatrical productions, live or filmed, for nationwide mass audiences. The theatrical productions of stories drawn from the modern revolution (rather than from distant history or legend) attract enthusiastic audiences everywhere of people mostly in working clothes. The visitor frequently hears people singing the songs as they walk in the streets or sit on buses, and sees posters from the ballet or opera in their homes.

Radio broadcasts and films involve the least amount of audience participation, and remain, therefore, in their original and most widely spread Mandarin versions primarily contributors to the passive knowledge of Mandarin. In dialect areas, however, it is possible to receive both Mandarin and dialect broadcasts of essentially the same material. This is especially true of news and political commentary, the abundance of which—presented bilingually—makes ideal material for bilingual education. More technical instructional material, such as advice or instructions on farming techniques suited to local conditions, also appears in the local dialect and in Mandarin.

Programming for the theater or films provides the most striking examples of de facto bilingual education. The Cultural Revolution saw the establishment of a canon of model revolutionary plays, opera, and ballet (often involving mixtures of speech, song, and dance) produced by national companies in Peking. Regional versions of performances from this canon—on stage or filmed—include dialect performances. The Cantonese version of one of the operas from the original eight in the vanon, Shajia Bang, was being produced in Canton during late 1971. The opera preserved, in translation, the libretto of the original production but was otherwise completely transformed from the Peking version into the very different Cantonese style of Opera. Shanghaiese versions of the same opera were also in production at the same time.

A film of the Cantonese version of the Shajia Bang appears among the advertisements of a wide variety of entertainments in the nationally distributed *Peoples Daily* on and about Jan. 21, 1974—the lunar New Year, a traditional time for all types of cultural activities and entertainment. There, as in the same or similar cases elsewhere of adaptations to local styles of theatrical as well as local dialects, the production is described as a "transplant into Cantonese" (Yizhi de Yueju) not as a "translation."[15]

The adjustment of the Peking to Cantonese operatic forms described above has taken place in a realm, the production of nationally distributed films, more easily subject (like radio broadcasts) to the guidance of national policy. The school system, particularly at the lower levels, is more at the mercy of local resources: the preferred language of instruction is Mandarin, but realization of this ideal is still sometimes limited by the shortage of Mandarin-speaking teachers.

Such teachers are ordinarily bilinguals, an asset in dealing with pressures to continue even classroom use of local dialects: at a November 1963 Conference on language reform,[16] complaints were heard about a Kwangtung Commune high school which asked its newly graduated Mandarin-speaking teacher (an overseas Chinese educated in China) to use the local dialect, Cantonese, rather than Mandarin because the students could not understand him well.

The "quality" of Mandarin can obviously vary with both local policy and local conditions. Numerous Fukien visitors from Southeast Asia anxiously tell travelers that Mandarin is even more widespread in their province than in Kwangtung, and of high quality too (an interesting example of nationalism in them as well as in their fellow provincials at home). Chou P'ei-yuan, Peking University President, noted that Fukien's mountain areas had an unusually good record in the spread of Mandarin simply because of greater determination on the part of the authorities or the masses in the area. On the other hand, the leader of a Chekiang tea commune not only did not speak Mandarin, but spoke a variety of Shanghaiese which even a native dialect speaker had enormous difficulty in following. It is possible that in the case of Fukien, the very distance of the native dialect from Mandarin has increased the incentives to learn the latter as a second language, while the relative proximity of Chekiang Shanghaiese to Mandarin reduced incentives. A passive knowledge of Mandarin would be easy to come by in the latter area, reducing interest in a truly active knowledge.

Subject to the availability of qualified and effective teachers, the elementary and higher schools use Mandarin. Children learn to read in Mandarin from texts with the Pinyin romanization added beside new characters, the principal current use, in fact, of romanization in the People's Republic. Taiwan likewise uses zhuyin fuhao, another form of romanization similar to the Japanese phonetic kana system. Recent foreign visitors have at times commented on the apparent heavy reliance in Chinese classrooms on reading aloud or recitations from memory and similar "traditional" pedagogic techniques. Few have realized that, apart from the impact the appearance of previously rare overseas visitors may have on performance during such moments, they have often been visiting what may be language classes. The classroom use of Mandarin by young students whose first language is another dialect is likely in fact to make most of their early education language education. Language teachers almost universally accept the necessity of memorization and recitation, and a huge number of teachers in China's elementary schools are in effect language teachers—however they may regard themselves.

Radio broadcasts, cultural performances (on stage, film, or increasingly, television), and classroom study all educate the Chinese population—responsive to the differing needs and tastes of their dialect audiences or students—toward increasingly common and accomplished bilingualism. They are part of networks of media, cultural, and educational organizations contributing to and maintaining the national solidarity which the spread of a national language measures.

At the same time, the persistence of proficiency in the nonnational dialects betrays sensitivity to a companion goal of social solidarity. For the visitor to China participating in group sessions in Peking—for example, banquets—it is always a great asset to be able to pass as a native speaker of Cantonese and Amoy as well as of Mandarin. And speakers of Mandarin as a second language are still happy to find visitors who can understand and use their home dialects. But what they enjoy with each other is a common similarity in being able to communicate with each other in both dialects or languages. The spread of Mandarin in a bilingual setting liberates people to enjoy their own dialects with no trace of uneasiness or inferiority.

Amateur—and some nearly semiprofessional—stage productions bring to schoolchild or worker performers (along with a knowledge of the Mandarin of original models) some of the poise and performance skills which find outlet in local dialect theater. But the most distinctive and pervasive occasions for self-expression provided individual Chinese in the People's Republic are the small "study groups" (xue-xi).

"Study sessions" are organized for small groups of usually 10 or 20 based on basic work, school, or residential units. They are composed of individuals whom the Chinese see most in their daily life next to family members. Ordinarily they meet regularly a couple of times a week to discuss problems of local life and work and to relate them to the larger national and social issues commonly through discussion of Mao's work or recent party directives. As in a well-run seminar or small classroom, every member is encouraged and required to participate actively in the discussions, with allowances for personality differences.[17] If classrooms have sometimes been criticized by recent visitors for giving students too passive a learning role, study groups have been faulted for the opposite trait: not allowing their members much opportunity to sit back passively.

Study sessions appear to be conducted in the language or dialect with which the members of the group are most comfortable. But this setting is also used for the promotion of the common language at times, and they are supremely well suited for the practice in discussing one's work and personal situation and relating them to general social and political questions which produces the oral fluency characteristic of so many Chinese in the new China.

So also the institution of the storytelling session, which persists from traditional China in all dialects and which has been enriched by some new practices. Chief among the latter are the "remember bitternesses and think of sweetnesses" sessions conducted by old people in neighborhoods and villages throughout China, sometimes at schools or factories, sometimes in study groups, sometimes informally. Old people are constantly brought into contact with children in China—and are encouraged to remind youth of the difficulties of times past as they contemplate the problems of the present in a "still very poor" nation and society. The stories, which old people delight in repeating and elaborating for their overseas guests, include much pride in surviving or transcending bitter situations and often humor in the form of self-mocking local aphorisms.

China has long had a rich oral tradition, with both elite and popular forms. There is occasional evidence, particularly in the New Year holiday season, of the persistence even of recitations from or retellings, if not of the Confucian Classics, of other "old books."[18] Convincing evidence of such continuities comes from the constant reappearance of stories about figures like "Monkey" (perhaps better translated "supermonkey"), whose exploits are recounted in the popular classic Voyage to the West. Though there is no evidence that the stories of Monkey appear in today's schoolbooks or theater, allusions to him colored the language, for example, of political debates in Szechwan newspapers during the Cultural Revolution. In China in 1971, I taped some lengthy and fluent recounting of Monkey's voyages told me by a seven-year-old schoolboy. When he finished, I told him and others present, that Li Chengtao, Chinese-American cowinner of the Nobel Prize for Physics (and a recent guest of Chairman Mao) drew on the same story in his Stockholm speech.

Though debate sometimes arises over the appropriateness of some stories as opposed to other or over interpretations, storytelling, like many other varieties of the oral tradition, goes on, with continuing admiration for both it and the gifts it requires.

UNIFORMITY OF THE WRITING SYSTEM

As we have seen, the use of a second dialect in different social situations is determined by flexible criteria and the pursuit of social solidarity through articulate participation in community discussion. While the formal educational system (apart from judgments of the quality as well as quantity of bilingual teachers available) allows least flexibility in decisions to use local dialects, the formal system must be seen in the setting of strongly supported and periodically reinvigorated informal educational facilities like the study sessions where dialects are used when more comfortable for the speakers and listeners. In this setting, dialects other than Mandarin—far from being suppressed—have been sustained, even to the point of national distribution of films of dialect versions of theatrical performances. The use of the dialects even in campaigns promoting Mandarin, let alone their protection in other settings, has made bilingualism integral to the spread of the national language. Yet there is little evidence of a self-conscious policy of bilingualism as distinguished from its acceptance as an example of the highly prized diversity of oral modes of communication in the society at large.

Historically, the rich diversity of the Chinese oral traditions has been facilitated by the uniformity of its writing system. The Chinese characters have always conveyed much less information about the sounds they represent than do other writing systems. This has naturally made literature written in characters less responsive to changes in speech. At the same time, however, the rather unphonetic script had less impact on oral practice, facilitating the wide variety of dialects we know today and the flourishing of vigorous oral traditions in relative independence of traditional writing. Classical literature (Wen Yen) when read aloud was read in local dialects. The reader was free to read it aloud with faithfully local sounds. And the very obscurity of the texts provided an occasion for an oral gloss or interpretation in local dialect for learners.

Nonetheless, particularly complex forms of the written characters combined with the nonspoken syntax of the classical literary style constituted a consistent impediment to literacy. Although literacy among premodern Chinese was not so low as has commonly been believed,[19] it was to such a degree as to alarm nationalistic intellectuals and political leaders alike. They recognized by the early 20th Century the necessity for mass literacy if China were to survive and flourish among modern nations. The result was a succession of efforts to promote new standards of vernacular in writing practices.

The Chinese Communist Party itself emerged during the "May 4th" movement, a movement of the early 1920s which had its origins, in part, in the conviction among influential Chinese intellectuals that a key to China's national political and social reconstruction was cultural reform or even revolution. The most concrete proposal for cultural change was the displacement of the classical literary style (Wen Yen) of written Chinese by the vernacular (Bai Hua) writing style. In fact, a vernacular writing style close to the common speech of the Peking area had been in use for a millennium[20] and was directly known to educated Chinese (and indirectly, through oral versions of the stories, to the uneducated) throughout the country. The adaption of this writing style, or approximations of this style, by most if not all of China's literary talent was a distinct characteristic of the "May 4th" and subsequent literary movements of the 1920s and 1930s associated also with mass literacy and other modern nationalistic movements.

As might be expected, the promotion (discussed above) of the national language and common language since that time has been closely associated with the promotion of vernacular writing. Versions of vernacular writing based on the common dialect of other areas than Peking have continued to exist during the 20th Century, and can be found even today in, for example, serial novels by Cantonese published in Hong Kong newspapers. But even in Hong Kong such writing remains a minor phenomenon. In both the mainland provinces of the People's Republic of China and in the province of Taiwan, cross fertilization through dialect borrowing is represented in vernacular writing almost exclusively to the extent that such writing reflects their direct contributions of lexical items and certain grammatical variations to the common or national language.[21]

Promotion of vernacular writing has, then, remained incidental in modern China to the promotion or spread of a uniform national language rooted in speech forms of the Peking area but successfully transplanted to other areas where it coexists with the local dialects in a bilingual situation. Experiments with reform also of the writing system—whether simplification of characters or the use of romanization—have in turn only followed promotion of the vernacular as part of promotion of a national language.

The goal of writing reform has consistently been mass literacy in a national language, in both pre- and post-1949 China; Chinese have consistently emphasized to this day the great difficulty for them of learning to write the alphabet. Discussions of the difficulty include complaints from students or their parents—much reminiscent of those from western students of Chinese—of loss for lack of practice of the hard-won ability to write alphabetically.

In contrast to the expectations of some Western proponents of writing reform for the Chinese, the Chinese case as yet provides no evidence of an advantage for the unilingual writer in an alphabetic over an ideographic system. Children are known to learn at least an initial small number of characters more rapidly than they can an equal number of words spelled with the alphabet, presumably because of the less abstract system of representing a single word or sound with a single ideograph.[22] As vocabulary expands, the point of diminishing returns for characters and increasing returns in the alphabet is eventually reached, but the syntactic complexity of the child's writing (as of his speaking) is governed by biological development.[23]

No one disputes the advantage of writing in *simplified* characters, and since 1952 the reduction of stroke counts has proceeded without controversy over its intrinsic merit. Pressure to adopt an alphabetic rather than ideographic writing system has meanwhile been kept low by success at radically reducing if not actually eliminating illiteracy; the Chinese have found it possible (using standards for literacy related to increasing emphasis on, for example, the universal study of agricultural technology) to speak of illiteracy as having been reduced to perhaps 10%.

Practical success in the promotion of literacy has reduced the importance of theoretical claims that knowledge of the alphabet *might have* accelerated the process more than reliance on simplified characters.[24]

The alphabet does, as a more nearly phonetic system, clearly confer certain advantages on the unilingual reader, if not writer. Most importantly, it greatly facilitates his eventual learning of a second, the national, language pronounced differently—whatever the structural similarities—from his original dialect. Practical experience has confirmed the desirability of the universal use in China of romanization as a pedagogical device: the speaker of a dialect other than Mandarin learns the national language from texts in which its pronunciation is printed next to the characters. The one conscious addition to this use of romanization of which I know (apart from labeling of goods destined for export) is its use on signboards in Shanghai: most storefronts in the big streets in Shanghai have romanization alongside the Chinese characters, possibly a problem due to dialect relations in the area, which would make even use on signs essentially pedagogical in character.

On March 25, 1974, the central broadcasting system inaugurated radio talks about romanization of the national language (Han-Yu Ping-Yin). This event follows an apparent revival of emphasis on reform of the written language signaled in 1972 by a commentary in *Red Flag*, the leading theoretical journal (in response to an inquiry from a reader), by Kuo Mo-jou, head of the Chinese Academy of Sciences. In 1973, the *Guangming Ribao*, the country's leading literary journal, resumed fortnightly columns on the topic discontinued in 1966 after having been published regularly from 1954.

Romanization remains, by all evidence, of interest primarily in the promotion of knowledge of the national language. The alphabet, that is, remains associated in Chinese minds thus far primarily with second language learning. This has been true from the inception of Chinese interest in the issue. When the romanization of dialects (as opposed to the national language) was revived in 1960, it was justified again,[25] as a means to bring speakers of dialects more quickly to a knowledge of the difficult and alien alphabetic writing system. Given the admitted advantages of a more phonetic system in learning a second language, this knowledge could then be put to use in learning the national language more quickly.

CONCLUSION

Language policy in the Han dialect areas is consistent with that toward the 6% of the population, about 50 million, who constitute ethnic minorities. The deeply rooted but often only implicit bilingualism of the former areas becomes explicit in the latter where historical antecedents are often lacking.

"Illiterates stand outside of politics; they must be given culture," Mao Tse-Tung noted in 1940. The term "culture" is synonymous with "education,"[26] but the problem was complicated by the absence in many cases of a written script. Accordingly, language policy in the minority areas passed through two more distinct stages than that in the Han dialect areas. Prior to 1958, work centered on creation of scripts for the numerous minority languages which had none of their own. After 1958, attention turned more to the larger groupings—diverse, some ten in all, though they are—into which the minority languages could be grouped: Zhuang-Tai, Tibeto-Burmese, and Miao-Yao of the Sino-Tibetan family comprehending about three-fourths of the minority population; Turkish, Mongolian, and Tungusic-Manchurian of the Altaic family, another fifth; and Mon-khmer, Slavonic, Iranian, and Korean, the remainder. At the same time, instruction in Chinese kept up its momentum. In contrast to the Nationalist government which preceded them, the Communists did not try to make minorities literate participants in national politics by teaching them Chinese alone. They sought to bring them in from "outside politics" by confirming, as it were, in script the oral diversity of the minorities which remains beneath the uniformity into which lessons in the national language, Mandarin, introduces them.[27]

Not enough time has elapsed to know whether or not the minorities will, like Han Chinese speakers of dialects other than Mandarin, prefer to write in the Mandarin rather than local vernacular. We would expect them not to share the

Han Chinese resistance to use of alphabetic scripts (including Pinyin, the script of the Mandarin vernacular) for other than pedagogical purposes—whether or not they share the Western aversion to the character system. For this reason they might, ironically, become more enthusiastic supporters of a Pinyin literature than Han Chinese.

The Chinese have consistently approached the alphabet with no less psychological terror (or obsession) than that displayed by Western students in their first contacts with characters. Additional evidence of special problems added to the learning situation by this obvious gap in writing systems is the very fact that this very (too) obvious feature of the Chinese mentality has been overlooked by Western students of the history of Chinese language reform efforts, most probably as part of a retrospective (or continuing) lament at the effort involved in the leap from the familiar alphabet to alien characters. Domestic application of the alphabet remains linked, in the mind of the Chinese user, to pursuit of facility in a second language, Mandarin.

The boundary between two writing systems like Chinese characters and the roman alphabet is obvious to all, but the attitudinal barriers associated with its discovery by a second (and first) language learner have been poorly understood. Wallace Lambert and his associates, working primarily on French-English bilingualism in Canada, have isolated and specified the attitudinal variables in second language learning situations with the precision allowed by the study of linguistic data. The present study of what may be called China's internal linguistic borders and border areas suggests the importance of attention to the larger social and political context of, and the illumination of that context by, the Chinese language, orally diverse and uniformly written.

In 1947, Y. R. Chao published in the introduction to his *Cantonese Primer* his statement, almost universally quoted when the topic comes up among specialists and nonspecialists on Chinese, that the various Chinese dialects, when one considers "mutual intelligibility," are "about as far from Mandarin and from each other as, say, Dutch or Low German is from English, or Spanish from French." Unfortunately, this passage has been used most frequently to suggest the approach of the Chinese dialects to the status of independent languages. What has lamentably been forgotten is the fact that Chao's remark is a comment on the closeness of European languages as well as upon the distance between Chinese dialects. It must be understood in the context of a more extended comparison along these lines which he has made, published in 1968 in his *Language and Symbolic Systems* (p. 133), discussing a trip he once made from France through the low countries and Germany to Scandinavia. He emphasized that "when crossing the national boundaries there was no noticeable sudden change of language except the language used in talking to foreigners."

Such tests of "mutual intelligiblity" devised for use in laboratory conditions of Morris Swadesh's or similar lists of "basic" words uproot the speech act from variables in language learning and using environments dominated by the existence of political and social boundaries. The basic question of mutual intelligibility is "how easy is it for the speaker of one language or dialect to learn and use the other?" It is a question which recognizes the creative activity, rather than assuming the passivity, of the speaker-listener.

A six-year-old whose speech I recorded in a Changsha, Hunan kindergarten in 1972, was a native speaker of Shanghaiese (his parents' dialect). He had acquired native speaker competence in Mandarin and then in six months an equal proficiency in the Changsha dialect. With the criteria of laboratory tests of mutual intelligibility it would be impossible to accept, as those about him or others like him in China do, that this child was normal rather than some kind of curiosity.

The intuitive response of a Chinese to such a child is to say (in somewhat different language) that "mutually unintelligible" dialects of Chinese can be learned very easily by anybody who speaks one of them. Some such natural (if originally acquired) intuition probably explains the delight linguists commonly take in saying of Roman Jakobson, that he "speaks fifteen languages, all in Russian." For some reason linguists have never accounted formally for the intuition suggested by their chuckles at this remark. They refer, of course, to the phonological uniformity of Jakobson's performance of fifteen differently struc-tured languages. Formal appreciation of the situation perhaps has been awaiting more careful study of the complementary Chinese case. In the Chinese dialects, the structure remains quite uniform; unlike Professor Jakobson, the six-year-old Chinese bilingual learner is required to perform differently only on the phonological level in a highly supportive social environment.

The Chinese case reminds us that a "dialect" is no less sufficient than a "language" to primary tasks of social communication, be they family table talk or local political meetings. Or as Akhmanova[28] states it formally, dialects are, no less than languages, "complete semiotic systems," dependent in complex ways upon a particular "language." Haugen[29] notes that a dialect is an "undeveloped" language, in that it is not regarded by users—speakers as well as listeners—as adequate to some situations or functions. Until 1971, although formally designated as an "official" language of the United Nations, Chinese in practice enjoyed no more status than an "undeveloped" or "dependent" language: the diplomats seated in the United Nations as China's representatives before 1971 ordinarily used English in debate.

Situations or functions appropriate or inappropriate for a language obviously extend to a scale as grandiose as their use in a diplomatic forum, preeminently perhaps the United Nations.

NOTES

1. Uriel Weinreich, *Languages in Contact*, Mouton, 1967. Weinreich defines bilingualism as the practice of alternately using two languages.

2. Einar Haugen, "The Stigma of Bilingualism," in *The Ecology of Language*, Stanford, 1972, on necessity as cause.

3. F. K. Li: "Languages and Dialects of China," *China Year Book*, Shanghai, 1937, reprinted

in *Journal of Chinese Linguistics*, vol. 1, no. 1, January 1973. See also Yuan Jia-hua, *Hanyu Fangyan Gaiyao*, Peking, 1960.

4. Ibid.

5. Y. R. Chao, *Cantonese Primer*, Harvard, 1947; *Mandarin Primer*, Harvard, 1948, introductions. Also Y. R. Chao, *Language and Symbolic Systems*, Cambridge University, 1968.

6. Wallace E. Lambert, *Language, Psychology, and Culture*, Stanford, 1972, and previously cited works of Chao, Haugen, Li.

7. Beverly Hong Fincher, "Chinese Society Today: The Return of a Native," *The Washington Post Outlook Section*, Feb. 13, 1972.

8. Beverly Hong Fincher, "The Chinese Language in its New Social Context," *The Journal of Chinese Linguistics*, vol. 1, no. 1, January 1973.

9. In addition to published material, sources for this article include observations during the author's trips to the People's Republic in 1971 and 1972 and interviews with numerous visitors to or people from China since 1971.

10. Urie Bronfenbrenner report on trip to China of Early Childhood Development Specialists Group in late 1973, to the Russell Sage Foundation, New York, Jan. 8, 1974.

11. W. Labov, "The Logic of Nonstandard English," in P. P. Giglioli (ed.), *Language and Social Context*, Penguin Books, 1972.

12. Tang Zhu Guo, "Shuo er iu ze shi," Central Daily News, Taipei, Taiwan, Apr. 8, 1974.

13. Jaroslav Prusek, *The Origin and Authors of the Hua-pen*, Prague, 1967.

14. Martin Whyte: *Small Groups and Political Rituals in China*, University of California, 1974.

15. *Peoples Daily*, Jan. 22, 1974, p. 5. See also the differing but complementary process of the presentation in local recitative styles of stories built around themes suggested by the Cultural Revolution models, e.g., text of Henan Zhuizi, Jingdong Dagu, etc., *Peoples Daily*, Jan. 18, 1974, p. 4.

16. *Guangming Ribao*, Feb. 5, 1964, p. 4.

17. See note 14.

18. *Peoples Daily*, Jan. 22, 1974, p. 1.

19. F. W. Mote, "China's Past in the Study of China Today," *Journal of Asian Studies*, November 1972, pp. 108-112, discussed underestimates of literacy in Late Imperial China; suggests the literacy rate as actually somewhere between 7 and 30%. John H. Fincher, "Political Provincialism and The National Revolution," in Mary C. Wright (ed.), *China in Revolution, 1900-13* (Yale, 1968), pp. 209ff., suggests use of literacy as a criterion increased eligible voters to perhaps 20% in the 1909-12 period.

20. Y. R. Chao, *Cantonese Primer*, p. 7.

21. See my discussion of the "nationalization" of Chinese in op. cit., *Journal of Chinese Linguistics*, January 1973.

22. Personal experience; accounts in discussions with Vivianne Alleton, Wolfram Eberhard.

23. E. H. Lenneberg, *The Biological Basis of Language*, Wiley, 1967. Carol S. Chomsky; *On*

Language Learning from 5 to 10: The Acquisition of Syntax in Children, Massachusetts Institute of Technology, 1971.

24. For a detailed chronology and description of post-1949 writing reform, see Constantin Milsky, "New Developments in Language Reform," *China Quarterly,* no. 53, January/March 1973.

25. *Guangming Ribao,* Dec. 1, 1960, p. 3.

26. As in "ta wenhua shuiping gao," meaning "he is well educated."

27. Li Fang-kuei, op. cit., for description of minority languages; I am grateful to Prof. David Deal, Whitman College, for letting me consult the summary of educational policies in a manuscript on Chinese minorities which he is preparing.

28. Olga Akhmanova: " 'Language' or 'Dialect'?" in S. Ghosh (ed.), *Man, Language and Society,* Mouton, 1972.

29. E. Haugen, "Dialect, Language, Nation," *The Ecology of Language,* Stanford, 1972.

IV

Multilingual Education

in India

Lachman M. Khubchandani

In the past few decades, Asia and Africa have been passing through a linguistic and literary upheaval, as a consequence of shift in the emphasis from colonial languages (English, French, Dutch, Portuguese) to the regional languages in education, administration, and other spheres of formal communication. The newly independent nations, representing many language areas, which were submerged by the dominance of European languages at a time when tremendous scientific and technological progress was achieved, are now becoming keenly conscious of their linguistic needs in a modern world.

India, like the other countries in South Asia, has a multiethnic and multilingual background. It was primarily during the Independence struggle that the language consciousness came to the fore on the social and political scene in the Indian subcontinent. Since Independence in 1947, various pressure groups and public institutions, with the strength of political power and educational expertise, have got entangled in polemics over language issues, leading to rival claims regarding language privileges in different spheres of interaction—conditioned by conflicting regional, economic, and sociopolitical interests. In a perpetual debate on the educational policy for a multilingual society, one notices a wide gulf in arriving at a broad consensus regarding the function of education in society, and of language in education.

LANGUAGE SCENE

India is a unique mosaic of linguistic heterogeneity with over 200 classified languages[1] spread throughout the country. In a land populated by over 600 million speakers, scores of small speech groups of a few thousand people still maintain their mother tongues in everyday life in various multilingual pockets. This exemplifies a degree of *tolerance* of linguistic and cultured variations in India's history.[2] There seems to be very little pressure of conformity on smaller groups from dominant speech groups. The acculturation process among migrants has, to a great extent, been voluntary and gradual. In this way, India as a language area is one of the most interesting laboratories of multilingual experience in the world today.

The federal setup of India (21 states and 9 union territories) comprises broadly 12 principal language areas, each dominated by a different language enjoying full or partial recognition in the spheres of public communication within that area. During the course of history, four language families—Indo-European, Dravidian, Austric, and Tibeto-Chinese—represented by different ethnic groups have acted and reacted upon one another, making for a fundamental cultural unity of the subcontinent. Much of the confusion in interpreting India's language scene comes from the tendency to deal with the subcontinent either as a whole or as a series of small linguistically isolated units. One can group those language areas together into *four* major linguistic regions—south, east, west, and north-central— which show many parallels in their overall communication environments, in spite of a widespread linguistic heterogeneity within each region. Table 1, presenting the statewide distribution of dominant languages and literary ratio, gives a glimpse of the linguistic heterogeneity in the country.

The complex segmentation of Indian society, frequent migrations, and conquests and internal colonization in the past have established conditions for extensive "folk" multilingualism in the country, despite the high percentage of illiteracy and absence of any strong tradition of systematic language teaching in the country (Pandit 1972, Khubchandani 1975a). One notices a general pattern of three major contact languages occurring prominently in most parts of the country: regional language, Hindi-Urdu, and English. These languages vary a great deal in their strength as contact languages in different states (Khubchandani 1975a, Table C).

The plural character of Indian society is well recognized. There is a shared core of experience despite several varying sociocultural characteristics—such as caste, religion, occupation, mother tongue—cutting across nearly 400 districts in 30 states and union territories. Such segmental identities find expression in diverse combinations through linguistic stratification (such as diglossic complementation, code switching, bilingualism) in everyday life. The intergroup language boundaries in many regions have remained fluid; and the masses at large are not overtly conscious of the speech characteristics which bind them in one language or

Table 1. State Population, Literacy Rate, and Dominant Language(s): 1971

Sr. No.	States and union territories (UT)	State language(s)	Total population: 1971 (in thousands)	Literacy ratio†	Dominant language(s)	Percentage of speakers of dominant language(s) to the state population
1	2	3	4	5	6	7
	India	Hindi/English	547,950	29.46		
South:						
1.	Andhra Pradesh	Telugu	43,503	25.57	Telugu	85.36
2.	Tamil Nadu	Tamil	41,199	39.46	Tamil	84.51
3.	Mysore	Kannada	29,299	31.52	Kannada	65.97
4.	Kerala	Malayalam	21,347	60.42	Malayalam	96.02
5.	Pondicherry (UT)	English	472	46.02	Tamil	88.98
6.	Lakshadweep Islands (UT)	English	32	43.66	Malayalam	84.38
East:						
7.	West Bengal	Bengali	44,312	33.20	Bengali	85.32
8.	Orissa	Oriya	21,945	26.18	Oriya	84.12
9, 10.	Assam (including Mizaram)	Assamese	14,958	28.72	Assamese	59.53
11.	Tripura	English/Bengali	1,556	30.98	Bengali	68.83
12.	Manipur	English/Manipuri	1,073	32.91	Manipuri	64.5 *
13.	Meghalaya	English	1,012	29.49	Khasi	45.5 *
14.	Nagaland	English	516	27.40	14 Naga langs.	98.4 *
15.	Arunachal (UT)	English	468	11.29		
16.	Andaman and Nicobar Islands (UT)	English	115	43.59	Bengali Nicobarese	24.35 21.9 *
West:						
17.	Maharashtra	Marathi	50,412	39.18	Marathi	76.60
18.	Gujarat	Gujarati	26,698	35.79	Gujarati	89.39
19.	Goa, Daman, and Diu (UT)	English/Konkani	858	44.75	Konkani	89.1 *
20.	Dadra and Nagar Haveli (UT)	English	74	14.97	Marathi (Varli)	58.11

Table 1 (continued)

Sr. No.	States and union territories (U T)	State language(s)	Total population: 1971 (in thousands)	Literacy ratio†	Dominant language(s)	Percentage of speakers of dominant language(s) to the state population
1	2	3	4	5	6	7
North-Central:						
21. Uttar Pradesh	Hindi	88,341	21.77	Hindi	81.42
					Urdu	10.50
22. Bihar	Hindi	56,353	19.94	Bihari langs.	35.4 *
					Hindi	35.11
					Urlu	08.85
23. Madhya Pradesh	Hindi	41,654	22.14	Hindi	78.92
					Urdu	02.37
24. Rajasthan	Hindi	25,766	19.07	Hindi	60.82
					Urdu	02.53
25. Panjab	Panjabi	13,551	33.67	Panjabi	79.65
26. Haryana	Hindi	10,037	26.89	Hindi	88.48
					Urdu	01.95
27. Jammu and Kashmir	Urdu	4,617	18.58	Kashmiri	52.48
					Dogri (Panjabi)	27.5 *
28. Delhi (UT)	Hindi/Urdu	4,066	56.61	Hindi	72.28
					Urdu	5.68
29. Himachal Pradesh	Hindi	3,460	31.96	8 Pahari langs.	79.8 *
					Hindi	55.64
30. Chandigarh	English	257	61.36	Panjabi	42.41
					Urdu	0.78

Sources: Tables 3, 6, and 12 in the Pocket Book of Population Statistics: 1971, Census Centenary Publication, Registrar General and Census Commissioner, India, New Delhi, 1972.

*According to the 1961 Census.

†Including population in age group 0-4.

another.[3] The patterns of verbal usage in the subcontinent are hardly coterminous with the political and administrative boundaries.

Contrary to the traditional Indian tolerance for linguistic heterogeneity, based on grass-root multilingualism which easily responds to situational needs, recent decades have seen strong drives for language *autonomy* in the name of language development.

MEDIUM OF EDUCATION

At present in the field of education, all states have the provision of teaching the students of major Indian languages through their mother tongue or through their language of formal communication (as Maithili and Rajasthani students get education through Hindi, and Kashmiri students through Urdu) up to the school-leaving stage. Many universities now provide instruction in the medium of regional languages at the undergraduate and graduate stages in arts and commerce faculties; but English still continues to be the principal medium for higher education, particularly in law, science, and technology faculties.

For a nation such as India with a multilingual and federal setup, education is made a responsibility of the states. The Constitution of India provides full freedom to the states to choose a language or languages in a region as "official" language(s) (Article 345). It also allows linguistic minority groups to receive education through their mother tongues and set up institutions of their choice for this purpose (Article 30). Hence, one finds wide variations in different states as far as the medium, content, duration, and nomenclature of educational stages are concerned. There is inevitable flexibility in the weight assigned to different languages in the total educational program, the framing of language curricula, prescribing textbooks, etc. A national policy of education emerges out of a consensus arrived at among the states constituting the federal polity. The role of the Union Government is therefore largely confined to promoting the national policies through seeking mutual accommodation from individual states, coordination of institutions for higher education and research, and for vocational and technical training, persuasion of language elites, and offering incentives of resources at its command for specific programs.

About eighty languages are being used as media of instruction at different stages of education. A large number of them are used only as *preparatory* media at the primary education stage (for classes I and II, often extended up to class IV; a few are stretched up to class VII as well), before a student switches over to any major language as the medium at the secondary education stage. Some tribal languages, spoken by smaller populations, are also promoted as *elementary* media by private institutions (missionary schools, monasteries, etc.). There are fourteen *principal* media languages, comprising eleven regional languages (including the pan-Indian Hindi), two languages without any region—Urdu and Sindhi, and one foreign language—English. Some prominent Indian Languages—such as Hindi,

Bengali, Telugu, Marathi, and Urdu—are now being extended as *alternate* media to English up to undergraduate and graduate levels in the universities of respective regions, depending upon their developmental stages. Foreign languages like Persian, Portuguese, and French are also retained as media in a few urban schools.

In recent years some multilingual states, mostly in eastern India, have introduced, as a state policy bilingual education in which a developing language in a region is used as a *partial* medium, together with English, Hindi, or the neighboring regional language as the major medium. Some states are initiating bilingual schooling for their tribal populations; various minority communities, particularly in urban areas, also prefer bilingual media. The Union Government has also introduced a "Central School" system in major towns throughout the country for the children of those employed in all-India services and those belonging to mobile occupations in business and industry where education is imparted through Hindi or English or both languages.

A list of languages used as media of education, in different regions, is given in Table 2.

Many distinct scripts are in vogue for writing these languages. Sanskrit, Hindi, and Marathi (also Nepali) are written in Devanagari script; Urdu, Kashmiri, and Sindhi in Perso-Arabic script. Other major Indo-Aryan and Dravidian Languages (also Tibetan) have distinct scripts derived from early Nagari system. Some vernaculars and tribal languages have adopted Devanagari, Roman, or regional scripts. Khampti in Arunachal uses a variation of Thai script. With the emphasis on literacy programs through mother tongue, many languages of small speech groups are now being committed to Devanagari or Roman writing, depending upon sectarian or regional pressures.

University Media

At the university stage, education through regional languages is being associated with "ordinary" tradition. The quality and prestige of "advanced" tradition still rests with the English medium. There are over twenty universities, which still maintain their unilingual character, and provide education only through English.

Many universities of Hindi and Bengali regions have been relatively more enthusiastic about providing regional language as an alternate medium along with English. Some universities in Gujarati and Marathi regions have liberal policies regarding media of instruction. Many universities in western India such as Baroda, Gujarat, Marathawada, Nagpur, SNDT Women, Sardar Vallabhbhai Vidyapeeth, Gujarat Vidyapeeth; and some universities in other regions such as Karanataka (Dharwar), Osmania (Hyderabad), and Visva Bharati (Shantiniketan) provide Hindi medium, along with English and respective regional language(s) media. Universities with Islamic tradition—Aligarth, Osmania, Jamia Millia—provide Urdu as an alternate medium along with English and Hindi. The Panjab University also provides Panjabi, Hindi, and Urdu media along with English. According to the

Table 2.   Medium Languages

Sr. No.	Language	Genealogical affiliation	Mother tongues grouped under the language*	Total speakers 1971 (provisional) (in thousands)	Percentage of total population	Dominant state(s)
1	2	3	4	5	6	7
A. Principal Media						
1.	Hindi	Indo-Aryan-central	97	162,578	29.7	Hindi-Urdu Panjabi (HUP) Region, and urban centers
2.	Bengali	Indo-Aryan-east	15	44,793	8.2	W. Bengal, Tripura
3.	Telugu	Dravidian-south	36	44,753	8.2	A.P.
4.	Marathi	Indo-Aryan-south	65	42,251	7.7	Maharashtra
5.	Tamil	Dravidian-south	22	37,690	6.9	Tamil Nadu, Pondicherry
6.	Urdu	Indo-Aryan-central	9	28,608	5.2	HUP region, A.P.
7.	Gujarati	Indo-Aryan-central	27	25,875	4.7	Gujarat
8.	Malayalam	Dravidian-south	14	21,938	4.0	Kerala, Lakshad-veep Islands
9.	Kannada	Dravidian-south	32	21,708	4.0	Mysore
10.	Oriya	Indo-Aryan-east	24	19,855	3.6	Orissa
11.	Panjabi	Indo-Aryan-central	29	16,450	3.0	Panjab
12.	Assamese	Indo-Aryan-east	2	8,959	1.6	Assam
13.	Sindhi	Indo-Aryan-northwest	8	1,677	0.3	Maharashtra, Gujarat, Rajasthan, M.P. Delhi
14.	English	Indo-European-Germanic	1	192	0.04	Urdan centers in India
B. Foreign Media						
1.	Persian			11		
2.	Portuguese			6		

Table 2 (continued)

Sr. No.	Language	Genealogical affiliation	Mother tongues grouped under the language*	Total speakers 1971 (provisional) (in thousands)	Percentage of total population	Dominant state(s)
1	2	3	4	5	6	7

Foreign Media (continued)

3.	French					

C. *Partial Media*

1.	Santali	Austric-Munda	11	3,797	0.69	Bihar, Orissa, W. Bengal
2.	Kashmiri	Indo-Aryan-Dardic	5	2,438	0.44	Jammu and Kashmir
3.	Nepali	Indo-Aryan-Pahari	4	1,287	0.23	W. Bengal
4.	Manipuri	Tibeto-Chinese-KukiChin	3	836	0.15	Manipur
5.	Khasi	Austric-MonKhmer	6	478	0.08	Meghalaya
6.	Garo	Tibeto-Chinese-Bodo	3	412	0.08	Meghalaya
7.	Lushai/Mizo	Tibeto-Chinese-KukiChin	2	270	0.05	Mizoram
8.	Tibetan	Tibeto-Chinese-Tibetan	14	66	0.01	W. Bengal

D. *Preparatory Media* (recognized by the state(s))

1.	Maithili	Indo-Aryan-east	9	6,122	1.12	Bihar
2.	Konkani	Indo-Aryan-south	16	1,531	0.28	Goa Daman and Diu
3.	Kurukh/Oraon	Dravidian-north	9	1,246	0.23	Bihar
4.	Sadan/Sadri	Indo-Aryan-east (pidgin)	1	807	0.15	Bihar
5.	Mundari	Austric-Munda	2	771	0.14	Bihar
6.	Ho	Austric-Munda	2	750	0.14	Bihar
7.	Bodo	Tibeto-Chinese-Bodo	2	544	0.10	Assam
8.	Tripuri	Tibeto-Chinese-Bodo	6	366	0.07	Tripura
9.	Kharia	Austric-Munda	5	88	0.02	Bihar
10.	Konyak	Tibeto-Chinese-Naga	3	72	0.01	Nagaland
11.	Ao	Tibeto-Chinese-Naga	3	65	0.01	Nagaland

Table 2 (continued)

Sr. No.	Language	Genealogical affiliation	Mother tongues grouped under the language*	Total speakers 1971 (provisional) (in thousands)	Percentage of total population	Dominant state(s)
1	2	3	4	5	6	7
12.	Sema	Tibeto-Chinese-Naga	1	65	0.01	Nagaland
13.	Ladakhi	Tibeto-Chinese-Tibetan	5	57	0.01	Jammu and Kashmir
14.	Angami	Tibeto-Chinese-Naga	2	44		Nagaland
15.	Hmar	Tibeto-Chinese-KukiChin	1	33		Manipur, Assam
16.	Lotha	Tibeto-Chinese-Naga	1	37		Nagaland
17.	Kuki	Tibeto-Chinese-KukiChin	3	30		Nagaland
18.	Mishmi (Digaru Taron)	Tibeto-Chinese-NEFA	4	20		Arunachal
19.	Sangtam	Tibeto-Chinese-Naga	3	20		Nagaland
20.	Phom	Tibeto-Chinese-Naga	2	18		Nagaland
21.	Nicobarese	Austric-MonKhmer	1	18		Andaman and Nicobar Islands
22.	Chang	Tibeto-Chinese-Naga	1	16		Nagaland
23.	Kheimnungan	Tibeto-Chinese-Naga	2	14		Nagaland
24.	Yimchungre	Tibeto-Chinese-Naga	2	14		Nagaland
25.	Zeliang	Tibeto-Chinese-Naga	2	13		Nagaland
26.	Rengma	Tibeto-Chinese-Naga	2	9		Nagaland
27.	Chakhesang	Tibeto-Chinese-Naga	3	8		Nagaland
28.	Karen	Karen (foreign)	1			Andaman and Nicobar Islands
E. *Elementary Media* (promoted by private institutions)						
1.	Bhili	Indo-Aryan-central	36	2,398	0.44	Gujarat
2.	Gondi	Dravidian-central	13	1,666	0.30	M.P.
3.	Halabi	Indo-Aryan-central (pidgin)	1	346	0.06	M.P.
4.	Korku	Austric-Munda	4	305	0.06	M.P., Maharashtra

Table 2 (continued)

Sr. No.	Language	Genealogical affiliation	Mother tongues grouped under the language*	Total speakers 1971 (provisional) (in thousands)	Percentage of total population	Dominant state(s)
1	2	3	4	5	6	7

Elementary Media (continued)

Sr. No.	Language	Genealogical affiliation	Mother tongues grouped under the language*	Total speakers 1971 (provisional) (in thousands)	Percentage of total population	Dominant state(s)
5.	Adi-Mishing	Tibeto-Chinese-NEFA	14	103	0.02	Arunachal
6.	Tangkhul	Tibeto-Chinese-Naga	1	58	0.01	Manipur
7.	Kabuli	Tibeto-Chinese-Naga	1	49	0.01	Manipur
8.	Thado	Tibeto-Chinese-KukiChin	19	42	0.01	Manipur
9.	Dimasa	Tibeto-Chinese-Bodo	1	38	0.01	Assam
10.	Dafla	Tibeto-Chinese-NEFA	2	28		Arunachal
11.	Paite	Tibeto-Chinese-KukiChin	1	27		Manipur
12.	Nocte	Tibeto-Chinese-Naga	1	24		Arunachal
13.	Mao	Tibeto-Chinese-Naga	1	20		Manipur
14.	Koch	Tibeto-Chinese-Bodo	1	14		Assam
15.	Apatani	Tibeto-Chinese-NEFA	1	13		Arunachal
16.	Mech	Tibeto-Chinese-Bodo	1	13		West Bengal
17.	Lakher	Tibeto-Chinese-KukiChin	1	12		Mizoram
18.	Vaiphei	Tibeto-Chinese-KukiChin	1	12		Manipur
19.	Lepcha	Tibeto-Chinese-Himalayan	1	11		West Bengal
20.	Tangsa	Tibeto-Chinese-Naga	1	7		Arunachal
21.	Anal	Tibeto-Chinese-KukiChin	2	7		Manipur
22.	Kom	Tibeto-Chinese-KukiChin	1	7		Manipur
23.	Zeni	Tibeto-Chinese-Naga	1	7		Assam
24.	Gangte	Tibeto-Chinese-KukiChin	2	6		Manipur
25.	Singpho	Tibeto-Chinese-Kachin	1			Assam
26.	Khampti	Tibeto-Chinese-Thai	1			Arunachal, Assam

+According to the 1961 Census, Annexture III, Mitra (1964).
†Appendix II, 1974 Census Mother Tongue (provisional figures), Nigam (1972: pp. 333-339).

1965 University Education Report, the provision of medium languages at different levels of university education is as shown in Table 3.

Table 3.

Medium languages	Preuniversity courses	Graduate courses	Postgraduate courses	Professional courses
English	38	55	61	64
Hindi	23	30	24	22
Urdu	5	4	1	4
Bengali	5	6	2	2
Marathi	5	5	2	3
Gujarati	4	4	3	3
Panjabi	2	2		2
Kannada	1	1		
Sanskrit	1	2	1	1

In recent years, some universities have introduced Tamil, Telugu, and Oriya as alternate media.

In the background of multiple-choice medium policy, the three stages of education have acquired distinct patterns of choice in the education system:

1. Primary stage:
   Dominant regional language.
   Pan-Indian language—English/Hindi.
   Other major languages.
   Newly cultivated languages (as preparatory media).
2. Secondary stage:
   Dominant regional language.
   Pan-Indian language—English/Hindi.
   Other major languages.
3. Higher education stage:
   English as developed medium.
   Hindi and regional languages as emerging media.

Though the policy of bilingual media is, by and large, not encouraged in "prestigious" institutions, in actual practice one notices a good deal of code switching and hybridization of two or more contact languages in informal teaching settings. In spite of the overwhelming state patronage to respective regional language media, there are many multilingual institutions with multilingual teachers catering to the needs of diverse populations spread in every state. Many minority institutions in every state impart education through minority languages, and/or pan-Indian languages like English and Hindi, depending upon the availability of textbooks, teachers, and the trends of language maintenance in a community.

Types of media are much diversified in character. Though many states have a policy of promoting the "exclusive" use of mother tongue as medium of instruction, in actual practice many students experience shift in language medium at one or the other stage of their education career, depending upon the context, domain, and channel:

1. *Passive and active media*: Students listen to lectures in one language and write answers in another.

2. *Formal and informal media*: Formal teaching in the classroom is conducted in one language, but informal explanations are provided in another language.

3. *Multitier media*: Elementary education is initiated through mother tongue as the *preparatory* medium, but when a student moves upward in the education ladder, he has to shift to a more cultivated medium.

In the present setup of education, a majority of students, mostly after high school stage, face the problem of switching over from their mother tongue to a common existing medium—English or, in a few cases, Hindi at the university stage. Success of the multitier system lies in the adequate preparation for shifting from one medium to another. To achieve this, it will be useful to introduce bilingual education *formally* at the higher secondary stage (classes XI-XII), based on a *combination* of the mother tongue and common language(s)—English or, in some cases, Hindi, the proportion of the latter gradually increasing till English, Hindi, or both become the media at the postgraduate stage (Khubchandani 1968).

LANGUAGE STUDY

For a nation such as India where no single language caters to all the needs of an ordinary literate citizen, pan-Indian languages like Hindi and, for some time to come, English occupy a significant functional position in the national life. Amid sharp controversies concerning the role of different languages in education, a broad consensus has been arrived at in the "Three-Language Formula" which provides a policy base for prescribing languages in the school education (Khubchandani 1967). The definition of mother tongue and the feasibility of teaching mother tongue to linguistic minorities in different states on the grounds of practicability have dominated the thinking of policy makers in assigning a language the *first* place for study during the primary and secondary stages of education. The introduction of *second* and *third* languages at the lower and higher secondary stages have remained tied up with the issues of language privileges, cultural prestige, and socioeconomic mobility.

The University Education Commission in 1949 first considered the teaching of regional language, general language (Hindi), and English in schools. The Secondary Education Commission in 1953, in a rather generous mood, suggested the teaching of five languages: mother tongue, regional language, two "federal" languages—Hindi and English, and also optionally a classical language—Sanskrit, Pali, Prakrit, Persian, Arabic. The Council for Secondary Education (1956) settled down to the Three-Language Formula, recommending mother tongue, Hindi, and English for the non-Hindi-speaking population, and Hindi, any other Indian language, and English for the Hindi-speaking population. The Central Advisory

Board of Education in 1957 also endorsed the Formula. But the tussle between the Hindi and English lobbies continued over the issue of *second* place in the education curriculum under the Three-Language Formula.

The Education Commission in 1966 recommended a liberalized version of the Formula, according to which it is expected that a student on the completion of his/her secondary education, would have acquired sufficient control over three languages: mother tongue and two nonnative modern languages, broadly, Hindi as official medium and a link language for the majority of people for interstate communication; and English as associate official medium and a link language for higher education and for intellectual and international communication. The choice of determining the *second* or *third* places for Hindi or English was left with the states.

But the Formula has been put to different interpretations by different states. On the one hand, Hindi states like Uttar Pradesh, Rajasthan, and Himachal Pradesh provide Sanskrit as the *third* language, in place of a "modern" Indian language, and on the other West Bengal and Orissa also favor Sanskrit at the cost of Hindi as the *third* language. Two states—Tamil Nadu and Mizoram—have backed out from the compulsory provision of the *third* language as envisaged in the Formula, thus avoiding the teaching of Hindi. For several linguistic minorities, it has virtually become a *four* languages formula, as many state governments insist on the compulsory learning of regional language.

Some states like Andhra Pradesh, Mysore, and Maharashtra are experimenting with the teaching of "composite" courses, by combining a modern Indian language, usually mother tongue, with a classical language, Sanskrit (or Urdu along with classical Arabic), to be offered as *first* language after the primary stage.

There are many minority languages confined to small pockets in almost all states. Some of these languages are proliferated widely in a state or are spread in more than one state. Generally the number of languages provided for teaching at the elementary stage is higher, and the number gets reduced as a student moves upward on the educational ladder. Various criteria are applied in different states for selecting languages a subject of study: number of speakers, spread of the speakers in different areas, cultivation of language, etc. Because of the prevailing antagonism over the language issue, many state institutions dodge the compulsory provision of teaching *second* and *third* languages (Hindi and English) by making passing in these languages optional.

In addition to the compulsory teaching of three languages under the Formula, many states provide for the teaching of one or two additional languages on an *optional* basis. Optional languages are usually the additional regional language(s) for linguistic minorities or a classical language (Sanskrit, Pali, Ardhamagadhi, Awestha, Persian, Arabic, Hebrew, Sriac, Greek, Latin) or Hindi or English or any other modern Indian or foreign language (French, German, Italian, Spanish). These are usually studied at the terminal stages of school education, stretching from three to six years.

In spite of heavy weight given to language learning in the education curriculum one notices general devaluation of language instruction, because of the lack of motivation and also of coordination. So far the general structure of language instruction has not been studied objectively and the linguistic content is not spelled out adequately. The allotment of more or less time to the teaching of a particular language is judged as a prestige or status issue for that language. In absence of a clear objective of learning a language, one notices many political pressures—literary prestige of a language, sociopolitical privileges of language speakers—being applied for incorporating specific languages in the curriculum. Some language programs are allotted out-of-proportion share in the total teaching priorities, in order to suit the climate of language privileges.

Different weight is assigned to different languages in the total instructional program. Generally schools in different states devote between a quarter and two-thirds of the duration of total teaching periods to the teaching of languages (Chaturvedi 1974).

The state Institutes of Education, the National Council for Educational Research and Training (NCERT) Delhi, the Central Institute of English and Foreign Languages Hyderabad, the Central Hindi Institute Agra, and the Central Institute of Indian Languages Mysore are engaged in conducting research to suggest methods of simplifying language teaching processes at various levels by introducing modern techniques. These institutes also help the state governments in preparing language curricula and in producing instructional materials for the teaching of language. Many states have established textbook research bureaus for publishing books in different languages according to the curricula.

LANGUAGE IN TRADITIONAL EDUCATION

Language in formal communication gets conditioned by the administrative and educational systems prevailing in society. Before the consolidation of the British rule on the Indian subcontinent at the turn of the 19th Century, there were two competing systems of education:

1. The *pāthashālā* (school), and *āshram* and *gurukul* (residential school) system of the Brahmins.

2. The *maktab* (primary school) and *madrasah* (college) system of the Muslims.

As in medieval Europe the language of education was Latin—the language of sacred literature; in India until the 19th Century, the language of education was Sanskrit for the Hindus and Arabic-Persian for the Muslims. Under the Muslim rule, certain Hindu elite made themselves conversant with both the systems of education. Significant characteristics of the traditional education setup in India can be described as follows:

1. Education was regarded as an *extension* of "primary" socialization imbibed through the immediate environments of family, caste, creed, and

tradition, providing a superstructure to the society in which an individual operates. It emphasized the personal "disciple" relationship between pupil and teacher. It was restricted to members of the classes that provided the priesthood, the rulers, and the merchants. Two patterns conditioned by the vocational relevance were prominently recognized in the education system:

    a. *Ordinary tradition* representing the "practical" education provided to the administrators and merchants to cope with the day-to-day needs of society (such as, for use in lower courts, for maintaining accounts) through locally dominant vernaculars.

    b. *Advanced tradition* representing the "elegant" education provided to the elite (priests, ruling class, and administrators) by reading of scriptures and historical texts, through sanskrit or Arabic-Persian.

    2. The education system was oriented to *preserving* segmental identities in the society through language *hierarchy* by catering to the needs of the "ordinary" and "advanced" traditions. A built-in hierarchical structuring of linguistic skills in the society promoted a chain of mutually intelligible speech varieties—from local dialects to subregional dialects, to a superregional network of dialects or languages, and "high-brow" styles—in different diglossic situations.[4] The education setup provided a measure of *fluidity* in the use of language according to the propriety of considerations of context and purpose, which is a characteristic strength of plural society.[5] Sanskrit and Arabic-Persian speaking elites acted as *liaison* between the rulers and the masses. To some extent, Hindustani in the north, Tamil in the south, and Bengali in the east also served this purpose for some of the princely states, and catered to the needs.

    3. Many regional systems of writing, varying according to locality and social group, for the same language were in use. Besides the regional varieties of Devanagari, and the Naskhi and Nastalik characters of the Perso-Arabic script, many variants of *mahājanī* writing prevailed among merchants. The scholarship, though limited to the privileged few, had to be acquainted with a variety of writing systems, distinguished according to locality, social group, and domain of use.[6] Sanskrit of the "advanced" tradition was in vogue in more than one writing system. Apart from the Devanagari writing system, Sanskrit was written in Grantha, Malayalam, and Telugu characters in the south; in Sharada script in Kashmir; in Bengali, Maithili variations of Nagari writing in the east; and other regional variations of Devanagari script in different areas.

COLONIAL LANGUAGE POLICY

In the early stages, the English rulers of the East India Company did not show any particular interest in undertaking the responsibility of education, as there was no state system of education in England itself.[7] The earliest efforts to introduce any form of education different from the indigenous systems emanated from missionaries, private societies, and individuals with occasional patronage from the Company. The rulers also took antiquarian interest in oriental learning, and established a *madressa*[8] in Calcutta in 1781, a Sanskrit college[9] in Benaras in 1792, and the Calcutta Fort William College in 1800. The missionaries ultimately succeeded in getting the first legislative admission in 1813 of the right of education in India and to participate in the public revenues.[10]

Phase I

The rival British education system, known as *schools*, soon eclipsed the traditional *pāthashālā* and *maktab* education systems in a large section of British India, though many princely states continued their patronage of traditional educational institutions. The colonial education policy for over one and a half centuries changed through many phases depending on the political expediency of times.

British administrators could not resolve the three basic issues of education: the content, the spread, and the medium (Dakin 1968: pp. 5-12). Initially, the change in the *content* of education from "traditional" to the "Western" knowledge represented little more than a continuation of the earlier system, as far as the *spread* and the *medium* of education was concerned. But soon a sharp contrast developed between the missionary system and the government system of education over the spread and the medium questions. The missionaries were keen to set up rural schools through local vernaculars, in opposition to the "advanced" tradition of education; whereas the rulers' stress on education was aimed at attracting "respectable" members of Indian society for manning administration through English medium.[11]

At the same time the British administrators themselves remained divided—the Orientalists represented by Princep and the Anglicists represented by Grant[12] and Macaulay[13]—over the basic issues of the education policy for Indian subjects. Because of the accruing privileges of economic status and social stratification, the Hindu and Muslim elites were easily attracted to accept English as their liaison language, abdicating or reducing the use of Sanskrit and Persian for such purposes.[14]

Macaulay's hard line concerning the triple question of *content, spread*, and *medium* of education echoed in the education programs of the British throughout their stay in the subcontinent. In his famous Minute of 1835, Macaulay recommended a policy of imparting Western knowledge through Western tongue (English) and then only to a minority: "We must at present do our best to form a class who may be interpreters between us and the millions whom we govern—a class of persons Indian in blood and colour, but English in tastes, in opinions, in morals and in intellect. To that class we may leave it to refine the vernacular dialects of the country, to enrich those dialects with terms of science borrowed from the Western nomenclature, and to render them by degrees fit vehicles for conveying knowledge to the great mass of the population" (Sharp 1920: p. 116). In the same year the Governor-General Bentinck, giving concurrence to the sentiments of Macaulay, made it explicit that "the great object of the British Government ought to be the promotion of European literature and science among the natives of India; and that all the funds appropriated for the purpose of education would be best employed on English education alone."[15] The Hardings proclamation of 1844 further divorced the objectives of education from the environment by spelling out preferential treatment in recruitment for service in public offices "to those who were educated in English schools."[16]

Phase II

In 1854, the British rulers modified their policy by accepting the responsibility for the education of the whole population, as recommended in the Wood's Despatch (Richey 1922: pp. 367-92). It suggested the use of vernacular medium "to teach the far larger class who are ignorant of, or imperfectly acquainted with, English." But the introduction of vernacular education was extremely slow, as in actual implementation when assigning resources the priority continued to be given to English secondary schools in cities and towns, to the neglect of the rural vernacular schools. Though the rulers often proclaimed their policy of secular and vernacular education, individual administrators at the district level were often enthusiastic in lending direct or indirect support to promoting English education under the missionary patronage.[17]

With the establishment of Calcutta, Bombay, and Madras universities in 1857, primary and secondary education became merely a step to fulfill the requirements of university pursuits. These universities adopted English as the exclusive medium of instruction, and the study of oriental learning as well as of the modern Indian languages was totally neglected. The British Indian Association of the North Western Provinces in a "memorial" (1867) urged the government of India to create a "Vernacular University" in which "the arts, sciences, and other branches of literature may be taught through the instrumentality of the Vernacular; and examination in the Vernacular be annually held in those very subjects in which the student is now examined in English in the Calcutta University" (Document No. 6, Naik 1963: pp. 21-28). The rulers, though conceding that the views of the memorialists were "fundamentally sound," felt the proposal was "too radical" as "the vernaculars of the country do not as yet afford the materials for conveying instruction of the comparatively high order contemplated by the British Indian Association" (Document No. 7, ibid.: pp. 29-32).[18]

A British educationist Howell (1872) very aptly characterized the rulers' approach: "Education in India under the British Government was first ignored, then violently and successfully opposed, then conducted on a system now universally admitted to be erroneous and finally placed on its present footing." The Hunter Commission in 1882, reviewing the implementation of the 1854 Despatch, recommended that priority should be given to primary education (through vernaculars) and it should be made the responsibility of provincial governments.

Shift in the rulers' policy to run their administration at the lower level in the vernacular required the setting up of committees to evolve a single script and establishing a single standard variety for Indian languages, for use in formal communication. The Education Commission in 1902 recommended mother tongue as the proper medium of instruction for all classes up to the higher secondary level. In actual terms, the British recognized three types of education:

1. English medium, in urban centers for the education of the elite, right from the primary stage.

2. Two-tier medium, vernacular medium for primary education and English medium for advanced education in towns.

3. Vernacular medium, in rural areas for primary education.

Thus, by the turn of the 20th Century, "although the official policy was that of the Despatch of 1854, it was Macaulay's policy of selective higher education in English that had achieved comparatively the greater success," under the plea of devoting the inadequate financial resources to improving the quality of education (Dakin 1968: p. 8).

During the long struggle for Indian Independence, the selective education structure was vehemently criticized by the leaders of the Congress. Gokhale and other intellectuals, influenced by the Western literature of the 18th Century Enlightenment, saw the need for *universal* elementary education,[19] and also put forward pleas for the use of mother tongue in administration. But the Hartog Report (1929) wanted to have "a drastic reorganization of the elementary system precede any wide application of compulsion."

Mahatma Gandhi in 1938 proposed a scheme for Basic Education which was practically the antithesis of Macaulay's policy concerning the questions of content, spread, and medium. It attempted to resolve the conflict between *quality* and *quantity* in education, by proposing to bring it into closer relationship with the child's environment and to extend it throughout rural areas without increasing the cost by integrating it to the rural handicrafts. Nobel laureate Tagore also rejected both the manner and the content of English education.

Though Gandhi's self-supporting rural education program was seriously contested by many Indian elite, it found eventual acceptance in the Sargent Report (1944), which envisaged universal, compulsory, and free education for children between the ages of six and fourteen. "But the gap between the ambitions and the achievement of the British administration on the eve of Indpendence (in 1947) was immense. Though nearly every state ('provinces' under the British rule) had passed a compulsory education bill, only one quarter of the school-age population was actually attending school in 1948-9." (Dakin 1968: p. 9.)[20]

As is evident from the review, the British policies made a significant impact on the concept of education itself and also on the role of language in education for plural societies of the subcontinent:

1. Contrary to "modern" values attributed to humanism, the country was rather confronted with a deliberate policy of *selective* higher education to train an elite class to mediate between the technologically superior "caste" or class. The English language, which was largely responsible for injecting "modern" thought

into Oriental life, took over the dominant position hitherto enjoyed by Sanskrit and Persian. The British system of education in India thus perpetuated the *dichotomy* of the privileged language (English) versus vernaculars, whereas accelerating modernization processes during the periods of Renaissance and Enlightenment in Europe had resurrected European languages from the dominance of classical languages—Latin and Greek (Khubchandani 1973b).

2. The Western Enlightenment imbibed through English contact radically changed the concept of education for the Indian elite. The "modern" conviction of the supremacy of mother tongue brought the demands for the use of Indian vernaculars for formal communication (i.e., administration, academic achievement, etc.). Dyanand Saraswati, in the latter part of the 19th Century, followed by Tagore (1906) and Gandhi (1916) were among the leading champions of the struggle for vernacularization in education. These trends, to a certain extent, shook the dichotomous structure of the liaison between elite and the masses which existed in the medieval period and was also perpetuated by the English rulers.

3. Diversification of language use prevailing in the traditional educational setup of South Asia was regarded by the colonial rulers as a "handicap." Many British administrators responded with a sense of bafflement to relatively fluid segmentation patterns in language behavior of the Indian society, and often expressed their annoyance concerning "the want of precision of the people" in identifying their language.[21] Axiomatically correlating their own values of social homogenization, the rulers laid great emphasis on clear-cut categorization and monistic solutions concerning languages and scripts. Many administrators engaged themselves in standardizing a single writing system, a single standard grammar, and a single style for every domain of use, in the name of bringing order into a "chaotic" situation.[22]

4. Indian languages have traditionally been characterized by "loan proneness" from the classical as well as spoken languages. Bilingual contacts with English have been greatly instrumental in cultivating various styles of expression in Indian languages to cater to the needs of modern society. The anglicization tendency in many languages is evident in the "high-brow" spoken styles among urban speech communities which are markedly different from the "high-brow" written styles. The introduction of the printing press also played a significant role in developing Indian prose through the publication of reference works, grammars, dictionaries, encyclopedias, and translations of creative literature and works of knowledge from different European languages.

AFTER THE INDEPENDENCE

University Education

When the British left the country in 1947, there were many schools in which education up to primary and secondary stages was given in major Indian languages of the respective regions. But at the higher education stage, the universities recognized *only* English as the medium with no alternatives.[23] During the

Independence struggle, in thrust for language autonomy and language privileges, many political and educational organizations had built up strong pressures to extend Indian languages as media at the university level.

Initially, the new Congress Government showed a good deal of enthusiasm for rapid change in the medium policy, and some universities expressed their willingness to introduce Hindi, Urdu, and other regional languages as media within five years (India 1948). The University Education Commission in 1949 also endorsed the view that the switch-over to the mother tongue education should be achieved within the next five years in all universities so as to promote cultural renaissance and social integration. But soon it became evident that, because of the conflicting ideological pressures among the national leaders and also the unenthusiastic response from the education experts who operated within the "established" system the government had to face an uphill task as far as the fulfillment of such aspirations was concerned.

In this tussle for leadership among the "established" and the "rising" elites, various language interest groups adopted rigid stands regarding language policy at the university stage:

1. The supporters of English claimed the virtues of having an "advanced" medium for technological and scientific progress.

2. The supporters of Hindi were motivated by the interests of cultural regeneration and cohesion at the national level.

3. The supporters of regional languages emphasized the facility of expression for students, and were guided by the claims of equal privileges and autonomy for their languages.

National leaders like Nehru, Azad, and Zakir Husain (1950) were the early champions of a common medium. Moderating over rigid postures in medium controversy, they suggested the *alternate* media policy, where Hindi serving the national interests could be adopted as the university medium along with English as a universally developed medium of knowledge. But the Terachand Commission (1948) rejected Hindi as a common medium for universities and suggested regional media in the states for administrative and academic purposes, restricting the common medium for the federal government.

The Official Language Commission in 1956 spelled out the criteria for the choice of medium at the university stage on the basis of the facility of expression, and the usefulness of such a medium for students. It endorsed the alternate media policy with regional language as the major medium. A variety of solutions cropped up in the dissenting notes:

1. English with alternative (Hindi, or dominant regional language).

2. Hindi with alternatives (English, or regional languages).

3. Sole Hindi medium.

4. Sole regional language medium.

The latter two suggestions were later dubbed "Hindi imperialism" and "language chauvinism," respectively, by the opponents of these solutions in the controversy.

The University Grants Commission in its 1960 Report pointed out the difficulties of students when moving from a mother tongue medium school to the English medium university education, leading to "parrot learning" and the crippling of original thought. It strongly pleaded that the sole dependence on English was widening the gulf between the educated few and the uneducated masses, which cannot be nourished in a democratic society.

During the fifties many sociopolitical and legal battles were fought over the university medium issue concerning Bombay, Gujarat, and Madras universities. The state governments' enthusiasm for switching over to Hindi, Gujarati, or Tamil was frustrated by the professional bodies. Hence, by and large, the states had to compromise their position, and leave the program of switch-over in the universities largely unimplemented. At the time of linguistic reorganization of states in 1956, it was strongly felt throughout the country that language tensions were undermining the national unity. The demand for a nationwide common medium got into momentum on the pleas that national loyalty requires free and rather intense communication within the nation, and regional languages as sole media will damage the administrative, judicial, and academic integrity and scientific pursuits of the country.

Hence, from early catholic stands of *sole* English, Hindi, or regional language, by 1961 a new approach promoting a *link* language had gained favor among national leaders. English and Hindi enthusiasts again seized the opportunity for claiming the "new" *link* status. Some southern and eastern states showed preference for English in place of Hindi as a common medium. The Link Language Formula was evolved by the Central Advisory Board of Education in 1962, suggesting that regional language medium would be necessary for removing the gap between the masses and the intellectual elites; and English as the "transitional," and Hindi as the "eventual" link languages will promote national unity, mobility among teachers and students, and the standards of education. The timing of the switch-over to the new system was left open. About the eventual adoption of Hindi as the link language, a veto was given to the states, and also to the professionals for the gradual and well-prepared change from English to the regional languages and Hindi.

Many professionals continued to emphasize the utility of highly cultivated media as precision instrument of thinking and communication through which students can be trained in logical thought and in the disciplined use of words. A UGC Committee reporting on Standards of University Education (1965) went to the extent of saying that: "A change is justified only when the university is confident of raising standards by doing so. Unless an Indian language has grown up to its full stature, with a good literature in science and other subjects, the move for its acceptance as the medium of instruction immediately would be a retrograde step." (p. 71)[24]

After the unsuccessful attempts of the fifties, the forces of hypersensitive language chauvinism are now considerably weakened, and rapid change in the media of education at the university level is ruled out. The status quo of English as a compulsory medium for some time to come is now being widely accepted in most of the university campuses, on the pleas that knowledge is more important than the medium, and standards are more important than the timetables. By hard struggle the Indian languages are now proving themselves increasingly practicable and acceptable for a wider range of study in the "elitistic" framework of education. Today after the lapse of over a quarter century, the citadels of higher learning have yielded only in providing an *alternate* medium of regional language usually associated with the "ordinary" tradition in education, for humanities and commerce courses up to the graduate level.

Thus the English status quo supporters won the battle of *time* and the Hindi and regional language supporters felt contented with the formal *recognition* of their viewpoint, and also with their claims over large funds for language development.

Mother Tongue in School

It is rather amazing to find, in a large nation committed to the gigantic task of eradicating illiteracy, that its intellectuals, with their political power and educational expertise, get entangled in the web of language privileges at the university level under the pretexts of the range and quality of education. During British rule the English medium indisputably remained a mark of superior "advanced" education, and the regional languages media were conceded a role for somewhat inferior "ordinary" education in rural and urban areas.

Many sociopolitical and psychological generalizations about the supremacy of mother tongue made during the Independence movement have, to a great extent, obscured the picture. The issues concerning the facility of expression in mother tongue have been highlighted in rather simplistic terms, by juxtaposing mother tongue against the foreign language—English. It is being taken for granted that a foreign medium hampers the growth of creativity and talents. In this conflict anti-Hindi lobbies regard even Hindi, along with English, as a foreign language. The advocates of mother tongue ideology have not cared to define the bounds of mother tongue; nor has adequate attention been paid to accounting for the diverse patterns of language hierarchy prevailing in multilingual plural societies. One notices several inhibitions among educationists concerning the problems of the wide gap between the hinterland varieties and the "elegant" urban-based standard languages, being imposed as *school* mother tongue.

The Central Advisory Board of Education in its 1930 Annual Meeting had accepted literary language of the region as the medium of education and made it quite clear that dialects are unacceptable as media of instruction (India 1960: pp. 39-40). In several elementary education curricula one often notices an over-emphasis on careful drilling in the "correct" forms of standard regional speech and pronunciation. Thus the acquisition of literacy in languages like Hindi, Urdu, Panjabi, Marathi, and Tamil becomes more like learning a "second" language. The vast Hindi-Urdu-Panjabi (HUP) region, comprising 46% of the country's total population, represents a unique case where identificational considerations of communication override the linguistic characteristics, and the Hindi, Urdu, and

Panjabi language loyalties in thrust for rival claims of solidarity incorporate many vernaculars of the region—Pahari, Lahnda, Rajasthani, Maithili, Bhojpuri, Awadhi, Chhatisgarhi—in their overall speech matrices. One notices a superposed homogeneity in communication patterns on the cline of urbanization in the entire region. Speech behavior of these people represents a pattern of the "divided joint family," where different languages enjoy hierarchical positions under a single umbrella but once again are split in diametrically opposite camps, namely, Hindi and Urdu (in some regions the split between Hindi and Panjabi is also more ideological than linguistic) (Khubchandani 1972a; 1974a).

So far there does not seem to be much realization of the difficulties which the rural population face arising out of the unintelligibility of the *instant* "high-brow" standards projected in mother tongue textbooks. This lack of recognition of the problem results in the wastage and stagnation in literacy programs. Most standardization devices in Indian languages today serve only to extend the "tradition-inspired" value system of small elites over all domains in the entire speech community. The pleas of language leaders for developing puristic "academic," "official" standards of language—on the lines of the 19th Century Latinized English, and the Sanskritized or Perso-Arabicized "high-brow" literary styles of Indian languages—puts a heavy strain on the users of language and contradicts in itself the concerns for the facility of expression of students through mother tongue education. The catholicity about the elite-acceptable diction of one's own speech often makes native speakers "alien" and "handicapped" in their own surroundings, unable to cope even with simple communication needs because of the new values and norms proclaimed for their speech behavior, especially in the domains of public communication—administration, education, mass media, etc. In heterogeneous plural environments, a child acquires language from everyday life situations where language behavior is guided by various implicit pressures based on close-group, regional, supraregional, outgroup, urban, and pan-Indian identities (for further elaboration, see Khubchandani 1974b). "One of the problems which should engage our (Indian) language teachers is the question of accepting what is standard over the whole linguistic area." (Katre 1959: p. 210.)

On the practical plane, with the professed policy of the Indianization of "alien" education system, the administrators were soon confronted with the demands of mother tongue education by the linguistic minorities. Initially the administrators' approach was of "harassed bureaucrats trying to impose a workable system on linguistic chaos." (Dakin 1968: p. 31). Eighty-seven percent of the country's total population is aligned with 12 major regional languages: 76% residing in their home states, and 11% staying outside their home regions. Once the dominant groups' right to mother tongue education was fully assured in their respective states, the new governing class did not lose much time in focusing its attention on the practical objectives of economy, utility, communication, and political cohesion, as far as it was concerned with the demands of the remaining 13% linguistic minorities, comprising a total of over 50 million speakers (at the time of the 1961 Census).[25]

The University Education Commission (1949) and the Official Language Commission (1956) felt that "the languages of the large advanced and organized groups with a current literature, practice and tradition" were the *only* fit media of instruction (OLC: p. 27). The first President of India, Dr. Rajendra Prasad, pointed out in 1961 that the costs of making separate arrangements of mother tongue education for different linguistic groups would be "colossal" and it "is feasible only if the linguistic group is of an appreciable size and forms a compact region. It cannot be reasonably demanded by those who are very small in number or are scattered in different parts of other linguistic regions." (India 1961: pp. 13-15.)

Different expert bodies on education such as Central Advisory Board of Education (1948), University Education Commission (1949), Official Language Commission (1956) gave greater weight to the *broad* interpretation of mother tongue, i.e., regarding all minority languages not having any written tradition as "dialects" of the dominant language in the region, by which there was implicit denial of equal rights to linguistic minorities on the ground of practicability.[26] Many protagonists of major languages pointed out that it is illogical to seek literacy in languages that have no literature. But during the past two decades, the linguistic minorities have shown greater vigilance in safeguarding their rights for mother tongue education, and have practically succeeded in getting the authorities to accept the *narrow* interpretation of mother tongue, by which the home language of each child, "the language spoken from the cradle" is accepted as mother tongue (1951 Census of India 1954: p. 1). Most of the state governments now show a sense of tolerance of the heterogeneity of education media in their multilingual pockets.

After initial reluctance, the narrow interpretation was conceded in favor of linguistic minorities who identified with a major language outside the region—languages which "transcended provincial barriers" (Azad 1949). But major languages without any specific region, such as Urdu and Sindhi, had to face initial discrimination in certain states like Uttar Pradech in getting the facilities of mother tongue education.[27] The concessions to the tribal and other such minority languages were slow in coming. The All-India Language Development Conference in 1953 and the Congress Working Committee in 1954 accepted tribal languages as media in the primary school stage.

The safeguards of mother tongue education at the primary school stage for linguistic minorities were also spelled out in the Three-Language Formula in 1956. Some concessions were even conceded for the continuance of secondary education through tribal languages media wherever possible. But the pace of implementation has been rather slow.

In a critical appraisal of the role of mother tongue in education, a study conducted at the National Council of Education Research and Training (NCERT) highlights wide disparities in sociocultural traditions of states, and consequently it points out that education through the minority languages, which hold subordinate position in society and are relatively less cultivated, is likely to produce uneven levels of achievements. Such a situation is bound to create unequal opportunities for higher education and employment for minority communities (Goel and Saini 1972). The Constitutional provisions for safeguarding the interests of the linguistic minorities being recommendatory and not mandatory, one notices lack of enthusiasm on the part of state authorities in their implementation of such programs.[28] Authorities still have not given up their hope that in practice the linguistic minorities will come to accept the advantages of the regional languages.

Similar to the British ambivalence in accepting the principle of *universal* education but directing their resources for *selective* education, the present policies of the state governments also seem to be ambivalent as far as giving lip service to the narrow definition of mother tongue but directing their attention and energies, along with their resources, to the development of regional languages, Hindi, and even English. Requirements of "elegance" in education, apart from slowing down the pace of switch-over from developed media to emerging media, also inhibit the introducing of literacy in an economical manner.[29] Common man has to be educated to use the language, quite unrelated to the facility in communication, of the academic.

LANGUAGE IDEOLOGY

Roots of the intense language controversies in South Asia can be found in the "schizophrenic" handling of education by the British rulers. They were responsible, to a large extent, for the mobilization of "native" pressure groups championing the cause of different languages by arbitrarily distributing favors or prejudices through language concessions or constraints (awarding or withdrawing recognition to one or another vernacular or writing system), just to bring some order into the "chaotic" diversity, or at times to serve imperial interests. Various instant, but often vacillating, decisions with regard to language education on the part of British rulers seem to have played a vital role in shaking the traditional fluid modes of language loyalty in South Asia (Khubchandani 1973c). The great debate about language policies among colonial administrators and the "native" elite for over a century has left deep imprints on contemporary language ideologies of different nations in the subcontinent. There are no two opinions regarding the *spread* of education. The eradication of illiteracy is regarded as the primary target of educational programs. But the *content* and the *medium* of education continue to agitate the minds of education experts. Out of the two, the politicization of language issue during the struggle for Independence dominated the medium controversy, pushing into the background the ideological issues concerning the content of the education.

Tagore (1906) and Gandhi (1916) pleaded for bringing education and life closer. The demand for vernacularization was associated with cultural and national resurgence, and eventually with the growth of democracy promoting equality of opportunity through education. All the maladies of "ineffective" education—lack of responsiveness, poverty of original thinking, prevalence of parrot learning—and other imbalances in the traditional societies which generated from the alien system were romantically attributed to the alien (i.e., English) medium. In spite of severe criticism of the content of present education for not being well integrated with the society, no formidable challenge has been posed to the white-collar-oriented, urban-biased education. The dichotomy, perpetuated by the education system between those who have education and those who have not, continues to prevail in the form of urban-elite standards as far as the medium and the content of education are concerned. Gandhiji's program of Basic Education, catering to the needs of rural masses, could not be pursued by the national elites wedded to the supremacy of "elegant" education. Hence the only salvation for rural illiterates appears to be by seating their way to the camp of the "privileged" urban literates.

One of the most intricate characteristics in the medium debate has been the uncritical acceptance of the Western education theories of the early 20th Century, mostly derived from the experiences of tackling the issues of relatively more homogenized societies, and also at a time when the thrust of technology was less pervasive than in the present times. Many modern education experts regard it as axiomatic that the best medium for teaching a child is its mother tongue. Several psychological, educational, sociopolitical, and historical arguments are advanced in support of this contention.[30] The Secondary Education Commission (1956) also endorsed this view: "Learning through the mother tongue is the most potent and comprehensive medium for the expression of the student's entire personality."

In the thrust for canvassing mother tongue medium, experts did not fully comprehend the plural character of Indian society at large, where a child's earliest firsthand experiences of life do not necessarily resemble the formal "school version" of his mother tongue. In societies where speech habits are not consistently identified with a particular language label esteem for a particular *ideal* of speech or a sociopolitical belief may lead individuals to identify with a prestigious major language group which need not necessarily be one's native speech.[31] In multilingual and multidialectal societies we often come across speech groups which have virtual native control over more than one language or dialect. One notices an inevitable measure of fluidity in certain regions in India and also among smaller groups throughout the country. In such situations one's total repertoire is controlled by more than one normative system, and language labels are not rigidly identified with fixed "stereotypes." A speech group associates the diversity of speech around it with different values in social interaction. A large gap between the speech patterns of a typical community and the socialization values promoted through school education is evident from the examples of Marathi and Santhali heterogeneous speech groups discussed elsewhere (Khubchandani 1974b).

In the linguistic and educational jargon, the terms "mother tongue" and "native speech" are often used indistinguishably, which leads to some indeterminacy when applied in different contexts. The term *native speech* can be distinguished as "the *first* speech acquired in infancy, through which the child gets socialized." It claims some bearing on "intuitive" competence, and potentially it can be individually identifiable. The term *mother tongue* is mainly "categorized by one's allegiance to a particular *tradition*, and it is societally identifiable." In the ingroup/outgroup dichotomy, a speech variety which members of a group (or, in extreme cases, even an individual) regard as their own is accepted as their mother tongue. Though the actual speech of an individual is marked by various *diverse* and *heterogeneous* characteristics revealing stratificational demands of the context, people perceive their own and others' speech in categorical terms as discrete language A or language B, as if it were *uniform* and *homogeneous*. This paradox of "heterogeneous" performance and "homogenized" perception (i.e., categorization) is one of the characteristic features of speech behavior (Khubchandani 1974a).

In various regions in South Asia different socialization processes identify the characteristics of a speech stratum—local speech, subregional, supraregional varieties, lingua franca, high-brow dictions—associating them with a variety of interactions on the cline: close ingroup → wider ingroup → intergroup → mobility → mass communication → urban contact → formal (model for prestige). In such diversified speech areas, education programs need to be geared to facilitate the scope of communication with the prevailing socialization values in a community extending from one's native speech to "associate native" speech, second language, and totally unfamiliar language.

Many speakers of the north-central region of India, who are not native speakers of Hindi or Urdu in the strict linguistic sense but claim Hindi/Urdu as their mother tongue in the census returns, command, by and large, native-like control over Hindi/Urdu, and either of the languages is almost an "associate native speech" to them. They are also called "adherent speakers," distinguishing them from "native" and "foreign" speakers (Kelkar 1968). For such people Hindi or Urdu represents a particular tradition. Most of the speakers in the region, particularly those in Uttar Pradesh, Madhya Pradesh, and Bihar, are quite unaware of their bilingual or multilingual behavior (Khubchandani 1972). For them switching of linguistic codes from native speech to Hindi/Urdu is similar to the switching of styles (such as informal/formal) in a monolingual situation. Kloss (1967) calls such vernaculars "near dialectized" languages: "Functionally as well as psychologically they are accepted by their speakers as dialect-like tools of oral communication (plus, at best, of unassuming poetry)."

The simplistic projection of mother tongue education as a means of establishing equality of opportunity for individual self-advancement has led to discarding the principle of language *hierarchy* in education. It has given way to the demands of language *autonomy*, i.e., "the promotion of full-fledged or autonomous status for a language as an exclusive vehicle for *full expression* in different fields of knowledge and in all walks of life." It is being taken for granted that the "high-brow" values of speech communication—uniformity, precision, elegance, purity of form, allegiance to literary tradition, elaboration of language through coinage of technical terms—are essential paths for developing a *medium* language (Khubchandani 1975d).

Theoretically, the arguments for mother tongue supremacy based on "elegant" urban standards hold very little substance as far as the facility of expression is concerned. The sudden imposition of a standard variety by a language elite on a community creates serious communication gaps (Pandit 1972). Such an "instant standard" remains unintelligible to the hinterland communities for a long time, and its tyranny hampers mass literacy programs.

So pervasive, in our times, is the distinction between developed and underdeveloped (euphemistically called developing) stages of economies, societies, and even cultures that many language experts are led to employ the same dichotomy for languages too. Many language elites, guided by the post-Renaissance European trends—such as creation of new standard languages, assimilation of neighboring dialects and tribal languages—regard such *homogenization* processes as inevitable in the contemporary modernization stages of Asia and Africa as well. In their thrust for "modernity," they either seek to get their speech recognized as a developed "absolute" language or abandon the "handicapped" speech altogether in favor of the one believed to be the "privileged" variety.[32]

In this dichotomous process, many less fortunately placed speech varieties—which may be dialects, vernaculars, or minority languages or may have nonelite styles—stand in danger of becoming totally extinct.[33] As the age-old, harmonious hierarchic patterning of different speech varieties (or languages) in one's verbal repertoire gets disturbed, it gives birth to disharmony among different speech groups (such as issues of language privileges in education and state boundary disputes over language identity in India). The dichotomous approach in "language development," in a way, depicts the futile race to catch up with the Joneses, as is evident from Macaulay's program (1835) of "refining the vernacular dialects," and also the British rulers' targets of vernacular development in response to the demand for Vernacular University in 1867. By the time the vernaculars struggle their way to acquiring the credibility of "developed" languages, the latter will have moved higher with additional honors, such as usability with computers, or space satellites and so on (Khubchandani 1973d).

The issue of "language development" merits close scrutiny to consider the chances of success of the present aspirations of language elite in developing nations, shaped in the "language autonomy" mold, to meet the needs of their heterogeneous pluralistic communities. Many typical problems confronting developing nations as a result of present language strategies are discussed in detail elsewhere (Khubchandani 1974b).

The magnitude of various linguistic and education problems in developing countries is quite outside the experience of most European countries either in the past or in the present. In most Western homogenized nation-states, identification of the standard core and demarcation of boundaries of a mother tongue are no longer sources of tension. Textbook standards of different languages, drawn from respective literary traditions, were stabilized along with the continuing process of urbanization. One does not find any apparent conflicts between the stabilized standard and actual speech variations in a language area. By and large, a speech community's *image* of language, its *identity* postures through language, and *actual use* of language have acquired some congruity within a language *territory*. But the intricacies of language behavior in the Indian context reveal apparent ambiguities in defining the concept of mother tongue itself. Mother tongue *identity* and its *image* do not necessarily claim congruity with actual *usage*, and these are again not rigidly identified with specific language *territories* (Khubchandani 1976a). The scope of mother tongue education, therefore, need to be reassessed in the light of recent insights gained from the studies of plural societies.

As already discussed, the issues regarding the *content*, the *spread*, and the *medium* of instruction have been matters of great concern to educationists for a long time. Contemporary thinking on the subject has come a long way from the early phase of *selective* education through the media of classical languages (such as Latin, Greek, Sanskrit, Persian-Arabic) and colonial languages (such as English, French, Spanish, Portuguese) to the later phase of *universal* education through the medium of the student's mother tongue. But the multiplicity of mother tongues in various regions has led to the reexamination of the supremacy of mother tongue medium stretched over the entire education career. In recent years, many political and academic agencies have lent their support to the claims of imparting education through either a single *dominant* language in the region, or through some sort of compartmentalized and *selective* bilingual media, in order to keep pace with the socioeconomic demands of rapid modernization.

Under various political pressures, it is now being conceded that the mother tongue cannot be the *only* language of education. But surprisingly very little research has been conducted in the country regarding the evaluation of mother tongue and nonnative languages as media of education. Experiments on bilingual education in the United States, Canada, the Soviet Union, Yugoslavia, and Singapore have shown favorable results among linguistically heterogeneous areas. But so far, little attention seems to have been paid to evaluating the differentiating roles of mother tongue and nonnative languages as media of instruction. Bilingual education requires a degree of planning, a proficiency in the language of the classroom and in the language(s) of learners, and a level of skill in teaching. The validity of these assumptions for a complex plural society such as India needs to be attested.

LANGUAGE INSTITUTION

In many developing countries, with overt language loyalty pressures in political and education setup, language is emerging as the most important element in identifying with a "group." It is displayed as an emblem of national or group solidarity.

Until the recent mobilization of pressure groups over language, one noticed that among many Indian communities the urge of belonging to a particular language group was often relegated to somewhat less significant status in one's subjective evaluation of social strata. Language consciousness on the Indian social and political scene, sharpened over the past century, is characterized by the lack of harmony and goodwill among different language interest groups. In the polemics over the language issue, one major confrontation is between the camps supporting English and those supporting indigenous languages in administration, education, public media, etc. At issue here are not only matters of a concern for modernization and of cultural regeneration, but also the tussle for leadership between the English-knowing westernized "established elite" and the regional "rising elite."

The dominance of English during the British rule has a reaction to the other extreme, i.e., total switch from English to indigenous languages in the post-British period. Champions of regional languages and Hindi, under the spell of a hypersensitive chauvinistic complex, are mostly guided by the presumption that Indian languages cannot be developed for full expression in different fields of knowledge until English is dislodged from its present privileged position. This demand for the creation of a "vacuum" in favor of Indian languages, apart from a concern for the optimal development of talent latent through the full use of mother tongue, is to a great extent motivated by the issues of employment and economic opportunities. Alienation of the established elite from the masses has been a great source of irritation to newly rising democratic forces in the country. Revolt against English, apart from having the overtones of national pride, is primarily the symptom of the revolt against this established privileged "caste."

The established elite, on the other hand, has a vested interest in maintaining the predominance of English in all spheres of life and has been clamoring for the status quo in the name of Indian unity and of the advantages for a nation in possessing a "world" language. Clash of interests between regional languages and Hindi, and the underdevelopment of Indian languages for modern needs are cited as factors necessitating the retention of English. The task of language transition could be somewhat smoother, if the English elite gave up the notion of "exclusive dominance" and worked in "partnership" with Indian languages in the fields of public communication. There is a good deal of truth in the charge that the westernized intelligentsia do not care to address their own people but seek an international audience and within the country move in the "clubs" of their self-restricted elite. The English-educated elite in India develop a "kind of dual personality." Their personal life is virtually sealed off from their drawing-room behavior acquired through education in "a kind of linguistic polythene bag" (Le Page 1964: p. 20).

Considering the linguistically heterogeneous composition of nearly half of the districts in the country—where minority speech groups exceed 20% of the district population (152 out of 330 districts, at the time of the 1961 Census)—the numerical majority of twelve regional languages in respective regions does not necessarily correspond with the language communication patterns in those areas (Khubchandani 1975a). Demands for the regional languages media during the Independence struggle merely signified the assertive attitudes of the pressure groups aligned with the numerically dominant language in a region. During the past three decades, with the politicization of language pressure groups, attention has been greatly focused toward legislating the roles of language in public spheres of communication, i.e., administration, education, mass media, etc. In this regard, national leaders show great mastery in tightrope walking, recognizing the strengths and weaknesses of diverse pressure groups in language politics. With a view to resolve the highly sensitized issues of language privileges, several language labels—such as home languages, regional language, link language, national language, official language, literary language, library language, world language—have acquired political salience in education programs (Khubchandani 1975b).

Many of the issues generating acrimonious debates at the national level, sometimes erupting into campus skirmishes, do not seem to have much relevance to the quality of education. Prominent axes over which the medium controversy have become polarized during the past 150 years are shown in Table 4.

In lang-drawn sociopolitical and legal squabbles over the medium, one notices various shades of opinions moderating between the two extremes. Eventually the status quo experts seem to have succeeded temporarily in their strategy by their insistence that the Indian vernaculars should first be cultivated through translations from advanced languages and, before even undertaking this task, they must equip themselves with the scientific terminologies appropriate for different subjects. Because of the "high-brow" elegant values in the formal language behavior, the task of cultivating urban-based standards has been the prerogative of the so-called "purists" of language. Ironically, in the elite parlance, the modern languages saturated with the instant derivation of terms from nonnative *classical* and neoclassical stocks—Sanskrit, Perso-Arabic, or classical Tamil—are regarded as *shuddha* "pure" languages, but those mixed with the everyday life terms borrowed from other *living* languages—such as English, Bengali, Marathi—matching with the newly acquired concepts from different cultures, are regarded as KhichRii "hotch-potch, potpourri" languages.

The preparation of textbooks for teaching technical subjects at the higher education stage is guided by the values set by ideological and literary leadership, and *not* by the exigencies of individual subjects, of professionals, and of the recipients of education. Thanks to the purists' antagonism toward endowing new concepts with expressions borrowed from real life, many scholars in various fields, finding the lofty coinages forbidding, are discouraged from making meaningful contributions through their native language.

Various programs of change pay scant regard to the reorientation limitations of the professionals, who in turn adopt the "obstructionist" attitude in implementation. Teachers who could play pivotal role in implementation programs are consequently reluctant to join in the processes of language shift, as most of them regard the issues concerning language policy as politically motivated and falling short on the test of practicability. One often notices a strong bias among them for leaning toward the rigid political stands concerning the functions and the content of different languages in the education curriculum. Against this background, teachers particularly of the advanced stages of education, who are themselves the product of *select* education systems remain, by and large, uninvolved in the developmental processes of language media, demanding the cultivation of Indian languages on the platter and waiting conveniently till the "developed" textbooks are produced by the language experts.[34]

The actual beneficiaries in this game are the multilingual elites who adopt language *postures* according to the ideologies preferring cultural resurgence,

Table 4.

Conflicting issues	Extreme stands professed by the "established" elite	Extreme stands professed by the "emerging" groups
1. Objectives of education	Universal values of knowledge	Knowledge in consonance with cultural background
2. Role of language in education	Autonomy of mother tongue as a full-fledged medium (from primary to advanced stages)	Language hierarchy with multitier media (preparatory, auxiliary, and major media—linked with the relevance of education)
3. Choice of medium	Common medium (national or universal)	Plural media (regional and minority languages)
4. Requirements qualifying medium languages	a. Advanced languages with "tradition-inspired" literary standards	Vernacular languages, with prevailing "situation-bound" implicit propriety controls
	b. Cultivated with "elegant" terminologies and translations	Endowed with uninhibited convergance resulting from pidginization, hybridization, code switching
5. Pace of change	Status quo or, if change at all, only after adequate preparation	Rapid change from dominating language(s) by creating "vacuum" in favor of vernacular languages

language autonomy in education, common medium, elegant styles, "vacuum" theory; but in actual *usage*, they feel at home in the prevailing patterns in education—cherishing universal knowledge, language hierarchy, alternate media, hybridization, code switching, and status quo. One is confronted with an interesting characteristic of regional "neo-elites" who have succeeded in manipulating the colonial education system to their advantage by aligning themselves with the masses through the demands of cultural resurgence and rapid change in education system, but at the same time professing the "elitistic" values of language autonomy, uniform medium, and elegant styles of "school" language. Hence in everyday verbal communication one notices enormous fluidity and diversity of codes dealing with the informal situations, whereas in the formal situations, particularly in the written form, one demands compartmentalized "appropriate" and "correct" usage according to the professed language policy.

LANGUAGE PLANNING AND EDUCATION

The heterogeneity of communication patterns in many regions, unequal cultivation of different languages for their use as media, demands of "high-brow" elegant versions of *school* mother tongue, nonavailability of personnel with adequate command over the *textbook* language, and the switching over to another medium in the multitier media system without adequate preparation are some of the difficulties faced by learners initiated to education through the mother tongue medium. As already pointed out, in actual practice one notices a wide gap between the professed language policies and actual practice in the classroom. It is not unusual to find institutions with anomalous patterns of communication where the teacher and taught interact in one language, classrooms are conducted in another, textbooks are written in a third, and answers are given in a fourth language/style.

Language identity in the present Indian situation is characterized by the demands of language privileges in different walks of life and consequently the "high-brow" content of privileged language is cherished for its "ornate" functions. But language as a means of communication in a plural society and as a means of social mobility acquires significantly different characteristics under the pressures of modernization. It is mostly the students who bear the total brunt of the imbalances arising out of the emphasis on language privileges and language elegance at the cost of communicability.

Thus one finds the linguistic needs and the capacity of learners are the greatest casualties in the present language education programs. Present education policies aim at replacing the easygoing *grassroot* multilingualism of the illiterate masses by the *elegant* bilingualism (or trilingualism) with standardization pulls from different directions, e.g., neo-Sanskritic Hindi, Perso-Arabicized Urdu, BBC or AIR English, medieval literary Telugu, classicized modern Tamil. One finds that even though considerable time is spent on the second and third languages in school these languages are either restricted for "library" use or find no application at all in meaningful communicative tasks during the *entire* school career. Thus the rigid demands on education turn the *effortless* gift of social verbalization among the illiterates into a strenuous, time-consuming task of learning the elite-acceptable diction of its own speech. This results in the depiction of IQ and other talent indexes through a skillful competence in a particular "tradition." In the so-called "advanced" speech behavior, spontaneity and creativity leading to hybridization is rationed through the standardization processes. Language boundaries become sacred. The contextual and functional fluidity in speech, which manages to go across the boundaries of languages or dictions is deprecated by the custodians of language.

The new values of autonomy and standardization have lured many language reformers toward the *exclusive* development of the dominant languages in each region. With the result, major language groups aspire for the educational setup where the student should *strictly* be conditioned to a single medium throughout his long career of education (from the age of 6 to 21 or so, roughly 15 years) and the teaching of two nonnative languages—Hindi and English under the Formula— to be conceded a place in the school curriculum as an "exercise" for eventual use in his adult life but having no immediate bearing in day-to-day communication of the student (just as classical and foreign languages are taught for limited functional value). But, in spite of the diverse speech patterns, the Indian society as a whole depicts a kind of "organic unity" resting in its pluralistic model of speech behavior. In pluralistic nations such as India, the principles of "situation-bound" language planning can provide a sound basis for bringing dynamic adjustments in response to the real-life communication settings (for a detailed discussion in the context of Indian education, see Khubchandani 1973d; 1974b).

Various constraints in the spread of education are attributed to the multiplicity of languages, whereas the real issues to cope with are the confrontation between "tradition" and "modernity" with regard to their role in education, and dogmatic rigidity in claiming privileges for different languages in the education curriculum. When dealing with the education for plural societies, we shall do well to realize the risks involved in *uniform* solutions.

One general concern of language experts in education for developing societies seems to be to adjust the patterns of speech behavior of a community to the new demands of modernization. The educated elite construes change as "replacement" of values, instead of "increment the existing order. Most of these efforts seem to imply the *handicap* model to achieve the determined targets of development. It may be more fruitful to consider the *adaptation* model and take into account the given assets as well as handicaps in meeting the new challenges. In order to counter the fractionalizing tendencies in these societies, it is essential to draw upon the traditional virtues of language tolerance promoted through language hierarchy grassroot multilingualism, and fluidity in speech behavior.

NOTES

1. The 1961 Census enumerates a total of 1652 mother tongues, returned by the population of 439 million; 1019 of the mother tongue, covering 438.6 million speakers are classified under nearly 200 languages; 103 mother tongues, covering 315,000 speakers, are of foreign

origin; and the remaining 530 are unclassified varieties, covering only 63,000 speakers, whose affiliations could not be determined (Mitra 1964, annexures I-III; pp. ccxxvii-ccxxxix).

2. "It is clear that in the West, specifically in the United States of America, the prestige of the old established English-speaking community works with such powerful pressure for conformity that the languages even of sizeable immigrant groups are generally wiped out in a very few generations. . . . In India immigrant situations often result otherwise than in America. After a period of at least fifteen centuries of migration Saurashtran still survives as the domestic language of the immigrant silk weavers in Madura (Madras State)" (Emeneau 1962).

3. A classic example is of bilingual Muslims oscillating between the *regional* and *religious* identities. One notices Muslims having much closer ties with Urdu than other religious groups. As Muslim population is mostly scattered throughout the country, so is Urdu. A large section of Muslims in many regions tend to have bilingual control over the language of the region (Telugu, Kannada, Marathi, etc.) and Urdu (Khubchandani 1972).

4. For a detailed account of the patterns of hierarchy in language loyalties in the Broad Hindustani region, see Gumperz and Naim (1960); Khubchandani (1972; 1974a).

5. The Collector of Bellary district in 1823 reported that out of 533 schools in the district, 235 schools employed Carnataca (Kannada), 226 Teloogoo (Telugu), 23 Mahratta (Marathi), 21 Persian, 4 Tamil, one English medium; besides, 23 schools were exclusively for Brahmins, teaching "some of the Hindoo sciences, such as theology, astronomy, logic and law, still imperfectly taught in the Sanscrit language" (Sharp 1920: p. 65).

6. Burton (1851) gives an elaborate account of the state of education in Sindh before its conquest by the British in 1843 (pp. 134-157). According to him, a Hindu child started with the Devanagari script from a Brahmin teacher for studying religious texts in Sindhi and also acquiring rudiments of Sanskrit. He also learned Gurumukhi characters to read the *Granth*—a sacred text of the Sikhs and Hindus in northern India. An *Amil* boy (belonging to the "courtly" Hindu class) then moved to an *Akhund* (a Muslim or Hindi pedagogue under the *maktab* system) and got initiated in popular Persian poetry. A few studied Arabic also. The *Amil* boy is "then taken to some *daftar* (secretariat) by a relation to be initiated in the mysteries of *arzi* (petition writing in Persian), simple calculation, etc." (p. 149).

7. A detailed survey of the language policy of British rulers in India is made in Khubchandani (1971, 1976b).

8. The Governor-General, Warren Hastings, founded the *madressa,* the main and special object of which was "to qualify the sons of Muhamadan gentlemen for responsible and lucrative offices in the State, even at that date largely monopolised by the Hindus." (Sharp 1920: p. 7).

9. The Resident of Benaras, Duncan, writing to the Governor-General Cornwallis, cites important advantages derivable from such an establishment: "its tendency towards endearing our Government to the native Hindoos; by our exceeding attention towards them and their systems." (quoted in Sharp 1920: pp. 10-11).

10. The East India Company Act 1813, Section 43, Document No. 7, quoted in Sharp (1920: p. 22). The clause concerning the improvement of literature and the encouragement of learned natives of India was differently interpreted by the Orientalists and the Anglicists, the controversy over which dragged on till Macaulay's Minute in 1835. See documents Nos. 27-34, ibid.

11. A plea of the Revenue Member, Fraser (1823) for establishing schools in Delhi "for the children of the peasantry of the country side, to instruct in English, Persian and the Hindee

languages" was rejected on the grounds that it was "expedient that the appropriation of any limited funds assigned for the purpose of public education should be chiefly directed to the best of means of improving the education of the more respectable members of Indian society, especially those who make letters their profession." Document No. 5, quoted in Sharp (1920: pp. 13-15).

12. Charles Grant, in the 1797 treatise, suggested the suppression of vernaculars and the diffusion of English as the vehicle of imparting Western ideas; he called them "our superior lights," and the knowledge of Christianity. Document No. 22, quoted in Sharp (1920: pp. 81-83). Later in 1805, when Charles Grant became the Chairman of the East India Company, he continued his efforts as a staunch supporter of the pro-missionary and the Anglicist views in determining the British education policy in India.

13. Macaulay, in his famous Minute of 1835, arguing the intrinsic superiority of the Western literature, claimed with a pungent rhetoric: "We have to educate a people who cannot at present be educated by means of their mother-tongue. We must teach them some foreign language. The claims of our own language it is hardly necessary to recapitulate. It stands pre-eminent even among the languages of the West. . . . What the Greek and Latin were to the contemporaries of More and Ascham, our tongue is to the people of India. The literature of England is now more valuable than that of classical antiquity. I doubt whether the Sanscrit literature be as valuable as that of our Saxon and Norman progenitors (pp 110-111)." Document No. 30, quoted in Sharp (1920: pp. 107-117).

14. Raja Ram Mohan Roy, in his petition (1823) to the Prime Minister William Pitt, citing the merits of the Baconian philosophy which displaced the system of classical schools "the best calculated to perpetuate ignorance," points out that: "In the same manner Sangscrit (Sanskrit) system of education would be the best calculated to keep this country in darkness, if such had been the policy of the British Legislature." Document No. 26, quoted in Sharp (1920: pp. 98-101).

15. Document No. 32, quoted in Sharp (1920: pp. 130-131). Princep, registering his protest to the resolution calls it "a rash act" and "a declaration of the mischievous and injurious tendency." Document No. 34, quoted in Sharp (1920: p. 139).

16. Quoted in the Secondary Education Commission Report, 1953, p. 8.

17. Johnstone, the Political Agent of Nagaland (1873-1874), opposed the adoption of the "effeminate ways and religious characteristics of the Assamese (language)," and desired that Nagas should be instructed in English language and the Christian religion under the clergy of the Church of England. Quoted in Barpujari (1973: pp. 24-30).

18. In 1877, on the occasion of the Queen Victoria assuming the title of the Empress of India, the Government of Punjab's plea for a separate university with Indian languages as media of instruction without neglecting the study of English was accepted. Eventually, the Punjab University was established at Lahore in 1882 with a provision for vernacular education in the statutes, but in practice English, by and large, continued as the medium of examination and instruction. Document No. 42, Naik (1963: pp. 185-187).

19. Pleading for a self-governing India on Western lines, Gokhale, the leader of the Moderates in the Congress Movement, argued: "the quality of education assumes significance only after illiteracy is liquidated." Quoted in Abid Husain, Saiyidain, and Naik (1952: p. 65).

20. An UNESCO Report calculated the costs of providing universal education for the Indian population—expansion of school establishments, the teachers' salaries, provision of books and food, the compensation of parents for loss of child labor, etc., at three-fourths the total revenue of the central and state governments, and thus pointed out the futility of the

expansion of education on the lines as designed for the upper classes in urban areas (Dakin 1968: p. 10).

21. One finds the language question in every decennial census from 1881 gave rise to various doubts and misinterpretations in the minds of people of different regions, as well as baffling the alien rulers. The Census Commissioner Gait, in his Report (1913), remarks: "(In the United Provinces), simply because they refused to define their terms before they argued, or rather because they would not take the trouble to understand the terms as used by the census authorities, the controversialists, who were really quarreling about the respective merits of certain styles as vehicles of instruction, succeeded in utterly falsifying a set of important statistics relating to something entirely different (p. 320)."

22. The Sind government in 1852 set up a committee for recognizing a *single* script for Sindhi in the midst of diverse usage. Though philologists like Stack and Trumpp agreed upon a modified version of Devanagari to suit the needs of the Sindhi language, the rulers because of political considerations ultimately decided in favor of a modified Perso-Arabic script. But till today Sindhi migrants in India continue to be divided over the formal recognition of one *or* another script. This controversy, going on for over a century among the Sindhi elite, provides useful insights to the consequences of such monistic assertions (Khubchandani 1969a).

23. Except the Osmania University at Hyderabad, the Telugu-speaking princely state of Nizam, which had continued to teach through the Urdu medium for catering to the traditional Muslim education.

24. It is interesting to note that this argument against Indian languages has been held by some Indian elite for over a century. The objection of the Lahore Indian association in 1876 against establishing a vernacular university at Lahore is couched almost in the same phraseology that the vernacular medium will be a "retrograde and reactionary step as there being in the vernacular languages a sad want of textbooks for the higher examinations" and "the English being dispensed with, the standard of instruction must necessarily be lower than that of other universities." Document No. 65, Naik (1963: pp. 283-296).

25. "A child bred in an area where the regional language is something other than its own mother tongue acquires the regional language with almost the same facility as that with which (he) acquires (his) mother tongue." (Mathai 1959: pp. 9-10.)

26. This view seems to have dominated in the post-Renaissance period in Europe as well, when language was claimed as a major criterion for stabilizing nationalistic states, e.g., French view of minority languages—Provinçal (another Romance), Breton (a Celtic,), and Basque (a non-Indo-European), treating them as dialects of the dominant French (a Romance language).

27. The exclusion of Urdu, one of the 15 major languages recognized in the Constitution, from the U.P. schools, was justified on the grounds that the use of the Urdu script would handicap the children who learned it since Hindi (in the Devanagari script) and English were the languages they would require at the universities and in the services. (CABE, 15th Meeting, 1949, India Government, Ministry of Education 1960: pp. 222-223.)

28. In 1956, Articles 350A and 350B were inserted in the Constitution by the seventh Amendment Act according to which: "It shall be the endeavour of every state to provide adequate facilities for instruction in the mother tongue at the primary stage of education to children belonging to linguistic minority groups."

29. The state of affairs can be visualized from a report (1971) of the Directorate of Education in Nagaland stating that textbooks (even for the primary education) are being "originally written in English and then translated in local languages" as "authors in the local languages are not available" (Sharma 1971).

30. A UNESCO Report (1953) justifies the use of mother tongue as medium of education on the grounds that "Psychologically, it is the system of meaningful signs that in his [the student's] mind works automatically for expression and understanding. Sociologically it is a means of identification among the members of the community to which he belongs. Educationally, he learns more quickly through it than through an unfamiliar linguistic medium" (p. 11).

31. Among the mother tongue claimants of Hindi in the north-central region, one prominent category is of those monolinguals (mostly rural) who speak languages altogether different from Hindi—such as Panjabi, Pahari, and many languages belonging to the Rajasthani or Bihari group—but testify "Hindi" is their mother tongue, as they regard themselves as part of the great "Hindi tradition." From a strictly formal point of view, their speech will be considered distinctly different from the so-called "Hindi" (i.e., Khariboli) as understood by structuralists, academicians, and other custodians of language standardization (Khubchandani 1972a).

32. The elitistic concern of national leaders finds expression in Nehru's statement (1957): "We are driven to English, principally because we know it a good deal, we have people who can teach it, and because it is the most important language in the world today. The whole success of our development schemes depends upon training manpower. It is patent to me that this manpower for industrial scientific and agricultural purposes cannot be trained in any Indian language in the foreseeable future (p. 62)."

33. Discussing the language problems of the Blacks and the Spanish-Americans, Spolsky (1971) points out the cases where "language is used as an excuse, like race or skin color or sex, for not hiring someone. No amount of language training will change this, for the discrimination exists in the hearer and not the speaker (p. 2). . . . A child going to school must be taught the standard language if he is to have access to the general culture and economy. At the same time, he has a right to be taught in his own language while he is learning enough English to handle the rest of the curriculum (p. 4)."

34. University teachers in Madras State at the Annual Conference in 1952 expressed their reluctance to make any change until "a large variety of books and journals in the national and regional language become available."

V

Problems and Prospects

for Indigenous Languages and Bilingual Education

in New Zealand and Oceania

Richard A. Benton

INTRODUCTION

In New Zealand, as well as in the rest of Polynesia, Australia, Melanesia, and Micronesia, which together comprise the "Oceania" referred to in the title of this chapter, learning a second language has become almost synonymous with schooling for those people who continue to use the local vernaculars at home and in familiar settings. This in itself constitutes bilingual education of a sort, but it rarely involves a sustained attempt at using two languages as media of instruction, a process which has come increasingly to be accepted as essential to bilingual education properly so called (cf. Saville and Troike 1971:4, Gaarder 1967:110, John and Horner 1971:178).

For most of the indigenous peoples of Oceania, formal education in the Euro-American tradition has at some point involved a home-school language shift for the individual student. For contemporary speakers of indigenous languages at least, schooling beyond the elementary level (and, as often as not, at even the lowest level) requires the acquisition of a European language which is the means both of instruction and of communication within the school. In this process, the vernacular language generally has a limited role, and is often regarded by educators as a problem they have to contend with, rather than an extra resource brought by the pupil to the school. Even where the indigenous language has been taught as a subject in the post-primary grades, it has seldom been regarded by school authorities as of any great intrinsic value, but is seen rather as a means of enhancing the self-concept (and thereby facilitating the general progress) of the children to whom it is available. Similarly, in those areas where local vernaculars are used to some extent as media of instruction in the elementary grades, their main function is often seen as simply facilitating the development of concepts and attitudes which will form the basis for later, more advanced, learning in the language of the most successful colonial power.

By and large then, "bilingual" education in Oceania and New Zealand has taken the form of what Mackey (1970) calls acculturative transfer, accomplished in either single- or dual-medium schools. Very recently, however, an interest in bilingual education as a means for maintaining or developing an indigenous language, as well as for teaching a metropolitan language, has developed in some of the countries and territories of the region.

In this chapter some of these newer developments and their possible outcomes will be discussed. Attention will be given to the current situation in most parts of Oceania, with notes on the historical and social background to the role of indigenous languages in formal education in selected cases. New Zealand will be singled out for special attention, as it is here that the debate over the educational status of the indigenous language has been most adequately documented, and has perhaps a longer history than in most other areas in the region.

AUSTRALIA

In many ways Australia is the "odd man out" in Oceania. Its indigenous people form a very small proportion of the total population of a continent whose land area is many times greater than that of all Polynesia, Micronesia, and Melanesia combined. The Australian aborigines do not speak Austronesian languages, and are culturally as different from the other indigenous peoples of Oceania as they are from the Europeans who now make up most of Australia's population.[1] Furthermore, in part because of the multiplicity of languages and the great difficulties experienced by Europeans attempting to learn them, and also because of the extreme differences between Aboriginal and Western cultures, there is no long-standing tradition of literacy in the vernacular among the various Aboriginal groups.

Until very recently, formal education available to Aboriginal children in private, state, or federal government schools has been almost entirely through the medium of English. This has, in part, been a practical necessity—the subject matter of the normal Australian school curriculum has so few points of congruence with traditional Aboriginal life that most of it could not be conveyed easily through the medium of an Aboriginal language. Linked with this, however, has been a widely shared belief that the future for the Aborigine lies in assimilation to the dominant European-based Australian cultural pattern (cf. Schonell et al. 1960:38-44). Proposals for improvements in Aboriginal education have, therefore, generally overlooked the possibility of bilingual education involving extensive use of Aboriginal languages in the school program, and have concentrated on ways of improving living conditions, raising the self-concept of Aboriginal children, making provision for the adaptation of the curriculum to the needs of Aboriginal children resulting from the assimilation process, preschool and parent education to help provide enriching experiences relevant to modern life, and the need to educate other Australians to accept Aborigines as equals (Schonell et al. 1960; Consultative Committee on Aboriginal Education 1966).

Quite apart from difficulties arising from cultural differences, the use of Aboriginal languages as media of instruction in a bilingual program is greatly complicated by the large number of languages (O'Grady et al. 1966 recognize at least 228 languages in 29 distinct families), with the number of speakers of individual languages ranging from less than ten to a few thousand. Furthermore, few if any of these languages have been adequately described for pedagogical purposes, texts are few, and dictionaries, where they exist at all, are mostly incomplete word lists (cf. Strehlow 1971).

Federal Government Policy

The many obstacles to any form of bilingual schooling for Aboriginal children notwithstanding, the Australian federal government made bold initiatives in this direction when the Labour government assumed office at the end of 1972. In January 1973 the Minister of Education set up an advisory group to make recommendations "for the implementation and development of a program of bilingual education in schools in Aboriginal communities in the Northern Territory." The advisory group's report (Watts et al. 1973) was published within two months of the group's first meeting, and has formed the basis of federal policy in this area.

The advisory group decided that "the optional educational, cultural and social development of the Aboriginal people can best be fostered through the institution of a programme of bilingual education" (p. 7), and adopted as their definition of bilingual education the one used in the United States Bilingual Education Act of 1968, i.e., "the use of two languages, one of which is English, as the mediums of instruction for the same pupil population," and the inclusion in the curriculum of "the study of the history and culture associated with the mother tongue." Like the framers of the American Act, the advisory group considered that through bilingual education Aboriginal children would be able to learn about and appreciate the dominant culture without damage to their own self-respect and to the growth of pride in their own ethnic identity. Furthermore, they held that through the implementation of such a program, the parents of Aboriginal children could be expected to respond more enthusiastically to efforts to involve them directly in their children's schooling.

Pedagogical reasons were also advanced for the use of Aboriginal languages as media of instruction. The group held, for example, that initial literacy was best approached through the first language, and noted that difficulties experienced with reading by many Aboriginal children could be traced to their being introduced to reading through a language (English) in which they had little fluency. It was also suggested that where reading was first learned through the vernacular, transfer of reading skills to English later would be greatly facilitated.

Literacy in English was, however, regarded as vital for Aboriginal social and economic progress. English was regarded not only as a vehicle for communication with the majority of Australians, but also as equally essential if Aborigines were to be able to communicate with each other. However, the advisory group did not advocate a policy of using Aboriginal languages simply as bridges to, and earlier substitutes for, English. The importance of the child's continuing to study in and about his first language was stressed, and the hope was expressed that, among other things, such an opportunity may assist in the evolution of a literature in the various Aboriginal languages.

After reviewing the current practices in Aboriginal schools (instruction basically in English, with varying ad hoc use of Aboriginal languages by some teachers to clarify matters for their pupils), the advisory group recommended a number of models for Aboriginal education, taking into account the sociolinguistic and demographic background of the pupils presently enrolled in Aboriginal schools. This background is sometimes extremely complex, so much so in many cases that any form of bilingual education employing an Aboriginal language presents many practical difficulties.

The large number of mutually unintelligible languages has already been mentioned. If speakers of each language occupied different geographical areas, this would be a problem for any materials development project, but a comparatively straightforward one. However, in many mission stations, as in towns to which Aboriginals have migrated from their original homelands, speakers of several different languages are to be found. In some cases, a particular language may have emerged as a lingua franca for part or all of the Aboriginal community. In others, many speakers may be bilingual or even polyglot. In others, a pidgin or creole language may have developed, drawing on elements from various Aboriginal languages, serving as a lingua franca. In all these situations, speakers of any given language are likely to speak a markedly different form of the language from that spoken by members of their original speech community who have not been exposed to the same kind of contact situation. Furthermore, although tremendous advances in this work have been made in the last decade, particularly by members of the Summer Institute of Linguistics, many Aboriginal languages remain inadequately described.

The advisory group warned against the imposition of an Aboriginal language on speakers of another language (or even of the same language) without the consent of the people concerned. They noted, however, that in some cases, where parents approved, it might be easier for children from one Aboriginal group to gain initial literacy through the medium of the language of another, rather than directly through English.

The models outlined in detail by the advisory group covered two situations in which one Aboriginal language was likely to be accepted by all members of the community: areas where the language concerned had been "analysed and recorded by linguists," and those where it had not. Of the 57 schools, attended by more than 5923 pupils,[2] visited by the advisory group, nine (1373+ pupils)[3] fell in the first category, and seven[4] (1119 pupils) in the second. Both models provided for extensive use of the Aboriginal language in preschool centers and the first two years of formal schooling. Where the language had been analyzed, the Aboriginal language and English would be used almost equally in the third and fourth years, with about one-fourth of the time in the remaining years of primary schooling, and also postprimary schooling, being devoted to Aboriginal language arts and Aboriginal studies through the medium of the Aboriginal language, with most other aspects of the curriculum being dealt with in English. In those schools where the Aboriginal language had not been described, the transition to an English-dominated curriculum (dual-medium differential maintenance in Mackey's typology, but with unequal treatment) is more rapid, being completed by the beginning of the fourth year of formal schooling. More importantly, in the latter group the establishment of early literacy would be achieved through *English*, so that the Aboriginal language would be used as an oral medium only. As linguistic work was completed, these schools would introduce programs of the first type, where reading and writing are to be introduced in the vernacular.

An indication of the complexity of the language situation in schools in the Northern Territory is given in Table 1. The advisory group recommended that bilingual programs be introduced into Aboriginal schools, and the existing single-medium programs phased out, in an orderly sequence, beginning with a first-year intake and following these through the various grades. It was suggested that five schools might begin such a program in 1973, but considerable work would need to be done on materials development. Requirements for materials development were outlined in the report, with suggestions as to how these requirements should be met and undertaken. Mention was also made of a workshop on materials development held in March 1973, in which members of the Summer Institute of Linguistics played a prominent part.

On the basis of the recommendations contained in the report, a program of bilingual education was implemented in five schools in the 1973 school year. After the scheme had been in operation for one term, the Inspector for Bilingual Education, W. J. McGrath, while remaining optimistic about its long-term success, noted a number of difficulties which had arisen. Chief among these were problems of personnel and materials: the effect on the program if the Aboriginal teacher left and a replacement could not be found, the lack of professional training among Aboriginal teachers, the scarcity of materials in most of the languages, and the strains imposed on the principal and staff of the school by the increased workload and the novelty of the situation. The accumulated effect of such problems make it likely that in one of the five schools the program would not be continued in 1974 (McGrath 1973a).

At the end of the first year's experience, a tentative list of objectives for bilingual education in Northern Territory schools was drawn up (McGrath 1973b). One aim was "to present the subject matter of the school program in the language

Table 1.   Aboriginal Languages Spoken by Pupils in Aboriginal Schools in the Northern Territory, Australia

Acceptability as media of instruction and state of linguistic analysis	Number of Aboriginal languages spoken in community							Total schools plus pupils
	One	Two	Three	Four	"Several"	More than four	Several, plus pidgin	
One language probably acceptable:								
Linguistic analysis completed	6 (973+)	1 (64)	..	1 (63)	..	1 (273)	..	9 (1373+)
Linguistic analysis proceeding	5 (839)	1 (253)	..	..	..	..	..	6 (1092)
No information on linguistic analysis	1 (27)	..	..	..	..	..	..	1 (27)
Subtotal	12 (1839)	2 (317)	..	1 (63)	..	1 (273)	..	15 (2492+)
No one language may be acceptable:								
Analysis of at least one language completed	..	1 (46)	2 (43+)	1 (92)	1 (16)	5 (1498)	..	10 (1695+)
Analysis of at least one language proceeding	..	2 (133)	..	1 (237)	4 (275)	1 (112)	1 (187)	9 (944)
No linguistic analysis reported	..	1 (24)	..	..	12 (335)[5]	7 (153)	2 (280)	22 (792)
Subtotal	..	4 (203)	2 (43+)	2 (329)	17 (626)	13 (1763)	3 (467)	41 (3431+)
Total	12 (1839)	6 (520)	2 (43+)	3 (392)	17 (626)	14 (2036)	3 (467)	57 (5923+)

Table compiled from data presented in Watts et al. 1973:24-31. Figures represent the number of schools and (in parentheses) pupils in each type of community.

most suitable for the instructional purpose, bearing in mind the language proficiency of the children and the special needs of specific subject areas." It was noted in this connection that while most subject areas could be first taught through the Aboriginal language, mathematics and related topics (colors, shapes, etc.) had to be introduced in English from the beginning. The stress on the bicultural aspect of the new approach to Aboriginal education was reflected in the use to which English and the Aboriginal languages would be put—operating within their own spheres of competence, with a limited degree of overlap. (In the past, the close identification between language and culture in Northern Australia has sometimes resulted in rapid loss of competence in English gained at school by Aboriginal pupils once they have returned to a traditionally Aboriginal environment—cf. Sommer and Marsh 1969).

Much thought has been given to the role of the teacher since the inception of the project. The employment of individuals with comparatively little experience of European Australian cultural norms was made necessary by the bilingual schooling program, and this in turn gave rise to a number of situations where the demands of the school, or assumptions of European teachers, conflicted with Aboriginal custom. Among these were the primacy of kin-based status over achieved status, and the various taboo relationships requiring the services of a third person for negotiations of any kind between siblings, relatives in law, etc. (Brandl 1973). The organizers of the new program have given much attention to the roles of principals and teachers in bilingual schools. The need for all teachers in such schools to cooperate much more closely than is usual in schools elsewhere in Australia, and the special and delicate nature of the relationship between Aboriginal and non-Aboriginal members of the teaching teams have been particularly stressed (McGrath 1974).

Subsequent reports indicate that considerable success has been achieved in coping with these and related problems (see Department of Education, Darwin Reports 1973a, b, 1974a, b; McGrath 1975; O'Grady and Hale 1974; Reading 1975; Tryon 1975; Willmot 1975).

Although the advisory group's report has been accepted as the basis for planning and action by the Australian federal authorities, the task of implementing it remains formidable. The abandonment of assimilationist policies in favor of an attempt to foster some form of biculturalism as well as bilingualism, with the school as "the agent of cultural continuity rather than of cultural discontinuity" (Watts et al. 1973:7) marks a change in government thinking the permanence of which is as yet uncertain. Although a major contribution to the program is likely to come from voluntary organizations like the religious groups operating the mission stations, and the Summer Institute of Linguistics, any scheme to infuse Aboriginal language and tradition into a substantial part of the primary and secondary curriculum is going to require massive and sustained financial support from the federal government. Not only have materials to be developed and printed—in small quantities and many languages—but teachers have to be trained capable of using the materials at various levels. Now that a start has been made, there is reason to hope that the momentum can be maintained. Overseas precedents give cause for some optimism. One legacy of the Johnson administration in the United States which does not seem to have suffered unduly because of a change of government is the bilingual education program, which continues to be extended to American Indian groups whose linguistic diversity and small numbers are reminiscent of Aboriginal communities in Australia.

THE ISLAND PACIFIC

Missionary activity in the Pacific during the 19th Century resulted not only in the widespread acceptance of Christianity, but also in the achievement of near universal adult literacy in the vernacular throughout Polynesia (including New Zealand), in many parts of Micronesia, as well as those parts of Melanesia where mission stations were established. Mission schools were established in many parts of Oceania, with the aim of teaching the arts of civilization, mainly through local vernaculars, and teaching the most promising pupils the missionaries' own language.

When the missionaries arrived, most Pacific Island communities were self-contained and exercised complete or near complete control over their own affairs. Several, most notably Tahiti, Tonga, Hawaii, and Fiji, had started to take on the characteristics of nation-states, a process reinforced by missionary advisers to the new monarchs. By the end of the 19th Century, however, or shortly thereafter the administration of almost all the Islands had been taken over by a European or quasi-European power, and emphasis shifted from the vernacular to the European language as the major vehicle for education. In French Polynesia, as in New Zealand, the native language had no place at all in formal education; in other areas it was relegated to second-class status.

For most of the 20th Century, education in the Pacific Islands has been almost synonymous with learning the dominant European language. Although in all cases the form of education, including the medium of instruction, has been imposed by a colonial government or the agents of a protecting power, the emphasis on a Western language has been generally accepted by the people involved. The European language is thought to be a source of the *mana* of the technologically, politically, and economically dominant European power. It is also essential for those who wish to share some of this power or affluence, whether as migrants to the colonial mother country, or as local functionaries or businessmen, to master this foreign language.

The great importance attached to European languages has altered the status of the vernacular in all Oceanic societies, but the nature of the alterations varies from one island group to another. In some, the local language has been severely devalued and is used, if at all, as an intimate language at home and between friends. Almost any discussion not concerned with concrete and routine experiences of daily life takes place in the European language if it takes place at all (this is alleged to be the case in parts of the Cook Islands, for example). In others, the local language continues to be used extensively in what are regarded as traditional spheres of activity, but the European language is used for certain types of technical discussion.

Whatever form this diglossia takes, however, or the reasons for it, attempts to give the vernacular a greater place in the school curriculum are often looked upon with great suspicion. The charge may be made that the Europeans are trying to prevent the local people from "catching up" by denying them a "proper" education. When there is also a strong desire to emigrate to the metropolitan country to secure economic and social advancement, any attempts to further differentiate the form and content of local education from that in the present or former colonial power are likely to be looked upon with great suspicion. This is especially so where language is involved, as it is often believed that proficiency in acquiring the esteemed foreign language is almost directly proportional to the time spent on learning and using it at school—a belief, it should be noted, which has been held by educators from metropolitan powers as firmly as by the colonial people among whom they have worked. (Many of these issues were undoubtedly discussed at a conference on bilingual education held at Pago Pago, American Samoa in December 1974 under the auspices of the South Pacific Commission; the report on the proceedings of the Conference had not been released when this chapter was prepared, but is now out.)

SAMOA

In the late 19th Century the Samoan islands were split into two political units, the larger portion, Western Samoa (present population about 130,000), being placed under German control, with smaller islands to the east being taken over by the United States of America. As a result of German defeat during the First World War, control of Western Samoa passed to New Zealand under a League of Nations mandate, and the country remained under New Zealand control until becoming an independent state in 1962.

Western Samoa

As a result of these divergent backgrounds, the role of the indigenous language in education has been very different in the two Samoas. Broadly speaking, policy in Western Samoa has been directed toward the development of an indigenous system of elementary education in which the vernacular plays the major role, leading to a more New Zealand oriented secondary system where English replaces Samoan as the medium of instruction. The basis of this policy was laid down at an educational conference held in Apia in 1923, at which it was decided that:

> It would be in the interests of the Samoans themselves if the teaching of English were not stressed. Europeanizing the natives was unanimously condemned. It was considered that by concentrating in the main on instruction in the vernacular, a better influence would prevail. It was not intended to give a less

useful knowledge to the Samoans, but to give a more comprehensive syllabus embracing with due regard the needs of the people. (Rutherford 1931:346)

Following the Second World War, however, emphasis on English tended to increase, at least in official thinking, and the use of Samoan came to be regarded as a bridge to English rather than as a medium of instruction in its own right (see, for example, the section on English teaching in the UNESCO *World Survey of Education* 1958:792). In the 1950s, it was explicitly stated that it was hoped "that as a result of having been taught in English all Samoans will become bilingual, with English as their second tongue." (ibid.)

This increased emphasis on English seems to have had considerable popular support. It is reported, for example, that "in 1947 it was announced that the medium of instruction in Samoan schools would be the vernacular. Next morning no one turned up at school." (Ma'ia'i 1956:386.) The medium of instruction in *most* Samoan schools had, however, always been the vernacular, and continued to be so. Under the rather complex educational system which had evolved in Western Samoa during the New Zealand administration three types of elementary schools had come into being: the "pastors' schools," where the medium of instruction was entirely Samoan; mission schools where the vernacular was used in the lower grades, with English taking over from the third or fourth year; and the government schools, for selected pupils thought to have high academic potential, where the medium of instruction was English. The majority of Samoan children attended the pastors' schools until they were eleven or twelve years of age, and thus, irrespective of their final scholastic destination, completed their early education entirely in the vernacular.

The development of the Tate oral language course under the auspices first of the New Zealand Department of Education and later of the South Pacific Commission made possible a systematic movement to a bilingual curriculum in all Samoan schools. This movement has received additional impetus with the appointment of Dr. Fannafi Ma'ia'i Larkin, an early advocate of an equal status approach to the teaching of and in Samoan and English at all levels of the school system (see Ma'ia'i 1956, especially pp. 386-396), as Director of Education in Western Samoa.

Despite the undoubted attraction of English as a world language, and its utility both in commerce and as a piece of essential equipment for would-be migrants to New Zealand, the Samoan language seems to have suffered far less than most other Oceanic languages in areas controlled by English-speaking administrators. This has sometimes been attributed to the innate strength of Samoan custom and the comparative weakness of the assimilatory and anglicizing tendencies which characterized official New Zealand policies toward the Maori at home and, to a lesser extent, to the Polynesians in the islands directly under New Zealand control. There is at least a grain of truth in the second explanation. Undoubtedly in part because of the comparatively large number of people involved, it was never a practical possibility for New Zealand, with its own small population, to swamp Samoa with English-speaking teachers and officials on the same scale even as the Cook Islands. With a large population, comparative isolation, limited opportunities for migration to a metropolitan country, and the prospect (and later realization) of political independence, as well as greater natural resources than most Pacific Island groups, Western Samoa has not been subject to the same kinds of pressures which seem to have resulted in a devaluation of the indigenous culture in many other Island territories, including neighboring American Samoa.

The strength of Samoan custom (whatever the reason for this) and the pervasiveness of Samoan language in everyday life notwithstanding, there remain formidable problems to the development of a bilingual school system where the Samoan and English languages receive in fact as well as in theory equal treatment. There remains a suspicion that education in Samoan is in some way second-class, and a resistance on the part of educators to the use of Samoan as a medium of instruction beyond the elementary school level. This resistance is often coupled with the belief, mentioned above, that every second spent teaching English and in English is of vital importance, and that the introduction of Samoan on any significant scale into higher education would have serious adverse effects on the quality of education at this level.

At Samoa College, the government high school for the most gifted students, as recently as 1972 there was a school rule banning the use of the Samoan language in the school grounds. This rule was retained by the principal, himself a Samoan, on the advice of the staff (and against the wishes of the Director of Education), as the whole curriculum of the school was geared to preparing pupils for New Zealand public examinations, and it was felt that to achieve this end pupils should be encouraged to think in English at all times while within the school precincts.[6]

Another problem, which the School Publications Branch of the Western Samoan Department of Education is making valiant efforts to solve, is the general lack of interest in a local literature. While there is (and has been for generations) universal literacy in the vernacular, what Ma'ia'i (1958:395) describes as the highly personalized mode of life and the absence of a reading habit militate against the creation of a vernacular literature. One very practical consideration is that the normal Samoan house, ideally adapted to its environment, has no convenient place for storing a collection of books. Furthermore, marked stylistic differences between formal and colloquial speech pose problems for writers. Most schoolbooks are of necessity written in the normal "low" language, but thereby lose a great deal of prestige. Yet, to be seen to be equal with English, Samoan must develop an indigenous literature as well as sets of textbooks and other materials of academic worth. Considerable progress has been made in the latter area (Western Samoan elementary schools are well provided with printed matter in the vernacular in all major subject areas, including mathematics), but arousing popular demand which could lead to a flourishing local literature in the vernacular is proving a much more difficult task.

American Samoa

The inhabitants of American Samoa have been subjected to much more intensive acculturation than their relatives in Western Samoa. English is the official language of the territory, and, according to a recent account by an official of the local Department of Education, "English is regarded by the general population as the most important course in every school." (Collins 1973.) Furthermore, all books used in schools, "except for a few Samoan readers," are printed in English (ibid.). Instruction in English as a second language begins in the first grade, and gradually replaces Samoan until in Grade 5 English is the medium of instruction in all subject areas.

Although the creation of a bilingual community has certainly been a major aim of schooling in American Samoa for some time (cf. UNESCO 1958:1287, Collins 1973:2), the relative status of English is very much higher than that of Samoan. The indigenous language is seen as having a value for a number of purely local purposes, with English being the vehicle for communication with non-Samoans and for most official business. Collins remarks, for example, that "Samoan has been given equal status in government business to clarify· any particular matter, but in practice, this policy is not widely followed." Furthermore, English seems to be regarded as superior to Samoan as a vehicle for thought: "English education should encourage students in rational ways of thinking so that they can choose wisely, and act independently in determining and solving problems." (ibid., p. 3.) By implication, Samoan language, like Samoan culture, is emotive and communal, in contrast to the rational and individualistic Anglo-American tradition reflected in the English language.

The dominance of English in American Samoan schools, and the strength of Samoan in Western Samoa, can be accounted for in large part by the differences between the political and demographic histories of the two areas. While American Samoa has been the colony of an English-speaking nation since the turn of the century, Western Samoa has, in the same period, passed from German to New Zealand rule, and thence to independence. Not only was American Samoa governed by English-speaking administrators, it was also a major base for the U.S. Navy, and, with the international airport at Pago Pago, has become an important point in the trans-Pacific communications network. As American nationals, citizens of American Samoa have unrestricted right of entry to the United States—a right that has been exercised by a very high proportion of the population. Schooling itself has also undoubtedly played a part. Not only have most Western Samoans completed their schooling in their own language, schooling itself has not been compulsory (although most people have probably attended school at some point in their childhood). In American Samoa, on the other hand, the smaller population has long been subjected to compulsory schooling, and thus also compulsory learning of and in English.

Bilingual schooling of the acultural transfer type has thus characterized education in both American and Western Samoa, affecting the whole population in the former, but only an academic elite in the latter. Most Western Samoans have experienced a curriculum directed toward the acquisition of basic English skills while maintaining and developing their own language—a trend which the present government policy seems to be encouraging. At the secondary level, however, there is at present little difference between the two Samoas: schooling is bilingual only in that the language of the school is a second language for most of the pupils.

THE COOK ISLANDS

Before the proclamation of a British Protectorate in 1888, the efforts of the London Missionary Society had produced in the Cook Islands a people that was both Christian and literate. Universal literacy in the vernacular was not, however, an accomplishment sufficient to satisfy F. J. Moss, the first British Resident, who was convinced of the need to Europeanize the Maori population as quickly as possible through the medium of a public school system in which all instruction would be given in English. Accordingly, in 1891 the first regulations for public instruction were issued, stating that "the purpose of the schools was the teaching of the English tongue and that no Maori was to be spoken during school hours, except by the teacher if necessary." (Coppell 1973:98.) This attitude was not atypical of European administrators of the time, nor was it unique in a Polynesian Kingdom: the medium of instruction in Hawaiian schools, for example, had been changed from Hawaiian to English more than thirty years previously. By 1898, however, the public school system had proved a failure, and the mission schools apparently returned to a policy of using the vernacular as the initial teaching medium.

The assimilationist policy found new advocates, however, after New Zealand took control of the Islands in 1901, and by 1920 all schools in the territory had been placed under government control. At the 1926 census 1491 people out of a total population of 13,550 were recorded as capable of reading and writing English, as compared with a further 6800 who could read and write Maori. The Superintendent of Education at this time was convinced that "the salvation of the native race" demanded "the use of English as the medium of instruction throughout the Cook Islands." (Binstead 1931:337.) In this he was supported not only by the New Zealand Department of Education's inspectors, but also by Sir Apirana Ngata, then Minister for the Cook Islands, who thought the English-medium schools in New Zealand were of great benefit to the Maori people (of whom he was one), and should be equally beneficial to Cook Islanders (see Coppell 1973:100-102). Superintendent Binstead, like many of his colleagues before and since in other parts of the Pacific, considered that English was the only suitable medium of instruction because there was no native literature (the only material in the vernacular available to the population being the Bible and the *Government Gazette*), dialect differences between the islands could cause complications, and there was no economic future for Rarotongan Maori. Even more to the point, he was able to quote approvingly from an anthropological textbook of the day passages to the effect that it was important to preserve native institutions, but not the language. Maori was not "analytic" enough, and would presumably, like other savage tongues, inhibit intellectual progress. English was essential to secure the liberation of the Cook Islander's mind.

Unfortunately, the expected results did not follow this enthusiastically applied policy of anglicizing the curriculum. In 1937, D. G. Ball, Senior Inspector of Native Schools in New Zealand, expressed concern at what he considered to be an overemphasis on the teaching of English and which seemed to be retarding rather than enhancing educational growth. Although material in the vernacular continued to appear in the *Cook Islands School Journal* (printed in New Zealand), the vernacular continued to have no official place in the school curriculum. The Beeby Commission (1945) expressed concern similar to that voiced by Mr. Ball seven years earlier in its investigation of the state of education in the Cook Islands, noting with disapproval that neither Maori language nor culture was included in the school program on the main islands of Rarotonga and Aitutaki, and that the schools continued to see themselves as agents of Europeanization.

This and later attempts by New Zealand to turn the Cook Island education system into one more responsive to local needs seem to have been continually frustrated by local administrators. In 1955, the Belshaw-Stace report on the future economic development of the Islands made various recommendations designed to decrease dependence on and orientation toward New Zealand. In the educational sphere these recommendations were largely ignored; by 1963, the vernacular was being used as a bridging medium in the first two years of schooling, but at the secondary level, the basic aim had become "to prepare as many pupils as possible for the New Zealand School Certificate" examination (Coppell 1973:105). This preparation is also, of course, a preparation for migration to New Zealand. (By 1971 the number of Cook Islanders in New Zealand had reached almost 14,000, including children of migrants; in the same year 21,317 persons were enumerated in the Census of the Cook Islands.)

Although the Cook Islands achieved full internal self-government in 1965, the status of the vernacular language in Cook Islands school does not seem to have altered. While they wish to have complete control of their affairs at home, Cook Islanders seem to have no desire to alter their status as New Zealand nationals (with unrestricted right of entry to New Zealand). This continuing orientation toward New Zealand closely parallels the relationship already noted between American Samoa and the United States, and has had similar effects on the relative statuses of English and the vernacular, to the relative disadvantage of the latter. As early as 1945, the Beeby Commission had noted that in the Cook Islands the ability of the people to use Maori had deteriorated.

From conversations with Cook Islanders and some scholars who have worked there, one gains the impression that this process has continued to the extent that Maori is fast approaching the state to which Binstead had confined it in the 1920s—a language for the least complicated domestic transactions, with English being used in almost all higher-level discussions and replacing Maori completely in many households in Rarotonga and Aitukai. So far no empirical evidence exists to support or refute this contention. It does seem clear, however, that increased use of the vernacular on the Western Samoan pattern has little appeal to those in control of education in the Cook Islands, at least for the time being. There seems little likelihood even of policies similar to those currently being introduced in Australia being politically acceptable in the near future.

NIUE

Niue was also placed under New Zealand control in 1901, and, after the transfer of the missionary schools to government administration, the close identification of schooling with instruction in and through English paralleled that already described in the case of the Cook Islands. By 1945, the effects of this policy were sufficient to cause concern to the members of the Commission of Enquiry, who noted that in Niue as in the Cook Islands facility in the vernacular appeared to have deteriorated without a compensatory gain in the form of a good general command of English (Beeby et al. 1945). Partly because of the anglicizing policy of the administration, but also because of the limited resources of the Island, the kind of orientation toward the metropolitan power which supports the dominance of the metropolitan language in the school system and consequent devaluation of the local language in this sphere has been quite as much a feature of life in Niue as it has in the Cook Islands and American Samoa. By 1971, there were almost as many Niueans resident in New Zealand (4264) as in Niue itself (4901).

The vernacular has been used in Niuean schools as the introductory medium, but the change-over to English has generally been completed by the time the children reach the third year of schooling. Although as long ago as 1945 the Beeby Commission remarked that the effect of this policy seemed to be a reduction of competence in the vernacular, with only a superficial grasp of English, the use of the English language as a medium of instruction in Niuean schools has been maintained throughout the postwar period.

In a report to the Niuean government completed before his departure in 1972, W. E. Christie, the outgoing Director of Education, advocated an intensification of this process: "The largest single step that may be taken towards the development of primary education, on which all later education is built, would be the dropping of the Niuean language teaching in the first four years of school." (Christie 1972: Pt. 1, 12.) This was a key recommendation in a report ostensibly directed toward a "policy of bilingualism and dynamic biculturalism," coupled with "practical integration" with New Zealand (Christie 1972: Pt. 2, 2-5). Mr. Christie's proposals, which are currently being studied by the government of Niue, advocate a home-school language shift approach to bilingual education: English is needed to enable Niueans to pass New Zealand exams and avoid difficulties when they migrate to New Zealand. Because at present Niueans still have problems with English [he notes, for example, that teacher trainees find abstract thinking in English difficult (Pt. 1, 7)], he thinks that more English earlier will help solve the problem. He points to several prominent Niuean leaders whose early education was almost entirely in English and who, he claims, have great facility in both English and Niuean, as a justification for an all-English program, adding that Niuean at present clutters the timetable and thereby reduces the time available in the early years of schooling for teaching the English language. It is not certain at present what action the Niuean authorities will take on the reorganization recommended by Mr. Christie; if his language policies are accepted, the vernacular language will lose its present toehold in the schools. It is possible, however, that a different approach to "dynamic bilingualism" may be taken, in which the local language would play an active role. The Niuean authorities are aware of the alternatives, and the final decision may well be determined by the relative weightings the administration of the newly self-governing territory gives to considerations of local development and Niuean identity as against ties with New Zealand and the strong desire of many Niuean residents to take advantage of the unrestricted right of entry to New Zealand which they continue to enjoy.

FIJI

Fijian, the native language of most of the 200,000 ethnic Fijians, is more properly considered as a group of closely related Austronesian languages (Schutz 1972) one of which, Bauan, has come to be regarded as "standard Fijian" for many purposes. Other "vernaculars" spoken in Fiji include various languages spoken by the 250,000 members of the Indian community, usually listed simply as "Hindi" on census returns, but including Hindi, Urdu, Tamil, Telegu, Malayam, and Gujerati (Hollyman 1962:312), as well as Chinese and Rotuman, the latter spoken by the Polynesian inhabitants of Rotuma (administratively part of Fiji) and Rotuman residents of Fiji proper. Only the Fijian and Rotuman languages are indigenous to the area.

At present, vernacular languages are used as the medium of instruction for the first three years of schooling. During this time English is taught as a second language until the fourth year, when it becomes the medium of instruction. This means that, in (ethnic) community based schools, Hindi, Urdu, or another Indian language, or a dialect of Fijian may be used as a bridging medium up to Grade 3. After this, Urdu, Hindi, or Fijian may be continued as *subjects* but not as media of instruction: in these classes the standard written languages are taught, which means Bauan in the case of Fijian. Although all three languages may be presented by secondary school pupils for the Fiji Junior Certificate examination, only Fijian is widely studied at the secondary level, and in some years no candidates have presented themselves for examination in Urdu. In government schools (which make up only a small proportion of the total number of primary schools) the medium of instruction is English at all levels.

In 1969, the Fiji Education Commission recommended that the situation mentioned in the preceding paragraph be continued as an interim measure, with the ultimate aim of introducing English as the sole medium of instruction in all schools. The conversion from vernacular to English medium in the lower classes would be accomplished as the supply of competent teachers increased and only with the consent of the parents of the children involved. Although stressing the key role of English in Fijian education, the Commission's report did note that "an increasing turn towards teaching English, however, must not mean the jettisoning of the mother tongue." (Sherlock et al. 1969:22.) The role of the mother tongues in school, however, was to be that of subjects of study as "cultural languages" (ibid.:28).

The Commission noted that Fijian had a special claim to importance as the indigenous language of Fiji proper, and also made reference to the fact that Fijian, rather than English, had established itself as a lingua franca among diverse ethnic groups in some areas (ibid.:22-23; see also White 1971). In the thinking of the commissioners, however, the fact that only about 250,000 people speak the language "rules out any very significant commercial publication and hence inhibits the growth of a literature." This problem was of some concern to them; they held that "unless it is possible to develop a literature, Fijian will *survive* as a 'Doric' or rustic language, but it can hardly live and grow." The commissioners recommended that "work for the standardization of Fijian should receive official support," that the development of a local literature should be stimulated by competitions and subsidies, and that efforts should be made to collect oral traditions. The Commission did not, however, see fit to recommend that attempts be made to extend the use of vernacular languages in the school system. Instead, as has been noted, it put forward as an ideal a home-school language switch type of bilingual education for speakers of vernacular languages, as far as the medium of instruction is concerned, without the benefit of the use of the vernacular as an initial teaching medium.

On the island of Rotuma, as in other parts of Fiji, the vernacular is used in the early years of schooling, with English taught concurrently as a second language. Rotuman is occasionally used after the third year of schooling to explain unfamiliar concepts introduced through English, but otherwise the switch over to English is complete by this time (Howard 1970:50). In the earlier part of this century, Rotuman played a more important part in the curriculum, somewhat similar to the role of the indigenous language in Western Samoa and Tonga at the present time. At least one Rotuman educator is of the opinion that the benefits of the switch over to English are somewhat doubtful. Mamao F. Managreve in his "Critical Examination of Education in Rotuma" (1970) notes that (as the Beeby Commission had earlier remarked concerning Niue and the Cook Islands) the chief effect of schooling mainly in English seems to have been to weaken the vernacular, without a compensatory growth in proficiency in English. He adds that "if the older generation cannot speak English because it was not taught when they were in school, then they can at least speak, read, and write in Rotuman." (Managreve 1970:178).

Calls for a more balanced form of bilingual education, in which both English and the vernacular would have the status of media of instruction in the upper levels of the primary school, do not seem to have gained much support in Fiji. Managreve's proposals for such a system applied to a small island with a homogeneous population, which had been comparatively neglected in respect to both subsidies and educational materials in the vernacular by the Fijian colonial administrations. In Fiji proper, however, the situation is much more complex. English is stressed not only because it gives the Fijian a "window on the world," but also because it is not associated directly with either of the major ethnic groups which make up the bulk of the country's population. The Fiji Education Commission, whose recommendations in the area of language policy seem to mirror current official thinking, favored the development of language *study* as a means not only of encouraging mother tongue maintenance but also of promoting intergroup understanding (e.g., by encouraging Indian students to study Fijian, and Fijian students Hindi and Urdu). Favorable comment was also given to a proposal for an optional course in basic Fijian for non-Fijians in the fifth year of schooling—one year being, in the Commission's view "enough to attain reasonable competence in a country where Fijian is so widely spoken" (Sherlock et al. 1969:25). As a medium of instruction, however, English was to be preeminent at all levels. While the possibility of limited use of local vernaculars in the earlier stages of schooling was conceded, the Commission also stated unequivocally that "as the medium of instruction in secondary schools, there can be no alternative to English." Thus while bilingualism is recognized as a fact of life in Fiji, and language study has a prominent place in the curricula of many schools, the use of languages other than English as teaching media beyond the most elementary levels seems to be considered either impractical or unnecessary by most persons with a voice in the making and implementation of the nation's education policies.

OTHER OCEANIC COUNTRIES AND TERRITORIES

The status of the indigenous languages and their role in the formal educational process in other parts of Oceania varies considerably, despite a common history of 19th Century missionary activity resulting in near universal adult literacy in the vernacular in most of Polynesia and many parts of Micronesia and Melanesia.

French has long replaced the Polynesian languages in French Polynesia and the Melanesian vernaculars in New Caledonia as the medium of instruction at all levels of the school system (see Thomson and Adolff 1971: Chaps. 16 and 35). The strongly assimilationist policies of the French administrations in these areas, and the general acceptance of school curricula similar to those of metropolitan France have left no place at all for the local languages in the school system. Nevertheless, according to Hollyman (1962:312), Tahitian still remains "in full use" in rural areas in Tahiti despite this lack of formal recognition, in marked contrast to Maori in New Zealand. The latter language seems to have steadily lost ground in rural areas, despite the tempering since the 1930s of a policy which was initially at least as assimilationist as that followed by the French.

Micronesia has been subjected to a succession of metropolitan languages over the past century: Spanish in the Marianas Islands from the end of the 17th Century (and in the Carolines and Marshall Islands, although much less pervasively, from the mid-19th Century) until 1899, followed by German (except in Guam) until 1914, when the Japanese government assumed control of the

Marianas, Marshall, and Caroline Islands from Germany. Guam was also under Japanese control between 1941 and 1944. In 1945, the United States, which had originally taken over the administration of Guam in 1899, was given administrative responsibility for the remainder of the Marianas Islands as well as the Marshalls and the Carolines under a United Nations Trusteeship. The Gilbert Islands have been administered by Great Britain since 1892, with a brief Japanese occupation during the Second World War.

In the Gilbert Islands, as in other island groups under the control of the United Kingdom, a school system has evolved in which the vernacular plays a dominant part at the elementary level. In American administered territories, however, the pattern described for American Samoa seems to have been followed until recently in the Trust Territory of the Pacific Islands, while in Guam the local language, Chamorro, received practically no recognition in the school system. In the first two decades of American administration of the Trust Territory, local demand for English language instruction in the schools was frequently so great that the local languages received even less use in the classroom than the official policy allowed, and even where local teachers may have been willing to use the vernacular, they were discouraged by the difficulties of obtaining suitable materials in their languages (Fischer and Fischer 1966:230). Materials in English were of course much more readily available.

The burgeoning interest in bilingual education in the United States has also had its repercussions in Micronesia. For several years an experimental program using Chamorro and English as media of instruction in Guam has been funded under Title VII of the Elementary and Secondary Education Act, and it is currently being evaluated by the Northwest Regional Education Laboratory (*Annual Report 1973*). Federal funds were made available by the United States government in the 1972 fiscal year to establish small demonstration projects using Palauan and Ponapean ($70,000 was granted for programs involving only 44 students), and a workshop for teachers and materials developers was held in Colonia, Ponape, in 1973. With a growing sense of nationalism and local pride, after three decades of cultural and economic dislocation (see, e.g., Wenkham and Baker 1972: Chaps. 2 and 4), it is likely that bilingual schooling will rapidly spread to the other major linguistic divisions of the Trust Territory (Yap, Truk, Kusaie, and the Marshalls). In fact, Professor Bernard Spolsky, who conducted the workshop seminar mentioned above, obtained the impression that the vernacular languages have in fact been used informally as media of instruction along with English by quite a number of Micronesian teachers at all levels of the school system for some time (personal communication). (See also Halferty 1974, Trifonovitch 1975.)

In other parts of Oceania vernacular languages generally play an important role in elementary education in territories under United Kingdom control or influence, i.e., in Tonga (formerly a British Protectorate) and the Ellis Islands (currently part of the Gilbert and Ellis Islands Colony) in Polynesia, and in the British controlled schools in the New Hebrides Condominium. In French schools in the New Hebrides, however, the medium of instruction is French at all levels and the curriculum is based on that of metropolitan France. In Hawaii the indigenous language is for all practical purposes extinct as a medium of day-to-day conversation except for a handful of speakers on the island of Niihau. The language is, however, available as a subject for study at the University of Hawaii; it was replaced by English as the medium of instruction in Hawaiian schools in 1854. In the Tokelau Islands, a group of small atolls north of Samoa and administered by New Zealand, the local language is used as the initial teaching medium, replaced by English in the upper levels of the primary school. Although large numbers of Tokelauans have been resettled in New Zealand, and all have unrestricted right of entry there (in 1971, 1655 persons were resident in the Tokelau Islands and 1195 Tokelauans resident in New Zealand) the Tokelauan language is possibly more extensively used in teaching than is Cook Island Maori in many parts of the Cook Islands. There is, however, little written material in Tokelauan currently available for use in Tokelauan schools.

In the field of elementary schooling, the countries of the Island Pacific may be placed along a continuum from the French policy of exclusive use of the metropolitan language at one end, to the dominant use of the vernacular in most of the British colonies, Tonga, and Western Samoa at the other. The policies followed in areas under the control of the United States and New Zealand have varied, with the United States generally closer to the French end of the continuum and New Zealand encompassing the whole range—from total exclusion of the vernacular at home to the toleration of its almost total use in nongovernment schools in Western Samoa. In all areas, however, secondary education has been the exclusive province of the metropolitan language. In this respect, recent developments in the United States Trust Territory, where the possibility of employing indigenous languages at the secondary level has been raised, are potentially the most revolutionary. It is also in the Trust Territory where active moves are now being made to develop a form of bilingual schooling at the elementary level where both the local and metropolitan languages have equal status. Up to now, even when the vernacular has been used extensively as a medium of instruction, facility in the metropolitan language has always been a prerequisite for higher education. This reality has led many Pacific Islanders to devalue their local languages, and regard education through the vernacular as a poor, if sometimes necessary, alternative to education exclusively through the medium of the language of the colonial or protecting power.

NEW ZEALAND

New Zealand Maoris, numbering 227,414 at the 1971 census, form the largest single indigenous ethnic group in Oceania, and make up 8% of the total population of the country. Since the census definition of "Maori" excludes those persons returned as of less than half Maori ancestry, the number of persons considering themselves to be Maori culturally may be considerably greater (at the 1966 census, 48,708 persons were enumerated as part Maori, in addition to those of half or more Maori ancestry: the detailed figures from the 1971 census are not yet available). Before World War II, the vast majority of Maoris lived in rural areas in the northern half of the North Island. Since the war, however, there has been a continuous migration to urban areas so that by 1971 slightly over half the Maori population lived in the 24 urban areas (*New Zealand Census of Population and Dwellings 1971, Vol. 1:10, Vol. 8 (Maori Population and Dwellings)*:4-7, Metge 1964; 1966:66-71).

The Maori Language

Maori is a Polynesia language, with its closest relatives in the Cook Islands, the Tuamotus, and Tahiti (Green 1966, Pawley 1966, Biggs 1971). Although there are regional variations in colloquial speech, these are not great enough to cause serious difficulties in communication to adult speakers, and many differences disappear in formal speech. Nevertheless, native speakers are aware of dialectical differences, however superficial these may be, and this awareness in turn has potentially serious implications for teaching the language—these are discussed further below.

The number of speakers of Maori is not known, although a major sociolinguistic survey currently being undertaken by the New Zealand Council for Educational Research will provide the first objective basis for estimates of this on a national scale.[7] It seems fairly clear, however, that before World War II the vast majority of Maoris were native speakers of the Maori language (cf. Keesing 1928:87, Andersen 1931a:10; Dale 1931), although during the 1930s a tendency toward the abandonment of the language in favor of English had already been noted (Sutherland 1940:413). Estimates in the postwar period have varied widely: Parsonage (1953) estimated that 55% of Maori children attending Maori schools could speak Maori, and a further 24% could understand the language (presumably the proportion of Maori-speaking children attending schools under the jurisdiction of local education boards would have been lower). Powell (1955) estimated that only between 5 and 10% of Maoris under the age of twenty could converse in Maori. Seven years later, Hollyman (1962) considered too low an estimate attributed to J. K. Hunn, then Secretary for Maori Affairs, that 14% of Maori children could speak the language. In 1966, I. P. Puketapu, in an article in the official *Encyclopaedia of New Zealand*, surmised that "probably only 60% of the young Maori population (possibly less) under 20 years of age can and do speak the language." (Puketapu 1966:439.) Some of these and other estimates were discussed by Biggs (1968), who noted that of those Maoris known to him personally, almost all over forty years of age speak Maori, but below the age of thirty Maori speakers constitute a minority diminishing steadily with age. In a study involving ten Auckland city schools Marie Clay (1970) did not encounter any Maori-speaking children in a randomly selected sample of five- to seven-year-olds whose parents both claimed to be Maoris.

The estimates of Parsonage and Hunn were based on questionnaires answered by teachers, who in some cases may have been deliberately misled by their pupils into thinking that the latter had little or no knowledge of the language (see Benton 1966:77-78). Biggs' intuitive assessment of the situation appears to be the most soundly based. From the data obtained so far in a sociolinguistic census of Maori households in North Island communities (see Benton 1975a, 1976), it is apparent that while in most communities a majority of adults can speak and understand Maori, there is a strong tendency even in areas where Maoris constitute a majority of the population for English to be used more often than Maori in the home. The result is that in many (but not all) communities a high proportion of the Maori population over the age of twenty is bilingual in Maori and English, but the proportion of children who are monoglot speakers of English increases sharply with each lower age group. The number of communities in which the Maori language is holding its own, i.e., where a high proportion of young children are native speakers of the language, appears to be declining rapidly.

The reasons underlying the shift to the use of English as the home language even when both parents are native speakers of Maori are probably similar to those causing language loss among immigrant and indigenous minority groups in many parts of the world. The shift of population from the countryside to cities and larger towns has put many Maori families in direct daily contact with speakers of English. With great improvements in all aspects of communication, few country areas are truly isolated from the mainstream of national life. Television, and all-English medium, has brought English into many Maori homes more forcefully than any other of the mass media. Generations of Maori parents have been taught that English is essential for economic success; now that subsistence farming is no longer a viable option for most Maori families, economic success has come in many ways to be equated with economic survival. "Mixed" marriages also have linguistic consequences. In one rural community, Ruatoki (about 25 km south of Whakatane Borough in the Bay of Plenty), a spouse who did not speak Maori at the time of marriage generally learned the language after settling in the district, where Maori is definitely still dominant. In most other communities, however, the language of the home is usually English when only one of the parents is a native speaker of Maori. Some elders in Ruatahuna (110 km southewat of Rotorua in Urewera National Park), which a decade ago was regarded as a Maori-speaking stronghold, attribute the increasing number of dominantly English-speaking children in the area to the effects of in-migration of former residents who settled in the towns, used English in their homes, and have carried this pattern back to their birthplace. In Te Tii (Bay of Islands), also formerly a stronghold of spoken Maori, the consensus is that the increased use of English to the exclusion of Maori in the younger age groups can be attributed to the influence of the Play Centre movement, reinforced by television and the school. In the mid-1960s supporters of the Play Centre persuaded themselves that they should prepare their children for school by talking to them in English rather than in Maori. With no prestigious outside institution to support the use of Maori, a switch back to the latter language, although desired by many adult members of the community, has proved difficult (cf. Dewes 1970, Reweti 1971, Sorensen 1973; the reverse of this pattern, where early pupils of Te Aute College who were not fluent speakers of Maori before entering this secondary boarding school for Maori boys were highly motivated to learn the language despite the fact that pupils were forbidden to speak Maori at school, is described by Fitzgerald 1970:51-52).

Maori-speaking communities have long been characterized by diglossia, where Maori is the language used at home and for what are perceived as Maori matters, while English is used for communication with outsiders and for Pakeha (New Zealand European) affairs. On certain occasions both languages may be needed to discuss certain topics from different points of view—Ritchie documents an interesting example of this type of situation in connection with a meeting about the future control of a local school (1956:23). Within the Maori language itself, there are clearly marked distinctions between formal or oratorical Maori, and colloquial Maori. Control of the first-mentioned group of registers requires a number of extralinguistic abilities: knowledge of traditional history, mythology, and poetry, knowledge of the rubrics appropriate in different situations, and so on. It is knowledge gained usually from prolonged observation of and informal tuition by experts, knowledge increasingly difficult to acquire in urban settings. Realization of the central importance of this "classical" variety of the language, and the ceremonial associated with it, in Maori social observances has led to the convening of *whare wananga* (schools of learning) in many parts of the country, where younger men and, in some areas, women are given intensive instruction in these matters.

Confusion between ordinary everyday language and the complex of skills demanded of the orator undoubtedly lies behind some of the statements made by and about contemporary Maori-speaking adults to the effect that they cannot speak "good" Maori, or that their children speak only "pidgin Maori." More often than not, however, such comments simply reflect the low status ascribed to the Maori language by the New Zealand community as a whole. Symbolic of this was the refusal of the New Zealand Broadcasting Corporation to require announcers to pronounce Maori place names or the names of Maori organizations correctly (i.e., using Maori rather than anglicized pronunciations). Many older Maoris who are native speakers of Maori also use these heavily anglicized pronunciations when speaking English. Examples: Ngaruawahia (ŋaːɾuawahia) becomes (Næɹəwɔhiɣə), Te Kauwhata (te kaufata) becomes (tiykʌwɔtə), Paraparaumu (paraparaumu) becomes (pæɹəpʌɹæm) or simply (pɹæm). Younger Maoris, many of whom are not native speakers of the language, are increasingly moving in the opposite direction, and the NZBC policy, described by Dr. P. W. Hohepa of the University of Auckland (himself a native speaker of Maori) as "an affront to the Maori people" has met with hostile reactions from some segments of the Maori population (see, e.g., *Te Kaunihera Maori* 1.4, 1967:4, 17), but, judging by the correspondence columns of the *Listener* and the daily newspapers over the last decade, has majority support among that segment of the Pakeha population which is concerned enough to express an opinion (mainly on the grounds that New Zealand is an English-speaking country, and Maori phonology must of necessity be modified when Maori words are used in English speech).[8]

On the other hand, moves to increase the standing of the language have had considerable success during this same period. For several years the national radio and television announcers have been in the habit of using Maori greetings to mark the beginning of major program segments (this despite the place names policy mentioned above), and, following the appointment of a Maori Advisory Committee in 1973, broadcasts featuring the Maori language have been increased (although they still occupy only a small portion—less than an hour a day—of total program time).

Over the last decade there has been a very rapid increase in the availability of the Maori language as a subject in secondary schools. In 1966, according to Department of Education figures, 1962 pupils, 96% (1886) of whom were Maori, were enrolled in secondary school Maori language courses, mainly in predominantly Maori rural and boarding schools. By 1975, the number of students had risen to 11,254, of whom only 59% (6595) were Maori, in 127 secondary schools, many of which were in predominantly European communities. The number of candidates in Maori for the national School Certificate examination, taken at the end of the third year of high school, has not, however, risen so dramatically, perhaps reflecting varying academic statuses of the language in different schools. Between 1967 and 1975, the number of candidates taking Maori as a subject in the examination had risen from 613 to 1225, doubling also in percentage of all candidates enrolled for the examination taking this subject (0.9 to 1.8%). The only other language subject to prosper similarly in this period has been German, rising from 1% (462) of candidates in 1967 to 2.2% (1300) in 1974, but dropping slightly behind Maori (1142 candidates, 1.6% of the total) in 1975. Although the numbers of candidates for examination in French have declined steadily, it is still much more firmly entrenched than Maori in the schools, with 7906 candidates (11.3%) presenting themselves for examination in 1975.

At the primary school level, Maori has been available officially on an informal basis for some years. In 1971, Department of Education figures showed 1158 pupils studying the language at intermediate schools, 637 (55%) of whom were Maori. This number is said to have jumped to "more than 9000" in 1975 [see *Education News (N.Z.)* 2.2, 1976, p. 3], but much of this language study is at the elementary level of greetings, simple commands, etc. However, the Department of Education appointed 30 itinerant teachers to coordinate Maori language programs at primary school level in 1976, and since 1973 has been training similar numbers of teachers of Maori for secondary schools at special one-year courses at various New Zealand Teachers' Training Colleges.[9]

In 1974, the Minister of Maori Affairs proposed statutory recognition for the Maori language "as the Folk Tongue of the indigenous peoples of New Zealand" (*Government White Paper* 1973). This proposal was incorporated in the Maori Affairs Amendment Act 1974, section 51 of which states "(1) Official recognition is hereby given to the Maori language of New Zealand in its various dialects and idioms as the ancestral tongue of that portion of the population of New Zealand of Maori descent"; the Act also authorizes the Minister to "from time to time take such steps as he deems appropriate for the encouragement of the learning and use of the Maori language." It is perhaps significant, however, that this recognition does not elevate Maori to the status of an *official national* language. It is not altogether surprising, therefore, that according to a survey made by the Inspector of Maori and Island Education in 1971, in many areas where the adult population was Maori-speaking only a minority of the Maori pupils in the Primary Schools identified Maori as their "preference language" (Hill et al. 1971: Appendix F, see also comment in Benton 1973a:25)—nor is it surprising that Maori writers feel constrained to call on the Maori-speaking community itself to take more pride in its linguistic heritage (see, e.g., Potatau 1973, Bosch 1967, Taepa 1972, Hau 1968, *inter alia*).

Bilingual Education in English and Maori

Almost from the beginning of the Colonial period, the New Zealand government followed a policy of Europeanization in respect to Maori education in which great stress was laid on the necessity to teach the native population English manners and the English language. In 1858, one of the conditions for government grants to mission schools, where the vernacular had been used, with great success, to teach initial literacy (see Parr 1963), was that English be made the medium of instruction (Parsonage 1956:6). The 1867 Native Schools Act set up a system of secular village day schools in which the medium of instruction was to be English and the curriculum "the ordinary subjects of English primary education." In 1879, control of these schools was transferred to the Department of Education (from the Department of Native Affairs), and for a time a modified form of bilingual schooling was encouraged under James Pope, the Organizing Inspector of the schools. He encouraged teachers "to use the Maori language in junior classes as an aid to the children's comprehension of English words and sentences." He also insisted that teachers in native schools should have some knowledge of Maori language, customs, and traditions (see Barrington 1966:2-5).

By the turn of the century, however, official attitudes toward the uses of Maori in schools had hardened, and under Pope's successor, W. Bird, the policies of the 1850s were revived. Bird commended teachers who had ceased to use the Maori language in their classes, and suggested that they encourage Maori children to speak only English in the playground. This "encouragement" in many schools took the form of negative sanctions, often involving harsh physical punishment, directed against children who were heard speaking Maori in the school grounds. A high proportion (often more than 50%) of the adult informants from rural areas interviewed in the current NZCER linguistic survey have reported being punished at school for speaking Maori (Benton 1975c:24).

During the 1930s considerable interest had developed in the teaching of Maori (outlined in some detail in the preceding section). The conclusion of the seminar-conference on Pacific Education held in Hawaii in 1935 that the peoples of the Pacific would in the future be bilingual or polygot and that both the vernacular and world languages should have a place in the curriculum (see Keesing 1937:172-3) was not, however, reflected in any change in official or unofficial attitudes toward using Maori as well as English as a medium of instruction in Maori schools. Douglas Ball, who attended the conference and who instituted many reforms designed to lessen the areas of conflict between the school and the Maori community, has said in retrospect that the idea of teaching in Maori was never taken seriously at this time for two reasons—first, the lack of interest in such an idea among Maori parents (discussed further below), and second the fact that the vast majority of teachers did not know Maori: "the [teachers'] training colleges were not interested in the Maori in those days at all. I don't think they knew the Maoris existed." (Ball 1973:12.) Like almost all administrators of his generation concerned with Maori education, as well as the majority of his successors, Mr. Ball himself did not speak Maori, which, as he says (ibid.) "probably had some influence" on language policies in this period.

The possibility of using Maori as a medium of instruction, along with English, in schools in Maori-speaking areas was not seriously raised again until the 1960s. By this time, the renewed interest in teaching Maori as a subject had received official support in the recommendations of the Currie Commission, although the latter had implicitly rejected any potential move toward an even more significant role for the language in the educational process. Such a role was, however, explicitly advocated in a report prepared for the Maori Education Foundation two years later, where it was recommended that "careful considera-tion should be given to the possibility of establishing bilingual schools in Maori-speaking areas." Possible models for such schools including "those in the Romansch-speaking areas of Switzerland," which had been suggested some years previously by Eric Schwimmer (1968), and the schemes outlined in the Report of the Central Advisory Council for Education (Wales) (Benton 1966:98, Recom-mendation 4)'

Although this particular recommendation had no effect whatever on policy making, it did appear at a time when traditional "establishment" attitudes toward the Maori language and bilingualism were being questioned from within the establishment itself. Ralph Hanan, then Minister for Maori Affairs, wrote in the *Journal of the New Zealand Maori Council* that early educators had been frankly assimilationist and "went as far as saying that the Maori language itself should be barred from the school and even from the playground. Today's thinking does not support such an attitude." (Hanan 1967:49.) Fears for the adverse effects bilingualism could have on the cognitive development of young children were still widely held, however. A writer in *Te Ao Hou* magazine, published by the Department of Maori Affairs and widely read in Maori communities, wrote, for example, that "many people do not realize what a handicap the speaking of two languages can be to a five year old just starting school. It has been estimated that the vocabulary of a child in such a situation is sometimes only half that of another who has only one language to contend with." (Loeffen 1966.) The writer offered the play center, where "the Maori child has an opportunity to get a good start in English before he begins school," as an antidote to this sad state of affairs. Although the play center movement itself never officially discouraged the use of the Maori language in centers attended by Maori-speaking children, play centers were widely regarded as means to combat Maori backwardness at school by providing the linguistic head start referred to. Several informants in one Northland community included in the NZCER linguistic survey claimed that many mothers in the community were persuaded by play center enthusiasts to stop speaking Maori to their children—a tactic which succeeded where attempted coercion by teachers had failed. The setting up of play centers in Maori communities was actively supported by the Maori Education Foundation, which regarded such preschool facilities as a significant first step in ensuring scholastic success for a greater proportion of Maori children.

Although the setting up of such facilities in Maori communities had the effect of creating a bilingual situation for Maori-speaking children at the age of three or four, instead of five or six, there was no complementary movement by the Department of Education to carry Maori into the early school years in the way that English had now been thrust into the preschool years. The New Zealand Educational Institute, the professional organization of New Zealand primary school teachers, had, however, by this time become quite sympathetic to the possibility of such an approach to Maori education. At its 1967 Annual Meeting the Institute adopted a report recommending not only "that the Maori language be introduced into as many schools as possible, at all levels," but also that experimental programs should be set up so that "in selected schools, where Maori is the first language of the home and community . . . Maori-speaking school entrants begin their schooling in Maori are taught English as a second language." (New Zealand Educational Institute 1967:25, Recommendations 47 and 49.) This recommendation notwithstanding, the Assistant Officer for Maori Education, at that time the highest-ranking official of predominantly Maori ancestry in the Education Department, wrote "from a Maori point of view" in *Te Ao Hou* the following year that "there is no doubt that the English language is the most important single subject in the curriculum" at all levels, and stated categorically that "all children must be subjected right from birth to the accepted language of the schools" (Royal 1968:25). There was no suggestion that the school might accommodate itself to the accepted language of the child; however, unlike other writers on similar themes, he did add that "all children are capable of handling two languages quite easily" and urged parents to teach their children "correct Maori and correct English" and thus give them "a better chance to succeed at school."

Meanwhile, the New Zealand Council for Educational Research had invited Dr. Byron W. Bender from the University of Hawaii to visit New Zealand as a consultant to assist the Council to determine whether there was a need for a special program of research into linguistic factors affecting Maori education. Professor Bender made two visits to New Zealand in 1968, and prepared a report containing seven recommendations for "a programme of research and action." One of these was "that reading and writing in Maori be offered as an optional subject in all primary schools having an appreciable number of students whose first or strongest language is Maori, and that schools having a preponderance of such students accomplish the initial teaching of reading and writing in the Maori

language, while building an oral language base for later transition of such skills."
(Bender 1971b:54, Recommendation 3.) In his comments on this recommendation, Dr. Bender also suggested that a special diploma course be established to
train native speakers of Maori in techniques of teaching through Maori and of
teaching Maori as a second language. "Holders of such a diploma," he noted,
"would be especially valuable in play centres located in predominantly Maori-
speaking areas where they could help children develop with respect to their own
language." (1971b:55.)

Although this particular recommendation had little direct effect on official
policy, it did come at a time when the Auckland, South Auckland, and Hawkes
Bay Education Boards had just taken over control of the remaining "Maori
schools"—i.e., those schools in predominantly Maori areas which had been
administered directly by the Department of Education from 1879 until 1968. The
inspectorate of the South Auckland board had become particularly sympathetic
to the idea of limited use of Maori in the classroom in Maori-speaking areas, and
had encouraged the informal use of the language in the infant (first year)
classroom in one school in particular. No attempt has yet been made, however, to
introduce a bilingual program systematically in any New Zealand school, or to
develop the materials necessary to support such a program.

In 1972, the head of the Maori Research Unit of the New Zealand Council
for Educational Research read a paper to a general meeting of the Wellington
Language Teachers Association, in which, after discussing approaches to bilingual
schooling in Wales, Ireland, Canada, and the United States, he advocated the
setting up of bilingual schools, where both English and Maori would be used as
media of instruction for all subjects with the same student body, wherever there
was community support for such a scheme. He argued that such a form of
schooling should be available to Maori children as of right, and advocated the
recognition of the Maori language as, along with English, the official language of
New Zealand. It was also argued that the official recognition of the Maori
language and fostering of Maori-English bilingualism might stand New Zealand in
good stead in its attempts to identify more closely with South East Asian nations,
several of whom also fell within the community of speakers of Austronesian
languages. Although, again, these opinions had little discernible effect on official
policy, the paper did create considerable interest. After about 2000 copies of the
mimeographed text had been requested by various individuals and organizations, a
new edition was printed (Benton 1973a); the paper was also reproduced in full in
a special edition of *Salient*, the Victoria University of Wellington student
newspaper, to mark Maori Language Day, 1973. A short speech in Maori by the
same author, read at the University of Waikato during the celebration of the first
Maori Language Day (Sept. 14, 1972), which urged Maori parents to accept
primary responsibility for maintaining the language, also met with a heavy
demand, and was also produced subsequently in printed form (Benton 1974). Part
at least of the interest generated by this material was its timeliness—the idea that
the Maori language was potentially of significance to all New Zealanders as a living

part of the country's national heritage had been expressed by several writers in Maori magazines in the preceding five years (see, e.g., Keen 1968, van der Schaaf 1971), and the then Minister of Maori Affairs, the Hon. Duncan MacIntyre, had in 1970 pointed out the value of the Maori language as a bridge to other Austronesian-speaking communities (*Te Maori* 1.6, 1970:9). H. V. George, Director of the English Language institute at the Victoria University of Wellington, had expressed grave concern at the lack of provision for teaching in the vernacular in Maori-speaking communities, describing the current policies of the New Zealand Department of Education in this respect as "disgraceful" (George 1968:5; see also George 1969). Jack Richards (1970) had urged a careful examination of the possible role not only of the Maori language, but also of Maori dialects of English, should the existence of these be established, in Maori schooling. (See also Benton 1970.)

A condensed version (Benton 1973b) of the first paper was written for the Department of Education's journal *Education*, at the request of the editor, as the introductory article in a series touching on the topic of "bilingual schooling for New Zealand children." This was followed in turn by articles by R. J. Dow, Theodore Andersson, Patrick McGrath, and Gabrielle Rikihana. The articles by Andersson and McGrath concerned overseas experience—Andersson's being a sympathetic review of recent developments in bilingual education in the United States, and McGrath's a generally negative account of his own experiences as a pupil in a bilingual school in Ireland. The two remaining articles by school inspectors with special responsibilities for Maori education within their respective Education Board districts, were direct commentaries on the initial article in the series.

While agreeing that "certainly for those new entrant children whose first language is Maori much more opportunity should be given for the use of this by pupils and teachers in the activities of the classroom," Dow expressed doubts about the feasibility of using Maori in a full-scale bilingual program. He considered that difficulties in developing materials, obtaining suitable teachers, and gaining parental consent (European parents, for example, might be unwilling to cooperate in a venture in which they felt that "their children would be at a decided disadvantage in efforts to become competent in a second language"), might prove insuperable. He also speculated that perhaps "the Maori language has disappeared to such a degree that the success of bilingual schooling in countries such as Wales and Canada may be impossible to achieve in New Zealand," a position which had been discussed and refuted by Ausubel (1970:113) in a review of arguments for and against the teaching of the Maori language, and welcomed the efforts of the NZCER to ascertain where and how widely Maori is now spoken.

The final paper in the series, by Gabrielle Rikihana, expressed doubts about the usefulness of bilingual schools in meeting the felt needs of Maori communities. She argued that "the conditions which encourage success in an overseas setting are not paralleled in New Zealand," claiming that the majority of Maori-speaking children now come from homes which want to be *monocultural,* and thus would probably be least receptive to the kind of intercultural exploration implied by the kind of bilingual education advocated in the initial article. She went on to claim that "some fields of knowledge present obvious barriers for interpretation in Maori; for example, mathematics and science subjects may be expressed more simply in English, although Maori may aid the refining of the idea," and asked, rhetorically, "how would students judge the integrity of such programmes?" Furthermore, she noted, many Maori families are quite emphatic that they send their children to school to learn English, not Maori.

The idea that the raison d'être of schools is to teach English has a long history in Maori education. As early as 1871, for example, a Maori member of Parliament had urged the government to enact legislation to ensure that Maori children be taught in English only, and in 1877 a petition signed by 337 Northland Maoris was presented to the House of Representatives asking that the 1867 Native Schools Act be amended to require that the teacher in a Maori school and his wife be persons "altogether ignorant of the Maori language," the use of which should be absolutely prohibited in any school (Barrington 1966:3). The intense desire to be able to secure the advantages of Pakeha society through schooling, despite the manifest lack of success of most Maori pupils in the schools, led many Maoris to resist the attempts made by D. G. Ball in the 1930s to bring the school a little closer to Maori society (see Hawthorn 1944:127-128). Sir Apirana Ngata, perhaps the most influential Maori politician of the first half of this century, laid great emphasis on the teaching of English; he is frequently alluded to as an example of Maori resistance to the notion of bilingual or any other form of education using Maori as a medium of instruction (see, e.g., Ball 1973:12). However, during the period of Ngata's greatest influence, Andersen was able to point out emphatically that while Ngata and other prominent Maoris emphasized the need for the Maori population to master English, they "do not say that Maori should not be taught, and that the Maori should be denied a share in the heritage of his own literature" (1931:9). Ngata's attitude, as he himself expressed it, was that "the best equipped Maori today must be bilingual and bicultural" (quoted in Fitzgerald 1970:57), and, while he first considered that the Maori mother could take care of transmission of the Maori language to her children, he later came to consider that the school, too, had a part to play. Other Maori writers of the day also shared the latter view—see, e.g., Smyth 1931.

More recently, the opinion of Maori leaders at least seems to be moving toward demands for more than token recognition of the Maori language in the schools. Maoris who have expressed a contrary view include P. B. Reweti, Member of Parliament for Eastern Maori, who noted that he "was one of those who went to school where the then policy was one of deliberate discouragement. In order that Maori pupils gained a faster grasp of English they were 'shamed' into it." (Reweti 1971, see also Dewes 1970, Walker 1972). He went on to advocate a new, bilingual policy to help not only to retain the Maori language as a living force in New Zealand life, but also as a step toward the development of a true sense of nationhood. Similar calls were made by other Maori writers including Hauraki

(1971), who wanted bilingual education to start at the preschool level; Dewes (1968), who called on the New Zealand Founders Society to support the wider teaching of the Maori language as a step toward the promotion of a bilingual, bicultural society; and Hau (1968), who, noting that "the present system operates against our language and culture surviving," called for the fostering of the language in the Maori home as well as its use in the schools. The latter writer felt that where schools were concerned Maori parents were at the mercy of the Pakeha majority, who did not understand their situation, but they could and should use their influence within their own families to ensure the maintenance of Maori language and culture.

The final report of the Working Party on Improving Learning and Teaching (Lawrence et al. 1974), a discussion document prepared for the Educational Development Conference (a series of national, regional, and local seminars and discussion groups aimed at overhauling the entire education system in New Zealand) recommended that "in appropriate subjects and to the greatest extent possible, Maori language and culture be included in the curriculum at all stages of the education system" (1974:198). Taken in conjunction with a preamble which noted that "where there are significant numbers of Maori children or where a community demand exists, Maori could profitably be used as a medium of instruction in appropriate subjects" (ibid.), this recommendation could be read as a mild endorsement of bilingual schooling. A report prepared for the Working Party by a study group under the chairmanship of the Party's only Maori member, R. Mahuta, was published separately at the Working Party's request. This report was quite unequivocal in its endorsement of bilingual schooling, advocating national bilingualism as a national goal (Mahuta et al. 1974:9) and recommending "that opportunity exist within the school programme for Maori to be used as a medium of instruction wherever there are significant numbers of Maori children or wherever there is a community demand," as well as "that steps be taken to ensure an adequate and continuing supply of teachers of Maori language" (1974:20, Recommendations 6 and 7). It is perhaps significant that among the members of the study group were T. K. Royal, now Inspector of Maori and Island Education, whose earlier views have already been discussed, and Alan Smith, the Department of Education's Officer for Maori and Island Education.

Should these recommendations find favor with the general public, and become part of the national educational policy, two sets of problems will arise. The first, development of materials and training of teachers, can easily be solved by careful planning and adequate funding. The second, gaining acceptance of the Maori community for this new approach, will present more difficulties. The fact that there are a number of regional (and tribal) dialects of Maori has already led to problems in teaching Maori as a subject. Although dialect differences are slight, speakers of one dialect often resent that of another group being presented as *the* Maori language to their children. In some communities Maori parents have failed to support attempts to introduce Maori language study in the school mainly because of the fact that one particular dialect area, not their own, has been unduly favored in the Department of Education's Maori language publications. Any future materials development project would need to take account of dialect differences, and make sure that no one dialect dominated the literature and recordings produced under its auspices.

A further problem, touched on in the remarks of Rikihana (1973) already referred to, is that of resistance to the bicultural aspect of bilingual education. This is not simply a resistance to European culture; much more importantly it may be a resistance to the sharing of Maori culture. It is almost certain that many Maoris who have clung to their own traditions despite the adversities they have suffered over the past century have come to look at their culture as that which sets them apart from the general population. The widespread teaching of Maori language and culture would be a direct assault on this irredentist mentality, and as such could well be bitterly resented by some individuals. To this segment of the Maori population, bilingual education in English and Maori available to all New Zealanders would be tantamount to a take-over by the Pakeha population of the last bastions of Maoritanga.

There is some evidence, however, that these difficulties may be more apparent than real. A student group, Te Reo Maori Society, founded in 1970 (see van der Schaaf 1971), seems to have thrived on a membership of Maori and non-Maori enthusiasts for the propagation of Maori language and culture, and contains among its Maori members native speakers of Maori from various tribal areas, as well as persons of Maori ancestry whose mother tongue is English but who are intent on reestablishing their cultural identity as "complete New Zealanders." In the course of about 3500 interviews conducted so far in the NZCER sociolinguistic survey, many comments have been made by informants about the desirability of teaching the Maori language in school. A few people have expressed a negative reaction to such ideas (from either separatist or assimilationist positions), but the majority have been supportive of recent moves to extend the availability of the language to pupils at all levels of the school system.

The fact that Maori has not been widely available in schools has had an adverse effect not only on the self-concept of Maori pupils, but also on the ease with which Maori adults employ the language in reading and writing. While a fairly high proportion of adults prefer to *speak* Maori, as opposed to English, those who prefer to *read* Maori are fewer, and those preferring Maori over English for writing are fewer yet. This tendency, which can in part at least be attributed to the fact that reading and writing in English have been learned and practiced extensively during at least eight years of compulsory schooling, whereas reading and writing in Maori have generally been self-taught in later life.

Professor Ralph Piddington of the University of Auckland, in a paper prepared in 1957 and later revised for republication in 1968, warned that failure to educate significant numbers of Maoris in the mastery of the Maori language could have serious consequences for leadership in future generations. Both Piddington (1968:267) and Biggs (1968:84) hold that although Maori may cease to be a medium of daily communication, its ceremonial importance will not be diminished, and that no individual is likely to be able to succeed in a leadership role who does not also have a firm grasp of the language and the oral tradition which informs it.

A more serious consequence of failure to make the language and culture freely available to the steadily increasing population of Maori ancestry in New Zealand is hinted at by Fitzgerald (1972:53), who remarks:

> We found practically no evidence for a firm racial identity among Maori graduates (contrast the blacks in the U.S.). Nevertheless, if the government persists in its present policy of cultural assimilation, i.e., the gradual eradication of the Maori subculture, it may yet precipitate the very racial problem it has tried to avoid. We are suggesting that a process of "forced acculturation" may lead to an overexaggeration of biological (racial) symbols as a source of one's identity, to compensate for the loss of cultural symbols.

A similar viewpoint was expressed by an amateur student of Maori language and culture, F. G. B. Keen (1969:49), who pointed out that it might be cheaper in the long run for New Zealand to spend money on teaching Maori in a serious effort to promote bilingualism than to continue with present policies and have to face up to combating minority problems in the future.

Whatever the final outcome of the present attempts to persuade or force the educational bureaucracy to establish some sort of program of bilingual education, it is likely that interest in the Maori language itself will continue to grow. In the words of Professor Biggs, "it is certain that scholarly study of the language will increase, for it seems in the nature of things that we value our treasures most as they pass from us" (1968:84).

BILINGUAL EDUCATION AND INDIGENOUS LANGUAGES IN THE SOUTH PACIFIC: PROSPECTS FOR DEVELOPMENT

Formal education in Oceania is dominated by what Fishman (1972) has called "Languages of Wider Communication," that is, the official languages of the present or former colonial power. In New Zealand and those areas of the Pacific under French control this domination is complete; in most other parts of the region, including, although only in a few schools, Australia, vernacular languages play a limited role in the educational process, either as initial teaching media, replaced by the metropolitan language after two or three years (as in the Cook Islands or American Samoa), or as the principal media of instruction in most schools throughout the elementary grades (as in Western Samoa and Tonga). Although in New Zealand and Fiji the indigenous vernaculars have long been taught as subjects in certain secondary schools, it is only very recently that moves have been made anywhere in Oceania to consider even a limited instructional role for indigenous languages beyond the elementary level.

The future role of indigenous languages in the school systems of the countries of Oceania is very much dependent on the relationship between these languages and national language goals, and the response of the speakers of indigenous languages to these goals. Joshua Fishman has proposed a very useful scheme for characterizing the language policies of developing nations, based on the presence or absence of an indigenous Great Tradition and the relative importance accorded to the metropolitan language and its associated Great Tradition (see Fishman 1972: *passim* and 206-207). He suggests there are three major patterns: *amodal*, where (at least from the perspective of the policymakers) there is no overriding indigenous Great Tradition, and the long-term aim is the creation of a society monolingual in the language of wider communication; *unimodal*, where there is a single indigenous Great Tradition and an associated language (which may be a special form of the vernacular language, or even a different language), and language policy is directed toward modernization of this language—the ultimate aim being the creation of a society where diglossia embraces the vernacular and elaborated indigenous languages, and the consequent phasing out of the language of wider communication; and *multimodal* where several Great Traditions are recognized, and the language of wider communication is accepted as a working language for certain kinds of national and intergroup activities, while the indigenous languages continue to dominate regional or intragroup affairs. Fishman also points out that some kind of functional specialization of language use seems to be necessary to ensure stable bilingualism in a society—one of the reasons for the failure of official policy in Ireland, when examined in terms of people's actual behavior, may be, he suggests, the functional duplication involved in the attempt to make the Irish and English languages equally available to all the people for all national purposes (see 1972:222-223).

Looked at in these terms, the development and direction of bilingual programs in Oceanic countries can be seen to be closely related to political decisions which have been or are being made by the governments of these areas, and to various social forces which affect the speakers of indigenous languages. French and New Zealand policy has hitherto been based on amodal assumptions, where the only valued Great Tradition has been that originating in Western Europe and expressed through the French and English languages, respectively. While the close economic, ideological, and political ties which exist between metropolitan France and the French territories in the Pacific are maintained, the importance of the French tradition is likely to increase and bilingual education will become correspondingly less relevant, even to the speakers of indigenous languages. The situation in New Zealand is less clear-cut. National policy has hitherto been of the amodal type, transformed perhaps into a unimodal policy as English has become indigenized. The existance of a second Great Tradition has long been recognized by some scholars, but not by the policymakers or by the bulk of the population. Even the increased official interest in the Maori language is often motivated by a desire to keep a potentially malcontented segment of the population happy, rather than by a recognition of any inherent value in the tradition of which the language is one expression.

In terms of national policy, bilingual schooling in New Zealand at present can be argued for on pedagogical grounds within the amodal framework (e.g., Bender 1971b)—i.e., Maori is used to teach initial literacy as a foundation for later work at a higher level in English—or in terms of multimodal criteria (e.g., Schwimmer 1968, Mead 1960, Benton 1966, 1975b, Hau 1968, Hauraki 1971, Lawrence et al. 1974, etc.), where, as the *Government White Paper* 1973 puts it, Maori is regarded as "the Folk Tongue of the indigenous peoples of New Zealand," and with the aim of bilingual schooling is to encourage language maintenance and give the Maori population increased access to its own Great Tradition, while retaining English as a "working language" for transactions with other segments of New Zealand society. Some recent proposals for the development of national bilingualism (e.g., Dewes 1968, Keen 1969, Benton 1973a, b, c, Mahuta et al. 1974) would necessitate, if they were to be carried through successfully to their logical conclusions, a shift in official policy and public support to a unimodal policy, aimed at replacing English by Maori in all spheres of national life, and retaining English as a second language for use in communication with the outside world. Both types of policy change present immense difficulties. Two generations ago, the Maori-speaking community had a number of solid regional bases where they formed a majority of the total population. The exodus to the cities and erosion of the Maori speech community by English influences in rural areas have greatly reduced the number of county-sized geographical areas which can be described as "Maori-speaking," and most of those which remain are isolated from each other. Unless the Maori speech community can somehow increase its geographical base through the recruitment of large numbers of families who are at present English-speaking, it is difficult to be optimistic about the long-term prospects of a multimodal approach to language planning (districts where there may be a remote possibility for such a renaissance of the Maori language would be the northern half of Northland, and the Bay of Plenty—East Coast area). The unimodal approach would require an even more revolutionary change in attitudes, although as the proportion of persons of Maori ancestry in the total population increases through intermarriage, and if ties with the Pacific and South East Asian nations continue to grow at the expense of those with Europe, an introspective nationalism may develop which would favor such a change. At present, however, there is little reason to suppose Maori will replace English in the daily lives of any appreciable number of New Zealanders. Given the present demographic trends, it seems that the prognostications of Biggs (1968) and Piddington (1968) concerning the likely future of the Maori language—its transformation from a vernacular to a purely ceremonial language—may well be realized. Keesing's remarks about Samoan (1931) that "in theory, the . . . language is capable of evolving to meet new experience. In practice, there is a margin of utility beyond which it becomes profitable to use the wider means of communication" seem, at present, to reflect more accurately the policies which have been adopted in many Maori households, in practice if not in theory.

Ironically, despite the great technical and administrative difficulties which have to be surmounted, the new multimodal approach to Aboriginal education in Australia may have more chance of success than any similar project in New Zealand. A clear distinction exists between the functions of English and of the Aboriginal languages, and in many areas, despite their small numbers, speakers of various Aboriginal languages do in fact have a clearly defined regional base. In this regard they occupy a similar position to the Polynesian speech communities in Niue, the Cook Islands, and the Tokelaus, where what in effect is at present a multimodal language policy in respect to New Zealand (where the vernacular is used for local purposes and English as the intergroup working language) could probably be successfully reflected in an extended bilingual program in the schools.

The areas in Oceania where bilingual education in a vernacular and metropolitan language based on multimodal language policies would have greatest chance of success are those where the population consists of a single speech community sharing a single recognized Great Tradition, but which also have strong political, economic, and demographic links (the latter through out-migration) with a metropolitan power. At present only two communities of any size fit this description—Tonga and Western Samoa. Although both these countries appear on the surface to be moving toward unimodal policies where the indigenous language will eventually replace English, in practice such an outcome is unlikely, given the recent emphasis in both countries in the development of tourism and the stress on the interdependence of the Oceanic community. In both countries the indigenous language is in a very strong position, local tradition acts as a powerful unifying force, and the advantages of English as a "working language" are sufficient to strongly motivate the learning of the language but no longer powerful enough to be a serious threat to the position of the indigenous language.

The Trust Territory of the Pacific Islands consists of a number of reasonably homogeneous speech communities (see Bender 1971a) which, taken individually, offer conditions somewhat similar to those obtaining in Tonga and Western Samoa. The situation in Fiji is much more complex. Here official language policy is, in fact, explicitly multimodal: the value of the indigenous Great Tradition, as well as these of the Hindi- and Urdu-speaking populations, and of the minority Chinese and Tamil communities, is explicitly recognized in the report of the 1969 Commission on Education, for example. In education, however, language policy is directed toward the phasing out of vernaculars as media of instruction, replacing them at all levels with the working language, English, but providing instruction in the languages associated with the Great Traditions as specific subjects on the curriculum. The cost of bilingual schooling in Fiji and the Trust Territory would be more than the economies of these countries could support without external aid, because of the multiplicity of vernaculars in both areas. A program of differential maintenance, using instruction in the vernacular for subjects related to the country, region, or ethnic group, and English for other subjects, might, however, be economically feasible and culturally rewarding. Such programs are being studied in the Trust Territory, which continues to have access to United States government funds. They have yet to be seriously considered as a practical possibility in Fiji.

The practical aspects of planning and evaluating bilingual programs have been succinctly outlined in a recent progress report from the Navajo Reading Study (Spolsky et al. 1974). In this report Professor Spolsky and his associates propose a model for the description and analysis of bilingual education consisting of seven factors (linguistic, psychological, sociological, economic, political, religiocultural, and educational) and three dimensions or levels (situational, operational, and the level of outcomes). The situational level is that existing before the introduction of bilingual education, i.e., the situation in most parts of Oceania at the present time, if the transitional use of the vernacular in the elementary grades is excluded from consideration. The operational level and the level of outcomes become relevant once the decision to establish a bilingual school program has been made. Some aspects of both these latter levels have been mentioned in the course of the discussion in this chapter, but in this concluding section it may be most useful to summarize the present situation briefly in terms of the seven factors listed above.

The *linguistic* factor includes such variables as the varieties of the language, existence of grammars, dictionaries, etc., domains and modes of use, literacy, existence of a literary tradition and/or a standard orthography, and the utilization of the language in the mass media. In Polynesia generally, there is a long tradition of literacy in the vernacular, and well-established standard orthographies. There is a strong oral tradition, but the early budding of a corresponding literary tradition has been frustrated in most areas by the cessation of higher education in the vernacular and a dearth of published materials. There is a large body of printed and manuscript material in New Zealand Maori, but much of this is accessible only to scholars; however, a literary tradition as such is probably far stronger in Maori than in any other Oceanic language. Australian languages are not associated with any literary tradition, and although in recent years linguists have developed orthographies for many of them, writing as yet has no place in the traditional and domestic activities within which the languages are used. The speakers of many Micronesian languages have been literate in the vernacular for generations, but a literary tradition, as against a tradition of literacy, has yet to develop. Problems have also arisen in the standardization of orthographies (see Bender 1971a; see also Blass et al. 1969 for a listing of grammars, etc., developed for the study of particular languages in various parts of the region). The vernacular languages are not generally used in the daily press in most parts of Oceania, but play a major role in radio broadcasts in Fiji and Western Samoa, and a very limited role in New Zealand. Although the major Polynesian and Micronesian languages are reasonably well described in abstract terms, little detailed information is available about the extent and significance of differences between different registers within each language, nor, in most cases, have dialect differences been systematically studied. The multiplicity of languages involved is a serious problem in many Aboriginal communities in Australia.

Psychological variables include attitudes held toward the language and its speakers by the speakers themselves, the wider community (where the speakers form a minority group), and by educators, as well as attitudes toward schooling and the "cognitive style" of the school and the students. The most extreme differences in cognitive style probably exist in Australia, where European approaches to education have little in common with traditional Aboriginal methods of transmitting knowledge. Even in New Zealand, where a temporary resistance to schooling after the Land Wars of the 1860s had disappeared in most areas by the turn of the century (see Barrington 1971), to be replaced by a general enthusiasm for European education (cf. Hawthorn 1944, also Beaglehole and Barrington 1974), the comparative lack of success of Maori students in the school system which has caused concern for many years suggests some lack of fit between the ways schools operate and the ways Maori pupils either learn or demonstrate their learning. Teachers may also be a problem group. John Watson (1967, 1973) has shown how New Zealand teachers are unwilling to believe that fundamental differences of approach may be needed in dealing with children from different cultural backgrounds—their training and general background have left them ideologically ill prepared to accept or even recognize linguistic and cognitive differences. Furthermore, the unwillingness of either the bureaucracy or the profession to encourage specialization has prevented the formation of a corps of teachers of the kind who would be most needed in a bilingual school. This kind of situation is probably present in most parts of Oceania, for even those members of the teaching profession who are members of the indigenous group are often individuals deeply affected by the assimilative pressures inherent in teacher education under the aegis of the metropolitan power. Other widely held attitudes likely to have an adverse effect on the development of bilingual education include belief in the inherent or functional superiority of the metropolitan language, and a desire to avoid contaminating the indigenous culture through its incorporation in an alien institution.

Among the *sociological* aspects of the situation are the social structure of the community, including the degree of ethnic interaction, and the socioeconomic status of the groups involved. In New Zealand, Maori speakers are found at all levels of the socioeconomic scale, but are proportionately fewer than non-Maoris at the upper levels. Although sometimes professing a separatist ideology, educated and affluent native speakers of Maori have often ceased to use the language in their homes, with the result that, if they speak the language at all, their children have learned it as a second language in early adulthood. However, it is interesting to note that while social pressures (including the mixing of English-speaking and originally Maori-speaking families in urban areas) have been responsible for language loss among the children of urban migrants in New Zealand, responsibilities of leadership in the Maori community have been equally powerful forces in causing many individuals to acquire or relearn the language in later life. Similar pressures probably exist in other mixed communities, including Australia, Fiji, and perhaps New Caledonia (at least as far as language loss is concerned). However, in relatively homogeneous societies like Tonga, Western Samoa, and the major islands in the Trust Territory such pressures would be slight—the advantages of both the local and metropolitan languages could perhaps be seen in a clearer perspective. Throughout Oceania, however, the language of wider communication has usually been closely associated with superior wealth and power, and the local language and culture with relatively depressed political and economic status.

Economic factors include the critical aspects of funding and employment.

Few Oceanic countries have the resources for adequate funding of educational programs of any kind, and development of materials for bilingual programs would place added strains on already overtaxed economies. The exceptions are Australia, the French territories, and New Zealand, which could finance such programs if it were considered politically expedient to do so, and Tonga and Western Samoa, where the development of materials in the vernacular is relatively well advanced. Australia has already made moves in this direction, and in doing so has opened up new employment opportunities for native speakers of Aboriginal languages. Similar opportunities have recently become available for native speakers of Maori in New Zealand, but in the field of second language teaching only.

Political considerations undoubtedly outweigh economic feasibility in French Polynesia and New Caledonia, and elsewhere in the Pacific a serious bilingual program would probably not be possible without considerable financial assistance from external sources; so far only the Trust Territory of the Pacific Islands is receiving such aid, and there is little evidence of demand for it in territories like the Cook Islands which remain oriented toward the metropolitan power although in full control of their own educational policies.

Religiocultural factors have had an important influence on movements within New Zealand for greater recognition of the Maori language, and the development of Maori liturgies and the generally high status accorded to Maori within the Roman Catholic and Anglican churches, as well as in the Maori-based Ratana and Ringatu churches has played no small part in the encouragement of language maintenance in certain areas. It was in the Anglican and Catholic boarding schools that Maori was first introduced as an academic subject. In most Pacific islands Christianity has been introduced through the medium of the vernacular, and most of the early dictionaries and grammars were the products of missionary labors. Mission schools have, however, tended to follow the policies most favored by the metropolitan power, and in New Caledonia, for example, both Catholic and Evangelical mission schools had abandoned Melanesian languages in favor of French well before the outbreak of World War II. On balance, though, religious forces in most Oceanic countries could be expected to by sympathetic to bilingual education. In Australia the possibility of religio-cultural conflict, from the Aboriginal side, is greatest, as certain forms of language and certain forms of knowledge are to be used and transmitted in particular ways to specified audiences. The "open" nature of the school may conflict with certain "closed" aspects of the culture—a problem with which the organizers of the present bilingual project in Australia are at present trying to cope.

The *educational* factor—as distinct from the other factors discussed above—relates to the availability of primary resources. Teachers have to be recruited and trained, materials developed, students chosen (if the program is to be an optional one), and buildings provided. These are complex problems in all Oceanic countries. If bilingual schooling were to be made widely available in New Zealand, for example, duplicate facilities would probably be required in many urban areas, as it is likely that at least as many parents would not want their children to be taught under such a scheme, at least in its initial stages, as would be willing to have their children participate. The problems would be least acute in countries like Western Samoa and Tonga, which have already gone a long way toward establishing their own types of bilingual schools.

Many of the problems, and some of the prospects, for bilingual education in vernacular and metropolitan languages in New Zealand and Oceania have been outlined in the preceding pages. The prospects seem reasonably bright in those countries which have a homogeneous population with a strong cultural tradition and control of their own affairs, and for those communities which, although small, are the recipients of adequate external aid for such programs. Four areas fall within this description at present—Western Samoa, Tonga, some Aboriginal communities in Australia, and parts of the Trust Territory of the Pacific Islands. In two other areas, New Zealand and Fiji, there are possibilities rather than prospects—at present, policymakers are committed to fostering bilingualism, if at all, through language study and second language teaching, coupled with a home-school language switch for native speakers of the indigenous vernaculars. Bilingual schooling using the vernaculars on an equal footing with the language of wider communication has yet to win official approval or the kind of public support in these two countries which could transform an idea into a reality.

NOTES

1. At the 1966 census, the total population of Australia was 11,550,462, excluding full-blooded Aboriginals. The latter were estimated to number 40,081 in 1961, when a further 39,172 persons were classified as half-caste Aboriginals. The total Aboriginal population is therefore less than 1% of the population of the Commonwealth, more than 98% of which is of European origin.

2. Figures for two schools were not available.

3. Figures for one school were not given in the report.

4. Includes one school (27 pupils) where the state of linguistic analysis on the community's language (Anmatjira) was not given in the report.

5. Includes one school (14 pupils). Linguistic analysis and number of languages spoken not specified.

6. This was reported to the author by the principal of the school during a visit to Western Samoa in 1972. Much of the information contained in this subsection and those on the Cook Islands, Niue, and Fiji, where not attributed to published sources, comes from conversations with government officials and educational administrators at the South Pacific Conference in Apia, Western Samoa, in September 1972, and subsequent visits to Tonga and Fiji in 1972 and 1973, as well as similar contacts with certain officials and scholars from these areas who have visited New Zealand in this period.

7. The first stage of this survey is a sociolinguistic census, begun in August 1973, similar to that undertaken by Joshua Fishman and his associates in their study of Puerto Rican bilingualism in Jersey City (see Fishman 1968). It is hoped to interview directly at least one representative from each of about 5400 households spread through the major areas of Maori population in the North Island, thus gathering information on the knowledge and use of

Maori and English of about 15% of the Maori population. It is aimed to complete the survey by 1977; up to May 1976 interviews had been completed in 3620 households covering more than 19,000 people in both rural and urban areas.

8. For comment on other aspects of the NZBC's treatment of Maori culture and Maori topics on television, see Armstrong 1967, 1971; Puriri 1967. The *Listener* is a weekly magazine published by the New Zealand Broadcasting Corporation.

9. Comments on the development, availability, and/or merits of Maori language courses in New Zealand schools can be found in the following sources addition to those cited in this section: Biggs 1968; Benton 1975b; Andersen 1931a, b; Dale 1931; Sutherland 1935; Ball 1940, 1973; Parsonage 1953, 1956; Laughton 1954; Powell 1955; Masters 1956; Anderson 1957; Mead 1960; Currie et al. 1962:427-428, 436; Barrington 1966; *Te Kaunihera Maori 3.2*, 1968:15; Ramsay 1969; *Education 21.3*, 1972; *Te Ao Hou 72*, 1973:34-37; NZEI 1973; Beaglehole and Barrington 1974; Beavis 1975.

Bilingual Education

in The Republic of South Africa

E. G. Malherbe

INTRODUCTION

As Professor Mackey[1] pointed out, the term "bilingual education" can mean different things in different contexts. It would therefore seem necessary to state clearly what it means in the South African context. It can, of course, mean simply the process by which a person learns a language other than his mother tongue. This could take place in a unilingual country and may remain a linguistic experience confined to that person as an individual.

In a country like South Africa, however, with two official languages, English and Afrikaans, geographically interspersed, bilingual education has important implications besides those of a purely linguistic or school nature. There are factors of a cultural, sociological, and political nature. These have had such a profound influence on bilingual education in South Africa that they will also have to be dealt with in this discussion. Because South Africans live in such a widely bilingual environment (at least as far as the white population is concerned), the process of acquiring two languages is greatly facilitated. For them it has become a political and economic necessity for effective citizenship, and when once achieved, it affords them access to two important cultures.

Of the two official languages English has had the advantage of being virtually a world language affording much wider contacts and a richer literary heritage than Afrikaans, which, like the Bantu vernaculars, is useful only in the geographic area of Southern Africa. Nevertheless, because Afrikaans is so closely associated with the rise of Afrikaner nationalism, a fierce struggle developed for dominance between English and Afrikaans in the school. Using the old Flemish slogan: *De Taal is gansch het Volk* (language is the entire nation), the Afrikaans language became for the Afrikaner the symbol of the struggle for national identity. In course of time the public (i.e., the state) school was seized upon as the means to foster that consciousness of a "nation with a God-given destiny."

In contrast, the consciousness of identity among the English-speaking South Africans was fused with sentiments of loyalty to Britain. This impeded the growth of a purely local English nationalism; and as far as the English language was concerned, the English-speaking group had little fear of loss of identity, speaking as they did a world language that ensured a world culture. In comparison, the Afrikaans language was a young and tender plant to be carefully nurtured.

Incidentally, Afrikaans is also the mother tongue of the Coloured population, who in the course of two centuries were as much creators of the spoken language as the Afrikaner. Yet, because of a matter of pigmentation, the Afrikaner will not regard the Coloureds as part of the Afrikaner nation. Thus, through *apartheid*, the much vaunted Flemish slogan has gone by the board.

As the school was regarded as the chief agency for transmitting culture from one generation to the next, it became for Afrikaner nationalism the strategic point of attack.

HISTORICAL AND DEMOGRAPHIC FACTORS

The Republic of South Africa is a multiracial and multilingual country consisting of nearly 23 million people of whom about 40% (mostly African) may be regarded as still "underdeveloped," i.e., in terms of Western European culture. It can almost be regarded as a microcosm of the world in its linguistic, ethic, political, and economic complexity.

Though English and Afrikaans are the two official languages with equal rights guaranteed by the Constitution, the following indigenous African (Bantu) languages are recognized as subjects and as media up to matriculation (university entrance) and as subjects at the university. They are spoken mainly by the following ethnic groups whose numbers are shown in parentheses: Zulu (4,026,000), Xhosa (3,930,000), Tswana (1,719,000), North-Sotho (1,604,000), South-Sotho (1,452,000), Tsonga (737,000), Venda (358,000). The rest of the Africans speak other Bantu languages not yet recognized at school.

When the white population (now numbering a little more than 4 million), who were predominantly of Dutch, English, French, and German stock, settled first at the Cape of Good Hope over 300 years ago, the indigenous African (Bantu) inhabitants of Southern Africa numbered less than a million. Now there over 16 million. Besides the whites and the Bantu, there are now also the following two groups: (1) the Coloureds (2,144,000), who are a mixed race of white and nonwhite blood and speak Afrikaans; and (2) the Asians (668,000), who are mainly descendants of Indian laborers imported between 1860 and 1911 to work in Natal sugar plantations. These speak mainly English, though there are still vestiges of Hindi and Urdu spoken by the older Indians.

EXTENT OF BILINGUALISM IN THE TWO OFFICIAL LANGUAGES

Of South Africa's total school population of 4,595,000 pupils, 93% attend state schools. In view of the fact that bilingualism, i.e., in terms of the two official languages, is so largely the effect of schooling, the following percentages of the total population in the respective racial groups who attend school (i.e., excluding university and technical institutions) may be relevant: white 22.5%, Coloured 27.2%, Asian 25.7%, African (Bantu) 19.6%.

The degree to which these four racial groups are able to speak the two official languages, English and Afrikaans, is reflected in diagrams A and B. The figures are in respect of persons of 15 years and older—an age at which schooling could have had an effect. They are based on the census of 1960, the last year that this item of "language spoken" was included in the census. It will be seen that the whites are the most bilingual group, with 79.5% speaking both English and Afrikaans. Next come the Coloured with 49.8%, the Asians with 15.4%, and last the Bantu, the most numerous group, with 12.0%.

About half the Bantu population live in their "homelands" where English and Afrikaans are hardly ever heard outside the schoolroom, if at all. The rest either live on farms in "white" rural areas or work in urban areas. Here they "pick up" by osmosis, as it were, the official languages, English and Afrikaans.

The figures in Diagrams A and B have been calculated from the returns made in connection with the 1960 Population Census, in which all *whites, Coloureds,* and *Asiatics* were required to complete the following item on the form:

If able to speak—
(a)   Both English and Afrikaans, state *Both*
(b)   English only, state *English*
(c)   Afrikaans only, state *Afrikaans*
(d)   Neither English nor Afrikaans, state *neither*

The form used for the *Bantu* concerning *languages spoken* was different:

Mark each square applicable with a cross, that is an X:
If able to speak:
A Bantu Language   □
English   □
Afrikaans   □

The above item concerning *languages spoken* in the case of whites, Coloureds, and Asiatics was for some unaccountable reason omitted from the 1970 census. This omission was most unfortunate because it broke the continuity

PERCENTAGE

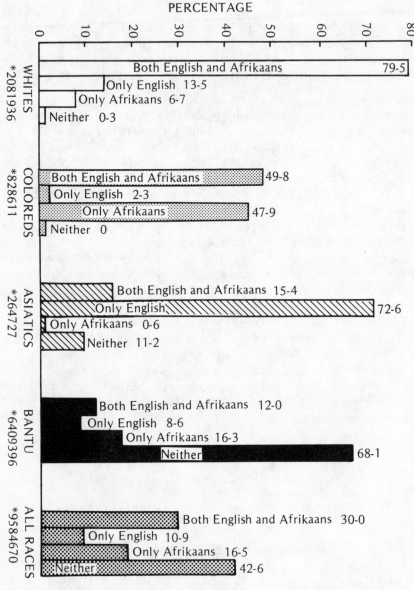

WHITES *2081936
- Both English and Afrikaans 79-5
- Only English 13-5
- Only Afrikaans 6-7
- Neither 0-3

COLOREDS *828611
- Both English and Afrikaans 49-8
- Only English 2-3
- Only Afrikaans 47-9
- Neither 0

ASIATICS *264727
- Both English and Afrikaans 15-4
- Only English 72-6
- Only Afrikaans 0-6
- Neither 11-2

BANTU *6409396
- Both English and Afrikaans 12-0
- Only English 8-6
- Only Afrikaans 16-3
- Neither 68-1

ALL RACES *9584670
- Both English and Afrikaans 30-0
- Only English 10-9
- Only Afrikaans 16-5
- Neither 42-6

*persons 15 years old and older

Diagram A   Percentage of people able to speak the Official Languages

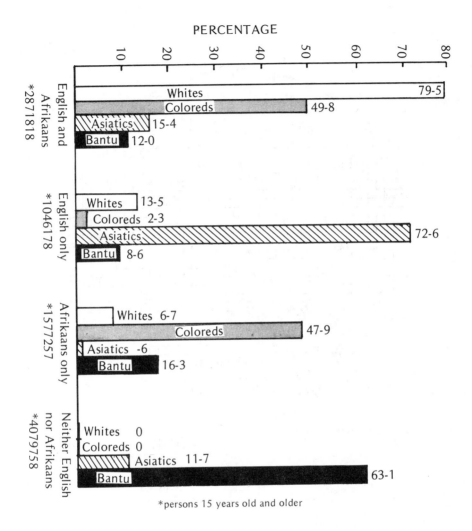

PERCENTAGE

English and Afrikaans *2871818

Whites 79-5
Coloreds 49-8
Asiatics 15-4
Bantu 12-0

English only *1046178

Whites 13-5
Coloreds 2-3
Asiatics 72-6
Bantu 8-6

Afrikaans only *1577257

Whites 6-7
Coloreds 47-9
Asiatics -6
Bantu 16-3

Neither English nor Afrikaans *4079758

Whites 0
Coloreds 0
Asiatics 11-7
Bantu 63-1

*persons 15 years old and older

Diagram B   Percentage of people able to speak the Official Languages

of the information gathered in the previous censuses from 1918 onward, and will now make future assessments of progress in respect of the knowledge of English and Afrikaans on the part of these three racial groups impossible. Curiously, however, the question was retained for the Bantu in the 1970 Census.

No specific indication is given on the Census form as to the degree of proficiency required in the spoken language. Presumably it is left to the person's judgment about his own proficiency and, in the case of very young children, to

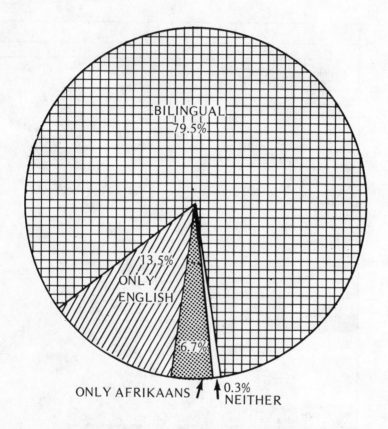

Diagram C   Percentages of white people 15 years old and older who are bilingual and who can speak only Afrikaans and only English (1960 census).

the parents' judgment. Obviously the degree of proficiency is a matter of degree and will vary considerably from one individual to another. However, whatever lack of validity there may have been in assessing bilingualism from these figures, the probable error in the totals of millions of cases can be assured to be fairly constant over the years, so that comparison between one census and the next would seem to be valid for practical purposes.

THE EFFECT OF SCHOOLING ON NUMBER OF BILINGUALS

In order to make the figures more meaningful, they are given in respect only to those of 15 years old and older. At that age the effect of schooling obviously has made itself felt, because both official languages are compulsory subjects at school.

In order to obtain a School Leaving or Matriculation Certificate all whites, Coloureds, and Indians must obtain a pass in both English and Afrikaans as subjects, at least one on a higher and the other on a lower grade. The Bantu may offer one Bantu language and one official language on a lower grade, at least. The degree to which schooling has had an effect can be gathered from the accompanying table in respect of the white population.

Ability to Speak the Official Languages among Whites According to Age Groups (1960 Census)

Percentage who can speak	Below 15 years	15 years and older	All ages	Total persons
Both English and Afrikaans	39.0	79.5	66.4	2,044,645
Only English	18.2	13.6	15.0	461,552
Only Afrikaans	42.2	6.7	18.1	558,401
Neither	0.6	0.3	0.5	15,361
	100.0	100.0	100.0	3,080,159*

*Including 200 "unspecified."

It will be noted that the percentage of those able to speak both English and Afrikaans is 79.5% among those 15 years old and older compared with only 39.0% of those below 15 years. The biggest gain in bilingualism was among the unilingual Afrikaans children where the percentage of unilinguals decreased from 42.4 to 6.7% as a result of schooling plus possibly wider contacts. There is a preponderance of Afrikaans children in the rural areas where they are largely isolated from contact with the English language in their immediate environment. It is here where the school exerts its greatest compensating influence. The same is observed in the case of the Coloureds, who are also mainly rural and Afrikaans-speaking.

The highest percentage (72.6%) of English unilinguals is found among the Asiatics. This is because the mobility of the bulk of them is restricted to the dominantly English-speaking Province of Natal. The Coloureds are the most unilingually Afrikaans group (47.9%). Next come the Bantu of whom 16.5% speak only Afrikaans, that is, they are called unilingual or bilingual only in respect to the white man's official languages. The Bantu speak a Bantu language as well. The "officially bilinguals" among the Bantu are in fact trilingual. This is becoming increasingly so because both the two official languages, English and Afrikaans, are taught as subjects in Bantu schools. This is in addition to the vernacular, which is the medium of instruction at the lower primary stages. One of the official languages is supposed to be introduced as an additional medium at the higher primary and secondary stages. Whether it is English or Afrikaans is largely dependent on which of the two official languages is preponderant and in the environment. In spite of these efforts 63.1% (4,364,499) Bantu 15 years old and older are still unable to speak either English or Afrikaans. As the Bantu are gaining independence in their own "homelands" they have shown a preference for English to be the additional and chief medium of instruction at school. One of the leading Bantu chiefs indicated this preference to me in the following rather picturesque language:

> If I know only a Bantu language, I am like a chicken picking at my food inside a pen. When, however, I know the white man's language (English) I can soar like an eagle!

AFRIKAANS: THE NEW ARRIVAL

In view of the fact that Afrikaans is probably the newest arrival as a full-fledged language among European languages, it is appropriate at this stage to give a brief account of its origin and present status as one of the official languages.

From 1652 and for nearly one and three quarter centuries, Dutch was the official language at the Cape of Good Hope. As a result of its isolation at the southernmost tip of the dark continent of Africa, the language as spoken by the inhabitants soon started to deviate considerably from the Dutch of their homeland. Not only did it incorporate into the vocabulary a number of new words as a result of contact with Malay-Portuguese and with the indigenous peoples, but living as it did mainly on the tongues of the people, the spoken language became linguistically streamlined by dropping many grammatical features of the Dutch of Holland. Moreover, being the language of pioneers, it was seldom written. As a result, it went during a period of about 200 years through much the same linguistic evolution that English did after the time of Chaucer. The Dutch, however, of the *Staten Bybel* of the Netherlands remained the language used mainly in church and religious exercises. It was also the language of the schoolroom. It was called "high Dutch," and the fact that it differed from the vernacular lent to scholastic exercises much the same artificial atmosphere which the use of Latin instead of the vernacular as a medium of instruction did in pre-Renaissance days. The history of the struggle of Afrikaans to be recognized as a scholastic language was similar to that which vernaculars in the schools and universities of Europe went through from the time of the Renaissance.

Afrikaans had to fight virtually on two fronts: against the traditional "high Dutch," on the one hand, and the powerful English language on the other. English had been made the only official language despite the fact that, including the 5000 English immigrants who had arrived in 1820, not one in eight of the inhabitants could speak English. The avowed object of the British Governor was to anglicize the population. Teachers and clergymen were imported from England in order to apply the policy to the schools. The original Dutch population, however, refused to give up their language, and it is from this period that bilingual education in South Africa dates. Both English and Dutch were taught as school subjects, and English was the sole medium where there were teachers competent enough to teach through that medium.

This policy of anglicization was frustrating and repressive in a number of respects. Nevertheless many of the persons imported to implement it were men of high moral and intellectual caliber. They were men who not only strove to learn Dutch and adapt themselves, but who were instrumental in setting up intellectual standards in a country which at that time was very backward educationally. They founded institutions and exercised a formative influence to which later many South Africans became greatly indebted. Without their contribution at the time, South Africa's cultural heritage would have been greatly impoverished.

EFFECTS OF TWO OPAQUE MEDIA OF INSTRUCTION

For the children, however, at that time the role of language as a school medium was a doubly unfortunate one. In the first place, English, which only a small proportion of children could speak properly, was used as the medium of instruction. In the second place, before the advent of Afrikaans in the schools, the alternative language was "high Dutch." This was by no means, as has been pointed out, the mother tongue of the children. They spoke Afrikaans. "High Dutch" was therefore in a sense virtually a foreign language; to a lesser degree than English, it is true, but nonetheless foreign to the child's out-of-school thoughts and experience. To the mind of the child, Dutch for many years remained a strange, stilted language, used only in connection with religion, prayers, the Bible and church, and to be learned with difficulty by means of a grammar book. This setup could not but generate a complicating dualism in the child's learning process. His schoolwork, if not in English, had to be assimilated through Dutch, another semiopaque medium.

The fact, too, that English was the language of government, something run by people who called England their home, made many of the Afrikaans-speaking inhabitants look upon schooling as something imposed upon them from without. Unconsciously, it set defense mechanisms going in their minds against education, and created an attitude which was often mistaken for intellectual heaviness. Education could hardly be a means of liberating the spirit of creative self-expression when schooling and learning generally were associated in their minds with the exotic and the unmeaning.

The learning and speaking of Dutch was difficult enough for the Afrikaans-speaking child. For the English-speaking child, it was a foreign language, like French or German, and far more difficult to acquire than English was for the Afrikaans-speaking child. Here we find one reason why the English-speaking section of the South African population was, until recently, less bilingual than the Afrikaans speakers.

AFRIKAANS AS WELL AS ENGLISH BECOMES ENTRENCHED

Section 137 of the Act of Union in 1910 legally entrenched bilingualism in South Africa. It laid down that both English and Dutch would be official languages of the Union and "shall be treated on a footing of equality and enjoy equal freedom, rights and privileges." In 1925, Afrikaans was declared by Parliament to be included in the word Dutch.

Educationally, this amendment was very necessary because by that time Dutch was hardly ever spoken by the people. According to the Census, Afrikaans was the language most commonly spoken in nearly 60% of the homes, English in 37% of the homes, and other languages in 3%. Both English and Afrikaans were compulsory subjects at the primary and secondary school level. In that specific sense, South Africa has a 100% bilingual education.

By the 1930s, Afrikaans had become standardized and dictionaries were published. The spelling was phonetic and was in consequence much more easily learned than English spelling. Afrikaans gained recognition as a matriculation subject for admission also to overseas universities. The stimulating effect of the change-over to Afrikaans from Dutch was unmistakable in church as well as in school. The translation of the Bible into Afrikaans had a great cultural as well as religious significance for the people. The British and Foreign Bible Society published the first complete Afrikaans edition in 1933.

The fine quality of Afrikaans literary efforts soon gained acclaim and recognition abroad as well as at home. South Africa's most prominent English poet, Roy Campbell, found Afrikaans as a medium of expression to be "as full of adventure for the bold and daring as ever any language in history and unique among contemporary tongues for youth and freshness." As a result of its phenomenal growth in literature, especially poetry, it can be regarded as the greatest single linguistic and cultural achievement on the African continent in recent times.[2]

What was important is the fact that Afrikaans was rooted in the soil and came to be regarded by the Afrikaner as peculiarly his own. By its virility and flexibility it came to be used to express aspects of human thoughts and life ranging from the most witty and earthy comedy to the profoundest of spiritual and scientific truths. Today there are in Afrikaans over 15,000 volumes covering a wide range of subjects including the technical and scientific as well as the purely literary. For example, in creating terminology in the physical and biological sciences Afrikaans could always fall back on its parent language, Dutch, by simply spelling the Dutch terms phonetically while retaining the common Latin and Greek roots which had already been incorporated generally in the Germanic languages. In this way Afrikaans has a big advantage over other vernaculars in Africa. In a few instances it has also borrowed an English term where it had become more current by usage than the corresponding Dutch term. At the most advanced academic levels, it replaced English as a medium of instruction at the universities of Stellenbosch, Pretoria, Potchefstroom, and Bloemfontein. Finally, its viability at all levels in South African life became assured and put beyond question.

Educationally, Afrikaans had a great liberating effect, for both Afrikaans-speaking and English-speaking pupils. The latter made more rapid progress in Afrikaans than they ever could have made in Dutch because they at least heard it spoken in common conversation in the environment. In 1975, the Nationalist Government inaugurated a monument on the mountain at Paarl to commemorate the hundredth anniversary of the publication of the first Afrikaans paper, "Di Patriot" in Gideon Malherbe's residence in Paarl. Its publication was sponsored by a group which called themselves Die Genootskap van Regete Afrikaners (The Association of Real Afrikaners). At the time of the centenary celebrations Gideon Malherbe's home was also declared to be a national monument.

LANGUAGE AND NATIONALISM

When fighting for political recognition, the Afrikaner instinctively seized upon the furtherance of that part of his national life, his language, which he regarded as most distinctive and therefore most precious. Without the Afrikaans language, there would have been no Afrikaner nationalist movement. Without the driving force of Afrikaner nationalism and the constructive efforts of great Afrikaner leaders, this distinctive and precious part of South African culture might easily have been swamped by the much more subtly powerful English culture, which had been socially as well as politically dominant for nearly a century.

There can be little doubt, however, that the prestige of the Afrikaans language will depend in the future, as it did in the past, far more on the quality of the creative work of its writers and poets than on the efforts of politicians who use it as a means of consolidating the political power of Afrikanerdom vis-à-vis the other cultural groups in South Africa. Such efforts tend to create a situation in which a fine language becomes associated in the minds of non-Afrikaans-speaking people with a particular political party or with an ideological issue.

South African history has shown that, once the propagation of a language becomes associated with power and ideology, reaction against the language sets in, as happened against the English language and under the domination of the British Empire.

In the minds of many of South Africa's nonwhites, the advent of Afrikanerdom, in recent years, has become associated with racial discrimination and repression. Such discrimination has caused even many Coloured people, who were the joint creators of spoken Afrikaans, and who have no other mother tongue, to turn their backs on Afrikaans, today the language of white officialdom, and to prefer English. It is little wonder also that some Bantu high school pupils, in referring to Afrikaans in a recent essay competition, used the expression: "The language of the conqueror in the mouth of the conquered is a language of slaves." This slogan was often used to rouse anti-English feelings among Afrikaners when English was forced upon the Transvaal and Orange Free State population after the Anglo-Boer War (1899-1902). History has repeatedly shown that when culture becomes the superstructure and the justification for power and privilege, the quality of that culture suffers.

Especially during and for many years after the Anglo-Boer War (1899-1902) the intrusion of emotional factors had a detrimental effect on bilingual education. For example, even as late as 1938 when the writer had found the pupils of a small

Afrikaans-medium school to be particularly backward in English, he asked the teacher to give an English lesson. He responded rather wearily and introduced his lesson with the remark in Afrikaans, "Come children, let us now once more wrestle with the enemy's language."

The educational experience in South Africa as well as in other countries has shown that the success with which a second language is acquired and used as a medium depends largely on whether that language is one which is eagerly sought after or whether the language is that of a people who are feared, hated, or despised.

If the attitudes prevailing in a particular school could be quantified and included as an additional set of variables to those that are listed in Mackey's *A Typology of Bilingual Education* mentioned above, the number of patterns under which bilingual schooling can take place would far exceed the 250 cataloged by him. In fact, if one considered each individual child (because emotional attitude is such an individual thing), the permutations and combinations of variables might become almost infinite.

In this discussion, however, we are dealing only with groups and average situations.

WHAT MAKES THE SOUTH AFRICAN SITUATION UNIQUE

In several respects the South African situation is unique. This is a fact which must be taken into account when comparing the methods and results of bilingual education with those in other bilingual countries.

Partly as a result of the fact that the study of both official languages as subjects is compulsory in all schools, and has been so for more than half a century, the percentage of white population able to speak both English and Afrikaans has grown since 1918 from 42½% to nearly 80%. (See Diagram D showing growth in successive censuses.) In Canada, for example, only 13% of its population speak both French and English.

Furthermore, unlike in other bilingual countries, the Afrikaans-speaking and English-speaking communities have become geographically interspersed and heavily linked by intermarriage. Then too, the whites in South Africa are not separated by religious affiliations (Protestant and Catholic) as, for example, in Canada or in Belgium.

Where English- and Afrikaans-speaking children lived in the same community, they usually attended the same school. In order, however, to give effect to the compulsory mother-tongue medium regulations, three types of school organization gradually evolved:

1. *Parallel-medium classes* in schools where there was a minority language group of at least 15 pupils. This meant a parallel set of classes under the same roof (at least at the primary level)—one set taught through Afrikaans and the other through English medium:

2. *Dual-medium instruction* where the minority language group was less than 15 pupils (that is, both languages were used by the teacher of that group).

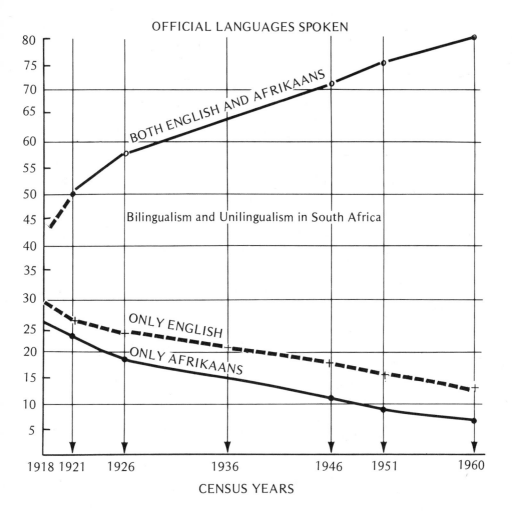

Diagram D   Growth in the percentage of bilinguals among the white population during about half a century.

3. *Single-medium schools.* These were usual in more or less homogeneous English- and Afrikaans-speaking environments and in metropolitan centers where the numbers warranted separate schools for the two language groups.

Whereas mother-tongue or home-language medium was compulsory at the primary level, parents could choose the medium of instruction at the secondary level. This was the practice in the Cape of Good Hope, Transvaal, and Orange Free State Provinces. In Natal, however, parents had the choice of medium of instruction at the primary as well as the secondary level. From 1970, however, home-language medium was made compulsory up to standard VIII in all four provinces.

Where English- and Afrikaans-speaking children attended the same school, they had the advantage of associating with each other on the playground and in other extracurricular activities. Thus, they picked up each other's languages in an informal way.

LANGUAGES AS SUBJECTS AND AS MEDIA

In bilingual education a distinction must be drawn between: (1) the teaching of the two languages as *subjects*, and (2) the use of these two languages as *media* when teaching other subjects.

Failure to make this simple distinction has been the cause of a good deal of confusion of thought on this matter not only in South Africa, but also in other bilingual countries. This confusion has unfortunately been exploited with a view to misleading the uninitiated. For example, whenever the introduction of the partial use of the second language as a *medium* was mooted, that section of the press which opposed such a step did everything in its power to make poeple believe that it meant doing away with the *mother tongue as a subject.*

In a bilingual country like South Africa the child obviously learns his first language as a subject from the start. It is also in nearly all cases the language medium of instruction generally in the classroom. But *when* and *how* a beginning should be made with the second language as a *subject* has been a matter of experimentation in South African schools with practices varying in detail between the different provinces.

There is general agreement, however, that the young child who is not acquainted with the second language should *hear* the language spoken first, then learn to *speak* it, and lastly learn to *read* and *write* it. As far as possible the method of acquiring the second language should follow the mode of acquisition of the first language.[3] This has been found to be best achieved in free association with other children who speak the second language. And failing the presence of such children, the second language should be introduced *conversationally* through games and other interesting experiences of intrinsically educational value to the child, e.g., simple stories from the field of history, geography, nature study, etc.

Used in this way, the language lesson (whether in the first or the second language) becomes ancillary to the other subjects, instead of being something sterile by itself. Afrikaans is written almost completely phonetically, whereas English spelling is anything but phonetic. That is why English-speaking pupils acquire the reading and spelling of Afrikaans (their second language) far more quickly than Afrikaans-speaking children can learn to read and spell in English. Consequently it has also been found that by the age of 12 years, Afrikaans-speaking pupils have a larger reading and spelling vocabulary in Afrikaans than English-speaking pupils have in their first language at that age. To the non-English speaker, English is actually a very difficult language.

NATIONALISTS AGITATE FOR SEPARATION

With the growth of Afrikaner nationalism came the movement to segregate English- and Afrikaans-speaking children into separate unilingual-medium schools, even where they lived in the same community. The movement began in the 1920s mainly in the large metropolitan centers where the Afrikaners at the time felt themselves insecure as a minority group. It spread to the smaller centers during the 1930s and 1940s. The protagonists of this movement knew that among the whites the Afrikaans-speaking population outweighed the English-speaking section on a ratio of roughly 60 to 40, and that, if through the schools they could apply the catch-them-young methods, they would, as a result of indoctrination, ultimately attain the political dominance of Afrikaner nationalism. At first this movement operated behind the scenes and was sponsored by a powerful secret organization known as the Afrikaner Broederbond. Later it was advocated openly as one of the planks in the political platform of the Nationalist Party.

Apart from the rather fanciful theories expounded by the church and party politicians, the following pedagogical arguments were officially advanced by the education departments and supported by professors in certain universities where future teachers were trained. They were to the effect: (1) that by linguistic contact the mother tongues of the respective language groups would become contaminated; (2) that any learning done by the pupil through the medium of the pupil's "other tongue" would have deleterious effects on his mental development; and (3) that, whatever antipathies and prejudices existed between the two groups, these would be exacerbated by contact on the playground, if they were put in the same school. If, however, they were separated, they would "find their own identity and respect each others' identities."

OBJECTIVE EVIDENCE ON BILINGUAL EDUCATION

As very little research of an objective nature had hitherto been done to prove or to disprove some of the generalizations in connection with the various aspects of bilingual education, and, as these issues had come so much to the fore during the 1930s, the National Bureau for Educational and Social Research (under the Union Education Department) embarked in 1938 on an extensive survey[4] in order to get at the facts. By means of standardized tests in English and Afrikaans the Bureau measured the school achievement[5] of pupils who had been taught respectively in single-medium, parallel-medium, and dual-medium schools and classes throughout their school careers. The schools were selected by the respective Provincial Education Departments so as to ensure that they would be representative of the province as a whole.

Full data were obtained from a total of 18,773 pupils in standards IV to X. (The median age of pupils is 11.6 years in standard IV, which corresponds roughly to the American 6th grade. The median age of standard X pupils is 17.6 years.) Each pupil was subjected to a battery of scholastic and intelligence (verbal and nonverbal tests)—twelve in all—administered personally by the investigators.

HOME LANGUAGE ENVIRONMENT MEASURED

Because the most important part of the child's linguistic experience is gained in the home, it was found necessary in this survey to gage more accurately the extent and nature of that linguistic experience than was usually done by merely asking a pupil what his home language was. This was done by putting the questions listed below to each pupil tested. The filling in of the replies was supervised item by item by the investigator.

These questions constituted part of a long list comprising an information test. Other questions elicited inter alia the names of books, magazines, and newspapers which were read in the child's home; the frequency with which he went to the cinema, the names of the principal towns he had visited, as well as lived in for more than a year at a time, etc. These questions were designed to give as complete a picture as possible of each child's linguistic background in his home and environment generally. In those days all films shown in the cinema were in English. From the teachers as well as from the pupil full information was obtained also regarding the general socioeconomic status of the home and the occupation of the father.

Because of the highly selective effect of these factors they had to be kept constant when comparing the scholastic achievement and progress of pupils under different medium conditions.

The influence of the pupils' general intelligence has also to be taken into account when comparing their language and other scholastic achievements. The number of cases was, however, large enough to make the correlations regarding the main variables statistically valid. At the time it was probably the most extensive investigation into bilingual education conducted anywhere in the world.

List of Questions Dealing with "Home Language"

1. Which language do you hear most at home?
2. (a)   Does your *father* speak to you in Afrikaans?
         Underline: (1) Always (2) Often (3) Sometimes (4) Never
   (b)   Does your *mother* speak to you in Afrikaans?
         Underline: (1) Always (2) Often (3) Sometimes (4) Never
   (c)   Do your *brothers and sisters* (if any) speak to you in Afrikaans?
         Underline: (1) Always (2) Often (3) Sometimes (4) Never
   (d)   Do you hear Afrikaans on the school playground?
         Underline: (1) Always (2) Often (3) Sometimes (4) Never
   (e)   Do you speak Afrikaans on the school playground?
         Underline: (1) Always (2) Often (3) Sometimes (4) Never
3. (a)   Does your *father* speak to you in English?
         Underline: (1) Always (2) Often (3) Sometimes (4) Never
   (b)   Does your *mother* speak to you in English?
         Underline: (1) Always (2) Often (3) Sometimes (4) Never
   (c)   Do your *brothers and sisters* (if any) speak to you in English?
         Underline: (1) Always (2) Often (3) Sometimes (4) Never
4. Which language do your parents consider the more important for you to know, English or Afrikaans?_____

5. Which language do your three best friends speak to you?
   (a) _____
   (b) _____
   (c) _____
6. What other languages do you speak besides English and Afrikaans?
7. Have you a wireless[6] set in your home?_____
   Which language do your parents prefer to hear in the wireless?_____
   You?_____
8. To which church do your parents belong: an English or a Dutch (Afrikaans)
   Church?_____
9. Do you go to Sunday School? _____ If so, do they speak English or
   Afrikaans to you there?_____

It was stressed that if "always" was underlined for English, "never" had to be underlined for Afrikaans, and so on; otherwise the evidence would be self-contradictory.

The following "weights" were given to the various items underlined in order to determine more specifically the child's *home* language:

		Always	Often	Sometimes	Never
(a)	Father	3	2	1	0
(b)	Mother	6	4	2	0
(c)	Brothers and sisters	3	2	1	0

To a certain extent these weightings were arbitrary. They were, however, arrived at after some experimentation with various values. The mother was given twice the weighting of the father because it was felt that in most cases the language of the mother was the strongest factor in the home determining the language of the children. After all, we speak of *mother* tongue.

The total weight, showing the language heard at home, whether English or Afrikaans, would in each case amount to 12 points. For example, a child who never hears Afrikaans at home would receive a total of $3 + 6 \times 3 = 12$ for English. If his father were to speak Afrikaans to him "sometimes," his score would be 11 English 1 Afrikaans. If his brothers and sisters also speak Afrikaans to him sometimes, his score will be 10 English and 2 Afrikaans.

The two scores had to be complementary; 6 and 6 would indicate a complete balance between the two languages heard at home.

In cases where the child's father or mother had died too early for the child to be influenced markedly by his or her home language, or if the child had no "brothers and sisters," the amounts of both languages heard in the home were reduced proportionately, so that the total again will be 12.

Where the children underlined (as they sometimes, but very rarely, did) words the values of which were *not* complementary, the replies obtained from the other questions dealing with the child's home environment, church affiliation, etc., were taken into account in adjusting the figures so that the child would be as nearly as possible in his correct language group.

In this way the linguistic structure of the pupil's home environment was measured on a scale of 12 units. When one, therefore, wanted to ascertain the relative strangeness of a language that was used as a medium of instruction and the effect it had on his learning, this provided a much more satisfactory measure than the all-or-none method usually adopted when assessing a pupil's school achievements in relation to the linguistic background of his home.

For convenience these units have been grouped into seven categories in the following table, e.g., (a) = 0 English 12 Afrikaans; (b) = 1 Eng. 11 Afr., 2 Eng. 10 Afr., and so on, as shown in the following table.

Linguistic Structure of Home Environment of Pupils Tested

			No. of pupils	%
(a)	Afrikaans unilingual	0 Eng. 12 Afr.	4736	25
(b)	Afrikaans unilingual with	1 Eng. 11 Afr.		
	slight English	2 Eng. 10 Afr.	2165	12
				37
(c)	Afrikaans bilingual	3 Eng. 9 Afr.	2333	12
		4 Eng. 8 Afr.		
(d)	Bilingual (50-50)	5 Eng. 7 Afr.	828	5
		6 Eng. 6 Afr.		
		7 Eng. 5 Afr.		
(e)	English bilingual	8 Eng. 4 Afr.	1165	6
		9 Eng. 3 Afr.		
				23
(f)	English unilingual with	10 Eng. 2 Afr.	1502	8
	slight Afrikaans	11 Eng. 1 Afr.		
(g)	English unilingual	12 Eng. 0 Afr.	6044	32
				40
	Total No. of pupils tested		18,733	100

From the above table it will be seen that only Afrikaans was spoken in 25% of the homes; only English was spoken in 32%, and *both languages were spoken in 43% of the homes in varying degrees of frequency.* These figures are graphically illustrated in the top part of Diagram E. It will be noted also that there were relatively twice as many Afrikaans homes in which a little English was heard as English homes in which a little Afrikaans was heard. If one groups these categories together in three main groups, one can say roughly that:

1. 37% of the pupils came from more or less *unilingual Afrikaans* homes.
2. 23% of the pupils came from more or less *bilingual* homes.

HOME LANGUAGE ENVIRONMENT OF PUPILS

MEDIUM OF INSTRUCTION

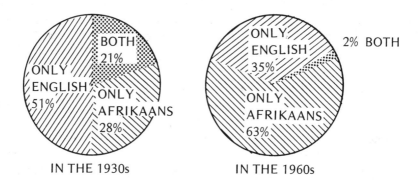

IN THE 1930s   IN THE 1960s

Diagram E   Comparison of home language of white pupils with their language medium of instruction. Note the decrease from 21 to 2% receiving instruction through bilingual medium (i.e., both English and Afrikaans) between the 1930s and the 1960s.

3. 40% of the pupils came from more or less *unilingual English* homes. These percentages will, of course, vary according to where one draws the lines demarcating the groups.

The percentage (23%) of bilingual homes ascertained by means of testing schoolchildren in the above-mentioned survey tallies very closely with the results of the 1970 Census, which included the whole population. In this census for the first time in history the question was put in a form so as to ascertain the number of homes in which both languages were spoken. A person had to say which was commonly spoken at home: (1) Afrikaans, (2) English, (3) both, (4) another language.

The above figures refer to *home* environment only. If one takes into account also the environment outside the home where in the country as a whole 80% speak both English and Afrikaans, one finds that there are many children who, while they hear nothing, or relatively little, of the other language spoken by the family members of their home, nevertheless have playmates who speak the other language or come into contact with the other language (outside the school) in other ways than in their homes. Actually, therefore, *the proportion of children with a bilingual background* (apart from school) *is larger than the above figures would indicate.*

When one studies the lower part of Diagram E, one sees that the percentage of pupils (21%) who were receiving their instruction through *both media* in the 1930s was much closer to the percentage of children who spoke both languages at home than became the case in the 1960s when the percentage receiving instruction was reduced to 2% as a result of the progressive segregation of the pupils into unilingual-medium schools according to the separation policy of the Nationalist government. If there had been any logic in the home-language-medium principle, according to which all children are today supposed to be taught, about 25% of the pupils should by rights be receiving their instruction through both English and Afrikaans, if not already at the primary level, then at least at the secondary level.

Moreover, it was not unreasonable to expect, where both languages are taught as subjects from the beginning of the primary school, that most pupils would at the time of entering the secondary school have acquired sufficient knowledge of the second language to be taught partially if not wholly through both media without suffering any serious damage to their educational progress.

This is, in fact, what the objective results of the survey proved. These results, it must be pointed out, are valid for white pupils in the peculiar South African situation, and would not necessarily obtain where the typology of patterns in school and environmental language situations is different. The many patterns which can arise from combinations of variables such as (1) the learner's home language(s), (2) the school curricula and methods of instruction, and (3) the language of the community and nation and their status, have been cataloged by William F. Mackey in *A Typology of Bilingual Education*, 1969.

He is quite right when he points out that "before any of the questions that arise can be answered with any degree of certainty, some means must be found of quantifying the variables within each type." This is what was attempted to a certain extent in the South African situation. In so doing we used "validated wide-mesh screens for quantitative analysis of large population samples," and the conclusions arrived at reflect the *average* position. One would need, as Mackey suggests, "fine-mesh screens for small laboratory-type studies and depth analysis of individual cases." South Africa offers unique scope for the latter kind of intensive study.

SUMMARY OF MAIN FINDINGS OF SURVEY[4]

The following were some of the main findings of the survey as regards language medium:

1. South African pupils gained considerably in their second language when that was also used as a medium and not merely taught as a subject.

2. Even where it was not used as a medium, there was a gain in the second language where English- and Afrikaans-speaking pupils attended the same school.

3. The proficiency of pupils in their first language was not adversely affected either by having the two languages represented in the same school or by using the second language as an ancillary medium.

4. As regards the effects on the mastery of "content" subjects taught through the medium of the second language, it was found that children did suffer an initial handicap when the second language was used exclusively as a medium at a very early stage, but that this handicap became progressively less and tended to disappear entirely with the increased knowledge of the second language as a compulsory subject and as children progressed to the higher standards of the primary school into the secondary standards.

5. This initial handicap, when it did occur, was directly proportionate to the initial relative strangeness of the medium used (as measured on a scale) and was practically nonexistent where the children's home and general environmental experience in the second language approximated that of the first.

6. Even with the duller pupils it was found, contrary to general belief, that their education was facilitated by using in the school both channels of communication available in the supporting environment.

7. Finally, there was no evidence of adverse effects of using two languages on the child's intelligence. In fact, there was a fairly high correlation between the children's intelligence and their bilinguality. This was probably due to social selection.

Obviously, exceptions did occur to each of the general conclusions listed above. These findings reflected the average position, however, and had a high degree of objective validity because of the large number of cases studied under every possible variety of conditions.

CHILDREN'S ATTITUDES TOWARD THE OTHER LANGUAGE GROUP

One of the important objects of the survey was to find out to what extent children's attitudes toward the other language group were influenced by being segregated into separate schools according to home language or, on the other hand, by being kept together in the same school in their communities, even though, because of medium regulations, they were taught in parallel classes.

The results are summarized graphically in Diagram F. The degree of social distance (antipathy) as expressed by the pupils is indicated on a percentage scale at the foot of the diagram. The vertical scale on the left indicates the school standards.

When children come to school, their initial feelings of social distance, prejudice, and even antipathy toward the other language group are usually a reflection of the attitudes of the home. By the time they got into standard IV, the degree of antipathy registered in the separate unilingual Afrikaans schools was 90% and in the unilingual English schools 84%. Where Afrikaans- and English-speaking children were kept together in the same (bilingual) school, the degree of antipathy was only 35%. This relatively lower percentage was obviously also a reflection of the attitudes they had brought from their respective homes, where the home attitude might, in certain cases, have been a factor in determining the type of school to which the child was originally sent as a result of parental choice.

In order to get as objective a measure as possible of the prevailing attitudes among schoolchildren, the questions pertaining to attitudes were casually interspersed among the scholastic tests and among the questionnaires of purely informational nature regarding their age, standard, occupation of father, etc. There was no separate ad hoc attitude test that might have affected the spontaneity of the replies. These questions were designed to elicit not only children's attitudes toward English and Afrikaans as school subjects but also the way they regarded these languages as media over the radio and their attitude toward various culturally oriented institutions.

After all the testing, which usually lasted a couple of days, had been completed, the pupils were each given a blank sheet of paper and asked to write down the reasons for their particular responses (already recorded) to certain questions pertaining to attitudes which had been interspersed among the other questions. This procedure was adopted because of the tendency of children to rationalize and to give a response for which they could supply the most plausible reason. Now, however, they had committed themselves and could not alter the choices already made. All the tests were marked "confidential," and it was stressed that neither their teachers nor anyone known to them would see their answers. They should therefore give their answers honestly and frankly. Quite apart from the responses themselves, the reasons afforded offer the best insight into the pupil's attitudes, often quite naïvely expressed.

An analysis of the results led to the following conclusions:

1. Adverse sectional discrimination was from three to four times as great in unilingual as in bilingual schools.

2. Of the unilingual schools it was greater in the Afrikaans-medium than in the English-medium schools. This was probably due to the fact that a considerable proportion of the Afrikaans unilingual schools were the ones that had been hived off because of extreme nationalist political pressure. By the same token some of

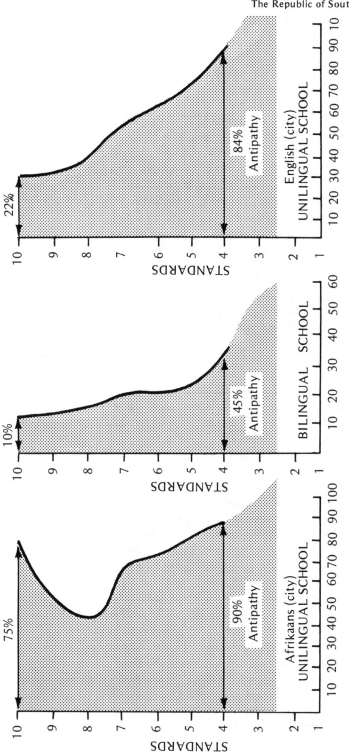

Diagram F   Illustrates the varying degrees (as measured on a scale of 100) of antipathy felt by pupils toward the other language group according as they go to unilingual or to bilingual schools. Note how the percentage of pupils with strong antipathies tend to decrease as they move up from lower to higher school standards.

the unilingual English schools were the "residual" ones, as it were.

3. Of the bilingual schools, it was slightly greater in those where English was predominant than in those where Afrikaans was predominant.

4. The children with bilingual home environments displayed the least adverse discrimination.

As will be seen from the diagram, in all three types of schools feelings of antipathy tended to diminish progressively as the pupils progressed to the higher standards. For example, in the English-medium schools, antipathy tapered off from 84 to 22%. In the bilingual schools it diminished from 45 to 10%. However, in the unilingual Afrikaans-medium schools antipathy tapered off from 90 to about 40% by the time the pupils got to standard VIII. From then onward, however, there was a recrudescence of antipathy against the English-speaking section culminating at 75% in standard X.

The relatively high degree of sectional discrimination as shown on the one hand by pupils of the unilingual Afrikaans-medium schools in the big cities in comparison with those in town schools, and in the city English-medium schools, on the other hand, might be attributed partly to the fact that the Afrikaans-speaking group, being generally in the minority in the cities, would tend to be on the defensive and to display inferiority reactions toward the English-speaking majority.

The English-speaking group in the large city is generally not so solicitous (at least not to the same extent as the Afrikaans minority) over their language or cultural distinctiveness. They tacitly assume that they are superior in other ways as well as numerically. Considering themselves in an unassailable position, culturally, they could afford to be tolerant, if not patronizing, to the Afrikaans minority group.

This attitude was revealed in the unconsciously naïve responses to the children who, as a rule, reflect fairly faithfully the social attitudes found in the home, or deliberately engendered in the school.

For example, in giving their reasons for preferring to have Afrikaans-speaking children in the same school together with English-speaking children rather than in separate schools, children of the Natal English-speaking majority group tended to be patronizing on general humanitarian grounds toward Afrikaans children: "Afrikaans children are also human beings." "They are also White people." "They might feel hurt if they were sent to different schools." And so these responses display discrimination by unconscious innuendo in varying degrees which can be graded on a scale in descending order until we come to ones that are simply and rationally tolerant like: "They are as nice as we are." "There is no difference between us except languages, and that does not matter, as we are all South Africans." "We have a lot to learn from each other."

The rather unnatural recrudescence of antipathy against the English-speaking section among the senior classes (standards VIII to X) of the large-city Afrikaans-medium schools might be accounted for by the fact that pupils at that stage were more susceptible to the anti-English propaganda at home and through the public press which was so strong at that particular time. Some of the replies made one suspect that it was due partly to the way South African history was taught at that stage.

Advocates of the unilingual-medium school advanced the theory in the most categorical terms that if one mixed the two sections in one school, one aggravated the antipathies which these children brought from their homes, and that it was consequently far better to isolate them in separate schools where each section would become conscious of its own identity, and would in consequence respect and appreciate the other section better. Theories like this were based on striking but isolated instances. What was far more common was the display of almost venomous hostility when two unilingual-medium schools (English and Afrikaans) met each other on the playing fields. Interschool rivalries are sometimes very strong and even healthy, but when they are exacerbated by cultural and political antipathies they can become very bitter and unpleasant and on (fortunately) rare occasions lead to violence.

In schools, however, where the Afrikaans- and English-speaking children were mixed together in fair proportions, a feeling of esprit de corps, of loyalty to the school, developed as a result of daily hearing each others' language spoken, playing in the same teams in sport, and associating in other extracurricular activities like school concerts and plays.

SCHOOL MEDIUM A POLITICAL ISSUE DURING WORLD WAR II

South Africa's participation in World War II on the side of the Allies was strongly opposed by the Nationalist Party. To the Afrikaner nationalist it meant consorting with the British, the erstwhile enemy and oppressor. Nazi propaganda cashed in on this and supported the Nationalist Party in their efforts to separate English and Afrikaans children in the schools.

While this was going on at the home front, the two language groups were fighting together in the closest comradeship and unity as South Africans on the battlefronts against the enemy in North Africa and in Italy. When they learned of this move on the part of the Nationalist Party to separate their children in the schools at home, they reacted very strongly against this artificial separation. How strongly the men felt about this issue can be gaged from their replies to a survey questionnaire to ascertain the soldiers' opinions about political, economic, and social questions with a view to their readjustment to civil life after the war. This survey, which was representative of both language groups, covered the whole of the South African Defence Force.

On the questions pertaining to bilingual education, they had to choose between the following statements, and their votes were as follows:

1. We shall have more national unity if English and Afrikaans children go to the same schools 93%
2. It is better for English and Afrikaans children to go to separate schools 6%
3. Don't know or no answer 1%
                                                                         ⎯⎯⎯⎯
                                                                         100%

As regards language medium in schools the votes were as follows:

1. Children should be taught only through the medium of their
   home language. The other language should be taught merely as
   a subject...   13%
2. Children should be taught mainly through the medium of their
   home language, but it is a good thing for them to learn some
   subjects through the medium of the other language...........   81%
3. Don't know or no answer..............................   6%
                                                                      ─────
                                                                      100%

Most of these soldiers had grown up in communities where English- and Afrikaans-speaking children went to the same school, and many of them had received their instruction through both English and Afrikaans at the secondary level. They were therefore averse to the idea that their own children should be segregated at home.

Even though the home-language-medium principle at the primary level was common cause between the two political parties, the Nationalist Party manifestoes gave the impression that the United Party was in favor of abolishing the home-language-medium principle entirely. However, despite these misrepresentations, the United Party under the leadership of General Smuts won the 1943 election with an overwhelming majority.

BILINGUAL EDUCATION TAKEN TO UNION PARLIAMENT

The outcome of the 1943 elections fought on the bilingual school issue was a great blow to the Nationalist Party and spurred it on to renewed efforts to continue the fight for the single-medium "mother-tongue school" by propaganda through their press and by holding protest meetings all over the country.

C. R. Swart M. P., one of the leading members of the party and destined later, after the Nationalist Party had come into power, to become the Republic's first State President, carried the fight even into the Union Parliament. This was rather unusual because school education was primarily a provincial function.

On Feb. 22, 1944, he introduced a motion before Parliament as follows:

> That this house declares itself unequivocally in favour of the educationally sound principle of the mother-language medium in Primary, Secondary and Higher Education, and emphasizes the fact that the single medium school in which a sound training in the official languages is also given is the most suitable for South African conditions.

In reply to Mr. Swart's motion, General Smuts brought in an amendment which, he said, far more truly expressed the wishes of the majority of the people as reflected in the recent parliamentary elections. Moreover, he said, it was in keeping with the tradition of good schools in South Africa in the past.

General Smuts' amendment[7] was as follows:

This house, taking account of the fact that the South Africa Act enshrines, as its fundamental principle, the conception of a united country and South African people, and to that end provided for a legislative union of South Africa, and for equal rights for both official languages, considers it necessary that everything possible should be done to foster national unity and to provide equal opportunities for all citizens to learn both official languages.

It, therefore, with a view to serving these objects, expresses the advisability that the government in consultation with the provincial authorities considers the amendment where necessary of the educational laws and regulations, and the revision of the educational machinery of the provinces so as to give effect within a period of five years to the following principles:

1. That the child should be instructed through his home language in the early stages of its educational career;
2. That the second language should be introduced gradually as a supplementary medium of instruction from the stage at which it is on educational grounds appropriate to do so; and
3. That such changes should be introduced in the system of the training of teachers as are necessary to make the ideals of bilingualism and of national unity in the schools fully effective.

In support of this amendment, General Smuts said, inter alia:

The mother-tongue must be the basis of all instruction. At the same time people must pass over at a certain stage to the other official language as a supplementary medium. This is what is meant by *dual-medium.*

While this "dual-medium principle" was equally as applicable to unilingual English medium schools as to unilingual Afrikaans medium schools, this part of his proposal was described by the Nationalists as merely a subtle means by which General Smuts wished to anglicize and denationalize the Afrikaners.

In the end General Smuts' amendment was carried by a large majority. Nevertheless, the debate showed how much the language-medium question was emotionally tied up with nationalism.

Little did General Smuts realize at the time that four years later the Nationalist Party would come into power on another issue (mainly the issue of the "black menace") and would put an end to his ideas of developing bilingual education.

Shortage of Bilingual Teachers

He was, however, fully aware of the fact that the main difficulty with the universal application of the dual-medium principle was the shortage of bilingual teachers at the secondary level. This applied also to unilingual English schools and especially to a number of private schools, which catered to about 3% of the total school population. Objections on this score came also from this quarter. This is why he made the training of bilingual teachers such an essential part of his proposals, and why he gave the provincial education departments five years to implement the proposal.

At that time over 70% of the teachers were from Afrikaans-speaking homes and a large majority of them had come up through unilingual Afrikaans-medium high schools and straight into unilingual-medium teacher training colleges. In consequence, the degree of bilingualism among both English- and Afrikaans-speaking teachers had deteriorated and it had, in fact, become difficult for them to use the second language effectively as a teaching medium at the high school level. This deterioration was the direct result of the gradual elimination of the bilingual schools brought about by the policy in three out of the four provinces (Cape, Transvaal, and Orange Free State) where the provincial education departments were Nationalist-oriented.

VARIOUS FORMS OF DUAL MEDIUM

In the South African practice, dual medium took on a variety of forms depending on the circumstances of the school:

1. Using English and Afrikaans alternately in the same lesson. This usually involved a certain amount of repetition. For this to be effective, the teacher had to be proficient in both languages. Other things being equal, the highest degree of bilingualism was usually attained under this system. It was found also that children's comprehension of subject matter was also enhanced under this system because it forced them to pay more attention when there was repetition through the second language than if repetition was made in the same language, as usually happens in all class teaching. There was also an enrichment of concept because of the different nuances of meaning coming out through the different media.

2. Teaching all subjects on alternate days in English and Afrikaans with short summaries in the language used the previous day. This procedure was known as the *alternating method.*

3. Teaching some subjects through English and others through Afrikaans medium. This was known as the *subject method.*

THE CAPE EXPERIMENT

The four provinces accordingly proceeded to implement the 1944 Resolution of Parliament as formulated by General Smuts. The Cape Provincial Education Department, however, approached these proposals empirically and proceeded to set up a series of experiments involving both the *alternating* and the *subject* methods.

About 6000 pupils were involved in experimental groups. Their attainments were eventually to be compared with about 4600 pupils in a selected control group. In some schools the experiment began in 1945 and in others in 1946. The experiment involved mainly pupils from standard IV to standard VI. The most significant results were obtained by means of the alternating method. There was a significant gain in the knowledge of the second language under this method, particularly among the English-speaking pupils. There was no serious retardation in the content subjects after the children had been exposed to this alternating method for more than two years. The use of the subject method, however, showed less positive gain in the knowledge of the second language than did the alternating method. This was partly due to the fact that in a number of schools nonexamination subjects like woodwork or physical exercises were taught through the second language. As regards the effect on the content subjects, there seemed to be no advantage or disadvantage either way on the whole. The biggest gains were obtained in the knowledge of the second language in environments that were unilingual. At the same time it was in unilingual environments that some adverse effects on the content subjects were recorded. In a number of schools the results of the experiment were not very conclusive. This was due in the first place to its short duration. In the second place those teachers who had wanted to make the dual system work succeeded very effectively. Those who were antagonistic or indifferent showed rather indifferent results. What is more, the experiment had barely got under way when in 1948 the Nationalist Party came into power and the whole experiment was called off at the beginning of 1949.

An official report on the uncompleted experiment was published in 1952. It concluded that children benefited by the use of the second language as a medium according to the degree that the teachers were: (1) dedicated to the project, (2) bored and indifferent, or (3) definitely hostile to the whole idea.

THE EVIDENCE OF HISTORY

In South African educational history there is ample evidence to show that the use of the second language as a medium of instruction does not have all the devastating effects which the propagandists against dual medium have claimed.

If one studies the cultural and linguistic background of those who have contributed most to the building up of the Afrikaans literature and language, one finds that the vast majority of them, and not only the earlier writers, have had their education almost exclusively through their second language, English. This was due partly to personal choice and to the educational policies prevailing at the time when they had their early education. One of South Africa's leading professors of Afrikaans observed recently:

> Strange as it may seem, practically all of the leading younger Afrikaans writers were trained at English medium universities. They have achieved a record in contributing to Afrikaans literature which surpasses that of the Afrikaans universities. There cannot be any doubt that South African cultural life in general and particularly Afrikaans literature have been stimulated and enriched by our dual cultural heritage.

The evidence is even more overwhelming where Afrikaners have shone in the fields of science, engineering, law, and medicine with an education which was received almost exclusively through their second language, English.

Professor Cecil Hourani, one of the leading educators in the Middle East, made the same point in regard to his country when he expressed himself as follows:

> To be a modern Arab man he must pass through the medium of other cultures. In order to be himself he must temporarily lose himself. The University of Damascus had become a failure because it did not allow for the refertilization of the Arab mind which comes only through contact from outside. That is with the French culture which has been very prevalent in the Middle East. Such a refertilized mind becomes more and more creative in its own language and culture.[8]

DEPRECIATION IN THE QUALITY OF BILINGUALISM

There is no doubt that in the Civil Service and in all semigovernmental organizations the predominating language used in correspondence and in other interdepartmental communications has become Afrikaans. In a number of departments the frequency has reached nearly 100%. This is largely due to the fact that the vast majority of civil servants, though they understand English and could even speak and write it in a fashion, have come to use it with difficulty and, therefore, reluctantly. This is because they did not learn to *use* it at school and subsequently in government service.

To sum up, it may be stated that, though there has been an increase in the *number* of bilinguals as a result of the prevailing system of bilingual education in which the study of both official languages is compulsory at school, a depreciation has come about in the *quality* of bilingualism measured in terms of the fluency and accent where English is the second language. For reasons already indicated, the opposite has taken place where Afrikaans is the second language.

RECENT BOOSTING OF AFRIKAANS

Bilingualism is Not Equilingualism

The requirement of bilingualism does not mean necessarily the attainment of equilingualism. There will always be a difference whether in kind or degree, between a person's mother tongue and his other tongue.

In a country like South Africa *the functional standards of bilingualism vary according to the job for which bilingualism is required.* One must always ask: bilingual for what? It is a matter of degree and as well as of kind. For example, the bilingualism that would suffice for a taxi driver, train conductor, or even an hotel receptionist will not meet the bilingual requirements of the teacher.

In his book, *The Bilingual School,* the writer has outlined six stages of bilingualism which must be attained respectively to meet some of the practical requirements of certain occupations in South Africa.

DUAL MEDIUM IN THE ARMED FORCES

Not long after the Nationalist Party had come into power in 1948, the fetish of separate English- and Afrikaans-medium training was pursued even in the armed forces. The active citizen force regiments were separated on the basis of home language. The Air Force was divided into English- and Afrikaans-medium squadrons. This dichotomy was based on a principle totally irrelevant to the situation when it came to defending the fatherland. It went also contrary to the practice which had obtained in the South African army during two world wars when such a wonderful spirit of unity and esprit de corps was developed between English- and Afrikaans-speaking fighters in the same units. They fought together as South Africans.

In the permanent force, however, the principle of dual medium has been followed by the alternate use of English and Afrikaans as media of correspondence as well as of training.

In 1972, new regulations extended the application of the dual-medium principle, alternating the instruction and correspondence monthly. Exceptions are made in the case of correspondence with foreign services. At present, however, for all ranks of the permanent force and the citizen force, the official languages are to be used on the basis of equal status and alternated daily during training. This principle, as far as possible, is to be maintained in every subject. Each lecture is to be given in full in one language and a summary thereof in the other language. Questions put by a student are to be answered in the language used by the student. All written examinations are to be set in both official languages. A candidate may reply to questions in the language of his choice.

At university level the only instances of dual-medium instruction were prevalent in the faculties of agriculture and particularly in the Pretoria faculty of veterinary science, operating the world-famous Veterinary Science Laboratory at Onderstepoort. Here the dual-medium method varied from time to time and from subject to subject. Sometimes English and Afrikaans were used on alternate days. Sometimes they were used alternately in the same lecture. Qualified veterinary surgeons had to be acquainted with the common terminology in both languages so as to function effectively when dealing with either English- or Afrikaans-speaking farmers.

THE TREND TOWARD UNILINGUAL MEDIUM TEACHING

In 1948, the Nationalist Party came into power and all dual medium was abolished up to standard VIII. Thereafter a change of medium was well-nigh impossible for a pupil.

When the education department had once decided what a pupil's home language was, it had virtually also committed him to a particular secondary school, which taught only through that one medium. Thus it often happened that a child from a bilingual home was sent miles away to (say) an Afrikaans-medium high school, when there was virtually next door an English-medium school which he could just as well have attended, if his parents had had the choice.

The following table as well as Diagram E on page 185 illustrates the trend toward almost complete unilingual-medium teaching at the secondary level during the last three decades.

Percentage of Pupils Receiving Instruction through Different Media at Secondary Level

Medium of instruction	Percentage	
	1932	1958
Only English	51.2	34.8
Only Afrikaans	28.2	62.4
English and Afrikaans	20.6	2.8
	100.0	100.0

Whereas in the past English had been the predominant medium in high school, Afrikaans has now become the predominating medium. The progressive segregation of English and Afrikaans pupils living in the same communities into separate schools greatly decreased for most pupils the opportunities of hearing the second language spoken in the schools outside the classroom.

The fact that the use of the second official language had been relegated to that one period a day in the classroom caused the pupils to regard it as a foreign-language subject like Latin, German, or French. This fact was repeatedly remarked upon in the annual reports of the Directors of the Provincial Education Departments, particularly in the Transvaal.

SALVAGING MEASURES

In order to salvage the situation, the Transvaal Education Department sent a number of its members overseas to study the latest methods in language teaching in order to improve the teaching of the second language in the schools. Apparently they did not realize the simple fact that language is not something which functions in a vacuum, as it were, that it is essentially an instrument—as a means of communication, and that this instrument improves with use at the spoken or the reading or the written level. Moreover, a pupil's interest in it will depend largely on whether such communication is meaningful to the pupil and on whether the pupil feels involved. There must be living content that goes beyond the sterilities of grammar and syntax which so often characterize the language lesson *qua* language.

Realizing apparently that segregation into separate schools diminished the opportunities of using the second language in a normal way, the Education Department exhorted teachers "to increase association between English and Afrikaans medium schools by arranging reciprocal visits and joint production of plays, folk dances, gymnastic displays as well as sports activities in schools."

The use of the second language in the school context was therefore by official decree restricted to extracurricular topics like sport. Any communication between teacher and pupil through the second language on subjects such as history or nature study was forbidden by law. No wonder that under such circumstances the oral use of the second language tended to become lacking in precision as well as importance on account of its being associated only with topics which had no academic status in the school itself.

Realizing probably what the social handicaps due to this very artificial segregation might be, the Education Department issued the following rather fatuous official injunction that teachers should see to "the efficient raising of the standard of bilingualism in the schools by encouraging the right attitude towards the other language and emphasize its practical value in the social relationship between Afrikaans and English members of the community and by affording ample opportunity for the active use of the other language."

Apparently these exhortations did not avail much. In order, therefore, to encourage pupils to become bilingual under such circumstances, the Executive Committee of the Transvaal awarded monetary grants as bribes. They were called bilingual merit grants. These went to pupils who attained a certain percentage of marks in each of the official languages. Attached to this award was also the condition that such pupils had to undertake that they would on completion of high school go to a training college in order to become teachers. In addition, monetary grants of 30 pounds each were given to teachers who satisfied the Director as to exceptional proficiency in the use of both official languages as media of instruction.

These salvaging measures did not prove very fruitful. It was the English language in particular that deteriorated. There were complaints from commerce and industry that the young people coming from the schools to seek employment were getting weaker in their ability to write correct English.

In 1953, the Public Service Commission commented on the grave decline in the standards of English as revealed by the Public Service Entrance Examinations.

In 1956, the Education Research Bureau of the Transvaal Education Department compared the results of standardized tests in English and Afrikaans obtained in that year with those obtained in 1938 and also in 1948. They found that while the standard of Afrikaans had shown an advance over what it was, in either 1938 or 1948, the standard of English had deteriorated in these years.

FURTHER EVIDENCE CONCERNING DETERIORATION OF SECOND LANGUAGE

Largely because of the general concern over the teaching of the official languages, the National Bureau for Educational and Social Research undertook a survey[9] of the position in 1965. The findings were based on the answers to questionnaires submitted to school principals and teachers of the two official languages in the secondary schools of the Republic.

The survey showed that a disturbingly high percentage of pupils did in fact regard the second official language as a foreign language. The main motivation for learning the second language was to meet an examination requirement rather than to provide an essential means of communication between citizens of the Republic. The report stated that: "Language instruction in the secondary school standards contributes very little to making the second language a living language. English when taught as a second language to Afrikaans pupils in the high school was considered by them to be a foreign language nearly twice as frequently as Afrikaans was considered by English-speaking pupils to be a foreign language."[10]

The large majority of teachers in the survey when asked to indicate the factors which contributed to the poor knowledge and faulty usage of English in the Afrikaans secondary schools attributed it to the "little opportunities of hearing and using English outside the English lesson period."

Nearly half of the respondents reported that: "English is mainly considered as a subject for examination purposes with few or no other advantages."[11] A great deal depended on the attitude of the teacher.[11]

The root cause, however, according to the report, is to be found in the limited educational and linguistic backgrounds of the teachers of English as a second language *at the primary as well as at the secondary level.* This background is even poorer in the former case than in the latter, particularly in the rural areas where the only English that the Afrikaans pupil will hear is from the mouth of the teacher.

If one of the functions of the school is to enrich the experience of the child by making good the deficiencies of the pupils' environment, the question arises how much compensatory effect the teacher can have on the limited linguistic environment of his pupils as regards the second official language, when the teacher himself is deficient in the fluent use of that language to which pupils are exposed only during that one lesson per day when that teacher is the sole source of that linguistic experience of the pupils.

THE LANGUAGE BACKGROUND OF TEACHERS

Seventy-five percent of the teachers in the Republic have Afrikaans as their home language. In the rural areas the percentage is 92%, in town schools 86%, and in the big metropolitan cities 61%. Most of them teach English in Afrikaans-medium schools and many of them teach English even to English-speaking pupils because of the shortage of English-speaking teachers.

An analysis of the home language of all language teachers at the secondary level showed that only 15% of the teachers who taught English to Afrikaans pupils had English as their home language. By contrast, 70% of the teachers who teach Afrikaans to English pupils had Afrikaans as their home language. While nearly all teachers at the secondary level have had some professional training, the academic background of those who teach English as a second language is much poorer than that of those who teach Afrikaans as a second language. The survey found that in the high schools only 45% of those who teach English as a second language at the secondary level have had at least two years' study of English at the university, while of those who teach Afrikaans 56% have had at least two years of Afrikaans at the university as an academic qualification. In this respect the children of the Republic in English-medium schools are much more fortunate in learning Afrikaans.

The home language of teachers of the two official languages would not have been of such crucial significance were it not for the fact that, by virtue of the compulsory home-language-medium regulations, the bulk of these teachers have themselves become isolated during their education in separate English- and Afrikaans-medium schools and training institutions where the normal oral contact with the second language is reduced to a minimum. It is here that the teaching of English in particular suffered in consequence.

Although about 39% of the white population of the Republic have English as their home language, only 22% of the full-time student teachers in training in the Republic have English as their home language. It seems, therefore, inevitable that, under the present system, the teaching of English will become increasingly the task of Afrikaans-speaking teachers whose competence in English is diminishing with every generation.

A VICIOUS CIRCLE

Not only is the disproportion of Afrikaans- versus English-speaking teachers in the profession far greater today than it was a generation ago, but as a result of the rigid application of the home-language-medium principle in segregating the children, those Afrikaans-speaking teachers who have to teach English have themselves now become the products of teachers who were poor exponents of the language. Thus has evolved a *vicious circle* of progressive deterioration as regards the second language, especially in English. As a result of artificially separating the country's children on the home-language-medium principle, we are also inbreeding the very type of teacher and school principal against whose one-sidedness, usually in English schools, the establishment of separate unilingual schools was a reaction and a supposed remedy. We are accordingly developing in our educational system what are practically two closed circuits of human association. This has had important political and social consequences, as recent political history has shown. This division has led to a position which is becoming more and more anomalous and irrelevant when viewed in the light of the Republic's future economic and political development.

NOTES

1. Mackey, William F. 1969. *A Typology of Bilingual Education.* Quebec.

2. West, Michael. *Bilingualism.* p. 70.

3. There is a full discussion on this aspect in the report edited by L. G. Kelly of the International Seminar held in 1967 on *The Description and Measurement of Bilingualism.* pp. 12-66.

4. This comprehensive survey was conducted in 1938. Owing to World War II, in which nearly the whole of the staff of the National Bureau for Educational and Social Research had become involved, the results were not published until 1943. A summary of the main findings was published in South Africa in a booklet, *The Bilingual School,* by the Bilingual School Association and later (1946) by Longmans in Great Britain.

5. Besides standardized vocabulary, composition, and reading tests, standardized arithmetic, geography, and generalized knowledge tests were applied to every pupil.

6. In those days there was no television in South Africa. There were English and Afrikaans stations on the radio, however.

7. *Assembly Debates of 1944.* Cols. 1739, 1740.

8. Address at University Congress, Tunis, 1959.

9. National Bureau for Educational and Social Research (Department of Higher Education), 1969 *Research Series* Nos. 40, 41, 42, and 43.

10. National Bureau for Educational and Social Research, *op. cit., Research Series* No. 41, p. 39; No. 43, p. 55.

11. National Bureau for Educational and Social Research, *op. cit., Research Series* No. 43, p. 445.

Bilingual Education and Social Change

in The Soviet Union

E. Glyn Lewis

THE BACKGROUND OF BILINGUAL EDUCATION IN THE USSR

Linguistic

The Soviet Union is preeminently a multinational-multilingual state where nearly 150 languages are spoken by ethnic groups of varying sizes and at varying stages of social and economic development. Some are still little more than tribal units while others are fully fledged and powerful nations. The languages, too, vary according to how far they have developed: some like the Pamiri are no more than a congeries of related dialects; others are standardized but vary to the extent of their standardization, since they may be fully modernized, like Russian or Georgian, or young standardized languages like Karakalpak, or they may be written languages at an early stage of standardization. Others have not been alphabeticized or, having been provided with a script, are no longer used for writing. Some of the standardized languages are associated with rich classical literatures while others are still tied to the folk literature derived from a threatened oral tradition.

The 1970 Census took account of only 90 languages, and of these only 14 had populations of under 10,000. The languages belong to several quite distinct families—Indo-European, Altaic, Uralian, Caucasian, and Paleoasiatic. Indo-European is represented by such East Slavic languages as Russian, Ukrainian, and Bellorussian, as well as by groups of Iranian languages such as Tadzhik, and by representatives of other subgroups such as Armenian or Moldavian (Romance).

Table 1.   Demographic Data Concerning Linguistic Groups, Their Degree of Language Maintenance and of Types of Bilingualism

Nationality	Nos. in thousands	% claiming national language	% claiming second language other than Russian	% claiming Russian as second language
Russian	129,015	99.8	3.0	0.1
Ukrainian	40,753	85.7	6.0	36.3
Uzbek	9,195	98.6	3.3	14.5
Bellorussian	9,052	80.6	7.3	49.0
Tatar	5,931	89.2	5.8	62.5
Kazakh	5,299	98.0	1.8	41.8
Azerbaydzhan	4,380	98.2	2.5	16.6
Armenian	3,559	91.4	6.0	30.1
Georgian	3,245	93.4	1	21.3
Moldavian	2,698	95.0	3.6	36.1
Lithuanian	2,665	97.9	1.9	35.9
Jew	2,151	17.7	28.8	16.3
Tadzhik	2,136	98.5	12.0	15.4
German	1,846	66.8	1.1	59.6
Chuvash	1,694	88.9	5.5	58.4
Turkmen	1,525	98.8	1.3	15.4
Kirgiz	1,452	98.8	2.3	19.1
Latvian	1,430	95.2	2.4	45.2
Daghestani	1,365	96.5	8.9	41.7
Avar	396	97.2	5.7	37.8
Lezgin	324	93.9	22.3	31.6
Dargin	231	98.4	2.8	43.0
Kumyk	189	98.4	1.2	57.4
Lak	86	95.6	3.5	56.0
Tabasarns	55	98.9	10.2	31.9
Nogai	52	89.8	1.1	68.5
Rutyl	12	98.9	18.8	30.7
Tsukhurs	11	96.5	43.5	12.2
Aguls	8.8	99.4	9.6	39.8
Kareli	146	93.0	15.1	59.1
Tuvin	139	98.7	0.4	38.9
Kalmyk	137	91.7	1.5	81.1
Rumanian	119	63.9	16.3	28.5
Karachai	113	98.1	1.2	67.6
Adygeis	100	96.5	1.4	67.9
Kurds	89	87.6	36.2	19.9
Finns	85	51.0	8.5	47.0
Mordvin	1,263	77.8	8.1	65.7
Bashkir	1,240	66.2	2.6	53.3
Poles	1,167	22.5	12.7	37.0
Estonians	1,007	95.5	2.0	29.0
Udmurts	704	82.6	6.9	63.3
Chechens	613	98.7	1.0	66.7
Mari	599	91.2	6.2	62.4

Table 1 (continued)

Nationality	Nos. in thousands	% claiming national language	% claiming second language other than Russian	% claiming Russian as second language
Ossetians	488	88.6	10.7	58.6
Komi	322	82.7	5.4	63.1
Permyak	153	85.8	4.6	68.5
Korean	357	68.6	1.7	50.3
Bulgarians	351	73.1	7.9	58.8
Greek	337	39.3	14.5	35.4
Buryat	315	92.6	2.7	66.7
Yakut	296	96.3	1.1	41.7
Kabardinians	280	98	0.8	71.4
Karakalpak	236	96.6	3.6	10.4
Gipsies	175	70.8	16.4	53.0
Uigurs	173	88.5	9.5	35.6
Abkhaz	93	95.9	2.8	59.2
Turki	79	92.3	31.2	22.4
Khakass	67	83.7	3.4	66.5
Balkar	60	97.2	2.5	71.5
Altai	56	87.2	3.2	54.9
Cherkess	40	92	2.5	70.0
Dungan	39	94.3	5.7	48.0
Iranian	28	36.9	12.7	33.9
Hungarians	166	96.6	9.8	25.8
Ingush	158	97.4	0.9	71.3
Gaguz	157	93.6	8.6	63.3
Peoples of the north including	151	67.4	7.1	52.5
Nenets	29	83.4	3.3	55.1
Evenki	25	51.3	7.5	54.9
Khanti	21	68.9	7.3	48.1
Chukchi	14	82.6	4.8	58.7
Even	12	56.0	17.6	48.4
Nanais	10	69.1	9.4	58.0
Mansi	7.7	52.5	5.4	38.6
Koryak	7.5	81.1	5.5	64.3
Dolgan	4.9	89.8	3.2	61.4
Nivkh	4.4	49.5	5.6	43.8
Selkup	4.3	51.1	8.6	40.8
Ulchi	2.4	60.8	7.0	56.8
Saami	1.9	56.2	9.3	52.9
Udegeis	1.5	55.1	10.1	46.0
Itelmen	1.3	35.7	4.3	32.5
Keti	1.2	74.9	2.0	59.1
Orochi	1.1	48.6	6.6	44.4
Nganasans	1.0	75.4	15.7	40.0
Yukagirs	0.6	46.8	32.8	29.1
Abazin	25	96.1	6.1	69.5
Aisors	24	64.5	14.7	46.2
Czechs	21	42.9	21.4	35.6

Table 1 (continued)

Nationality	Nos. in thousands	% claiming national language	% claiming second language other than Russian	% claiming Russian second language
Tats	17	72.6	15.3	57.7
Shortsi	16	73.5	5.9	59.8
Slovak	12	52	31.3	39.3
Others	126	69.4	12.8	38.4
USSR	241,720	93.9		

The Altaic family has three branches—Turkic, which includes Uzbek, Azerbaydzhan, and Turkmen, etc.; Mongolian, which includes Mongolian itself, Buryat and Kalmyk, etc.; and Manchurian, which includes the languages of the small groups such as Orochi, Eveni, and Ulchi. The third major family, the Uralian, like Altaic has three branches—Finnic, which is represented by Karelian and the almost extinct Vespian and Vodian; Mari (in a separate Finnic group); and Permyak and Komi (in a third Finnic group). The second and third main subgroups of Uralian are Ugrian (represented by Hungarian, Khnati, and Mansi) and Samoyed (represented by Nenets, Nganasan, and Enets). Caucasian languages constitute a fourth major family, and this consists of three subgroups—the North East (Chechen-Ingush), the North West (Abkhaz-Adygei), and the South (Kartvelian or Iverian). This last subgroup includes Kartli, Iverian, and Zan. The fifth major group is usually regarded as a conglomerate rather than a family of languages and

Table 2. Ethnic Composition of Union Republics and Percentage Contribution of Each Nationality in 1970*

Union Republic	Nationalities and percentage contribution
Russian SSR	Russians (82.8), Ukrainians (2.6), Belorussians (0.7), Tatars (3.7), Kazakhs (0.4), Azerbaydzhan (0.1), Georgians (0.1), Moldavians (0.1), Jews (0.6), Chuvash (1.3), Peoples of Daghestan (0.9), Mordvin (0.9), Bashkir (0.9), Udmurt (0.5), Chechen (0.4), Mari (0.4), Ossetes (0.4), Komi-Permyak (0.4), Buryat (0.2), Yakut (0.2), Kabardinian (0.2), Karakalpak (0.2), Armenians (0.2), Peoples of the North (0.1), Karelians (0.1), Turvin (0.1), Ingush (0.1), Kalmyk (0.1), Karachai (0.1), Adygeis (0.1), Khakass (0.05), Altai (0.04), Balkar (0.04), Cherkess (0.03), 20 other nationalities (1.3)
Ukraine SSR	Ukrainians (74.9), Russians (19.4), Belorussians (0.8), Moldavians (0.6), Jews (1.6), Poles (0.6), Bulgars (0.5), 10 other nationalities (1.6)
Belorussian SSR	Belorussians (81.0), Russians (10.8), Poles (4.3), Ukrainians (2.1), Jews (1.6), 8 other nationalities (0.6)

Table 2 (continued)

Union Republic	Nationalities and percentage contribution
Uzbek SSR	Uzbeks (64.7), Karakalpak (1.9), Russians (12.5), Tatars (4.8), Kazakhs (4.6), Tadzhiks (3.8), Koreans (1.3), Ukrainians (1.0), Kirgiz (0.9), Jews (0.9), Turkmen (0.6), 18 other nationalities (3.0)
Kazakh SSR	Kazakhs (32.4), Russians (42.8), Ukrainians (7.2), Tatar (2.2), Uzbek (1.6), Belorussians (1.5), Uigur (0.9), Korean (0.6), Dungan (0.1), 20 other nationalities (10.7)
Georgian SSR	Georgians (66.8), Ossetes (3.2), Abkhaz (1.7), Armenians (9.7), Russians (8.5), Azerbaydzhanis (4.6), Greeks (1.9), Jews (1.2), Ukrainians (1.1), Kurds (0.4), 19 other nationalities (0.9)
Azerbaydzhan SSR	Azerbaydzhanis (73.8), Russians (10.0), Armenians (9.4), Lezgin (2.7), 12 other nationalities (4.1)
Lithuanian SSR	Lithuanians (90.1), Russians (8.6), Poles (7.7), Belorussians (1.5), Ukrainians (0.8), Jews (0.8), 6 other nationalities (0.5)
Moldavian SSR	Moldavians (64.6), Ukrainians (14.2), Russians (11.6), Gagauz (3.5), Jews (2.7), Bulgars (2.1), 7 other nationalities (1.3)
Latvian SSR	Latvians (56.8), Russians (29.8), Belorussians (4.0), Poles (2.7), Ukrainians (2.3), Lithuanians (1.7), Jews (1.6), 8 other nationalities (1.1)
Kirgiz SSR	Kirgiz (43.8), Russians (29.2), Uzbeks (11.3), Ukrainians (4.1), Tatars (2.4), Uigur (0.8), Kazakhs (0.8), Tadzhiks (0.7), 14 other nationalities (6.9)
Tadzhik SSR	Tadzhiks (56.2), Uzbeks (23.0), Russians (11.9), Tatars (2.4), Kirgiz (1.2), Ukrainians (1.1), Kazakhs (0.3), 9 other nationalities (3.9)
Armenian SSR	Armenians (88.6), Azerbaydzhanis (5.9), Russians (2.7), Kurds (1.5), 9 other nationalities (1.3)
Turkmen SSR	Turkmens (65.6), Russians (14.5), Uzbeks (8.3), Kazakhs (3.2), Tatars (1.7), Ukrainians (1.6), Armenians (1.1), 12 other nationalities (4.0)
Estonian SSR	Estonians (68.2), Russians (24.7), Ukrainians (2.1), Finns (1.4), Belorussians (1.4), Jews (0.4), 7 other nationalities (1.8)

*Source: 1970 Census—reported in *Izvestiya 17*:4.1971.

includes the "fishing and reindeer languages" of the northeast—Chukcha, Koryak, Itelmen, Chuvan, and Yukagir. They are grouped as Paleoasiatic languages.

Though the speakers of these several languages have their own "core locales," they tend to be spread over considerable distances and to live not simply in contiguous areas but to be intertwined or intermingled with each other. This is the case of the Gagauz, generally thought to be of Turkic origin. They live for the main part in southern Moldavia but they have smaller numbers in the Ukraine,

Kazakhstan, and Central Asia. In the Moldavian Republic itself they have contact with Ukrainians, Bulgarians, and Rumanians as well as Moldavians, and in the recent past they have mixed with speakers of Greek and Turkish (Baskakov 1973). The Mordvin, again, though they are a relatively large nation are so scattered that 60% of the total population of the group do not occupy their original habitat. Similarly the Lezgin have very close contact not only with Russian but with several other Daghestani languages so that the level of bilingualism and of multilingualism among speakers of Lezgin is very high. The Nganasans have long been in close linguistic contact with speakers of other Samoyedic languages, and like other communities with fairly similar levels of development and size (the Khanti, Kareli, and Mansi, for instance) they have more than average knowledge of other languages and especially of Russian.

The speakers of the major languages do not require and do not in fact extend themselves to learn a second language other than Russian. Apart from speakers of Belorussian, Armenian, and Ukrainian, who have a very high dispersal level, none of the major groups has more than a 5% level of non-Russian-related bilingualism, and most are in the 2% range. However, this overall low level of bilingualism tends to disguise very heavy concentrations of bilingualism in particular areas. The Russians themselves are notoriously unwilling to learn the language of the area to which they may immigrate within the Soviet Union, although, because of the nearly fifty languages groups represented within the Russian Republic, the Russians have had a long history of bilingualism involving the acquisition of the languages of minorities such as Chuvash, Nogai, and Bashkir. Speakers within the Soviet Union of such major European languages as Polish, Hungarian, Greek, and Czechoslovak tend to have very high levels of Russian and non-Russian-related bilingualism. However, this tendency to supplement the mother tongue with the local as well as the Russian language is not confined to representatives of language groups normally situated outside the Soviet Union. For instance, in Latvia 96% of the population know Russian and 24% of other minorities know Lettish. Of the Lithuanian minority in Latvia, 70% know Russian and 54.7% know Lettish. Of the Jews in Latvia, who normally speak Yiddish, 98% know Russian and 43% have a knowledge of Lettish as well. Among the Estonian minority 62% know Russian and half of these know Lettish (Kholmogorov 1970: Tables 3.1 and 3.9). Finally, though there is no predictable or consistent correlation between the extent of bilingualism among a particular group and the possibility of selected individuals being bilingual, the fact is that the probability of a particular individual of whatever nationality being bilingual and even multilingual is fairly high. This is especially true of all cities such as Tashkent, with over 10,000 and sometimes as many as 50,000 representatives of over 15 language groups. Alma-Ata and Tbilisi have representatives of 9 major language groups. This degree of heterogeneity is also true of noncity areas if they have relatively high population densities, as in the Dzhambul Oblast with 12 minorities each represented by over 5,000 people. There are 9 such major language groups in the Ferghana Valley.

The Background of Social and Cultural Change

Demographic Mobility

In the last resort the types of school and their relative status reflect the broad sweep of change in Soviet society. Several aspects of this dynamism of bilingual education in the USSR may be identified. First, bilingualism itself, an element in "the culture fund," is on the increase. This is partly due to improvements in communication and intensified population movement. Second, traditional forms of bilingualism are being superseded or supplemented by new forms; for instance, the ability simply to speak two languages has been transformed to literacy in at least one language and usually in both, and this literate bilingualism is being extended to the great masses of Soviet people and not restricted to the elite. Third, contacts on a massive scale are being formed between linguistic/ethnic groups which hitherto were hardly aware of each other's existence. And finally, the contemporary forms of bilingualism in the Union are becoming increasingly important in social theory and are a major consideration in political strategy for the nationalities.

For all these reasons it is hardly possible to understand the nature of bilingual education in the USSR or its contribution to Soviet general educational theory and practice without considering the impact of changes in society on the cultural basis of the languages in the Union. One of these changes is the considerable degree of population movement, which has operated in three ways. First it has helped to accelerate and intensify long-standing or historical language contacts. For instance, the Kazakhs in their native Republic have been in contact with Russians, Ukrainians, Tatars, Uzbeks, Bellorussians, Uigurs, Dungans, and many other peoples over many decades and in some cases centuries. Between 1959 and 1970 the proportions of these long-established nationalities relative to the indigenous Kazakhs increased and the quantity of bilingualism involving Kazakh with other languages grew enormously. Again, because the Kirgiz have become a minority in their own Republic as a result of immigration, the importance of the Kirgiz language relative to the other languages in education has declined. In 1970, the Tadzhiks constituted only 56.2% of the population of that Republic, and the speakers of the language are now increasingly influenced by the introduction of new languages. The same is true of areas like the Altai and the North Caucasus. Between 1913 and 1968, approximately twelve and a half million people, mainly from the West, immigrated to the Central Asian Republics. Consequently the hold which the native languages of Central Asia had on the indigenous populations tended to relax and there has been increasing evidence of language shift. There is similar evidence from other areas. Between 1926 and 1970, over 16% of the speakers of Udmurt have shifted to other languages; over 10% of the Ossetians, 15% of the speakers of Khanti, over 36% of the speakers of Tat, and over 31% of the speakers of Abazin have ceased to claim those languages as their native tongues.

The prevalence of certain types of bilingualism has been affected by the fact that it is not the local language alone which suffers from increased immigration: in many instances the relative size of existing minority groups has been affected by the arrival of new ethnic groups. This has been the case in Transcaucasia, where in 1959, 10% of the population were native speakers of Russian. In 1970, their share of the population had dropped to 8%. In Tashkent the proportion of Russians fell from 44% in 1959 to 41% in 1970. As a result it has been claimed that a de-Russification of these areas has set in, with obvious implications for the pattern of bilingualism and bilingual education.

Second, immigration has accelerated the decomposition of hitherto stable language communities. The long-standing traditional relationships of some ethnic and language groups have been upset. Immigration has tended to substitute unstructured heterogeneity for fairly stable pluralism, and this has meant that the schools have had the burden of stabilizing the linguistic situation by providing an institutional base for sociolinguistic rationalization. Because the rates of language decline tend to be far higher among emigrant groups than among others, minorities are easily assimilated. For instance, while 96% of the stable Nogai population continue to speak their language, less than 65% of the migrants do so. The respective figures for the Lezgin are 92% and 69%, among the Karachai 96% and 65%, and among Avars 97% and 79%.

The effect of such movements on both the stable and migrant language groups is reinforced so far as bilingualism is concerned by the increase in interethnic marriages. Since the Revolution the taboos against such marriages have tended to be ignored and migration has served to offer greater opportunities to do so. For instance, in Ashkabad between 1951 and 1965, 29% of the marriages involved men and women of different nationalities. Twenty percent of the marriages in Tashkent and Samarkand belong to the same category. In Frunze the percentage rose between 1953 and 1962 from 22.4 to 27%. In Tataria marriage between Tatars and members of other nationalities amount to 13.2% of the total number of marriages (Busygin and Zorin 1973). "In zones of ethnic contacts with multinational populations (borderlines between different ethnic areas, bit cities, areas interspersed with populations of different nationalities, etc.) mixed marriages produce families which prove microenvironments for the processes of integration and natural assimilation. Among the factors determining the ethnic development in such families the leading role is played by the language and national self-consciousness" (Gantaskaya and Terentieva 1973). The result is a long period of bilingualism, since in most cases the spouses speak different languages even though they may share knowledge of the Russian language. Where one of the parents is of European Soviet origin, though the children may continue to use the local language with their grandparents, the main language is Russian. In the two districts of Tashkent a 1963 survey showed that where one of the parents was a native speaker of Russian that language became the normal means of communication in 79% and 47% of the families, respectively. In 86% and 54% of the cases in the two districts the children adopted Russian as their native language. In Latvia the number of 10th grade students who claimed Russian as their native tongue was found to be considerably greater in mixed families whatever the nationality of the parents than in families where both parents were of the same language group: 33% of such students were bilinguals claiming Lettish and Russian (Kholmogorov 1970). Often Russian becomes the basic language of the families even though neither of the parents is a native speaker of the language.

However, the tendency toward Russian is not equally strong in all such families—a great deal depends on the locality and the linguistic environment. In Kazakhstan when both parents were Slavs (Russians, Ukrainians, or Bellorussians) 85 to 100% of the children in most areas chose Russian. But when one of the parents was a Kazakh though the other might be Russian or Tatar, because of the local influence, 67 to 90% of the children chose Kazakh (*Nauchnyi Komm. 73*, 4:2834). In mixed Daghestan families where one parent was a member of the indigenous nationality 82% of the children chose the native language of the area and 17% chose Russian. Where both parents were members of different nationalities though still indigenous to Daghestan, the choice tended to be evenly divided between the two nationalities. Where one parent was Russian though the other was a member of a nation indigenous to the North Caucasus though not of the ethnic group among whom they lived two-thirds of the children chose Russian as their native tongue (Sergeeva and Smirnova 1971:4). Busygin and Zorin (1973) conclude from their data on the middle Volga that "Russian is the basic language in bi-national families. This is the case with 85% of all the surveyed inter-ethnic families. The remaining 15% use both Russian and the national language." The children inevitably become bilingual, and mixed marriages tend to consolidate the influence of Russian in such cases of child bilingualism.

A third aspect of population mobility which favors Russian among potentially bilingual children is the fact that the immigrants of whatever nationality tend to be young and better educated than the average. For instance, the percentage of those over 60 in the Central Asian in-migration areas is about half that of the European Soviets. In 1970, while the proportion of the total Soviet population under 29 years was 49%, the proportion of that age group in Central Asia was over 63%. Since 1959, the proportion of the total Soviet population in the same age group has fallen by 5.5% but the proportion in Central Asia has risen by approximately 1% (1959 Census, 1962-1963 and 1970 Census reported in *Komm. Tadzh.*, May 6, 1971). Already more than half the youngest citizens of the Union live outside the Russian Republic, although the population of the RSFSR represented over 54% of the total population of the Soviet Union. Sixty percent of the immigrants between 16 and 29 became urbanized in 1964. Of the age groups 15 to 24 in a Novosibirsk village approximately 35% moved into large towns and cities (*Vest. Stats* 7:1965). Most of the parents involved in such moves had a higher or complete secondary education. Only 13% of those studied in a 1972 survey (Topilin and Gilinskaya) had not continued beyond the elementary level. About 40% were engineers, technicians, or office workers. These were highly motivated young people whose ambitions for their children are not likely to be met if they receive an education which is principally in the national language. Furthermore a willingness to speak a local language when a prestige language is also part of the child's repertoire does not usually characterize young people in bilingual countries. In fact among non-Russians the younger the age group the more likely it is to claim Russian as its native language. Generally speaking, twice as many young people between the ages of 10 and 19 compared with men and women between 25 and 29 tend to shift away gradually from their native tongue.

Table 3.   Percentage of Population Claiming the
Russian Language as Its Native Tongue,
1959 Census Returns

Ages	Chuvash	Mari	Mordvin	Udmurt
All ages	16	16	22	23
10-19 years	34	28	58	36

It has been pointed out that "the predominance of small elementary and 8-year secondary schools . . . hinders the organisation of the normal pedagogical process. . . . For this reason there is urgent need to press on with consolidating schools, especially rural schools. In the last few years . . . the location of the network of schools and especially boarding schools has been rationalized and over 700 of the smallest schools have been closed" (Kotliarov et al. 1971, 34). Consolidation means drawing children from a much more extensive geographical area where several different ethnic and language groups may be dispersed. In the 25 nationality schools of the Nenetz National District, Nenetz children pre-dominated in 8, Komi children in 12, and Russian in 5 (*Narod. Obraz*, 1969). Rationalizing the network of schools in such an area produces a far more heterogeneous school and facilitates the use of Russian as the lingua franca. This is the case with the secondary school in Providenie, the capital of the Chukot District, attended by Chukchi, Eskimos, Russian, and other nationalities.

Not all factors favor Russian against the national languages. The relative importance of the latter in extending bilingualism among school-age children especially in Central Asia is affected by differences in the birth rates of the nationalities, of immigrant and nonimmigrant populations, as well as of rural and urban groups. The birth rate is especially low in European regions. In 1967, the reproduction index for the Baltic Republics was less than 1. In 1959, the rates for the Russian, Ukrainian, and Bellorussian republics were 2.3%, 2.0%, and 2.4%, respectively, whereas the average for the Central Asian Republics and Kazakhstan was approximately 3.8%. Azerbaydzhan and Turkestan had rates of 4.2% and 4.1%, in each case. This tendency for the non-Russian populations to increase more rapidly than the Russian tends to neutralize the influence of massive Russian immigration into Central Asia. The educational significance of differences in the size of language communities is not to be underestimated, since planning processes in the Soviet Union recognize its importance. To take an extreme case, the Abazin language is spoken by fewer than 20,000 people and will not be used in secondary or higher education (Desheriev 1973:31). Furthermore the fact that the birth rate in the rural areas of Central Asia, the stronghold of the nationality languages, is higher than in the heterogeneous towns and cities also tends to neutralize the effect of Russian immigration and assimilation arising from contact.

Linguistic Heterogeneity in Schools

The factors we have considered help to explain the very high incidence of schools where the ethnic/linguistic composition is heterogeneous. For instance, people belonging to more than 100 nationalities live in the Georgian Republic and there are schools where the instruction is organized in separate tracks to provide for Armenian-, Azerbaydzhan-, Greek-, and Ossete-speaking children, and where in addition the different groups all learn Georgian and Russian. The children in some Bashkir schools are taught in six languages, Russian, Tatar, Bashkir, Chuvash, Mari, or Udmurt according to their ethnic origin. In the city of Kzyl-Orda (Kazakhstan) the Saken Seifullin School is attended by representatives of 30 nationalities while School No. 23 in Frunze has 18 different language groups. In 1964, there were 317 such multinational schools in Kirgizia.

All the schools in the cities of Daghestan recruit children from 5 to 25 nationalities. One school in Maikop (Krasnodar region) is attended by children from 12 linguistic groups. In the 1966-1967 school year there were at least 400 such schools in Daghestan, some of them in relatively small villages like Tataiurt in the Babaiurt region. The 508 children of the village represented 16 nationalities, and every class in the village school was a complete cross section of the heterogeneous village community. The school in the Daghestanie Ogni settlement was attended by Ossetians, Avars, Laks, Tatars, Ukrainians, Kumyks, Mountain Jews, Rutuls, Armenians, Bellorussians, Greeks, and Aguls as well as by the native Dargin children. Such complexity not only makes a bilingual/multilingual education necessary but puts a premium on the use of the lingua franca as the teaching language, as was the case in Derbent, School No. 4 (Garunov 1970).

Sociocultural Homogenization

Conflicting cultural justifications for bilingual education. The Soviet system of education, whatever concessions it may make to the historical traditions of the nationalities, is committed to facilitating rapid modernization characterized by industrialization and extensive mechanization, together with consequent high levels of urbanization. It involves the creation of one national state, however multiple its components may be. It is dedicated to uniformity of political and educational organization and cultural homogenization. The differentiation of courses together with the provision of "electives," which have not hitherto been a notable feature of Soviet education, are aimed partly at offering opportunities of specialization in the sciences. The 1966 decree on Measures for the Further

Improvement of Work in the Middle General School stated that "it is permitted to have general schools and classes for more fundamental theoretical and practical study in the 9th and 10th (or 11th) grades of mathematics, computer techniques, radio electronics, chemical technology, agrobiology and the humanities." The Soviet student tends to take at least two sciences for 4 years and possibly three sciences for 5 or even 6 years. They also tend to follow courses in mathematics, algebra, geometry, and trigonometry for the whole of their secondary schooling. In comparison fewer than 33% of American high school students are taught more than a year of chemistry, approximately 25% are taught a year of physics, and fewer than 14% take the whole range of mathematics for more than a year.

Clearly such an intense drive toward a scientifically oriented society in the Soviet Union reflects a considerable degree of social change and envisages more, involving a reconsideration of the place of the national languages in education. In multinational as much as in any other type of state, modernization tends to imply a growing identification with a specified national language (or a lingua franca which serves as a surrogate for the national language). The lingua franca, Russian in this case, tends to appropriate more and more social functions even when in the past the other national languages have been able to discharge such functions and are still able to do so satisfactorily. Where bilingual education is concerned, this leads to unilateral bilingualism—only the non-Russians need to learn and to use a second indigenous language. Bilingualism is for the nationalities alone.

On the other hand, where a society is moving from a traditional to a posttraditional phase as is the case in many Soviet nationalities, the tendency is to seek, however temporarily, some haven from the harshness of social change, especially since such changes involve not simply the secularization of hitherto intensely religious communities like the Muslims of Central Asia, but their adoption of an abrasive atheism. Therefore, traditional values receive a possibly exaggerated emphasis. Because of the conflicting tendencies inherent in modernization, the justification of a bilingual education tends to differ according to whether it is regarded as a means of ensuring change—participating in a dynamic society—or as an aspect of the conservation of a traditional way of life with limited communication patterns. In this chapter we are concerned with bilingual education as an aspect of change.

Types of traditional cultures—the pristine culture. Bilingual education in the Soviet Union reflects the tensions between application to the several types of culture—those with which the Russian language and the nationality languages respectively are associated. Attitudes to the different types of culture, and even more the attitudes to how the cultures relate to each other may conflict. Bilingualism in education, insofar as it involves the maintenance of nationality languages, has usually been justified as necessary to the preservation of the associated "pristine" culture; and in spite of the claims about their growing together and of their eventual merging, nearly all aspects of these pristine cultures, intellectual, spiritual, as well as material, remain strong. So far as Transcaucasia and the Central Asian communities are concerned, the success of the attempts to popularize Slav or Western culture in literature, the mass media, the visual arts, theater, and ballet is seldom commensurate with the effort involved. The indigenous populations of Central Asia are still reluctant to participate in atheistic propaganda and the survival of traditional habits is remarked upon critically (Allworth 1973:68). Islamic marriage rites and observances continue. The work of classical Persian poets such as Rudaki (b.858) is claimed with pride as an undisputed contribution to present-day Tadzhik culture. Among Tatars there is considerable interest in Tatar-language radio programs from Kazan (46% of the people listen to them). Tatar folk music is popular not only in rural areas but among professional people in the towns and cities. Tatars are increasingly interested in reading literature originating inside the Republic and especially in the native language. Of the Tatars, 63% read Tatar only, 25% (usually professional people) read Tatar and Russian literature, and only 11% confine their reading to Russian (Savoskul 1971:3-13). The strength of the positive attitude to national cultures is often derived from a rediscovery of their historical roots, and this is especially true of the Central Asian nations. "Tadzhik and Uzbek writers often reach back to Arab, Iranian and Central Asian scholars and writers for support. Central Asian musicologists and art critics frequently point to Al Farabi (d.990), Ibn Sina (d.1037) and Bezhad (d.1505) among others as outstanding contributors to classical Uzbek and Tadzhik arts" (Naby 1973:112). All those who reach back to the past are equally concerned to identify their cultural heritage with their immediate locality—their national as opposed to the much publicized concept of the "Soviet homeland."

One consequence of all this is the conscious and deliberate use of educational institutions and linguistic scholarship to isolate Russian language influences as much as possible. Representatives of the centralizing tendencies in Soviet life allege that there are "nationalist tendencies and erroneous theories which give rise to a desire for language isolationism. . . . Borrowings, including such as have already struck root are replaced by words of native stock, this very often without the least need. Special accent is placed on purist tendencies" (Desheriev 1973:9). To circumvent such attacks, Uzbek writers claim the support of Lenin in safeguarding the Russian language as well as their own. "We are corrupting the Russian language by using foreign words out of place and improperly. . . . Has not the time come to announce a struggle against corrupting the Russian language?" (Allworth 1973:17).

Traditional international or contact cultures. It is questionable whether the pristine culture can continue much longer to be even a partial justification for the maintenance of the national languages in a bilingual education. Most of these pristine cultures have been contact cultures for many centuries, and have flourished in multilingual areas. Many are variants of regional or supranational ways of life. The resurgence of Islam not only supports the specifically national cultures (vis-à-vis Western influences) but strengthens the international characteristics of Central Asian life. Many members have left the Communist Party because its materialist world view is uncongenial to Islam (*Ozbek. Komm.* 1970). Central Asians tend to welcome Oriental and Middle Eastern influences from outside the Soviet Union. Similarly the peoples of the Caucasus emphasize the interaction of their various national cultures, so that in addition to maintaining the peculiar characteristics of those separate national cultures, a typologically single regional cultural milieu exists. The national and ethnic cultures of the Soviet Union are individual and unique, but they are also the products of close contact within a broader culture context. "The ethnic culture is made up partly of characteristics specific to a particular nationality but partly also of characteristics which they share with others because of mutual influence" (Kholmogorov 1970:26).

The most powerful of these contact cultures is mediated by the Russian language. Central Asian themes are set to Russian music and are expressed in Western dance and ballet. Popular Russian images and Tadzhik inscriptions in Cyrillic lettering are found in paintings inspired by Middle Eastern carpet designs and based on the execution of Middle Eastern delicate abstract patterns or floral designs (Nahy 1973:119). The present tendency in official circles is to stress the multinational and contact features rather than the intrinsically national, and the argument for maintaining a particular national language as the expression of a multinational or contact culture has lost a considerable degree of cogency in the Soviet Union. The stress on regional cultures makes the linguistic assimilation of peoples easier and undermines the stability of a reciprocal bilingual education.

Modified-urbanized national cultures. An urban way of life tends to exert two conflicting influences. Though urbanization facilitates cultural convergence and homogenization, it also tends to intensify ethnic or national consciousness and an awareness of the uniqueness of the national language. This conflict is crucial in the development of bilingual education in the Soviet Union, especially since increasingly rapid urbanization is a major aim of Soviet policy and an important element in its ideology. Lenin regarded it as a progressive phenomenon: "It raises people's literacy and consciousness and imbues them with new culture habits and needs" (Lewis 1972:99). The increased rate and intensity of interpersonal as well as group communications in towns and cities together with more general aspects of social change help to create an unpredictable linguistic situation the result of which is to promote the emergence of a koine where that is possible, or a lingua franca.

On the other hand, urbanization in circumstances of culture and language contact, at present as well as historically, is identified with intensification of ethnic, national, and linguistic self-consciousness which tends to run counter to uniformation. The traditional cultures of Bukhara were essentially urban. Royal and princely patronage drew artists, musicians, and poets from all parts of Central Asia to the cities of Bukhara, Khiva, Samarkand, and Tashkent. It is the same today: "New Tadzhik literature like other evidence has shown that industrialization and urbanization . . . have provided the Tadzhik with self identification" (Rosen 1973:71), for "the gravity of ethnic consciousness has gravitated from the countryside to the cities" (Pokshishevskiy 1971:53). The customary view that it is the village which is best able to preserve distinctive linguistic and cultural traits and values, and therefore best facilitates the maintenance of the national language as an element in a bilingual education is true only if the nationality is identified with the "folk," and the maintenance of the language is tied to the continuance of the folk culture. A literate culture tends to be urban, and a literate bilingual education also tends to be supported by an urban consciousness. Furthermore, the cities are in any case the centers of ethnic language publishing and broadcasting, and their schools set the standard by which all others are judged. To this extent, though the rural areas may remain as the storehouse of the "culture fund" and of the local language as an element in that fund, the "consumption of culture" and bilingual education as the principal means of ensuring a high level of "culture consumption" is increasingly a function of urban life.

Though the towns and cities are the centers of national culture and language consciousness, the culture with which the language is associated is no longer the pristine national culture: it is an urbanized-modified national culture, and the role of national languages in education depends on their adapting themselves to an urban way of life. Already a shift of attitude has been observed which "reflects the emergence of a new society with its own imperatives. . . . In a positive sense perhaps the fact that young Central Asians are not saying anything—at least not anything couched in the old vocabulary, about the nationality questions is the principal new message. They de-emphasize the nationality principle (ethnic, multi-ethnic or other) while redefining the country . . ." (Allworth 1973:18).

The three types of culture we have sought to distinguish up to this point—the pristine culture, the contact culture within a regional context, and the modified-urbanized culture of the Soviet Union—are all national. They are ranged along a historical and unbroken continuum leading from the folk to the urbanized but nevertheless nationally conscious community. Until comparatively recently bilingual education has sought its justification in association with each of the first two in turn. In the circumstances of the Soviet Union committed to general modernization, industrialization, and an urban way of life such a justification is becoming increasingly inapposite.

The technological and nonethnic culture. Soviet writers stress the emergence of a new culture, though they seem to have different views about its relationship to the existing national culture of whatever kind. Disjunction or fragmentation, as well as convergence, are equally important aspects of ethnic development and equally significant in the development of bilingual education. Since the beginning of the Soviet regime and until comparatively recently, working on the principle of divide and conquer, it is fragmentation of linguistic communities which has governed policy. In the 1920s the Young Bukhuarans aimed at the unity of their related language groups; but contrary to their demand, Kirgiz and Karakalpaks were separated from Kazakhs, and the traditionally associated and culturally closely knit Uzbeks and Tadzhiks became two distinct nations. In order to foster this separateness, the Karakalpaks were given schools in their own language when much larger linguistic groups, like Kabardinians, Chechens, Avars, and Ossetians, were not. Similarly Uigurs and Dungans, relatively small linguistic groups within the Union, were granted their own nationality schools in order to foster their sense of identity as against large numbers of their kinsmen in northwest China. The same is true of the early Soviet attitude to the nationalities of the North Caucasus.

At present the contrary ethnic process, convergence, is encouraged. "Voluntary assimilation of small ethnic minorities and enclaves in the large nations takes place and this is drawing the nations together not spontaneously but through a policy of centralized state planning" (Davletshin 1967). The Batsbi tribe are ceasing to speak their native tongue, being absorbed by Georgian, which is also assimilating Mingrelians and Svans. In Daghestan speakers of Avar are assimilated by several other linguistic groups, and in Uzbekistan the same fate is overtaking Kipchaks. In Tadzhikstan the Pamiri group of dialects is ceasing to be functional. Though the results of convergence are most obvious in the case of the small language groups, it is a process which is encouraged among the larger languages also. The results are being interpreted in three ways by Soviet observers. First, a new culture is said to emerge "synthesizing the true richness and diversity of the national elements . . . giving new and progressive direction and development to the national process." The productive element in this synthesis is the "rich experience of Russian literature and its revolutionary tradition, which is the real university where nationality writers attain their mastery" (Barrett 1973:25). Such a process of synthesis "does not at all imply denationalization" of the languages and cultures" (Groshev 1967:21).

A second group of writers, however, emphasize that in developing the new culture there must be a "muted treatment of the usual identifying nationality traits" (Barrett 1973:29). To some non-Soviet observers denationalization appears to be inevitable because "allowing for geographical variants there must be an effacement of those ethnic distinctions including differences in family relationships, religion and workview" (Dunn and Dunn 1973:62). A third group asserts that convergence creates possible conditions for an entirely new culture, requiring a new pattern of linguistic affiliations to support it. This is a "USSR wide culture" (Kholmogorov 1970:57). While it is conceded that for some time to come national cultures will continue to coexist with the Soviet-wide culture and will therefore ensure the use of the national languages in bilingual education ultimately, it is stressed that the one-type culture will supersede all national cultures and the languages will merge. The Soviet-wide culture is therefore discontinuous with national cultures as they are known at present, and a system of bilingual education which allows for the use of elements of those cultures is merely transitional, a palliative measure. Ethnic culture and ethnic language alienation is not simply one of the consequences of this view—it is one of the principal aims.

The rise of the social functions of the lingua franca and the strengthening of unilateral bilingualism at present do not justify the conclusion that a new language community is already in being. But the "areas of traditional culture with its ethnic associations (including language) are receding, and the ideological content of the culture is becoming more uniform" (Savoskul 1971:8). Because it is so general, the basis for participation in such a culture is not ethnicity but citizenship—a civic culture. It is for this reason that official critics of national language affiliation and of national literatures demand that "more attention should be devoted to the obligations of Soviet citizenship in such literature" (Khaimov 1971:16). The main thrust in the advocacy of bilingual education at the present time is to gain acceptance of the one-type Soviet culture and therefore to ensure 'that Russian, the lingua franca, predominates. Modernization in the Soviet Union places ethnic languages and cultures at an almost prohibitive disadvantage compared with the lingua franca, especially in education. Ethnic and national cultures have always changed, albeit slowly and almost imperceptibly, but the problems now facing them have a new dimension because innovations implied by the Soviet-wide culture are no longer fragmentary but embrace most if not all aspects of science, of social awareness and communication, simultaneously. Innovation is no longer simply experienced or endured but is actively pursued as an independent value. Consequently modernization results in the increasing alienation from ethnic and language affiliations. In many ways the new knowledge necessary to and produced by modernization is expressed and communicated in such abstract terms that nationality languages cannot sustain important roles.

The new one-type Soviet culture is a response to a system-transforming demand just as ethnic cultures are system-sustaining responses. One of the crucial features of a traditional society is the acceptance of the tradition as "given"— primordial and self-justified. This is equally true of the ethnic language: the simple existence of the language is the justification of its maintenance, and a bilingual education requires no further defense than the existence of the national language. The nonethnic Soviet culture because of its technological base tends not only to level out differences between languages but also to require a justification for their maintenance in the system of education. Bilingual education has to be supplied with a rationale, and the arguments being advanced by Soviet educationists and sociologists in respect of the nationalities is an attempt to provide such a rationale.

The "one-type culture of the Soviet Union" (Arutyunyan 1973:10) is the distillation of a "civic" as distinct from a communal awareness, and as such is a "professional culture" (Arutyunyan 1973:4). It arises from relationships to political institutions, like the Party, rather than relationships within and between historical communities. Part of the influence of the "civic" culture is due to the existence of an authoritarian central government which controls the whole Soviet system, has created a uniform political organization and educational organizations and institutions, and has promoted a single uniform ideology. The result is, it is claimed, "a single system of social and moral standards and values which is typical of every nation and nationality in the Soviet Union" (Arutyunyan 1973:8). To the extent that the center predominates, it tends to justify bilingualism only to the extent that it promotes the acquisition of Russian as a second language. Reciprocal bilingualism, involving the speakers of Russian acquiring a nationality language, has little interest for most Soviet educationists.

Differentiation of the Structure of Society

The separation of functions among Soviet languages. Modernization, while it promotes convergence and homogenization in the area of cultures, simultaneously tends to promote differentiation on the level of social structures. This offers even minority languages the opportunity to appropriate new social functions derived from the restructuring of society. In the Soviet Union this tendency toward differentiation helps to make explicit the relationships between nationality languages in contact, as well as relationship between the nationality languages as a category and the lingua franca. These problems are reflected in the linguistic policy for schools. In traditional societies, like some of the minorities of the Soviet Union, activities tend to be characterized by functional diffuseness: few such activities have a single or specific role but each tends to become the focus of multiple interests. Productive activities like harvesting may have religious associations as well; religious observances and festivals have recreational aims and serve the purely secular functions of holding a society together. In such a case there is little reason for a language to evolve a system of subcodes suitable for specific or specialized roles, or for different languages to have differentiated functions. In Daghestan or the Ferghana Valley bilinguals and multilinguals until very recently used their whole linguistic repertoire across the whole range of social activities. Both (or the several) languages in a person's command were used indifferently and with considerable switching on any occasion. Similarly, until the Soviet Revolution and the rapid acceleration of the process of modernization most bilinguals in the traditional Bukharian emirate used Turkic (Uzbek) and Persian (Tadzhik) indifferently to cover the same range of social functions.

In posttraditional and modernizing societies the roles adopted by individuals tend to be more specialized. Within a homogeneous language group this tends to intensify the need for differentiated subcodes of the single language. In modernizing multilingual societies the different languages spoken by any one person tend to be regarded as subcodes within his total repertoire, some occasions demanding one language and other occasions a different one. For example, not until after the revolution and the beginning of rapid modernization late in the twenties did Uzbek and Tadzhik each come to be identified with a separate national consciousness, or each to be used to promote a different ethnic destiny—an innovation and a separation of function which was facilitated by the intrusion of Russian. In Daghestan the Russian language is assuming an almost exclusive role in administration, as well as in science and higher education, and exerting a pressure on bilinguals to associate their other languages more specifically and habitually with other social functions. This means that the schools tend to associate some languages more closely than others with particular areas of the curriculum, for instance, science and mathematics with Russian as compared with history or geography. In Georgia while Russian and the national language are both used in teaching physics the former is used more frequently because "all aspects of science were extremely developed in the past and today in Russian while this was historically not the case with Georgian" (Desheriev 1973:22).

Some languages have an important role in only one or two social activities, everyday life and religion, for instance, where even the unalphabeticized languages are necessary. The same is true of legal administration, where it is obligatory to permit the use of any language and if necessary to employ an interpreter. However, some languages have more numerous and more important roles to play in the administration of justice: some have Soviet-wide currency, some have Union Republic currency, and others have Oblast currency only. In education, too, the use of all the alphabeticized languages is permitted, though here again some are used for elementary teaching only, some for only early grades, and some for all grades of secondary education. Only one language is used throughout the Soviet Union at all stages of education from preschool to university. In technology and especially for the purposes of international translation between Soviet languages, and to make non-Soviet literature available within the Union, only the basic languages of the largest Union Republics are called upon. Many of even the long-standing literary languages have only a very slight part to play in this field. In sociopolitical activities, too, only the basic languages of the Union Republics and especially Russian have wide-ranging functions to perform, though in communicating at local levels the languages of even the small minorities may be called upon, and political announcements may be circulated in them. The same is true of trade and commerce: while all languages are used at the local level, transactions are recorded in Russian and the basic languages of the Union Republics. Russian is the language of international trade within the USSR and between the USSR and the rest of the world. So far as industry is concerned the more advanced the processes the greater the role played by Russian. Graduates from specialized and technical secondary schools may have difficulty in finding satisfactory employment and permanent residence permits unless they speak Russian and the language of the Republic where they intend to work (*Mol. Est.* 22:8-73). Only in agriculture and in some face-to-face communication situations among low-grade workers are unalphabeticized languages used. So far as the theater and films are concerned, only the Union Republic languages, especially Russian, tend to be used, and this is true, though to a lesser extent, of the press. Radio and TV, because they are forms of face-to-face communication, tend to give greater currency to nationality languages, to some minority languages, and even to unalphabeticized ones. Generally speaking, members of the professions and those with higher levels of education tend increasingly to extend the social functions of Russian and the major languages of Union Republics even when the other languages can fulfill the same roles as satisfactorily. Those with lower-level professional and educational standards, though they too use the major languages for many social functions, tend to use those languages less frequently and to reserve important social roles for minority languages (*Sov. Ped.* 4:73).

The system of bilingual education makes several vital contributions to the rationalization of this extremely complex sociolinguistic situation. In the first place the schools tend to reflect the local situation, but not necessarily so. Often the choice of language of instruction is determined not by the relative position of the several languages in the community but by adherence to a centrally determined policy. For instance, parents are frequently said to demand transference to Russian as the teaching language even when the majority of the children speak a non-Russian language (Carunov). Second, the school may reinforce the position of a particular nationality or a minority language. Even if this is limited to elementary grades, it improves its status locally and helps to refine the quality of the language used outside school in such activities as the village theater. Third, the language policy adopted for a particular school helps to implement the main thrust of dynamic bilingualism which, whatever its disadvantages, does facilitate the necessary modernization of Soviet society and ensures a greater opportunity for more varied social experience for most of the children. Finally, the system of education is the principal means of rationalizing the relationships existing among the several languages. In spite of possible disadvantages and inevitable distresses to those who are affiliated to small language groups, this is a very necessary development in such a vast multilingual society. To the extent that the various languages have institutional support linguistic heterogeneity can be transformed into a structured linguistic plural society, which is basically the aim of the Soviet Union. An unstructured linguistic heterogeneity is rich soil for potential conflict between languages.

Potential conflict. The probability is that no social unit exists in which convergent (homogenizing) and divergent (differentiating) trends are not insepa-rably interwoven, but the different direction of these processes may be more likely to lead to conflict in multinational/multilingual developing communities than in homogeneous, advanced societies. The complex structure of linguistically heterogeneous developing societies increases the number of relatively disparate contexts of social action, and at the same time increases the instances where there has to be differential valuation of the languages associated with the different spheres of action. Such possibilities of conflict arise from the fact that segments of traditional areas of experience coexist with intrusive and unintegrated aspects of more modern areas of social experience. In the Soviet Union, "The drawing together of nations in the economic, social and political ideological spheres has proceeded faster than in the cultural-linguistic sphere ... aspects of spiritual culture retain a large degree of their original national colour" (*Vestnik Akad. Nauk 11*:72, 3-11). In the new and expanding Soviet cities the varying rate of development of ethnic groups moving in from neighboring rural areas and coexisting ecologically with linguistically heterogeneous elements originating in areas with very different culture and language development levels creates tension. Related to this is the fact that the unintegrated areas of social experience are associated differently with the lingua franca or the nationality languages.

The more highly differentiated a society is the more emphatic is the distinction between the levels of traditional generalized values and the social structures with their very specific norms of action (Williams 1971). In the modernizing nationalities of the Soviet Union the ethnic languages tend to be associated with the generalized values of the traditional cultures which change very slowly rather than with the norms of the very clearly articulated and centrally controlled system of social action and government which have changed and are changing rapidly. Bilingual education is interpreted differently, therefore, according to whether it is looked at from the standpoint of the needs of a dynamic political and social system or of the values which have helped to guide traditional, conservative communal behavior, including religious behavior for many centuries. This kind of conflict in a linguistically complex society is only an exaggeration of what occurs in the schools of a homogeneous society between the concept of education as a means of inculcating humanist values on the one hand and on the other the need to ensure a scientific technological advance. The conflict in a linguistically heterogeneous society is more apparent and apt to create social as well as educational conflict because the two tendencies are associated with two languages, the ethnic language and the language of wider communication or the lingua franca.

THE DEVELOPMENT OF SOVIET BILINGUAL EDUCATION

Pre-Soviet Bilingual Schools

The present policy for bilingual education is the product of developments which have their roots in the 19th Century, though clearly the social and political changes which have occurred in the last fifty years have markedly affected both the policy and its implementation. Nowhere is it more apparent than in the USSR that bilingualism reflects changes in the structure of society and that bilingual education not only reflects but mediates such changes, especially those which affect the languages of the "nationalities" in their relationship to the Russian language. "It is as if history has staged in the Soviet Union a large scale experiment of interaction of different cultures and languages which had formed on a different social, economic and ideological basis" (Arutyunyan 1973).

The general picture of the bilingual education of the "alien populations" (inorodtsy) of Russia under the Tsars was bleak: without question the policy was ultimately to engineer "fusion with the Russian people ... State schools cannot have an alien character" (D. Tolstoy, quoted in Sovetskin 1958:14). Among the Peoples of the Far North, for instance, what teaching was available was in Russian, a language with which very few of the children were acquainted. Even so, for those who attended school and had some knowledge of Russian, education consisted of little more than committing prayers and biblical texts to memory. Children were taught in either secular Russian language schools or in mission schools of the Orthodox or other faiths. Some of those who attended secular schools might be taught in a non-Russian language, although in such cases the teachers had only a poor command of the language. Generally speaking the mission schools were more favorable to the national languages. The pioneer educationist Ushinsky had attacked the "tyranny which deprived so many generations of their heritage ... and of their mother tongue, which they cannot recover once it has been taken from them" (1939:11). Ilminsky, tthe founder in 1872 of the teacher training college at the Kazan Theological Seminary specifically for the "inorodsty," took the same line, and his college proved the prototype of several colleges catering to teachers among Udmurt and Bashkir children and others.

In 1905, the report of a Commission of the Ministry of Education claimed that being deprived of instruction in their native language was "creating a stupid inorodsty, and provoking their antagonism to schooling." In 1911, the First All-Zemstvo Congress on Public Education proposed that the native language should be used during the first years of the non-Russian schools. In 1913, the First All Russian Congress on Child Upbringing adopted several suggestions bearing on bilingual education: first, the educational rights of the various nationalities of Russia should be protected; second, the native languages and the national literatures should be taught; third, the Russian language should be taught from the third year and earlier if it was appropriate to do so; and finally, all non-Russian schools should be staffed by teachers who spoke the local language fluently and could use it confidently."

The oppressive Tsarist policy had some escape routes for the minorities. Leaders of the Georgian nation, for instance, exploited to the full the provision for "alien schools" in which the national language was taught and which ensured attention for Georgian traditions by regarding the schools as private establishments. The Tsarist statutes permitted private schools and allowed their promoters to stipulate the language of instruction so long as Russian and Russian literature were also taught (Tumin and Zelenko 1915:76, 77). The Armenians were "guilty" of using the parochial school system simply to ensure that instruction was conducted in the national language (Malinovsky 1914:19). The Muslims adopted the same strategy of providing a "general education in the mother tongue" in nominally religious institutions, *maktab* and *madrash*, but teaching many of the subjects which were part of the secular curriculum in the national language. In addition there were among the Muslims of the present-day Uzbek, Turkestan, and Kazakh Republics a considerable number of Russian schools in which the local languages had a place. There were 350 schools where Kazakh was taught, and many Kazakh language textbooks, printed like those of Turkestan in an Arabic script, were employed (Sembaev 1958:21, 22).

For the 19th Century these were rather eccentric educational developments, and it required a set of major changes in society to make the education of bilingual children a central consideration. It is therefore only natural that these social factors should remain foremost in the minds of Soviet teachers for whom education has a dominant role in manipulating a complex social environment to ensure intergroup (and especially international or interethnic) adjustment, and accelerating such groups toward predetermined goals. These may be subsumed under the following heads—mobilization and uniformation of the total population, modernization (including economic, industrial, and technological advance) together with the formation of a secular, urban proletariat. Changes which are consequent on the struggle to achieve these aims affect ethnic processes throughout the USSR and determine the availability and the content of education as well as the relationships between national languages in the system of education. Changes in the occupation of territories and in political conditions, an increase in the number of interethnic marriages, adaptation to a sedentary as opposed to a nomadic life, alphabetization of nationality languages and dialects as well as their introduction into the system of education, have all served to break down historical barriers between clans, tribes, and even larger ethnic groups. The dialects they speak tend to be leveled out or to disappear; there is considerable language shift as well as modification and intensification of ethnic awareness. These changes have affected the broader structures of society and such microstructures as family life, which is crucial in the maintenance of a mother tongue and therefore of bilingualism. For example, the economic and social life of the Pamirs have undergone significant transformations which have meant that the old established (kindred) family group and closed pattern of marriage are being replaced by looser ties and fewer restrictions on the acceptance of strangers into the ethnic group. In consequence the bonds which tie together the language and the traditions of the group are relaxed and the opportunities for assimilation to Tadzhik multiply.

The Administrative Framework

The problems of providing bilingual education are somewhat less extreme than the complexity of the situation might lead us to expect. One reason is that the schools in which this education is provided are part and parcel of a uniform state system of education—there is nothing special about their administration. Schools for bilingual children are governed in the same way as all the other schools. This means that they have been set the same tasks as those facing the normal type of school, i.e., "giving the pupils a general education that corresponds to the present day demands of socialist, scientific and technical progress," as well as "moulding the Marxist-Leninist world view in the younger generation." Consequently bilingual education, whatever the traditions of the nationality with which a particular language is associated, must aim to provide an education which will enable the student to live in an industrial society. Basically the rationale of a bilingual education is conceived to be identical with that of any other form of general education.

The length of compulsory education is 8 years, but a large percentage of students complete 10 years. There is an additional year for those who receive their instruction in a language other than Russian. Primary schools (*nachal'nye shkoly*) cater to grades 1 to 4 (ages 7 to 10), and these elementary schools may be entirely separate from secondary schools though not necessarily so. The tendency is to reduce the length of the elementary stage from 4 to 3 years so as to enable children in small village schools to have a year longer in large "consolidated schools." Consolidation of several small village schools may produce secondary schools that are more heterogeneous linguistically, since they have a wider catchment area. Secondary schools, which may have two or more parallel grades, are of two kinds—those that cater to grades 5 to 8 only, *nepolnoe srednee obrazovanie* (incomplete secondary) and *polnoe srednee obrazovanie* (complete secondary) catering to up to grade 10. So far as concerns the timetables and other aspects of the organization of these schools, some concessions are made to bilingual children. Sometimes a preparatory class is provided to enable those who do not speak Russian to become acquainted with very elementary Russian vocabulary and the sounds of Russian. Then, as we have noted, such students are required to attend for an extra year (9 years of incomplete secondary and 11 years of complete secondary education). The hours of instruction are normally 24 in primary, 30 in incomplete secondary, and 32 in complete secondary schools, with the stipulation that 2 or 3 hours per grade may be added each week in the "national schools of the Russian Republic and in the schools of other Republics where instruction is in the local language." The other types of institutions which are involved in providing some form of bilingual education are the boarding and specialized schools (*srednee special'noe obraz.*), and institutions of higher education, including universities and higher technical schools (*vyshee obraz.*).

Bilingual schools experience, albeit in a more exaggerated form, most of the problems with which the nonbilingual schools are faced, such as the gap which exists between the quality of education in rural and urban schools. Since the local languages are usually strongest in the rural areas, this bothersome issue is almost inextricably bound up with bilingual education. The Soviet aim is "to eliminate differences between the countryside and the town" (*Prog. Komm.* 1961, 76), but because the urban schools are better staffed and have more and better equipment and books as well as specialized facilities, education by means of local languages, insofar as this is typified by the rural school, tends to have a poor image. For instance, it is extremely difficult for them to teach foreign languages satisfactorily if at all."Urban in the Soviet context is a good surrogate for the attributes of an advanced society: industrialization, higher education institutions, skilled employment and services. The participation of a group in urban life is a good measure of participation in the advantages of a technically advanced society." In the Central Asian area there are two "separate spheres of population, indigenous and non-indigenous. These are characterized by dichotomous levels of urbanization, dispersion, education and skilled employment" (Clem 1973:39, 42). The indigenous tend to predominate in the rural areas. Some aspects of bilingual education in the Soviet Union as elsewhere are almost coterminous with the problems of rural education.

Development of Soviet Bilingual Policy

Soviet policy for the development of bilingual education is a crystallization of political attitudes toward the nationalities of the Union—it is an aspect of "nationality policy" and is governed at all times by the *political* aims of the rulers of the USSR. In the process of developing the Soviet multinational and multilingual state the operative principles, it is claimed, have been "first, the safeguarding of both the large and small nationalities; second, the equality of all the soviet languages; third, the right of the nationalities to . . . determine the place of the relevant languages in their administration; fourth, acceptance of Russian assistance as a leading factor in national development; and finally, movement towards full integration between nationalities and 'rapprochement' of national languages and cultures in the creation of a 'Soviet nation' as opposed to a large number of ethnically limited nationalities" (Kulichenko 1972). In the light of these aims and the general direction of Soviet education toward a technologically advanced society, there are at all times two conflicting tendencies at work in the formulation and periodic revision of policy toward national languages. There is first of all the drive toward a "proletarian internationalism and rapprochement of socialist nations" and on the other hand a recognition of the need as well as a sincere desire to preserve as much as possible of the great variety of Soviet languages and traditions. From time to time the relative importance attached to these two aims is reviewed. The first phase is nationality policy, lasting from the beginning of the Revolutionary period to the early 1930s was characterized by a determined effort to carry into practice the principles of the prerevolutionary discussions affecting attitudes toward nationalities. In the main these favored a "pluralistic" concept in which the native languages would be used in all aspects of life—the administration of justice, the press, and education especially (Resolution, Tenth Congress, 1921). Even Stalin supported the pluralist standpoint in this first phase. The aim, he argued, was to "make the Soviet regime . . . not merely Russian but also multinational. . . . It is necessary that not only the schools but also all institutions should operate in the languages understood by the masses . . . and function in conditions appropriate to the way of life of a given group or nationality" (*Soch.*, vol. V, 257-258).

The encouragement of national languages even in this first phase stopped far short of tolerating the concept of "national culture" or national languages as the expression of nationalistic ideas. It was Lenin's view that "the slogan of *national culture* is false and expresses only a bourgeois, narrow minded understanding of the national question" (Lenin 1958:88). While he favored the use of national languages in education, he opposed separate schools for national languages and promoted the formation of integrated schools where the two or many different languages might be used to teach different ethnic groups.

The second phase, from the middle of the 1930s to the 1950s saw a sharp swing away from linguistic pluralism toward centralism. This was the time of Stalin's most repressive measures. He criticized "deviation towards local national-isms, including the exaggerated respect for national languages" (Stalin 1961). The tendency to emphasize uniformity in education at the expense of the unique contribution it was possible for the national languages and cultures to make coincided with constant insistence on the teaching and use of Russian. In 1938, the teaching of that language in all schools in the Union was made compulsory, and the process of changing the alphabets first to Latin and then to Cyrillic was commenced. The consequences of this drive toward uniformity became evident in Daghestan, for example. In 1928, 12 local languages were used in the schools of that area, but by 1948 the number had been reduced to 7. One administrator from Daghestan expressed his regret that "for fifteen to twenty years the position of the languages has been endangered. They have not been used in schools or elsewhere."

The death of Stalin and the rise of Khrushchev inaugurated the third phase. Pressure toward centralization was relaxed so far as language policy was concerned, but only hesitantly. The 1960 and 1961 Party Programmes, while emphasizing the separate identities of the several nations and nationalities, still gave the main emphasis to "the growing together of the nations of the Union and the achievement of their complete unity." Khrushchev proposed to ease the burden of linguistic studies carried by students who might have to study the basic language of their Union Republic (as it might be Georgian), the lingua franca (Russian), their own mother tongue if it happened to be neither of these (Armenian, for instance), and a foreign language. But pedagogically constructive though these proposals were, they were not appreciated by those who feared the competitive power of Russian over the national languages if parents were allowed to choose between them, as Khrushchev suggested. His policy of balancing competing interests did not succeed in establishing a modus vivendi for the lingua franca and the national languages in the Union Republics.

As general disaffection with Khrushchev increased, the antipluralist interests were able to regain control of nationality and language policies. This was reinforced when Brezhnev came to power and the reversal of policy constitutes the fourth phase of the development of bilingual education policy. In 1971, after making the expected reference to the "diversity of to-day's Soviet reality" Brezhnev claimed that the problems raised by that diversity had been solved and had been irrevocably consigned to the past" (*Pravda 11*:4.71). Clearly the justification of attempting to reconcile the interests of those who favored centralism and Russian and those who favored the diversity which alone makes sense of any policy for bilingual education was questioned at the highest level. But whatever the leaders might wish to believe, the realities of Soviet life make it difficult for questions concerning bilingual education to be relegated to the limbo of history. To secure universal literacy in a multinational/multilingual state necessitates the teaching and use of the mother tongues of a large diversity of ethnic groups, and this has to be continued generation after generation. The fact that the present generation of Soviet citizens are literate is no guarantee that the next will also be literate unless the national languages continue to have a place in the system of education. This implies that the problems raised by diversity are permanent. Consequently so long as the provision of education *in general* is to be extended or even to be maintained at its present high level the problems connected with bilingual education will occupy a central area of Soviet educational thinking.

The Extension of Bilingual Education and Language Planning

Bilingualism and Bilingual Education

Arutyunyan, in his discussion of the interaction of cultures among the peoples of the USSR, distinguishes between on the one hand the "cultural fund" which corresponds largely with the sum of cultural traits or the contents of the cultures, and on the other "the consumption of culture," namely, the extent to which the people are able to take advantage of the culture. The important task he argues is to "analyse the consumption of culture and not the cultural fund, to analyse how widely some or other features of culture are spread among the people" (1973). This is a useful distinction so far as the study of bilingual education is concerned. Bilingualism itself is an element in the cultural fund, while bilingual education is an aspect of the consumption of culture, a means by which the advantages of the fund can be appropriated by the people and extended. However, insofar as institutions are employed to ensure that the advantages of an element of the culture are enjoyed by more and more people, the nature of the element itself is transformed. For instance, bilingualism as an element of the culture is usually fortuitous, the results of the accidents of history, of war and other forms of conflict, or cooperation. But bilingual education is nothing if it is not planned at almost every level of social life, political, economic, and demographic as well as linguistic. In turn planning modifies the nature of the phenomenon which it handles: fortuitous bilingualism within the system of education changes from oral to literate, and forms of bilingualism which were hitherto experienced by a few, for instance, bilingualism based on the acquisition of French among the Russian elite, becomes the possession of large masses of young people in secondary schools.

In any analysis of bilingual education in the Soviet Union, therefore, what we are necessarily concerned with is the impact of various types of planning on the original cultural element. Educational planning in the Soviet Union has the same characteristics as economic planning: it is planning within the context of highly centralized control for development, and for a high rate of growth as well as for the transformation of the structure of society. So far as bilingual education is concerned, such planning influences not only the physical provision, buildings, for example, and the production of sufficient teachers of the respective languages, but also the research and development programs which affect pedagogy strictly so called, new methods and new teaching materials. Conversely the planning of bilingual education is judged in the Soviet Union by its success or failure to produce a scientifically oriented generation as well as social uniformation. The study of Russian by all Soviet children is not simply a pedagogical issue but "a powerful means of educating the rising generation to Soviet patriotism, proletarian internationalism and devotion to the Communist party" (*Uch. Gaz.* *11*:12.69). The nature of bilingualism in the Soviet Union is determined by the success attending social aspects of planning, especially educational and linguistic planning.

Vernacular Literacy

It is not only because of the Communist Party's wish to raise the educational level of the peoples of the Union as an end in itself that the expansion of bilingual education was planned, but also because it was realized that only by ensuring reasonably equal opportunities for all nationalities could a modernized, socially mobilized multinational state be created. This meant that some nationalities would have to be brought on faster than others simply to catch up with the more advanced. The candidates for more rapid advancement were the nations most concerned with the interaction of several cultures and languages, like those in Central Asia. The success of their plans can be judged by the fact that by 1969 while the number of students in general education schools in the whole of the USSR was five times the number in 1914, among some nationalities the development was even greater. In Buryat Mongolia there were only 48 schools in 1914, but within 20 years the number was 700. In the Far North the very few and sparsely attended schools of the prerevolutionary period increased to 600, with boarding schools for all the children of hunters, fishermen, and reindeer breeders. In Bashkira the increase between 1914 and 1930 was 200%, and by 1969 the 1914 figure had been increased tenfold. Even the very large nations, such as those of the Transcaucasus and Central Asia, showed only slightly less rapid advances. While the RSFSR student population increased from over 5½ million in 1914 to over 28 million in 1969 and the advance of the Ukraine and other developed European Soviet countries was roughly of the same order, the number of school places in Uzbekistan in 1969 was well over 150 times greater than in 1914. In Tadzhikstan it was 1200 times greater. In Kazakhstan the figure in 1969 was 24 times greater than in 1914. When we consider differences not in the total increase of school places but in the rate of growth of secondary education in the European Soviet countries and the countries of Central Asia, the picture is very favorable to the latter. Between 1939 and 1970, the number of children of 10 and over who obtained secondary education in the USSR as a whole increased from 1.1 million to 4.8 million. In the Uzbek, Kirgiz, Tadzhik, and Turkmen SSRs the average increase was twice as great (*Tadzh. Sov.*, Apr. 18, 1971). The difference in the rate of development of education has meant that the national languages have been able to adapt themselves to new roles in education and in other aspects of social life as well.

To enable themselves to fulfill these new roles the speakers of the national languages needed to become literate, and the increase in literacy in the several languages is even more pronounced than the expansion of general education. The campaign to develop vernacular literacy was waged from the beginning of the

Soviet era, although the amount of literacy in some even small nationalities like the Chuvash and the so-called Baptist Tatars of the Volga was not inconsiderable even before the Revolution. This was true also of the Oriots of the Altai, the Abkhazians, Kabardin, and Ossetes. Some Finno-Ugrian groups had also developed a literature, and the level of literacy among them was higher than elsewhere. But generally speaking the overall picture of literacy in the Soviet Union even in 1926 was gloomy. For the whole of the USSR the percentage was 56.6 and in the European countries of the Union approximately 60%. Among the Transcaucasians and Central Asians the levels were exceedingly low—Azerbaydzhan, 28.2%; Kirgiz, 16.5%; Tadzhik, 3.8%; Turkmen, 14%; Armenian, 38.7%. Of this group only the Georgians exceeded 50% literacy. In 1959, however, the lowest level of literacy was 95.4% (the Turkmen SSR), and this is only 3% below the level for the Russian Republic.

The increase in vernacular literacy was even greater among the smaller nationalities, the figures for 1926 and 1959 being as follows in some of these: Karakalpaks, 13 and 51%; Uigur, 4.5 and 55%; Yakut, 2 and 96.3%; Chukchi, 6 and 54%. It is true that a great deal still remains to be done in reducing the gaps between the levels of literacy in some of the major languages and the languages of the smaller nationalities, but the present position is such that large proportions of all those ethnic groups whose languages have been alphabeticized can if they wish be educated in their mother tongue. Previously these languages could be ignored by educationists and the only kind of bilingualism open to the speakers of most of the languages was entirely oral. Making the national languages the foundation of universal literacy has helped to ensure the high percentages claiming the national language as their mother tongue (Table 1). Consequently however desirable to political strategy merging nationalities and the creation of a uniform Soviet people as well as a one type culture may be, it is recognized by sociolinguists and educationists that the "path to the future rapprochment between nations lies through a prolonged and many faceted development of . . . their languages. The CPSU acknowledges that in the area of mutual national relations haste . . . is particularly inadmissable" (*Pravda*, Oct. 17, 1966). In other words, long-term provision for bilingual education is inevitable.

Language Planning

The extension of bilingual education and the increase in vernacular literacy could be achieved only after intensive planning. In the Soviet Union such planning has affected the development of languages in several ways. Decisions were taken which meant virtually the extinction of some languages. Where steps were taken to maintain languages, planning helped in some instances to extend and in other cases to limit the range of their social functions, so that they became available for only the early stages of education and for only restricted use in mass media. Finally, the extent to which two or more languages interacted and influenced each other and the manner in which that influence was exerted were consciously planned within the context of highly centralized research organizations and other academic agencies. In the first place alphabets were created for some languages that had previously not been written. In the case of almost as many more languages "unsuitable" alphabets were modified. Though alphabet reform had begun about the middle of the 19th Century, it was not until the need for universal education as the foundation for social mobilization became imperative that such reform made any significant headway. Because of pressure to promote social unification from the center rather than to attempt to realize a pluralist concept, a single alphabetic base was approved, Latin in the first instance (as a means of dissociating the Central Asians from closely related non-Soviet literature and cultures) and subsequently Cyrillic (as a means of reinforcing the influence of Russian).

The second necessary step was to standardize languages like Buryat, which at the beginning of the Soviet era consisted of a number of dialects which differed greatly, like Khorin, Selenga, Tsongal, and others. Only a very few Lamaists possessed a written approach to Mongolian languages of which Buryat is one. Buryat itself had no written form and was unstandardized. Its alphabeticization was completed in the 1920s and the standard literary language was evolved on the basis of the Khorin dialect. This meant that the Buryats were consolidated as a self-conscious nationality, aware of a national language and anxious to extend its use. Similar processes have been observed among the Altaians as a result of the standardization of their language on the basis of the southern dialects. The past decades have seen the standardization of the Khakass language, thus creating a self-conscious nationality of the five Tiurk-speaking tribes, the Kachin, Koibal, Sagai, Beltir, and Kyzyl. Some of the major languages also experienced the same planning. Uzbek was standardized in the first instance on the basis of the South Kazhakstan dialect, for which the dialect of Tashkent was later substituted. In the case of Tadzhik the northwestern dialect, Plains Tadzhik, was selected.

In the case of the North Caucasus none of the languages had become standardized, in none of them was a literature available, and none could be used in schools. Even those of Daghestan, such as Avar, Dargin, and Lak written in Arabic characters, could be read only by a small erudite group of scholars. In other areas of the Caucasus, especially the eastern and central districts, none of the languages such as Chechen, Ingush, Kabardin, Adyge, Balkar, and Osset had progressed beyond the oral stage. In many of these languages during the process of standardization new phonological and morphological elements were introduced. The syntactic structures of the standardized language were constantly regulated in many cases; consequently the standard language had to be acquired in ways that were very different from the customary casual and fortuitous oral fashion—the languages had to be taught in school. Furthermore many of the new elements were the result of contact with other languages. This happened with Udmurt, which introduced 12 supplementary consonant phonemes from Russian. The Kabardin and Yakut languages, when standardized, went through the same process of assimilating contact elements. The study of these contact languages became necessary in order to ensure that the separate languages developed according to their own inherent characteristics. Thus standardization was necessary to the possibility of bilingual education and the latter in turn ensured the satisfactory development of those languages which were involved.

It is in the "augmentation" of the lexical content of the languages that planning, especially planning with the intention of promoting the influence of Russian, is most evident. The process of "lexical augmentation" affects the most well-developed languages such as Georgian and Armenian as much as it does the languages of very small minorities. For instance, by 1950 a Special Terminology Commission had approved 18,000 new medical terms and 13,000 new legal terms together with other specialized items, most of them from Russian or borrowed from international sources via Russian. A Terminology Commission in the Kirgiz Academy of sciences has been systematizing scientific vocabulary and has published 70 different lexicons on 44 branches of learning. "Maximum use is made of native language resources, but at the same time priority is given to keeping international words with wide use of their untranslated Russian forms, thereby fostering unification of all national terminologies and bringing Kirgiz closer to Russian" (*Sov. Kirg. 10*:4.73). It has been claimed that in "most Soviet languages 70 to 80% of the new terms have been borrowed from Russian" (*Vyshka 20*:6.72). The language planners work on the "principle of minimum discrepancy" (*printsip minimal'nykh rashkozdentsiy*) so that the standardization and augmentation of other languages operate in such a way as to ensure that all languages are brought closer to Russian (Desheriev and Procenko 1968).

Finally, the publication of literature in the nationality languages is an integral part of language planning in the Soviet Union. Publication is one way of justifying planning processes while the publications themselves reinforce the aims of language planners to establish close links between nationality languages and Russian. Books and periodicals are now published in languages which are spoken by fewer than 100,000 people, or as in the case of Eskimo fewer than 10,000, and which prior to 1920 had no alphabets. The greatest impact of publishing has been on the Central Asian languages, which although they might have Arabic scripts were rarely used for general publishing. For instance, within the 50 years between 1913 and 1963 the number of new titles appearing in Kazakh rose from 40 to 187. By 1964, this figure had risen to 500 and in the next 3 years the total had been raised to 557. No books were published in Kirgiz before 1920, but by 1947, 4.5 million copies of new books had been published. By 1967, the number of copies produced had become 2.8 million. Publications in Uzbek rose from 37 titles in 1913 to 700 in 1957, and this figure was raised to 794 by the end of 1966. At present the Uzbek SSR has 234 newspapers and 51 magazines distributed in the Uzbek, Russian, Tadzhik, and Karakalpak languages (*Pravda Vostoka 5*:5.72). Equally significant are the publishing figures for the smaller nationalities like Mari, Mordvin, and Bashkir with 135 titles in 1966 where there had been none prior to 1925. In Daghestan many of the small linguistic groups like Lak and Dargin had 28 publications each in 1966 (*Nar. Khoz.* 1968). Without these publications, many of them designed specifically for teaching, there would be little possibility of bilingual education and little point in attempting to provide it.

THE ORGANIZATION OF BILINGUAL EDUCATION—
TYPES OF SCHOOLS AND PROGRAMS

Dynamic Aspects of Bilingual Education

The Soviet Definition of Bilingualism

Bilingual education in the Soviet Union, depending on whether it is looked at from the standpoint of the bureaucracy as a means of promoting the Russian language or from the standpoint of the local intelligentsia as a safeguard for the nationality language, is simultaneously dynamic and conservative. However, in most of the literature concerned with the subject it is the dynamic aspects which attract attention, to the extent that bilingualism tends to be limited to the acquisition of Russian as a second language rather than comprehending all cases where two or more languages, whatever their status, are acquired by the student. For instance, Desheriev and his associates, in listing "the questions posed by the existence of the multinational Soviet State," refer to "bilingualism—the cultivation of the native language and the cultivation of the Russian language among non-Russian populations of the USSR" (*Kommunist 1965*:13, p. 55). Baskakov makes a distinction between "bilingualism (local language and Russian)" and what he refers to as "more complicated inter-lingual relationships . . . of minorities who in addition to the local and Russian languages also know the language of the basic indigenous Republic they reside in" (Baskakov 1973). The most explicit identification of bilingual education with the learning of Russian as a second language appears in *Vestnik. Akad. Nauk SSSR 11*:72, 3-11, where integration is referred to as "the development of bilingualism, i.e. the non-Russian mastering Russian." The scholarly discussion of bilingual education does its best to limit the concept to the promotion of Russian.

There are several reasons for this dynamism of Russian-related bilingualism apart from the demographic factors to which reference is made later. In the first place, the percentage of Russian-speaking bilinguals is much higher in every Republic than bilingualism arising from the acquisition of local languages only, and this disparity is increased by the fact that the latter type of bilingualism would involve the mother tongue and one of several and not simply a single local language in any Republic (Table 1). Second, the Russian language is *the* language of the Communist Party wherever that Party operates in the Union. It is the one language which has an entry to all party discussions and therefore the one language which carries political influence. "The process of voluntary study not only of one's native language but of Russian has a positive significance as it promotes mutual exchange of experience and familiarization of each nation and nationality with the achievements of all the other peoples of the USSR" (CPSU

Programme, p. 115). While all languages are equal by statute, "this should not be confused with equality of social function, which cannot be the case in a multinational state" (*Cina 8*:9.72, p. 2). Russian has appropriated more of the important and prestige social functions than other languages and is continuing to do so: "It would be wrong not to see that the study of the Russian language is progressive, that it must be encouraged and supported as the seedling of innovation" (Rogachev and Suerdlin 1963).

Third, Russian has a dynamic role because it is the foundation for the "free interchange of cadres." The policy of exchanging administrators and functionaries as well as technologists between the Union Republics was well developed in Khrushchev's time: it is one of the characteristics of student life also. During 1963-1964, to take a period of only moderate exchange rates among students, over 139,000 students were enrolled for higher education in Uzbekistan, 25,000 in Kirgizstan, 24,000 in Tadzhikstan, and 17,000 in Turkestan. Less than half the students in the institutions of higher education in these Union Republics were indigenous; and even allowing for the permanent settlement of nonnationals in these areas, very high student exchange rates appear to be implied.

A fourth aspect of the dynamism of the Russian language is entirely linguistic. "The experience of the USSR peoples has shown that the Russian language has played and will play a historically important role in the development of the national languages," both directly and as the "intermediary of the influence of other world languages" (*Vyshka 20*:6.72. pp. 2-3). It is more and more apparent that there is a tendency in the Soviet Union to rely on linguistic as distinct from ideological integration as the means of creating a "Soviet nation and a one type culture." It is the Russian language which is regarded as the spearhead of uniformation: "It is important for educational reasons and because it is inseparable from the unifying work of the Party" (*Okutucilar Gazetasi 14*:7.68). Because of this dynamic characteristic of Russian-related bilingualism, Soviet social scientists have recommended that the linguistic assimilation of non-Russians should be attempted at progressively early ages and especially at a "pre-competitive stage of personality formation" (Arutyunyan 1969:39). According to this view, the Russian language is conceived as entering into a bilingual relationship only temporarily and as the first phase of eventual linguistic assimilation.

Education is the principal agent of this dynamism, and it is here that the promotion of Russian is most carefully planned. One effect is the elimination of other languages from the system of education. For instance, according to the 1927 Belorussian School Census, there were 213 Jewish schools in the Republic—202 in which Yiddish was the only language used, 7 in which Yiddish and Russian were used, and 4 where Yiddish and Belorussian were the languages of instruction. In the Ukraine in 1930 there were 786 Yiddish schools, and over 830 in 1931. The numbers increased everywhere, except in the Russian Republic, until the middle of the 1930s. Nevertheless Yiddish is not used or even taught in any part of the USSR at present, although the total number of Soviet Jews in

1970 was 2.15 million, of whom 18% claimed Yiddish or another Jewish language as their native language. In the Russian Republic there were over 800,000 Jews, of whom 12% claimed Yiddish or another Jewish dialect as their native tongue, while 9.6% claimed it as their second language. The great majority of these receive their education in Russian and the rest in a local language. There are, of course, several reasons for the elimination of Yiddish from the schools, some of them connected with divisions among the Jews themselves about the acceptability of secular schools and the relative importance of Yiddish and Hebrew. Some of the causes are connected with the urbanization and dispersal of the Jewish communities; but the main reason is a policy decision to remove Yiddish from the curriculum. The Jewish case is only the most extreme example of the general tendency to promote the Russian language at the expense of other languages.

Even if it is claimed that the teaching of Russian is not planned actually to replace a national language in the school, aspects of the teaching of that language are geared to facilitate the acquisition of Russian as a second language. For Galazov a "well organised teaching of the national language promotes a deeper mastery of the Russian language and consequently all the subjects of the curriculum taught through Russian" (1965:53). Similarly Baskakov reminds those who are concerned with language planning that while "it is essential that the orthographies should be based on the phonetic and grammatical structures of the national languages, at the same time they should not depart too abruptly from the existing features of the Russian orthography. The formulation of such an orthography would help to a considerable degree in avoiding difficulties in teaching Russian in national schools" (Baskakov 1960:40). The second edition of the Great Soviet Encyclopaedia comments that "transfer . . . to the Russian script not only helped to improve the national languages but also served greatly to facilitate the acquisition of Russian by speakers of those national languages" (vol. 33, 99).

The Russian Language in Bilingual Education

Teaching Russian as a second language. Twenty years after the resolution of the 7th Russian Conference of the Communist Party in April 1917 had called for the "abolition of a compulsory state language" it was decreed that Russian should be taught to all students of the Soviet Union whatever their nationality. For some time after 1938 the teaching commenced in the third grade, but it has been common practice for a long time for Russian to be introduced in the middle of the first class, and not later than the second. In spite of this early introduction, the professional journals as recently as 1972-1973 have given space to considerable criticism of the quality of Russian among students who are nonnative speakers of the language. The Minister of Education for the Uzbek SSR, having stressed the fact that Russian is taught from the first to the tenth grade in all schools, that 14% of school time is devoted to the language, and that there were nearly 12,000 Russian language teachers in the Republic, concludes that a great deal remains to be done to raise attainment in Russian to even a moderately satisfactory standard (*Pravda Vostoka 19*:3.73). The Collegium of the USSR Ministry of Education criticized the quality of the results in Estonia and Turkestan and instructed all non-Russian schools to broaden the *use* of Russian in school work and extracurricular activities (*Nar. Obraz. 6*:1972, pp. 114-115). The same criticism was voiced in Azerbaydzhan where the teachers are criticized for their reluctance to attend refresher courses in the language (*Uch. Gaz. July 18*:1972, p. 2). In Kirgizia the indifferent quality of the Russian teachers is stressed as well as the lack of such teachers, good or bad, especially in the rural areas. More than 50% of the girls (Kirgiz, Uzbeks, Uigurs, Dungans, and Tatars) entering the first-year course of the language faculty of the Kirgiz Pedagogical Institute for Women and preparing to become teachers of Russian have a very limited knowledge of the language, and a sizable number of even fourth year students are unable to construct a Russian sentence correctly. Only those who had received all their secondary education through the medium of Russian could be regarded as satisfactory (*Uch. Gaz. 1*:2.72. p. 2).

The attitude to Russian studies in the Georgian SSR lends itself to the most sustained attack of all. An editorial in *Zarya Vostoka* (10:7.73) follows a report of the February meeting of the Central Committee of the Georgian Communist Party in which a long list of shortcomings were itemized. The editorial maintains that the quality of Russian teaching has deteriorated in the last 15 years and the training which the teachers receive is unsatisfactory. The University of Tbilisi has ceased to take an interest in the problem, and other measures are called for to retrain (*perepodgotovka*) the teachers of Russian and Russian literature. New textbooks and ancillary materials are called for. So bad is the position of Russian in Georgia, it is maintained, that members of the highest professions, leaders of the Komsomol and experts in economics, have a very poor knowledge of Russian. The effect of this kind of situation in Georgia and other Republics is that the planned program of transfer from national language instruction to Russian medium is delayed because knowledge of the language does not reach the minimum standard necessary. Desheriev (1968:60-61) criticizes efforts that were made in the Volga and North Caucasus regions to transfer pupils from classes where teaching was in the native language to Russian-medium classes not because this step was undesirable but simply because it was impracticable—the "level of bilingualism in Russian and the national language was too low to make the transfer a practical proposition."

Partly because of this unsatisfactory position at the end of even higher education the teaching of Russian has been brought forward into preschool classes. Six-year-old children are introduced to Russian in informal ways but before they receive formal instruction in the mother tongue. In 1946, the establishment of these classes was approved in Daghestan as well as among Buryats, Kabardins, and Yakuts. In 1965, Tbilisi saw the establishment of the first of these classes in Georgia, and although the step caused some controversy (*Izvestia*, Apr. 24, 1972) it was envisaged that the provision would be extended.

In Kirgizia classes in Russian for non-Russians have been established since 1965. Although preschool nursery classes for children between 2 months and 3 years, and kindergarten for those between 3 and 7 years are voluntary, they are an important part of the preparation for bilingual education. In 1968, there were nearly 9 million places. Nevertheless the provision is said to be inadequate.

The intention is that they should enable a language other than the mother tongue to compete with the influence of the home and the immediate neighborhood in establishing which language is dominant in a child's linguistic repertoire, and they "help to avoid failure later in the school course. Teaching occurs during 35 weeks of the year and the Russian classes last 35 minutes daily" (*Uch. Gaz. 15*:2.73). In October 1971 at a conference held at Frunze, teachers reported on their experience of these preparatory classes, and it was evident that many teachers objected to what they conceived to be one of the results of such classes, namely, the increasing tendency to transfer from the national to the Russian language as a medium of instruction (*Sov. Ped. 6*:72, 148-150). One variant of the preschool provision is adopted by many if not most rural schools. They organize courses of about 6 weeks' duration immediately prior to entry to the elementary school so that the children may familiarize themselves with a basic Russian vocabulary and the sounds of the language (*Russ.yaz.v nats.schk.4*:65, 45-47).

Russian language schools for non-Russians. Even during the period when the national languages were favorably regarded in education, schools where Russian was used as the sole medium of instructing nonnative speakers of the language were popular and formed one of the most important strands in the pattern of bilingual education. Theoretically, nevertheless, Lenin argued that "the tendency to make Russian the language of teaching rather than the subject of study . . . is harmful and wrong" (Sovetskin 1958:36). In spite of this caution the percentage of Russian-medium schools for non-Russians increased so that by 1956, 14% of all Ukrainian schools, 27% of Moldavian schools, 27% of the schools in Latvia, and over 40% of Kazakh schools were of this character. In the Transcaucasus and Central Asia the proportions tended to be much lower, averaging 3%. In the Tadzhik SSR, although these schools constituted only 2% of the total, they accounted for 16% of the pupil enrollment in the Republic. Among Turkmens the number of children attending Russian-medium schools for non-Russians constituted 20% of the total in 1964 and among Azerbaydzhanis 24%. In the cities the proportion of non-Russians attending Russian-medium schools tended to be higher than the average. In Ashkabad in 1964, 87% of the schools belonged to this category. Naturally, they tended to attract most if not all the children of Russian immigrants, but often the percentage of non-Russians was equal to them. In Georgia and Azerbaydzhan the number of children attending Russian-medium schools was twice as high as the number of Russians in the Republic would appear to justify. In Lithuania 11% of all students were taught in Russian, though the percentage of Russians in Lithuania in 1959 was only 8.5%. In Latvia the respective percentages were 33 and 26% and in Estonia 22 and 20%.

Even if students begin attending elementary schools where they are taught in their native tongue, the tendency is for them to transfer to Russian-medium instruction sometimes in the elementary school but most frequently when they enter or during early grades in secondary school. In 1958, the majority of minority children in the Russian Republic transferred at some stage from national language instruction to Russian. The only exceptions were Tatars and Bashkirs. Generally speaking, the children of nationalities living in autonomous oblasts did not receive any secondary instruction in their own language. Smaller nationalities usually transfer to Russian after the first two years of elementary school (Sovetskin 1958:23). In 1965-1966, the transfer of all teaching from the native language to Russian was decreed in the Kabardin-Balkar ASSR, and this began with the transfer of 50% of the second grade in all schools (*Russ.yaz. v nat. schkole* 4:65). In North Ossetia all students transfer to Russian-medium instruction in the fifth grade (*Nar. Obraz. 12*:1962; 6; 1964). In some Autonomous Republics the transfer begins in the third grade, although the practice in most areas is to arrange the transfer in grades 4 to 8 (*Sov. Ped. 6*:72).

The exclusively Russian-medium schools for non-Russians and the schools where transfer to Russian at some point is a regular feature of the organization tend to be in the urban areas. This is true of the Tatar ASSR (*Russ.yaz. v. nat.schkole 6*:1963) and Daghestan (*Sov. ethnog. 6*:1965, 98-99). Therefore, the students who are taught in Russian profit from the advantages of equipment and teaching facilites which urban schools enjoy whatever their language of instruction may be. This purely urban advantage appears to parents and administrators to have a necessary association with Russian, and this impression is fostered. The Minister of Education for North Ossetia, for instance, claimed that "children having instruction in Russian from the first grade onwards receive a better general education" (*Narod. Obraz.* 1965:78). The main advantage derives from the reluctance of teachers to go into the rural and national language schools. In 1973, it was complained that teachers trained to teach Russian used every subterfuge to avoid going outside the urban areas. In Armenia in 1972, for instance, 297 of the 453 students graduating from the Erevan Institute of Russian and Foreign Languages did not undertake any kind of pedagogical work rather than go into rural schools; and of those who became teachers very few taught in rural schools. The Party Central Committee and the USSR Council of Ministers issued a document "On Measures for the Further Improvement of Conditions for the Work of the Rural General School" (*Pravda 6*:73), which referred to the serious shortcomings of such schools. Generally speaking, they are the non-Russian schools and in consequence the use of a national language as a teaching language acquires a low prestige by association with rural education. The converse of this is that Russian-medium schools in urban areas reinforce attitudes favorable to Russian. The extent of a person's general education, the level of his knowledge of Russian and especially graduation from the Russian-medium school produce very favorable attitudes to the Russian language and culture (Arutyunyan 1969:12, 129-139).

The "integrated school" or parallel medium instruction. In countries where the main thrust of bilingual education is exerted by minorities seeking to safeguard their language against the penetration of a major language which is already entrenched, the dynamics of bilingual education is reflected in nationality schools. In the Soviet Union, where outside the Russian Republic and the Ukraine the national languages are maintained very strongly by the vast majority of the people, the main thrust is toward the establishment of Russian as a subject and as the language of instruction. In this case the dynamism of bilingual education is most characteristic of the rapid expansion of Russian-medium schools and classes for non-Russians, and more recently in the expansion of integrated schools where Russian and one (sometimes as many as four or five) other language may be used to teach the different nationalities.

The rationale which is offered for the integrated school is complex. In the first place, these schools bear the hallmark of Lenin's approval. In 1913, with reference to the Jews of Odessa, he opposed separate schools, whether Russian or nationality schools. "It is in the interests of the working class to unite children of all nationalities in integrated schools" (*Soch. XVII*:108-109). Following this lead, parallel-medium schools were popular in the 1920s. In the Ukraine, 7% of the children attended such schools, and in Kharkov province the figures were as high as 49% (*Stat. Ukr. 1928*). These schools were and still are regarded as the cradles of international understanding. Secondary school No. 55 in Riga was reported in 1966 as having provided parallel Latvian and Russian classes for over 6 years, with the result that more than 1000 Latvians had learned to live as one family. This estimate of their achievement is confirmed by the experience of foreign observers. One of these, visiting Central Asia in 1965, agreed that the "multinational co-education/integrated school apart from its primary aim of Russification and *sblizhenie*, in practice means that from their earliest years young Slavs, Kazakhs, Kirgiz, Tadzhiks and many other Asian nationalities . . . are working together and playing together. This co-education may go far to destroy the racial and linguistic barriers among Central Asian nationalities which were formerly endemic here" (*Central Asian Rev. 1965*:13).

Other reasons than the promotion of international understanding are held to justify the establishment of integrated schools. Some schools carry instruction in three or more languages, and in these cases, where the numbers in any one ethnic or linguistic track are too small to make separate schools possible and where the parents are disinclined to opt for the lingua franca there is no option but to organize parallel classes. This is one of the main reasons for the establishment of such schools in Lithuania where, in 1964, the Minister of Education stated that in "every Lithuanian and Polish school . . . the children are taught in one of three languages—Polish, Russian and Lithuanian" (*Izvestia Feb. 1964*). Children in some Bashkir schools are taught in one of six languages—Russian, Tatar, Bashkir, Chuvash, Mari, and Udmurt. However, although it may be administrative difficulties which make the establishment of integrated schools necessary, it is not denied that the result is to promote the Russian language, and that this is one of the aims. It was reported in 1965 that even though the children may not be taught in Russian, since the language of play is Russian and Russian is also the language of the school administration and of extracurricular activities, the integrated school is a useful instrument in the advancement of Russian-related bilingualism (*Narod. Obraz. 1965*).

The Baltic Republics, especially Latvia, are the areas where integrated schools have flourished most successfully. They were started there in 1946 when approximately 30,000 school places were provided. By 1965-1966 the number had been more than trebled, representing over a third of the total school population. The number of integrated schools in the Republic during the same school year was 240 (*Pravda*, 1966:5, 4). However, there was considerable difference in the treatment of Russian and Lettish as second languages in these schools. In the Lettish-medium classes Russian was taught for 1685 hours annually while Lettish in Russian-medium classes was taught for less than half that time, 830 hours annually. In spite of these differences, over 80% of the Letts surveyed in 1966 (Kholmogorov 1970) approved of integrated schools in preference to other types of bilingual schools. Among the non-Letts surveyed the percentage who approved was even higher, 84.5%. Only 3.8% expressed their disapproval of the integrated school.

In the thirties in Turkestan, 12% of the pupils attended integrated schools, but by 1965 the percentage had dropped to 7% (*Kulturnaya Strana 1956*:186). The number of parallel Azerbaydzhan and Russian schools increased from 158 in 1940 to 183 in 1953, 231 in 1959 and to over 300 at present (*Azer. v tsifrakh 1970*). In Uzbekistan the proportion of pupils in such schools was nearly 20% in 1963 (*Voprosy Filologii* 6:11). In the Tashkent Oblast, 50% of the children attended integrated schools, while in Kirgizia there were over 300 such schools in 1964 (*Kommunist 1964*:12, 19). Kazakhstan in 1962 had nearly 2000 schools with classes which were taught in Russian and one or more of the national language. The boarding schools were often similar to integrated schools (*Pravda 1962*:29, 5). In the schools of the Nenetz National District of the Northern Territories, "Parallel primary grades have been established in schools with a mixed national composition. In classes with Nenetz or Komi children teaching is conducted in the languages of these nationalities. From the third grade on children of all nationalities are no longer educated in parallel classes but together (*Narod. Obraz. 1967*:6).

Conservative Aspects of Bilingual Education

Attitude to Nationality Schools

The constitution of the Soviet Union, Article 121 (1960 ed.) reaffirms the 1936 enactment of the right to use the nationality languages in education. In 1962, the USSR ratified the UNESCO Convention against Discrimination in Education which obliged all its signatories to recognize the right of members of national minorities to carry on their own educational activities including the maintenance of schools and the use or teaching of their own languages. This has always been the policy of the Soviet Union, however much it may have departed from the strict interpretation of that policy from time to time. With their rights so enshrined, it is hardly surprising that among the nationalities and especially among the core nations of the Union Republics there should be the strongest attachment to the native languages. Among educationists the most widespread expression of this attachment occurred during the discussions of Thesis 19 of Khrushchev's proposed Law on the Strengthening of the Relationship of the School and Life and on the Further Development of the System of Education in the USSR (*Pravda 1958*:25.12). The Thesis stated, "Instruction in the Soviet School is carried on in the native language"; and having made the expected reference to the importance of Russian, it draws attention to the position of the national schools which have to offer three languages, the basic language of the Republic, Russian, and a foreign language together with the mother tongue of any of the students if it does not coincide with the language of the Republic or Russian. The Thesis then proposes that parents should be allowed to select from among these languages—that is, to omit the study of the mother tongue, or the language of the Republic or Russian. It must be conceded that whatever other motives there may have been the net effect of this suggestion, if adopted, would be advantageous to students heavily burdened with linguistic studies. But there was little inclination to accept the suggestion at its face value, and the discussions served only to emphasize the fear of the further penetration of Russian into the system of education, as well as the deep-seated attachment to the national languages among representatives of the Union Republic Ministers of Education.

Many of those who took part in the Moscow Conference proposed "that in schools of the Union and Autonomous Republics the study of Russian and the native language should be obligatory on all pupils" (*Izvestiya 24*:12.58). This certainly reflected the mood of the Armenian delegation who argued that by far the greater proportion of students remained to work in their respective Republics, so that knowledge of the basic language of the Republic was a major consideration for them. The Azerbaydzhan press supported the arguments in favor of the teaching and use of the national language in the Republic schools, often in preference to Russian. The First Secretary of the Communist Party in Georgia supported obligatory teaching of Georgian as the "language of the Republic in which a young boy or girl will be living and working." This, he argued, would make a positive contribution to the "international upbringing of the new generation and not simply reinforce their local affiliations" (*Pravda 1958*:2.12). In some Republics it was proposed that the national language should be safeguarded by delaying the introduction of Russian until the fifth grade. The strongest expressions of support for the national languages came from the Ministers of the Baltic Republics, who went on record as stating that any change adversely affecting the use and teaching of Latvian, for instance, would endanger the friendship of the Latvian and Russian People. Nevertheless the 7th Plenum of the Latvian Communist Party condemned the intention which was strongly approved by supporters of the national language to make Lettish a required subject for non-Letts.

Even though the support at all levels of a particular Republic for the national language might be very strong, the "conservative" nature of the arguments in favor of the use and teaching of the language could not be disguised.

Few if any of the protagonists of the national languages employed more than two arguments—first, that the national language would remain the only language which most of the workers would need since they were unlikely to work in other areas; and second, that the nationalities were tied by strong historical associations with the Republic languages. One aspect of this "conservative" attitude is the adoption of a linguistic policy which sets out to limit the social development of national languages. "The correct policy in the linguistic development of the national languages of the multinational state," Desheriev argues, "should be to promote the vital *internal* or *local* needs of each people, while the study of Russian should be extended so as to provide for all the wider, international communication demands" (Desheriev et al. 1966:81). The Republic Ministers of Education would not have dissented from this limited view.

This is still Desheriev's standpoint. Basing his thesis on the assumption that "Planning the development of any language's social function hinges on . . . the level of the people's political and economic development, its possession of statehood, the size of the population speaking the language, the existence of a second language that performs extensive social functions, etc.," his attitude suggests that the future of the Soviet languages should be planned to allow for the extension of Russian. There is no suggestion that Georgian or Ukrainian might develop extraterritorial functions. Among the most important patterns in the development of languages at present Desheriev lists the advancement of national languages that have historically achieved a high level of development and have become widespread, e.g., Russian; the conversion of the most highly developed literary languages used in multinational states into languages of international intercourse, e.g., Russian; and the reduction of the number of smaller languages as they are assimilated by the larger literary languages (Desheriev 1973). At no point is the progressive extension of the role of Soviet languages other than Russian envisaged. The languages of nations with classical traditions of their own like some of the Central Asian languages which have developed out of Middle East classical cultures do not appear to be candidates for the extension of their social functions. The case of the smaller languages is even more bleak. Khanti, Mansi, Nannai, and Nenets, though they have been provided with alphabets, "will not become languages of instruction at high school" and will perform "only limited functions in elementary education" (Desheriev 1973:38). So far as the national languages are concerned, this is conservative planning. Progressive planning is reserved for Russian. In these circumstances bilingual education involving only two national languages has no future, while from the standpoint of the national language even bilingualism which involves Russian is only palliative, meant to alleviate the limitation of function imposed upon it and to mitigate any possible distress likely to be caused by its decline.

Extent of Provision for
National Languages in Education

At present 57 languages are used at different grade levels of education in the Soviet Union. The number of nationality schools in the Russian Republic in

Table 4.   Languages of Instruction 1959

Republic	Language used	Total
Russian SFSR	Russian, Tatar, Chuvash, Mordvin, Bashkir, Udmurt, Mari, Komi, Komi-Permyak, Avar, Buryat, Ossetian, Yakut, Lezgin, Kabardin, Dargin, Kumyk, Adygei, Azerbaydzhani, Lak, Khakas, Altai, Nenets, Evenki, Khanti, Chukchi, Koryak, Abazin, Nogai, Tabasaran, Balkar, Kalmyk, Karachai, Ingush, Mansi, Tuvinian, Finnish, Chechen and Even	39
Ukrainian SSR	Ukrainian, Russian, Moldavian, Hungarian, Polish	5
Belorussian	Belorussian, Russian	2
Uzbek SSR	Uzbek, Russian, Kazakh, Tadzhik, Kirgiz, Karakalpak, Turkmen	7
Kazakh SSR	Kazakh, Russian, Uzbek, Tadzhik, Uigur, Dungan	6
Georgian SSR	Georgian, Russian, Armenian, Azerbaydzhani, Ossetian, Abkhaz	6
Azerbaydzhan SSR	Azerbaydzhani, Russian, Armenian, Lezgin	4
Lithuanian SSR	Lithuanian, Russian, Polish	3
Moldavian SSR	Moldavian, Russian, Ukrainian	3
Latvian SSR	Latvian, Russian	2
Kirgiz SSR	Kirgiz, Russian, Uzbek, Tadzhik, Kazakh, Turkmen	5
Tadzhik SSR	Tadzhik, Russian, Uzbek, Kirgiz, Kazakh, Turkmen	6
Armenian SSR	Armenian, Russian, Azerbaydzhani	3
Turkmen SSR	Turkmen, Russian, Uzbek, Kazakh	4
Estonian SSR	Estonian, Russian	2

1955-1956 was 11.8 thousand, and these were attended by approximately one-third of the non-Russian population of the Republic. In the Russian Republic in 1972, of the 42 indigenous ethnic groups, 16 did not have schools which used the nationality language at any stage. These included Kabardin, Balkar, and Kalmyk, smaller groups like Adygei and Cherkess, and very small ones like Mansi and Eskimo. Of the rest only the Bashirs and Tatars had schools where the national language was used from elementary through all secondary grades. Some, like Yakut schools, used the language through grade 8 or grade 7 (Tuvin) or grade 6 (Buryat). The remaining nationalities, where they did make use of their national language in education, confined them to the elementary grades, and some only to the first grade. Two groups which are not indigenous to the Russian Republic, Armenian and Kazakh, have their own schools where the national language is used through grade 10. The situation has deteriorated since 1958, mainly in the sense that transfer to Russian-medium instruction occurs earlier in all schools except those of the Bashkirs, Tatars, Armenians, and Kazakhs where there is no transfer at any point, and in the Yakut schools where the use of Yakut in 1972 occurs a grade later than in 1958. In all other national schools the use of the nationality language in 1972 ceased two or three grades earlier than in 1958 (Sovetskin 1958 and Danilov 1972).

During the early years of the Soviet regime the national languages had a very prominent place in education. In 1927, over 93% of the Ukrainian-speaking children received their elementary education in that language and 83% received their secondary education in Ukrainian, accounting for 73% of the total child population of the Ukraine (Bilinsky 1968:418). Since 1959, the number of schools using Ukrainian has declined from 84 to 82% in 1968 (*Pravda Ukr. 1968*:3. 11, 20), but not all these schools made use of Ukrainian for more than two or three grades. The decline has been greater in urban schools. In 1965, there were only 56 schools in L'vov in which Ukrainian was used for some part of the course, and these constituted only 65% of the total. In Kiev, although speakers of Ukrainian represented 60% of the total population, the schools in which Ukrainian was used provided for only 41% of the child population. In Belorussia in 1927, the situation was similar to that of the Ukraine—90% were taught in their national language. In Georgia and Armenia, 96 and 98.5%, respectively, were taught in their native tongue. Among the Azerbaydzhanis (93.8%), Tatars (77%), and Tadzhiks (54%) the percentages tended to be lower but were still higher than they are at present if we take into account the fact that the schools which employ the national language for some grades at present transfer to Russian much earlier than they did. The decline is apparent also in the number of national languages that may be used in a Union Republic. Thus, in the Uzbek SSR Russian, Tadzhik, Kazakh, Tatar, Korean, Armenian, Yiddish, and several other languages were used as well as Uzbek, in 1935. In 1960-1961 only Uzbek, Russian, Tadzhik, Kirgiz, Turkmen, and Karakalpak were used, and this is the present position.

Schools for Non-Russian Minorities

Some of the nationality languages are not indigenous to a particular Union Republic, and they may be spoken by groups of immigrant populations of varying sizes. We have referred to some of these already, for instance, Armenians and Kazakhs in the Russian Republic. The following languages, whatever proportion of their speakers may be dispersed outside their eponymous Republics, are taught and used only within those Republics—Estonian, Latvian, Lithuanian, and Belorussian. In some cases, like those of the Autonomous Republics, they may be minority languages when considered against the total population of the Union Republic, but within their own limited areas or Autonomous Republics they tend to be the major language. Where this is the case, the use of the language is confined to the Autonomous Republic of which it is the basic language. Russian is the only language where the immigrant Russian minority has its own language schools in every Republic. Of the other languages Uzbek has minority schools in four Republics, Kazakh in four, Tadzhik in four, Tatar in two, and Armenian in two. But in almost every one of these cases the minority schools are on the borders of the Republic where the language is normally spoken. Of equal significance are the number of nationalities with considerable dispersed populations constituting minorities who have no schools in which the language of the dispersed minority is either taught or used. For instance, according to the 1970 Census there were 578,000 Tatars in the Uzbek SSR, 284,000 in Kazakhstan, 69,000 in Kirgizia, and 71,000 in Tadzhikstan, but they ceased to have minority schools before 1959. The same is true of Uzbeks (50,000), Kirgiz (21,000), and Azerbaydzhanis (96,000) and Turkmens (23,000) in the Russian Republic. The position was summed up, with barely disguised critical overtones, by Khanazarov (*Voprosy razvitiya 340*:1960): "During the period of developing Socialist construction in 1938-9 Uzbekistan provided schools where instruction was offered in 22 languages ... The provision even made it possible for a single Polish family to have its child taught .in the mother tongue. The change of policy has recently led to parents sending their children not to minority schools but to Russian medium schools (which may also be minority schools). In Uzbekistan at present there are schools for only 7 language minorities and these are limited to Central Asian languages in addition to Russian. At the same time 50% of the children in schools for the Russian minorities consist of Ukrainian, Belorussian, Jewish, Armenian, Mordvin, Kazakh and other minorities."

Training Teachers for Nationality Schools

We have referred to the fact that most of the nationality schools are in the rural areas and suffer from the disinclination of teachers to work there. But the question is not simply a matter of a sufficient number of teachers but of teachers who know the language of the nationality and have been trained to teach it and to use it in teaching other subjects. This is exemplified in the case of Abkhaz. In 1945, it was decreed that elementary schools in which Abkhaz was used should be closed. In 1953, it was announced (*Zarya Vostoka 20*:10.53) that this decision had been reversed and that Abkhaz could be used in elementary schools, with either Russian or Georgian after the first four years. However, this reversal of policy had little effect because few teachers could be recruited who were competent to teach and use the language (Bennigsen 1961:51).

The same is true of the nationalities of the Far North. It was reported in 1949 that 60% of the teachers in those schools were recruited from outside the area and special bonuses were paid to attract teachers (*Nar. Obraz. 1966*: September). In the schools of the Evenki there were very few more teachers who spoke the language as their mother tongue in 1947 than the 12 who were there in 1935. Because of this shortage of qualified teachers, the Institute of the Peoples of the North was established on the foundations of the Leningrad Institute of Geography. The Institute became incorporated into the Herzen Institute which has been the prototype for other institutes concerned with training teachers of nationality languages. By 1960, the Institute was able to recruit a hundred students annually, five from each of the main northern ethnic groups. These are tenth grade students, and at the Institute they follow a 3-year academic course and subsequently a 3-year professional teacher's course to which a fourth year is added to prepare them for the specific problems of bilingual education in the Far North up to the eighth grade. In 1967, the situation had shown a measure of improvement. One-tenth of the teachers working in schools of the Chukot National District were Chukchi or Eskimo, Evenk, or some other Northern nationality. In the Nenetz National District Nenetz and Komi teachers comprised a quarter of the staffs of the schools, and of these up to 80% had higher or secondary specialized education (*Nar. Obraz. 1967*:6). In addition to being able to continue their education at the Herzen Pedagogical Institute in Leningrad or at Krasnoiarsk Magada or Kharovsk, the students may be trained as teachers in Nar'ian-Mar, Salekhard Igarka, and Anadyr.

There is similar provision for teachers of other nationality languages at the Tashkent Institute, The Tbilisi Institute, and the Pedagogical Institute in Erevan which like the Institute at Tbilisi has separate sections for the basic language of the Republic and for Russian. All these institutes work in close association with the Academy of Pedagogical Sciences in Moscow which, in 1949, set up a Scientific Research Institute of the Nationality Schools. This has contributed greatly to the understanding of problems connected with bilingual education, the teaching of Russian as a second language, and the use of minority languages in schools. At one time it had four branches in the various Autonomous Republics of the RSFSR, and experimental schools for children who speak Mordvin, Buryat, Chuvash, and Kabardin.

CONCLUSION

Bilingual education in the Soviet Union is interesting from several points of view. Its very complexity is baffling. It involves considerable numbers of languages belonging to different language families. The languages are at various stages of development, and the ethnic groups and the nationalities with which they are associated also differ enormously in respect of social, political, and economic development levels. Yet these languages and their associated societies are held within a very tightly organized system which tends to discount the need for or the possibility of the flexibility we regard as normal in bilingual education. Second, the system of bilingual education in spite of the existence of some important experiments in the pre-Revolutionary period has been virtually created within the last 50 to 60 years and has been made available universally within the Union. This in itself is a phenomenal achievement, which has required the cooperation of linguists of the highest eminence in the Soviet Union. Third, the developments have changed many aspects of bilingualism itself in the USSR. Bilingualism of the most traditional type, that which exists among small groups in Daghestan, for instance, is no longer fortuitous as once it was, arising from the unorganized relationships and contacts of individuals. Although this fortuitous bilingualism has not been superseded, it is supplemented by planned bilingualism which extends over the whole field of education as well as to other areas of communication. Where fortuitous bilingualism might be most likely to create conflict, as in the large towns and cities with large numbers of immigrants, the eystem of education exists to stabilize the situation.

Fortuitous bilingualism was normally entirely oral, whereas it is now literate in respect of at least one of the languages and in millions of cases in respect of two and sometimes more languages. Clearly this is the consequence of the system of education, as is also the third change in the type of bilingualism, namely, that from elitist to mass bilingualism. Historically bilingualism when it occurred appeared to the person involved as unavoidable and inevitable. The bilingual did the best he could with the necessity. However, with the penetration of Russian as a lingua franca, together with the teaching and the use of the basic languages of the Union Republics as well as the mother tongue where it is different from them, bilingualism is *promoted*; it is part of planned social change. At the same time the tendency is for such planned and promoted bilingualism to become unilateral bilingualism as opposed to reciprocal bilingualism. Historical and fortuitous bilingualism was normally reciprocal, since the population tended to have equal status and the languages equal prestige. This is no longer the case: a planned bilingualism is part of the general planning of society, and this ensures that some languages are organized to deal with different levels of social activity. The speakers of the most prestigious languages tend not to learn the languages next below them in the range of social roles they are expected to fulfill—this is the case with speakers of Russian in relationship to all other languages and with speakers of the Union Republic languages in respect of the languages of Autonomous Republics, etc. The tendency toward unilateral bilingualism if it continues will eventually create a linguistically homogeneous state.

Among the most interesting questions about which a considerable amount of discussion has occurred is first whether future bilingualism, which it is assumed will be mainly Russian-related bilingualism, is to be a "vehicular bilingualism," the second language being acquired for the purposes of social communication at the "surface level" in the main, or cultural bilingualism where the second language is learned as a means of assimilating the world view associated with that language. And second, if the second alternative is adopted what world view is in fact associated with the bilingualism which is to be acquired—is it to be a synthesis of all the national cultures, or a culture which is evolved by muting the national characteristics and building upon the minimum that is common to them; or is it to be a new type of Soviet culture which owes nothing to national cultures and is discontinuous with them historically and qualitatively? The probability is that this question, which is fundamental to all Soviet thinking, is likely to be the most intriguing for students of bilingual education in the Soviet Union for a long time to come. And since it is in effect a discussion of the rationale for a bilingual program in any kind of modern highly industrialized urban society, the nature of these discussions is of interest in every bilingual country.

Bilingualism in Education

in Wales

E. Glyn Lewis

INTRODUCTION—THE BACKGROUND

According to the 1971 Census, the total population of Wales is nearly 2.6 million. Parts of the country, South and North East Wales especially, are highly industrialized and densely populated. The South West is rich agricultural land, while North West and Central Wales are mountainous and sparsely populated. The Welsh language is spoken by just over 20% (542,000) of those who are over 3 years of age. Just over 1% (33,000) claim not to be able to speak English, half of those being under 4 years or over 65 years of age. There is virtually 100% literacy in one or the other of the two languages, and of the 20% who are bilingual nearly 95% are able to read (449,000) both languages and write (397,000) both languages. Together with Scots Gaelic, Breton, and Irish the Welsh language belongs to the Celtic group of Indo-European languages; and, again like Irish, it possesses a rich classical literature dating from the 14th Century and earlier, as well as a lively and varied contemporary literature.

Two waves of speakers of Celtic dialects descended upon Britain in pre-Christian times, Brythonic in the 6th Century and Goedelic in the 4th Century. After the coming of the Romans there was considerable Celtic/Latin bilingualism, both in society at large and in the schools which were available to the children of Roman functionaries and the Romanized aristocracy (Lewis 1976). When the Roman occupation ended in the 5th Century, Welsh was still the native language of nearly all the inhabitants, but by the 7th Century the greatest part of England had been conquered and dominated linguistically by the English and Saxons. The speakers of Welsh had been pressed into the northern areas of England, west into what is now Devon and Cornwall, but mainly into the Principality of Wales as it became. Four centuries later, after the Welsh language had been established as the language of nearly all the population of Wales, a new threat was posed by the military campaigns of the Normans which resulted in the occupation by speakers of English and Norman French of the low-lying lands of South Wales, the border with England, the northern coastal strip, and the lines of communication into the heart of Wales along the Severn Valley. But in spite of the military occupation, the Welsh language remained the native tongue of the great majority of the population and was sustained by the native aristocracy. In the 15th and 16th Centuries the Tudor dynasty of England, which was of Welsh origin but devoted entirely to a ruthless centralizing policy in legal administration and in religious affairs, deprived the Welsh language of its aristocratic support by drawing the gentry to London. The language gradually became the prerogative largely of the unlettered and the underprivileged. It had no official standing in any of the spheres of public affairs, though it was used sometimes in the local courts because it was the only language litigants would probably know.

The demographic if not the social status of the Welsh language was high when industrialization began to revolutionize the Welsh way of life at the beginning of the 19th Century. Even in 1840 an observer claimed that over two-thirds of the population, including the most anglicized, still spoke Welsh and half of them were monolingual. In 1858, a representative area of North Wales with a population of 52,000 claimed nearly 90% monoglot speakers of Welsh, while the remaining 10% spoke Welsh more often than English. Even in anglicized South Wales in the same period 75% spoke Welsh habitually. Between 1811 and 1911, largely because of the flow of English immigrants to the coal mines and iron works of South Wales, there was a nearly fourfold increase in the total population of the country but the proportion who spoke only Welsh dropped to 19%; those who spoke only English accounted for over 47% and bilinguals contributed 33% of the population. At present those who speak English represent only 69% and bilinguals approximately 30% of the total population. This condition has been produced by a succession of military conquests, political subordination, and administrative disregard of the Welsh language. But in the last analysis the Welsh language had survived all these vicissitudes. It was industrialization and a killing rate of English immigration which made the most telling contribution to the development of bilingualism and English monolingualism in Wales (Lewis 1974).

The demographic and social preponderance of English is reflected and reinforced by differences in the institutional support for the two languages, especially in the press, broadcasting, and education. English is the only official language in *all* spheres of public affairs, like law, local and central government, and publicly owned industries or corporations. There is no daily Welsh language newspaper, though several English periodicals carry Welsh contributions from time to time. In recent years there has been an increase in the number of books published in Welsh. The annual production approximates over 200 new publications, of which well over 60 are meant for school-age children. Radio and TV in Wales are regional departments of the British network, though they make significant contributions in the Welsh language. In religion 66% of the Non-Conformist communicants attend Welsh services and 6% bilingual services. Twelve percent of the communicants of the Church in Wales (corresponding to the English Established Church) attend Welsh services, 3% bilingual services, and 85% entirely English services.

THE RATIONALE OF BILINGUAL EDUCATION IN WALES

The Place of English

The system of bilingual education in Wales, its motivation, recent developments in creating new types of schools and extending the availability of existing types of bilingual programs, together with the polarization of attitude among adults and students to the teaching of the two languages can be understood only in the light of the long history of severe social and political as well as linguistic oppression. This is the reason why bilingual education is governed strictly by the wish of a minority to maintain the Welsh language and its associated culture. The place of English in the curriculum has seldom been questioned until recently, and even then solely by representatives of the extreme nationalist intelligentsia, themselves fluent speakers of English, who "fear and seek to avoid bilingualism. . . . Monolingualism is the only policy consistent with the welfare of the Welsh people" (Lewis 1962). If ever the day dawned, this group continues to argue, "when everybody in Wales spoke English reasonably well our Welsh culture would have disappeared and been destroyed completely" (Bebb 1960). These views have not commanded support in the past nor do they at present: the vast majority "assumed the fact of the continual and necessary existence progress of the English language among the population of Wales" and this served as the sheet anchor of any proposal for a bilingual education. The intellectual leaders of Wales in the 19th Century contemplated with equanimity the disappearance, even, of the Welsh language. In an address on the training of teachers for schools in Wales one of the foremost educationists of the time, while expressing his attachment to the Welsh language, maintained that "few would wish to postpone its euthansy" (Griffiths 1845). The language had outlived its usefulness; "The golden days are done . . . and there is little point in regretting their disappearance" (Rees 1858). In spite of their patriotism, English is the language to which such writers are pledged, and so far as concerns the learning of Welsh by those who do not speak the language, "let them do as they wish" (Rees 1858).

Just as extreme nationalists among the contemporary Welsh intelligentsia entertain the dream of a monolingual Welsh Wales, so conversely the discussions among 19th Century leaders envisaged equally unrealistically a monolingual English educational system. Bilingualism was not feasible to their way of thinking: "Intelligent and educated Welshmen put forth the bilingual theory as a last resource to secure the perpetuity of the Welsh language. But such a theory that a whole population will for all future time keep up two languages where one only is necessary is proof of intellectual perversity merely" (Royal Commission 1886-1887). Even if such a society were conceivable, "a bilingual education could not be grafted on the present system of elementary education" (Lewis 1887), and in any case it entailed too great a sacrifice. If the Welsh student is "encouraged to think in Welsh he will have to sacrifice the advantage which he has of learning English" (Lewis 1887). But over and above all these considerations the main argument of those who opposed bilingualism was that the whole community of Britain should be bound by a uniform language: "under a common sceptre, a common code of laws with common interests it were desirable if but one common language prevailed" (Blackwell 1851).

The place of English in a bilingual education was argued for on more strictly educational grounds however. In the first place a knowledge of English was a liberating force because "the Welsh have been too long committed to the Welsh language excessively" (Rowlands 1886). There were "no books for general reading, or by which information on any branch of modern knowledge might be acquired; nor did the Welsh language contain a nomenclature adequate to the requirements of the modern world in science or art" (Royal Commission). For these reasons "the Welsh scholar needs to be taken out of his own groove" (Lewis 1887). Among leaders of Welsh thought, "even those who loved our nation saw *then*, no less clearly than we see *now* that the thing that weighed down our countryman was ignorance of English" (Davies 1882). The knowledge of English "would liberate the now poor, depressed monoglot Welshman from his mountain prison" (William Williams). English was the language of the higher social strata, and in acquiring it the Welsh would have the chance to avoid the "dirty and arduous labours which they are forced to undertake when the prestigious and less exacting work is available only to English men and Scotsmen" (Rees 1858). Even those who were distressed by the allegedly offensive criticism of English administrators (Royal Commission 1847) conceded that "the need to acknowledge the importance of English increased daily" since it was the necessary means of rising in society. The young Welshmen "were admonished to master the language and culture of the English thoroughly. Ensure that you are able to speak English eloquently and elegantly. To this extent make yourselves English" (Derfel 1864). But such advice was hardly necessary: it reflected a lack of facilities to acquire English rather than a disinclination to do so. Among nearly all Welsh parents "a strong prejudice prevailed universally against teaching children to read Welsh" (Davies 1886). One witness to the Royal Commission on Education (1887) maintained that he "had never yet come across a parent who wished the Welsh language to be taught to his children in school; on the contrary, every Welsh parent is most anxious . . . . that his children should learn English" (Lewis 1887).

The Endurance of Welsh

But whatever the prejudice of parents or the arguments of educationists, the Welsh language was a fact of life: in 1848 it was stated that "the greater part of the children of Wales never hear or utter a word of English but during the hours of instruction and within the walls of the school" (Royal Commission 1847). Forty years later the position had not changed much: 55% of the children above 7 years were reported as speaking Welsh habitually at home in the most anglicized areas of South Wales and 72% in the remainder of that part of the country. In North Wales "the language used by the children out of school is exclusively Welsh" (Evans 1887). The headmaster of an elementary school argued that English was "certainly a foreign language to children in my school as if a Frenchman were to teach French in an English school" (Morris 1887). Therefore, "while no Welsh child ought to be excluded by want of instruction from access to those means of cultivating his mind or bettering his worldly condition which the English language supplies, neither ought he to be entirely dependent for his education on that language and in the meanwhile be debarred from all such benefits as he might derive certainly from the use of books in his mother tongue" (Phillips 1849), a point of view which had been expressed over two centuries earlier: although acquisition of English ought to be the aim of all Welsh men, "Can we be satisfied to remain an ignorant nation," the writer asked, "until we have actually learned that language?" (Quoted in Welsh in Ed. & Life, 13). Many, nevertheless, considered that some aspects of a bilingual education would be disadvantageous, while others argued that advantageous or not it should be the province of the Sunday School, which had always used Welsh (Derfel 1864). However, the consensus was that reliance on English as the sole means of education would be too precarious a strategy: "What length of time," asked the pioneer of bilingual education in Wales, "how many hundreds of years must be allowed for the general attainment of English and of the dying away of Welsh? and must they not be taught in the things which concern their salvation till they be instructed in a language they do not yet understand?" (Jones 1744.)

Simply because it was the only available language, and by implication only until the English language became the possession of the majority, the Welsh language should be taught and used jointly with English in elementary schools: "While we confess the existence of a disadvantage we cannot see a remedy. A nation cannot change its language in a day; it must be the work of centuries. . . . Shall we then allow our countrymen to sink into barbarism and spiritual ignorance while the process of change in the language goes on?" (Blackwell 1851.) However, once it has conceded that the system of education should be bilingual, it followed almost of necessity that both languages should be not simply taught but *cultivated*. "So long as the language is spoken it should be taught . . . and not casually but systematically" (Derfel 1864). Though the argument continued, invariably the teaching of Welsh was a secondary consideration: "If one of the two languages is to be sacrificed the Welsh language certainly must be that language, and if the teaching of Welsh were to hinder the teaching of English, support for that language," it was emphasized, would decline: "Children ought not to be taught Welsh exclusively but be encouraged to acquire English; and where it may be desirable to be versed in both it is preferable that they should first learn to read English" (Hughes 1882). One way of avoiding the necessity of choosing between the two languages was to secure for each of them its own specific and acknowledged area or domain of usage: "If the Welshman has anything to say about philosophy and law, administration or science, he may prefer to use English. . . . But in communicating about those things which have to do with the arts and religion why should he need to use the English language?" (Darlington 1891.)

Bilingual education was conceived as a severely limited and temporary expedient, a compromise between the permanent advantages which were offered by a knowledge of English and, to even the most patriotic Welshman, the apparently embarrassing fact that Welsh survived and could not be ignored. Even the leaders of the bilingual education movement never argued consistently for the equality of the two components of that system of education.

The Social Argument for Bilingual Education

The inclusion of the Welsh language was justified for less negative or apologetic reasons. There was, first, the association with a long tradition and a rich literary heritage. In a period of unprecedented social change it was only natural in Wales that the emphasis should be placed on the more stable factors and traditional values. The Welsh language, "the most notable for its antiquity and its endurance" (Alun 1851) had the greatest significance among the historical factors. The Welsh reminded themselves that it was absurd to dream "luxuriously of the past while the world continued to advance" (Mills 1838) and were not unaware of the dangers of insularity and isolationism. Yet, it was argued, "they would never again achieve pre-eminence among nations if they ignored their historical language" (Darlington 1891). The agencies which spearheaded the propagation of these views in the campaign to develop bilingual education were the traditional national institutions like the National Eisteddfod and The Honourable Society of Cymmrodorion, but they were supported also by new local organizations like the Cambrian Institute (1854), The Cambrian Society of South Wales and Monmouthshire (1885), and the Cardiff Welsh Society (1886). From the membership of these societies came the most active supporters of the new Welsh Language Society which was formed to press for the use of the Welsh language in education.

The literature produced by or for these societies emphasized the importance of Welsh as a key to a classical culture, and it is this argument which tended to appeal to English supporters of bilingualism in education. The historian H.A.L. Fisher, when Minister of Education, spoke of the "great national possession represented by the Welsh language . . . which enshrined so great and imaginative a literature. . . . Your schools should take it up, refine it and make it a substantial part of the inheritance of every Welsh child" (Fisher 1920). But even more important has been the function of the language in promoting a sense of national identity. "The Welsh," it was argued, "rather than assimilate an English culture should nourish their intellectual life in accordance with the inherent characteristics of the Welsh nation and this depends to a great extent on teaching the Welsh language" (Darlington 1891). A nation tends to "mould its language according to its peculiar national requirements and to associate it in a consistent and ineradicable fashion with emerging national attitudes and ideas" (Rees 1858). The centrality of the Welsh language in any attempt to preserve national identity is the pervasive argument: "Our language is the foundation of our distinctiveness.... To lose our language would be to lose part of our claim to be a nation" (Derfel 1864). Support for this view was sought in the writings of Romantic philosophers and writers like Schlegel and Mazzini.

But the traditional associations, the historical continuity, and the cohesive value of the Welsh language were not the only social aspects of language maintenance which were advanced as arguments for a bilingual education. Of course, there were many opponents who saw a bilingual education as "strengthening the ancient differences between Wales and England" (Turner 1887), and many otherwise very enlightened educationists thought that it was not the place of a state system to encourage linguistic or cultural pluralism. Even Matthew Arnold, the greatest humanist among them, argued "that the acquisition of the English language should be more and more insisted ... as the one object" of the state grant for education. "Whatever encouragement individuals may think it desirable to give to the preservation of the Welsh language on grounds of philological or antiquarian interest, it must always be the desire of a Government to render its dominions ... homogeneous and to break down barriers to the freest intercourse between the different parts of them" (Arnold 1853). Others, however, sought to rebut this contention. The proposition exaggerated the efficacy of the schools in producing a change in the language of the country. "Schools, however well conducted, must of themselves be almost entirely powerless for such an object, where the language is taught for a few hours in the day is one which the children neither think in nor use at any other time" (Thirwall 1848). In fact, the teaching of Welsh might do much to obviate disunity, first of all between homes and the surrounding society and within the general fabric of that society: "What is taught in school influences profoundly the character of the child and in turn the character of society.... Ignoring and despising the Welsh language, the child's mother tongue, will tend to make the child despise the things which are associated with that language, namely his home, his parents and his country" (Evans 1887).

Because a bilingual education was not available to all social classes, "Evil circumstances arise ... wherein one side is disposed to depreciate whatever is Welsh while the other looks with suspicion on whatever is English" (Royal Commission 1881), a polarization which, in fact, has not been eliminated by the advance of bilingualism in education. Furthermore, this evil condition meant that "the majority of our countrymen are ignorant of the very language of the laws they are required to obey.... Punishments and rewards are alike esoteric and consequently alike uninfluential upon those who most require their help" (Griffiths 1848). Many people who had no interest in the Welsh language and little interest in the nation nevertheless realized that a bilingual education was the most likely means of ensuring social tranquility: "It ought to be borne in mind," stated one commissioner who had been sent to enquire into the state of education in the industrial bilingual areas," that an illeducated undisciplined population such as exists in the mines of South Wales is one that may be found very dangerous to the neighbourhood in which it dwells, and that a band of school masters is kept up at much less expense than a body of police or soldiery" (Tremenheere 1840).

Economic considerations were also advanced to support the claims for bilingual education. Welsh educationists appealed to the self-interest of the English. If the children were taught exclusively in English, "If all of us spoke the same tongue with you, the common labouring people would desert their callings in low life here" and compete with the English for better job opportunities. This would deprive the Welsh land-owning aristocracy of those hands which were wanted here to cultivate our grounds" (Jones 1744), an unexpected argument in favor of what is so generally regarded as a progressive education. But generally speaking it was the welfare of the Welsh which was the main objective of the program. Of course, the English language, as part of such an education, was emphasized, for "The shadows of coming events warn all Welshmen to prepare themselves by a superior English education so that they may not be mere hewers of wood and drawers of water" (Jones 1859). But English was not the only requirement for social and economic advance. At a time when Wales was rapidly becoming an important industrial nation, "Had we made a knowledge of Welsh a sine qua non in the Principality we should not now have had so many strangers among us to take our bread" (Jones 1859). Therefore, knowledge of both languages, "English and Welsh is becoming equally necessary for the young . . . if they are to succeed in professional or official occupations in the Principality" (Evans 1889).

The Moral and Intellectual Argument for Bilingual Education

A bilingual education was seen as the necessary foundation for confident personal development and sound moral behavior. Because of the inappropriateness of an exclusively English education, "The Welsh had lost faith in themselves . . . and were convinced that others had ceased to believe in them also" (Derfel 1864). Only by "nourishing the language which was fitted to express the Welshman's most intimate reflections" (Blackwell 1851) could the foundations of self-confidence be laid: "If it is the design of Education to make people good citizens and good Christians . . . that education must be dispensed in the language of the people" (Rees 1868). This was not a hypothesis to be entertained at the level of abstract argument so much as a fact to be observed daily: "Where the Welsh people retain their own language . . . their morals are superior to those who have thrown aside this national privilege and become amalgamated with other nations" (Griffiths 1887). The significance of this "moral argument" was all the greater because of the conclusions of the 1847 Commission on Education that "The Welsh language is a vast drawback to Wales and a manifold barrier to its moral progress" (Royal Commission 1847). It was natural, therefore, for those who led the campaign for bilingual education to maintain that it was the Welsh language that "had prevented the licentiousness of the English press" from invading Welsh homes. Not to include the Welsh language in a bilingual education would mean "that much of our national simplicity would disappear" (Alun 1851).

Bilingual education was associated with two aspects of a more specifically religious or ecclesiastical character. To a considerable extent the claim for greater prominence for Welsh in education reflected the evangelical movement within and outside the established Church of England in the 19th Century. It was the conservative element among church people "who set up the foolish cry and talked about a bilingual difficulty" (Davies 1887), and because of this alleged difficulty insisted on an exclusively English education. The evangelical party did not ignore the difficulties but felt that the people, if they were refused a bilingual education "might not, then, be taught the things which concerned their salvation" (Jones 1744). Then again, because the exclusively English instruction, the only one available, was conducted in the schools of the established Church, the "people stand aloof and either leave their children entirely untaught or obtain for them an education which ... is less effective" (Bowstead 1856). The tendency therefore was to insist on the separation of the educational and the ecclesiastical systems, and to provide within the proposed secular program a bilingual component. "It was for the English to decide what kind of schools are wanted in England; but as for Wales the only schools should be those in which secular instruction alone would be communicated" and this in both languages (Jones 1859).

Because of the very strong Non-Conformist commitment to a secular education the demand for a bilingual education stressed with increasing force the academic and intellectualist argument as against the traditional and aesthetic values associated with Welsh. As it stood, the English language could not enable the Welsh child to acquire knowledge and information or help him to develop his intellectual faculties. Instruction was purely mechanical, devoted entirely to the training of the child's memory. At the same time it was acknowledged that the Welsh language itself did not possess the literature or whatever else was necessary to satisfy the need for new knowledge. It was because of the realization that for different reasons neither English nor Welsh alone offered the chance to educate the Welsh child, that the newly formed Society for the Utilization of the Welsh Language insisted that the aim of teaching Welsh was to improve the teaching of English. Education depended in the last resort on the use of English, but English itself in Wales depended on the teaching of Welsh. "In the hands of a skillful teacher a systematic training in Welsh could be very helpful to the acquisition of English. If I did not think so," stated one of the main supporters of the Welsh Language Society, "I should not support the bilingual society at all." Moreover, "What we want is not to develop the speaking of Welsh, but by means of it to teach the classics and modern languages" (Davies 1887). Of the two languages, English and Welsh, "If one is to be sacrificed the Welsh should be that language" (Williams 1887).

Conclusion

The provision of bilingual education in Wales was obviously associated with a desire to preserve the Welsh language, but the principal intention was to use the best means, English if necessary, to ensure a satisfactory education for children who would inevitably be bilingual in any case. The promotion of the bilingual movement coincided, perhaps necessarily, with the gradual emergence of the dispossessed, the fulfillment of whose demands for education happened to necessitate the use of the vernacular in the circumstances of those times. The provision of bilingual education in Wales must be seen, then, as reflecting the interaction of five factors in the 19th Century which were European in the extent of their operation. There was first of all the Romantic movement, which stressed the idea of the fundamental and universal value of "the folk" and of ethnic languages whatever their status. This was reinforced by the fact that the ethnic language of the Welsh possessed a rich classical literature. Related to the Romantic revival in the realm of ideas was the evangelical movement, which sought to articulate the religious needs of the "folk" and which promoted literacy as an important if not a necessary contribution to salvation. This was reinforced by the fact that the Bible had long been translated into Welsh and there was a valuable corpus of original religious literature and of translation. Third, the rise of political nationalism in Europe popularized the concept of the uniqueness and distinctiveness of even small linguistic communities, and the right of each to self-determination. This was reinforced in Wales by a sense of injustice and by the fact that conquest which motivated that sense of injustice had nevertheless failed to eradicate or even significantly to diminish the demographic status of the vernacular. Fourth, rapid social change and especially intense industrialization required a working force which had been provided with fundamental education as the basis of their incorporation into the whole society, and with the literacy which a developing industrial economy required. So far as the vast majority of Wales was concerned, fundamental education in the 19th Century could be offered in Welsh alone. Finally, the extension of a democratic system of government which meant the gradual recognition of the lower and middle classes together with increasing tendencies toward centralization made inevitable the provision of a state system of universal education rather than a voluntary ecclesiastical provision. A voluntary system could have gone on ignoring the advantages of a bilingual education, but once the system of education was "codified" and regulated by statutory obligations, the demands of even a hitherto unregarded minority had to be taken into account. It was no longer simply a question of making ad hoc arrangements for the use of Welsh when the benevolence of the local school managers permitted it, but of systematizing the programming just as the provision for English was regulated and codified.

THE PRESENT POSITION

Evolution of Bilingual Education Policy

While the day-to-day conduct of educational administration is left to local education authorities, the duty to determine general policy as well as to ensure the effective implementation of policy, however modified to meet local needs, is that of the central government—it is a "dual system of education." The Ministry of Education, however, has usually tended to initiate policy changes only as the result of commissions of enquiry or advisory councils. So far as bilingual education is concerned, five such commissions or advisory councils are of outstanding significance. The first was the "Commission of Enquiry into the State of Education in Wales (1846-1847), which was directed to examine "especially the means afforded to the labouring classes of acquiring a knowledge of the English language." In spite of its extremely unfavorable reception in Wales, arising from its unwelcome realistic portrayal of the educational destitution of the country, it is probably the most influential of all the enquiries. It was clearly concerned mainly with English, but its clinical account of the effects of an exclusively English education ensured that such a system would not continue to command confidence even among the English.

The second important enquiry was conducted by the Royal Commission on Education in England and Wales (1886-1887). This, unlike the Commission of 1847, was only partly interested in Wales and its peculiar problems. But it did receive evidence from Wales, and much of this evidence, naturally enough, was concerned with the two languages. It was upon this Commission that the newly formed Welsh Language Society pressed its demands for recognition of Welsh in the "Codes" which governed the administration of education and the curriculum of elementary schools. To all intents and purposes the Report of the Commission was favorable to the demands for a bilingual education, and this was the first major advance. The next enquiry was specific to Wales, The Departmental Committee of the Board of Education to Enquire into the Status of Welsh in the Educational System of Wales (1927). The Welsh Committee reported 3 years after a similar English Committee had reported on the Teaching of English in England (1924). The Welsh report is a classic account of the vicissitudes of the Welsh language in "Education and Life" and continues to inspire Welsh educationists on account of its exalted view of the function of the language. But it would be difficult to identify any major specific recommendations which contributed to advances in bilingual education in the Principality.

Two more enquiries were entrusted by the Ministry of Education to the Central Advisory Council for Education (Wales). The second of these enquiries covered the whole field of primary education in Wales and to some extent duplicated the enquiries simultaneously conducted into primary education by the Central Advisory Council (England). The second report referred to bilingualism in the primary schools, but its contribution to this problem largely recapitulated that of the Report of 1953, which was produced by the Central Advisory Council set up to consider the bilingual situation exclusively and specifically—"The Place of Welsh and English in the Schools of Wales" (1953). In addition to a historical account of the development of bilingual education in Wales, this report gives a detailed statistical analysis of the incidence of the Welsh and English languages among various age groups in each of the local education authorities, outlines the psychological and cultural arguments and research evidence for bilingualism, makes specific recommendations to ensure the extension of bilingual education, and indicates methods of implementing the recommendations. It would not be unfair to say that the recommendations of the 1953 Council carry the proposal for bilingual education in Wales as far as it is realistically possible to do so. It recommends that "the children of Wales and Monmouthshire should be taught Welsh and English according to their ability to profit from such education. . . . A second language, English or Welsh, can and should be taught with advantage to all children of Wales and Monmouthshire" (Advisory Council 1952). The teaching of the two languages was taken to include their use to teach other subjects where appropriate, in primary, secondary, and higher education.

The Ministry of Education, either centrally or through the Welsh Office, has issued pamphlets and guidelines to teachers and local education authorities. The first which was of immediate significance to language policy was Suggestions for the Consideration of Education Authorities and Teachers (Memorandum I, 1929). This was followed by Language Teaching in Primary Schools (1945), Bilingualism in Secondary Schools in Wales (1949), The Curriculum and the Community (1952), and Language (1953) which was written for England and Wales and has a separate chapter on Wales. Some local education authorities have conducted their own surveys of the linguistic characteristics of their areas, and they have also published materials on policy issues. The most interesting of these materials have emanated from the Welsh-speaking counties of Caernarvon, which have published four such surveys between 1949 and 1953, and the Denbighshire, which has published one (1953). Altogether the official Ministry of Education publications, together with the reports of the various commissions of enquiry and advisory councils and local education authority reports constitute probably the most comprehensive and detailed study available anywhere of bilingualism in the schools over a period of over a hundred years.

The Extent and Distribution of Bilingualism Among School Age Children

According to the 1971 Census, less than 20% of the total all age population of Wales are bilingual, representing an inexorable decline each decade (see Table 1).

Table 1.   Proportion of Bilingual Children According to Age Groups

Ages	1911	1921	1931	1951	1961	1971
All over 3	35.0	30.8	32.8	27.2	25.0	19.6
3-4	17.4	15.5	12.5	8.5	8.3	7.3
5-9	26.5	21.6	20.5	15.9	16.7	13.2
10-14	33.7	27.5	27.5	20.6	18.9	16.2

There are considerable real differences in the incidence of bilingualism among school children. From these figures in Table 1 it can be appreciated that there are considerable differences in the impact of the general policy for bilingual education—there is no uniformity in the implementation of policy. Table 2 shows that in only five authorities is the proportion of bilingual children above 50% and these are all in the extreme west of the country where the population is sparse and therefore the number of bilinguals comparatively small. The six authorities in South Wales account for over 60% of the total school age population and nearly one-third of the school age bilingual population of the whole of Wales. At the same time the proportion of the school population of South Wales which is bilingual is under 5%. Recommendations for bilingual education in schools are usually related to three types of local authority areas—those where between 45 and 55% of the school age population are bilingual, areas where the proportion is between 20 and 45%, and the other areas where there is very little or no bilingualism.

The Bilingual Competence of School Children

The decennial census returns do not enable us to ascertain the competence of the bilingual children in either of their two languages, or whether English or Welsh is the native language. Two investigations have been reported which allow us to draw some conclusions about this question, and a third investigation has yet to be reported definitively. In 1951, as part of the enquiry into the Place of Welsh and English in the Schools, all children between the ages of 5 and 15 were classified according to which was their native language, and within these two categories according to the level of their command of the second language. Four levels of bilingualism were specified in each case: A = minimal bilingualism; B = ability to understand less simple statements in the second language; C = ability to understand and conduct simple conversations in the second language; D = reasonable fluency in the second language. This statistical enquiry was repeated 10 years later (1962). A preliminary analysis of a very small sample enquiry along the same lines conducted in 1972 indicates little change in the tendencies revealed by a comparison of the 1952 and 1962 analyses (Table 3). The rapid movement away from Welsh monolingualism as the child grows older, and the change in the overall position between 1951 and 1961 are very apparent. Taking the total of pupils of all age groups in 1951, only 9% of Welsh children were monolingual compared with 79% of the English children. In 1961, the figures were 6.1 and 70%. In 1951, 11% of the Welsh and 15% of the English were included in the lowest effective bilingual rating (B). In 1961, the figures were 8 and 22%. The native speakers of Welsh were becoming better bilinguals and more English native speakers of children acquired only a poor command of the second language. Among the native speakers of Welsh there were nearly twice as many moderate bilinguals as there were poor bilinguals. Native speakers of Welsh constituted also twice the number of moderate bilingual English speakers, in both 1951 and 1961. There was over 60% effective bilingualism (category D) among native speakers of Welsh in 1951 and 1961, and little more than 2.5% among native speakers of English, who tended to become bilingual with great reluctance as they grew older, and showed even less inclination to do so in 1961 than in 1951. In the County of Caernarvon, for instance, where support for Welsh might be expected to ensure an equitable and reasonable adjustment between the two languages, the difference is very

Table 2.   Distribution of Bilingual Children According to Local Education Authorities (In thousands)

		Counties						
Total population	3-14 population with bilinguals	Wales	Anglesey	Brecon	Caernarton	Cardigan	Carmarthen	Denbigh
Total population		2618	56	51	118	53	156	176
Total bilingual		508	35	11	68	34	99	46
% bilingual		19	62	22	57	66	66	36
Total 3-14		518	11.7	9	20	9	27	33.5
Bilingual 3-14		518	11.7					
Bilingual 3-14		78	6	1.5	11	5.2	13.5	6
% Bilingual 3-14		15	51	16.5	55	58	50	18

marked. The percentage of Welsh monolingualism at ages 5 to 8 is 20; in the groups 8 to 11 and 11 to 15 it is 2½ and 0% respectively (Lewis 1974). There is a decline among the English monolinguals from 46% at 8 to 14% at all, and 12% at 15 years. Among native Welsh-speaking pupils there is a regular, continuous and rapid rise from one age group to the next not only in the number of bilingual pupils but also in the level of their ability in English. This is reflected by the fact that the percentage of pupils in categories B and C declines in each successive age group and rises in category D. In other words, Welsh-speaking pupils as they grow older tend to shift quickly and uniformly from categories B and C (low-level ability in English) to category D (high-level ability in English). In Carmarthenshire as the children become older the amount of poor and indifferent English declines from 25 to 0% and the percentage of those with nearly native English moves from 28% at 5 to 8 years to 85% at 11 to 15.

Among the English-speaking children, however, after the initial step away from virtual monolingualism, nothing like the same development toward effective bilingualism occurred. For instance, in Caernarvon after the initial departure from monolingualism 25% of the 5 to 8 age group remained in category B, 12% of the 5 to 8 age group remained in category C, and only 12% of the 5 to 8 age group were in category D. By and large the bilingual development rate among English-speaking pupils was slow, and tended to stop considerably short of effective bilingualism. For instance, the great majority of English children did not progress beyond category B in Breconshire, Carmarthenshire, Flintshire, Montgomeryshire, and Cardiff. In the case of Anglesey it will be seen that there was a slight decline

Table 2 (continued)

| | Counties (continued) | | | | | County boroughs | | | |
Flint	Glamorgan	Merioneth	Monmouth	Montgomery	Pembroke	Cardiff	Merthyr	Newport	Swansea
167	714	34	333	41	94	266	53	107	166
23	23	22	9	11	19	12	5	2	20
14	13	64	3	27	20	4	2.3	2	12
34.5	145	6.6	70	8	20	55	6.4	23	32
3.6	10	4	0.6	1.5	2.5	1.5	4	0.15	1.3
10	7.7	64	0.8	19	12.5	2.8	64	0.5	4

from the position of 1951 when the percentages in categories C and D were fairly even at 25 and 23, and in 1962 showed a marked decline from category D (22 to 12%) and to increase the percentage in the lower category C (33%).

The position of Welsh in Glamorgan should be noted because of the numerical importance of the area, which produces nearly a third of the whole of the school population of Wales. As would be expected from the 1951 analysis, the Welsh-speaking pupils in 1961 were bilingual at a very early age and 88% of them were thoroughly bilingual at 15. The position of the English-speaking pupils was very different: 78% were monolingual English and only 1% became thoroughly bilingual. The highest level of bilingual attainment for the great majority of the English children who have some knowledge of Welsh at 15 years was no higher than category B, 30% in 1951 but only 18% in 1961.

From the 1952 and 1962 returns and the preliminary analysis of the small 1972 samples none of the conclusions we are able to draw offer much comfort to those who seek to maintain the existing level of Welsh in Wales. These conclusions take on added significance because at all points they reinforce those we have been able to draw from an analysis of the total population of all ages. There is a rapid rise in the number of Welsh-speaking children who achieve increasing competence in English, to the extent that over two-thirds are thoroughly bilingual before they leave school. This would not be an unfavorable phenomenon were it not accompanied by two other tendencies. First the progress of the Welsh child in English is nowhere even remotely matched by the English child's competence in Welsh. In 1961, only 2.3% knew Welsh thoroughly, and only an additional 3.8%

Table 3.   Categorization of Bilingual Children According to Their Native Language and Competence in the Second Language (1952 and 1962)

Area	Total No. of pupils, thousands		Percentage of totals		First language Welsh					
					Level of competence					
					% in each category					
					A		B		C	
	1951	1961	1951	1961	1951	1961	1951	1961	1951	1961
Anglesey	6.6	7.6	79	67	9.1	5	13	12	22	20
Brecon	6.9	7.7	18	12	0.2	4	4.9	3	14.5	5
Caernarvon	15	15.5	74	67	10	7	13	10	20	19
Cardigan	6.7	7	76	67	12	9	11	9	20	22
Carmarthen	20.7	22.2	62	53	10	10	14	9	19	18
Denbigh	22.1	24.9	25	19	6	4	8	6	14	11
Flint	19	22.4	8	6	0.1		0.1	1.3	0.8	4.7
Glamorgan	92.0	113.4	7.2	3.5	8	1.4	9	3.3	17	7.3
Merioneth	4.8	5.2	83	75	4.3	5	10	10	22	22
Monmouth	43.2	51.5	0.2	0.1				10	20	
Montgomery	6	6.5	25	19	10	4	12	8	22	14
Pembroke	11.9	14	20	16	14	3	12	8	24	20
Radnor	2.7	2.6	1.2	0.6	3			36		10
Cardiff	30.7	40.2	0.4	0.3	70		1.5	0.5	8	2.5
Merthyr	8.2	8.9	1	1.3	1.2					5
Newport	12.4	16.1	0.1	0.1						1
Swansea	19.7	23.4	4.5	2.6		0.5		1.5	6	1
Wales	335.4	389.5	17.7	13.4	9.0	6	11.0	8	19	17

knew it moderately well; 69% never learned any Welsh at all. Furthermore there is every evidence of a decline between 1951, 1961, and 1972.

Second, Welsh children not only became competent bilinguals but increasingly transferred to English as their mother tongue. Thus in 1951 only 17.7% claimed Welsh as their mother tongue, and this figure fell to 13.4% in 1961—a decline of 25% in 10 years. The evidence for this decline is most apparent in the areas of "high-intensity" Welsh speech—Anglesey (79 to 67), Cardigan (76 to 67), Carmarthen (62 to 53), and Merioneth (83 to 75), because it is those areas which possess the highest potential for loss. But it is, proportionately, even more devastating in the industrial areas: for instance, in Glamorgan where the decline was of the order of 50%, from 7.2 to 3.5%. It is noteworthy that Merthyr, the focal point of early industrialization, claimed no more than 1.3% of its school children as speaking Welsh as their mother tongue. These tendencies produce the situation that increasing proportions of those who make any claim to speak Welsh have learned it as a second language. In 1951, according to the Census, the percentage of bilinguals between 3 and 16 years was 27.2%, of whom it is

Table 3 (continued)

		Percentage of totals		First language English — Level of competence — % in each category							
D				A		B		C		D	
1951	1961	1951	1961	1951	1961	1951	1961	1951	1961	1951	1961
53	63	25	28	32	25	28	27	73	33	22	12
82	88	86	90.2	70	52	15	35	6.4	11.3	3.8	2.7
57	64	33	44	23	22	35	3.3	20	21	20	21
58	61	28	42	40	31	2.9	22	19	2.7	13	19
58	63	44	57	28	32	36	40	16	14	17	14
70	79	78	84	64	53	19	33	8	9	4.5	5
99	95	93	96	83	56	12	32	3	5.9	1.5	1.3
66	88	95	96.7	64	78	30	18	4	3	1.7	1
52	62	24.8	37	20	28	26	18	27	22	28	27
70	100	99	99	97	99	1.8	0.3	0.5	0.07	0.1	0.03
56	74	79	83.5	82	66	12	28	4	3.5	3	2.6
50	70	80	87	87	88	7	5.7	3	3ı	2	3.2
50	100	99	99	99	99	0.5	0.5	0.25	0.3	0.1	0.1
80	97	99	99	98	42	0.25	54	1	3	0.1	0.2
93	100	99	99	95	91	4	6	0.8	2.2	0.4	0.8
100	90	99	99	99	99						
98	97	98	98.5	95	70		23		4		0.1
61	69	84.4	87.3	78	69	1.5	20	8.6	3.8	2.5	2.3

estimated 3.3% claimed English as their mother tongue. In 1961, the overall percentage fell to 25% but the percentage of those claiming to have learned Welsh as a second language rose to 4.2%. In 1971, the percentage of bilinguals fell still further to 19.6%, but the percentage claiming Welsh as their second language had risen to 6.1%. An increasing proportion of those who learn Welsh as their second language live in the urbane south of the country while in spite of their fewness the rural minority combine to acquire Welsh as their mother tongue.

Impact of Bilingualism on Individual Schools

Up to 1967, several reading ability surveys were conducted in England and Wales. In all but the last two of these Wales was included with England in the total school sample. However, in 1957 and 1967, it was decided to deal separately with Wales and to draw separate samples of schools. In order to obtain a satisfactory stratification of the sample, it was necessary to classify individual schools according to their linguistic character. The Welsh reading surveys were based on schools where a sufficient level of bilingualism enabled tests in both languages to be administered to a large enough number of children. Ninety-four schools in ten areas with the highest incidence of bilingualism were included. Even in areas with a generally high level of bilingualism there were considerable differences between schools. In Anglesey the percentage of bilinguals varied between 80% in some schools and 94% in others; in other areas the range was as follows: Breconshire, 0 to 47%; Caernarvon, 5 to 100%; Cardigan, 76 to 100%; Carmarthen, 6 to 100%; Denbighshire, 0 to 100%; Merionethshire, 60 to 100%; Montgomeryshire, 0 to 95%; Pembrokeshire, 0 to 91%; West Glamorgan, 30 to 96%.

It was also found that between 1957 and 1967 the total number of children in the same sample of schools had increased by 16% but that the proportion of bilinguals among them had increased by only 3.8%. In fifty schools the proportion of bilingualism had declined, in 28 it had risen slightly, and in 16 there was virtually no change, largely because of a zero return on each of the two occasions. This is itself of interest, but of equal significance is the identification of the factors which produced the results. Schools were asked to account for the change if any in their linguistic situation, and among the main influences to which reference was made is industrialization and the still rapid growth in the importance of English as the language associated with technological advance. Some schools referred to the influence of two world wars and the effect of prolonged, and in some cases intensive evacuation of monolingual children from English cities or from anglicized areas of Wales during the second of these wars. Others referred to improved communication and the influence of mass media and tourism. Intensive afforestation of the highland areas has meant that very small one-teacher, monolingual Welsh schools might become predominantly bilingual if not monolingual English almost overnight because of the employment of immigrant English forestry workers. The same is true of farming: some schools which originally had no more than 15 children, all Welsh-speaking, have been known to have received children from two or three families, in some instances Poles or other European refugees, none of them Welsh-speaking and contributing nearly as many as the original number on the school registers.

Apart from the changes brought about by the immigration of English children, there has been a steady movement out of the Welsh-speaking countryside. Intermarriage between Welsh-speaking and non-Welsh-speaking men and women is responsible for considerable changes in the linguistic pattern within families and schools. Rehousing of the existing populations of Welsh-speaking areas may mean that Welsh-speaking children are moved to schools where the dominant language is English, and the same result is seen to occur when schools are reorganized at the primary level, usually because of decreasing numbers, or at secondary level when children from several primary schools in sparsely populated areas are recruited to a central secondary school, which may be situated in an anglicized area or be comprised of a predominantly non-Welsh-speaking school population. Finally, attitudes, though they may be the most imponderable and fugitive factors to analyze, appear to be among the most influential in modifying the character of schools.

THE PROVISION OF EDUCATION FOR BILINGUAL CHILDREN

Limited Bilingual Education

Bilingual education is provided on one of two levels: it may be "limited" in the sense that the two languages are taught though only one is used to teach other subjects. It is a "complete" bilingual education only to the extent that both languages are taught and used. In view of the complex pattern of distribution of speakers of Welsh and English in Wales, authorities differ as to whether their aim should be a "limited" or a "complete" bilingual education. Even where they propose the former, there are difficulties to surmount, principally those of obtaining sufficient satisfactorily qualified teachers of Welsh. So far as primary schools are concerned, four authorities appoint only those teachers who are themselves bilingual. Some require that half the teachers in any one school should have this qualification, while others are willing to accept that at least one teacher in every school is thoroughly bilingual. In some areas the tendency is to offer even a limited bilingual education only as a special program for some classes. There is a wide variation between authorities in the allocation of time to the teaching of Welsh as a first or second language, ranging from 100 to 300 minutes a week.

There are also considerable differences in the ages at which Welsh is introduced formally. Among primary age children sampled in the NFER/WJEC Survey (1970:120), of the 55 schools in the Welsh-speaking areas which responded to a questionnaire all taught Welsh from the age of entry. In the English-speaking areas Welsh was introduced under the age of 5 in 10% of the 100 schools sampled, in 18% under the age of 6 years, and in 22% under the age of 7. In approximately 71% of the English-speaking schools Welsh was introduced at or slightly over 7 years of age. Some of these schools introduced Welsh as second language as late as 9 and 10 years of age. Where English is concerned, there are considerable differences. In the English-speaking schools English is taught from the beginning, but this is also the case in a less formal fashion of English in the Welsh-speaking areas, too. When it comes to the formal introduction of the language, however, the tendency is to introduce English as a second language later than Welsh as a second language: only 10% (as against 18% for Welsh) introduce English as a second language below the age of 6 years. The difference is accounted for by the belief that Welsh requires an earlier introduction in order to compensate for a weak societal support for the language in the English-speaking areas.

So far as the secondary schools are concerned, the same survey reported that 30% of the Welsh-speaking schools taught Welsh for the whole of the period of secondary schooling, 60% taught the language for 5 years, and 10% taught Welsh for 3 years. Where the secondary schools taught Welsh as a second language this was done for 5 years in 42% of the schools, for 4 years in a similar proportion of the schools, and for 3 years in the remainder. It is also noticeable that where Welsh is offered as an alternative some schools make it available only to the abler pupils of the secondary schools (the top stream) and some only to the least able (the bottom stream). Where Welsh is offered as an optional subject some schools provide the necessary time for Welsh out of the basic allocation for such subjects as drama or music or physical education. Other schools make Welsh a straight alternative to another subject, which may be another modern language, or Welsh may be included in a group of four subjects from which students may choose any three. Where Welsh is taught in anglicized areas, whether in primary or secondary schools, classes may be organized for native speakers of the language separately from native speakers of English. It is seldom that the teaching of English is differentiated in this way—it is usually taught as if it were the native language of all students. The amount of time available for Welsh in the secondary schools of the Welsh-speaking areas tends to be the same as for English. In the English-speaking areas Welsh is taught usually for approximately 3 periods of 40 minutes each week compared with the 5 or 6 for English. Where bilingual education is "limited," the teaching of Welsh as a second language tends to be academic, and as most informed observers agree, the standard after 4 or 5 years of secondary instruction, sometimes following a period of 3 years of instruction in primary schools, is apt to be unsatisfactory.

Complete Bilingual Education

The most interesting developments have occurred in the use of Welsh to teach all or some of the subjects in primary and secondary schools, as well as in institutions of higher education. Until fairly recently the great majority of even thoroughly Welsh-speaking children were taught in English after the age of 7, frequently even in the infants' school. Where they had been taught in Welsh below the age of 7 the only problem was the speed at which instruction might be transferred to English. In some cases, especially where infants' and junior schools were in separate buildings or were organized as separate departments, a total transfer might be made immediately the child reached the junior school. In other instances, especially where the Welsh language was stronger than usual, the transfer might not be completed for 2 or even 3 years. However, where instruction was entirely in English the Welsh-speaking child might have explanations offered him in his native language. As late as 1930, the Ministry of Education considered it necessary to draw attention to the need to use Welsh as a teaching language more frequently with thoroughly Welsh-speaking children, but qualified its insistence by admitting "that the immediate introduction of Welsh throughout the school would be difficult. . . . English has become a more effective means of expression" (Ministry of Education 1932:41-46).

Although the establishment of schools in anglicized areas where the medium of instruction was predominantly Welsh had been suggested as far back as 1927

(Ministry of Education 1927), the idea did not receive appreciable support until 1939, when the first step toward a complete bilingual education for children in anglicized areas was taken by the parents of a small number of children. The Welsh League of Youth (Urdd Gobaith Cymru), a voluntary organization whose aim it is to mobilize interest among the young in Welsh culture and especially the Welsh language, established a class for Welsh-speaking children at the request of parents who were disturbed by the interruption of their children's normal education on account of the arrival of considerable numbers of "evacuees" from English cities or anglicized areas of Wales at the commencement of war. This school opened with seven children of various ages and one teacher. It was soon taken into the state system, and the idea spread. Between 1947 and 1951, over 12 similar schools were set up, and the largest authority, Glamorgan, set up two such schools annually up to 1955. Some of the schools increased in size from about 40 to 50 pupils to 240 or 300 over 15 years. By 1962, 40 such schools had been established with a total recruitment of nearly 5000 children. They were all within the state system of education. Apart from establishing new schools, some authorities "designated" some schools as Welsh-medium schools (Ysgolion Cymraeg) and transferred the children of parents who favored a complete bilingual education from neighbouring non-Welsh medium schools. Nursery schools or kindergarten outside the state system were also established, many of them for one or two days a week or for only part of a day. This movement to create "complete bilingual schools" affected primary and secondary schools alike, and authorities adopted the same attitudes in establishing them. Some secondary schools were purposely built "Welsh" secondary schools; some were the result of the reorganization of two or more schools in the same area. A parental survey conducted as part of the Advisory Council enquiry (1967) tended to suggest that support for these schools is greatest among professional and middle-class parents.

In the meantime, of course, the schools in the thoroughly Welsh-speaking areas continued to develop their use of Welsh as a teaching language without necessarily having to undertake reorganization of schools or departments.

Table 4 shows the results of an enquiry among a small sample of primary schools throughout Wales. Even in the least anglicized areas less than 65% of the schools use the Welsh language for 50% of the time. In the most anglicized areas the use of Welsh in the schools included in this sample is negligible. Among the specially created Welsh-medium schools (Ysgolion Cymraeg) throughout Wales 12.5% used Welsh for up to 50% of the time, a similar number used the language for between 50 and 75%, and 75% used the language for between 75 and 100% of the time.

It is significant that the subjects which are taught in Welsh are generally speaking not those which are required to ensure material success. In secondary schools religious instruction and physical education tend to be taught throughout the course. Some teach handicraft, music, and homemaking for a good portion of the time. Welsh history and aspects of local geography are frequently taught for part of the time in Welsh. Mathematics, the natural sciences (most of the

Table 4.   Proportion of Time in Which Welsh is Used as a Teaching
              Language, According to Linguistic Area

Type of area	Total No. of schools		No. of schools with indicated %			
			1-25%	26-50%	51-75%	76-100%
Least anglicized	57	9%	25	30	28	8
Moderately	41	29%	20	15	15	21
Most	26	96%	4			

Source: Schools Council (1973) p. 219.

secondary schools teach at least three sciences), English, as well as other languages
are all taught almost exclusively in English. Preuniversity (sixth-form) classes tend
to be taught almost always in English.

There are single-medium English schools in areas where Welsh is spoken by
an appreciable number of native speakers of the language. There are few if any
schools which use Welsh exclusively even in the thoroughly Welsh-speaking areas.
In most areas of Wales there are "dual"-medium schools where both languages are
used to teach some subjects to mixed classes of native speakers of Welsh and
native speakers of English for part of the time. There are also dual-medium
schools where the two linguistic groups are separated into parallel streams or
tracks. Where dual-medium primary schools do not stream the students according
to their linguistic affiliation but have heterogeneous classes, the medium of
instruction may alternate either each day or each week.

However, where in the linguistically mixed areas the demand for
"complete" bilingual education is taken seriously, the tendency is to separate the
two language groups and provide different schools for them. Where there are
insufficient pupils to establish two schools in the same neighborhood two or more
secondary school catchment areas are amalgamated and the students anxious to
attend a Welsh-medium school are brought together into one school, transporta-
tion being provided for students who may have as many as 10 or 15 miles to travel
to school. In other countries, the USSR, for instance, the tendency is to create
"dual-medium schools" by bringing together the local nationality school and the
Russian language school. The reason for the difference reflects the different aims
of bilingual education in the two countries. In the USSR the main push is toward
the establishment of the "international" language, namely, Russian, as the major
or dominant partner in bilingual education. In Wales the main thrust is to preserve
the "nationality language," Welsh, against the "international" language, English,
which is so firmly established in all schools (Lewis 1972, 1974).

Higher Education

The seven constituent colleges of the federated University of Wales have a total of
something over 15,000 students drawn from many countries but mainly from
England and Wales. Ability to understand Welsh is not necessary for entry, and
the proportion of students who are able to speak Welsh is approximately 25% and

declining as the University grows. However, the influence of the native speakers of Welsh among the university population is far greater than their numerical status would allow us to expect. Some of the colleges have residential hostels which are reserved for Welsh-speaking undergraduates. Some departments of the University, for instance, Philosophy, History, Theology, Politics, and Sociology, but in particular Education, teach some of the courses in Welsh and they have appointed members of the respective faculties with this purpose in mind. There have been prolonged discussions in the governing body, the Court of the University, about the feasibility as well as the desirability of establishing a separate University College which would teach all or most of the courses in Welsh. This discussion was intensified after the publication of the Advisory Council recommendation (1953:74). But there does not appear to be any possibility of this being implemented soon, and Welsh students have tended to identify the oldest of the Colleges, Aberystwyth, as the most congenial to their way of thinking, and the one which is most concerned about advancing a bilingual higher education policy.

The same pressures have been exerted on the Colleges of Education (the former Normal Colleges) established exclusively to prepare teachers mainly for primary and the lower grades of secondary schools. The Advisory Council (1953:60-61) proposed advanced courses in bilingual education for experienced and qualified teachers; second, the addition of one year to the course of intending teachers who wished to teach in Welsh-medium schools—primary and secondary; and third, a separate College of Education to specialize in Welsh studies. From 1956 onward the use of Welsh as a teaching language was firmly established in two of the nine colleges. In one of these a student must follow the whole course in English or Welsh; in the other he may follow only part of the course in Welsh or the whole course in English. In both colleges a student who elects to follow a Welsh language course is required to follow a modified English course. Where students do not choose to pursue their general course either partly or wholly in Welsh, they are offered the opportunity to prepare for an endorsement of their teacher's certificate—a bilingual endorsement. This entails a concurrent 3-year course in the theory and practice of bilingualism in education, and it certifies that the holder of the endorsement is able to teach Welsh as a first and second language and English as a second language. It is assumed that he is able to teach English as a first language. Approximately 80% of the Welsh-speaking women students and 60% of the men pursue the course each year. Finally, whether they elect to study in Welsh or not, and whether they wish to obtain the bilingual endorsement or not, all students are required to follow a general course in the education of bilingual children with special reference to Wales.

Pedagogy

Language Instruction

Steps to improve language pedagogy in Wales as it affects first or second languages tend to parallel developments in England and elsewhere. They reflect the same kinds of controversy that characterize other bilingual and linguistically homogeneous countries (Lewis 1974b). One of the main problems connected with the teaching of Welsh (as a second language especially) arises from the fact that there are still considerable differences between the several dialects (Richards 1949:46). The written language had been standardized, apart from finalizing the orthography, as far back as the 17th Century. For various reasons a great disparity has emerged between dialectal colloquial Welsh which was ignored and disparaged by the intelligentsia and the rather formal literary Welsh of the pulpit. Writers and Welsh academics placed "so much emphasis on correctness and so much effort went into the attempt to conform to a standard of purity in writing that those who have not followed higher academic courses in colleges fear to use the language either in writing or speech" (Cymraeg Byw, 6). Until very recently the cultivation of an appropriate standard of oral Welsh had been ignored. At the same time speech levels had deteriorated because of considerable English immigration while the need for a uniform oral standard for the whole of Wales had become more important because of increased mobility. Furthermore the shift in emphasis toward an oral approach to language learning whether as a first or second language and the need to ensure that the materials that were used in oral instruction were equally suitable in all parts of Wales and by teachers from very different dialect areas made the standardization of oral Welsh an urgent pedagogic consideration. Two processes were involved: a filtering or leveling of dialects weighing the leveled forms against any competing written forms. These processes were facilitated by the work of teachers of Welsh in schools and colleges. Their aim was to suggest oral standards which would be acceptable everywhere in Wales. At the same time standard oral forms were related as closely as possible to literary standard Welsh (Cymraeg Byw, 8). Without this work and the earlier efforts of the Board of Celtic Studies of the University to bring to a fruition the long-continuing work of Welsh scholars to finalize the orthography of Welsh, it would have been far more difficult to teach Welsh or to use the language to teach some subjects.

So far as concerns language pedagogy strictly so called, perhaps the most valuable work had been undertaken at the University of Wales, Aberystwyth. It has published several general guidelines to teachers (1961) and initiated fundamental research (1968). The most promising as well as the most linguistically competent work has been produced by R.M. Jones at Aberystwyth. Dodson had suggested the use of what he terms the bilingual method, which is a modified translation method and is probably better suited to teaching a foreign rather than a second language (1962, 1966). Watkins (1961) has helped to acquaint teachers of Welsh, especially those of the more academic schools and colleges, with contemporary linguistic theory. More recently Thomas, together with Morris Jones, has been engaged on producing a more suitable teaching grammar for Welsh taking into account the most recent advances in linguistic analysis (Thomas 1973). The Schools Council for England and Wales has promoted various research and development projects on aspects of bilingual education one of which has been concerned with attitudes to the two languages (1973) and the other, recently inaugurated, is concerned with teaching English in the Welsh-speaking areas.

Broadcasting to Schools

The comparative status of the two languages in Wales is reflected in the total broadcasting provision for the country. In 1972, the two broadcasting agencies, BBC and the independent commercial ITV together broadcast 94½ hours of programs on all channels to Wales per day. The division according to language and type of medium is as shown in Table 5. This provision includes the exceptionally

Table 5.   Provision of Welsh and English Language
Broadcast 1972

Type	Welsh	English	Total
Radio	2 hr, 9 min	63 hr, 24 min	65 hr, 33 min
TV	1 hr, 48 min	27 hr, 16 min	29 hr, 4 min
Total	3 hr, 57 min	90 hr, 40 min	94 hr, 37 min

useful and well-produced schools broadcasts in both languages. The latter are integrated into the total provision for schools in England and Wales, but there is a separate Schools Boardcasting Council for Wales which is responsible for the Welsh language programs and those English language programs which reflect aspects of Welsh life. The programs cater to school children of all ages from infants to preuniversity classes. Two programs on Welsh as a second language have been broadcast for several years—Early Stages in Welsh, and Second Stages in Welsh—based on some very useful research on the selection and grading of vocabulary and the selection of syntactic forms. Apart from their value to the students themselves, the programs and the accompanying literature have helped to acquaint teachers of the second language with progressive ideas about classroom practice. Equally significant has been the contribution of programs in the Welsh language about Welsh cultural and industrial life and about the geography and history of Wales. There are also several programs in Welsh which are meant to stimulate activities such as music and movement in the classroom among infants and juniors. All these are supplemented by English programs about Wales. The programs in Welsh amount to 2 hr 20 min on radio and 1 hr on TV each week. The English language programs for Welsh schools amount to 1 hr on radio and 20 min on TV each week. In addition there are out-of-school broadcasts for children in the Welsh language on matters of general and leisure time interest.

Books and Related Materials

There is no lack of schoolbooks in English for native speakers of that language in Wales any more than there is elsewhere. Books prepared for English as a second language are a different matter. An attempt was made in the 1950s when the teaching of English as a second language became a major preoccupation of several important English publishing houses to adapt productions which were meant for the overseas market for use among the native speakers of Welsh. The attempt was unsuccessful partly because the linguistic situations in the countries for which the materials were prepared and that in Wales are so different, but mainly because the level of educational sophistication is so much higher in Wales and the range of childhood interests not only different but much greater. Nevertheless, the teachers who discussed and attempted to use the materials learned a great deal about teaching English as a second language. In some cases the English publishers allowed teachers in Wales to use the lavish illustrations as the nucleus for the preparation of their own materials.

By far the more pressing problem has been the provision of books for the teaching of Welsh at all levels, books in Welsh on subjects such as geography and science, and books of general interest for use in and out of school. The government set up the "Ready Committee" to investigate the state of Welsh publications (1952), and this reported that only 5.2% of the total spent on books by local education authorities for school use went to buy books in Welsh and the figure varied from 3% in one authority to 30% in another. It recommended that a Welsh Books Foundation financed by central and local government funds be formed to help supply schoolbooks and to stimulate interest in the publication of books of a general interest in the Welsh language. In 1954, the Welsh Joint Education Committee launched a scheme to increase the supply of Welsh schoolbooks, and at present upward of forty new titles are issued annually. In addition nine local authorities cooperate with the Joint Committee to encourage books of more general interest in Welsh for children of school age. Since 1956, the central government has made an annual grant, administered by the University of Wales Press Board, which is intended to encourage the publication of books of general interest for older age groups and especially adolescents. The original grant of 1000 pounds has been increased to 25,000 pounds. The Welsh Arts Council (an integral of the Arts Council of Great Britain) provides the bulk of the patronage of Welsh language literature in Wales, and there are now seven organizations also concerned to promote the publication of books in Welsh for school age children and others.

It must be emphasized, however, that whatever has been achieved in the way of Welsh books for bilingual children in Wales depends upon the work of those who have set out to augment the vocabulary of Welsh especially in those domains of use where it had fallen into desuetude. The Board of Celtic Studies has published lexicons for Homemaking, Crafts, History, Mathematics, Technical Vocabulary (including Grammar, Phonology, Metaphysics, Aesthetics, Logic, Music, and Chemistry). The Faculty of Education of the University have issued lexicons for Physical Education and Athletics, Geology, Principles of Education, Physics, and Mathematics; and the Ministry of Education (The Welsh Department) published a lexicon for nature study. The task of those who have written textbooks in Welsh would have been immensely more difficult if not impossible without agreed specialist vocabularies.

A major step was taken in 1968 to add to the materials, books, and other aids required to teach Welsh as a second language. The National Language Unit, administered by the largest education authority (Glamorgan) on behalf of the Welsh Joint Education Committee, was founded to prepare audio-visual aids in the first place and it has so far prepared a course for junior schools entitled "Llafar a Llun" (Sound and Sight) which consists of teachers' handbooks, nearly 90 film strips, and accompanying taped dialogues. By September 1973, a second audio-visual course was completed based on the most popular language textbooks for secondary schools. A third course designed for infants' classes consisting of children whose first language is Welsh has just been completed, and this is intended to reinforce an existing command of the Welsh language in anglicized areas. Its format is similar to the courses already prepared for junior and senior classes. The language unit, which is a research and development institute, has commenced the preparation of a new teaching grammar for the Secondary Leaving Certificate, together with reading materials which accompany the course. For the very young film strips and accompanying taped recordings of Welsh folk tales are being produced as well as material which it is hoped will help the independent acquisition of Welsh by very young children.

BILINGUAL EDUCATION AND ASPECTS OF CHILD BEHAVIOR—RESEARCH IN WALES

Schoolmasters in Wales were among the first to undertake admittedly modest investigations of the consequences of bilingualism for school children in school. The earliest studies (Saer 1922, 1928, 1932) were concerned with the relationship of bilingualism and intellectual development and bilingualism and verbal ability measured by formal objective tests. Sociological variables were taken into account only when serious reservations had been expressed about the validity of this type of investigation arising from the repeatedly conflicting conclusions as well as about its limited relevance to the practical problems of conducting bilingual schools and implementing a bilingual policy. Of greater practical import have been the several surveys undertaken by the Advisory Councils, the Welsh Joint Education Committee, and the National Foundation for Educational Research, the Schools Council for England and Wales, and the Ministry of Education. These surveys have provided necessary information about the incidence of bilingualism and the relationship of variabilities in attainment in key areas of the curriculum like reading in the two languages and mathematics on the one hand, and degrees of bilingualism in individuals and in different parts of Wales.

Bilingualism and Intelligence

For three years Saer (1922) investigated 1400 bilingual children between the ages of 7 and 14 years in seven Welsh-speaking rural and urban areas, together with one school in an anglicized area. In all the schools English was the teaching language. The children were classified according to the level of their bilingual competence and were administered tests of ability to reproduce pure rhythms, tests of manual dexterity, the Stanford Binet-Simon, and the Burt Scales of Intelligence (translated into Welsh), as well as vocabulary and English and Welsh composition tests. Though this early work has been criticized for faulty statistical techniques, it compares not unfavorably with later investigations in Wales. Saer's results were confirmed by Frank Smith (1923) using different techniques. A summary of these studies concluded "that under present day conditions and the organisation of schools in Wales the child who has learned two languages at an early age . . . by learning the second language during play and in association with other children suffers less disturbance than those who are obliged to learn the second language at school and continue to use their mother tongue in their association with other children" (Saer, Smith, and Hughes 1924). Smith, from his investigations of the development of bilingual children over 3 years, concluded that "monoglot children between the ages of 8 and 11 years make better progress than bilingual children in their power of expression, their choice of vocabulary and their accuracy of thought. So far from bilingualism being an intellectual advantage it seems to be exactly the reverse at least under present day conditions in the schools of Wales" (1923:282). These severely qualified conclusions governed attitudes to bilingualism in Wales for many years and reinforced the reluctance of educationists to promote the teaching of Welsh among native speakers of English.

A study of monoglot English and bilingual children from Welsh families was conducted in 1938 (Jones) using nonverbal, concrete verbal, and abstract verbal tests as well as tests of linguistic attainment of a general nature. It was found that "bilingualism did not seem to be a hindrance to thinking carried out in verbal terms" (pp. 10-18). Another study by the same investigator collaborating with Stewart (1951) modified the conclusions. They used adapted English tests to compare the performance of monoglot English and bilinguals and found in the "results a highly significant difference in favour of the monoglot group on the verbal and non-verbal tests." But when the results were adjusted to a common nonverbal basis the difference was substantially reduced but still remained statistically significant. It was therefore concluded that the bilingual children were significantly inferior to the monoglot children even after full allowance had been made for initial differences in nonverbal intelligence" (pp. 3-8). This second set of results only served to confirm the very much earlier studies of Barke (1933), and Barke and Williams (1938). They found very little difference in the performance of monoglots and bilinguals on nonverbal tests but concluded that the bilinguals were distinctly inferior on verbal tests, especially when the verbal tests were administered in the child's mother tongue.

More recent investigations have tended to reveal a consistent inclination for scores on nonverbal tests of intelligence to increase as the linguistic composition of the group became more English and less bilingual (Jones 1955, 1957, 1959, 1960 and Lewis 1959). This conclusion was supported by a later study using largely the same techniques. It has also been suggested that these tendencies continued beyond the early university stage. In 1952, W.R. Jones investigated the performance of Welsh-speaking bilinguals on verbal and nonverbal tests and how their performance on the two types of tests compared with their English reading performance. This was the first study which even tentatively included any sociological variables, namely, parental occupation. He concluded that because of their inferior English reading attainment Welsh-speaking children could not be assessed satisfactorily on verbal tests given in English. This appears to have been the most conclusive though not unexpected result of a long series of studies into the relationship between bilingualism and intelligence among Welsh-speaking children. In 1959, a further study elaborated the treatment of the social background variables in an attempt to correct earlier misconceptions (Jones 1959). On this occasion it was found that the crucial variable in the test performances of bilingual children appeared to be the type of locality, urban or rural, and the occupational status of the parents, and that everything else being equal, bilingualism need not be considered a disadvantage.

Bilingualism and Attainment in Welsh and English and in Other Subjects

Some evidence of the reading attainment of bilingual children is available from some of the researches to which reference has been made already, but in 1955 (Jones) an investigation was undertaken in order to compare the reading attainment of mainly Welsh-speaking and mainly English-speaking bilinguals. The Welsh groups were reported as significantly inferior on the silent reading tests, and this was attributed to insufficient opportunity to acquire satisfactory aural and oral skills in their second language, English. Furthermore, the mainly English-speaking bilinguals were reported as inferior to monoglot English groups, and this was attributed to the fact that the bilinguals were required to learn Welsh as a second language. It was also suggested that even children of superior intelligence were handicapped because of the need to learn a second language. Among the 10-year-old students it was found that the average reading age of the mainly Welsh group was 9.47 months lower than that of the mainly English group of the same age. Among the 11-year-old students the difference was 10.8 months. When mainly Welsh bilinguals were compared with a mixed English/Welsh group the figures were 8.85 and 10.46 min, respectively.

Other studies have been conducted by the local authorities, and it is significant that most of these are concerned with estimating the English reading attainment of students rather than their attainment in Welsh. Monmouthshire published a Survey of Reading Ability in 1953, and since this county is intensely English, there is no real reason why it should have been concerned with reading attainment in Welsh or with comparing the standards of the monolingual English and the bilingual English. The most thoroughly Welsh-speaking authority, Merionethshire, undertood surveys in 1958 and 1961. It was reported that attainment in Welsh as a first language was extremely good and that the mainly Welsh-speaking bilinguals achieved a much higher standard of reading in their second language, English, than did the English bilinguals in Welsh, their second language. There was considerable difference between the standard of reading among urban groups, where the parents appeared to be on professional and nonmanual grades and the rural groups where the parents were mainly engaged in agriculture. The 1961 follow-up survey was concerned with the same students, now in secondary school. It was reported that, judged on the average scores for the whole county, the standard reached by the students at the age of 13, especially in English reading comprehension, was not significantly below that usually associated with monolingual English children in England, though the majority of the Merionethshire students had a predominantly Welsh background and English was the second language. This is largely attributable to the very heavy pressure on students to learn English in the Welsh-speaking areas.

Following the three surveys described in "Standards of Reading 1948-56" (Her Majesty's Stationery Office 1960) which were conducted in 1948, 1952, and 1956 by the Ministry of Education, it was decided to undertake a separate study in Wales taking into account not only standards of English reading as had been the custom but standards of reading in Welsh also, among bilinguals in different linguistic areas. This study was carried out in 1968 (see Table 6). The samples

Table 6.   Standards of Reading in English

	11 years	15 years
All Wales	12.0	20.8
Pupils whose first language is Welsh	9.4	18.0
Other pupils	12.4	21.4
All England	13.3	21.7

Source: Lewis 1968. Extracted.

were drawn for Wales—boys and girls whose first language was Welsh and those whose first language was English. The same measures were used for testing English, namely, the Watts Vernon test as had been used in all previous England and Wales surveys. For the specifically Welsh survey a reading test similar to the English test was constructed in Welsh. For all Wales pupils aged 15 score 8.8 points more than pupils aged 11; for all England, 8.4 points more. This gives a rough equation of 8 points to 4 years of average progress or one point for every 6 months. The difference of 3 points between junior pupils whose first language was Welsh and the other junior pupils in Wales can be regarded as a difference of 18 months, and the difference of 1.3 points between the average junior score for all Wales and that for all England as a difference of 8 months. For senior pupils the difference is somewhat less—0.9 points or 5 months. The difference between English-speaking bilinguals in Wales and English-speaking pupils in England has been reduced considerably by the age of 15, though there is still a slight inferiority. There is an appreciable difference in favor of the English-speaking bilinguals in Wales at the junior and senior levels, though as one would expect the rate of progress of those who are learning English as a second language is slightly greater than that of those of the native speakers of English whether these are bilinguals in Wales or monolinguals in England. The rate of progress of the

English-speaking pupils learning Welsh as a second language is hardly impressive: the level of attainment at 15 years is well below that of Welsh-speaking pupils at 11 (see Table 7). Furthermore, if the progress of the two languages, the Welsh-speaking bilinguals and the English-speaking bilinguals, is compared, the former advance more rapidly in their second language, English, than do the latter in their second language, Welsh.

There is some evidence also of the relationship of attainment in other subjects and levels of bilingualism. Jones and others (1957) administered a mechanical arithmetic test, a problem arithmetic test, a test of silent reading in English, and a Moray House English test, together with a Welsh silent reading test and a Welsh adaptation of the Moray House test, to 11-year-old pupils of schools in the most thoroughly Welsh-speaking areas. The total sample was divided into four groups—Predominantly Welsh speaking (W), Moderately English speaking (We), Predominantly English speaking (E), and Moderately Welsh speaking (Ew).

Table 7.   Standards of Reading in Welsh

	Pupils whose first language was		All Welsh-speaking pupils
	Welsh	English	
Pupils aged 15	22.9	13.6	20.5
Pupils aged 11	16.7	10.5	15.4
Difference between A and B	6.2	3.1	5.1

Source: Lewis 1968. Extracted.

It was found that the four groups did not differ significantly in mechanical arithmetic, though this was uniformly presented in English. There was a significant difference in problem arithmetic between the Welsh (W) group and the English (E) group in favor of the latter, the test having been administered in English. But the performance of the Moderately English speaking group (We) was better than the performance of any of the others. So far as concerns the English reading and the English usage (Moray House) test the Predominantly English (E) group had higher scores than any of the others. The Welsh group's (W) performance on the Welsh language tests was superior to the performance of the Moderately English speaking (We) group. Bilingualism tended not to have any significant association with mechanical arithmetic and only a slightly adverse association with problem arithmetic. The influence of bilingualism on attainment in English and Welsh varies according to the degree of the student's bilingualism.

The most thoroughgoing assessment to date of the attainment of bilingual children in Wales has been the National Foundation and Welsh Joint Education Committee Co-operative Investigation (1969). Samples of pupils aged 7, 10, and 14 were drawn from the whole of Wales (see Tables 8 to 10). The sample was stratified according to type of school and intense linguistic character of the area in which a school was located. The 7-year-old pupils were given tests in number concepts (English and Welsh versions), mechanical arithmetic, problem arithmetic (English and Welsh versions), English reading, and Welsh reading. The 10-year-olds were given English or Welsh versions of concept arithmetic and problem arithmetic and mechanical arithmetic where instructions for the administration of the test were in English and Welsh. The language tests consisted of an English usage test, an English reading test, and parallel tests in Welsh. The 14-year-olds were given the same language tests in English and Welsh as the 10-year-olds. The mechanical arithmetic test was also identical. In addition to these tests, a mathematics problem test and a mathematical insight test were available in both languages.

The differences in the Welsh and English reading tests generally coincided with the linguistic character of the area—the English regions performing better in English and less well in Welsh. So far as concerns problem arithmetic there were no significant differences between linguistic areas. This was not the case with mechanical arithmetic or number concept tests, the Welsh linguistic region tending to have higher scores in both tests than the moderately Welsh-speaking area, and the thoroughly English-speaking area performing better on problem arithmetic than either of the other two areas.

As among the 7-year-olds, performance in the language tests varied according to the linguistic character of the area. The more English the area the better the performance in English and the poorer in Welsh. On the other tests the English area schools tended to have higher scores, though in some cases the differences were only slight.

Performance on the language tests again varied with the character of the area. On the other tests the moderately Welsh-speaking area B obtained higher scores than the other two areas, though the variations are not very great. When we consider all three age groups, some interesting conclusions may be drawn. It is clear that standards in English tend to be higher than those in Welsh especially where the two are second languages. School performance varies among different bilingual strata according to age. The influence of differences in linguistic background appears to be least at age 7 and then increases as the pupils reach 10 and 14 years. When the pupils in the thoroughly Welsh-speaking area (A) were further classified according to their specific home background, the differences in achievement between children from thoroughly Welsh, moderately Welsh, and thoroughly English homes appeared to conform to the differences between the broader linguistic areas. Where bilingualism has an important effect on performance, it appears to be confined to those aspects of the curriculum where language is the key factor. Where language is less important, as in certain types of mathematical skills, the influence of bilingualism in Wales declines.

Attitude to English and Welsh among School Age Children

Three substantial investigations into attitudes toward the two languages have been conducted fairly recently. The Advisory Council (1967) submitted a series of

Table 8. 7-Year-Old Pupils in All Schools According to Linguistic Area

| | Sampling areas | | | | | | Wales | |
| | A | | B | | C | | All schools | |
Test	Mean	SE	Mean	SE	Mean	SE	Mean	SE
Number concept:								
Boys	99.75	0.84	95.94	1.23	99.21	2.03	98.83	1.97
Girls	101.73	1.48	100.02	1.52	101.18	2.20	101.11	2.05
Mechanical arithmetic:								
Boys	102.48	1.39	98.7	1.23	98.02	1.30	98.73	1.24
Girls	106.06	1.46	102.70	1.69	100.77	1.34	101.64	1.21
Problem arithmetic:								
Boys	100.22	1.10	98.47	1.10	101.51	1.58	100.91	1.53
Girls	98.16	1.44	100.34	1.75	100.18	1.62	99.96	1.51
Reading comprehension:								
Boys	94.90	1.08	95.57	1.12	98.17	2.08	97.36	2.01
Girls	97.76	1.34	101.92	1.00	103.31	1.64	102.48	1.56
Welsh reading (Prawf Darllen):								
Boys	93.85	1.47	77.97	2.50	74.08	1.12	77.33	1.05
Girls	95.13	1.40	83.05	2.14	73.32	1.19	77.07	1.21
Number of children:								
Boys	369		374		428		591	
Girls	314		303		439		575	

Sampling areas: A = LEAs with 62 to 100% Welsh-speaking children.
B = LEAs with 17 to 25% Welsh-speaking children.
C = LEAs with less than 8% Welsh-speaking children.

Source: WJEC/NFER 1973: p. 34.

Table 9.   10-Year-Old Pupils—All Schools According to Linguistic Areas

| | Sampling areas | | | | | | Wales | |
| | A | | B | | C | | All schools | |
Test	Mean	SE	Mean	SE	Mean	SE	Mean	SE
Concept arithmetic A:								
Boys	98.20	1.05	98.78	0.72	100.83	1.29	100.14	0.95
Girls	96.93	0.79	97.00	0.75	101.51	1.29	100.22	0.92
Concept arithmetic B:								
Boys	98.78	1.16	98.60	1.08	100.22	1.29	99.77	0.95
Girls	100.35	1.18	98.72	1.17	101.74	1.20	101.14	0.89
Problem arithmetic:								
Boys	99.47	1.10	101.38	0.93	101.08	1.19	100.86	0.87
Girls	99.00	0.89	100.24	0.78	101.10	1.28	100.66	0.93
Mechanical arithmetic:								
Boys	98.66	1.21	98.88	0.91	98.92	1.06	98.92	0.78
Girls	100.41	1.06	100.54	0.95	101.86	1.19	101.63	0.88
English:								
Boys	92.78	1.05	95.49	1.03	98.88	1.32	97.45	1.02
Girls	94.24	1.00	96.23	1.06	102.56	1.60	100.45	1.02
English reading:								
Boys	91.90	1.06	95.67	0.83	100.68	1.45	98.60	1.13
Girls	90.49	0.94	94.18	0.76	101.32	1.24	98.72	0.99

Table 9 (continued)

| Test | Sampling areas | | | | | | Wales | |
| | A | | B | | C | | All schools | |
	Mean	SE	Mean	SE	Mean	SE	Mean	SE
Welsh:								
Boys	89.19	1.76	56.93	2.82	53.63	3.21	59.77	2.22
Girls	90.92	1.68	58.65	3.13	53.95	3.32	60.36	2.45
Welsh reading:								
Boys	89.27	1.98	61.05	1.98	58.88	2.15	64.04	1.60
Girls	89.21	1.97	61.08	2.10	58.63	2.47	63.76	1.77
Number of children:								
Boys	537		441		478		677	
Girls	509		398		468		653	

NOTE: Sampling area as defined in Table 8.
Source: WJEC/NFER 1973: p. 36.

Table 10.   14-Year-Old Pupils—All Schools According to Language Area

| | Sampling areas | | | | | | Wales | |
| | A | | B | | C | | All schools | |
Test	Mean	SE	Mean	SE	Mean	SE	Mean	SE
Mathematics:								
Boys	99.46	0.84	104.05	2.81	103.99	2.84	103.39	1.26
Girls	98.37	0.93	98.71	0.63	97.37	1.35	97.71	1.28
Mathematics insight:								
Boys	97.94	0.86	102.50	2.60	102.20	1.04	101.67	1.27
Girls	99.52	1.23	99.89	0.60	97.81	1.30	98.35	1.19
Mechanical arithmetic:								
Boys	98.40	1.05	100.06	2.10	99.78	1.18	99.64	1.23
Girls	100.83	0.65	101.37	0.65	101.58	1.54	101.45	1.99
English:								
Boys	94.93	0.78	99.34	2.84	99.48	0.76	98.85	1.23
Girls	99.98	1.51	100.29	1.12	99.96	1.40	100.01	1.06
English reading:								
Boys	94.48	0.55	100.23	2.62	101.85	1.25	100.61	1.31
Girls	95.36	1.49	97.02	1.14	98.22	1.20	97.66	0.98
Welsh:								
Boys	88.03	2.29	65.82	2.69	58.98	2.22	63.92	1.42
Girls	94.03	2.50	71.41	3.93	62.59	3.96	68.15	1.94
Welsh reading:								
Boys	86.82	2.86	62.57	3.44	56.10	2.41	61.21	1.56
Girls	91.88	2.63	66.92	4.98	57.76	4.15	63.73	2.00

Source: WJEC/NFER 1973: p. 37.

questions to the parents of children in all parts of Wales concerning the possible advantages or disadvantages of learning Welsh, and about the degree of their satisfaction or dissatisfaction with the teaching of the language (Table 11).

Table 11.   Parental Attitude to the Teaching of Welsh as a Second Language According to Linguistic Area

	Intensely Welsh areas	Moderately Welsh areas	Glamorgan	Most densely urban
Percentage who saw advantages	67	60	49	45
Percentage satisfied with instruction in Welsh	59	77	68	72
Percentage satisfied with pupil's progress in primary school Welsh	44	54	35	25

Source: Central Advisory Council (CAC) 1967: p. 237.

It will be seen that attitude to the language is more favorable the less anglicized the area. Yet it is noteworthy that even in the most thoroughly Welsh areas there is considerable doubt about the usefulness of bilingualism. When it comes to satisfaction with the teaching of the language, it appears that attitude is more favorable in the areas where the usefulness of the language is most in question; in other words, concern about the quality of instruction declines as the attitude to the language becomes less and less favorable or a matter of indifference. When the parents in all areas were classified according to their linguistic affiliation, 46% of the mothers who were not bilingual and 74% of the mothers who were bilingual saw advantages in their children being bilingual. Where both parents were bilingual, 85% saw the advantage of their children learning Welsh.

A second survey (see Table 12) was specifically concerned with the attitudes of children in junior schools toward Arithmetic, English, and Welsh (WJEC/NFER 1973).

Clearly negative attitudes to Welsh as to the other two subjects tend to be quite low in all three linguistic areas, but they are higher in respect of Welsh than they are for arithmetic or English. Attitude to the latter is very favorable in all three areas and not appreciably lower in the thoroughly Welsh-speaking area than in the other two. Generally speaking, attitude toward Welsh improves with the degree of bilingualism in the area, but it does not attract high levels of support even in the thoroughly Welsh-speaking area.

A much more exhaustic enquiry into attitudes to the two languages was conducted between 1967 and 1971 under the aegis of the Schools Council for England and Wales (1973). A stratified sample of 57 junior schools yielded 1750

Table 12. Percentage of 10-Year-Old Pupils with Positive, Indifferent, or Negative Attitudes to Arithmetic, English, or Welsh, According to Linguistic Area

Subject	Percentage of bilingualism								
	60%			16-25%			0-15%		
	Positive	Indiff.	Negat.	Positive	Indiff.	Negat.	Positive	Indiff.	Negat.
Arithmetic	57.0	33.9	9.1	52.8	38.9	8.3	46.1	43.6	10.2
English	70.5	19.0	10.6	74.1	18.6	7.3	71.2	19.7	9.1
Welsh	59.0	20.8	19.1	43.1	28.1	28.8	32.6	29.1	28.3

Source: WJEC/NFER 1973: pp. 91-93 (extracted).

children in three localities of varying bilingual intensity. Twenty-seven secondary schools yielding 3650 students were also selected, twenty-one from the three linguistic areas referred to, and six, irrespective of area, from among the total of schools which have been created in recent years to give Welsh a more prominent place in the curriculum and to use it more frequently and intensively to teach other subjects. Thurstone-type tests were administered to all junior and secondary school students, and a Semantic Differential Scale to the secondary school students only.

The investigation brought out marked differences in the pattern of attitude among those represented in the different strata of the sample (see Table 13).

The attitude to Welsh becomes increasingly less favorable in all areas and types of schools as the students grow older, and increasingly favorable to English. In the areas where English is generally favored (category C) the disparity between Welsh and English attitudes is increased. In areas where Welsh is generally favored (categories A, B, and D) the disparity decreases to the extent that at 14+ there is an attitudinal switch from Welsh to English except in category D (Table 13).

Table 13.   Mean Scores of Attitude to Welsh and English on Thurstone Tests According to Age and Linguistic Area

| | Type of linguistic area | | | | | | | |
| | A, 68-81% Welsh | | B, 48-55% Welsh | | C, 3-26% Welsh | | D, Welsh-medium schools | |
Ages	Welsh	English	Welsh	English	Welsh	English	Welsh	English
10+	3.97	5.87	4.22	5.66	5.39	5.06	3.21	6.75
12+	4.26	5.45	4.78	5.16	5.50	4.82	3.55	6.43
14+	4.86	4.81	5.16	4.92	5.92	4.58	3.70	5.76

*The lower the mean the more favorable the attitude.

From an examination of the percentage response to each of the items in the Thurstone-type tests together with the results of the Semantic Differential Test it becomes more evident than ever that the nature of the response, from item to item in the questionnaires, varies consistently with the area from which the subjects were drawn. Where the percent responses of students in categories A, B, and C to the item "English should be taught all over the world" was in the range 40 to 60%, varying according to age and area, the percentage response in category D was half that, in the range of 23 to 33% varying according to age. The "English is a beautiful language" produced a range of 40 to 60% in all students except category D, where the percent was 21. Attitude to the two languages and especially Welsh is a function of the linguistic character of the locality, and individual variance within localities is limited.

Attitude to Welsh among children, as it can be interpreted from an examination of the Thurstone test results, appears to have four major components. The first of these is a factor which we may term "general approval"—"I would like to speak Welsh for the fun of it," "Welsh is a language worth learning," "I like speaking Welsh," etc., where the average response is favorable 60 to 75%. The second factor is "commitment to practice"—represented by such statements as "I want to maintain Welsh to enable Wales to develop" (50%); "I should like to be able to read Welsh books" (45%), "Likely to use Welsh" (40%); "There are more useful languages than Welsh" (38%). While general approval was very favorable, response to items which might be taken to imply a practical decision to implement approval was relatively unfavorable. One indication of the apparent reluctance to take practical steps to promote Welsh is the fairly high percentage of responses in favor of individual choice in deciding to study Welsh, "Welsh should not be forced upon non-Welsh-speaking pupils" (75%); "The learning of Welsh should be left to individual choice" (78%).

The third factor in attitude to Welsh is "national tradition," represented by "The need to keep up Welsh for the sake of tradition" (68%); "We owe it to our forefathers to preserve Welsh" (78%); "The Welsh language should be preserved because it is a sign of Welsh nationhood" (65%). This, together with the first factor of "general approval" is the most important aspect of attitude to Welsh. The fourth factor, "economic importance," plays a much less significant role. For instance, the percentage who considered Welsh offered advantages in seeking good job opportunities was as low as 41% in Welsh-speaking areas, and in the English-speaking areas the percentage who thought that Welsh was important in Welsh economic life was below 50%. So far as Welsh is concerned, therefore, two factors—"general approval" and "traditional nationalism" produce favorable responses, and the two other factors, "a commitment to practice" and "economic importance" produced unfavorable responses on the whole. The components of each pair of factors appear to relate to similar or closely related aspects of attitude to Welsh, so that we can speak of a favorable "emotional attachment" to Welsh, which contrasts with a "realistic and unfavorable appraisal of the use of Welsh," which exert strong pulls in opposite directions.

Attitude to English also has four major components, three of which correspond closely to components of the attitude to Welsh—"general approval," "commitment to practice," and "economic and educational importance," all of which receive very favorable responses. The fourth component of attitude to Welsh, "traditional nationalism," finds no place in the attitude to English, and is replaced by a factor we may term "necessary bilingualism." This factor is expressed in favorable responses to such statements as "I should not like English to take over from the Welsh language" (65%); "The English language is killing the Welsh language" (80%); "The Welsh should speak both languages" (72%); "English should not be more important than Welsh in Wales" (68%). The existence of this fourth factor in attitude to English is in line with the nature of the curve of distribution of total responses to English (Table 13), which is unimodal and to that extent is devoid of extreme antipathy to Welsh or extreme commitment to English in Wales, but displays a degree of tolerance which is remarkable among relatively young children.

Insofar as the attitudes of children toward Welsh take the form of a general emotional response, either to the aesthetic (musical and "magical") attributes of the language or to its claims upon their loyalty, those attitudes show a remarkable consistency both within individuals (measured by the correlation of item scores) or between different age and area strata (measured by the correlation of means). Furthermore the two areas of the emotional response to Welsh, the "aesthetic" and the "affiliative," whether that response is negative or affirmative, reinforce each other in the sense that high or low scores on items related to one aspect are supported by high or low scores on items related to the other.

From one point of view the attitude to English is also, generally speaking, internally consistent, though several more attributes of English are identified as evoking the emotional response. Among children drawn from Welsh-speaking areas (A and D especially) there are high scores favorable to the use of English because of its universality and prestige. These characteristics of English, though they are given greater prominence among some age groups and in different language areas, appear in the profiles of all such groups.

A kind of inconsistency characterizes attitudes to both languages among children. This derives from the fact that attitude to either language reflects, though in two very different ways, attitude to the other language as well—there are two conflicting points of reference or sources for both attitudes. Neither attitude is unequivocal, and this is true of subjects who are monolingual English or bilingual. So far as attitude to English is concerned, the ambivalence is articulated openly. For instance, the two statements in the English scale on which there was greatest agreement are "I should not like English to take over from Welsh" and the statement which follows immediately, "English will take you further than Welsh." We have noted earlier the awareness of the value of both languages which emerges in the responses to the English test, and the degree of tolerance which characterizes that awareness.

So far as attitude to Welsh is concerned, the awareness of English expresses itself quite differently, because it helps to exaggerate the potentially favorable or unfavorable response—to polarize attitude. There is evidence of far greater conflict between attitudes to Welsh and English in the Welsh-speaking categories of schools (A and D) than in the English areas. The conflict is least in category C—the most English-speaking. The impact of the awareness of the English language is to force an unequivocal choice upon the subject, while in the case of attitude to Welsh on the part of the English child it is to encourage an attempt at compromise. This is only to be expected, since the English language is nowhere felt to be threatened and attitudes of the majority can therefore afford to be moderately favorable. Welsh, especially in the Welsh-speaking category schools, is seen to be, and in season and out of season is said to be under threat, so that the attitude to it hardens among the minority, and becomes more tolerant among the majority.

CONCLUSION

Bilingualism is an integral part of the system of education in Wales, and however little Welsh may be spoken in an area there is the consciousness that it was the dominant language there once and in consequence a sense of guilt that no more is being done to promote the minority language. But whether Welsh is spoken or not it affects the teaching of several other subjects—like history, music, homemaking, and crafts where a sense of Welsh tradition may still be imbued. Bilingualism is in fact more significant as a climate in which education is facilitated than as the actual teaching of the two languages. There is no doubt that even if the decline of the Welsh language continues, "bilingual education" in the more general sense will continue to exert a significant pressure upon educationists. However, as the state of Welsh becomes more precarious there is likely to be even greater pressure to obtain a more prominent place for the Welsh language in all kinds of schools and at all ages, with the intention of making the language an obligatory subject. But even here bilingualism is not a pedagogical issue. No amount of research concerning the influence of bilingualism on attainment and no amount of information about the way children and parents feel about the two languages will carry much weight, and ironically a conviction that teaching Welsh is not very successful simply feeds the fire of militancy. If there are disadvantages, it is argued, then the school system needs to be modified to minimize them. If instruction is unsuccessful, there should be more of it. Bilingualism, since it is almost exclusively a matter of maintaining the minority (but at the same time traditional national) language, is associated with the intense desire to assert one's distinctiveness and the uniqueness of a particular way of life. The problem is that the way of life is no longer that which the language has been associated with traditionally. Wales is no longer a "traditional" society, but part of an extensive industrial complex. It is predominantly an urban society, with the great majority of even the Welsh-speaking population living in areas of high population density. The rationale for a bilingual education which has been appealed to during the last century and a half is no longer relevant and the question for the future is to discover a rationale for bilingualism in which Welsh can justify a place in a culture which is almost indistinguishable from the culture of the western world as a whole and, apart from the Welsh language, identical with the culture of England.

Part II

SOCIAL PERSPECTIVES

Bidialectal Education:

Black English and Standard English

in the United States

J. L. Dillard

In the United States, bidialectal education does not enjoy the status or the development accorded to bilingual education. For one thing, the principle has not yet been generally accepted that American English dialects vary enough to cause educational difficulties. As a matter of fact, the whole process of dealing educationally with dialects is often slandered with such opprobrious terms as *doublespeak*.[1] In one extreme case, bidialectal educators have been charged with complicty in an alleged plot to stamp out dialects.[2] The entire topic remains a matter of debate—often acrimonious, and more often politically oriented than linguistically based (Stewart 1970). One special reason is, of course, that the speakers of the most radically nonstandard dialect in the United States are the Black descendants of plantation field hands (Dillard 1972).

Whatever theorizing has been done about bidialectal education in the United States follows the transitional orientation toward bilingual education. The eventual aim, in all clearly articulated cases, is monodialectal education for both native speakers of Standard English (and of the less radically deviant dialects) and of Black English. No one has presented a plan for anything like a full program of education in Black English, or parallel education in both Black English and Standard English, which would be a more perfect parallel to the programs advocated by a great many bilingual educationists. Some Black militants have advocated complete education of ghetto youngsters in Swahili or in some other African language (overlooking the historical inappropriateness of Swahili). In one extreme case, the Universal International Catholic Church of Brooklyn, N.Y.

[according to a personal communication from His Holiness M. Zidonee Hama-theite, Presiding Archepatriarche (sic) No. 1] is attempting to "write a New African Language, based on the general syntax of the more than 800 languages which are now being spoken by various African ethnic groups in Africa."

The lack of educational attention to Black English can be traced, in part at least, to the delay in recognition of the language variety. Although there were some important forerunners (Bloomfield 1933:474, Wise 1933), the debate as to whether a Black dialect exists apart from general Southern speech was a product of the late 1960s, and the topic remains controversial. There is grudging recognition—or none at all—of ethnically correlated dialects on the part of many dialectologists and of almost all dialect geographers (Dillard 1974). It has long been a part of general linguistic knowledge, however, that there are two language varieties in the United States which are spoken almost exclusively by Blacks and which differ strikingly from the standard languages and from European nonstandard dialects. One of these is Louisiana French Creole, studied by Morgan (1959, 1960) and observed by Read (1931) and Tinker (1936). Even more relevant is the case of Gullah, best known through the work of Turner (1949) but less formally reported by Jones (1888), Gonzales (1922), Smith (1926), and others. McDavid and McDavid (1951) flirted with the notion that the same processes which produced Gullah may once have been more widespread; but the notion had been discarded until Bailey (1965), Dillard (1964), and Stewart (1965, 1967, 1968). R. McDavid (1967) rejected the "creolist" theory, as it came to be known, and virtually repudiated his earlier viewpoint in an Addendum to a reprint of the earlier McDavid and McDavid paper (McDavid 1971).

Despite the opposition of the dialect geographers, those with orientation toward the creole languages and with experience in West African English have generally adopted some version of the "creolist" theory (Dalby 1969, Hancock 1972). Hancock (1972 and ms.) calls into question the direct relationship of Black American English to Gullah while still asserting the existence of the former variety, its difference from other varieties of American English, and its relationship to the Afro-Caribbean varieties. Dillard (forthcoming) reviews the historical evidence, presenting a kind of compromise between the viewpoints of Hancock and Stewart.

Other researchers, not involved in either of these historical controversies, have found considerable evidence of an ethnically correlated Black language variety. Baratz, Shuy, and Wolfram (1969), Baratz (1969a), Bryden (1968), Buck (1968), Labov et al. (1968), and Tucker and Lambert (1969) show that respondents are capable of differentiating Black and white residents of a given geographic area from tape-recorded cues only.[3] Not all of these agree that syntactic differences are involved; indeed, it seems impossible to make any such determination from listening tests only.

Exponents of the view that Black English has a different syntactic system from that of Standard English, differing to a degree that cannot be described by a few low-level derivational rules, are Stewart (all references), Dillard (all references), Loflin (all references), Fickett (1970 and forthcoming), and Bailey (1965). Berdan (1973) finds that "the facts of Standard English seem best described by positing a rule of Got-Insertion. There is no evidence for such a rule in Black English." Berdan's evidence is the most extensive task-oriented evidence for the existence of syntactic differences (virtually the only report except for Baratz 1969a and a few other reports of repetition tasks), but it examines only the relatively trivial matter of Black English *he got* (negated *he don't got*, or *he ain't got* in later age-status grades) in comparison to Standard English *he has/he has got* (negated *he hasn't/he hasn't got*, also *he ain't got* in white nonstandard dialects). Stewart (1964) pointed out the syntactic difference involved in the rules which produce *he don't got*, along with differences in the preverbal auxiliary structure and other more superficial differences, but offered only observational evidence.

Stewart (1964) also pointed out that Black English has a systematic difference in that its zero copula (*he busy*) contrasts with an invariant *be* form (*he be busy*) which has often been called a "durative" or "habituative" form; *be* co-occurs more normally with time adverbs like *all time time* whereas zero copula occurs more normally with *right now*. (There are, of course, complications to these central grammatical tendencies.) Loflin, Sobin, and Dillard (forthcoming) offer some evidence from co-occurrent time adverbial forms, in sentences like *He be dancing last Friday*, where *be* could not possibly be a substitute for Standard English *is*, **He is dancing last Friday* not being found in any "white" variety. The *be*-durative difference between Black English and Standard English is now rather generally accepted in linguistic circles, although there are differences of opinion about its exact description (Fasold 1969).

In addition, Stewart (1964) called attention to the fact that the zero copula (or the "missing" auxiliary in *he going* as against Standard English *he is/was going*) could not be the result of phonological deletion, since Black English has sentences like *Doris stupid* where Standard English contraction rules do not permit **Doris's stupid*. Labov (1969a) wrote rules of such complexity that they would allow for such forms even in a context of contraction and deletion, and this article has become a kind of rallying point for those like Houston (1969), Fasold and Wolfram (1970), and Wolfram (1971) who have insisted that the differences between Black English and Standard English are exclusively or primarily phonological. Labov's rules seem unnecessarily complex, however, when many phonological rules may be saved by the introduction of one category into the syntactic base component (Luelsdorff 1970:I:11). In addition, Stewart (1964) pointed out the existence of structures like *Im is*, which further complicated a contraction-deletion description and which argued that *Im* (as in *Im right*, versus *you right*) was best regarded as an alternative form of the first person pronoun *I* and not as a contraction of *I* and *am*, where the Black English usage was concerned.

Stewart (1964), Dillard (1967, 1972), and Fickett (1970) have also emphasized the use of preverbal *been* as an anterior time marker.[4] Fickett, especially, gives elaborate data on the use of *been done* and *done been*, with intricate shades of meaning difference. Fickett's description is the most extreme statement of the differences between the preverbal systems of the two varieties. Labov (1972:53-54) now acknowledges that the structure exemplified in *I been know your name*, where *been* is said to mark a "remote present perfect," is a syntactic difference; according to this most recent statement by Labov, "It is not normally understood by speakers of other dialects." It must be assumed, therefore, that the existence of syntactic differences between Black English and Standard English is coming to be accepted.

There is, however, a further problem in that, even if it is accepted that there are syntactic differences, the precise function of syntactic structure in understanding remains subject to some controversy. Ficket (1970:117) quotes a charming anecdote about a Black junior high school student in Buffalo who, upon being told that his white contemporaries did not understand the difference between *been V* and *done V*, responded "those kids gotta be dumb." While it is relatively certain that speakers of Black English or of Standard English habitually classify the other group as "dumb," there is little evidence as to the degree of actual misunderstanding which takes place. Even Labov et al. (1968) present no quantitative data on this very important consideration. Loflin, Sobin, and Dillard (forthcoming) isolate a few instances in which the time reference is ambiguous and hypothesize that misunderstandings are more likely to take place at such ambiguous points than elsewhere. Fasold and Wolfram (1970) assert that *be,* as in *Sometimes he be there and sometimes he don't*, occurs only in Negro dialect and is usually misunderstood by Standard English speakers. Roberts (1969) stresses the handicap faced by a child who speaks Black English when it comes to taking the Wechsler Preschool Intelligence Test, which in effect assumes "full socialization into the culture of the speakers of the dominant dialect of English." Haskins (1973) presents, although no more formally than many popular efforts of this type, the "Dove Counterbalance Intelligence Test," a man-bites-dog IQ test which promises to make for lower white than Black scores but which is entirely Standard English except for some items of ethnic slang. Crawford and Bentley (1973) and Baughman (1971) present equivalent efforts.

The problem of mutual intelligibility is equally vexed where earlier historical stages are concerned. Horsmanden (1744:127) remarked that one of the ringleaders of the alleged New York Plot of 1744 spoke English which was "so perfectly Negro and unintelligible that it was thought it would be impossible to make anything of him without an interpreter." Two young (white) men were found who could serve as interpreters, and it may be that such strategems were frequently employed in the early years of slavery in the United States. When such historical evidence of the degree of mutual intelligibility is considered, it should also be remembered that Horsmanden and his fellow judges of the supreme court of the colony of New York were dealing with adults only; the creolist theory of Black English history stresses age-grading, most adults and even adolescents having learned to make some accommodation to other varieties of English. Smyth (1775), who, like Horsmanden, dealt with adults only, found that he could not understand "a single word" of the language of one slave whom he bought. He apparently understood the second perfectly well, although that slave's recorded speech is also obviously creole. Douglass (1855) reports the difficulty of native-born slaves in understanding those who had come directly from Africa. Douglass himself was a relatively privileged slave, who among other things taught himself to read and write with the involuntary aid of his master's children, with whom he played; the possibility that the field servants, as suggested by Frazier (1957), were more like the recent African arrivals linguistically should not be discarded. Jones (1832) wrote of the language of the Blacks as "broken English" but asserted that they were capable of understanding Standard ("good") English and that his preachers should avoid the use of the slaves' variety. Benezet (Brookes 1937) thought that his Indian and Black students of the mid-18th Century needed special language instruction, but no details are given.

The question of the degree of linguistic difference is crucial to the matter of bidialectal education. If the only differences are those of a few prestige pronunciations, like the learning of *mother* instead of *muvver* (and perhaps the substitution of lexical items like *tough character* for *bad muvverfucker*), bidialectal education concerns itself with matters of linguistic etiquette or linguistic snobbery—matters with which very few workers in the field would be willing to concern themselves. Sledd (1973) questions the teaching of, for example, *bathe* instead of *bave* and strongly hints that "bidialectalists" are attempting to divert attention from important social issues (as, for example, whether poor Black babies have an equal chance to be "baved"). If, on the other hand, there is a real basis for questioning the mutual intelligibility of the two varieties, especially on the part of a six- to eight-year-old child who has not had a lifetime of practical experience in accommodation, then the issue is a serious one of great practical and even of paramount importance for American education. It is well known that Black children, particularly in the inner city, do poorly on standardized reading tests (Coleman 1966, NAEP 1970-1971) and that their rate of dropping out from school is high (Baratz 1969b). If the explanation is to be anything except genetic inferiority (Jensen 1969), then the possibility that poor Black children and middle-class teachers do not understand each other—especially the possibility that a tenuous understanding is lost at critical moments—remains a very important factor to consider.

For those who recommend some form of bidialectal education, there are two alternative (although not contradictory or competing) solutions and a kind of application of the first to composition teaching. The first is the teaching of Standard English as a second dialect (SESD). This approach would be in a sense bidialectal because proposals (e.g., Stewart 1964, 1965; Allen 1967) have always called for teaching the instructor about Black English as well as for development of teaching materials on the principle of contrastive analysis. The other is the use of nonstandard dialect in initial reading instruction. Several projects of this type have been carried out (Board of Education, City of Chicago 1968, 1969; Rystrom 1970). Some of them, like Rystrom's, have involved so little exact data on the dialect that their results hardly have much bearing on the advisability of dialect reading instruction. Others, like that of the Chicago Board of Education, have not been completely reported. The sociopolitical climate has prevented ideal, or even acceptable, experimental conditions for some projects (Johnson and Simons 1973). Composition teachers have dealt with the use of Black English and with the contrastive approach to teaching Standard English (Crystal 1972, Ross 1972, Schotta 1970).

Historically, there have been two branches of the Standard English as a Second Dialect approach, similar on the surface but different in underlying philosophy. One of them looked upon the language of Black inner city children as a "deficient" language and sought to teach them an "adequate" language (Bereiter and Engelmann 1966). The second regarded Black English as adequate for all communicative purposes but asserted that most Americans face the need of learning Standard English as a kind of dialect of wider communication. For many, mastery of the "unmarked" dialect followed almost automatically from participation in business or professional activities (Fishman 1971). Many Blacks are, however, trapped in the vicious circle in which they cannot get the kind of job needed to provide the opportunity to learn varietal switching unless they are already speakers of Standard English.

The "deficit" model, which considers Black English as an inadequate language, is not a live issue among linguists. However, it has profoundly affected the school system and therefore the climate in which a pedagogically oriented linguist must work. A teacher in the elementary schools will be likely to have read Bereiter (1965) "[if the child] does not know the word *not* . . . he is deprived of one of the most powerful tools of our language." The same teacher may be somewhat less likely to have read Baratz (1971), who points out that *ain't no* is as effective as *not* insofar as negating power goes. But the teacher is least likely of all to have read Fickett (1970) or Stewart (1964), where the differential functions of *he not working* and *he ain't working* are pointed out. The teacher cannot, then, be reasonably expected to know of the extra "powerful tool" which the Black child has—to differentiate *not* (immediate present negation) from *ain't* (general negation). Linguists who advocate a form of bidialectal education, like Baratz (1969b), as well as those like Labov (1969b) who regard such strategies noncommittally or even unfavorably, have unanimously attacked deficit theory. Baratz (1973) reviews the evidence for language deficit among Black children, including some of her own studies which show difference rather than deficit. Baratz (1969a) showed that, whereas Black children did worse at repeating Standard English sentences than did middle-class white children, the Black children were significantly better at the repetition task when the sentences presented were in Black English. Linguists have, of course, felt themselves in agreement with such relativistic conclusions, whether based on experimental evidence or on speculative theory. A few linguists, like Houston (forthcoming), have apparently associated all bidialectal education with deficit theory; her rejection of such programs is apparently based on an identification of the two.

Those linguists who have advocated the teaching of a second dialect in the school system have been very much aware of the sociolinguistic work on diglossia (Ferguson 1959, Fishman 1971). Stewart, one of the first in the field, drew heavily on his own work on diglossia in the Caribbean islands, particularly Haiti (Stewart 1962a, 1962b). Furthermore, his insights into age-grading gained from those studies proved applicable to the Black American situation (Stewart 1964, Dillard 1972). As Stewart has frequently pointed out (1964, 1965, 1967, 1968, 1969, 1970) dialect studies made with adult informants—or even with adolescents as in Labov et al. (1968)—almost necessarily fail to capture basilect,[5] and thus fail to discover how much language difference exists between the dialect of the Black children in the first grade or in the preschool and the dialect of which their teachers expect them to be masters.[6]

Educationally oriented studies, often with slightly older children than those preferred by Stewart, have frequently tried to determine the extent of the difficulty in varietal switching. Wood and Curry (1969) tested the extent to which Black children do not learn to adapt to school. They found that linguistic adaptability is limited and that the children are not suddenly transformed into middle-class children. These authors report that there was a great difference between the speech of a welfare Black child and a middle-class Black child when asked to use "school talk" as opposed to "everyday talk" in answering questions. In the case of the use of "everyday talk," the differences between the two groups were not quite so apparent. A Black field worker spoke with ninth grade girls in both socioeconomic classes, using the type of speech that she wished to elicit from her students. The field worker found that "everyday talk" was more down-to-earth and free, but generally negative and pessimistic in terms of attitudes, whereas the "school talk" was more inhibited, idealistic, optimistic, and more reluctantly used by the lower-class girls. Egocentric speech patterns were more prevalent in middle-class speech (contrary to what has often been asserted about lower-class children and their "restricted codes") and more common in everyday speech for both groups. In addition, the more informal the situation, the greater was the use of more complex speech patterns. This type of research has often raised the point of how the Black child's everyday speech patterns differ from what is the expected norm in school and also just how inhibiting an experience schooling must be to the Black child from a lower-class background. Except, however, insofar as "inhibition" can be taken as a possible index of understanding, such research says nothing about the degree of mutual intelligibility. Houston (forthcoming) supports the conclusion, paradoxical enough from a doctrinaire school point of view, that Black children use more complex structures in their familiar "everyday" talk than they do in "school talk," which they do not master comfortably.

Research of this type, like the frequent statements of the linguists, has been diametrically opposed to the assumptions of many schoolteachers, for whom "school talk" (roughly, Standard English) has been automatically assumed to be more expressive and structurally more complex. A stereotyped schoolteacher (the "Miss Fidditch" of Joos 1962) might be expected to consider "everyday talk" (including Black English and other nonstandard dialects) as inherently less expressive, even lacking in potential for conveying information or in "logic." Works attacking the purism of the schools became especially abundant in the pedagogical linguistic literature of the late 1940s and early 1950s (Fries 1927, 1952). By the middle of the decade of the 1950s, however, many linguists were beginning to suspect that some of "Miss Fidditch's" recommendations had a kind of practical utility—if they were generally made for the wrong reason.[7] The teaching of a second dialect was recommended, then, as a linguistically more defensible alternative to the schoolteacher's outright condemnation of non-standard dialects as well as to the sentimental primitivist's notion that everyone should continue to speak the language variety which he was so to speak born with. It was felt, moreover, that there should be incorporated some of the sociological knowledge which led many practitioners of the newly developing sociolinguistics to believe that "Your Language Is Good Language," while a noble slogan, did not take sufficiently into account the social problems which might be encountered by one holding to the first language variety which he happened to have learned as a child. It was also felt that the second dialect should not be learned as the stiff, formal, essentially inexpressive "good" English upon which the schools had long insisted but as a linguistic instrument with as much expressivity as the child's native variety. SESD programs, ideally, aim at enabling the child to use a second type of "everyday talk."

Earlier workers in the field of SESD either practiced or advocated the dominant foreign language methodology of the time for teaching: pattern practice, repetition, overlearning, and the extensive use of the language laboratory (Lin 1963, 1965). Stewart (1965) advocated, implicitly at least, such measures: Hurst (1965), with whom Stewart debated extensively, also utilized something like the same procedures in order to get rid of what he called "dialectolalia." The Urban Language Study of the Center for Applied Linguistics (Dillard 1966) developed and tested a fairly large number of drills of the conventional FL type in 1967-1968. Feigenbaum and Carroll, who developed the drills, came to hold the opinion that drills of the length usually utilized in FL classes were boring and not really necessary for the purpose (Carroll 1967). Feigenbaum eventually published a book of lessons (1970b) based indirectly on the Urban Language Study drills. Johnson (1968) reports successful results of an experiment in SESD in Los Angeles.

It quickly became apparent, however, that an immense amount of teacher retraining would be necessary before any such program could be put into effect in the schools. There were also continuing criticisms of the equating of second dialect learning with second language learning (Allen 1969). For students of a junior high school level, Feigenbaum (1970a) worked out a set of modified techniques which still fell fairly well within the boundaries of FL teaching:

A. "Presentation" exercises in which students compare Standard English sentences to their Black English equivalents.

B. "Discrimination" drills in which students are given two sentences and must determine whether they are the same or different, such as *He work hard* and *He works hard*.

C. "Identification" drills which consist of translating a given Black English sentence into Standard English and vice versa.

D. Response drills which expect the student to negate given sentences in the same dialect, such as *Your best friend work after school—No, he don't* or *The Teacher gives too much work—No, she doesn't*.

Feigenbaum also advocated phonological discrimination drills, in which students were asked to judge whether *teef* and *teeth*, for example, were the same or different, or to evaluate them as standard or nonstandard.

An obvious objection is that, in the material printed at least, Feigenbaum does not deal with the deeper grammatical differences. "Translating" *he work hard* as *he works hard* may be harmless enough in itself. But the student who is taught simple Standard English substitutions for Black English has been done no service. Knowing that Black English *Yesterday he work hard* is acceptable, he may be tempted to produce *Yesterday he works hard* as Standard English. Fickett (1970:98) observes that learning to substitute Standard *have* for nonstandard *done* produces pseudo-standard *I have seen him a while ago*.

Although it never led to the production of pedagogical materials on the scale of Feigenbaum's materials, Stewart's approach recommended a more detailed involvement of the structure of the Black English vernacular, including the age-grading factor and the recognition that intermediate (mixed) stages were regularly reached which would be stigmatized by the schools as nonstandard while actually representing an effort on the part of the Black child to achieve Standard English. Stewart (1969:270) asserted: "Instead of being ignored or made the target of an eradication program, Negro dialect should actually be used as a basis for teaching oral and written Standard English." Stewart's proposal is worth looking at in some detail. He recommends using Black English as a foundation upon which one can acquire Standard English in graduated steps, taking advantage of the fact that a roughly similar process takes place in age-grading. One example of such a series is given:

Stage 1: Charles and Michael, they out playing

According to Stewart, the grammar of sentences used at this stage should be pure basilect, the most extremely "deviant" form of Black English grammar. The vocabulary will also be controlled so that no words will appear which seem strange to a Negro dialect-speaking child.

Stage 2: Charles and Michael, they are out playing

At this stage, the most important features of Standard English structure are introduced. In the example, there is one such feature—the copula *are*. It is important that such Black English features as the "pleonastic" pronoun *they* be left in at this stage.

Stage 3: Charles and Michael are out playing

The remaining grammatical adjustments are made at this stage, so that full conformity with Standard English is reached.

It is important, however, that no actually artificial sentences be presented in the sequence. The dialect mixing which regularly goes on, in the school situation and outside, makes all three of these quite probable utterances. Neither the student nor the teacher should feel that any "gaps"—whether linguistic or cognitive—are being filled in. It is better that the student think of himself as becoming bilingual than that he consider himself to be becoming "better" in one language variety. It should not be asserted that Stage 3 is in any sense "better" than Stage 1. Neither should there be disapproval, on the grounds of some kind of inverted purism, of Stage 2. Rather, the whole process involves a transition from one linguistic system to another in the most natural progression which can be achieved.

Stewart places no special emphasis on the three-stage paradigm, and other progressions can easily be formulated:

Stage 1: John, he don't got no money.
Stage 2: John, he ain't got no money.
Stage 3: John ain't got no money.
Stage 4: John hasn't got no money.
Stage 5: John hasn't got any money.
Optional Stage: John doesn't have any money. John hasn't any money.

Again, any intelligent SESD approach would have to be very careful to avoid stigmatizing the intermediate stages. There would, of course, be considerable difficulty in persuading puristic teachers not only not to stigmatize but even to encourage the production of those stages.

In all such approaches, the syntactic system of Standard English has been emphasized, although phonological drills have been provided as integral parts of or in addition to the courses which have been developed (Luelsdorff ms.). There came to be, however, a feeling that pronouncing English "the man's" way involved a great deal of linguistic, perhaps even racial, snobbery. Most linguists agreed that teaching from the spoken word to orthographic representation would affect reading only to the extent that dialects differ on syntactic and lexical levels. (There is implicit, however, an assumption that the need for Standard English exists only with respect to the school situation.) It is generally felt that differences in phonological rules need not be stressed, and Fasold (1969a) provides a rationale for using an orthographic system in which dialect materials would not differ from Standard English at that level.

It will be noted that the stage procedures of Stewart (1969) referred to above contain a provision for having nothing lexically strange to a Black child in an essentially syntactic lesson framework. Observers, most of them complete amateurs linguistically, had long perceived that Black ethnic slang had a lexical content greatly different from that of Standard English and that a "hip" speaker from Harlem could contrive to make himself unintelligible to a white while still communicating to his own in-group. Folb (1972) discusses the function of such terms in ghetto subcultural activities like drug traffic and pimping and gives examples of terms "unknown to any white informant." Crawford and Bentley (1973:80) present contrived texts:

> Man, dig it, I'm gonna pull your coat tail to this, this chick's shuckin' and jivin',
> and that dude gonna go upside her head.

Beck (1967) found it necessary to include a glossary in his book on pimping, although he specifically attributes the words to prostitution and pimping rather than to the Black community. The approaches utilized pedagogically have deemphasized this ethnic slang and have preferred simply to require that nothing lexically unfamiliar to the child be involved. Stewart (1964) asserts that slang terms are characteristic of adolescent and older Blacks and are not a major part of the problem in educating younger children. Most of the linguistically sophisticated approaches to SESD have, therefore, not given primary emphasis to slang and in-group vocabulary in considering the amount of mutual intelligibility between the two varieties.

Implementation of Standard Dialect teaching techniques of any sort has been inhibited by opposition like that of Sledd (1973), who has "travestied" the entire movement through a superfluous syllable in his designation *bidialectalism* and has frequently questioned the motives of both the linguists and the educators who are involved in the movement. Sledd, who likes to use the ridiculing synonym *doublespeak* for what is also called *biloqualism*, rejects the goal of making Black citizens upwardly mobile and of helping them to "make it" in mainstream culture as "corrupt motives" (1973:584). Since Sledd also asserts that "there is not, and there has never been, a serious proposal that Standard English should not be taught at all" (1973:583), and since he agrees that "We should know and respect our children's language as we demand that they know and respect ours" (1973), his continued resistance to bidialectal education (or "bidialectalism") seems logically ill-motivated. Sledd himself asserts that "the opposition [to biloqualism] rests on traditional notions of a just society which our society does not approach." One wonders what Sledd, and other less articulate opponents to SESD and other manifestations of the bidialectal approach, would say about instruction in, say, mathematics in such a nonideal world.

Opposition to the use of Black dialect in initial reading instruction comes not only from the idealists represented by Sledd but also from reading specialists like Cohen (1969) who are oriented toward the methods of behaviorist psychology. Cohen, who tends to lump together dialect differences and minor speech impediments, devotes his book (aside from deficit theory) to a plea for pedagogical reform and to an elaboration of the methods that might be used in such a reform. Within such a scheme of things, the linguistic content of basal readers would make little or no difference. Fishman and Lueders-Salmon (1972) report that there "is little concern" about nonstandard dialects in Germany, and extend the analogy to suggest that dialect readers might by "dysfunctional" among Black Americans. Paradoxically, however, they stress the social differences between Germany, where a dialect speaker can easily support himself within his own rural community, and the Black ghetto, where a resident "has to go outside in order to be self-supporting" (1972:72).

Most linguists have, of course, held to different ideas (UNESCO 1953). Dialect readers, a natural offshoot of concern with primary education in the vernacular, were first given firm advocacy for the Black American community in Baratz and Shuy (1969a), especially in Stewart's contribution (Stewart 1969). He based his predictions of greater success from the use of Black English initial reading materials on an anecdotal account of the success of Black children of his acquaintance who found it easier to read his translation of "The Night Before Christmas" in Black dialect than in the original. Besides the orthographic considerations presented by Fasold (1969a), the collection contained an important position paper by Baratz, who discussed the relationship of reading failure to deficit theory and discarded the latter as an effective explanatory device. It should be emphasized, however, that the only reading specialist among the contributors was Kenneth Goodman (1969).

Goodman, like Serwer (1969), felt that teaching the standard dialect before teaching reading, writing materials in the dialect of the learner, and letting the reader use his own dialect forms in reading a text (i.e., not objecting if the child reads *his book* as "he book," because of the invariant possessive pronoun in Black English) were key approaches. Following the orthographic representation of his own dialect, the child would learn to recognize larger units first, then individual words, and finally sound-sign correspondences by the process of "analytical phomics."

The actual use of initial reading texts in Black English was the approach of Stewart (Education Study Center, 1968). The Education Study Center's experimental readers, *Ollie, Friends,* and *Old Tales,* were actually written in basilect, with simple illustrative drawings which actually looked like ghetto children (down to the uneven number of plaits in the hair of the little girls) and which, in the first two at least, concerned the children's actual activities like the game of "kick the can." *Old Tales,* translations of classical myths, seemed like a perhaps unnecessary concession to more traditional educational practice. A few project disagreements developed, over matters like the use of *big momma* "grandmother," which Stewart (personal communication) feels should not have been included.

The Education Study Center texts were designed for an experimental project, and were not intended to be complete even as initial readers. After some publicity in the national magazines in the summer of 1972, however, Stewart and

Baratz (personal communication) received great numbers of requests for the texts from teachers and from school systems. Unfortunately, the NIMH project for which the texts were designed was abortive; sociopolitical factors, like those described in Stewart (1969b), prevented the actual carrying out of the research design.

The Psycholinguistic Reading Series: A Bidialectal Approach utilized by the Chicago Board of Education (Board of Education, City of Chicago, 1968, 1969) were greatly different in design. Not so authentic in dialect as the Education Study Center texts (there was an excessive dependence on the invariant be), the Chicago texts made considerably less effort at ghetto authenticity in the other design features. Pictures, which were attractively and brightly if not realistically colored, presented Black children but not in any special kind of ghetto-culture detail. Parallel texts ("everyday talk" and "school talk") were developed, much as in the Education Study Center materials. Rather than giving diagnostic tests to determine which kind of language the child should start to read, however, the Chicago texts apparently assume that each child will have both and that he will make whatever progress he can in reading with whichever one happens to suit his fancies or abilities. The pedagogical apparatus associated with the Chicago readers is also much more elaborate than that of the Education Study Center; in fact, it is quite probable that the "psychological" aspects of the texts outrank the linguistic in emphasis.

With no experimental results from the Education Study Center project and with only fragmentary results from the Chicago project, the use of dialect readers must be judged from such small-scale projects as have actually been completed. Schaaf (1971) had eight Black students in the third grade read texts written in both Black English and Standard English. She found that the subjects had better comprehension of and made fewer reading errors in the Standard English stories. They also, in reading orally, shifted from Black English to Standard English. Thus, the Schaaf study failed to support the hypothesis of grammatical reading interference from Black English. It should be noted, however, that Schaaf used an excessively small sample (eight children) and that she failed to equate and balance the standard and dialect stories both for difficulty and for dialect features. Sims (1972) had ten second grade Black children read stories written in Black dialect and in Standard English, using the Education Study Center readers and thus achieving a better dialect balance than did Schaaf. Sims found that the children did better on the Standard English versions of the stories, although she made no comparison by features. Nolen (1972), like a rash of graduate students in various schools,[8] studied reading recall by Black and white students who read selections in both Black English and Standard English. She found no reliable differences related to the dialect used.

Melmed (1970) studied the effects of phonological interference on reading in forty-five Black children, "the majority" of whom "could be characterized as being from a lower socioeconomic environment." He found that "differences in dialect phonology appear to interfere with comprehension largely in the absence of grammatical clues. This may indicate that BE and SE are so similar on the syntactic level that they are easily comprehended by black youngsters." Melmed's data do not, however, include anything on syntactic systems. In view of the many findings of syntactic differences (Loflin, all references; Loflin, Sobin, and Dillard ms.; Fickett 1970) it should more probably be concluded that Melmed's experiment has no bearing on that matter. Melmed did find some phonological interference in reading, but he considered it so slight as to be insignificant. Such interference as he found consisted of "additional homonyms." Melmed did not consider his own experiment to offer the final answer. His recommendations for further research conclude:

> A research project should be conducted to determine whether Black students' scores on standardized reading tests improve if items are written in dialect. A related study would be to make content of the tests environmentally relevant to the subjects being tested.

There should be general consensus in the field that such a study is eminently desirable and that it has not so far been conducted.

The one study which shows a positive correlation between dialect factors and reading ability is Politzer and Hoover (1972). Politzer and his associates have conducted a series of experiments with Black and Spanish-speaking children in California. They have especially concerned themselves with the effects of Spanish phonological interference and dialect phonology on audio discrimination tests of the standardized type. Politzer and McMahon (1970) found that the Wepman test (1958) contains

> phonetic discriminations which are simply not found in Negro dialects or in other dialects usually associated with lower socioeconomic status. An examination of the Wepman test reveals at least seven such discriminations on each of the two forms of the test.

This finding is important, since low performance on the Wepman test was one of the earliest findings which led to a deficiency explanation (Deutsch 1964).

Politzer and Hoover (1972) extended the test to include the ability of subjects to distinguish dialects—Standard English (spoken by educated Blacks) and Black English. They found that Black children scored better than white middle-class children in discriminating Black Nonstandard English and Black Standard English. They hypothesize that this finding is indicative of reading success:

> For Black children, by contrast, making the distinction between standard and nonstandard English is related to reading achievement from the very beginning of their school career.... The Black child must become highly skilled in recognizing the standard/nonstandard distinction in order to succeed in a Standard English reading program. The white child does not face a comparable task.

If they are correct, the discrimination drills provided in certain SESD programs (Feigenbaum 1970) may prove to be extremely valuable teaching tools.

A few studies, like Mitchell-Kernan (1969) present interesting materials on speech behavior in the Black community without providing any real data on linguistic similarity or difference. Some of these, unfortunately, draw conclusions about mutual intelligibility, universal dialect switching ability, and even educational policy to which the research is not relevant. The statements, therefore, constitute no more than the opinions of the researchers. Mitchell-Kernan asserts "It is the unhesitating opinion of this writer that, whatever difficulty some BE speakers exhibit in producing SE variants, there is not a corresponding difficulty in comprehending SE." It is but a step to a statement like "Whatever difficulty BE speakers may have in scoring high on standardized reading tests, there is not a corresponding difficulty in reading."

Cazden, Hymes, and John-Steiner (1972) collect some articles which purport to show that "language behavior" is more important than grammar in educational activities and that some (only vaguely, if at all, specified) educational policies should be implemented because of such alleged conclusions. Like Mitchell-Kernan (1969), Kochman (1969) presents interesting material on "rapping," "capping the rap," and other interesting ghetto discourse strategies. Insofar as such articles may help teachers in verbal interaction with ghetto students, these articles may have some positive educational value. But the rewrite of Kochman's article (1972) draws some educational conclusions which do not seem to follow from his observationally collected data. Kochman argues that the school should concern itself not with "*how* the child says something but with *how well* he says it." His own data, however, seem to indicate that *how well* a ghetto youngster plays the dozens is completely independent of anything the school can do. Furthermore, Labov et al. (1968) have shown that ghetto adolescent boys have a rank in the dozens and other such verbal activities which is the direct inverse of their ability to read and to excell in school activities.

Horner and Gussow (1972) classify recorded speech data from ghetto preschoolers into Skinnerian mands and tacts, finding that John and Mary (children from the same family) "sound alike" (i.e., apparently, they speak the same dialect) but that they have "strikingly different verbal techniques for dealing with life." Apart from reservations about the validity of classification into mands and tacts (Chomsky 1959), one could object that Horner and Gussow offer no clear picture of how the school could deal with these techniques. An even more severe criticism would be that their data are based exclusively on indoor contacts, primarily with adults, and not at all on outdoor contacts. The latter would tell about interaction with peers, which is a much more valid index of language behavior (Weinreich, Labov, and Herzog 1968).

Like Kochman (1972), Silverman (1971) apparently has opted for monodialectal education—or for a haphazard distribution of dialects in the educational process. Silverman asserts that the children should read texts written in Standard English but should be allowed to produce them in Black English. He does not say, however, how such procedures differ from those current in the schools today nor how such unaltered educational practices are going to solve the problem of Black children's reading failures. Since Silverman's data do not bear on either of these issues, his assertions must simply reflect a distaste for bidialectal teaching methods (or for monodialectal teaching in Black English). Bailey (1970), a teacher of Silverman, phrases her objection to bidialectal education primarily in terms of inappropriate cultural climate in the United States.

A few writers and researchers have concerned themselves with the problem of the Black student in composition classes either in integrated high schools or in open enrollment college classes. Schotta (1970) aimed to make available to the teachers at Prince Edward County (Virginia) High School relevant English-as-a-second-dialect theory, methods, and materials. Information was to be provided concerning linguistic items which deviate from Standard English, optimal ranking and sequencing of these items, and procedures which are optimal given the cultural and linguistic context of Prince Edward County. The actual publication desctibes mainly the grammatical structures found in a written corpus. Ross (1972) prepared a description, again from a written corpus, of elementary school Black children's grammar in California. He found less evidence of age-grading than claimed in Stewart (1964) and Dillard (1972), but found the grammar of Black English as outlined in those sources. Ross also remarked upon the evident restraint on written expression exercised by the school's demand for Standard English. Finding *ain't* only a very few times in a large corpus, Ross remarked that such a situation "ain't natural."

The Brooklyn University project, funded by the Ford Foundation, was one of the most active projects in attempting to aid Black students in an open enrollment school with their English composition courses. The project drew the attacks of no less an organization than the National Association for the Advancement of Colored People (1971), which suffers from the very prevalent misconception that anyone who incorporates Black English materials into an educational program must be trying to teach that language variety to Black students. Reed (1973) expresses great enthusiasm for the goals and even the procedures of the project; but, as in many other cases, no quantitative results are available.

Kligman, Connell, and Verna (1972) studied the relationship of Black English phonology to spelling difficulties. They found that "pronunciation differences in BE are significantly related to the spelling output" but that "only selective features cause enough difficulties to justify pedagogical concern." In view of Fasold (1969a) and other statements, it seems unlikely that research into spelling errors can offer any special insight into the reading problems of Black children.

The case of bidialectal education in the United States thus stands at an impasse. Such research as has been reported is inconclusive, and most of the projects have been so badly planned that even positive results from one of them would be virtually meaningless. The one really significant project, where reading is concerned, the Education Study Center project funded by NIMH, was blocked for political and emotional reasons. It is possible to cite the analogy to Osterberg (1961), whose experimental group of dialect-speaking Swedish children profited enough from initial reading instruction in their own dialect to score better than the control group, which was given instruction in standard Swedish from the beginning, on the Reading Achievement Test *in standard Swedish*. The test was given, however, only after the end of the fourth year of instruction.

The present political and emotional climate in the United States will hardly permit students to be given instruction in what parents, school boards, and political leaders regard as "bad" English for even one year. When fourth grade students in the United States are presented with a comprehension or recall test involving texts in both Black English and Standard English, indoctrination into what the schools label "good" English introduces a bias against the Black English text. Many teachers (personal communications) are able to influence their students to declare that "nobody talks like" the Black English texts. Labov et al. (1968:197-216) have shown, however, that self-report procedures are extremely unreliable where Black English speakers and outside investigators are concerned.

At the present time, then, we have opinions and possibilities rather than facts and relative certainties. Everyone knows that something is wrong with the education of Black children, and the very earliest observers found a language deficit to blame. Now that the notion of such inadequacy of language has been effectively discarded, no one seems seriously to want to tackle the problems posed by a fully adequate, completely expressive, but different language system. Instead, we are told that English instruction should be concerned with pollution control and with the bringing about of universal peace and justice (Sledd 1973).

Those who believe that certain goals of literacy and academic education are in themselves worthwhile, even in the absence of the achievement of a perfectly just society, are a small but vociferous minority. Their aims will not be achieved, nor begin to be achieved, anywhere in the near future. Nevertheless, the topic of Black English is no longer taboo in academic circles, and a few independent researchers, like Berdan (1973), are beginning to discover that statements about linguistic differences of "disadvantaged" Black children are not merely the wild-eyed accusations of racists.

There are enough limitations traceable to the climate of opinion, however, to render virtually impossible any kind of educational research about which there are not serious reservations. Linguists who advise the educationists have not yet provided the kind of information which the latter can actually utilize. Even though all who have worked on Black English analytically have given lip service to the elementary principle that description should focus on the system, all have given way to some degree to the dialectologist's working method of treating isolated features. It is not surprising, then, that pedagogical researchers like Rystrom (1970) and Nolen (1972) have come up with insignificant and even irrelevant conclusions. In some few cases, nonstandard forms have simply been incorporated into teaching materials without regard to whether they are the specific nonstandard forms used by that child population. No one should be surprised that such procedures have not established the value of bidialectal education in the United States.

The present state of affairs, deplorable as it is in many respects, has come about in just one decade. Before the 1960s, there was virtually nothing which could be regarded as reliable information about Black English. Although educational progress has been slow, it may well be that another decade or two will see more proficient application of our knowledge about Black English to educational programs.

NOTES

1. James Sledd, "Doublespeak: Dialectology in the Service of Big Brother," *College English 33* (1972); 439-456. Sledd's Orwellian criticism of "biloquialist" approaches (which are extended to a rejection of the use of dialect texts for initial reading instruction, relying exclusively on Labov and Cohen 1968 for evidence against the feasibility of such a program) is based on the "immorality" of such procedures and on his discovery of some unfelicitous phrasing in the writings of some of the proponents of bidialectal education. One would ordinarily not think that such *ad hominem* arguments would have much effect on large-scale educational policy, but Sledd and others like him are relatively influential. More importantly, they probably reflect the emotional reaction of the educational Establishment to any really new suggestions. The continuing debate over such matters in the periodicals *College English* (Sledd 1973) and *Elementary English* is indicative of the radical differences in approach between bidialectal and traditional American language education. For such reasons, the articles which appear in those publications are often more immediately diagnostic of current trends than articles in higher-level periodicals devoted to specialized research.

2. Wayne O'Neill, "The Politics of Bidialectalism," *College English 33* (1972): 457-460. The only way to combat such an assertion is to label it untrue, since the writings of the advocates of SESD and initial reading texts in Black English are full of statements about the value of the child's dialect. See, for example, Gross (1972:ix), and no program of eradication has been proposed by any of those authors cited by O'Neill. For an equally ill-tempered article, as little grounded in fact, see Robinson (1973). If, however, the "bidialectalists" are somehow going to stamp out dialects by printing dialect texts, their subtlety is so diabolical that they should be kept under constant surveillance.

3. Most of these tests have, fortunately, involved more sophistication than the question (the *first* in a series!) recommended by Shuy (1970):

> 1. What is the race of this speaker
> Negro ( )   White ( )

One more indication of the great variation in competence among those who advocate bidialectal practices is provided by this failure to observe a basic requirement like the embedding of sensitive questions, in an attitude survey, and the other methods of indirect inquiry.

4. More complete lists of syntactic differences, provided in sources like Baratz (1973), often fail to achieve the desired result, since they give fuel to the belief that "otherwise, Black English and Standard English are the same." My position is that, if there are *systematic* differences, then everything in Black English is to some degree different from Standard English. In spite of the fact that I have some differences of opinion with Loflin insofar as the

data are concerned, his works (all references) embody the best formal statement of this position.

5. Stewart (1964) defines basilect as the lowest variety in a sociolinguistic (attitudinal) hierarchy. The topmost variety in the same hierarchy is referred to as *acrolect,* and acropetal switching occurs in transition between the two extremes. Although Stewart applied the terms to Negro Nonstandard Dialect, he obviously meant for them to apply to a large number of other situations as well.

6. The slight attention given to variable rules (Labov 1969a) and panlectal grammars (in the sense of articles by C.-J.N. Bailey and others in the *Lectological Newsletter*) here is intentional rather than an oversight. It is held that these strategies, although of course they are of great interest in the field of speculative linguistics, have no effect in deciding the empirical question as to whether speakers of two varieties (or two versions of one variety), differentiated by some exponent from the alternative possibilities expressed in a variable rule), understand each other "perfectly." In the terms of Luelsdorff (1970:I) both panlectal grammars and variable rules would be "grammars which relate the speech behavior of individual speakers" rather than "grammars underlying the speech behavior of individual speakers." It seems entirely probable that, given the requisite expenditure of ingenuity, a "panlingual" grammar, relating language behavior of speakers of languages as diverse as English and Chinese, could be written; that is, in fact, the premise upon which most theories of language universals are built. The fact that a grammar of English-Chinese would be written would not of course affect the fact that monolingual speakers of Chinese cannot understand monolingual speakers of English and vice versa.

A few empirical studies (Baratz 1969a, Troike 1970) show that speakers of one dialect often have a receptive competence in the other (as represented by a corpus of sentences selected by the experimenter) and readily reincode stimuli presented in the standard dialect (*I don't know if he can go*) into their own nonstandard forms (*I don't know can he go*). While this factor of receptive competence obviously means that not every dialect difference which can be expressed in syntactic rules leads to automatic misunderstanding, it remains unproved that *all* syntactic differences are *within* receptive competence simply because they are *outside* productive competence. Some indications have been given, but full studies of mutual intelligibility remain to be done.

7. Something of this attitude was actually expressed in Joos (1962). In many cases, what the teacher regarded as "good" English had many points in common with the standard variety (in the sense of Garvin 1959), and many students had access to the standard dialect primarily or only through the school system. Although a red herring issue is often made of the matter, it is probable that almost no one referred to in this article conceives of Standard English in terms of the "good" English of the Fidditch-type school teacher. For an honest attempt to cope with the standard/nonstandard problem on the part of a literature specialist not indoctrinated into the linguist's attitudes, see Morse (1973), who sincerely believes that nonstandard dialect—specifically Black English—is intellectually limiting to its speakers.

8. Several experiments concerning the use of Black English and Standard English texts for reading instruction were made by my own students at Ferkauf Graduate School of Yeshiva University, especially during 1972-1973. Several of those showed "trends" toward advantages from the use of the Black English materials, but none of them produced statistically significant results.

X

Yiddish Schools

in North America

Sandra Parker

INTRODUCTION

The Yiddish secular school movements, the Hasidic groups, and the non-Hasidic orthodox movement have used Yiddish in their schools or given instruction in it. Non-Hasidic orthodox schools[1] have increasingly turned to English as the language of communication both because the maintenance of Yiddish is not for them a high priority and because declining levels of comprehension among students make it difficult to use the language to any significant extent. Exceptions to this trend are to be found in old orthodox schools in areas of large metropolitan cities that still contain a Yiddish-speaking population. Only within Hasidic schools (which by definition are day schools) and in secular movement schools has there been great interest in the Yiddish language as a vehicle for strengthening and perpetuating a sense of ethnic community.

In spite of an apparent common interest in perpetuating Yiddish language use and knowledge, Hasidic Jews, known as Hasidim,[2] and Yiddishists have, historically, held extremely conflicting ideological views, and thus even their advocacy of Yiddish has stemmed from a vastly different set of assumptions and objectives. These differences and their effects upon the type of educational experiences provided within the respective school systems constitute the focus of this chapter. All those in the secular movement perceived the Yiddish language as *both* a language of communication and an object of instruction, while among Hasidic groups extensive instruction in the language was rare and use of the language received the primary stress. Because of these distinctions an examination of the role of Yiddish in the secular schools and in Hasidic schools cannot be given the type of parallel structure that would be the case if one were comparing and describing institutions with more congruent objectives.

BACKGROUND

Fears of the assimilative effects of Americanization upon the Jewish masses[3] served to reinforce the Yiddishists' commitment to Yiddish. They increased their efforts to ensure its survival through the establishment of secular (nonreligious) educational systems whose goals were perpetuation of Yiddish culture and Jewish peoplehood as well as of the ideals of social justice and human dignity. Strong convictions relating to specific ideological emphases within these broad goals[4] prevented any possibility of establishment of a united Yiddish secular school movement in the early days of activity within the United States.

According to Niger, the first Yiddish secular school in the United States was opened in Brownesville in New York City in 1906.[5] By the second decade of the 20th Century, similar instutitions were established in Canada as well. These first attempts to provide a Yiddish secular education were tenuous, lacked organizational support and they were frequently forced to shut down after a brief existence owing to lack of funds, the wrath of the local orthodoxy,[6] or competition from other secular schools in the neighborhood.

The first organizations to support the notion of Yiddish secular schools were the Jewish National Workers Alliance, or Farband, and the Poele Zion, both Yiddishist Labor Zionist organizations, who in their conferences in Rochester, N.Y., and Montreal, accepted resolutions to found National Radical Schools. The first such school was established in 1910 in New York City with class sessions on Saturday and Sunday, and the following year two more schools were founded in Canada, one in Montreal and one in Toronto.

In the period between 1910 and 1918, conflict arose between Socialist-Zionist factions about whether or not Hebrew should be included in the curricula of their children's schools and the quantity of time that should be devoted to it. Poele Zion supported Hebrew and the Socialist Territorialists, a Yiddishist faction within the Farband, opposed it. The rift caused a split from which the Sholem Aleichem Schools (1916) (supporters of Yiddish) and the (Jewish National Worker's Alliance) Farband Schools (supporters of both Yiddish and Hebrew) emerged as independent and separate offshoots of the original National-Radical movement.

While the Farband school movement retained its Socialist-Zionist affiliation and a bilingual emphasis, the new Sholem Aleichem movement emphasized only Yiddish and maintained a humanist, nonpolitical posture. Members of the latter group focused primarily upon the needs of the child and the creation of a Yiddish secular environment.

The Jewish Socialist Bund, another Jewish fraternal organization, formed the Workmen Circle. At the turn of the century it was primarily occupied with universalist, working-class concerns, and although members used the Yiddish language, they considered it primarily an effective means of communicating with the Yiddish-speaking Jewish masses in order to achieve larger ideological objectives. They therefore established, in their earliest period of educational activity, not Jewish or even Yiddish children's schools, but adult evening programs which emphasized the Yiddish language, Socialism, and free thought. Adult members who were influenced and impressed by the success of the National Radical School experiments began to demand Workmen Circle schools for their own children. Socialist Sunday schools were established, and in the course of a few years their content became more Jewish and their structure more intensive.[7]

In the period between 1919 and 1926, labor groups in the United States became more radical, and as a consequence of this fact pro-Soviet elements within the Workmen Circle were strengthened. By 1926, a rift occurred in this movement and the majority of schools and teachers left the parent body and formed the Nonpolitical Children's Schools. These later became the school movement affiliated with the International Worker's Order (IWO; in more recent years it has changed its name to the Jewish People's Fraternal Order).

These four movements (in order of establishment), (1) the Farband, (2) the Sholem Aleichem, (3) the Workmen Circle, and (4) the IWO, became the main Yiddish secular school movements in the United States. The ideological issues which separated them were language loyalty (to Yiddish, Hebrew, or both), cultural or territorial nationalism, and extent of commitment to and emphasis upon Socialist as compared with ethnic content and experience.

Most of the extant schools of the movements are to be found in New York City, Philadelphia, Chicago, Los Angeles, Montreal, Toronto, and Winnipeg. Of these, only New York City and the Canadian cities support day schools, and those in Canada tend to have much larger student enrollments than those in the United States. A national census of Jewish schools taken in December 1967 indicated that of all children attending Jewish schools, 1% were in Yiddish secular schools and 0.4% were in Yiddish secular day schools.[8] Prior to World War II it was claimed that up to 15% of all Jewish children attending Jewish schools were enrolled in Yiddish secular institutions.

No remnant of the many small supplementary Yiddish secular schools which were scattered throughout the southeast (in such cities as Atlanta, Chattanooga, and Memphis) and the midwest during the prewar period remain, although at one time they were active, flourishing schools whose students contributed prose and poetry of varying degrees of quality to their elementary and secondary Yiddish school journals.

While Hasidic groups had existed in the United States before World War II, the period prior to the holocaust (the murder of six million Jews by Hitler) and the years immediately following it saw a great influx of Hasidim of various sects to the United States. As a consequence the headquarters of some groups shifted to this country when their respective "rebbes" (rabbinical leaders) took up residence here, as in the case of Lubavitch and Satmar, whereas other Hasidic groups now have their main centers in Israel. Many Hasidic sects exist, and they differ in geographic origin, degree of religious isolationism and extremism, and in some cases on political issues related to their theological positions. They tend, however, to maintain similar community structures and patterns and to support their own "rebbe," who is frequently the most recent in a hereditary family chain of leaders of a particular sect.

Some of the Hasidic movements,[9] whose schools had been concentrated in New York City, Montreal, and hamlets in the Catskill Mountains of New York, have in the last three decades sent personnel to establish schools in towns and cities beyond the areas of heaviest Jewish population concentration. A successful orthodox day school which currently has a student body of about eighty and is administered by a follower of Lubavitch has existed in Nashville, Tenn. since the fifties.[10] Boston has a Lubavitcher Yeshiva with a student body of three hundred that includes preschool and a girls' school. However, these schools use English rather than Yiddish as their language of communication because the children who attend do not usually come from homes in which Yiddish is the spoken language, nor, in many cases, are the parents Hasidim. Therefore, it can be said that Hasidic *Yiddish* schools are at present concentrated primarily in New York state and Montreal, Canada.[11]

Exact statistics on numbers of Hasidim within each sect, size of schools, and amount of Yiddish used in schools of the various sects is difficult to gather for a variety of reasons. Rabinowicz says there are about two hundred thousand Hasidim throughout the world and that between forty and fifty thousand of them live in New York City, where 8.1% of Jewish children attending Jewish schools are to be found within Hasidic institutions. In the United States, 10% of all day schools are Hasidic.[12] Location and the degree of homogeneity of the school population, as well as the extent to which the particular Hasidic sect welcomes children from non-Hasidic homes into their schools, are major factors in choice of language used for instruction. Extremely conservative Hasidic sects use Yiddish not only because it is a distinctive characteristic of their ethnicity but because they view English as a vehicle of assimilation and Hebrew as too holy a language for everyday use. These groups have reluctantly agreed to use and teach English in their general studies departments encouraged by the existence of state regulations governing the education of children in day schools.

PHYSICAL PLANT AND RESOURCES

The great majority of secular movement schools that were established in the first three decades of activity were founded "on a shoestring." Their primary source of support was local members of the four movements, mainly struggling garment workers and small shopkeepers without funds to spare.[13] The competition among the movements in the establishment of new schools and the need for local neighborhood elementary schools (for this was before the now common family car) encouraged the development of many small schools rather than more stable, regional institutions with larger student bodies and a more viable economic base. Consequently, the mortality rate was high as some schools shut down, reopened, and closed again, always sensitive to the slightest financial reverse or change in the socioeconomic complexion of a neighborhood.

Financial support from the parent fraternal organizations was minimal during the first decades of the 20th Century. Contributions from Jewish community chests were not always offered to working-class Yiddishists by the more middle-class Jews who administered these funds, nor were they frequently solicited owing to a fear among some of the members of the movements of external bourgeois control. Even tuition could not be counted upon as a constant source of income because economically hard pressed parents were frequently advised by school workers, eager for new pupils, to pay whatever tuition they could afford or not at all. To meet one financial crisis after another, local members often taxed themselves voluntarily, ran benefits, concerts, and raffles, and sold greetings and advertisements in yearbooks and journals. In spite of these earnest efforts many schools existed on the brink of bankruptcy at all times.

Consequently, the secular schools were maintained in apartments, stores (in which the larger, front area might be used for assemblies and the smaller stockroom area, in the rear, served as classroom space), or even in basements. Surroundings were dingy and facilities ranged from limited and inappropriate to unhealthy and unsafe. Ironically, in the post World War II period, as pupil numbers dwindled and many schools closed, support for existing schools increased from both the parent fraternal organizations and Jewish community chests. Many present-day schools are housed in buildings owned or rented by the parent organizations, in space rented in public schools which are not in session during late afternoons, or on weekends, or in school buildings designed and erected specifically for their use.

Because the greatest growth of the Hasidic movements in the United States and Canada occurred immediately before and after World War II, with the influx of eastern European Jewish refugees, a different set of conditions prevailed while their movements' schools were growing. In areas with large concentrations of Jewish population, the prevalence of automobiles and the acceptance of the notion of transporting children to school made possible the growth of regional schools. Although small Hasidic schools, of the type that were operated by Yiddishists during the first decades of the 20th Century, do exist, a number of Hasidic schools have student populations that exceed five hundred boys or girls.[14] (These groups tend to separate the sexes in different educational institutions.)

TEACHERS

The Yiddish secular school teacher, product of the same working and lower middle-class origins as his pupils' parents, assumed a pivotal and multifaceted position when he accepted a job within the Yiddish secular framework. The extreme poverty of most Yiddish schools imposed many tasks upon the teacher that were not necessarily instructional. He was, simultaneously, administrator, secretary, public relations expert, spiritual counselor, music and drama specialist, and sometimes custodian as well. For all these responsibilities, in addition to teaching, he was poorly and irregularly compensated.

> The only certainty that he has was that at the end of the year the school would owe him back salary of the pitifully small amount he was to receive in the first place. No one spoke of old age security. It was an issue that idealists were embarrassed to discuss. But the Workmen Circle is now doing something about it. As of January, 1967, Workmen Circle teachers will receive a lifelong pension on reaching sixty-five if they teach a minimum of ten hours in the Workmen Circle schools.[15]

These teachers (predominantly men) were in the main individuals with little formal secular education beyond the secondary level, but imbued with great enthusiasm and a fondness for children.[16] Many of them pursued their own education at night or studied on their own.[17] Chanin, an educational director of one of the movements, suggests that the demands of the teaching role in a cultural-center type of school stimulated the teacher to develop intellectually in order to prepare for a variety of tasks which included, in addition to instructing children, lecturing to adults on such subjects as Jewish history, literature, and ideology.[18]

The numbers of Yiddish secular school teachers have dwindled because of the decline in numbers of schools and children attending each school, the relative nonattractiveness of Yiddish teaching as compared with other professions available to Jewish youth, and normal attrition resulting from retirement and death. Consequently, there is inadequate personnel for existing schools and for schools that might have continued to function or might have been established had competent teachers been available.

In Hasidic schools, the teachers who teach the secular subjects are subject to state requirements. In the girls' schools of the more conservative Hasidic denominations, the women teachers of Jewish subjects, teaching in Yiddish, tend to be graduates of the same or similar institutions. In spite of limited academic and pedagogical preparation, they seem totally familiar and comfortable with the requirements of the program. Men teachers who instruct in Yiddish on Jewish subjects in the boy's schools have a more extensive background in Jewish studies. Numbers of them are rabbis, whose careers are devoted to teaching rather than to leading congregations of their own. Since these men and women do not perceive themselves as competitive, mobile members of the mainstream of American society who seek access to careers that produce great status or wealth, the modest remuneration of the Hasidic teacher is not as negative a factor as it might be to others.

STRUCTURES AND ORGANIZATION

The predominant structural pattern of Yiddish secular schools in the United States was the afternoon school which children attended three to five times a week for an hour to an hour and one-half after public school. The day-school pattern which prevailed in eastern Europe and remains quite prevalent in Canada did not attract sufficient support. The absence of a universal public school system, rather than the coercive power of governmental forces, was probably a factor contributing to the interest in day schools in Canada.[19]

Because of growing concern in recent years with the need to guarantee some degree of intellectual sophistication about their culture to future generations of Jews, many Yiddish educators who in earlier years had been the greatest adversaries of the day-school structure (because of their opposition to parochialism) have in the past two decades revised their position and suggested the opening of day schools.[20] As the individual secular movements declined in numbers (but resisted unification except for limited purposes) and ceased to attract young people who wished to make Yiddish teaching a career, the suggestions of opening day schools remained for the most part in the realm of Utopian planning. Indeed, as old neighborhoods emptied of Jews, suburbia (with its dependence upon the automobile) grew, and other competitive activities claimed the time and attention of young children. The one-day-a-week Sunday school which no longer necessarily met on Sunday regained the popularity that it had had in the earlier part of the century, and two- and three-day-a-week schools began to decrease in numbers.

CURRICULA

Yiddish

It is clearly evident from the ideological as well as the promotional literature which streamed from the Yiddish secular school movements in the period prior to World War II that they saw Yiddish, Yiddish culture, and particularly the Yiddish secular literature that flowed in the 19th and early 20th Century as the means by which Jewish children might understand their past, communicate with Jews throughout the world, and become a productive link in a chain which would perpetuate their cultural heritage and ethnic and ideological identity.

> There is a national and deep-seated desire of every man to teach his children the language of his people and race. A language contains more than a set of words; it embodies the history of a people, its experience, its accumulated wisdom and folklore, its philosophy of life. He who truly wishes to understand a people must first learn its tongue. Since Yiddish is the native language of about three-quarters of the Jewish people throughout the world, it is but natural that they should desire their children to know it.[21]

After the dimensions of the holocaust became apparent in the middle and late forties, an additional rationale began to acquire prominence, namely, the importance of an intimate knowledge and appreciation of "lashon Hakdoshim," the language of the six million Jews murdered by Hitler.

By the early fifties, although new Yiddish-speaking centers had not arisen to replace those which had been destroyed, many Yiddishists still refused to compromise the Yiddish language on the altar of translation and continued to press for the maintenance of language and literature instruction as the main focus of their schools.[22] This resistance stemmed undoubtedly from the conviction that a culture known in translation could not long endure and that the need to resort to it would signal the demise of a cherished heritage.

In 1956, Leibush Lehrer, ideological leader and educational director of the Sholom Aleichem Folk Schools, wrote an essay in which he categorically rejected the advocacy of Yiddish language instruction for merely sentimental reasons, i.e., that it was the language of six million martyrs or that of forefathers. He saw value in positive Jewish separateness, while admitting the existence of increasing evidence which indicated that it was fast disappearing. He maintained that the Yiddish language could become a powerful tool (if Jews wished to remain Jews and have their children continue to be Jewish) in the struggle for ethnic survival.

> The Yiddish language can therefore act as a psychological wedge in perceiving a synthesized, unique world, a world which is ours and with which our destiny wills us to ally ourselves. A normal Jewish life is possible only if this will is echoed in each of us.[23]

By this period, Lehrer no longer denied the possibility of benefiting from various levels of immersion, including translation, although he did make a plea for as much contact with Yiddish as possible (his own schools oppose translation up to the present time) indicating that one gets

> a sense of one's flesh and blood. Even partial acquaintance with the Yiddish idiom can pay rich dividends by unsealing and illumining the depths and recesses of Jewish thought which remained sealed from the stranger.[24]

Aware though he was of the factors in modern society which, in concert, act to weaken ethnicity and "the clear delineation of a separate Jewish existence,"[25] Lehrer steadfastly asserted the power of language and, in particular, of Yiddish as a weapon in this struggle.

The Hasidim also saw Yiddish as one powerful tool among others, which included dress, observance of ritual, and isolation, to help maintain a distinctive ethnicity. Their orientation to Yiddish was primarily to preserve it rather than to generate and to create in the language and thus they focused upon the specific portion of it spoken in the particular area from which they had come (Russia, Poland, and Galicia). For them, the term Yiddish literature referred only to the wise sayings, essays, parables, legends, and philosophic reflections of the great Hasidic rabbis and not to the Yiddish secular literature. This they ignored in their schools and rejected as impious and in some cases indecent.

The Yiddish secularists, particularly in the first three decades of the 20th Century, emphasized Yiddish literature and culture in their schools and took ethnic language competence on the part of the Jewish immigrant for granted. The language material which was included within the curricula of the Yiddish school was geared to make it quicker and easier for adults in the evening programs and children in the afternoon schools to start reading Yiddish literature and appropriate selections from world literature in Yiddish translation.[26] Through this exposure it was thought that bonds with the Jewish people and humanistic-universalistic values would be strengthened.

During the early period of the secular schools, little difference was recognized between the approach necessary for teaching literature based upon ethnic language competence and that which is crucial for teaching a foreign language with literature as a goal. This was undoubtedly because the student body was, to all intents and purposes, already bilingual, and in those cases in which individuals were not, their native tongue was Yiddish and not English. Therefore, the importance of discrete, vertical teaching strategies with emphasis upon carefully sequenced grammatical structures as well as vocabulary which provided opportunity for practice and review, was not part of the conscious awareness of the Yiddishists working feverishly to establish as many schools as they could as quickly as possible.

Recognition of the change in the level of knowledge of Yiddish among Jews in the United States came slowly. Some evidence of this awareness can be seen in the calls of many Yiddishists for stress on the spoken language. Yiddish should not become foreign to the tongue of the immigrant Jewish child who was under much pressure in public school and elsewhere to avoid using his mother tongue. By the end of World War II it became apparent that Yiddish was strange not only to the tongue but also to the ear of many pupils attending Yiddish secular schools. In the postwar period, therefore, many published texts included a stronger emphasis on structural aspects of the Yiddish language. The desire to stress literature did not decline, however, and efforts to maintain Yiddish literature as a focus of the school programs continued, but reduced comprehension of textual material and inability to express ideas in substantive discussions dramatically affected the interest and motivation of the student body as well as their achievement.

Hasidic objectives for Yiddish language learning have not been altered in recent years because the unchanging quality of life within the geographically concentrated Hasidic, Yiddish-speaking communities did not generate a need for any new pedagogical adjustments or modifications. In areas where no Hasidic communities previously existed and Hasidic day schools were established, no real effort was made to introduce Yiddish as a language of communication and only limited time was allocated to teach it to the English-speaking student body. In the Boston Lubavitcher day school, for example, a brief experiment in teaching Yiddish to the girls was initiated but was terminated after a short time because of a lack of competent teachers and the pressures of other curricular priorities. A Lubavitcher rabbit indicated that youth from non-Hasidic families who are attracted to various Hasidic sects often move to an area in which an indigenous Hasidic community exists. They then learn Yiddish very quickly through both study and natural immersion in the social environment.

After World War II Yiddish pedagogical journals began increasingly to include articles which summarized and described research on approaches to the teaching of foreign language. The various movements began to publish beginners' texts which were intended for children with no background at all in Yiddish. Some of these texts emphasized a limited concrete vocabulary, and the stories in them utilized this vocabulary in a programmed, sequential manner. An effort was made to make the format colorful and attractive, and to provide some opportunity for written practice of new material either in the textbook itself or in an accompanying workbook. Long overdue, in terms of fulfilling an important need, some of these materials, though they reflected an acknowledgment of the true level of Yiddish competence among children, had distinct weaknesses that were not overcome by their sequential structure. These included too heavy a reliance on material that was limiting and infantile because it was based upon the mistaken notion that simple vocabulary and structure inevitably result in content appropriate only for young children. For students beyond the first or second grade level, such material is frequently inappropriate and uninteresting. (Most children do not begin supplementary Yiddish schools until they are in the third or fourth grade of public school.) In some of the texts the sentence patterns that were selected did not permit use of as broad an array of vocabulary as might have been possible. These factors in combination with a shrinking Yiddish language community in which the language might be heard and used, and the scarcity of talented teachers made Yiddish instruction less substantive and stimulating than it had been prior to World War II. Teachers, working in one or two day a week programs, frequently tell stories from Yiddish literature in English and occasional use is made, at least in Workmen Circle schools, of *Yiddish Stories for Young People*.[27] In spite of the assertion made by Goldberg, the editor of this anthology, that children must acquire the treasures of their heritage in whatever form they can, and that the figure of Sholem Aleichem's Tevye is as important to their understanding of that heritage as was the biblical figure of Job, there seems to be marked resistance to producing appropriate literature material in translation for children in the secular schools.

Instead they are generally offered only that Yiddish material which, with the help of the teacher, they can comprehend. During the last two decades the result has been, except in a few rare cases of five-day supplementary schools, the almost total disappearance of substantive literary confrontation in the afternoon schools of the movements.

In a study of various types of Yiddish secular schools, I sought data on learning or psychological problems resulting from a bilingual or multilingual program. Of all the schools I visited,[28] the day schools appeared to be the ones in which ethnic language learning seemed to be the most natural and most significant to the children involved.[29] The day school framework also seemed to be capable of promoting the integration of general and Jewish knowledge when this goal was identified as important and the staff and materials necessary to implement it were available.

Clinical data gathered in a Yiddish day school in Montreal, Canada,[30] where a quadralingual program is in operation, as well as findings offered in *A History of*

Jewish Education in the Soviet Union by Dr. Elias Schulman on similar schools in the Ukraine, tend to suggest that most children participating in these intensive multilingual programs were not adversely affected by them.[31] A further conclusion that can be inferred from the available data is that the most crucial factors for pupils who are intellectually equipped to handle a multilingual program are the emotional tone of the learning environment (conducive to building a strong self-image through the provision of pleasant, successful experiences) and the level of expectation which is conveyed by adults with whom the children are closely identified.

Yiddish textbooks for primary level children used by the Hasidic movements reflect the same type of assumption manifested in early texts produced by Yiddish secularists, namely, that the pupils who use this material are familiar with Yiddish but do not yet know how to read and write it. Thus, *Unzer Buch*, a common text used by the Lubavitcher Hasidic movement, contains a sequenced presentation of the letters of the Yiddish alphabet in cursive and printed form and an enormous variety of vocabulary words that contain each letter. Attention is also given to proper verb conjugations. But here again the vocabulary offered to illustrate a particular conjugation pattern and the stories related to this material would totally bewilder pupils who had not had prior contact with the Yiddish language. In the case of Hasidic schools in the New York and Montreal areas where these texts tend to be in use, the assumption referred to earlier is valid. A substantial amount of Yiddish language comprehension is acquired in the homes and the neighborhoods from which the children come.

The content of the texts relates to the customs and daily routines of an observing Hasid and implicitly directs pupils toward an acceptance and perpetuation of this life style. For example, one story in the first section of the beginner's book mentioned above gives an account of a sabbath on which the whole family goes to synagogue. The father and sons sit in the men's section and the women in their section.[32] It should be noted that only among orthodox Jews is this separation of the sexes during prayer maintained. Attitudes and values, such as showing respect and sitting quietly, are also stressed.[33] The vocabulary and sentence structure are fairly complex and include the following: "In school they learned that a synagogue is a holy place where people come to pray, to pour out their hearts to their father in heaven."[34]

In later portions of the text bible tales, stories stressing such values as concern for all living things and respect for parents, and accounts of the early life of famous rabbis are included. Similar material in monthly magazine form is published for children and young people by the Lubavitcher movement and by others.[35]

Through such materials and constant use of Yiddish in the classrooms, pupils in Hasidic schools within Hasidic communities expand their knowledge and use of Yiddish. In some cases their command of Yiddish, in spite of the existence of a general education program within each school, may be better than their command of English.

The oral Yiddish used in the Hasidic schools varies greatly and the dialect used is a reflection of that used in the region of Europe from which the particular group emerged. The Satmar Hasidim came from the general area of Hungary, and characteristics of their Yiddish include a great number of German words and a smaller number of Hebrew words than might be evident in the speech of other groups. Among the Lubavitcher Hasidim who come from Russia, and were thus geographically more remote from Germanic influence, the reverse is true. The Yiddish of groups from Poland and other areas seems to be somewhere between the two extremes in terms of Hebraic and Germanic characteristics.

Once children in the Hasidic schools acquire the rudiments of reading and writing Yiddish and a smattering of grammar, Yiddish becomes a tool for the comprehension, in the case of the girls, of bible stories and legends, and in the case of the boys, of rabbinic talks and essays, and philosophic writings by the great Hasidic rabbis of the past.

Customs, Ceremonies, and Ritual

The place of ritual grew in importance and became an educational priority in the secular schools as both Yiddish language competence and the habits and patterns of the eastern European traditional life style disappeared from Jewish homes. Yiddishists not only sensed the significance of filling a growing vacuum but appreciated the value of ritual at a time when other ethnic and socioeconomic manifestations of uniqueness and solidarity were rapidly declining. Furthermore, holiday practice and the customs and ceremonies relating to them could be taught in English, and even in some instances in transliteration, without losing as much of their quality and nuance as Yiddish literature might lose. And finally, though rituals and customs might be superficial, limited, and without substantive depth, they could quickly provide a sense of continuity and ethnicity through active participation in group experiences.

In the first years of educational activity in the United States, the movements' attitudes toward religion, ritual, and holidays varied from appreciation of the quality of the religious experience and of Jewish holidays and traditions on the part of the Farband to total rejection on the part of the IWO. First the Scholem Aleichem, then the Workmen Circle, and ultimately the IWO became more tolerant of religion in Jewish life and began to emphasize its historical, cultural, and symbolic importance in their curricular materials. Under pressure from their members to include some emphasis on holidays and traditions because of their developmental significance for the child and their power as tools for the maintenance of ethnicity, the Sholem Aleichem, Workmen Circle, and IWO (the Farband had always had a more accepting attitude) started to celebrate holidays whose theme was national liberation, and then slowly began to commemorate in some form almost all the other Jewish holidays as well. Holiday observance within the secular schools was not usually traditional in either form or content but stressed national, secular elements such as the role of man in improving his own lot, social justice, and ethical behavior. A great deal of Yiddish literature was woven into the adapted ceremonies that were developed for the holidays.

The degree of universalist (as opposed to Jewish) emphasis was directly related to the ideology of the particular movement. The Passover Hagaddah (a book read on Passover containing historical background, prayers, commentary, and songs), as used by the various movements,[36] is an example of secular adaptations of a traditional source for the celebration of a Jewish holiday.

The desire to develop a Yiddish secularist tradition and ritual was obstructed by the duplication and fragmentation resulting from the felt need of each of the movements to produce independent materials. A basic ingredient of a successful tradition or ritual would appear to be acceptance of its standardized form, whatever that may be, by a group large enough to give it stability and some degree of continuity. In the case of the Yiddish secular school movements no effort was made to achieve a unified ritual, and this in combination with the categorization of Americans by religious affiliation, which was common in the forties and fifties, and the absence of a standardized secular ritual, gradually caused a return among most of the movements to some of the elements of the standardized orthodox ritual which did exist. This trend in combination with the disappearance of a working-class identification and Yiddish language distinctiveness (as most of the supplementary Yiddish schools became English-speaking, except during language instruction periods) removed a large measure of the separate environmental quality which had in earlier years prevailed even in the afternoon Yiddish school. The sense of a unique school environment and community, to the extent that it exists, seems (except in a rare case or two) to be present in recent years only in the day schools.

Except in the Lubavitcher movement which attempts to serve a broad spectrum of non-Hasidic Jews and to attract them to Lubavitcher principles, the Hasidic educator's tasks are simplified by the existence of a total and complete congruence of values shared by the school and the home. The responsibility for initiating pupils into customs, ceremonies, and rituals is assumed by the family, and children are taught implicitly through parental models. The school needs merely to elaborate, reinforce, and afford time for further practice of desired behaviors in communal and peer group settings. Many Hasidic sects in areas like New York City isolate their children from what they feel are the undesirable stimuli of mainstream American culture by forbidding the use of television and radio in the home.[37] Perfect congruence of values between the school and the home is thus almost totally assured at least in the early, most impressionable, years of a child's life. It was not surprising, therefore, to observe the complete acceptance of lengthy prayer sessions in a fourth grade class of girls in the B'nos Yaakov school. The children continued unperturbed and undistracted while I was talking to the teacher.[38] Indeed, the pupils seemed perfectly independent of any need of guidance or supervision. In a later Yiddish discussion in the same class of a legend about how the Torah came to be given to the Jewish people rather than to any other people, the quality of attention displayed by the children was remarkable and the pure and innocent acceptance of the content as fact was unmarked by a single question, reservation, or qualification. Although the teacher might have permitted some degree of objective analysis, the children, by their comments and additions, tended to reinforce and to strengthen rather than to weaken the original supernatural premise upon which the legend presented by the teacher was based.

Customs, ceremonies, ritual, and religion do not require formal presentation in the Hasidic schools as they might in other Jewish and non-Jewish ethnic schools where the practices are unfamiliar and are in competition with conflicting ideas or life styles that attract students strongly.

Jewish History

The Yiddishists saw Jewish history as a body of content which, if transmitted properly, would help develop strong identification between the Jewish child and the Jewish people in addition to providing greater historical perspective. Because of limited resources, the priority that was given to Yiddish literature and later to Yiddish language study, and the inappropriateness of textual materials for the elementary level, an oral approach to history was used by Yiddish teachers in the secular schools. Without the aid of any effective manipulative or concrete materials to help develop social studies skills and concepts, and unable to rely on any consistent source of guidance or supervision, the Yiddish teacher attempted to transmit the Yiddish secularist view of Jewish history and create a positive emotional reaction to it. While primary level children responded with interest and absorption to tales presented in simple Yiddish[39] of heroes of the biblical and postbiblical period, topics that needed to be treated in a more conceptual and analytical manner posed more serious cognitive and language comprehension problems for older pupils.

In the first decades of the secular movements the creative and expressive arts and Yiddish literature in recitation, choral reading, play and skit forms, were much used to augment objective historical data and to generate strong, positive feelings in students. Frequent Yiddish presentations provided many opportunities for children to use the Yiddish language in aesthetically pleasing and psychologically charged contexts.

As Yiddish competence declined in the Yiddish school and Yiddish teachers became scarce, Jewish history was increasingly taught by people without a movement background or Yiddish language competence, using English texts published by the Jewish Conservative or Reform movements. The IWO was the only one of the movements that published its own history textbook series in English. This series was not utilized as much as might have been expected by other movements, probably because of hostile feelings that stemmed from earlier ideological conflicts. Consequently, in many schools the distinctive orientation of the secular movements is not as clearly present d during history instruction as it was in earlier times when committed Yiddish-speaking teachers were able to utilize both cognitive and affective Yiddish materials with children who were capable of comprehending them. English resources of the quality and kind which had been used in Yiddish in earlier years were not produced to replace those that became incomprehensible.

Although the Ghetto fighters of the World War II period, the martyrs and the builders of Israel, were heroes that the secular schools continued to use effectively in teaching Jewish history, there were, and are, no American Jewish heroes that could evoke the degree of identification generated in the 1920s and 1930s by dealing with the American Jewish proletariat. None of the movements or other Jewish organizations have produced much effective material that deals with the postimmigrant era in the United States.

Jewish history as a separate entity is not emphasized by most Hasidic schools. The Lubavitcher movement publishes a history series in English, and secondary pupils are encouraged to pursue the subject independently through available sources. In other movements, students gain their knowledge of Jewish history from intensive study of the bible, the talmud, and writings of the great Hasidic rabbis. Familiarity with these sources provides an awareness of the significant periods in Jewish history, although the presentation may not be sequential, comprehensive, or objective. At the elementary level, history is limited to tales of biblical heroes, martyrs, and great Hasidic rabbis.

SENSE OF COMMUNITY

The roots of the deep commitment of the Yiddish secularists to humanism and universalism clearly stemmed on the one hand from their socialist and proletarian origins in Europe and immigrant working-class experiences in the United States, and on the other from the ethnical and social teachings of Judaism. Unlike other radical movements in which the leadership was frequently drawn from the middle or upper classes rather than from the masses, the Yiddish secularists were indigenous "ethnics" of the Jewish working classes and many of their leading figures were poets and novelists who earned their living during most of their adulthood in the sweat shops they described so vividly.[40]

Belief in the unity of "Mentsh un Yid" (human being and Jew), that the Yiddishist Zchidlovski referred to in his goals for a Yiddish secular education, was commonly accepted by the Yiddish secularists who established the school movements in the United States. In the first three decades of activity (1910 to 1940), their universalism was reflected in the curricula of their schools. It was not, however, an aspect which paralleled or was superimposed upon the distinctively Jewish elements of their program. Quite the contrary; in the view of movement educators both the Jewish and the universal content were part of an integrated whole. Concern for Jews in various parts of the world and interest in the welfare of oppressed groups everywhere were extensions of the same humanitarian perspective and sense of community.

The strong behavioral and affective features which, in earlier decades, had characterized the Yiddish secular neighborhood community school and gave the young child his most intimate and dynamic contact with, and concern for, a group beyond his family, seem to have suffered most from the decline in movement activity and in the Yiddish "sviva" (environment) as a whole.

Paradoxically, whether as a reaction to the holocaust and assimilation or because of an altered perspective stemming from new social and economic identifications, the curricula of all the secular schools now show a declining emphasis on universalism[41] and a greater focus on Jewish content.

One of the most conspicuous characteristics of Hasidic groups is their strong internal sense of community, with the "rebbe" (rabbi) as the focal figure of the group. Degree of interest in affairs beyond their own community varies but is generally severely limited, particularly among extremely conservative sects. The Lubavitcher group have, as indicated earlier, opened their schools to children of non-Hasidic families. Many of them also support Zionism and the state of Israel. On the other hand, Satmar Hasidim, even those living in Israel, are opposed on religious grounds to the establishment of a Jewish state prior to the coming of the messiah. Interest in universal or humanistic causes or problems, except in the most general way, is not apparent in terms of directed activities or concerted forms of intervention or help and is therefore not reflected in the curricula of the schools.

CONCLUSIONS

It is unwise and possibly even counterproductive to evaluate the Yiddish secular school movements in terms of their long-range historical or sociological influence. Although these are important dimensions and frequently determine the survival or demise of an educational system, they should not become the primary focus for purposes of evaluation. This approach is particularly unfair to a group that, at least in its early years, supported ideological openness and contact with mainstream culture, and thus increased its vulnerability to strong educational and cultural forces that drained its strength and vitality. But more important than any other consideration is the idea that the primary criteria for judging educational institutions should be educational criteria which illuminate the cognitive and affective inner climate of a school rather than merely environmental circumstances and relationships which, while important, are not fundamental to an educational examination. This is true for all educational systems, but it is particularly so in the case of ethnic institutions which are culture- and value-oriented and whose external impact is difficult to quanitify and to measure.

At its best, an education in a Yiddish secular school was probably a relevant experience for pupils because it provided a sense of continuity, group identity, and pride, all of which are necessary to emotional stability and a positive self-image. In addition, there was strong emphasis within the educational programs of the schools upon behavioral and affective elements. Abundant opportunities were provided for meeting children's developmental needs through perceptual, emotional, aesthetic, and cognitive experiences. Close relationships with teachers and community workers in many curricular and extracurricular settings resulted in a high level of visibility for children who received warmth and acceptance from familiar adults who were somewhat less emotionally involved with them than their own parents.

The decline in Yiddish language comprehension led to a loss of the Yiddish secular school's uniqueness, since it relied heavily upon linguistic distinctiveness as the vehicle through which it presented many of the social, ideological, and value-oriented elements that are essential components of a good ethnic and, it might be argued, any good education. Although they, at least initially, demonstrated this type of strength, they always lacked some of the qualities that provide an educational institution with internal stability, namely, the existence of appropriate structure, personnel, materials, and methods to sustain a program without excessive reliance on the existence of conducive external factors. The proper balance of idealistic and practical elements within a school system is difficult to achieve, and many large, financially well supported public and private schools suffer more from a lack of the idealistic values that the movement schools had in such abundance than a lack of the institutional stability in which the Yiddish secular schools are weak.

It is difficult to say whether a united secular school system with bigger, more stable schools capable of sustaining an inner community life might find itself in a stronger position than the movement schools find themselves in today. However, it is clear that in order to increase their chances of survival, ethnic schools must offer an education that is of superior quality both in objectives and in organization and implementation. Otherwise, they will neither be able to withstand the impact of competitive social and educational forces nor be able to provide the quality of ethnic education which they feel is desirable and attainable.

The Hasidic schools and the secular day schools have the kind of structural control over hours and schedules which increases institutional stability and independence. Their program is not influenced by extensions or curtailments of the public school day or by other external variables. Inferior status is not associated with ethnic language study as it is in Jewish schools in which these subjects can be scheduled only during late afternoon hours when children are already fatigued from a full day of activity at their "main" school. Administrators are not forced to fit their extracurricular activities around primary commitments to other institutions.

The expectations related to Yiddish language in the curricula of the Hasidic schools may be said to focus upon language maintenance as a tool for the preservation of a unique Jewish life style closely associated with the 18th and 19th Century eastern European shtetl. Facility with Yiddish also enables boys studying in Hasidic schools to have more direct contact with the writings of the great rabbis of the Hasidic movements and to benefit from talks and lectures given at various religious and social occasions by the current "rebbe" of their respective community. Girls from Hasidic families need Yiddish to assume their roles of wife and mother (the only acceptable roles) in a Yiddish-speaking community.

The congruence of outlook and values which exists among Hasidic parents and school officials, as well as the closed quality of the Hasidic society, fosters a sense of continuity and acceptance of tradition which is intentionally kept unhampered[42] by the temptations of alternative sets of values. It is interesting to note that many Hasidic groups reside in poor areas in which the quality of life would not be attractive enough from an external perspective to pose a threat.

Hasidic schools are thus less vulnerable to external educational and social influences than are secular schools, and the precarious condition of many supplementary secular schools is more a reflection of this factor than of any other.

Because there are no longer secular Yiddish-speaking communities, children of secular background who were not exposed to a Yiddish education in their early years do not have later opportunities similar to those of Hasidic youth to study Yiddish in a natural linguistic environment. Those Jewish pupils who did study some Yiddish in secular schools have no framework in which to use it or expand their knowledge of it. Consequently, even the Yiddish language competence which still exists, limited as it may be among Yiddish secularists in the post World War II era, is largely invisible and its potential influence is further diluted by the absence of a concentrated, active Yiddish secular community.

Frustration and disappointment with the quality of modern Jewish life has grown, and in sharp contrast to rising statistics on intermarriage and other forms of assimilation, there is evidence of increased interest in language, ritual, and culture among previously indifferent Jewish groups.[43] If this trend in the direction of increased ethnic identification continues to grow, future prospects for both the Yiddish secular schools and the Hasidic movements may be brighter than is now predictable.

NOTES

1. The Yeshiva of Flatbush in Brooklyn, N.Y., is one such example.

2. Hasidism was a branch of the Jewish Orthodox movement in Europe which traditionally placed a greater emphasis on prayer and emotion in their definition of piety than did the Mitnagdim (the other major branch of European Orthodoxy), which placed a greater emphasis on intellect. Followers of these groups are now dispersed throughout the world.

3. S. Parker, "Inquiry into the Yiddish Secular Schools in the United States: A Curricular Perspective" (doctoral dissertation, Harvard University, 1973), pp. 15-16.

4. The leaders of the four secular schools held strong ideological convictions that were in some measure related to their earlier experiences in eastern European reform and revolutionary movements.

5. Parker, *op. cit.*, p. 21.

6. *Ibid.*, p. 21.

7. *Ibid.*, p. 23.

8. *National Census of Jewish Schools.* New York: American Association of Jewish Education, 1967.

9. The Lubavitcher group in particular.

10. According to Rabbi Posner, principal of the school in a discussion in Nashville, January 1974.

11. Small enclaves of Yiddish-speaking Hasidic groups do exist in other cities.

12. Harry M. Rabinowicz, *The World of Hasidism*. London: Vallentine, Mitchell, 1970. Pp. 237-238.

13. Parker, *op. cit.*, p. 24.

14. According to Rabbi Fogelman, the principal, B'nos Yaakov, a girls' school with a pupil population of 700 in Brooklyn, N.Y., operated by the Bobover Hasidim, is an example of such a large regional school.

15. J. Mlotek, "Concerns about the Yiddish Teacher," *Kultur un Dertsiyung*. New York: Workmen Circle, January 1963. P. 3.

16. Parker, *op. cit.*, p. 34.

17. *Ibid.*, Appendix E.

18. N. Chanin, "Kultur Tetikait in un Arum Die Schulen," *Kultur un Dertsiyung*. New York: Workmen Circle, April 1944. Pp. 6-7.

19. The Jewish People's School in Montreal, Canada, had over 700 students in 1971, according to its principal, Mr. Wilesky. Other large Yiddish day schools exist in Canada. In the United States the Kineret School in New York City is one of very few remaining Yiddish day schools. Most of these, in both the United States and Canada, were established by the Farband and taught or teach Hebrew as well as Yiddish.

20. I. Goldberg, "Jewish Secularism in the Year Two Thousand," *Jewish Currents*. New York: Jewish Currents, Inc., July-August 1971.

21. *Give Your Child a Progressive Yiddish Education*. New York: Workmen Circle.

22. S. Yefroiken, "The Y.L. Peretz Schools of the Workmen Circle, *Bleter Far Yiddishe Dertsiyung*. New York: Congress for Jewish Culture, June-September 1951.

23. L. Lehrer, "The Role of Yiddish in the Yiddish School," *Why Yiddish for Our Children?* New York: Sholem Aleichem Folk Institute, 1956, p. 5.

24. *Ibid.*, p. 4.

25. *Ibid.*, p. 5.

26. These selections had humanitarian or nature-oriented themes, and early editions of the literature anthologies used in the secular schools include them.

27. According to Jack Noskowitz of the Workmen Circle, who offered this information during an interview in April 1972.

28. More than ten in Montreal, New York City, Philadelphia, Los Angeles, Boston, and Whippany, N.J.

29. This may have been due to the fact that, for example, in the Montreal Jewish People's School, the French, Hebrew, and Yiddish teachers used the languages in conversing with one another in the corridors. Some children in this school were observed making efforts to use Yiddish in responding to questions for which teachers would have accepted answers in English.

30. Parker, *op. cit.*, pp. 101-106.

31. Pupils attending the Jewish People's School in Montreal were reputed to have been of average or above average intelligence. Schulman's work did not provide data on ability levels.

32. I.I. Lifskitz, *Unzer Buch: A Ler Buch Far Yiddish,* Part I. New York: Gross Brothers Printing Company, Inc., 1969. pp. 18-19.

33. *Ibid.,* p. 19.

34. *Ibid.*

35. *Shmussen Mit Kinder un Yugent.* New York: Mercaz Leinyanei Chinuch, August 1973.

36. Parker, *op. cit.,* Appendix H.

37. This information was offered by a teacher at B'nos Yaakov School, a Bobover Hasidic School in New York City, during an interview and class observation in March 1973.

38. Observed in March 1973 in the B'nos Yaakov School in New York City.

39. Yiddish words that were not understood were explained with a whole Yiddish phrase, and if this failed, an occasional English translation was offered.

40. Morris Rosenfeld and Mani Laib were two such writers.

41. The more recent editions of Yiddish literature anthologies published for secular school students reflect this trend. See Wiseman's *Dos Vort* and texts by Yefroiken.

42. A Hasidic rabbi told me of his resolve to keep his young children away from contact with Jews who did not fully observe the Sabbath.

43. "Nov. 11," *New York Times,* 1973, p. 35.

XI

American Indian

Bilingual Education

Bernard Spolsky

INTRODUCTION[1]

American ambivalence toward its aboriginal population is clearly reflected in attitudes to Native American languages and to language maintenance efforts. While linguists found the American Indian languages a rich mine for study, they generally felt little responsibility to preserve them except in grammar books and archives. In similar vein, they generally chose to study the languages rather than how they were used. The paucity of studies of sociolinguistic questions—of languages in contact or being destroyed—is most regrettable. With a few distinguished exceptions, the student of an Amerindian language has made no mention of these matters, except to complain how few speakers are left, or how poorly they recall the language (cf. Spolsky and Kari 1974).

Official policy toward American Indians and their languages has swung from virtual genocide to moderate acceptance, from the encouragement of assimilation or relocation to the support of some degree of maintenance of ethnic and linguistic identity. This chapter will concentrate on a recent trend to the direction of maintenance: it will not be able to predict future directions or efforts. It will record in the main recent federally supported initiatives to encourage one form or another of bilingual education. This will be shown to be interpretable in various cases as language maintenance, language revival, or more efficient language loss, depending on the sociolinguistic situation in which it is developed. It will be seen to represent in some cases support for local impetus toward Indianization of education, in other to remain an undigested and uninfluential modification of curriculum. Some common principles will emerge and some practices will be seen to have wide currency, but bilingual education will appear as multifaceted a concept for American Indians as for other cases.

A brief historical sketch will set the background. John Collier, Commissioner of the Bureau of Indian Affairs in the administration of Franklin D. Roosevelt, reversed earlier forced assimilation programs, and made a number of basic changes in education policies. Among these were the establishment of day schools, the recruitment of Indian teachers, and the start of some bilingual programs.

Collier's declaration that an Indian has as much right as anyone to his native language, was, according to Beatty (1944), greeted with scorn. Older teachers in the Service predicted that the already difficult problem of teaching English to their charges would be made more difficult.

The wording of the 1941 Manual for the Indian School Service in which Collier's new policy was finally detailed is of interest:

> *Use of English and Native Language.* It is self-evident that the first step in any program of instruction must be to develop in the children the ability to speak, understand, and think in the English language. Every effort shall be made to provide activities and other forms of encouragement for children to use English in their daily association in the classroom and on the playgrounds. As language expression is essential to the development of thought, the use of native languages by Indian children may not be forbidden or discouraged.
>
> Experimental teaching in the native languages of several of the larger Indian tribes is contemplated in the near future and textbooks and other material in the native language are being prepared to aid in this work.
>
> The Indian Office desires to staff such experimental schools with teachers who are interested in the project, and if possible, who speak the native language. Requests for transfers to such stations would be appreciated.

First emphasis is on English, which is to be taught thoroughly and "encouraged" in classroom and playground. At the same time, the native language is to be neither "forbidden" nor "discouraged." There is to be "experimental" teaching of the native language, and material preparation is to be started. Finally, the shortage of teachers is referred to. Clearly a somewhat lukewarm and hesitant commitment to bilingual education, but a start.

The effect of such a program among the Navajo has been described by Young (1972). In 1936, John P. Harrington of the Bureau of American Ethnology was asked by Willard Beatty, Director of Indian Education under Collier, to develop a practical alphabet and produce primer material. Harrington worked on this with Robert Young and William Morgan: an orthography was developed, and several primers were written but never published. In 1940, Young and Edward Kennard were employed by the BIA to develop reading materials In Navajo and to teach literacy. A preprimer, primer, and reader were translated into Navajo and published in 1940, followed by another reader. In 1941, William Morgan joined the literacy team, and Kennard moved on to work in Sioux and Hopi. In 1941, Young and Morgan produced a book called *The World and Its People* in Navajo and English; in 1940-1943, a four-volume series of bilingual readers by Ann Nolan Clark was published; in 1942, a new set of bilingual reading materials based on Navajo stories was prepared by Hildegard Thompson and published; in 1943, Young and Morgan published *The Navajo Language* (still the basic grammar and dictionary) and an account of the events leading up to World War II, and started publishing a monthly Navajo newspaper. Materials written for adults and for the accelerated postwar program continued to be produced until 1957, when with a new stress on the teaching of English, the BIA removed support from the use of written Navajo and discontinued the newspaper.

The programs that are described in this paper often owe something to the earlier BIA programs but are generally the result of two new initiatives, the developing movement for local control, and the availability of federal funds, especially through the Bilingual Education Act. Other important federal funds that will be mentioned in the course of this account are Title I and Title IV. A word of background and explanation of each will perhaps be useful.

The three main sources of federal funds for Native American Bilingual Education are often referred to as Title I, Title VII, and Title IV. *Title I* is the Elementary and Secondary Education Act of 1965, officially known as Public Law 89-10. Its basic aim was to provide aid to local educational authorities for the education of low-income children, supporting programs "which contribute particularly to meeting the special educational needs of educationally deprived children." A 1966 amendment expanded the law to apply to a number of specific groups including American Indian children. Title VII of the Elementary and Secondary Education Act, passed in 1968 as Public Law 90-247, is the Bilingual Education Act. It was designed "to meet the special educational needs of children who have limited English-speaking ability, who come from low-income families." Primary emphasis is on the acquisition of English: it is also recognized "that the use of the child's mother tongue in school can have a beneficial effect upon their education." *Title IV* of the Education Amendments of 1972, Public Law 92-318, is the Indian Education Act. It provides grants to local educational agencies, federal schools, Indian tribes and organizations, and institutions of higher learning, for programs designed to meet the special needs of Indian children. It requires that any program be developed in open consultation with the parents of Indian children.

Other bilingual activities are supported with funds under the Johnson O'Malley Act of 1934, which provided for federal reimbursement to states for the education of Indian children. In one or two cases referred to in the descriptions that follow, there is specific earmarking of state educational funds for bilingual programs; at the moment, however, it is the general rule that the programs are dependent on additional externally provided support.

CURRENT BILINGUAL PROGRAMS

In the section that follows, an attempt will be made to describe in general terms each of the existing American Indian bilingual education programs. Some words of caution, of the type more usually relegated to footnotes, are in place. The descriptions are based on sources of varied detail and accuracy. A good deal has been obtained by reading continuation proposals for Title VII grants. These, unfortunately, follow fairly rigid guidelines according to the criteria developed by the Office of Education, and tend to be written in what might be called "proposalese." There are seldom data on language maintenance or the sociolinguistic situation, although there usually are statistics of poverty. There are usually large and complex charts and lists dealing with such matters as "process" and "product" evaluation, and pages detailing who will report what, when, and to whom. Much of the description has been gleaned or interpreted from these proposals, and while the description has in most cases been checked by local program staff, there may still be inaccuracies. A good deal of other information, more difficult to document, has been obtained from educators with experience in the programs. Again, inaccuracies of fact or interpretation are possible.

Every effort has been made to describe the state of the programs and of their plans in the spring of 1974. But the very newness of the activities, and the speed with which they are developing will mean that many changes will have taken place by the time this chapter is published.

In particular program descriptions, I have chosen to concentrate on those features which seem distinctive. The list is exhaustive insofar as Title VII programs are concerned; it also includes every other bilingual program that I have been able to find in progress in the spring of 1974. It does not necessarily include a number of Title IV supported Indian cultural programs or a number of places where some bilingual activity has started or is planned for the coming year. The descriptions are arranged alphabetically according to language name, except that all Alaskan programs are treated together as is a Wisconsin five-language program.

ALASKA[2]

Bilingual education has become rapidly established in the many Native American languages in *Alaska*. Given that there are a score of different languages at all stages of maintenance or loss, three education systems, and half a dozen different kinds of funding source, it is not surprising to find that the term "bilingual education" covers a multitude of aims and policies.

Aleut is still spoken by about 700 of the 2000 Aleutians living in villages or native towns. In one village, Atka, where there are children who still speak the language, a bilingual program with two language aides and eighteen students began in 1973. Support is from the State General Fund, which for the last two years has included money for bilingual education.

Some of the strongest programs are those with the Eskimo languages, backed up by the work of the Eskimo Language Workshop at the University of Alaska. There are close to 15,000 speakers of all ages of *Central Yupik*, which is still widely spoken by children. Four bilingual programs started in 1970 with Title I support; Title VII programs started in 1970 and 1971 at four locations, and in 1973 at another, and there are now a total of 24 schools with programs supported by Title I, IV, or VII, Johnson-O'Malley or State Funds. The programs affect about 900 children, mainly in the first three grades but in many cases up to eighth grade, and employ about 45 bilingual aides. At four schools, Clarks Point, Ekuk, Levelock, and Newhalen, there are complete oral programs in Central Yupik. The Eskimo Language Workshop is engaged in material and curriculum development and in teacher and paraprofessional training. There are five classes in Central Yupik at Kuskokwim Community College and Yupik is to be required for the AA degree. There are also classes at Bethel High School.

To provide closer leadership and coordination for the programs, it is planned soon to move the Eskimo Language Workshop from the University of Alaska at Fairbanks to Kuskokwim Community College at Bethel. With this move, the importance of the Yupik program as the vanguard of bilingual education in Alaska will be confirmed. As Central Yupik accounts for the close to half of the speakers of Native American languages in the state, and two-thirds of the children still speaking their language, its successful maintenance will establish a model for the others.

Inupiaq, a second Eskimo language, has close to 6000 speakers; in some parts, children still speak the language, but in others they come to school speaking English only. There are fourteen programs in Alaska state-operated schools (ASOSS) supported from the general fund, and one in the Barrow BIA school supported by Title IV funds administered by the Alaska Native Education Board. Twenty-eight language aides work in these programs; in some cases they run their own classes, in others work as part of a team, in still others work with children taken out of the class. Teacher training started last summer.

Pacific Gulf Yupik Eskimo (also known as *Sugcestun Aleut*) is spoken by about a third of the 3000 estimated native population; generally, most of the speakers are over 30 years old, but there are children speaking the language at English Bay and teenagers at Port Graham. At each of these locations, in schools part of the Kenai Peninsula Borough system, there are Title IV bilingual programs. At the other schools, under ASOSS control, there is Johnson O'Malley support for bilingual work.

Most of the 1000 Eskimos in St. Lawrence Island still speak their language, *Siberian Yupik*. A bilingual education program began in 1972 in the two BIA schools with Title IV support. The first grade at one school and the first and second at the second are taught in Yupik, except for one hour a day of oral English. Next year, kindergarten and second grade will be taught in Yupik. Materials are being prepared in Siberian Yupik, with English translations being made available to the English teachers. A particularly interesting point is the potential comparison with the situation on the mainland of Siberia, where the same language is spoken. Materials in the language started to be printed in 1932 in the Soviet sector, and there has been a bilingual program since then (Krauss 1974). The Soviet books use the cyrillic alphabet, and show signs in their various editions of developing modernization and Russification of Eskimo life.

A *Haida* culture course is taught at the high school and elementary school in Hydaburg, with Johnson-O'Malley funds. Only one hundred of the five hundred

Haida speak their language, and most are over the age of 50. But there has been strong interest in language revival. The Ketchikan Haida Language Society has held two workshops, completed a noun dictionary, and has regular classes. But there is no school support for the language programs in Ketchikan.

Tlingit is also a revival program with few of the 2000 speakers under the age of 30 (there is a total population of about 9000). At Hoonah, the language has been taught for three years; at Angoon and Yakutat programs are in their first year; there are no other language programs. At some schools, aides and untrained native speakers are teaching culture and some language: a touring bilingual specialist is working through the Alaska Native Brotherhood, school boards, and other agencies trying to encourage language revival work. The elementary school Tlingit program involves teaching words and phrases and some reading. There is a shortage of materials.

The situation with the eleven *Athabaskan* languages varies considerably from case to case, but some progress has been made with each. Orthography has been established, literacy workshops started, word lists and dictionaries are in preparation, and a core of native speakers is being trained for linguistic work and as a potential staff for bilingual programs. In *Ahtena* (500 population, 200 speakers generally over 30 years of age), a score or more people attend evening classes, and there are plans to start language revival programs in two schools in the fall. With *Tanaina* (1000, 300 mainly over 30), there is a program at Nondalton, but not elsewhere. There is a Title I and state-supported program in *Upper Kuskokwim*, where all of the 100 people still speak the language. The program is supported by an SIL linguist. There are seven schools with *Koyukon* programs (2000, 700 over 30), all with the language taught as a second language. In *Minto* and *Nenana* (350, 100 speakers over 30), there is a Title I program at Minto. In the *Tanacross* language (175, 135 speakers including some children), there are Title I bilingual programs at Tanacross and Dot Lake. In *Upper Tanana* (300, all ages) the BIA school at Tetlin has one language aide and the ASOSS school at Northway has two. In the case of *Kutchin* (1000, 700 and many children speaking the language), there is a Title I program at the BIA school and Title I and state-supported programs in three ASOSS schools. A number of books have been prepared, and seventeen stories transcribed by Sapir are to be published. The language has been taught at the University of Alaska. A program is planned for *Han* (65, 30 over 50 years of age), and literacy work (but no school program is starting with *Ingalik* (300, 100 over 30) and *Holikachuk* (170, 20 over 30).

Support for these programs comes from a number of sources. The Alaska state-operated school system has state general funds and has its own bilingual staff; the BIA uses various funds; the Alaska Native Education Board administers a Title IV (Indian Education Act) grant; the Alaska Native Language Center at the University of Alaska, set up by legislative action in 1972, provides basic linguistic support, material development, and teacher training for many different languages; the Eskimo Language Workshop provides similar backing for the Yupik programs; linguists from the Wycliffe Bible Translators are working with Siberian Yupik, Inupiaq, Kutchin, Upper Tanna, Upper Kuskokwim, and Koyukon and assist locally with the bilingual programs; the Alaska Native Language Program at the University of Alaska offers majors in Yupik and Inupiaq, a minor in Alaska Native Languages, and courses in the various languages; the Sheldon Jackson Community College offers aide training and plans a post-AA teacher training program. The strength of this general statewide commitment to the native languages is demonstrated by the 1972 legislation establishing bilingual programs in any state-operated school with at least 15 pupils whose primary language is other than English, appropriating $200,000 for this, and a further $200,000 to establish the Alaska Native Language Center.

CHEROKEE[3]

While the Cherokee had developed a high standard of literacy in their native language during the 19th Century, the dissolution of the Cherokee Nation in 1907 was followed by a rapid decline in the language. By the 1960s, only the older people could read and write the syllabary that Sequoyah had developed, and only a third of the 30,000 Cherokee living in Oklahoma and the 3000 in North Carolina were believed to be able to speak their language fluently (White 1962). Very little is written in Cherokee now: tribal council minutes, for instance, are kept in English, and there is only one Cherokee typewriter in Oklahoma. Studies by Wahrhaftig (1970) and Pulte (n.d.) have shown that a good number of children still speak the language, although Pulte finds reason to believe that in some areas the language will soon be lost. In any case, all research supports the need for some bilingual education.

Based on the belief that one of the major causes of language decline was the lack of reading materials in Cherokee, a revival program started in 1961 with a newsletter and some reprinting. An ACLS grant in 1962 made it possible to have the Cherokee syllabary set in type again, and some literacy classes were set up (White 1962). The impetus was picked up by the Carnegie Corporation Cross-Cultural Education Project of the University of Chicago, which included among its various activities the development of a Cherokee primer, radio programs, the newsletter, and courses in Cherokee in various public schools (Walker 1965).

A Cherokee Bilingual Family School Project was established with USOE support in Adair County, Oklahoma, in March 1968 with aims of providing bilingual preschool experiences for the children and of involving parents in the school. The program included instruction in Cherokee for the parents.

In 1969, Northeastern State College at Tahlequah, Okla., established the Cherokee Bilingual Education Center, which works with Cherokee bilingual programs at four schools within close range. The programs are supported by Title VII, and involve the use of bilingual aides who "not only do the kinds of things that aides normally do, but . . . also serve as interpreters between the children and the teachers." The aides now teach in Cherokee using Cherokee materials. There is a teacher training program, hampered reportedly by the College's unwillingness to give credit for knowledge of Cherokee. There is strong emphasis on the teaching of English as a second language. In 1972, permission was received from the Oklahoma State Department of Education to do some teaching in Cherokee, although Oklahoma law requires that all instruction must be in English (Holland 1972).

CHEYENNE[4]

The Northern Cheyenne Bilingual Education Program is a joint project of the Lame Deer Public School and St. Labre's Mission School for Indians. About 200 of the 800 children in the schools are reported to be dominant in Cheyenne, and another 150 are said to understand it. The program was developed originally as part of a combined Crow-Cheyenne bilingual Follow-Through program. There were fears that bilingual education might disrupt the procedures of the Follow-Through model: a separate Cheyenne program was therefore set up. In its first year of operation in 1972-1973, some basic surveys were carried out. A questionnaire given to teachers and aides in the schools revealed initial doubts about bilingual education: most knew little about its goals, and more than half were indifferent to the program. Most of the first year seems to have been spent overcoming these fears and doubts, and a great deal of emphasis went into explaining the program's merits to the teachers and parents. A policy advisory board, consisting of respected bilingual members of the local community, is given "weight and authority," with the director of the project, in preparing policy recommendations for the local school board. The bilingual program is being integrated into the Follow-Through classroom as one of the activities children may choose. The Tribal Council has shown a keen interest in the program: they receive regular reports at each of their meetings, and have provided some financial support. A bilingual day camp is planned for the coming summer in order to give the children more experience speaking Cheyenne. In a recent handout, the program reports its results as follows:

> Most dramatically, a reversal in the Cheyenne attitudes toward the Cheyenne language: three years ago, young children absolutely denied being able to speak Cheyenne; today, Indian and white children alike are being given daily culture and language lessons, and enjoying them. The Cheyenne language now has a solidly based, useful writing system capable of displaying its true nature and keeping up with its complex variations—and the best in language research is yet to come. Sporadic language classes are being given for non-Indians to learn Cheyenne, and plans are being made for literacy classes to teach Cheyenne speakers how to use the new system. And perhaps best of all, the Elders of the Tribe are again becoming useful and respected participants in the education of their grandchildren—through participation in the Culture Advisory Board, clasroom visits, and night-time story-telling sessions.

CHOCTAW[5]

The Choctaw Bilingual Education Program began in 1970 with Title VII support, and operates in four elementary schools in McCurtain County, Oklahoma, with its headquarters at Southeastern State College. An orthography has been developed and materials are being written in the language. The program has three main purposes: the encouragement of the self-concept of the Choctaw children, the teaching of English as a second language, and the encouragement of recognition of individual differences. Bilingual aides are used in the classroom. In addition, some sixteen local Choctaws in teacher training programs at Southeastern work with the program as coordinators: their training includes work with Choctaw language and culture. The program thus aims to develop bilingual teachers whose role in the maintenance of the Choctaw language and culture is clearly recognized.

CREE[6]

The Cree Bilingual Education Project is part of the activities of the Rocky Boy School. The school is Indian-controlled, the district having become independent after some years of effort. From the beginning, there was a bilingual program, and in 1973-1974, literacy in Cree was reported up to the third grade. There is evidence of considerable community interest in the program: a bilingual parents' advisory council meets every two weeks, observes classes, and plays an active role in direction. While none of the certified teachers are Cree, all have undergone extensive training in Cree language, culture, and values, attending weekly classes in Cree language and culture. In grades 1 to 3, classes are divided into three kinds of groups: two groups of Cree speakers, two of Cree "listeners," and four of children monolingual in English. In the second and third grades, children who are dominant in Cree are in a separate group, receiving more of their instruction in Cree. The project is developing its own materials, and is recording the stories and legends of the Chippewa Cree tribe in English and Cree. Classes receive instruction in Cree culture half an hour a day. There is already one Cree certified teacher working with the program, and five more graduating in the near future. In a few years it is expected that it will be possible to staff the school with Crees. Teacher training is carried out by Northern Montana College.

CROW[7]

The Crow Bilingual Education Program has been operating since 1971 in one of the larger public schools on the Reservation. A study conducted by Dracon (1969) established that 82% of the 1102 Crow students examined spoke Crow as a "primary" language, 8% spoke it as a "secondary" language, and 10% were monolingual in English. This strong language maintenance appears related to a number of factors: the size of the reservation and its comparatively sound agricultural economy, the fact that it is on ancestral land, and the strength of native traditional elements in religion. While the language is strong, literacy in it is virtually restricted to the school's bilingual staff. The orthography has been fairly well established for two years, but some details are still in dispute.

Language maintenance is generally considered to be a task of the home rather than the school: only parents one of whom does not speak Crow seem to believe that school should teach the language. The bilingual program then can focus not on language revival or maintenance, but on attempting to overcome educational disadvantages of Crow children. It follows the principle of education in the vernacular: an initial reading program in Crow, and a program for oral language development. An extensive and intensive evaluation project has shown consistent improvement on various achievement methods by children in the bilingual programs when they are compared with other Crow-speaking children: the 1972-1973 results showing effects beyond the first year are summarized:

> Achievement tests given at Crow Agency school last year indicated a much higher level of performance than had ever been obtained for the grade levels in which the bilingual program had been implemented. Most scores were at or above the national grade equivalent for the first time in the school's history. While differences could still be observed on some sub-tests between bilinguals and monolinguals, they were being reduced by second grade.

However, these encouraging results have not been repeated on some of the formal standard tests now being used, raising questions about the exact nature of the improvement. While there are very few bilingual Crow teachers at present, a number are in training and twenty are expected to receive teacher's certificates in the next two years. The development of a unified program is hampered by the fact that several school districts are involved. The program at the moment is dependent almost entirely on federal support, and would be unlikely to survive its loss.

KERESAN[8]

The Acomita Day School Title VII Bilingual/Bicultural Program started in 1972. The children in the program come to school having heard Acoma *Keresan* spoken at home, but already speaking English. The project and the tribal council have moved toward agreement on an orthography: a dictionary with 2500 entries and a first primer have so far been prepared, large numbers of visual aids are in preparation, and thirty folk stories and twenty songs have been underway. Local Acoma people work as paraprofessionals in the schools, and some are enrolled in on-site teacher education programs conducted by the University of New Mexico: four of the aides in the program have just completed AA degrees. The program appears to have good community support.

LAKOTA (SIOUX)[9]

The Lakota Bilingual Education Project has been operating at Loneman Day School, Oglala, S.D., since 1971, but its work has been hampered by the political tensions in the community and with the BIA. The corporation to whom the original grant was made was removed, and a new administration established. The nonbilingual teachers have been learning Lakota, and are assisted in their teaching by bilingual assistants. There has been emphasis on community participation:

initially, there were objections to bilingual education which have been overcome. In spite of these difficulties, the program continues. Teachers are being trained, and there are prospects of having Lakota certified teachers in the next few years. About 15% of the children are reported to be dominant in Lakota and another 35% can understand it: half are monolingual in English.

MICCOSUKEE[10]

The Miccosukee Bilingual Education Project was begun at the Miccosukee Day School, Ochopee, Fla., in 1972 with Title VII funds. The school is operated by the tribe under BIA contract; the Miccosukee tribe is small (about 400 members) but isolated and influential. Almost all the children come to school speaking Miccosukee. As part of the program, elders of the tribe come to school to pass on traditional knowledge. The project has obtained authorization to claim copyright over material in the language, for the tribe considers its language a treasure that may not be stolen. An orthography is being developed. The aides teach Miccosukee language and culture and help the children with other subjects.

NAVAJO[11]

Navajo bilingual programs, virtually extinct after 1957, were revived in the mid-1960s as part of the general resurgence of ethnic awareness and specifically in association with the growth of Navajo control over education. There are in fact two distinct trends that coalesce in the present activities. The first, educationally motivated, may be characterized as the attempt of local educators (BIA in particular) to improve instruction by a policy of teaching in the vernacular. To these people, bilingual education is seen as one method of overcoming the obvious disadvantage under which Navajo children work in a completely English environment. The policy has been translated into action, with the support of federal funds separate from the BIA regular educational budget, to develop a bilingual kindergarten and first-grade curriculum, to provide support for development of Navajo reading materials, to encourage the use of Navajo aides, and to start a program for training Navajo teachers. The second trend is more political or economic in its motivation: it is the establishment or encouragement of bilingual programs as part of a movement for tribal or community control of Navajo education. It is manifested in the bilingual programs developed by the four community-controlled schools (Rough Rock Demonstration School, Rock Point Community School, Ramah Navajo High School, Borrego Pass School), the dissemination activities of DBA, the Navajo Education Association, and the myriad of activities including a major teacher training program undertaken by the Tribal Division of Education in the last twelve months.

The Rough Rock Demonstration School Bilingual/Bicultural Project is now in its fourth year of Title VII funding, although the program began in 1966. As a recent position paper suggests (Division of Education, The Navajo Tribe 1974), "One of the most significant aspects of the first community controlled school on the Navajo Reservation was its exploration and initiation of a bilingual/bicultural program for its student body." The program is guided by a Navajo Language Committee, and its philosophy stresses the use of Navajo in instruction from an early age, with subsequent teaching of English as a second language. As one might expect, the project has been a pioneer in developing curriculum and materials. Teacher training is carried on at the school through the University of New Mexico.

The Rock Point Bilingual Education Project is in its third year of operation at the Rock Point Community School. The basic approach, developed before extra funding was available, is described as "coordinate bilingual instruction," with the students learning to speak in Navajo to the Navajo Language Teacher and in English to the English Language Teacher. These two teachers form a team. Instruction in Navajo is given in the primary grades in language arts, social studies, and mathematics, and there are Navajo social studies and science classes in the third through sixth grades. Most of the Navajo Language Teachers are working toward university degrees and teacher certification. Classroom material and workbooks have been produced, and the University of New Mexico is preparing a number of books written by Rock Point staff for publication. The school is under complete local control; the bilingual project is not autonomous, but is "an integral part of a community-controlled school attempting to evolve a quality Navajo education program."

The Ramah Navajo High School Bilingual Education Program is in its third year. The school came under community control in 1970, and the Title VII project set out in 1972 to raise the competences of its seventh grade pupils in both Navajo and English. In the second year, the bilingual program added the eighth grade, and the next year ninth grade was included. Emphasis has been split between an oral approach and Navajo literacy. During the first year, all non-Navajo speakers on the school staff were required to study elementary Navajo, offered for University of New Mexico credit. As the second Navajo community controlled school, and the first high school under complete Navajo control, the program had special problems: all its students have spent six years in English-only programs, and few materials are available for high school age pupils. The school is offering a course in Navajo law and another in Ramah Area Studies.

At Borrego Pass Community School, which has been an independent community controlled school since 1972, the combined first and second grade is taught mainly in Navajo with some teaching of English by English speakers. In the third grade, the main language of instruction is English, with a Navajo specialist for reading and writing. New curriculum is being developed, teacher training for aides is underway, and a special education program has been established.

The BIA-supported bilingual education programs are at Sanostee Boarding School, Toadlena Boarding School, Cottonwood Day School, Greasewood Boarding School, and Pinon Boarding School. At these schools, there are kindergartens and first and second grades with Navajo-speaking teachers following a bilingual-bicultural curriculum. The curriculum was written by Muriel Saville in 1970; it is at present being revised. The efforts of the program are hampered by a shortage of certified teachers (many of the bilingual classes are under the control of uncertified instructors), the shortage of materials, and the absence of supervisors experienced in bilingual education or able to understand what is happening in the classroom. To remedy these situations, the BIA Area Office established a Title VII teacher training program at Sanostee and Toadlena and has found funds to support material development activities at the University of New Mexico.

A few of the many public school districts with Navajo children have so far started bilingual programs.

The Gallup-McKinley County Schools Title VII Bilingual Project started in 1972. It involves 12 classes (K-2) at four schools, reaching about 300 Navajo children. Materials are being developed, and Navajo aides are being trained by the University of New Mexico.

San Juan School District, Monticello, Utah, began its Navajo Bilingual Education Project in 1969 with Title VII support, and aims to integrate a new proposal with other funds to develop a curriculum for Indian students. One of the principal activities of the project has been to develop a series of film strips and animated films in Navajo. The project's initial aim of raising the academic standards of Navajo children appear not to have been met in the first few years: while the evaluation results are confused, there is no evidence that experimental bilingual classes did better than controls. Navajo parents responded positively to questions about their attitude to the program, but expressed the desire to have more influence in school policy.

Tuba City Public Schools have a Navajo Cultural Center, funded through Title IV, that provides resources and support for Navajo studies at all grade levels. Using Title I funds, a single pilot class has now had a bilingual program with the same teacher for three years. But concern has been expressed that the students in this class are not learning enough English; the program is to stop. A new program with more moderate emphasis on Navajo is planned to start at the kindergarten level next year and follow through until second grade.

There has been increasing emphasis on training of bilingual teachers. From the beginning of the use of Title I and other funds to hire Navajo aides, provision was made for career training, and a number of AA degree programs have been operated in BIA and contract schools. In 1971, the BIA obtained Title VII funds to establish the Sanostee-Toadlena Title VII Navajo Bilingual Teacher Training Project. Five trainees were selected by a committee of local community members at Sanostee Boarding School, and another five by a similar committee at Toadlena. Training is conducted on site at the two schools. For the first two years, instructional support was provided by Antioch College. In summer 1973, the subcontract was transferred to the University of New Mexico. The ten trainees are following a program toward a BS in Elementary Education, and should graduate with degrees and certification in 1975.

The Navajo Teacher Education Development Project was started in 1973 by the Division of Education of the Navajo Tribe with funds under Title IV. There are about one hundred trainees in the program, all Navajos with a minimum of two years of college credit who want to work for a university degree and certification as elementary teachers. The program is conducted on-site, in New Mexico by the University of New Mexico, and in Arizona by the University of Arizona, under contract with the Division. The trainees are generally working as paraprofessionals.

PAPAGO[12]

The Papago Bilingual Education Project started in 1967 with local funds and since 1973 has been funded through Title I. In earlier years, emphasis was on English as a second language. In 1973, it moved to bilingual education, with an aim of teaching reading and writing in Papago before English. There is evidence of strong language maintenance, and the program has begun at Kerwo BIA Day School, where, because of isolation, very little English is spoken. There is a separate program at a public school, funded by Title IV through D.Q. University. Materials are being prepared in Papago by a native linguist, in-service training for aides has begun, and there is evidence of community support.

PASSAMAQUODDY[13]

The Wabnaki Bilingual Education Program operates in one school in Maine: its aim is to "reinforce Passamaquoddy values ... and expand the Passamaquoddy culture." In its third year (1973-1974), it involved 71 children, 64 of whom were said not to be English-dominant. The evaluation report for the second year reveals average gains, over five months, of 13, 28, and 43 new Passamaquoddy words for the K-1, 2-3, and 4-6 grades, respectively. In October testing, children spoken to in Passamaquoddy replied mostly in English: in January, they were starting to use Passamaquoddy words and phrases, and there are reported impressions of more Passamaquoddy used in regular conversations. A great deal of emphasis is placed on material development: there is training of the bilingual aides (some for credit from the University of Maine), and more Indian teachers have been studying Passamaquoddy. There has so far been little success in involving the community: a bimonthly community newspaper and a language committee were planned.

POMO[14]

The Ukiah Indian, Mexican American Bilingual-Bicultural Program established in 1969 includes a component for the Pomo Indian children in the schools covered. None of the teachers are fluent in Pomo, and the goals are cultural rather than linguistic. Attempts to obtain statements of priorities from the Indian parents have met with difficulty: the Indians consulted have given individual opinions, but have not been willing to represent others. For the 1973-1974 year, it was planned to include more Pomo culture in the curriculum, "including language." It was hoped to find some way for staff to learn "linguistics, second language teaching and learning, and hopefully, Indian languages." There were also plans to train a group of three Pomo parents to develop language and culture materials.

SEMINOLE[15]

The Seminole Bilingual Project, funded through Title VII ESEA, has been operating since 1972 in six elementary schools in Seminole County, Oklahoma. It is reported that the Seminole language is still used by adults speaking to each other, in church services, and in other community activities. About 90% of the students come from homes where someone speaks Seminole, but most parents speak to their children in English. Teachers claim that the children speak English poorly, and have no more than a passive knowledge of Seminole. A survey of parents has shown that 129 out of 315 involved in the programs in grade K-3 are "bilingual," many of them understanding Seminole but speaking English. The main thrust of the program seems to be to revive the status of the Seminole language and to encourage the children to use it. There is one bilingual certified teacher. Teaching in Seminole is also done by bilingual assistants, who are in a teacher training program conducted by East Central State College. The regular class teachers, themselves not Seminole, are learning the language. The bilingual program involves teaching Seminole for a set period each day to all students Seminole or not: the bilingual assistant can use the language at other times. The Seminole orthography was developed by missionaries in the 19th Century: various religious texts were printed, but there is little adult literacy now. The project therefore is writing its own materials, and has printed so far reading books for each of the first three grades, two phonics books, two language workbooks, a number of readiness workbooks, three coloring books of legends, and a book of "Seminole Haiku." Curricular objectives have been established for the first three grades: the highlights of the kindergarten and third grade objectives are listed below to give some idea of the goals:

Kindergarten

1. Seminole greeting.
2. Names of two days of the week in Seminole and English.
3. Counting to ten in Seminole and English.
4. Names of weather conditions in Seminole.
5. Six basic colors in Seminole.
6. Eight animals in Seminole and English.
7. Three Seminole leaders.
8. Seminole words for head, arms, feet.
9. One song in Seminole.
10. Ask "What is your name" in Seminole.
11. Say "This is a_____" in Seminole.
12. Say "I want_____" in Seminole.
13. Recognize Seminole tribal dress.
14. Make two craft objects, or explain a Seminole custom.

Third Grade

1. Addition and subtraction in both Seminole and English.
2. Circles, squares, rectangles in Seminole and English.
3. U.S. coins in Seminole and English.
4. Time in hours and half hours in Seminole and English.
5. Simple sentences.
6. Simple questions.
7. Seminole possessive pronoun prefixes.
8. Story or poem about animal.
9. Parts of body in Seminole.
10. Major solar bodies in Seminole.
11. A Seminole custom.
12. A craft object.
13. A rhythmical activity.
14. Occupations.

In addition, children at all levels will be expected to make a gain on a wide-range achievement test and to make "more positive statements about themselves."

It will be seen then that the bulk of the instruction in the school will continue to be in English, with the teaching in Seminole focused on the improvement in self-image thought to come from recognition by the school of the native culture. The project is controlled by the school and the local State College: project staff are concerned to obtain community support, but are not under the control of the Seminole community. The fact that Seminole parents have come to speak English with their children is a reflection of their understanding of what the school wants: the reversal of policy will take time to be believed and to have effect. But community reaction to the program is reported to be favorable. There is some objection to the notion of teaching the language to non-Seminoles, and some Seminole leaders do not see why the language is important: some do not speak it themselves and fear that Seminole language and culture may hinder success in the dominant English-speaking society. Hope is expressed that the program may help produce jobs nearer home for some of the young people.

TEWA[16]

The San Juan Pueblo Tewa Bilingual Project may be characterized as a language revival program. Over recent years there has been a steady decline in knowledge of the language: fewer than half the children in school speak Tewa, and only one child in this year's kindergarten class speaks it. With support from a linguist from the Summer Institute of Linguistics and a native SIL-trained linguist, adult literacy classes have been started. The bilingual project, under the control of the Pueblo and directed by a local Tewa man, operates at the BIA school with Title IV funding and at the local public school with Title I support. In each class, there are Tewa-speaking aides, who are themselves all working toward teacher's degrees through the University of New Mexico. At the BIA school, Tewa is taught an hour a day, while in the public school, a Tewa resource room is used for language teaching. The tribal council appears satisfied with the positive effect of the program on the children.

UTE MOUNTAIN UTE[17]

Project SUN is a multilingual project in five public school districts in the Four Corners area of Southwest Colorado working with Spanish, Ute, and Navajo. Both Ute and Spanish are used at Monaugh Elementary School. The project worked with the Ute tribe in developing an orthography, and sponsored training for a Ute linguist who is now developing booklets, a dictionary, and tapes in the language. The project has as its goal the development of mutual respect among the various ethnic and linguistic groups involved. Half an hour a day is specifically devoted to language development, arts and crafts, and other cultural activities. The project stresses the need for parental decision, arguing that a bilingual program can be of benefit to all kinds of children: to those monolingual in a language other than English by providing a co-instructor who can help the child; to those monolingual in English by teaching them more than one language; to bilingual children whose native heritage is retained; and to children who speak English but understand one of the other languages by restoring their bilingualism. The program is funded through Title VII, with partial support from school districts: it is assumed that districts will take full responsibility by 1975-1976. Working with Project SUN is a full-time Ute linguist, who visits the Ute classroom periodically and works on the development of materials. Filmstrips prepared in Ute Mountain Ute await approval by the Tribal Council.

THE WISCONSIN PROJECT[18]

The Wisconsin Native American Languages Project was established in 1973 with a Title IV grant to the Great Lakes Center Tribal Council. Of the five languages involved, Winnebago and Potawatomi are the most viable, with a strong tie between religion and language: but neither these two nor the others (Oneida, Chippewa, or Manominee) have children speaking them as a first language. The speakers of these languages, all of which are spoken also outside the state, are scattered all over it, and attend public schools with white majorities and under white control (there is a community school at Menominee). No bilingual programs have yet started, but the Project, based at the University of Wisconsin, Milwaukee, is developing materials and carrying out training in preparation for a second language instruction program. Four teams of linguists and native speakers are at work.

ZUNI[19]

A bilingual education program in Zuni is conducted by the Gallup-McKinley County Public School at Zuni Elementary School under this Title VII grant. In its second year, the program affects 75 children in grades k—2. Zuni parents speak the language to their children at home, and the children know little or no English before they come to school. Instruction starts in Zuni, with transfer to English as soon as practical, and translation back to Zuni when there are problems of comprehension. The English teacher works with two Zuni aides. Five Zuni textbooks have been written, and a number of English texts translated in Zuni.

The Acomita Day School Title VII Bilingual/Bicultural Program started in 1972. The children in the program come to school having heard Acoma Keresan spoken at home, but already speaking some English. The project and the Tribal Council have moved toward agreement on an orthography: a dictionary with 2500 entries and a first primer have so far been prepared, large numbers of visual aids are in preparation, thirty folk stories and twenty songs have been underway. Thirty local Acoma people work as paraprofessionals in the schools, and are enrolled in on-site teacher education programs conducted by the University of New Mexico: four of the aides in the program have just completed AA degrees. The program appears to have good community support.

A DESCRIPTIVE MODEL

Even from these brief sketches, it will be clear that bilingual education for Native Americans is a complex and varied phenomenon. While on some levels the programs look similar, the similarity is often superficial, arising from the terminology and phrases used in order to follow Title VII or other guidelines. The range of variation in situation, programs, and goals may be shown if we look at the programs according to a model proposed for the description and analysis of bilingual programs (Spolsky, Green, and Read).

The model tries to map all relevant factors onto a single integrated structure and to suggest some of the lines of interaction. It is based on a hexagonal figure. Each side of the hexagon represents a set of factors that may have a bearing on, or be affected by, the operation of a bilingual program in a particular situation. The six sets of factors are labeled psychological, sociological, economic, political, religio-cultural, and linguistic. Not all the factors will be equally—or even at all—relevant in an individual case but, since the aim is to make the model as universally applicable as possible, the full range of factors is presented, with no special concern at this stage for their relative significance.

In the center of the figure are located a seventh set of factors, the educational ones. This is not done to assert the primacy of these factors. In fact, a purpose of the model is to show how relatively insignificant educational considerations may be, both in the decision whether or not to establish a bilingual program and in the evaluation of a program's "success" in reaching its goals. However, we are engaged in the study of an educational activity and it is appropriate to recognize this by placing education in the middle as the focus of the figure, while the other factors circumscribe and shape it on all sides.

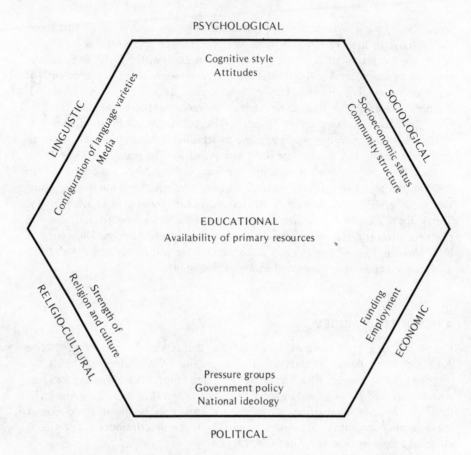

Figure 1a.   The Situational Level

The model comprises three of these hexagons. The first hexagon (Figure 1a) represents the total situation of a community before a bilingual program is introduced. Here "community" should be understood to include any relevant socio-educational entity, ranging from a village or neighborhood through a school district, a geographically focused ethnic group, a province, or a region to a whole nation (Spolsky 1974). The model is intended to be broad enough to deal with the consideration of bilingual education at all these levels. It sets out the whole range of factors that should, ideally, be taken into account in deciding on the establishment of a bilingual program.

It is at the situational level that one could make something of a case for a seven-sided figure, so that educational factors would be placed on a par with the others. This would emphasize that, although an educational decision is being made, educational factors are not necessarily the most important ones, even when the decision is ostensibly made on the basis of them.

The second hexagon (Figure 1b) incorporates those factors which are more or less under the control of the people administering a bilingual program, or which

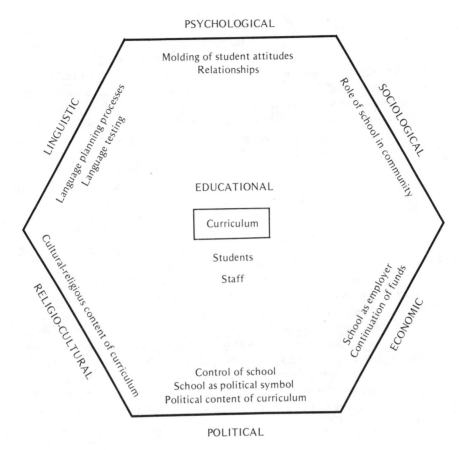

Figure 1b. The Operational Level

may be directly influenced by the operation of the program. The prime factor here is the central element of the whole model, the sine qua non of bilingual education: the use of the two languages as media of instruction and, in particular, their distribution in the school curriculum. One would like to think that this is a purely educational matter, but even this decision may be subject to the influence of other factors. There may be pressure from outside to restrict the use of one of the languages, because "undue emphasis" on one is interpreted as a denigration of the culture and people to which the other language belongs. Or, one language may have insufficient linguistic development to be used in the teaching of certain subject matter; the necessary range of books written in the language may be lacking.

The fact is that there is a considerable interpenetration of the school and the wider community. Educational activities affect the life and constitution of the community, while social factors have their influence on the school. Even in stable polities in which a right to academic freedom and independent inquiry is recognized, it may be misleading to assume that any educational decision is made in isolation from noneducational factors. In many countries, the link between education and national ideology is quite explicit.

So it is crucial to know who the decision makers are and the framework in which they operate. They may be the superintendent of a school district, his specialist advisers, and the principals of the schools in the district, who are seeking to improve the educational performance of a large number of their pupils whose mother tongue is not the normal medium of instruction in the schools; or they may be the top educational bureaucrats in a nation, decreeing that bilingual education shall be instituted nationwide in terms of a directive from their political superiors, who are in turn responding to pressure from ethnic groups demanding recognition of their languages in the education system and elsewhere; or perhaps they are a group representative of the community that a particular school serves—local politicians, ethnic group leaders, parents, educators, ordinary citizens—who desire for the children an education rooted in the values of the local community and one that will allow them to contribute to the maintenance and development of the community in the future.

These various groups of decision makers will have different priorities, according to their motivation and their goals. This will affect the nature and level of the interchange between school and community in ways that the second hexagon is intended to indicate.

The first hexagon, then, represents factors that predate and are independent of a bilingual program, whereas the second one deals with factors involved in the interaction of the school with the outside world upon the introduction of bilingual education. The latter includes the sources of the program's basic needs (funds, personnel, materials), the constraints within which the administrators have to work, the program's contribution to the community, and potential reasons for the program's failure.

The third hexagon (Figure 1c) sets out the effects of a bilingual program. The effects may be on the individual participant or on the community at large. Included here are both the explicit goals of those who have planned the program, and unintended outcomes or by-products of it. It is important to make this distinction, because the planners often have too narrow an appreciaiton of what the program involves. Unforeseen outcomes may go unrecognized or be misinterpreted if they are not related systematically to an outline of the total situation such as the one we present in our first hexagon. For example, the planners of a program may establish as their primary goal an improvement in the children's educational achievement as measured by standard intelligence tests, but find that no such improvement results from the program. They may interpret this in terms of a lack of educability or genetic deficiency or the ineffectiveness of bilingual education. However, it could well be that they were unaware of strong attitudes against the program among the parents, attitudes that the children translated into a passive resistance to learning. Such a situation is aggravated if there is a linguistic or cultural barrier between the educators and the parents.

The content of the third hexagon takes us well beyond the classroom, in both space and time. It deals with the effects of bilingual education on the wider

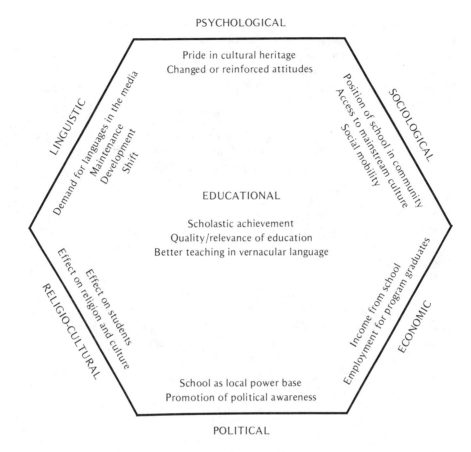

Figure 1c.   The Level of Outcomes

society, including people who have not participated in the program. In the case of those who have participated, it is concerned with their later work life and adult experiences generally, just as much as their educational attainment.

To make the distinction between the second and third hexagons clearer: the second contains factors that have a direct bearing on the operation of a program, things that the administrators can manipulate, or that they must take into account, in the day-to-day activities of the staff and students. The third one takes a broader view of goals and outcomes including those which the administrators may not recognize or over which they have little direct control.

OVERALL VIEW

Using this model as a guide, then, we can see how different the programs we have described are in detail. Take first the linguistic factors. There are cases like Navajo, Crow, and Central Yupik where the language is strongly maintained, spoken by a large population of all ages, and with developing literacy and modern life. At the other extreme, as with Pomo or Haida, there are few speakers left; most of the children coming to school were brought up by parents who have spoken only English most of their lives. The number of speakers of the languages concerned ranges from close to 140,000 with Navajo to about 30 with Han. Some languages like Cherokee have a strong literacy past: others like Tanaina are still involved in developing their first written materials. Given this situational range, language planning activities vary from the first stages of orthography development, through the range of adult literacy training needed to provide teachers, to the advanced problems of language standardization and modernization exemplified by Navajo (with its planned Navajo Language Institute) and Yupik. Linguistic goals vary accordingly. In those cases where children no longer speak the language, like Tlingit or Tewa, the only meaningful goal for bilingual educators is language revival: the traditional language is taught as a second language, usually with related cultural training. In cases where children still speak the language, the aim will always be to add English. As mentioned earlier, the basic design of the Bilingual Education Act is to provide for transition from the native language to English. Some programs, like Northern Cheyenne, Choctaw, Ute, and Zuni, seem so far to have accepted this transitional goal completely: others, like Navajo, Yupik, Cree, and perhaps Crow and Papago, emphasize native language maintenance, planning already to carry the language program well beyond third grade.

It is not simple to disentangle psychological factors from the general situation in which they occur. All bilingual programs speak of developing pride in cultural heritage enhancing the students' self-concept; those (like Project SUN and the Pomo project) which have multicultural emphasis make a great point of how they will reduce ethnocentrism and increase ethnic and racial understanding.

The attitudes of Indian parents and community leaders to bilingual education make up a complex patchwork of varying influences and beliefs. In very few cases do parents or community have any real control of the school or the bilingual program. While Title VII guidelines insist on the use of advisory boards and extensive community liaison work, these activities do not necessarily lead to any real change in authority. Thus the bilingual program, often with a white or assimilated Indian director, is still seen as an externally imposed method of dealing with Indian children. Additional complexity is created by the makeup of the local advisory board. It can easily be the case that the board is made up of people whose qualification for election is knowledge of English and of Anglo ways. One result of such a case will be that the board, whose members would be considered progressives, will fail to reflect the opinions of the traditional members of the community whose support is necessary to an effective bilingual program. There again, these same progressive leaders, whose success may well have depended on their own learning of English, are often hard to convince of the value of maintaining the native language. There are paradoxically two opposing points of view from which the use of the native language in school may be opposed: from that of the progressives, who feel English is more important, and from the traditionalists, who feel their language is too sacred for school use. A third point of opposition is generally serious: the fear of many parents that bilingual education is a method of preventing their children from learning English well enough, a way, in other words, of keeping Indians as second-class citizens.

The opposition from the educational establishment, whether administrators or teachers, is likely to be equally strong. First, the proposal to teach in the native language can only be interpreted as rejection (or at least strong criticism) of all the past and present educational programs and practices. It is a fundamental attack on the validity of the education that America has provided for its Indian peoples. That there is good evidence supporting such an attack does not make it any more acceptable to the people who have been responsible for educating Indians. And the implications of the bilingual proposal are clearly more radical than others. To establish bilingual education is not just changing the curriculum: it leads to basic changes, not just of philosophy but of teachers and control.

Compare the alternative strategy often proposed for U.S. minority groups, the more effective teaching of English as a second language. The ESL approach is easily assimilated by a school system: a few new materials are bought; a few extra specialists are hired; some extra in-service training is provided. In actual practice, there are comparatively few cases where this approach has been adopted wholeheartedly, and fewer where it has had any success. A well-documented study of its difficulties is provided in the case of the ESL program on the Navajo Reservation. An evaluation of English as a Second Language Program in the 1969-1970 school year (Harris 1970) found "dull, mechanical, and unimaginative" classes, "taught in a kind of vacuum" without integration with the rest of the curriculum, by inadequately trained teachers resentful of the materials they used and with low opinions of their students. But ESL is a *curricular* option.

Bilingual education is a greater threat to the educational establishment, for it requires native speaking teachers and administrators. It aims thus to change not just the curriculum but also the staffing of schools for Indian children. In very few cases are qualified native speaking teachers available. When the Bureau of Indian Affairs decided to use fully qualified, college-trained teachers for its schools, it automatically blocked all but a few local people from participating in the education of their children. The results are most strikingly evident in the case of Navajo. In 1974, there are close to 3000 teachers in Bureau, Public, Mission, and contract schools on the Reservation; of these no more than 200 are Indians, and probably no more than one hundred are speakers of Navajo. To establish even a minimal transitional program for the first three grades will require that a thousand Navajo-speaking teachers be found. One way this might theoretically be accomplished is by the Anglo teachers learning Navajo, but there is little likelihood of this occurring in more than a handful of cases. The second is of course to replace a thousand English monolingual teachers by Navajo bilinguals. Nor will it be enough to replace teachers: there will clearly be need for teacher-supervisors and principals able to understand what is happening in a bilingual class.

The threat of bilingual education is thus a direct economic one to the present teachers and administrators. However much they may sympathize with a bilingual education program, and however much they may agree on an intellectual level with its logic and its goals, they cannot remain for long unaware that their own jobs are at stake. In these circumstances, it is not surprising that bilingual programs often face opposition from teachers and administrators.

The most widely adopted compromise has been to set up programs using bilingual aides, who, as one teacher put it, "do what aides usually do and also act as interpreters." Often, fine relations develop between the classroom teacher and the Indian aide. But it is not unusual for the monolingual college-trained teacher to feel resentful of the more effective rapport the bilingual aide has with the children. As long as the aide can be kept in her (or his) place, it is not too bad. But all Title VII programs involve starting to train the aides as teachers. These programs have not yet reached the stage of producing many certified teachers: they generally terminate at the AA level. But some programs (the Navajo is most notable here) are now developing strong training components that will soon start to produce certified bilingual teachers. As this happens, it would not be surprising to find even stronger opposition developing from white educators.

The description of the sociological factors can only be sketchy. Common to almost all American Indians is their lower socioeconomic situation: the Bilingual Education Act recognized this with its double linguistic and economic criteria. In a great number of communities, there is a strong contrast between the poverty of the indigenous Indian population and the comparative affluence of the white school teachers, with their regular and often high government salaries. Generally, too, in most cases, the maintenance of an Indian language will reflect the absence of what Fishman calls "interaction-based social mobility." Where there has been physical, religio-societal, or social isolation, there is less English; where there has been more or less easy integration, English will be weaker and the Indian language stronger. In the Alaskan cases, it is generally a fact that language maintenance has depended on physical isolation. In the case of Navajo, it has been shown that there is a correlation between the accessibility of a community and the tendency of children to know English (Spolsky 1970, 1974). The Pueblo languages, Winnebago and Potawatomi, are examples of religious influence on language maintenance.

There is a clear potential conflict in the affirmed sociological goals of most bilingual programs. On the one hand, they aim to teach English and in other ways permit access to the mainstream, or in the terms used by Lews (to appear), the supranational, technologically based, civic culture. On the other hand, they work toward integrating the assimilating instrument (the school) into the community. One of the permanent effects (and sometimes goals) of the American Indian bilingual programs has been to slowly and slightly reduce the alien nature of the school, but breaking down the linguistic and personal barriers that parallel the actual fences that separate many school compounds from the surrounding reservation. More of this later.

The economic situation of almost all programs is similar in one revealing factor: in virtually no cases are bilingual programs part of the regularly funded educational system. Almost every program is supported by special federal funds. In Alaska, there is a special state appropriation for bilingual education: in New Mexico, there is a similar state appropriation, but none of its funds support Indian programs. Only in the few community schools like Rough Rock and Rock Point is it likely that there would have been a bilingual program without federal funds. And it remains to be seen how well the programs are carried on when federal support ceases.

One of the most important economic effects of a bilingual education program is in its potential for immediate benefit to the local community. The size of this benefit varies from the possible thousand well-paying teaching jobs on the Navajo Reservation to the part-time job for an older speaker of a dying language, but its impact on a local poor community cannot be underestimated. Economic motivation alone could lead to strong support from the local community.

The political factors are closely related to the economic ones. The initiating source of American Indian bilingual education in the 1970s is the federal government, reflecting a growing acceptance of pluralism, or perhaps as a palliative to minority groups. There are so far only a few signs of indigenous linguistic pressure groups, but those that exist range from the Tanaina Language Society with its weekly language revival classes for adults, to the Navajo Education Association (DDA) with its strong thrust toward political action. The political situation then shows more pressure from outside than from inside.

But when one comes to the operational effects and the goals or outcomes of the programs, the case is different. The movement for bilingual education has become very closely associated with the movement for local Indian control of education. The local school boards set up through BIA initiative in the late 1960s seldom developed much power: personnel and curriculum decisions were out of their scope. But the advisory boards concerned with Title VII programs often have gained some real authority in hiring program staff and aides, and in making curricular decisions. These boards then come to be the main liaison between the community or the tribal council and the school, and in a number of cases have become the focus of the movement for local control.

The various forces involved can be seen in some of the discussions at the 1972 National Indian Bilingual Conference. A participant from Ramah Navajo High School explained that the school board was given as much power as possible, but that Civil Service still had authority over hiring and firing at the Ramah BIA Dormitory. Similarly, at Acomita it was hoped that the school board would "in a couple of years" obtain similar power; in the meantime, the board has authority from the Governor of the Pueblo:

> The Governor feels he doesn't have time to deal directly with the school, so this is his way of dealing with the school (via the board). The School Board chairman meets with the Tribal Council about once a month or if anything comes up the chairman goes directly to the Governor. . . . Three (of the school board members) are appointed by the Tribal Council and the Governor and three . . . are elected by the Parent Teacher Organization (Proceedings).

The school boards at the contract schools like Rough Rock and Borrego Pass have become models for many others who seek power. One of the key questions raised about these boards is whether and how they should be paid. At Acoma, board members are not paid at all; at other schools, they are paid about $25 per diem for their meetings.

One of the key effects of more local control is to break down alienation of the school from the surrounding community. As one participant in the conference summed up the position, the local people "identify the school as a white institution, . . . like the doctor." Another replied, "Well, in our situation, since the School Board has taken over, they really feel it's their school."

The Navajo situation provides the most striking example of this development in action. The move for Indian control developed first around Rough Rock school and its Navajo program; from here, it moved to the Navajo Education Association whose 1973 Bilingual Education Conference showed the strength of this backing and is now focused in the attempts to assert the power of the Navajo Tribal Division of Education. Political factors then are of considerable importance in American Indian Bilingual Education; bilingual programs not only assert the need for Indian control of schools, but provide a way of gaining part of that control.

Language, culture, and religion are often closely tied for American Indian as for other groups. While great numbers of Indians belong to one Christian group or another, many have managed to Indianize their new religion, linguistically, ritually, and sometimes theologically. Religious factors play an important part in language maintenance in such cases as Potawatomi, Keresan, and Crow. And these factors often lead to difficult problems for those trying to use Indian languages and cultural materials in school.

One of the critical problems many American Indian bilingual programs face is the question of ownership of material. Under federal policy, the government has the right to reproduce any materials produced with federal grants. Many Indians feel that the traditional and religious material they might provide for local programs needs to be kept under strict local control. One member of a project staff describes the situation:

> We found that we had to very strictly observe tradition. For example, some of our stories can only be told in the winter time and we had to make very definite agreements with the old people that we would not tell these stories other than in the winter time. We also had to make definite agreement that anything we made that was semi-commercial would not contain anything religious in nature. These things could then be disseminated to other organizations. But we have a collection of things that nobody knows about at our school. There are religious things that we use in the classroom. Our basic problem in the beginning was that they didn't want to give us anything because we didn't have ultimate control over our materials. . . . So often we made the agreement that certain things would never leave the community, under any circumstances, and they saw that we did observe traditions and did use the pipe, then we started to get quite a lot of community participation (Proceedings).

The basic conflict created when a white, alien institution is being used to maintain local indigenous culture is fundamental to many of the difficulties. It explains why there are many communities still where language maintenance is high, but the Indian community opposes a bilingual program. It explains, conversely, the eagerness of communities whose language is dying to have the school preserve it for its religious role.

Finally, we come to the educational questions. The failures of the educational system to provide for American Indian children has been often fully documented (cf. e.g., Fuchs and Havighurst 1972). Children have long bus rides or live in dormitories; facilities are inadequate; there are few if any local teachers, and curriculum and materials are prepared for English-speaking middle-class children. When it came to starting bilingual programs, the general situation for all Indian languages was the same: no material, no curriculum, no bilingual teachers. In every program, therefore, there has needed to be material and curriculum development and the use and training of previously unqualified native speakers. Depending on previous literacy and the resources available, some programs are well along with the printing of material: the Navajo and Yupik cases are outstanding. And the programs have brought bilingual aides into the classroom, and are engaged in providing them with some kind of training. The function (and title) of the aide is closely correlated with the key educational factor, the distribution of languages by time and subject. The range is complete. In three Yupik schools and in a couple on the Navajo Reservation, all teaching is done in the language except for an hour a day for English as a second language. The middle of the range is perhaps represented by the coordinate bilingual program at Rock Point. The extreme in programs where children are monolingual in the Indian language are classes where aides do more than act as interpreters; in programs where the children do not speak the language, it is a few minutes a day learning Indian words and phrases as part of a cultural program. It is not easy to tell from available documents, but my guess would be that most of the programs described here tend in reality to lean toward the minimal end. In very few are there yet qualified certified bilingual Indian teachers; in a few more, the bilingual aide (or instructor, or paraprofessional) has virtually complete authority in the classroom; in a few more, the English language teacher and the Indian language teacher have authority and share the teaching equally. While almost every program includes provision for paraprofessional training, up to the stage of the AA degree, only a few are already engaged in training teachers to the level of the bachelor's degree and certification. All programs assume that bilingual education will result in better instruction and general improvement in the quality of education; the special (and somewhat unhelpful) evaluation design required for Title VII disguises the varying emphasis on English-related goals or goals related to the native language.

The various programs that have been lumped together in this paper to portray current trends in American Indian bilingual education make clear the heterogeneity of the phenomenon. Because it is so varied and so recent, it is difficult to arrive at any clear view of the whole process. If there is a common factor, it is probably in the use of language-related activities and arguments to support a program of "Amerindianization" of the schools. The first and most critical effect will be to make possible the integration of the school into the Indian community, by leading to a continuity of language, people, and even values and culture. All the time that schools for American Indians stay in their compounds, controlled and conducted by what seems not unlike an occupying army of outsiders, the community has no chance to use the school to help it handle the difficult transition to modern technological life. Whatever its other ultimate effects, American Indian bilingual education seems to be a step toward this end.

NOTES

1. The preparation of this paper was supported by a grant from the Ford Foundation to the University of New Mexico. Given the scattered sources on which it had to be based, I am more than usually indebted for a great deal of assistance from others. First, I thank my graduate research assistants John Read, Joanna Green, and Kathryn Manuelito who found facts, checked guesses, and argued conclusions through all stages of preparing the paper. Second, I am grateful to those associated with programs who provided information; they are named in the notes below, but in particular I thank Robert Rebert, Harry Berendzen, Michael Krauss, and Elaine Ramos. Third, I thank all who read the manuscript in one of its earlier versions, and suggested (or insisted on) corrections in fact or interpretation. Of these, I mention in particular Harry Berendzen. Finally, I must mention the technical skills of Judy Benedetti and Maia Cramer that turned scribbled drafts and messy handwritten additions into the final legible version.

2. Data on language maintenance and language names and spelling are taken from the 1973 report of the Alaska Native Language Center written by Michael Krauss, with some corrections made by Krauss in May 1974. For each language, the report gives an estimate of the population living in villages or predominantly native towns (excluding any living in Anchorage, Fairbanks, and many other nonnative communities), an estimate of the number of speakers of the language, and an indication of the language status expressed in terms of the age of the youngest speakers. For details on bilingual programs, I am indebted to a statistical chart prepared in April 1974 at the Alaska Native Language Center. Much of the information in this section was collected at a meeting of the Center's Advisory Board in April 1974. Of particular value was the report prepared by Elaine Ramos, administrative director of the Center.

3. For this section, information was gathered from papers listed in the References (Holland 1972, Pulte n.d., Wahrhaftig 1970, Walker 1965, White 1962) and from a personal communication from Agnes Cowan.

4. For this section, information was gathered from the 1973 Title VII Continuation Proposal and from personal communications from Wayne Sypert and Herbert Swallow.

5. This section is based on a pamphlet issued by the program.

6. For this section, information was gathered from the 1973 Title VII Continuation Proposal and from personal communications from Robert Murie and Lynn Baker.

7. For this section, information was gathered from various Title VII reports, including the

Final Report for 1971-1972 and the Interim Evaluation Report of March 1973, and from personal communications from Steve Chesarek.

8. This section is based on the 1974 Title VII Continuation Proposal.

9. For this section, information was gathered from the 1973 Title VII Continuation Proposal and from a personal communication from Michael Madden.

10. This section is based on personal communication from Cyrin Maus, Minnie Cypress, and Robert Rebert.

11. For this section, information was gathered from the 1973 Title VII Continuation Proposals for Rough Rock, Rock Point, Ramah, and San Juan County, and from personal communications from Roby Leighton (Rough Rock), Agnes Holm (Rock Point), Tom Cummings (Ramah), and Marjorie Thomas (Tuba City).

12. This section is based on a Title VII proposal for 1973-1974 and a personal communication from Joe Sturgeon.

13. For this section, information was gathered from the 1973 Title VII Continuation Proposal and from a personal communication from Robert Leavitt.

14. This section is based on the 1973 Title VII Continuation Proposal and personal communication from Pamela Mitchell.

15. For this section, information was gathered from the 1973 Title VII Continuation Proposal, from mimeographed material and a pamphlet on the project, and from personal communications from Ronnie West and Susannah Factor.

16. This section is based on personal communications from Arthur Ortiz and Harry Berendzen.

17. This section is based on the 1973 Title VII Continuation Proposal.

18. This section is based on personal communications from John Beaudoin and John Nichols.

19. For this section, information was gathered from the 1973 Title VII Continuation Proposal.

XII

Teaching in Chinese

Outside China

Robert L. Cheng

The author expresses his thanks to Professor Jason B. Alter for reading this chapter and offering helpful suggestions.

INTRODUCTION

Purpose and General Premises

This is a sociolinguistic study of the Chinese language as a medium of instruction outside of the People's Republic of China (PRC).

The general premise of the study is as follows: In the making of school-language policy, political considerations usually outweigh educational concern for the children's immediate linguistic environment and future needs of survival in their multicultural and multilinguistic communities. Education in the policy-makers' language, be it Thai, Indonesian, English, etc., prevails rather than education in the mother tongue. In schools where Chinese have the freedom to choose, Mandarin tends to be selected as the medium of instruction, even though this dialect may differ drastically from the children's mother language. Ties with the Nationalist government before and after its move to Taiwan, conflicts with non-Chinese communities, and pride in Chinese culture, leading to a strong desire for Chinese solidarity, are major factors in such a selection. The Chinese traditional view that sees education as a means of advancing individuals on the social ladder by their studying the classics and preparing themselves for service to the emperor or the central government rather than to better understand and serve the local community is the major reason for parents' lack of support for education in their own mother tongue. In places where the Chinese population is small in proportion, Mandarin education at the expense of vernacular education has in fact served to accelerate the extinction of the mother tongue as a functional language of the mass, though it has created a small Mandarin-speaking elite. The elite undoubtedly have a wider prospective Chineseness and greater pride in Chinese culture than a vernacular education could have produced. They, however, tend to manifest too much Chinese nationalism, and know too little of their own communities to cope with the problems that are facing their diversified, changing interests and identities. They orient themselves too much to the greatness of an idealized, remote China and have too little confidence in or esteem for their own community's culture.

The Term "Chinese"

The term Chinese is generally understood by linguists to refer to a collection of mutually unintelligible dialects or languages, the major groups of which include Mandarin, Wu, Cantonese, Hakka, South Min, and North Min. The same definition is adopted in this chapter, except that we include in our discussion any written system that represents spoken Chinese. Since spoken Chinese varies greatly according to time and locality and since the fit between the spoken language and writing is usually far from perfect, Chinese writing can in effect be the representation of any vernacular at any stage of its development or of a written tradition that represents no real vernacular of any time, but is itself a product of development through long years of mutual influence between writing and different vernaculars. (Written classical Chinese and modern written Chinese are examples.)

Teaching in Chinese and its Sociolinguistic Implications

The phenomenon of teaching in Chinese calls for some special comments. Teaching in a language and the teaching of a language are usually easy to distinguish in the case of other languages, say Japanese. One would usually draw the line between the two in Japanese by saying that the former included teaching various subjects and not the teaching of the Japanese language. Such a qualification and delineation of one's topic is necessitated by the desire to have a coherent topic. To define the topic of the present paper meaningfully with regard to teaching in Chinese is not so simple, because the term "Chinese" refers to mutually unintelligible vernaculars; and schooling in Mandarin can actually be the learning of Mandarin and the culture associated with the Mandarin world. Another complication is that the gap between the writing system and the spoken language is so wide that the mastering of the written language itself takes more than ten years.

In many Chinese schools outside the PRC and Taiwan, the main purpose of instruction is to teach Mandarin, together with its writing, as a second language. In quite a few schools in Singapore and Hong Kong, subjects related to China are taught in Mandarin, but other subjects are taught in English. Teaching in a language seems to have at least the following sociolinguistic implications:

1. A language is used in class because it is the mother tongue of the majority of the students.

2. A language is used so that it may replace the students' language in their community life.

3. A language is used so that it can be used side by side with the students' mother tongue(s) in the community. (In other words, the intent is to promote bilingualism in the community.)

4. A language is used so that students may have a sense of cultural or national identity or solidarity in the language.

5. A language is used so that students may in the future receive their higher education in the language of their own country.

6. A language is used in class because it is the subject matter of the course.

Teaching in a second language, as in case 6, is an effective way of improving students' language ability. The purpose is for the students to acquire a native-like proficiency in the language so that they may use it with native speakers of the target language (and possibly to attend college in a foreign country). As long as such teaching is not intended or likely to change the sociolinguistic situation in a community, this teaching should be treated under foreign-language education rather than as a sociolinguistic study.

Whether case 5 has any sociolinguistic significance or not would vary from country to country. When the language in question is also an official language, as in the case of English in Singapore, and not merely a language which is used in schooling because it is a convenient link with universities in other countries, the sociolinguistic significance cannot be belittled. Quite a few Chinese in Southeast Asia have complied with the idea of teaching in Mandarin so that they can send their children to college in the PRC, Taiwan, Hong Kong, or Singapore for their Chinese education. The impact of these students on the sociolinguistic situation within their communities is almost nil in places like Thailand and the United States, but it may not be insignificant in Hong Kong, the Philippines, and Malaysia.

Mandarin is in prevalent use in most Chinese schools in Southeast Asian countries, in both teaching in Mandarin and teaching Mandarin. Mandarin had for a long time been merely a school language in Chinese schools and had never been a community language, until recently when it became in some limited areas one of the several lingua francas among Chinese who have had sufficient Chinese schooling. In many places, Mandarin can never be a community language, in spite of proclaimed intentions. In places like Thailand, such does not seem to be the intention.

Whatever effect such schooling in Mandarin may eventually have on the language of the Chinese minorities, if it is a reflection of the desire of the overseas

Chinese to form a united front for solidarity among different linguistic groups, such a desire is in itself a sociolinguistic phenomenon.

The teaching of written Chinese (whether taught in Mandarin or Cantonese or Hokkien) is rather unique in its sociolinguistic implications. In spite of the fact that some linguists tend to exclude writing from language, I am inclined to include it as an indispensable part of any sociolinguistic study. Overemphasis on writing has been one of the main reasons why the Chinese people regard themselves as the same and do not mind their children's receiving education in Mandarin, even when this tongue is completely unintelligible to them. The Chinese commonly believe that literate people can understand each other through writing even though their dialects may be mutually incomprehensible. One cannot overemphasize the psychological impact of such beliefs.

Teaching in Chinese and Chinese Communities

Unlike English and other European languages, Chinese is seldom learned or used by non-Chinese outside of China's territories. We find many Chinese in Southeast Asia who do not speak any variety of Chinese at all. This is a great change from the past. Chinese history is one of continuous expansion and sinicization. In some three thousand years, the Chinese have expanded from a small area in the Yellow River valley to the vast territories of the Chinese mainland we know today.[1] The population has grown to 800 million, a figure which cannot be surpassed by any other people in the world. Such territorial and population expansion has been mainly due to emigration, preservation of the Chinese culture and language, and sinicization of non-Chinese peoples. Immigration and sinicization took place regardless of the military policies of the Chinese government. It took place even when non-Chinese (the Manchus and the Mongols, for example) conquered and ruled the Chinese, who outnumbered the invaders.

Since the rise of the Western powers and Japan in the 18th and 19th Centuries and the emergence of nationalism in the developing countries in the 20th Century, the long-standing trend of Chinese to expand by emigration while preserving their own culture and sinicizing non-Chinese has encountered great rivalry and resistance. The trend has either halted or been reversed. In spite of their economic success and significant numbers, the Chinese are being assimilated rather than assimilating the non-Chinese. Unlike Westerners in their colonies, who were protected by the military strength of their government, the Chinese moved abroad and had to adapt to economic and political conditions where they settled.

Today, not all Chinese outside of China (whether Chinese by law or by blood or by family name) learn or use Chinese. As Murray (1964:64) has pointed out, it is in many cases very hard to tell who is Chinese and who is not. Many overseas Chinese have correctly insisted that whether one is to be counted as Chinese or not should be determined by culture and not by law, blood, or family name.

Rather unique to the Chinese people is the concept of the Chinese as one people as held both by Chinese themselves and by non-Chinese. As a matter of fact, there have been other peoples, such as the Slavic and the Germanic, who have expanded even faster than the Chinese in the past few centuries. These people have evolved into different peoples and used new names for the "new" peoples, such as "German," "Dutch," "British," "American," and "Australian." The Chinese are not different from any other people with respect to changing their culture patterns or developing into subgroups as changes take place. This has been the case for Chinese within China and even more so for those outside China. What makes them special is the fact that among non-Chinese or between Chinese and non-Chinese, the Cantonese, Hakka, Hokkien, etc., groups are seldom referred to as "Cantonese," "Hakka," "Hokkien," etc., but rather indiscriminately as Chinese; whereas we hear "German," "British," "Australian," and rarely "Germanic," perhaps from specialists concerned with the classification of people or languages. The contrast is even more striking when we note that the internal differences among the subgroups of Chinese are even greater than those within the Germanic, Slavic, or Romance groups. Some linguists in fact believe that the whole Chinese language group can be compared to the whole European family as a group. Whatever the reasons and whether or not such unity is real, the *concept* of unity has a magical effect on the behavior of Chinese, as well as of non-Chinese people. One could not conceive of German children's being taught in English in Germany. People, however, whether they are Chinese or non-Chinese, seldom question the practice of using Mandarin as the only medium of instruction in primary schools attended by Chinese students, the majority of whom speak Hokkien or Cantonese at home.

Scholars specializing in Europe would not be so bold as to claim that they know the "European" language if they knew only English or French. The Spanish would feel very much insulted if a scholar claimed to know the Romance languages well and yet knew only French and Italian. Today, many China specialists claim that they can converse with "the Chinese people" while they understand only classroom Mandarin.[2] To the many non-Chinese, especially Westerners, the Chinese are a species of creatures, who all look and behave, talk, and write alike.

Among the Chinese themselves, political and linguistic differences are very important. Today, Chinese in Malaysia and Singapore insist that they be called "Huaren," a term with an ethnic connotation, as opposed to "Chungkuoren" (People of the Middle Kingdom of China), which would imply that they are nationals of the PRC or the Republic of China. Taiwanese in exile who advocate independence for Taiwan refuse to be called "Chungkuoren," preferring to be called "Taiwanese" or "Formosan," though they do not mind being referred to by the term "Huaren" or "Hanren."

The study of what variety of Chinese is being used in Chinese schools outside of China, together with the factors responsible for the choice and the implications for the social, political, and economic life of the Chinese community, are as important as the study of whether or not some variety of Chinese is used in schooling at all.

From a political point of view, the study is relevant to the question of whether or not the overseas Chinese in general identify themselves with China and place the interests of their "mother country" before those of their own community, and/or their countries of residence. From a sociolinguistic point of view, the study can cast light on development of relations among the Chinese in the same country, between the Chinese and indigenous peoples, and between the Chinese outside of the PRC and those within the PRC. From an educational point of view, only a study that takes a close account of the student's specific mother tongue can serve as a useful basis for evaluating whether or not a language-education program takes into account the student's sense of dignity and confidence as a member of his family and community, and whether the school provides the student with proper opportunities for him to appreciate and participate in the cultural life of his country of residence by making the best of his own cultural and linguistic resources.

The life of overseas Chinese has attracted enormous scholarly attention for several reasons. There are more than 18 million overseas Chinese in the world,[3] not including the more than 15 million dwellers of Chinese ancestry in Taiwan. These Chinese are scattered all over the world and have been in contact with a wide variety of peoples and cultures. They have played a significant role in the developing countries. There has been anxiety over economic domination by overseas Chinese communities and the fear of Chinese expansion through political ties with China.[4] The Communists in China and the Nationalists in Taiwan have been competing for the support of overseas Chinese, for political reasons. Overseas Chinese have been regarded as very conservative in maintaining their culture and have been regarded as a problem in various countries.

Past works on the overseas Chinese vary greatly[5] in emphasis. Some focus on the political implications (international or domestic) of schooling in Chinese, some on anthropological aspects, and some on the socioeconomic life of the Chinese settlers. Even though few of these treat teaching in Chinese as the main theme, quite a few dwell on schooling in Chinese wherever it is relevant to their main theme.[6] These works have been the major sources for the present study.

Main Focus and Arrangement

Since teaching in Chinese is essentially limited to Chinese communities and since the present study is a sociolinguistic one, our study on teaching in Chinese cannot be divorced from the Chinese communities. This chapter will focus on major factors that are responsible for the choice of the media of instruction in various Chinese communities outside of mainland China. Educational programs in which Chinese is used for instruction will be described, with special reference to what varieties of Chinese are chosen and how teaching in Chinese is balanced with teaching in non-Chinese languages. The sociolinguistic implications of such particular choices will be discussed in connection with nonsociolinguistic goals as identified by the Chinese themselves and their respective governments.

Although the situation in each of the communities is unique and in many ways very complex, discussion of each community as a separate entity may not expose all the generalities that are involved. For purposes of convenience, I shall divide all the Chinese communities outside the PRC into four groups.

1. The Chinese communities in Taiwan and Singapore.
2. Those communities in Hong Kong and Macao.
3. Those in other Southeast Asian countries.
4. Those in other areas.

The Chinese communities in the first two groups constitute the majority of the total population in their respective political entities. Those in the first group differ from those in the second in that the governments in the first are run by Chinese. Those in the third and fourth groups are minorities in their respective countries. Those in the third represent a higher proportion of the population in their countries of residence and have more problems with the host communities than those in the fourth, owing to bigger size, the shorter distance to China, and the existence of fear of Chinese expansion.

FEATURES COMMON TO CHINESE COMMUNITIES
OUTSIDE THE PEOPLE'S REPUBLIC OF CHINA

Aside from the fact that Chinese communities in each group are outside the reach of Peking's sovereignty, there are several significant features that distinguish the Chinese communities from the Chinese within the People's Republic of China. Some features developed after the Communist takeover of the Republic in 1949, but most of them are the result of long years of separate socioeconomic, linguistic, and political history.

1. Unlike the population in the PRC, the majority of whom speak different varieties of Mandarin, the majority of the population of each Chinese community outside China speak southern Chinese dialects, each of which is quite different from Mandarin.[7] In fact, except for Taiwan, where more than 10% of the population speak Mandarin as a mother tongue, there is no community outside the PRC that has more than 1% speaking Mandarin "natively."

2. There is only a very limited written tradition that attempts to represent vernacular dialects. Among the Chinese in and out of China, the only two established writing traditions are the Wenli (or classical Chinese) and written Mandarin, which is based on the northern dialects of China. In learning either of these, a speaker of the southern dialects has to learn, in addition to several thousand characters, a different set of vocabulary items and sometimes grammatical rules which, though related to those of his native tongue, are in many cases different enough to cause errors or failure in understanding. In most schools outside China where children have to learn to read and write in Mandarin, they have to learn the Mandarin sound system and the pronunciation of all the lexical

items. Learning to read and write with proficiency in Mandarin is much harder for speakers of these dialects than for Mandarin speakers. There have traditionally been limited colloquial, written versions of many Southern Chinese dialects, which differ significantly from Mandarin, but these have not been widely accepted by the speakers themselves and therefore are not used in the academic or official circles. Even in schools where Cantonese is the only medium of instruction, the textbooks are generally in written Mandarin.

For wider circulation and for more serious discussions, people generally write in Mandarin; and for this reason, those who are able to write for and communicate with their fellow men through the mass media are limited in number. Written mass communication therefore tends to be monopolized by an elite minority. It is common for the press in overseas communities to hire editors from Taiwan, Hong Kong, and the People's Republic of China because people competent in written Mandarin are not available.

There is almost a universal tendency among the Chinese to overemphasize the importance of the written language. Accompanied with such an overemphasis is the belief that knowing "the Chinese script" enables one to read classical Chinese as well as modern, written Chinese and to communicate with any literate person no matter what dialect one speaks. Such a belief is true only so far as the representation of etymons is concerned. The same etymons are represented by the same characters even if they are pronounced differently at different stages in different dialects. It would be a serious mistake for one to think that the grammar and the lexicon of the Chinese language at different stages and in different dialects are so alike as to warrant mutual intelligibility.

Thus, most people educated in written Mandarin do not have much difficulty in studying classical writing, especially that of the later periods, because written Mandarin incorporates many classical elements, and learning written Mandarin also involves learning classical Chinese.

There has been universal agreement that mutual intelligibility is nonexistent if each Chinese "dialect" is written in romanization. When "dialects" such as Cantonese and Taiwanese are written in Chinese characters, the writing will not be understood by a person without a substantial process of orientation. The individual characters are mostly familiar to him, as Roman letters are familiar to all Westerners. But so far as comprehension is concerned, the chances are that he would be at as much a loss as a French reader trying to understand a piece of Spanish writing.

Among the three components of a spoken language (phonology, lexicon, and grammar), the major dialects differ from each other most in phonology and least in grammar. But a speaker of one dialect has to spend most of his time in learning the lexicon of another dialect, since this task is by far the most time-consuming among the three components. With regard to a writing system for a Chinese dialect, the three components will be Chinese characters, lexicon, and grammar. Given a knowledge of the written and spoken language, a reader in Mandarin will have to learn the Cantonese lexicon and grammar plus a few hundred additional Chinese characters that are common in Cantonese but almost unknown in written Mandarin, although most of them may also be listed in big dictionaries of Chinese characters which include characters used by the Chinese sometime in the past 3000 years for various vernaculars. No dictionary can be exhaustive enough to include all the characters that have ever been used by the Chinese.

To my knowledge, there is no good way of measuring the degree of similarity or difference among the lexicons and grammars of different vernaculars. Y. R. Chao's remark that Chinese "dialects" are similar in grammar can be understood in various ways by different readers. A comparison of written Mandarin with written Cantonese or Taiwanese will help one understand how lexicons and grammars differ from one dialect to another.

The relationship between the Wenli, or classical Chinese, and its users who speak mutually unintelligible tongues can be compared with the relationship between Latin and its users during the Middle Ages. In either case, there was a written language which was quite different from the spoken language of its users. For quite a long time, the written language, which represented the language of the dead, enjoyed the sole recognized, prestigious status among the living. Any writing that represented the language of the living was looked down upon as unworthy to describe serious matters. In Europe, writings in various living languages acquired higher status, and slowly and eventually replacing Latin for one after another in their respective countries.

In the People's Republic of China, classical Chinese has been completely replaced by the Paihuawen (or colloquial writing), which is based on Mandarin. Outside the PRC, classical Chinese still has some status, in competition with written Mandarin, especially in official documents and business correspondence. Even the written Mandarin is not pure Mandarin. Classical elements prevail so much in the written Mandarin that Huang (1974) has pointed out that one cannot be a good writer of Mandarin unless he is also versed in classical Chinese. Aside from conscious efforts to preserve the culture of Old China for political or sentimental reasons by Chinese outside of China, the fact that the Paihuawen (or colloquial writing) is based on Mandarin and is almost as strange to the Min, Cantonese, and Hakka speakers as classical Chinese is a factor in the survival of the classical writing and the abundance of classical elements in the written Mandarin outside the People's Republic of China. Whether the existing colloquial writings based on Cantonese, Taiwanese, Hokkien, etc., will acquire a higher status in the future after Mandarin as the English, French, and German orthographies did after Italian is anybody's guess.

It is common sense that the closer the fit between the spoken language and its written language, the easier it is for the speaker to learn the writing, and the more effectively a speaker can read and write it, especially in literature which describes the feelings and emotions of the native speakers themselves. It was on this basis that Hu Shih advocated colloquial writing during the May Fourth Movement in the 1920s. Today, intellectuals in China are proud of the success of the colloquial writing movement, taking it for granted that any colloquial writing is a close representative of speech. It has seldom been pointed out that non-Mandarin speakers have not been able to enjoy the benefits of writing as they speak. In view of the distance between Mandarin and the major southern "dialects" of China, there is no doubt that there should be some sort of writing representing closely the student's own speech for a more effective pedagogy. However, the question of whether to introduce written Cantonese or Taiwanese— for example—in schools is also determined by such factors as how much the Chinese communities outside the PRC are willing to sacrifice their own sentiments and interests for the political and/or cultural unity of the Chinese people, how much the leaders of various governments are determined to cultivate a self-confidence and self-respect among their fellow countrymen, to counteract the tradition of the Chinese outside China proper to look toward the latter for cultural and political leadership, and how much the educators and intellectuals can value efficient and sufficient intracommunity needs over intercommunity needs.

There are already a few signs of divergence from the People's Republic of China in the development of Mandarin writing. Many lexical items have been created because of the rapid social change in China. There is the influence of Western writing styles, as well as the simplified Chinese characters which characterize the writing of the PRC but are not imitated by Chinese outside of China. (Such characters are in fact banned in Taiwan.) The way written Chinese has been influenced by non-Mandarin vernaculars outside China has been quite different from that in China. The Wu dialects and northern dialects have been dominant in this respect in China, whereas Cantonese or Hokkien have been the major source of such influence outside China. In addition, influence from non-Chinese languages on written Mandarin has taken place in many different ways outside China.

Most communities outside China have been or still are under the political domination of modern powers, and each has had or still has close contacts with one or more non-Chinese cultures and peoples. There is a high proportion of bilinguals and trilinguals or polyglots. As a reaction against alien domination and assimilation, there has been a conscious effort to preserve some features of old China which are already regarded as obsolete in the People's Republic of China (i.e., in regard to funeral customs, Chinese characters, etc.). On the other hand, because of new environments and influences from non-Chinese peoples, innovations in their ways of thinking and life styles can be found everywhere which are foreign to peoples from the PRC.[8] No matter whether the differences can be attributed to changes on the part of the people in the PRC or outside of China,[9] there is a general lack of understanding on the part of both the Chinese outside of China and those in China on the exact nature and content of such cultural and linguistic differences.

The actual differences that have developed after the Chinese left their motherland are usually greater than the Chinese on both sides realize. Nostalgia for the motherland and pride in Chinese culture are widely shared and especially intensified when there have been bitter experiences of hostility and discrimination in the host community. Such feelings have been regarded as Chinese nationalism. They make people forget how the Chinese outside China have changed. The differences will not be felt until people from both sides have closer contacts. Whenever there are close contacts between old settlers and significant numbers of newcomers in an overseas community, there is usually group conflict between the two.

The relations between the Taiwanese and the "mainlanders" (i.e., the "newcomers" from the Chinese mainland in Taiwan after World War II) can best illustrate the point. After a joyful welcome over the idea of "returning to the mother country," the Taiwanese discovered that there was something in themselves that was different from the newcomers. Many Taiwanese claim that not only their skill at using the Japanese language but also any cultural changes which had resulted from adaptation to a non-Chinese environment and modernization were entirely unappreciated and even ridiculed by the newcomers. The newcomers thought that the Taiwanese had been "poisoned by a Japanese imperialistic education" and needed to be completely "re-educated."

The Taiwanese viewed the mainlanders as backward in modernization and resented them for their ignorance of and defiance of the customs and language of the place in which they wanted to live. The war between China and Japan might have heightened the mainlanders' dislike of the ability of the Taiwanese to use Japanese. The ability to use non-Chinese languages has been observed to be a cause of friction elsewhere. In Boston, for example, bilingualism in English and Cantonese and cultural changes on the part of earlier immigrants are also often found to be the cause of conflict with newcomers who speak Cantonese and very little English.

It is noteworthy that newcomers from Fukien (or Hokkien) province who speak a dialect very close to that of the majority of Taiwanese often got along better with the other mainlanders who spoke Mandarin than with the Taiwanese. The relations between the two groups are improving as children of both groups speak no Japanese but pick up Mandarin and Taiwanese or Hakka.

3. Within each overseas Chinese community, there is a certain degree of linguistic heterogeneity. Its members therefore have, on the average, more exposure to fellow Chinese and non-Chinese peoples from other villages or towns than the average people in China. Linguistic changes, therefore, have been faster there than in China. In many places, a new lingua franca has emerged to satisfy needs in new lands. For example, the Chung Shan variety of Chinese has been learned and used by speakers of dialects such as Hakka, Lung-tu, etc. in Hawaii, while Taiwanese has developed as a mixture of Amoy, Chaochou, Chouanchou, and Teochiu. There is a general pattern of change in the direction of sociocultural orientation which can be described in terms of three stages of development.[10]

During the first stage, the Chinese generally thought that their stay in the new world was temporary. The economic situation back in China was miserable when they left, but they dreamed of a comfortable life when they went back to China someday with the money they would earn in the new world. Their life during this stage was naturally oriented toward their respective families and villages in China. The abundance of family and home-village organizations reflects this attitude. They reached the second stage as their "sojourner" attitude gradually changed to a "settlement" attitude and they began to identify themselves more and more with the whole Chinese community in the new land. A change was required by the need for survival amid the competition and discrimination in their respective host communities, along with the establishment of schools for *all* Chinese children rather than only for those of specific areas or dialects. The development of a dominative Chinese "dialect" into a lingua franca among speakers of different dialects reflects such an attitude. Hokkien in most Chinese communities in Penang, Cantonese in Kuala Lumpur, Hawaii, and San Francisco was used by Chinese who speak other "dialects" at home (Chan 1975). The third stage is one in which the Chinese are conscious of their own status as members of the country of residence. They are at least partially assimilated or integrated into the new world. When they travel outside their country of residence, they identify themselves as Singaporeans, Malaysians, Americans, and so on, with or without the qualification that they are ethnically Chinese. Such an attitude is reflected in their mastery and constant use of the language of the host country.

4. Because of rapid linguistic and cultural change and various types and degrees of bilingualism and educational background, each community is divided more than is the case in China.

In spite of the cultural differences from the motherland, the history and culture of these communities is seldom included in the curriculum of their own children. Much of the content in the education concerns the remote past of China or the Mandarin world which is of little immediate use to their own communities. In Singapore and the United States, efforts are being made to incorporate the history and culture of their own communities for their immediate needs, but such programs have been started too recently to have had much effect on the majority of the population. Because of the lack of systematic, uniform orientation to their own communities, and overemphasis on their "motherland" or the motherland of the colonial power, such as Great Britain and France, the cultural and political identity of members of Chinese communities in the respective countries of residence are very diversified though there is a widespread sense of being Chinese. The members of each of the communities are divided as to what should be the goals of their political and educational efforts, and even more divided as to how to achieve these goals. Even if there is agreement on these matters, there is a general lack of united action in implementing an agreed-upon plan owing to a lack of common educational backgrounds that might be oriented toward their own needs in the new world.

5. Most Chinese communities have failed to work out a language plan that could help to realize political and educational goals for the community as a whole.

In many cases, the educational goals of Chinese schools are not directed toward their own needs.

Two major goals have been the incentive for Chinese education everywhere outside China: (1) elevation of the social and economic status of the individual; and (2) acquisition and preservation of the "superior, authentic" Chinese culture.

The first goal has been the dream of every parent in traditional Chinese society, where children from poor families could obtain high government positions by passing civil-service examinations. Concerned parents and ambitious children, instead of aspiring for success in the traditional civil-service examination, look forward to graduation from a reputable university, which almost guarantees a certain social and economic status.

Pursuit of the second goal is the result of a long tradition of Chinese education which builds in the minds of students as a utopia as conceived by the ancient sages of China. Culture change is either not clearly known to the community leaders or viewed as a phenomenon of deterioration. What exactly is the authentic culture is never known or agreed upon. What seems to have been agreed upon, however, is the idea that the overseas community's culture has been contaminated by the non-Chinese environment and that anything worthy of a description of Chinese culture should be taken from ancient writings.

To achieve such goals, most overseas communities copied the educational system and curricula of China under the Nationalists or Communists, used the textbooks used in China or those compiled by the Nationalists or Communists (particularly for Chinese schools abroad), and looked for China to supply the teachers or the training of teachers. As a result, students knew more about the history of China as presented by the Nationalist or Communist governments than about the history of their own countries of residence. Few people knew how they should interpret their own interests or how to solve their own community's problems.

Compared with the Peking government the Nationalists in Taiwan have played a much more significant role in developing a Chinese education aimed at cultivation of love for "great and glorious China." Teaching of and in Mandarin has in fact been regarded as a very important task, since it was interpreted as an indication of overseas Chinese loyalty for China, which in theory was represented by the Nationalist government. The Nationalist government has a great stake in overseas Chinese education because moral support from overseas communities will make the claim less embarrassing that the Nationalists are still ruling China, and not merely Taiwan. It is an irony, however, that young Chinese who have received Mandarin education tend to support the Peking government because of their hope for great and glorious China, and the older generations who hardly know Mandarin tend to either support the Nationalist government or stay neutral between the two Chinas. Nationalist control over overseas Chinese schools has been decreasing, especially since its recent diplomatic setbacks. It still has, however, a great influence on overseas Chinese education through supplying textbooks and teachers and offering scholarships for higher education in Taiwan.

There has been a growing awareness of the need for change. Increasingly stressed are such goals as improving the relations among members of the Chinese community, the relations between members of the Chinese community and the host community, the ability to recognize the interests and problems of their immediate community, and the cultivation of happy, useful members of their own families and communities. Community leaders in general, however, are so divided that reforms are hardly possible. Interference by the government often severely impedes the development of sound educational programs that meet the needs of children in a multicultural society.

6. The total lack of a pan-community literature that can be enjoyed by all members of the same Chinese community regardless of difference in educational background, occupation, sex, or dialect group is a problem shared by all communities. With such a literature, dignity, confidence, and respect for one's own community and one's own way of life can be cultivated. Most Chinese outside of China read too much about China, especially its past. They read and write too little about themselves and their own environments and share too little of their own aspirations, anxieties, joy, suffering, failures, and achievements through writing. They do not know to what extent they understand, respect, or trust their fellow members in the community. The need for cooperation and solidarity is much felt for the survival of their culture. But they have been oriented too little toward themselves, and they often fail to achieve it.

There are obvious reasons for the meagerness of such literature. Writing in Mandarin is a skill that takes a long time to master, even for the educated elite; consequently, there are relatively few literary works reflecting the life of overseas Chinese. Reading in Mandarin is an ability shared by a relatively large proportion in each community, but is seldom used for enjoyment because of the gap between the writing in Mandarin and that in their own dialect. Writing in the vernaculars is rather limited. For example, few have tried to write in Taiwanese or Cantonese. But such a literature has not had a large legion of readers and has not been welcomed by their respective governments.

7. In spite of the size of various vernacular groups, especially Cantonese, South Min, and Hakka, the status of each vernacular is dubious amidst either a Chinese or a non-Chinese government. In many places, Mandarin has replaced the vernaculars as the medium of instruction. In Hong Kong, Macao, and North America, where Cantonese is the medium of instruction in Chinese schools or bilingual educational programs, the textbooks are written in Mandarin.

The neglect of vernaculars in primary- and secondary-school education affects the students and communities in various ways. Generation gaps are extremely large, especially when the parents do not understand the language used in their children's schools. The parents cannot command the respect or confidence of their children. The children fail to learn of their parents' experiences of life in China and settlement in the new world. Only a few talented elite can develop the power of self-expression. The lack of real understanding of their own people and culture results in a lack of ability to solve their own social, cultural, and political problems.

When students are taught to use nothing but a second language at school, they may be made to look down upon features of their own language and lose the power of evaluating sensibly the features of their own community in comparison with those of the other communities (i.e., they may either denounce or glorify emotionally the original cultural features of their own community or the new cultural features from another community). During the beginning period of schooling, too much of the school day is devoted to a language which has no direct use at home or in the community, and the students may lose interest in school. Since the students are using their second-best tool to learn, the learning of various subjects is ineffective. Communication in the second language is adversely affected in school.

8. Chinese curricula outside the People's Republic of China are not regarded as complete unless the students read the classics. More than half of the selections of literary works selected as textbooks for secondary Chinese education are written in classical Chinese. Unlike the case in the West, where students read Western classics in their native language, the Chinese read Chinese classics in the original text.

Since the graphic shape of Chinese characters has been the same for some three thousand years, the Chinese regard classical Chinese as part of the one Chinese writing system, which often implies that a modern literate person in Chinese should be able to read classical Chinese. Defenders of the inclusion of classical Chinese in secondary education object to the idea of having the students read in modern translation, claiming that the Chinese classics are best understood in the original texts and that any translation tends to distort the meaning. Implied in such a claim is the assertion that while there have been changes in lexicon and grammar, there have also been changes in the semantic structure in the development of Chinese—which is an accurate observation.

Often overlooked is the fact that in order to develop the semantic structure of Chinese in any period in the past, a student had to be exposed to many pieces of writing of the same period, accompanied by sufficient orientation to the cultural backgrounds. This is an impossible task for any secondary-school student to undertake because of the lack of time, given the absence of adequate research in the past on the semantic structures of different stages. Therefore, most students, when they read the classical texts, in the pronunciation of Mandarin or any other modern vernacular, are not even aware that the semantic structure used by writers of the texts is different from that used by contemporary writers. Neither do they know that the pronunciation has changed. The results are generally negative. The texts are often vaguely or wrongly understood. The language of classical Chinese influences the student's grammar and lexicon of Mandarin. Its study results in less time to devote to studying other subjects.

When an English student reads Homer's epics or Dante's *Divine Comedy* in English translation, he enjoys reading these becuase he understands the contents without difficulty. He explores a wide world through the tool of his native language, and his ability in English to describe a wide range of experiences is also increased. He also has no illusions that he is reading in the original text. He may imitate the style, the grammar, and the vocabulary of the translation, which would have no undesirable effects on his English composition. When a Chinese student reads the *Book of Songs* or *Mencius*, he needs his teacher to explain the text sentence by sentence. He may learn to use phraseology from the classical text without really understanding it or being understood himself. He is reading the original texts without knowing that he does not have the correct semantic structure to perceive the message conveyed in classical parlance. He is convinced that he is not interested in or competent in the Chinese language.

9. Students' achievements in written Mandarin are generally low. Attending Chinese schools for nine or even twelve years does not guarantee the ability to read and write. The reasons are numerous: gaps between written Mandarin and spoken Mandarin; the gaps between the student's native language and spoken and written Mandarin; irrelevance of the contents to immediate needs; introduction of classical Chinese to students who have not mastered written Mandarin; and the difficulty involved in the learning of thousands of Chinese characters.

TAIWAN AND SINGAPORE

Major Similarities between Taiwan and Singapore

Taiwan and Singapore are the only two places outside of China that have an overwhelming majority of Chinese population (see Table 1) and a government run by Chinese. Therefore, the governments in these two places can exercise their full power in their language policies without external interference. For this reason, a comparison of their language policies with those of the PRC would be interesting and fruitful. Such a comparison, however, requires a much longer space than allowed in this study. The language policies of the two governments are in both

Table 1.   Comparison of Chinese and non-Chinese population in Singapore and Taiwan

Singapore*		*Taiwan*	
Total population	2,167,200*	Total population	15,424,000*
Chinese	76%†	Chinese	99%
Malay	15%	Austronesian	1%
Indians	7%		
Others	2%		

*Figure based on Britannica Book of the Year 1974 (1973 estimation).
†% based on Spector's interpretation of 1947 census. See Stanley Spector in Fried (1958:21).

cases explicitly expressed so far as schooling is concerned. Singapore has declared a policy of multilingual, multicultural education in the hope of achieving the goals of equality, harmony, and integration among all the ethnic groups in the country. The Taipei government has been implementing a policy of Mandarin monolingualism in school education with the assumption that Taiwan is a part of China and Mandarin is the national language of China.[11] In both places, a South Min vernacular is the one most widely used in the communities (see Table 2). Mandarin, however, is the medium of instruction in all Chinese schools, though the reasons, motivation, and implications of using Mandarin are quite different in each of the two communities. A new variety of Mandarin is developing among the younger generations in either place which is quite distinctive as compared with the Mandarin of the PRC. The differences have been due to the drastic changes in the Mandarin of the PRC chiefly because of social changes since its establishment in 1949, and also because of changes in Singapore and Taiwan which have been brought about by non-Mandarin speakers' using it in the new separated environments. Since neither government regards the cultural and linguistic changes that have been taking place in the PRC as models to be copied by their population, since both are very fearful of infiltration by the PRC, and since both governments need to cultivate confidence in and respect for their own cultures and language, especially vis-à-vis the traditions of the past to encourage those Chinese far away from China proper to look toward the latter for cultural and political leadership, there is a need to establish a norm for the spoken as well as the written Mandarin of their own.

Table 2.   Comparison of Chinese language groups in Singapore and Taiwan*

Singapore		Taiwan	
South Min	(69%)	Taiwanese	80%
Hokkien (Amoy,		(Amoy,	
Chuan-chiu,		Chuan-chiu, Chiang-	
Chiang-chiu)	40%	chiu, Teo-chiu)	
Teochiu (Chaochou)	22%	Hakka	10%
Hainanese	7%	Mandarin and other	
Cantonese	22%	Chinese dialects	10%
Hakka	5%		
North Min	(3%)		
Hinghua	1%		
Hakchia	1%		
Hokchiu (Fuchou)	1%		
Other Chinese dialects	1%		
Total 1,647,000	100%	Total 15,270,000	100%

*See Table 1 for source of data.

Both places have a complete educational system in Chinese, from kindergarten to university levels. In such schools, Chinese textbooks are used except for highly technical subject matter for which Chinese textbooks or translations in Chinese are simply not available.

Both places have experienced the problems of confrontation and reconciliation between different speech groups, between different immigrant groups arriving at different periods, and between groups with different ability in the Japanese or English language of the past colonial power. Both have benefited more than other Chinese communities from such experiences and from the sharing of each other's ideas. Bilingualism as a human resource has contributed to the recent economic progress in both places.

Substantial use of a non-Chinese language makes Taiwan and Singapore different from the PRC but similar to other Chinese communities outside the PRC.

A comparison between Taiwan and Singapore also deserves a separate study and will not be discussed in any detail here.

In Singapore, education in English has been flourishing, at the expense of Chinese education, whereas in Taiwan, Japanese education was stopped overnight. In both places, the governments have implemented Mandarin education. But the Mandarin education in the two communities differs from the other greatly. In Taiwan, Mandarin education has been aimed at making the population culturally and linguistically an integral part of China. In Singapore, Mandarin education has been continued not because of Chinese nationalism or a desire to have cultural identity with China, but mainly because there is no single speech group powerful enough to impose its language on the other groups. A multilingual approach for the various tiny vernacular groups (see Table 2) is viewed as impractical, and a need for unity is strongly felt in order to compete with the political force of the Malays and the cultural, economic, and technological power of the English world.

Compared with Taiwan, Singapore has had some difficulty in using the non-Mandarin vernaculars at school because there is a greater multiplicity of dialects among the Chinese population in the same city-state. Each major vernacular is less stable because of constant contacts with other vernaculars in the same city. Each group is less uniform because the dwellers have not been settled there long enough and the speakers of each vernacular are relatively few in number. The largest group in Singapore, which is the Hokkien group, is even smaller than the smaller groups (the Hakka and the Mandarin groups) in Taiwan. Mandarin certainly serves to unify the diversified vernacular groups, without favoring any particular group, though it does put each group in an equally disadvantageous situation.

There are several important reasons for the Singaporeans to feel happier than the Taiwanese about the idea of having their children receive education in Mandarin, a tongue which is strange to themselves. In the first place, Mandarin was chosen of their own will, through a democratic process. Second, a number of options were open to the parents: the Mandarin medium, Hokkien medium, Mandarin and Hokkien medium, English medium—all these schools were available to them.[12]

The recent trend of increased enrollment in English education and decline in Mandarin education on all levels of schooling in Singapore should be surprising to those who keep in mind that Mandarin is a Chinese tongue which is much closer to the native tongues of 76% of the Singaporeans. The following reasons can be given to account for such a trend.

1. English has been more useful than Mandarin in the cosmopolitan city-state, whose economy is oriented toward trade or trade-related industries.

2. While spoken Mandarin is easier than English for the Chinese population to learn, there is the serious problem of establishing a norm. It is the native language of nobody, and there are many internal differences when it is used as a second tongue.

3. While spoken Mandarin may be easier than spoken English, written Mandarin is much harder than written English. Written Mandarin is hard not only because of the logographic Chinese characters but also because its syntax and lexicon differ from those of spoken Mandarin greatly, owing to influence from classical Chinese and different localities of Northern China.

4. Though there is no doubt that Mandarin is closer to the native tongues of the population than English is, Mandarin is still an alien tongue. It may unite the elite of different groups, but it may separate the quick students from the dull, and alienate the young from the old. Therefore, the question of linguistic loyalty or cultural identity plays a minor role for many parents when they choose between English and Mandarin for their children. Some even shy away from a Mandarin education because Chinese-communist infiltration once made use of Chinese nationalism fermented through Mandarin education. As for the official policy, it is doubtful that the government would take effective steps to prevent the emerging trend of English from becoming the lingua franca not only between non-Chinese and Chinese but also among various Chinese speech groups.

HONG KONG AND MACAO

Among the overseas Chinese communities, Hong Kong and Macao are unique in that the overwhelming majority in the two places are Chinese; and yet, as two political entities, they are both under non-Chinese governments, British and Portuguese, respectively. These two Chinese communities differ from others in several other respects. They dwell in places very near China, and most of them have moved from places very near the two city-states. This means that continuous communication with the people of China is physically easier for them than for those in other communities. Unlike other Chinese communities, in which the influx of new immigrants stopped some time ago (especially as of 1949), legal or illegal immigration into these two places has been continuous. Immigration into other overseas Chinese communities is sporadically noticed, but Hong Kong and Macao almost invariably have been the stepping stones of such immigration. The majority of such immigrants had stayed in Hong Kong for several years before they moved to other places. The ratio of newcomers to old settlers has always been much higher than that in other Chinese communities. There is no other Chinese community outside China that has a linguistic situation so homogeneous. Cantonese speakers represent more than 95% of the Chinese populace in Hong

Kong. There are some Min (Hokkien), Hakka, and Tanka speakers. However, Cantonese is universally understood among the Chinese.

In Europe and on the two American continents, there are quite a few Chinatowns where Cantonese is exclusively used among the Chinese; but there are also usually some non-Cantonese speakers living in the same country who do not learn Cantonese at all.

The sizes of the Chinese population in Hong Kong (4,000,000) and Macao (280,000) are also remarkable for such small areas. Hong Kong has the second largest population—Taiwan having the largest—of all the Chinese communities outside of the PRC. (Because of lack of information on Macao, my discussion in this section is limited to the teaching of Chinese in Hong Kong.)

Language and Writing Outside Schools

The linguistic situation in Hong Kong reflects the political relations among the speech groups in an interesting way. English had been the only official language until 1972, when Chinese was eventually recognized as one of the official languages inside the British colony. Outside government circles, English is also widely used, because the whole economy of Hong Kong depends on trade and trade-related industries. Among the Chinese population, written English is used much more than spoken English. English writings are readily available to the average Chinese, but English speakers are not. Occasionally, Chinese will converse in English with other Chinese. There have been complaints by Mandarin speakers that Chinese visitors who speak no Cantonese find themselves more readily accepted if they use English rather than Mandarin. The Chinese written in Hong Kong, as in all Cantonese speech communities, includes three major types: (1) classical Chinese, which uses a large amount of modern vocabulary; (2) written Mandarin; and (3) written Cantonese. Classical Chinese is used mostly in personal and commercial correspondence and official announcements. This is understandable to people who can read classical Chinese no matter what dialect they speak. It is usually read in the native dialect of the reader. Very few people, however, can understand it if they listen to the reading of classical Chinese without seeing the texts.

Written Mandarin is used in most magazine and newspaper articles.

Mandarin speakers can understand the content when they hear something read in Mandarin without seeing the text. For people who do not understand Mandarin, written Mandarin is usually read in Cantonese with whatever grammatical and lexical adjustments are needed for Cantonese listeners. Hong Kong people literate in Chinese are mostly capable of reading and writing in written Mandarin because they have been constantly exposed to it. If written Cantonese and classical Chinese were the only two types of Chinese used in Hong Kong and if written Cantonese were taught in school instead of written Mandarin, the Cantonese speakers there would not be able to read Mandarin at first sight, especially if the written Mandarin were in purely colloquial style; that is, if it had few classical elements.

Written Cantonese which represents spoken Cantonese syllable by syllable is found in novels[13] and in magazine and newspaper articles that describe the daily, casual life of Hong Kong. Written Cantonese is more established in Hong Kong than any other non-Mandarin writing in any Chinese community. Cantonese is understood by almost everyone in Hong Kong who can read Chinese characters. Written Taiwanese or Hokkien, by contrast, is understood by those who are used to folklore books, hymn books, and manuscripts for television and theater shows. The written Cantonese in Hong Kong is rather uniform. The characters chosen for morphemes peculiar to Cantonese are relatively identical among different authors, unlike the case in Taiwan where different authors may choose different characters for the same morphemes. If there were to be any written vernacular that would emerge as a well-recognized written tradition after written Mandarin—comparable with Spanish and French after Italian, it is safe to predict that it is likely to be written Cantonese.[14]

Compared with Singapore, Hong Kong has a much smaller percentage of Chinese who cannot read Chinese and who speak Chinese only on casual topics and must use English for more serious topics. More homogeneous linguistic situations, a higher rate and constant influx of newcomers from China, and the closer distance to China are all factors for such a difference. A more direct cause for the more universal ability to use Chinese in Hong Kong than in Singapore is the fact that Cantonese, the students' mother tongue, is used as the medium of instruction in every school in the beginning years and continues to be one of the media of instruction even in the Chinese-English schools. Spoken Mandarin is taught only as a subject and is used occasionally as a medium of instruction but not until college years, when the students' ability in their native language is fully developed.

Language and Writing in Schools

As to the media of instruction used, the schools of Hong Kong can be divided into three categories: Chinese schools, Chinese-English schools, and English schools. The first two types are for Chinese children, whereas the last is for non-Chinese. In Chinese-English schools, the medium of instruction is Cantonese in the beginning but is gradually switched to English. Toward the end of primary school, both English and Chinese are used as media of instruction. When the students enter high school, they have all their classes conducted in English except courses on Chinese and Chinese history. The secondary schools of this type are also called "English secondary schools." Hong Kong University is an English university intended for graduates from this type of secondary school. In Chinese schools (including the Chinese university, which is made up of several Chinese colleges), English is also taught but only as a subject, and the language is never used as a medium of instruction in other courses.

As to manners of support from the government, the schools in Hong Kong are divided into four categories of schools: public schools, aided schools, subsidized schools, and unsubsidized schools.[15] Public schools are operated and fully financed by the Hong Kong government. It is worth mentioning that Hong Kong has a low ratio of students enrolled in public schools as compared with the total enrollment in all types of schools; about 10% in primary schools in 1970 (UNESCO 1974). The other three types are private schools, which are free from governmental interference unless they violate regulations on safety, sanitation, political association with foreign governments, or qualifications of teachers.

The aided schools differ from the subsidized schools in that the latter receive more restricted financial support from the government. It goes without saying that the government can influence the language education of private schools through control of its financial support. Control has been based mainly on the standards of facilities and teachers' qualifications.[16] There have been few restrictions on the instruction of the culture or the media of instruction which the local leaders deem proper and desirable. English is taught at least as a second language in every Chinese school, not so much because Hong Kong is a British colony but because English has been widely taught as a subject in secondary education in China under the Nationalists or the Communists. English as a subject is introduced in the elementary schools, not because it is required by the government but because a need is felt. An environment has been created such that people sense the need to learn English in order for individuals to survive and prosper.

One can point out that the Hong Kong government has encouraged English-medium education in private schools by making it attractive through financial aid. One should also point out that teaching facilites in English have been developed very well elsewhere in the world and that teaching the ability to use English and teaching in English can be made quite effective by simply utilizing teaching materials and methodology developed elsewhere.

Other than this, the British government in Hong Kong has been quite consistent in the policy of noninterference in the culture and language of the school curriculum. Restraint from dictating the future culture and language of the colony through control of school education is seen not only in not prescribing which language is to be learned by the younger generation but also in not even requiring school-age children to receive an education. It is rather rare for an industrialized state like Hong Kong not to have compulsory education for children of a certain age group.

In summary, the language policy of the British government in Hong Kong is as follows: Environments are created so that English ability is considered highly desirable for individuals who aspire to greater success in a free economy. Alternatives in English and Chinese education are offered to meet the needs of various language abilities in the community. Parents have complete freedom to choose either alternative or the option of not sending their children to any school at all.

Two trends can be observed as a result of this policy. First, language education has been flourishing, as can be seen from the increase in the total enrollments.[17]

Second, English education is getting more and more attractive, whereas Chinese education has been declining, as can be seen in the enrollments in Chinese schools.[18] Aside from the fact that opportunities for higher education and better-paid employment are more available for students with English educational backgrounds than those with Chinese educational backgrounds, the relative effectiveness of Chinese and English education has been an important factor.

Among those who have attended or are attending Chinese schools, one finds a low ability in reading and writing Chinese and a general lack of interest in learning or using Chinese.[19]

Reasons often cited for such a decline include the following (Liu 1970a and 1970b, Ts'ai 1970):

1. Written Mandarin is not only taught in Cantonese but also read in Cantonese. The gap between the spoken language and the written language causes difficulties in learning.

2. Writings of different periods of classical Chinese are included in the textbooks without considering their effects on the students' grammar and vocabulary.

3. The existing written Mandarin taught in schools incorporates plenty of classical usages from different stages of Chinese and dialectal elements from many localities.

The second and third problems are shared by all schools outside China that do teach in Chinese. The first problem is not so widely shared. For textbooks written in Mandarin in most other overseas Chinese communities, teachers read in Mandarin (and explain in the students' mother tongue) or even teach and read in Mandarin.

For centuries, the Chinese have learned to read texts written in classical Chinese which had grammars and vocabulary very strange to their own language. They also have learned to write in classical Chinese, though their writings tended to be more uniform in grammar and vocabulary than the texts they read. Even Japanese scholars in the past had a long tradition of reading classical Chinese texts in Japanese. The grammar and vocabulary of Mandarin is closer to those of Cantonese than to those of classical Chinese (except the contemporary "classical Chinese" which is written with comparatively modern vocabulary and classical grammar). Reading written Mandarin in Cantonese is therefore not hard in the eyes of those teachers and educators who have experienced the hardship of learning to read and write in classical Chinese. This is even more so when they believe that written Chinese is alike all over China because all etymons are unmistakably identified through the use of Chinese characters.

It is quite true that the art of reading written Mandarin in a different dialect is an art which once acquired is an enjoyable and easy activity. It should be borne in mind, however, that the process of acquiring the skill is a tedious, painstaking one. Even more difficult is the skill of writing in Mandarin at a stage when one does not know how to speak Mandarin. Unlike the learning of a mother tongue, the individual difference in acquiring such a skill at school is so great that some may acquire it in a few years while others may never be able to do so. The situation can be compared with one in which a student has to read French texts in Spanish. It is an easy, enjoyable art for those who have mastered the two languages, both spoken and written. The process of learning to read and write French, however, is certainly quite demanding for a Spanish speaker. What is inconceivable is to learn to read French texts in Spanish without learning how to read and write in Spanish first.

Reading in Cantonese would be easier to teach if there were a system of indicating Cantonese pronunciation for Chinese characters. Such a phonetic device is very desirable from pedagogical and sociolinguistic points of view because it has the function of aiding the students to recognize Chinese characters and standardizing the pronunciation. A system of phonetic symbols for Mandarin, like Pinyin or the National Phonetic Symbols, will enable Cantonese children in a few months to learn the Mandarin sound system from scratch together with the graphic symbols. A system of Cantonese phonetic symbols could be learned in a few weeks, since the children know the Cantonese sound system already.

It is hard for those concerned with language teaching to understand why the Hong Kong government has failed to select one of the available systems of phonetic symbols for Cantonese and introduce it in schools in Hong Kong to improve the teaching of reading Chinese texts in Cantonese. To introduce phonetic symbols to teach Chinese characters more effectively should not be so controversial as introducing them to replace fully or partially the Chinese characters already in use.[20] Even the conservative Nationalists have introduced a system of phonetic symbols for the teaching and learning of Mandarin pronunciation. One could fault the Hong Kong government, saying that it has failed to introduce a system of pronunciation aids because it does not want to boost Chinese education to compete with English education in Hong Kong. One could, on the other hand, defend the government by saying that it wants to avoid dictating the future of the sociolinguistic situation of Hong Kong and risk the danger of being accused by China of attempting to divide the Chinese by introducing Cantonese romanization to upgrade Cantonese, which is "merely a Chinese *dialect*" in the official view of the PRC.

Alternatives to Achieve the
Principle of Writing as One Speaks in Schools

There are two alternatives to solve the problems involved in learning to read written Mandarin in Cantonese. One is to introduce written Cantonese in school. The other is to have the students read the existing written Mandarin in Mandarin as they do in Taiwan. Either approach has a series of social, political, and educational implications: One may regard the selection between the two as a matter of choosing between the desire to cultivate respect and confidence in their way of life and a natural love of their own mother tongue on the one hand, and the desire to obtain unity among the Chinese of various communities at least through writing on the other hand.

The undesirability of neglecting the students' mother tongue has been discussed earlier and elsewhere by the writer (1973b) as well as by others (UNESCO 1953).

For a practical person, the choice between the two is a matter of choosing between learning to read and write effectively a variety of Chinese that can be used very satisfactorily within the community and learning to use a variety rather ineffectively (and rather insufficiently for most people) that can be used widely in and out of the community. It is interesting that some authors who recognized that the reading of written Mandarin in Cantonese causes serious problems in learning to read and write effectively did not even mention the introduction of written Cantonese as an alternative (Liu 1970b, Ma 1970a).

In the 1968 Report of the Committee on the Teaching of Chinese, it is recommended that instruction should be in Mandarin. It added, however, that until there are enough teachers who can teach in Mandarin, Cantonese may be used for instruction. According to Liu's view (1970b:56), the Hong Kong government will never train a large number of Mandarin teachers, and the present practice of teaching in Cantonese by every teacher no matter where he is from or whether he can speak Mandarin now or not will continue indefinitely. Liu thinks that teaching in Cantonese has its merits and that teaching in Mandarin should be introduced gradually and naturally.

With recent developments in the techniques of language teaching and a more systematic understanding of relationships between Cantonese and Mandarin as advocated by Chou (1970), language educators should be able to develop a program that can achieve the merits of both approaches. Namely, the schools could introduce written Cantonese in the beginning stages of school and Mandarin in the later stages.

It might be argued that if the mastery of written Mandarin is indispensable, it is more economical to introduce it from the beginning since the learning of two systems (written Mandarin and written Cantonese) is an additional burden on students. Switching from written Cantonese to written Mandarin, however, is not very difficult because the Chinese characters used in both are the same except 1 or 2% of the commonly used ones that are peculiar to Cantonese morphemes. There are many more similarities than differences in vocabulary and grammar. Textbook compilers, in fact, can emphasize the common elements by avoiding characters and lexical items that are peculiar to Cantonese except for the limited, essential ones. These elements can be presented in romanization in order to reduce the number of Chinese characters.[21]

This approach will enable the student to pay due attention to the similarities and differences between Mandarin and Cantonese; and, therefore, problems of confusing the former with the latter can be reduced. The approach also enables the students to experience the actuality of writing and reading as they speak and hear in Cantonese as well as in Mandarin.

It can also cultivate respect for and confidence in their own community and people—a people that are civilized and cultured enough to put their own speech into writing. The allegation that the existing written Cantonese is vulgar and hence unpresentable in school curricula is unsound from an educational point of view. To those who put the first priority on the political or cultural unity of the Chinese people or those who put primary emphasis on the desirability of being able to read and write in a variety of Chinese that is also used by a greater number of people, one can point out that a more effective learning of written Cantonese will enable more people to master it and that a higher ability in written Cantonese acquired by more people will result in more people capable of better Mandarin.

CHINESE COMMUNITIES IN
SOUTHEAST ASIA (EXCLUDING SINGAPORE)

Chinese communities in Southeast Asia (excluding Singapore), unlike the Chinese communities in the first and second groups, are minorities in their respective countries of residence. Compared with those in the fourth group (those in other areas of the world), their proportions in the host communities are, in general, much higher (see Table 3). The size of this Chinese population is second only to the first group (Taiwan and Singapore). Except in Thailand, the Chinese communities and their host communities were once under the rule of Western colonial powers. The impact of colonial rule on the sociolinguistic situation of the Chinese communities has been manifold. Chinese children tended to receive Chinese or Western education (French in Vietnam, Laos, and Cambodia; Dutch in Indonesia; Spanish then English in the Philippines; and English in all other countries). Most children picked up the vernaculars of the indigenous peoples, but just enough to get along with their indigenous playmates and engage in business with them in the future. Chinese history and culture were seldom included in the school curricula. Chinese children who attended Western-language-medium schools had chances to mingle with special classes of non-Chinese communities.

Because of their larger sizes, their greater economic success in comparison with the indigenous peoples, their closer ties with the motherland, past colonial policy of ethnic autonomy, and more heterogeneous linguistic situations in the host community, the Chinese in these communities have been more motivated and able to preserve their Chinese identity than those in the fourth group. Preservation of Chineseness is reflected in the maintenance of Chinese schools, which are likely to grow with their Chinese communities if no restrictions are imposed by the government.[22] Chinese schools in other areas are likely to decline even though there is no government interference. More than any other group, Chinese of this group have problems with their respective countries.

Under colonial rule, the Chinese were able to prosper and preserve their ethnic autonomy without serious open conflicts with the indigenous population. No sooner did the emergence of these colonies into independent countries occur than the assimilation of the Chinese into their host communities became a hot political issue everywhere. The Chinese were then "victims of post-independence nationalism, political suspicion and economic jealousy" (Murray 1964:67). There

Table 3.

Country	No. of Chinese	
Malaysia	3,555,879	(1973 Yearbook)
Singapore	1,579,866	(1973 Yearbook)
Thailand	3,500,000	(estimate for 1972)
Burma	540,000	(estimate for 1972)
North Vietnam, South Vietnam, Khmer Republic, Laos	910,000	(estimate for 1972)
Indonesia	3,500,000	(estimate for 1972)
Philippines	733,688	(estimate for 1972)

were fears and suspicions that the Chinese would eventually control the economy of their countries of residence, taking the place of past colonial masters in economic exploitation, that they would never be loyal to their host countries and might even serve as a fifth column for the Peking government or serve the cause of either the Communist or Nationalist government against the interests of both the Chinese communities themselves and the host country.

Chinese were viewed as being always united, stolid, and determined to preserve their Chinese identity.[23] They were often accused of being ethnocentric, arrogant, contemptuous of the indigenous peoples, and reluctant to be integrated into their communities.[24] As a result, the Chinese of this group have been severely repressed by the governments of their host countries. In the Philippines, Vietnam, Laos, Cambodia, Indonesia, and Thailand, the Chinese are barred from a long list of trades and professions. Almost everywhere, restrictions of some sort have been placed on Chinese schools (Murray 1964:68).

The history of a significant amount of Chinese immigration into Southeast Asia is longer than those of all other areas except Taiwan. Different categories of Chinese families can be established by early immigration, which implies different degrees of acculturation. In Indonesia, for example, the distinction between "peranakan" and "totok" Chinese is important. The peranakan were the descendants of the earliest Chinese who had married local women; the Indies language became the rule in these "Chinese" homes, Dutch being used in many elite families. They are highly acculturated, though they remain a distinct group. Totoks were the new arrivals from China who live a more typically Chinese way of life. "They no longer moved automatically toward the peranakan way of life, but with the rise of Chinese nationalism, the reverse often occurred" (Murray 1964:75).

According to Murray's (1964) estimate, there were about 1,050,000 ethnic Chinese students attending over 3400 schools in Southeast Asian countries, including Singapore (see Table 4). In such schools, Mandarin was the main medium of instruction and taught to all students as the second language (Fitzgerald 1965:83).

These schools are, in general, private schools. A few as in Malaysia, are sponsored by the government. Financial subsidies for nonprofit schools may come from organization dues (such as syndicates of businessmen, Chinese speech groups, surname or district associations) or, where permitted by the government, from mainland China or Taiwan (Murray 1964:70). In most countries, Chinese schools can qualify for government assistance while remaining private, although restrictions on teaching often accompany the aid. In Malaya by 1963, about 90% of the Chinese schools had become fully government-aided.

Table 4. Murray's (1964) estimate of Enrollment in Chinese schools (Schools in which Chinese is the medium of instruction, or taught as the second language)

	Year	Schools	Enrollment	% among Chinese population[d]
Malaya[a]	1962	1,239	423,950	16.0
Sarawak[c]	1961	260	49,200	21.0
No. Borneo	1962	122	28,100	25.0
Brunei	1960	8	4,470	20.5
Indonesia	1960	490	100,000[b]	4.0
Thailand	1962	167	71,000	2.9
So. Vietnam	1960	228	60,000[b]	7.0
Philippines	1963	165	64,000[b]	5.5
Burma	1962	259	39,000	10.0
Cambodia	1962	200	(30-40,000?)[b]	12.0
Laos	1963	14	5,000	12.0
Total		3,152	875,000	

[a]Excluding 101 night schools, enrolling 8000 students. The 1963 total enrollment was 416,150.

[b]Murray's own estimates.

[c]Excluding 5 to 10 private and estate schools; including these, total enrollment probably reached 51,000.

[d]These percentages are best appreciated with reference to age distribution. Approximate figures for school-age populations in most *hua ch'iao* areas in 1962 were as follows: ages 5 to 14, 23 to 25%; ages 5 to 19, 33 to 36%.

Major events in China have had some related effects on the growth of Chinese education in this area. The 1911 revolution that overthrew the Manchu government and the victory in the war against Japan both gave the Chinese people pride in their culture and confidence in themselves as a people who were assuming power and prestige. But the boom in Chinese education in Southeast Asia was mainly due to the new arrivals who fled the turmoil in China before and after the 1911 revolution and during the war against Japan. These new arrivals took active roles in promoting Chinese education and sending their children to those schools. The Nationalist government has also been instrumental in improving the quality of Chinese education by supplying teachers, textbooks, and other teaching materials, as well as training teachers and giving guidance on curricula and school administration.

The rise of Mao's China as a superstate has had mixed effects on the growth of Chinese education in Southeast Asia. Increased fear and suspicion of Chinese schools as a tool of Chinese expansion and world revolution resulted in harsher restrictions on Chinese education.[25]

In order to woo the support of overseas Chinese, both the Communist and Nationalist governments have given more support to overseas Chinese education than each would if there were no such rivalry. Higher education was made especially attractive for Chinese students from Southeast Asia. This rivalry, however, has been destructive rather than constructive. Hostility and disharmony often stand in the way of effective instruction, and education in some schools tends to become too political for local governments to tolerate. It also gives them a good excuse to place more restrictions on Chinese schools. Policies on overseas Chinese education vary greatly and are often subject to change.

Today, owing to the policy to naturalize and assimilate the Chinese, Chinese schools as defined above have been declining since their peak in the early sixties. Gradually, higher percentages of Chinese school-age children are attending non-Chinese schools exclusively, or combining Chinese education with English and/or national education.[26] Primary education in separate Chinese schools is still available in all Southeast Asian countries. Almost everywhere, some national subjects are required in the curriculum. In Indonesia, nationalized Chinese are not alllowed to attend such schools. In Thailand and Vietnam, the number of hours of Chinese subjects allowed is hardly enough to develop adequate ability in written Chinese.

Teaching in Chinese has encountered several problems for reasons peculiar to Southeast Asia as well as for reasons common to all Chinese communities outside China. Two problems are especially grave: the problem of coordinating teaching in Chinese with teaching in the indigenous language as well as some Western language (English or French) and the problem of teaching a variety of spoken and written Chinese so that teaching can be conducted in that medium effectively in various subjects.

The need for teaching in Chinese as well as in the language of the host country is shared by Chinese communities in most countries elsewhere. The problem of satisfying such a need is greater in this area because education in the respective national language is still in the developing stages and because in addition to the national language, instruction in English or French is regarded as highly desirable by both the indigenous people and the Chinese. The problem is harder to solve because in this area, it is viewed merely as not a purely educational problem, but a political problem between peoples who have lived side by side without knowing each other at all.

People who would like to see the elimination of teaching in Chinese as soon as possible often argue that the Chinese in Southeast Asia make up a "Third China,"[27] which is uniform, unchangeable, and unbreakable, where Chinese education serves to perpetuate such an existence. The theme that the Chinese are uniform, unchangeable, and unbreakable is not well founded. The Chinese have developed linguistic differences that cause mutual intelligibility through speech to be almost impossible. Speech groups are still an important factor in organizational behavior of the Chinese anywhere outside China.[28] Communication through writing is possible only after long years of learning to read and write in classical Chinese or written Mandarin, the grammar and lexicon of which is entirely strange to them, and the memorizing of thousands of Chinese characters. Love for and pride in one's own language and culture are by no means a peculiar feature of the Chinese but are universal to all peoples. Under certain circumstances, Chinese have been assimilated into their host communities as easily as most other peoples and much more quickly than Westerners outside of Europe.[29] In Japan, Korea, and many other parts of Southeast Asia, we see Chinese without any trace of Chineseness. The fact that the Chinese did not receive education in the indigenous language was not because they were Chinese, but because of past colonial policies and because of the attractiveness of Western education as well as a Chinese education. If they have tended to stick together, it is because they have been forced to do so in order to protect themselves against the impatient indigenous peoples who blame the Chinese for their failure to solve the problems of emerging nations overnight. The booms in overseas Chinese education in the past have coincided with the rise of nationalism in the motherland, but this has been mainly due to an influx of China-born Chinese who tend to find acculturation difficult as do other peoples in similar situations. It is true that the content of Chinese education was invariably oriented toward China; and, as a result, those receiving Chinese education tended to know very little of themselves or their host communities. But the Chinese are also capable of and even eager to receive a non-Chinese education, nor is slavish admiration for the prestigious educational establishment peculiar to the Chinese. There is, in fact, quite a high proportion of Chinese who were educated under the English or French system, and their life styles and values have been oriented toward London or Paris rather than Peking or their countries of residence. Pursuit of prestige and economic security via education is a feature common to developed communities. The fact that the overseas Chinese relied on Peking or Taiwan for their supply of teachers and educational materials was not due to their political loyalty to either government but rather to some explainable factors: the early immigrants, being laborers, were barely educated themselves. They were eager to have their children get educated, but hardly knew how to teach them. Chinese education has not been very effective in producing enough graduates who were competent and interested in teaching Chinese. There was a tendency for ambitious Chinese children to receive Western education, which resulted in a shortage of Chinese teachers.

The view that the Chinese are concerned only with the preservation and expansion of Chinese culture is true only with regard to a few of those who were educated in the old tradition. Enloe (1968) observes, for instance, that the Chinese in Malaysia are more preoccupied with opportunities for advancement than with the survival or expansion of communal institutions. Howell has observed that mental commitment to Taipei or Peking is greater among those who have received Chinese education than among those who have received non-Chinese education (1973). It is rather obvious that this was due to the content of Chinese education in the past and not due to the use of Chinese as the medium of instruction. It goes without saying that the same language can be used to teach Chinese about China, about their own Chinese communities, and about the country in which they live. Given that teaching in Chinese can orient the students toward their own communities as well as the host communities and can best satisfy the needs of Chinese communities as a minority in the respective countries, the problem of teaching in Chinese and teaching the national language and a Western language can be solved rationally from an educational viewpoint.

Finally, Chinese—like any other people—need to have a linkage between generations and confidence in themselves and their own culture in order to survive with dignity, to win respect from other ethnic groups, and to participate in the building of new nations. When they suffer from political suspicion and cultural suppression, they themselves and their countries as a whole will also suffer from racial disharmony, retarded social progress, and political unrest. The goals of education should be social progress, racial harmony, and national unity—not the elimination of differences in language and culture.

The problem of a discrepancy between language in school and in the communities is greater in this area because of a relatively more complex dialect situation in most Chinese communities. Now that Chinese children cannot receive education entirely in Chinese, there may not be enough time for them to learn spoken and written Mandarin so that other subjects can be conducted in Mandarin. Teaching in Chinese is likely to result in teaching spoken and written Mandarin with hardly anything else, because of lack of time. Insufficient learning of spoken and written Mandarin is likely to lead to decreased use of the language. It has already been observed that as a result of requiring the introduction of Malay into the Malaysian school curriculum, Mandarin is less widely spoken by the younger graduates and their ability in written Chinese is generally lower. Unless attention is paid to the students' mother tongue in schools while teaching Mandarin, or unless the students' mother tongue replaced Mandarin as the medium of instruction at least in the beginning years, Mandarin and the Chinese dialects throughout Southeast Asia may disappear in the near future, as is already taking place in Thailand (Puyodyana 1971, Tanapatchiyapong 1973). It is likely that the use of Mandarin will fade first in the communities because few people can speak Mandarin without learning it in school for several years. For communication between different Chinese speech groups, the national languages or English can take the place of Mandarin easily. Various Chinese vernaculars are likely to stay longer, since their acquisition needs no formal education and their function as a linkage between generations in the same speech group will have no substitute for a while.

CHINESE COMMUNITIES IN OTHER AREAS

The Chinese in this group are smallest in number, though they are scattered over the largest area. The proportion of Chinese seldom reaches 1% of the total population of their respective countries. Just as the Chinese in Southeast Asia are predominantly Cantonese South Min speakers, those in this group are predominantly Cantonese speakers. The number of Chinese tends to be greater in countries that had a colonial history during the Industrial Revolution (see Table 5). Immigration of Chinese laborers into the colonies during the latter half of the 18th Century was partly due to the need for labor for industrial development and party due to miserable living conditions in China.[30]

Quite different from this group of Chinese immigrants are those intellectuals and professionals who left China to avoid the turmoil of civil war, revolution, and the war against Japan during the first half of the century. The earlier immigrants arrived in groups from the same places, often as contract laborers. The recent immigrants, who arrived after the ban on the importation of Chinese laborers, have been very small in number because of very strict visa restrictions and limited job opportunities. They speak Cantonese, Mandarin, Taiwanese, and other dialects. Because of their different linguistic and educational backgrounds, they usually do not mingle with the earlier immigrants. Since they are smaller in number and usually live in non-Chinese neighborhoods, their children tend to speak less Chinese than the older settlers, who often stick together in Chinatowns.

The earlier settlers still preserve features of prerepublic China. The later immigrants, who left China after having been influenced by cultural and social changes that took place after the 1911 revolution, reflect more features of the new China, modern-minded and nationalistic. The early settlers are more conscious of their traditional way of life and their own speech group. The later immigrants are more conscious of China as a nation because of the influence of rising nationalism when they were in China. The fact that Chinese schools in this area teach mostly in Cantonese and not Mandarin as in Southeast Asia can be explained by the insignificant impact that the new settlers have on established residents.

If the Chinese in this group are regarded as "problems," it is not because they are feared as a political or economic threat, but because they are viewed as a minority that adjusts poorly to the environment because they are cohesive, distinctive, and almost impossible to acculturate. The view that the Chinese do not acculturate may result from the existence of Chinatowns that are so conspicuous. Outside Chinatowns, Chinese in this group do acculturate, though at different rates. In Hawaii, where the Chinese have been accepted without much discrimination in the past few decades, have prospered economically, and have been free to preserve their culture and language, including establishing a Chinatown and several Chinese schools, acculturation has been no slower than that of other ethnic groups.[31] In San Francisco, New York, and other big cities

Table 5. Chinese and Chinese schools outside Southeast Asia, China, and Taiwan*

	No. of schools	No. of Chinese
Korea	54	24,000
Japan	12	46,000
India	11	46,000
Sri Lanka	1	500
Canada	8	58,000
U.S.A.	36	237,000
Mexico	3	10,000
Cuba	3	31,000
Dominican Republic	1	1,000
Guatemala	1	5,000
Panama	1	3,000
Trinidad	1	12,000
Jamaica	3	19,000
Ecuador	1	4,000
Surinam	1	6,000
Peru	2	30,000
Chile	1	3,000
Fiji Islands	2	5,000
Society Islands	4	7,000
United Kingdom	2	12,000
Malagasy Republic	11	9,000
Mauritius	15	23,000
Reunion	6	3,000
Mozambique	6	2,000
South Africa	7	5,000
	193	601,500

*Data based on 1962 Overseas Chinese Statistics by Overseas Affairs Commission, 1963. Only countries with Chinese schools are included here.

where social acceptance of the host communities and economic opportunities are not so favorable as in Hawaii, acculturation has been slower.

Unlike the Chinese in Southeast Asia, those in this group generally have fewer restrictions imposed by the government on the education of their children. They can send their children to public schools to receive education in the language of the host community, or establish their own schools to educate their children in Chinese.

There is no doubt that children need to develop language ability to function satisfactorily as members of the Chinese communities and host communities. There are three ways by which the Chinese meet such a need.

1. By relying on school education only for development of knowledge of Chinese language and culture. This was common among Chinese communities in the early stages of immigration who still had the sojourn attitude. Since staying abroad was temporary, the children should be versed in Chinese language and

culture so as to prepare them to return to China. The sojourn attitude gradually changed into a settlement attitude, and school tended to be used for orientation to the host countries. When Chinese do not have much contact with members of the host communities, such as in the case of isolated Chinese communities in New York and San Francisco in the recent past, or when the Chinese feel that there is not much to learn about the language and culture of the host community in school (since it can be learned through daily contacts), such as in the case of some Chinese in the Fiji Islands, the situation may continue even though they have no intention of going back to China.

2. By relying on school education only for acquiring knowledge of the language and culture of the host countries. This is most common for those who have acculturated or discovered Chinese schools very ineffective, uninteresting, and not usefully oriented toward their own communities. In many places where the number of Chinese is too small to have a separate Chinese school or Chinese programs, the Chinese find no other alternative. There are those who regard schooling in Chinese as unnecessary because their children have picked up their parents' language already. The accomplishment of home instruction in written Chinese is usually very limited, and many children as a result have no knowledge of written Chinese. The Chinese have a long tradition of emphasizing the written language, however; and the difficulty of mastering Chinese is widely known. If Chinese schooling is available and parents do not require their children to attend, it is usually because of the ineffectiveness and impracticality of the Chinese education rather than because of the intention to teach Chinese to their children at home.

Chinese schools today are generally very poorly supported financially. The teachers' qualifications are low because the salaries cannot possibly attract good teachers. It is common for new arrivals to teach in Chinese schools, partly because they cannot find a better job and partly because teachers competent in Chinese are otherwise not easily available. New arrivals are regarded as desirable for their possession of "pure" and "uncorrupted" Chinese. However, they often make ineffective teachers because of their lack of knowledge of life in the new lands, especially as to the minds and aspirations of the children—which even their own parents cannot fully understand.

3. By relying on school education to acquire the language and culture of the host communities and those of the Chinese. There are many ways in which the parents have relied on school education. One variable is whether they send their children to the same or different schools. When children attend different schools, the usual pattern is to attend public schools for education in the host country during the regular hours and then Chinese schools afterward. This has been the practice of many Chinese children in Hawaii and other places. Under such circumstances, the role that Chinese schools play for the mental growth of the children is rather peripheral. When parents know mostly English and quite a few even use it at home, and when it is clear that English is more useful than Chinese even in the Chinese community, learning Chinese at school is for the purpose of identification with fellow Chinese rather than for communication in daily life.

The symbolic value of being identified as Chinese might be important for parents who have experienced benefits from various Chinese institutions, but not for the children who have no such experience. Lack of coordination between Chinese and regular schools often results in a conflict of values for the students. Neglect of a student's particular linguistic and ethnic background in regular schools tends to foster the value judgment that maintaining Chineseness is inimical to the trend of integration. In Hawaii, the major content of such an "after school" Chinese schooling goes hardly beyond the learning of written Mandarin with Cantonese pronunciation. The level of reading ability achieved by a student has been getting lower and lower as fewer and fewer children speak Cantonese at home or in the community. Most children in Chinese schools have only a passive knowledge of Cantonese, and they use English with each other even in Chinese schools. Learning a language is not very effective when the language taught is not used in school or at home and when it is not recognized by the regular school system. This arrangement has had a great impact on students, however, when the community used Chinese frequently in their daily life. With students having a firm knowledge in spoken Cantonese, classes were conducted effectively in it to teach written Chinese and things about China. Chinese education after regular school has played an important role in slowing down the extinction of the Chinese language, in letting the members of the Chinese community compare Chinese and non-Chinese cultures, and in preventing a big gap between generations.

When children attend the same school to acquire and improve in both Chinese and the language of the host country, the most important factor is who runs the school. When the schools are run by Chinese, the total education tends to focus on Chinese. In the Chinese schools which are run by Chinese in Japan, for example, all the courses are on Chinese or taught in Chinese except for the courses on the Japanese language and society—which usually take less than five hours a week.

To the writer's knowledge, no public school in this area group of Chinese communities, except a few schools in the United States, offers teaching in Chinese.

4. Depending on bilingual and bicultural programs in a school in which language courses are taught in both Chinese (usually Cantonese) and English. Unlike the Chinese schooling described above, which is invariably financially supported by Chinese communities without government subsidies, the bilingual programs that are known to the writer are offered in public schools using the parents' tax money or in private schools financed by church organizations. Such programs are still in the experimental stage and available only in some chosen areas in such big cities in the United States as San Francisco, New York, Chicago, Boston, and Los Angeles. This arrangement has several advantages over other ways of developing students' language and cultural skills in Chinese and the language of the host community:

1. Students' needs for ability in Chinese and English can be coordinated in an integrated, balanced program. Excessive emphasis on one at the expense of the other can be recognized and rectified from a purely educational point of view.

2. Since students can get credit for what they achieve in Chinese courses in the regular school system, they are more highly motivated to learn the language and culture of their own parents.

3. Since the Chinese courses are offered during the regular school hours, students do not feel that learning Chinese is an additional burden on a minority group. Learning during regular hours, moreover, is more effective than "after school" when students are tired.

4. Since bilingual education is offered in the same schools which children of other ethnic groups also attend, there is ample opportunity for Chinese students to share their knowledge with other students; and there is no danger of ethnic isolation or the apprehension of being suspect or looked down upon. Some Chinese-English bilingual programs even have 40% of the non-Chinese students participating in "learning Chinese culture, spoken Mandarin and, eventually, Chinese reading and writing" (San Francisco Unified School District, Chinese Bilingual E.S.E.A., Title VII Program 1974).

5. Since bilingual programs do not merely teach Chinese and English but also teach in English as well as in Cantonese, the students' ability in both languages is quite likely to develop.

6. Since the bilingual educational programs are supported by tax money, there is a feeling of a minority's participating in the government of a nation on an equal basis and in determining the future cultural makeup of their country of residence.

7. Since Chinese schools are generally inadequately financed, government financing of bilingual programs can result in better facilities, better-qualified teachers, and more suitable educational materials.

Where two or more alternatives are available, the prestige of the school system of the host country seems to be very important among many factors in determining the selection from available alternatives. Thus, in developed countries where there are universities with high reputations, the parents tend to select education in the local system. In countries where the language used in school is not used beyond the boundaries of the country, Chinese education is usually the choice.

Among all non-Chinese languages, English is the most attractive and desired because there are more opportunities for higher education and economic advancement in the minds of Chinese. Japanese is also regarded as desirable because many political leaders, professionals, and entrepreneurs in China and Taiwan have received Japanese education. Thus, in Japan, those Chinese children who attend Chinese schools are much fewer than those who attend Japanese schools; but in Korea, the opposite is true.

There are also Chinese who send their children to receive education without seeking a general knowledge of the language of either the Chinese community or the host community. This is common in places where there is no Chinese school and the education in the language of the host community is not attractive (i.e., Africa, India, and some Pacific Islands). The writer knows quite a few cases of Chinese who attend American schools in Japan for primary and secondary education. The reason often given is that it is hard for a foreigner to be naturalized in Japan unless his own government approves first,[32] and the parents plan to send their children to America for higher education.

The teaching of Mandarin in order that teaching can be conducted in it can be described as a case of using school education for purposes other than preparing them to be effective members of the parents' community and of the host community. As China rises as a big power and as Mandarin becomes a more popular foreign language in universities and even in high schools, there have been suggestions to replace Cantonese in some Chinese schools. While the idea may sound attractive to some Chinese in the beginning, it has seldom been carried out with success. In reference to the present linguistic situation in Hawaii, there is still some possibility that half the students who attend Chinese schools may become proficient in Cantonese if the Chinese schools improve their program of teaching in Cantonese. This is so because Cantonese is still functional in some sectors of the community. When Mandarin is used, because it has no proper environment for actual practice, the chances are that less than 3% will graduate with even minimum ability in Mandarin. Even these students will have to continue studying Mandarin in college and/or visit and stay in Taiwan or China for a while eventually to develop sufficient skill in Mandarin.

The introduction of Mandarin into public schools in Hawaii has had the effect of accelerating the extinction of Cantonese as a functional minority language. Failing to distinguish a foreign language from a functional minority language, some educators have begun to think that Mandarin will soon replace Cantonese in the community. Neglect of Cantonese in public schools in Hawaii has a discouraging effect on those who wish to preserve it in the community. It is safe to predict that replacement of Cantonese by Mandarin as a community language in Hawaii is impossible unless a huge number of Mandarin speakers migrate in the future. The two-hour-a-week Mandarin program on TV did not last long in 1973. Two out of the four public schools that started Mandarin courses discontinued them because of low enrollments. Cantonese may die out in the Chinese community, but it will be replaced by English and not Mandarin in Hawaii as well as in many other Chinese communities in this group.

The boom to learn Mandarin by Chinese-Americans in fact has been influenced by the rise of China as a major power as well as the growing tendency to view it as desirable for American-Asians to maintain their cultural identity because of their oriental appearance, which can never be changed into a Caucasian one. When Chinese college students find themselves embarrassed without the ability to speak any variety of Chinese, they are apt to learn Mandarin rather than their community language. The obvious reason behind the choice of Mandarin over their parents' language is that ability in Mandarin can also provide a Chinese identity, at least among non-Chinese; and it is more fashionable and prestigious than Cantonese (at least in areas where Cantonese is being replaced by English). A deeper reason behind the choice is that these young people have been using English in their daily life without feeling any inconvenience either because they are living outside the Chinese community or because the Chinese community has dissolved as a result of integration. For these people, the learning of Chinese is for its symbolic value as a token of identity rather than for its practical value as an essential means of communication in their environments. When Mandarin is learned with such motivation, the result is usually poor, since language learning takes a much stronger motivation than acquisition of a token identity. The tendency to choose Mandarin as a foreign language benefits those who can speak Cantonese much more than those who cannot. When a student has a firm Cantonese background, the learning of Mandarin is much more successful than among those without this background. Such a student can usually function in Mandarin after one year of instruction at the college level.

CONCLUSION

In this chapter, I have described the conditions under which media of instruction are chosen for Chinese children outside the People's Republic of China. Among the factors that are responsible for the selection of any variety of Chinese, of a non-Chinese tongue, or of both, as media of instruction, the two most important are government policy and the size and proportion of the Chinese community in the total population of the host country. Except the Taiwanese children who had to study all courses in Japanese, Chinese children under colonial rules were able to have schooling only in Chinese during the colonial period; but today they have to receive their education either bilingually in Chinese and non-Chinese or entirely in a non-Chinese medium, chiefly because of changes in government which result in changes of language policy. Among all the Chinese communities that have witnessed these changes, the most thorough and most drastic implementation of changed language policy was found in Taiwan. The size and proportion of the Chinese population to the total population of the host country is as important as government policy. Most of the Chinese in Southeast Asian countries constitute significant proportions of the total populations and are still able to send their children to Chinese schools in spite of government policies to impose national languages in school. However, Chinese in many countries are unable to do so in spite of the absence of governmental restrictions, because of their small populations.

Other major factors[33] for selection of media of instruction for their children's schooling are economic opportunities, opportunities for higher education, and sufficiency and effectiveness of alternative educational programs. English is becoming even more attractive than before, mainly because of better job opportunities and a better future for higher education. Indigenous languages are still not very attractive because of fewer opportunities for economic and/or educational advancement. Whether Chinese education is effective enough to produce graduates who are found to be useful members of Chinese communities involves many variables. One such variable is whether the students' mother tongue is properly treated so that schooling can have a direct bearing on the students' daily life. If Mandarin is taught and used as a medium of instruction, an important variable is whether Mandarin education is effective and sufficient for students to function in Mandarin. Cantonese schooling continues to flourish in the United States in spite of the attractiveness and necessity of English-medium education, whereas Mandarin schooling in Southeast Asia is declining after the peak in the early sixties because it has less impact on the students' life than schooling in English or the national language of their countries of residence.

Selection among varieties of Chinese is determined somewhat differently. In Singapore and Taiwan, the governments dictate that Mandarin is to be used in Chinese education, and such a language policy overrules all other factors. Elsewhere, the government is hardly concerned with the problem, and the choice is usually determined by factors such as linguistic homogeneity within a Chinese community, educational traditions and facilities, and conflicts with the peoples of the host countries and ties with China. In Southeast Asia, most Chinese schools shifted from various Chinese vernaculars to Mandarin because of the multiplicity of Chinese vernaculars used in the same country, the tie with China (which was still strong, at least among the China-born), and the need for solidarity, which was strongly felt among the Chinese because of conflicts with the non-Chinese peoples. In other areas, it is usually the vernacular of the biggest speech group that is used as the medium of instruction in Chinese schools. Ties with China were once a very important factor in choosing Mandarin as a medium of instruction.[34] As the overseas Chinese become increasingly aware that their future lies in their countries of residence, and neither Taipei nor Peking can give them enough protection against the educational policies of their indigenous governments, ties with China diminish as a factor in the selection of Mandarin as a medium of instruction. Tradition and educational facilities, such as textbooks, pronunciation aids, and a desire for unity among the Chinese community in a hostile community, have been the major reasons for the continued use of Mandarin. As more and more overseas Chinese denounce their ties with China and become affected by the growing tendency to learn English as an international language on the one hand, and the tendency to seek knowledge of a minority culture and language on the other hand, Mandarin education is likely to continue to become less attractive. On the other hand, Mandarin may be more widely studied as a foreign language by overseas-Chinese college students, especially for those who have firm backgrounds in their mother tongue.

Coordination and cooperation among Chinese communities of various countries is an important factor in determining the selection of the medium of instruction. As more overseas Chinese become better educated and more aware of the fact that they have some cultural features, sentiments, and community interests which are not shared by other Chinese communities, especially the Chinese of the motherland, the past pattern of the Chinese government's supervising Chinese education abroad will definitely change. While the pattern can no longer serve the interests of the government of the motherland or of the overseas communities, it does arouse the suspicion and fear of the governments of the host countries.[35]

There is growing recognition that the past policy of copying everything in the educational system of the motherland is impractical and unfruitful. There is an obvious need for cooperation among the Chinese communities for the sharing of their experiences to work toward better educational systems to enable their children to understand themselves, their past, and their immediate environments, to improve relations among Chinese and relations with the host communities, and to make contributions to the well-being of the host communities. When such cooperation exists, bilingual and bicultural education are likely to last. When there is no such cooperation or when the ties with the motherland go beyond fulfilling such a need, there will be a less likely chance of developing a healthy language-education program.

NOTES

1. William Mackey's *Preface to Chiu* (1970: v-viii).

2. The lack of ability to converse in non-Mandarin is quite a drawback for specialists on Chinese communities even though most of them read Chinese quite well. The most desired information is not available in writing because there are many things which the Chinese do not write down and written descriptions are often understood to be different from reality. This might be why Pye (1954:20-21) has remarked that Chinese rely on rumor more than on writing for information and entertainment.

3. This figure is based on *China Yearbook* 1969-1970. Taipei: China Publishing Company, 1970:394.

4. See Fitzgerald (1972), Pye (1954), and Howell (1973) as examples on treatment of overseas Chinese and ties with China.

5. Fried (1958), Simoniya (1961), Purcell (1965:575-610), Fitzgerald (1972:257-263), and Uchida (1960)—for bibliographies of works on overseas Chinese.

6. Works directly on overseas Chinese education, including Chinese University of Hong Kong (1970), Murray (1964), Ch'iao Wu Wei Yuan Hui (1971).

7. For discussions of distance between Chinese dialects, see Wang (1960) and Cheng (1973a). For statistics on speakers of various dialects, see Chan (1975).

8. The problem of the integration of returned overseas Chinese is also an example of culture change among Chinese in and out of the People's Republic of China. For a study of the problem, see Fitzgerald (1972:69-73).

9. Fincher (1972, 1973) claims that changes over the past quarter of a century in the People's Republic of China warrant discussion of a new distinction: that between modern and what might be called "trans-modern" Chinese.

10. The three stages of development have been discussed by Yu (1971:2) for the Chinese community in Hawaii.

11. See Cheng (1973b) for a more detailed description of sociolinguistic situations in Taiwan.

12. According to a source the writer cannot yet identify, in 1945 the number of students receiving education in their vernaculars was about the same as that of those receiving their education in Mandarin.

13. See Wu (1963) for bibliography of works done on the vernacular.

14. See Cheng (1976) for a statistical study of literature of various Chinese dialects. This study clearly shows that Cantonese has the widest vernacular literature written in Chinese characters among the non-Mandarin Chinese vernaculars.

15. According to Ma and Chen (1958:42, 50), enrollments in various types of schools are as follows:

	Primary Schools	Secondary Schools
Public schools	19,541	7,363
Aided schools	6,626	9,265
Subsidized schools	75,549	17,022
Nonsubsidized schools	143,891	35,707

16. See Ma and Chen (1958:11).

17. See UNESCO (1974).

18. Ma and Chen (1958:7).

19. Ma and Chen (1958:7), Ts'ai (1970:33-34).

20. The sentiment against romanization of Chinese fully or partially is quite strong among conservative overseas Chinese. The Nationalists, who proclaim to be defenders of Chinese culture, are especially against it. The Communist government has declared it to be their eventual goal of language reform (Milsky 1973). For a study of language reform in China, see DeFrancis (1950).

21. Such a writing will be similar to the present Japanese orthography, which mixes Chinese characters and kana.

22. Restrictions on Chinese education are seen in many variations: establishment of new Chinese schools (Thailand, Cambodia, Indonesia, the Philippines); maximum hours for Chinese courses (Thailand); minimal hours of courses on national languages (almost all countries); citizenship of principals and teachers, contents of textbooks (Thailand, Malaysia, Indonesia); enrollment of indigenous children or local-born Chinese children (Indonesia, Cambodia). See Chou (1961:74-87).

23. Cf. Fitzgerald (1965:81-82). For an opposite view, see Chan (1975).

24. Engstrom (1966).

25. For a detailed discussion of Peking's policy on overseas Chinese, see Fitzgerald (1972:162-184).

26. It is noteworthy that throughout Southeast Asia today, Chinese children receive more formal education than indigenous children, yet nowhere today, except in Malaysia's Borneo States, are the majority of school-age Chinese enrolled in Chinese schools (Murray 1964:71).

27. For the term "Third China," see Fitzgerald (1965:84).

28. For a description of organizational behavior of Chinese in Malaysia, see Li (1970).

29. Francis L.K. Hsu, in Fried (1958:68), has made a similar remark.

30. Cf. Fried (1958:60).

31. See Yu (1971) for an account of acculturation of Chinese in Hawaii.

32. Before the Japanese government recognized the PRC, the Nationalist government of Taiwan had the policy of not approving the abandoning of Chinese citizenship (Chu 1967).

33. See Le Page (1964) for a discussion of factors which affect the choice of a national language.

34. Engstrom (1966:13).

35. See Fitzgerald (1972:185-195) for an analysis of Peking's policy toward overseas Chinese and of the tendency for the overseas Chinese to become independent of China.

XIII

Language Education

in a Post-Creole Society

Dennis R. Craig

FORMATIVE CONDITIONS AND ATTITUDES

The term post-creole (De Camp 1971) is used to designate a speech community where the coexistence of an original pidgin-creole language and a dominant official language has resulted in the development of a dialect continuum linking the two. On this continuum, the presence of an intermediate area of language, or mesolect (Stewart 1964), between the two extremes (acrolect and basilect) distinguishes a post-creole speech community from an otherwise bilingual or multilingual one, since the structural gap between discrete languages that is present in strictly bilingual and multilingual communities is absent in a post-creole situation. In other words, without a mesolect, there would be no significant difference between post-creole and bilingual situations since, in the former, the acrolectal and basilectal extremes, taken by themselves, tend to remain mutually unintelligible in the same way as discrete languages tend to do.

The way in which post-creole speech communities come into existence has much to do with the necessary form of language education in such communities. Commenting on processes that produce post-creole communities, DeCamp (1971) has pointed out that:

> It would appear that a speech community can reach post-creole status only under two conditions. First, the dominant official language must be the same as the creole vocabulary base; if it is different, then the creole either persists as a

separate language with little change (e.g., the English creoles of Surinam and the French creole of St. Lucia and Grenada) or becomes extinct, as Neger-hollands is now doing. Second, the social system, though perhaps still sharply stratified, must provide for sufficient social mobility and sufficient corrective pressures from above in order for the standard language to exert real influence on creole speakers; otherwise the creole and the standard remain sharply separated as they do in the French areas. These corrective pressures (radio, television, internal migration, education, etc.) do not operate uniformly on all speakers, of course; otherwise the result would be a merger of the creole with the standard rather than a continuum.

The two conditions here referred to as being necessary for the development of post-creole speech communities have separate as well as joint implications for language education in such communities. An examination of some of these implications will be attempted here with special reference to the set of post-creole speech communities that comprise the "English-speaking" West Indies, Guyana and Belize, and that for all practical purposes may be regarded as comprising a single post-creole society.

In some of the latter speech communities, like Trinidad and St. Vincent, for example, the original and basilectal form of the creole that probably once existed has all but disappeared, and what remains is what would otherwise be the mesolect that is intermediate between creole and standard language. In some other communities, however, such as Jamaica, Belize, and Guyana, there is a basilect that is relatively further removed from Standard English and close to, if not identical with, the creole that must have existed originally. In all these communities that comprise the wider post-creole society already referred to, a social-class classification would put most basilectal and mesolectal speakers within the levels of the lower-working, working, and lower-middle class; and the structure of the society as a whole is such that the latter speakers can be estimated to form about 70 to 80% of a total population of about 5 million speakers. Throughout the society, the language-education problem that is posed by basilectal and mesolectal speakers is experienced mainly in the public system of primary, all-age, and post-primary schools for which the governments of the respective countries are responsible. In fee-charging preparatory schools, and secondary high schools to which entry is gained by either competitive scholarships or the payment of fees, the language-education problem is much less, since the latter schools are the ones in which middle and upper social-class children coming from homes where some form of internationally acceptable English tends to be spoken are mostly found. This situation has not changed much in recent times, although, in all the countries referred to, government policies are directed toward creating egalitarian educational systems.

One characteristic of educational policy in the countries mentioned is that, traditionally, creole or creole-influenced language has been treated in schools as if it did not exist, or as if it should be eradicated if it existed. One reason for the development of this attitude to creole is to be found in the fact mentioned already that the first condition that is necessary in order for a community to become post-creole is that the dominant official language must be the same as the creole vocabulary base. In the society being considered, because of the common vocabulary base of creole and standard, it was easy for educational planners in the past to feel that creole was merely a debased form of the standard language and that this debasement could be corrected merely by a sustained exericse of carefulness on the part of the creole speaker. The common vocabulary made it appear that the basilectal or mesolectal speaker was merely being careless about a grammatical inflection or a grammatical particle or other element here and there, but that the speaker was operating essentially the same linguistic system as the Standard English speaker. This attitude of educational authorities toward creole has been widespread from the earliest times until quite recently and is still found in some localities at present. It is an attitude that took root despite early scholarly descriptions of creole (e.g., those of Russell 1868, Thomas 1869, Van Name 1870, Schuardt 1882), and also despite a steady growth of popular literary interest in creole throughout the society over the past fifty years (see Craig 1976 for further reference to this).

Since 1950, the attitude referred to, if not changed, has tended to become better informed, mainly because of the growth of studies of Caribbean creoles. (For a discussion of these studies and their significance to language education, see Craig 1976, 1974a). The advent of these studies (e.g., LePage 1952, 1955, 1957, ed. 1961; LePage and DeCamp 1970; Allsopp 1958a, b, 1962; Bailey 1953, 1962, 1966; Stewart 1962, 1967; Hall 1966) created an awareness of the nature of the surviving Caribbean creoles (even though it was the Jamaican community that received the most thorough treatment); as a result it became impossible for creole to be ignored as persistently as it was before. The fact began to be more generally understood that the lexical affinities between creole or creole-influenced speech and Standard English often helped to disguise significant differences between the syntactic-semantic systems of the two types of language, that the creole or creole-influenced speaker, in making an approach to Standard English, was faced with the task of acquiring a new language system, and that merely "being careful" would not be sufficient to achieve that task. Craig (1976) refers to early evidence of this improved understanding on the part of educators and quotes Walters (1958), which, in examining the teaching of reading in Jamaica, said incidentally about English teaching:

> A gradual change of attitude is being noted, however ... when teachers are warned not to begin corrections too early and stifle spontaneity. A further step takes us away from the concept of "correcting wrong speech" towards learning a new way of saying things.

But this increased understanding of the nature of the educational implications of basilectal and mesolectal speech came at a stage in the evolution of Caribbean society when the major trends of language policies had already been firmly set. The second condition for the development of a post-creole society (namely, that the social-mobility pressure of the official language must be just so strong as to influence creole speakers, without at the same time eradicating creole) had operated long enough for even basilect creole speakers themselves to accept firmly that the acquisition of Standard English was a socioeconomic sine qua non. Craig (1971), referring to this attitude toward Standard English in Jamaica, quotes Bailey (1964) as follows:

> It is possible to move from one social class to another by changing one's linguistic norm. This is of course due to another factor, the correlation between a good education and acceptable English, which makes it possible to assume that ability to manipulate SJE (Standard Jamaican English) is indicative of a good education, in addition, of course, to birth in a higher caste or class.

The result of this prolonged conditioning, throughout the society, toward a high regard for some form of internationally acceptable English has had the effect of making it impossible at the present time for the society to consider any language policy other than that of having Standard English as the language of literacy and instruction in schools.

It is certain, for example, that any attempt at the present time to use language and reading materials in creole in schools would meet with the same hostility and rejection that Wolfram (1970) comments upon in relation to the recent attempt to use dialect readers in some communities in the United States. It seems to have been the certainty of a result such as the latter that prevented educational authorities in the West Indies from even taking seriously the suggestion, in the UNESCO (1953) study of the role of vernacular languages, that some of the creole English dialects in the West Indies were feasible for use in formal education. Factors of cost and problems of implementation such as those discussed in Bull (1955), and methodological questions such as those reviewed in Engle (1973), for example, entered very little, if at all, into the consideration of whether the official language or the creole or both would be used for literacy in Caribbean post-creole society. The issue was clearly resolvable on the basis of a single fact: the attitudes of basilectal, mesolectal, and standard speakers alike were such that literacy and instruction in the official language was the only policy that the society as a whole would easily accept in its schools.

POSITION WITHIN A TYPOLOGY
OF BILINGUAL EDUCATION

A language policy which requires schools to use a language different from that of the home is necessarily a policy that seems to create a bilingual or bidialectal situation for the child. However, because of the traditional definitions that belong to the terms "language" and "dialect," it could possibly be held incorrect in a technical sense to regard the Caribbean post-creole society with which we are here concerned as being either bilingual or bidialectal. It would certainly be correct, however, to regard that society as *biloquial*, since the official language differs significantly from the normal speech of a majority of the population, no matter how that normal speech is categorized in terms of "language" or "dialect." When the practical manifestations of the *biloquialism* in the society are considered, however, it becomes clear that patterns of language behavior in the society are similar to those of genuinely bilingual societies in some cases and bidialectal societies in others. For example, a basilectal creole speaker in Guyana, Jamaica, or Belize who might say, for example,

> / a waak mi bina waak /
>   ena
>   de
> "What I was doing was walking"

would be mutually unintelligible to a monolingual speaker of internationally accepted English. On the other hand, a mesolectal speaker in the same communities who might say

> / is waak ai woz waakin /
> "Is walk I was walking"

is likely to be intelligible to both the basilectal and the standard speaker, since the mesolectal vocabulary, morphology, and pronunciation would be sufficiently close to English for there to be some communication, although the structure of the sentence remains creole; at the same time the characteristics of the sentence are not so far removed from creole as to render communication with a creole speaker totally impossible. The basilectal and the standard forms of speech in such cases are, for all practical purposes, in a bilingual relationship, while the mesolect, on the other hand, seems more to be in a bidialectal relationship with either extreme of the continuum.

It seems clear then that a language policy which, in situations such as have been just illustrated, requires some form of internationally accepted English as the language of schools is one which is classifiable within a typology of bilingual education, despite whatever distinctions can be drawn between terms such as bilingual, bidialectal, and biloquial. However, it also seems clear that the special characteristics of the post-creole language continuum can be expected to differentiate between post-creole and other language-education situations within that part of the typology that best fits the language policy already referred to. We shall therefore briefly examine the bilingual nature of language education in the post-creole society as a preliminary to discussions of how the special characteristics affect educational procedures that can be considered appropriate.

A simple but effective typology of bilingual education is that suggested in Fishman and Lovas (1970), which may be represented as follows:

> a) Transitional bilingualism, in which the home language of the child is used in school only to the extent necessary to allow the child to adjust to school and learn sufficient of the language of school to permit the latter language to become the medium of education.

b) Monoliterate bilingualism, in which both languages are developed for aural-oral skills, but literacy is aimed at only in the one language that happens to be dominant in the community.

c) Partial bilingualism, in which aural-oral fluency and literacy are developed in the home language only in relation to certain types of subject-matter that have to do with the immediate society and culture while aural-oral fluency and literacy in the school language are developed for a wider range of purposes.

d) Full bilingualism, in which the educational aim is for the child to develop all akills in both languages in all domains.

From what has been said already, it is obvious that within this typology only alternatives (a) and (b) are possible in Caribbean post-creole society, given the general policy of having internationally acceptable English as the language of schools. The implementation of this policy makes it imperative that at least some form of transitional bilingualism be accepted in those communities where a basilectal form of creole survives. It is well known, for example, that in some localities young children coming to school for the first time find difficulty in understanding simple commands like

"Stand!"

because they are accustomed to hearing

/ tanop /
"Stand up!"

or like

"Tell me your name."

because they are more accustomed to hearing

/ a wa dem kaal yu /
Literally: "What do people (they) call you?"

or perhaps a more mesolectal alternative:

/ a wa yu niem /
"What is your name?"

in their home environments. In such localities, it is difficult to see how native schoolteachers can avoid a policy of transitional bilingualism, although such a policy is not overtly prescribed in official guidelines, and there are still some schoolteachers who, because of the traditional attitude of disapproval of creole speech, would deny that they use such speech (even transitionally) in school, until they happen to be confronted with the tape-recorded evidence. In most of the relevant Caribbean countries, situations of this kind where some form of transitional bilingualism is imperative will be found in early education in practically all urban working-class and in all rural schools.

In the absence of a declared official decision on the subject of the type of bilingualism that is aimed at in the educational system, the difference between transitional bilingualism as referred to above and monoliterate bilingualism merely has to do with the period of school life over which the child is allowed to use the home language in school. In the transitional situation, the use of the home language comes to an end relatively early and gives place to the official language. In the monoliterate situation, oral usage of the home language continues indefinitely in school and develops parallel to the development of speech and writing in the official language.

Since the mid-1960s, again without any overt official prescriptions or guidelines, what can be regarded as tendencies toward monoliterate bilingualism seem to be increasing in many parts of the society. As the individual countries began achieving self-government and political independence in the 1960s, the language of the common people became an aspect of the cultural heritage to which a higher regard began to be paid. Especially in the more rapidly developing countries—Guyana, Trinidad, Barbados, Jamaica—there has been an increased use of basilectal and mesolectal language in literary creation, in popular drama and song, in the news and advertising media, on radio and television. National interest in the folk tale, the anancy story, and "dialect" verse has been increasing significantly and is reflected all over the region in competitions (national festivals, independence celebrations, and the like), many of which are specially for schoolchildren. The result is, among the young especially, a more active use of basilectal and mesolectal language and a more receptive attitude toward such language. In the writer's experience, it is now becoming increasingly common throughout the region to find secondary high school students who, as a form of rebellion in many cases, have consciously rejected spoken Standard English, and who on all occasions tend to use some form of the basilect. In the context of this kind of development in the use of creole and creole-influenced language, it seems that monoliterate rather than merely transitional bilingualism will probably become increasingly present in schools.

However, the educational systems in all Caribbean post-creole countries leave a maximum of autonomy to schools to formulate their own curriculum and methodological procedures. Such uniformity as can be found in schools tends to come about merely because the schools work within the same system of examinations and the same type of national administration and organization. The result of this operational freedom is that it is quite possible to find schools near each other in the same locality, and even different teachers in the same school, each having different opinions of and different methodological orientations to the language situation. In some countries (e.g., Guyana, Jamaica), the Ministries of Education have from time to time put out guidelines for teachers, but such guidelines have generally been regarded as suggestions rather than regulations so far as curriculum content and methodologies are concerned. The result of this is that no uniformity is likely to be found in schools in respect of whether the general policy of English as the language of school is being implemented within a framework of transitional or monoliterate bilingualism. The point is that the former framework is often inevitable and the latter is probably tending to become so as well.

Because of the lack of uniformity referred to, there is also a third possible framework for the implementation of the general language policy. This framework possibly precedes the development of the other two in point of time, since it is the traditional one of monolingualism in English, the official language. The latter framework might appear at first sight to be an alternative that lies outside the sphere of bilingual education altogether; however, since the children concerned would, within this alternative, still remain in a virtually bilingual situation, it seems relevant to consider it here. Moreover it is an alternative that merits renewed consideration in view of recent studies such as the St. Lambert Experiment (Lambert and Tucker 1972) in which children were introduced to reading and instruction completely in a second language in the primary school.

Lambert and Tucker found that a monolingual primary school program in a second language had no adverse effects on children, that skills such as reading learned in the second language were transferred to the first language without any handicap, and that the learning of the second language was either improved or not in any way impaired. However, it would seem that one has to be very careful in trying to act upon these findings in situations that are different from the St. Lambert situation. For one thing, the St. Lambert children were middle-class children whose home environments probably supplied the necessary stimulation both for learning the second language and for the transferring of acquired skills to the home language. Second, the two languages (English and French) involved in the St. Lambert situation were both internationally accepted languages and the attitudes of home and school to those languages would have had a relatively favorable effect on how children were influenced in that situation. In the post-creole language situation, on the other hand, the children who would be involved in the monolingual school program are predominantly working-class children with home environments that give no help in the acquisition of the school language; second, these children and their homes and schools are aware of the home language as a stigmatized form of speech, and this awareness would only be strengthened and made more harmful psychologically by the monolingual school program. Unlike the St. Lambert children, therefore, the children in the post-creole situation are likely to be stifled in the development of their home language, while at the same time they are likely to fail to acquire native fluency in the language of school; in their situation, it would not be surprising if they are adversely affected in terms of cognitive development, like the children referred to in Eichorn and Jones (1952) and Anastasi and Cordova (1953); the conclusion from the latter studies was that the restriction of the normal development of the home language in bilingual situations tends to produce a cognitive handicap, although bilingualism under fairer conditions need not itself be a handicap.

It seems clear, then, that Caribbean post-creole society can implement its language policy within three alternative frameworks: transitional and monoliterate bilingualism and English-language monolingualism, with the last alternative acting to reinforce traditional attitudes of stigmatizing and probably stifling creole and creole-influenced language. In whichever of these frameworks the policy is implemented, however, the educational system is faced with the task of teaching English and literacy to creole or creole-influenced speakers; and in order for that task to be carried out with adequate efficiency, due consideration has to be given to certain aspects of the competence of speakers in post-creole speech communities.

LANGUAGE COMPETENCE IN A CONTINUUM SITUATION

All investigators of Caribbean post-creole language situations have remarked on the ability of speakers in those situations to code-shift from one level of the speech continuum to another. The writings of LePage, DeCamp, Cassidy, Bailey, and Stewart already referred to are full of references to this ability. In addition, Craig (1966, 1971) and Cave (1970) among others have discussed specific examples of this ability and have looked at some of its consequences in language education. Code shifting can arise out of the speaker's awareness that varying degrees of "careful" or "casual" speech (Labov 1964, 1966) are or are not appropriate. Some types of code shifting may be characterized in terms of *diglossia* as in Ferguson (1959). The awareness of the speaker that is responsible for code shifting is obviously related to the attitude of high regard for the standard language of the society; this attitude has already been discussed, and the discussion has been supported by citation from Bailey (1964). However, it would be an unrealistic simplification to suggest that the social-mobility value of English, referred to by Bailey, is necessarily present in the speaker's awareness when code shifting occurs. What is obviously present in speakers is an awareness of relationships between contexts and the form of language, as analyzed, for example, in Hymes (1967). Thus, because of the speaker's awareness of his role as narrator to a prestigious audience, the introductory sentences to stories, as in LePage and DeCamp (1960), will tend to be as acrolectal as the speaker can make them until his awareness subsides and he becomes his more habitual self; or a grandmother, probably because she is more aware of contextual roles, will maintain, as in Bailey (1971), a more acrolectal sequence of language than her 14-year-old grandson cares to do; or young children becoming aware of being overheard as in Craig (1966, 1971) and Cave (1970) will make successive modifications to basilectal sentences so as to bring them closer to the acrolect.

The ability to code-shift does not mean that the speaker can necessarily move from basilect to acrolect or vice versa. It simply means that the speaker can move from some given point to another on the continuum; most speakers are unable to command the full range of the continuum from basilect to acrolect. It is now known also that the range of language variation that is referred to as the continuum is not produced merely as a consequence of code shifting in speakers; such variation exists rather as a consequence on the one hand of idiolectal variation between speakers, and on the other hand of intra-idiolectal variation that cannot be explained by code shifting. Labov (1971, 1973) has shown how the latter types of variation may be described by variable rules which would state that a particular form of a variable, if not fully co-varying with an alternative form, is likely to occur more frequently in a given environment; DeCamp (1971a), Bailey (1969, 1970), and Bickerton (1972, 1973), on the other hand, have worked toward developing techniques that would rank speakers on scales according to the variation of their idiolects, and thus show their position on a continuum and the detailed structure of that continuum. It would seem that the two sets of techniques are descriptive devices with different ends in view and that each has its specific purposes, and more will be said about this subsequently. What is important is that they both show that speakers in general, though probably more so in post-creole continuum situations, are continuously operating with language variation, receiving and interpreting it and producing it, sometimes with purposive strategies, and at other times unself-consciously, apparently in the process of automatic linguistic change.

LePage (1972) raises a question concerning the concept of competence that has to be entertained by linguists if that concept is to apply to speakers in the latter kinds of situations; LePage points out that competence in the sense in which he wishes to use the term (which is not the same as Chomsky's sense) consists in having available a code and the knowledge of how and in what contexts to use the code. Bickerton (1972, 1973) raises a similar question and points out that the Chomskyan notion of competence was contingent on the existence of static and unvarying language systems and now needed to be replaced by a different one that would conceive of language as being dynamic and in a state of variation. Bickerton's emphasis differs from that of LePage by focusing on morpho-syntactic form to the exclusion of context. It is an emphasis which is unsatisfying from the viewpoint of an adequate sociolinguistic theory; but at the same time it is one that needs to be tolerated in the interests of adequate morpho-syntactic explanations. It is an emphasis, however, which by its method of scalogram analysis tends to represent the speech community in terms of a catalog of the individual variation of speakers. Labov (1973) is critical of this aspect of Bickerton's proposals. In the latter context Labov pointed out that the Labov variable rule is, unlike Bickerton's proposals, an attempt to approach the description of individual variation from the viewpoint of the speech community as a whole. Whichever of the latter emphases or approaches is accepted, however, it seems clear that the notion of competence, as being the speaker's knowledge of his language, has to be comprehensive enough to include contexts and the continuous production and reception of language variation that has already been referred to.

It has sometimes been suggested, as in Fraser (1973) for example, that data on language variation and on the speaker's abilities in post-creole types of situations can lead to no new inferences about the speaker's underlying knowledge, except insofar as such data can be related to the general phonotactics and syntactics of language conceived as a static system. Investigators of language variation have helped unconsciously to strengthen suggestions such as the latter, since their attempts to explain variation within grammatical formulations usually begin and end at those points of grammars where necessary inferences about the underlying knowledge of the speaker have already been established. Thus, for example, the polylectal grammar suggested in Bickerton (1973), apart from a minor peculiarity, deviates from a standard generative model chiefly at the level of morphophonemics. This question has been discussed in Craig (1975), where it is argued that some types of morpho-syntactic variation that are observable in post-creole speakers cannot be explained in a generative grammar which has a standard phrase-structural base. It is shown (Craig 1975), for example, that creole-influenced speakers, while using invariant lexical labels, seem to be processing simultaneously (in a string of related sentences) references that denote persons by occupation as well as the behavior that constitutes the occupation itself, so that a single lexical label is often being comprehended simultaneously, for example, as a *+human* concrete noun, abstract noun, and verb as the labels /nors (nurse), tiicha (teacher), taipis (typist)/ in the following conversations illustrate:

1) A. ai waan tiicha / sor.
      "I want to be a teacher, Sir."

   B. ai waan nors.
      "I want to be a nurse."

   C. enihou ai di hier . . . di-man-dat
      "Anyhow I heard . . . that man

      . . . se dat wi na-a torn nors//
      . . . say that we'll not turn nurses.

      aid sie no chilron in seven-yu kyanot
      I'd say no children in 7U cannot

      turn nors biko / wat dem gain tek
      turn nurses because—what are they going to take
          (i.e., what are they going to do in)

      torn it?
      (and) turn it?"
      (order to turn nurses?)

2) ai waan taipis
   "I want to be a typist."
   . . . .
   shi lorn tu duu taipis
   "She learned to do typist."
       (i.e., "to do typewriting"
            "to be a typist"   )

It would seem that an adequate grammatical explanation of the speaker's competence in cases such as the latter and in many more general cases such as the treatment of transitivity and the passive voice in creole-influenced language, for example, would need to start at a level of description where grammatical categories are not discrete and there are prelexical operations; as pointed out in Craig (1975), however, the proposals known as generative semantics do not yet seem adequate, as they now stand, to supply the required explanation. The point is, however, that the concept of the speaker's competence that seems necessary relative to post-creole situations has implications for fundamental questions in grammatical theory, and does not merely involve a superficial, morphophonemic departure from standard notions of competence.

So far as language education is concerned, this question of the nature of the speaker's competence is of crucial importance for the formulation of a language-education theory. If the speaker's competence in post-creole situations is conceived as being limited to knowledge of a static language system, or even to two or more static language systems, then the language-education theory that will derive from it will be different from what will derive if that competence is conceived in terms of a facility in the simultaneous processing of undiscrete grammatical categories under invariant lexical labels, and of operating under conditions of continuous variation at several linguistic levels. The language-education theory that derives from the latter conception, relative to the use of the standard language in Caribbean post-creole society, will be discussed subsequently. Before such discussion is undertaken, however, it seems necessary next to consider certain questions relative to the relationship between the form and function of language, since such questions have constantly plagued educational policies in a standard language for nonstandard speakers, especially where language differences are correlated with social-class stratification as they are in Caribbean post-creole society.

SOCIAL CLASS, LANGUAGE FORM, AND LANGUAGE FUNCTION

Since the 1960s particularly, there has been considerable discussion of the relationships among social class, language, and cognitive performance. By far the most important aspect of that discussion is that which emerged out of work such as that of Reissman (1962) in the United States and Bernstein (1961a, b, c; 1962a, b; 1965, 1966) in Britain. The former expanded on the thesis of the limited mental and learning capacities of the "culturally deprived child"; the latter gave an apparently sociolinguistic basis for this thesis by suggesting that the different patterns of socialization in lower and upper social-class environments gave rise respectively to restricted and elaborated linguistic codes; the elaborated code assumedly indicated a "more extensive and qualitatively different order of verbal planning" as compared with the restricted code, which limited its users to a relatively narrow range of mainly concrete and face-to-face linguistic functions. The Bernstein thesis has been generally supported in researches such as those of Lawton (1963, 1964, 1968), Robinson (1965, 1968), Coulthard et al. (1968), and Hawkins (1969). The main additional proposition emerging from these is that low-social-class subjects, influenced by education, sometimes have an elaborated code available for selected purposes; but this does not alter the main thesis that on the whole, the lower social class is habitutated in a mode of language use that puts it at a disadvantage in the performance of certain linguistic and intellectual operations.

Preceding the Bernstein theory and also contemporaneously with it, much work had accumulated to demonstrate that measured intelligence and educational achievement are determined by environment, and are biased toward middle- and upper-class norms. Some of the relevant researches are Nisbet (1953), Ferguson (1954), Floud and Halsey (1957); Vernon (1955, 1965a, b, 1966, 1967); Bruner et al. (1956, 1966); McClelland et al. (1953, 1958, 1961); Douglas (1964); John (1962); Klein (1965); Goodman (1968). In the light of this work, wnat the Bernstein theory appeared to do was to show that language, through its link with socialization, was the main factor in the demonstrated disabilities of the lower social class. This suggested role of language seemed credible as well on the basis of findings such as those in Luria and Judovič (1959), Luria (1961), and Vygotsky (1962), where it is shown that the possession of appropriate language facilitates performance of many types of cognitive tasks that, on the surface, might even appear to be nonverbal.

The preceding viewpoint of lower-social-class linguistic and cognitive disabilities has had a marked influence on educational programs from the 1960s to the present. It is well exemplified in writings such as those of Corbin and Crosby (1965), Crow et al. (1966), and Bereiter et al. (1966) which have exercised a strong influence on early education practices in the United States and elsewhere, and certainly in the post-creole Caribbean. The doctrine and practices of "compensatory education" for the lower-social-class child is evidence of the strength of the influence referred to. In more recent times, however, even Bernstein (e.g., 1972) has come to doubt the validity of the inferences on which compensatory education is based; but at the same time, no careful attempt has been made to revise and reinterpret the findings of earlier work that gave rise to the theory of elaborated and restricted codes.

The main opposition to the suggestion of linguistic and cognitive disabilities in lower-social-class children has come from sociolinguistic work such as that of Labov et al. (1965, 1969) where it is shown that lower-social-class language in natural and uninhibiting circumstances is accompanied by much creativity and efficiency in the treatment of logical relationships and the processing of ideas; it is shown, on the other hand, that the expression of meaning in upper-social-class language can often be accompanied by much vagueness, empty verbosity, and lack of conciseness; it is also shown that the contexts in which upper- and lower-social-class children are studied: classroom types of situations and topics, talking about pictures, obviously upper-class interviewers and testers, and so on, militate against lower-social-class children who cannot help but be uncomfortable and anxious in such contexts, and who are thereby induced to minimize their language production.

In Craig (1971, 1976) and elsewhere, I have argued that the discussion about social class, language, cognitive behavior, and education outlined in the preceding paragraphs is relevant to the English-speaking Caribbean. This relevance exists for the following three reasons. First, as said earlier, the society is socially stratified in a manner not widely dissimilar from that found in the metropolitan countries that have been under discussion; second, the relationship between social stratification and the distribution of standard and nonstandard speech is likewise not widely dissimilar, although there are some differences owing to the creole-language background in the Caribbean; third, and most important, however, basilect creole speech bears, as compared with Standard English, most of the formal characteristics that Bernstein has attributed to restricted codes, and the question ought to be squarely asked as to whether the Bernstein theory is incorrect or whether creole speakers must necessarily suffer a natural linguistic and cognitive disability because of their language.

The likelihood, just referred to, of a natural disability in the creole speaker can be argued against purely on the basis of what we know about natural languages, their structural adequacy, and their flexibility in expanding or changing to meet the demands of their cultural contexts. All investigators of basilect creole agree that it is a full-fledged language system; as such it is capable of meeting a full range of communicative needs and creating or absorbing new vocabulary as all other languages do in order to deal with any incursion of new concepts that need labeling; there is no doubt that basilect creole has been doing this historically, like all other language systems and continues to do it now. Essentially this argument is the one put forward in Labov (1969) and in the 1972 L.S.A. Bulletin to rebut the views of Jensen et al. (1969) and Eysenck (1971) that a cognitive inferiority has been genetically transmitted in the deprived black minority in the United States. But views such as the latter and the theory of restricted and elaborated codes cannot be rebutted on a linguistic basis alone, since they suggest that it is not merely language but the process of socialization of which language is merely a part that is responsible for the suggested disabilities of the lower social class. However, although there is a need for more comparative studies of the linguistic correlates of socialization at different social-class levels, sociolinguistic descriptions such as those of Labov (1969) and Shuy et al. (1967), studies of black American lower-social-class speech events such as those referred to in Kochman (1972), and studies such as those of Abrahams (1977) of the oral cultural traditions of the lower social class in Caribbean post-creole society do not support the view that socialization in post-creole and similar situations promotes any restriction in language capabilities; on the contrary, the strong oral orientation of lower-social-class culture in the relevant communities justifies a hypothesis that natural capabilities in the use of language, except and excluding literacy itself, might be more highly developed at the lower than at the upper social levels.

An illustration that seems to support such a hypothesis is seen, for example in Craig (1974), where a comparison is made of peer-group conversations of upper- and lower-social-class children of the same age. The lower-social-class children were creole or creole-influenced speakers, and it was found that obviously because of the conditioning they had received from their subculture, they showed a greater preoccupation and acquaintance with the world of adults, and with the themes and topics of adult life than their upper-social-class counterparts did; there was no indication that the patterns of their socialization would have accustomed them to a narrower range of experiences and intellectual modes of treatment of experiences than their upper-social-class counterparts were accustomed to; in fact, the exact opposite seemed to be indicated. That the latter should be so is not at all surprising; children of low social class, under stringent socioeconomic circumstances such as those that apply in North America and the Caribbean, varied as these are, would from a very early age be more stimulated than their upper-social counterparts to look after themselves, to be independent, to assume responsibilities of various kinds, to survive through situations of physical and intellectual competition linked to everyday living, and so on; such children at an early age need to be skillful and mature in the use of language, and it seems highly unlikely that their environment could ever determine that they should develop the restricted capabilities that have been assumed to belong to a restricted code.

Yet, on the indications of most studies, the formal characteristics of the language of that kind of child will tend to be those that have been suggested as indicating a restricted code. In the study of peer-group conversations (Craig 1974) referred to earlier, the latter was found to be the case, but at the same time an explanation of the apparent contradiction was provided; it was shown that the suggested formal characteristics of restricted coding (short, simple sentences; concrete as distinct from abstract vocabulary; a greater use of agglutinative rather than other linguistic processes; fewer adjectival modifiers that represent evaluation, and so on) were accompanied by certain other characteristics (a greater volume of words over a given period of time, and a greater reliance on the nonliteral use of concrete vocabulary) which gave to the ostensibly restricted code all the functional possibilities assumed to belong only to elaborated coding. What generally happens is illustrated by the following pairs of sentences taken from Craig (1974) in which the (a) sentences are formulated as they would be in creole or creole-influenced English, while the equivalent (b) sentences are in a form approximating what has been suggested as characterizing an elaborated code:

1. (a) He doesn't do things when you want him to and he tells lies and steals.
   (b) He is *untrustworthy*.

2. (a) Everybody sends their children to school and you don't send yours.
   (b) You *ought to* send your children to school.

3. (a) You hit him and he didn't do you anything.
   (b) You hit him *although* he didn't *interfere* with you.

4. (a) That is the one; he came here yesterday and you gave him ten cents, and now he has come back again.
   (b) That is the one *to whom* you gave ten cents yesterday and who has *now returned*.

5. (a) / it iizi wen yu a klaim di trii / "It is easy when you are climbing the tree."

      (b) Climbing the tree is easy.

6. (i) (a) / . . . wen (taim) rien fall (plenti) /
           " . . . when the rain falls (plenty)"
      (b) . . . in the *rainy season.*

  (ii) (a) / . . . wen di (skuul) bel ring / "when the (school) bell rings"
      (b) . . . at the end of school

Within the (b) sentences in the preceding examples, the specific items which have often been categorized in relevant previous work as evidence of elaborated coding have been italicized; in the kind of analysis that has usually been attempted in the Bernstein and similar studies, speakers of the (b) sentences would be regarded as performing a higher level of linguistic-cognitive operations than speakers of the (a) sentences, even though the two sets of sentences are intended to communicate an equivalent content; in reality what is represented in the two sets of sentences is two different styles of communication, not two different orders of capability in linguistic and cognitive operations. I have suggested (1974, 1975, 1976) that the existence of these contrasting styles of communication has implications for linguistic theory, and that not only social-class but even age-developmental linguistic differences seem capable of some explanation in terms of them.

    The recognition that social-class differences in language and patterns of socialization are accompanied by differences in communication styles rather than differences in cognitive or intellectual capabilities is exceedingly important for a language-education theory in post-creole and similar societies. The latter recognition gives a strong rationale to the conclusion that formal school education is unjustifiably biased toward the standard-language style of communication and the criteria of linguistic achievement that go along with it. In addition also, it is now made clear that the practice of compensatory education often involves an erroneous perception of lower-social-class children. Such children are normally not linguistically or intellectually deprived in any absolute sense; what happens is that the school system, curricula, and educational methodology of the dominant upper-social culture make no use of the natural linguistic and cultural orientation of the lower social class; instead, they aim from the outset of formal education to remold lower-social-class children into replicas of the upper social class.

    In reality, what is suggested here is that educational practices have in general been distorted by the kind of sociocultural relativity that has been the concern of some anthropological studies ever since Malinowsky (1923) and that has been discussed more recently, for example, in Hymes (1961a and b, 1962) and much of Gumperz and Hymes (1972). In terms of such cultural relativity, it would be justifiable to regard both sets of children here being considered as being culturally deprived relative to each other, with each set having certain strengths and weaknesses that the other does not have. It has been suggested (for example, Craig 1974, 1976) that were it not that literacy and the upper-social communication style tend to be acquired and perpetuated together, the lower-social language-culture would probably be more prolific than the upper in creative literature, where the details of personal experience are perceived and expressed in a very direct way, and in close correlation with emotive and imaginative responses; on the other hand, the upper-social language culture, with the communication style that it promotes, is probably more efficiently oriented toward the generalizing of large quantities of basic information and the discarding and suppressing of inconsequential, though interesting, experiential details. In short, if language education in post-creole and similar societies can avoid a discriminatory sociocultural bias, its aims ought to be consistent with the development of the natural attributes to be found in the contrasting language cultures at both ends of the sociocultural scale.

THE THEORY OF STANDARD LANGUAGE
TEACHING IN POST-CREOLE SITUATIONS

The issues discussed in the preceding sections of this paper combine to produce a theory of standard-language teaching in post-creole and similar situations. Relevant to these issues, factors that have to do on the one hand with the attitudes of speakers toward standard English, and on the other with the language-education choices open to the society determine that school programs will vary, as pointed out already, between transitional bilingualism, monoliterate bilingualism, and Standard English monolingualism. Whichever of these alternatives becomes operative in particular school situations, Standard English will have to be taught against a background of basilectal or mesolectal speech in children. In order for Standard English to be taught against such a background, however, note has to be taken of the fact that the competence of the learner generally extends, as has been explained already, over at least a part of the range of the language continuum, and cannot be described in terms of a static language system.

The last-mentioned fact has been shown in Craig (1966, 1971) to have a particular significance for the creole-influenced learner of English. This significance is that the creole-influenced learner of English needs to be considered as having an English repertoire that is stratified as follows:

1. Structures that are common to creole as well as English and that are therefore fully within the production repertoire of the learner.

2. English structures not usually produced in the informal, nonstandard speech of the learner, but which are known to the learner and which are produced under stress in prestige social situations.

3. English structures which the learner would recognize and comprehend if they are used by other speakers (especially in meaningful contexts) but which the learner would be unable to produce.

4. English structures totally unknown to the learner.

The special implications of this stratification of English relative to the creole or nonstandard learner of English have been discussed in Craig (1971, p. 378; 1976) where it is shown that, because of the 2 and 3 strata, learners often fail to perceive new target 4 elements in the teaching situation, unlike learners of a foreign language; consequent upon this, the reinforcement of learning which derives from the learners' satisfaction at mastering a new element, and knowing they have mastered it, is minimal, unlike that accruing to learners of a foreign language; and because of the ease of shifting from Standard English to basilectal or mesolectal speech or vice versa, post-creole and similar learners, again unlike the learners of a foreign language, resist any attempt to restrict their use of language exclusively within the new language elements being taught to them. Because of the obvious similarity of the determining conditions, there is no doubt that the suggestion here made relative to learners in the Caribbean post-creole situation applies as well to learners of language and literacy in the United States such as those considered in Wolfram (1969, 1970), Shuy et al. (1967, 1972), Baratz and Shuy (1969), and Fasold and Shuy (1970).

In the context outlined above, it is not surprising that many creole-influenced and other nonstandard speakers, taught by foreign language methods, continue to show a very low rate of acquiring standard language. Kochman (1969, p. 87) in discussing this point, felt that the "efficiency quotient" of standard-language teaching, i.e., the result that comes from an input of time and effort, is so negligible that the wisdom of at all attempting to teach the standard under conditions such as those relevant here has to be questioned.

Usually, the reasons for such poor results have been ascribed completely to social factors and the unfavorable attitudes of learners; this is done, for example, in Fasold (1968) and Abrahams (1970). There is no doubt that social and attitudinal factors are exceedingly important and obviously play a part, but slow or negligible acquisition of the standard is not restricted to poorly motivated learners or to learners below the age of social awareness (referred to in Labov 1964, p. 91) at which some motivation might develop. The suggestion here made therefore needs to be seriously considered: that the very nature of post-creole and similar speech situations produces strictly linguistic and nonattitudinal factors that derive from the stratification of the learner's repertoire, and that have a bearing on the poor results of standard-language teaching. The suggested stratification also explains the behavior of nonstandard speakers in sentence-repetition tests in some of the work of Labov (1964) and in reading tests such as those of Baratz (1969) and Goodman and Buck (1973). In the last mentioned work it is suggested that rejection of nonstandard speech and not linguistic structure is the barrier that hampers the acquisition of reading. What Goodman and Buck say about rejection is undoubtedly true, but the results of their research throw no light on what happens to the nonstandard reader who encounters patterns that fall exclusively in stratum 4 here suggested rather than in strata 2 or 3; the suggestion that linguistic structure is not a barrier would hold only for such nonstandard readers as possess a stratification that ends at 3 rather than at 4.

The first discussion of the notion of a stratification of the learner's target repertoire (in Craig 1966, and subsequently in Craig 1971) introduced the correlated notion that language in a post-creole or similar society could be considered as consisting of two contrastive polar forms with an "interaction" area between them; the interaction area was described as a region of complex language variation in which learners, aiming at the polar target, reacted creatively and produced various types of mixtures and mutations on their way toward acquiring the target. Craig (1967, 1969) discussed some early indications of learning a second dialect and showed experimentally that the learning of standard language by creole-speaking children proceeded by a process of mixing and mutating of contrastive language forms and not by an instantaneous acquisition and production of the standard at a single point in time. Subsequent to these developments, Selinker (1972) discussed the notion of "interlanguage," and Richards (1972) and Schumann (1974) discussed the relevance of this notion to pidginization and creolization, nonstandard-language situations generally, and language learning; but Selinker, Richards, and Schumann do not seem to have realized that similar notions had already been developed relevant to the Caribbean language situation several years before; only Richards (1972:172), referring surprisingly not to the previously published work but to an undated and unpublished paper, had the awareness which make it possible for him to remark:

> In describing the Jamaican situation, Craig proposes a model with a creole component, an interlanguage, and the standard local variety of English. He uses the interlanguage concept to describe the area between the creole and the standard which is the end point for the majority of young people in Jamaica.

However, work such as that of Selinker, Richards, and Schumann has served to generalize more widely than is done in the earlier formulations the principles which seem to apply in post-creole and similar situations.

The four-way stratification of the learner's target repertoire in post-creole and similar situations and its suggested effects on the further learning of standard language creates the necessity for some special methodology to be devised for approaching the language-education problem in the post-creole society with which we are here concerned. Obviously the appropriate methodology cannot be the strategy of teaching by correction, especially when that strategy is grounded in the attitude seen, for example, in Crow et al. (1966:124); in the latter it is stated that the language-education problems of socially disadvantaged children are similar to the problem of poor listening habits, and arise from the home where parents do not realize that their own speech is incorrect, and where parents are too unconcerned to correct their children's speech; a different attitude underlying this same strategy of teaching by correction is seen in Brooks (1964), however, where an individualization of second-language teaching methodology is recommended to suit each particular learner who already knows some of the standard language that is being aimed at; the drawback of the latter procedure is that, because it involves an intensive one-to-one relationship between the learner and the teacher, it can be applied only on a small scale and cannot be used for the vast majority of children in the entire school system of a society.

On the other hand, the appropriate methodology (for the reasons already discussed) cannot simply be that of teaching a second language to a class of learners at a time, although modified forms of second-language methodology so as to make it appropriate for teaching a second *dialect* rather than *language* can possibly have some effect (subject, of course, to the poor results in comparison with efforts, already commented upon). An awareness of the need for applications of second-language methodology developed in the Caribbean, as pointed out earlier, soon after the revival of creole language studies in the late 1950s. The most important writings that point to such a need apart from those already cited in this chapter are the U.W.I. Faculty of Education Report (1965), Allsopp (1965, 1972a, 1972b), Armstrong (1968), Bailey (1953, 1962, 1963, 1964), Carrington (1968, 1969, 1970, 1969, 1972, 1972a), Cave (1971, 1972), Craig (1964, 1966a, 1971), Cuffie (1964), DeCamp (1972), Figueroa (1962, 1966, 1972), Gray (1963), Grant (1964), Hughes (1966), Jones (1966), Knight et al. (1972), Lawton (1965), Steward (ed. 1962, 1969), Trotman (1973), Tyndall (1965, 1973), and Wilson (1968). All these writings make direct references to language-educational needs in the society with which we are concerned; the individual territories directly referred to include Jamaica, Guyana, Belize, and several of the smaller Eastern Caribbean territories, but the issues discussed are relevant to many other territories in the region that might not have been treated individually. There are, in addition to the latter, a number of other writings which examine specific basilectal or mesolectal linguistic structures and which although not primarily concerned with education present data that have educational implications. Among these are Allsopp (1958b, 1962), Alleyne (1961, 1963), Bailey (1971), Berry (1972), Bickerton (1971, 1971a), Carrington (1967), Cassidy (1967, 1972), Christie (1969), Edwards (1972), Lawton (1963, 1971), LePage (1952, 1955), Reisman (1961, 1965), Solomon (1966, 1972), Spears (1972), Taylor (1945, 1952, etc.), Warner (1967), and Winford (1972).

Most of these writings, except those which are concerned mainly with structural descriptions, imply a recognition of the relevance of a second-language methodology for the teaching of standard language in the post-creole Caribbean; they also imply a recognition of the need for that methodology to be adapted in some way consistent with the fact that the standard language, to most speakers, is in reality neither a foreign language nor a mother tongue but has a dichotomized status; it is this dichotomized status of the standard language, however that is captured by being described in terms of the four-way stratification of the learner's repertoire earlier suggested. In Craig (1976) consideration is given to the kind of teaching program that is dictated by the suggested stratification of the learner's repertoire and by the implications of that stratification. The principles of the required language-education program may be outlined as in the following paragraphs.

1. Relevant to a given set of learners, the structures of English are classified into 1, 2, 3, and 4 categories according to the stratification already suggested.

2. Topics for classroom treatment in languages are selected so as to reflect the interests, maturity, and immediate cultural environment of the learners, but at the same time so as to permit adequate use of the specific 3 and 4 structures that form the goal of teaching at any specific point in time.

3. The learners are led by the teacher to explore the topic fully at first in whatever language the learners possess. The teacher may speak the basilect, the mesolect, or the standard itself, so long as the learners are able to comprehend

easily; and the teacher accepts whatever language the learners choose to produce, including such new language as is infiltrating into the learners' competence. This part of the program is completely oral and may be designated "free talk." The purpose of this part is to promote normal growth and development of the learners in whatever type of language is most natural to them. This part of the program is also expected to develop in the learners an increasing flexibility in the use of the communication style to which they have been most accustomed.

4. The teacher next uses the selected topic, or aspects of it, as the basis of systematic quasi-foreign language practice. Because of the high rate of recognition and comprehension of the standard (through the learners' possession of the language strata 1, 2, and 3) teaching procedures need not make intensive use of imitation drills, but need rather to make more use of substitution and transformation practices, controlled dialogues and dramas, a heavy reliance on simulated situations for forcing learners into a creative use of specific linguistic structures in the 3 and 4 strata, and as much sheer immersion into the standard language as is possible. The aim here is not merely for learners to acquire the morpho-syntax of standard language, but that they should also acquire, for use when they wish, the style of communication that goes with it. This part of the program may be designated "controlled talk," and a persistent effort is made to use only the standard language.

5. For teaching in (4) preceding, linguistic structures are selected so that, relevant to the 1, 2, 3, 4 classification of structures already discussed, the learners are forced to use target structures selected from 3 or 4 (which, for practical purposes, may be combined into a single class).

6. Language learners who are also learning to read use reading materials consisting only of such linguistic structures as they have already learned through the procedures outlined at (4) or as already belonging in any case to the 1 and 2 strata. Language learners who can already read may use materials that are linguistically uncontrolled (and the more such learners can be saturated with reading, the better). The purpose of this set of measures is to ensure that the acquisition of and interest in reading is not hampered by standard-language deficiencies, and that reading and language learning should reinforce each other; once the specific techniques of reading are sufficiently acquired, however, there is no longer any point in linking reading to the formal learning of language structure.

7. For all learners, writing is controlled so that it requires and uses only such linguistic structures as have already been learned through procedures as at (4). By this means writing is closely linked to a productive knowledge of English structure, and the one reinforces the other.

8. The various subject areas of the total school curriculum enter into the selection of topics as explained at (2), so that aspects of these curriculum subject areas get reworked in controlled speech, reading, and writing in the same way as other experiences of the learners.

The difference between what is outlined in the preceding paragraphs and strictly foreign-language teaching procedures lies in what has been termed free talk and the way in which controlled talk, reading, and writing are linked to it and to one another; the different parts of the program have to be planned together and be well integrated. In this way, learners get the kind of stimulating education that ought to be present in a first-language program; but at the same time, linked to this stimulation and arising out of it, there is a concentration on the ordered and sequential teaching of new language elements; the natural resistance of the nonstandard speaker to such teaching is countered by the carry-over of his free-talk interests into standard-language learning, by the constant reinforcement passing from one type of activity to another, and by the encouraged possibility of newly learned language gradually infiltrating into free talk and becoming a part of it. This last mentioned possibility is in fact more than just a possibility, since it has been shown, as already discussed, to be the inevitable way in which language learning proceeds in this situation, i.e., as a gradual mixture, replacement, and mutation of items along the post-creole continuum.

This does not mean that learners can be expected necessarily to lose their original vernacular; rather they can be expected to retain their original vernacular for such occasions as it is needed in their home and peer-group environment, but at the same time they can also be expected to acquire an increasing ability to shift their formal speech into the standard-language end of the continuum until they achieve some acceptable proficiency in standard speech. On the way toward the achievement of such proficiency, many compromises are inevitable: some learners might persist in retaining certain of their original speech characteristics in the most-nearly-standard language they learn to produce; others might achieve good native proficiency in reading and writing the standard language but at the same time persist in their original nonstandard speech even on the most formal occasions; and so on. It would seem that this kind of variation in the response of learners has to be expected in post-creole and similar situations and is a reflection of tendencies that are universal. Such variation, for example, is well known, as has been suggested already, in the nonstandard speech situations in the United States; and Fishman and Luders-Salmon (1972) have shown that German dialect speakers react to the necessity as well as the experience of learning High German in some of the same characteristic ways.

One consequence of the recognition of the inevitability of variations in the response and achievements of learners in these situations is that educators have in turn to recognize the necessity of varying their standard-language aims for different types of learners. This, together with the lack of uniformity, already referred to, in the choice of bilingual alternatives (limited though those alternatives are) means that a considerably diversity in the emphases of English-teaching programs can and ought to be found throughout the Caribbean post-creole region. However, the principles here outlined form the basis of some language-education programs developed in the University of the West Indies in Jamaica and used with teachers in several parts of the region, sometimes at the special request of Ministries of Education.[1] In addition, adapted second-language methods, similar in many respects to those outlined here, have been the basis of language programs in the Eastern Caribbean (see references to Carrington et al.), and Guyana (see references to Cave, Armstrong, Tyndall, Trotman, Wilson).

NOTE

1. The writer's work in this respect was assisted by Grant 690-0664 from the Ford Foundation to the University of the West Indies for Language Education Research, between 1971 and 1976. Preceding this, from 1969 to 1972, the work of the writer was also assisted by a grant from Esso Standard Oil (Jamaica) to the Institute of Education, University of the West Indies, for a study of the language of young Jamaican children.

XIV

Church, State, and Marketplace

in the Spread of Kiswahili:

Comparative Educational Implications

Ali A. Mazrui and Pio Zirimu

The spread of Kiswahili in Eastern and Central Africa has taken place against a background of interaction between church and state and between economics and politics. Missionaries, merchants, and administrators, politicians as well as educators, have all played a part in this drama of linguistic spread.

We propose to draw a sharp distinction in this chapter between Kiswahili for political and administrative purposes on one side, and Kiswahili for economic functions on the other. But the story of the language touches not only politics and economics but also religion. We shall address ourselves to all these three domains of social experience—spiritual considerations, political considerations, and considerations related to the business of earning a living and to the balance of cost and benefit.

We shall further argue that the role of Kiswahili as an economic medium is, in some respects, older than its role as either a political or a religious medium. After all, the language initially spread as a result of expansion of trade in Eastern Africa. We hope to demonstrate that the role of Kiswahili as an economic medium has been the most spontaneous and the most natural of its three historic functions. Because the spread of Kiswahili for economic purposes has been the most spontaneous, it has also depended least on formal education and lessons in schools. Where Kiswahili is needed purely for purposes of trade, marketing, and employment, the language has not fired the imagination of educators. Certainly in Uganda in the last forty years Kiswahili has played a major role in important sectors of the economy, but this role has not persuaded successive Ugandan educational authorities to introduce the language formally in schools on any significant scale. Yet the economic role of Kiswahili has been important in horizontal national integration, fostering contacts across ethnic groups at the grass-roots level. The political role of Kiswahili has, on the other hand, promoted vertical integration, creating links between the elite and the masses.

It is when Kiswahili is needed either for a political function or for religious purposes that educational policymakers become inspired, and governments or missionaries move with despatch toward giving the language a role in the formal structures of training and socialization.

Let us now look more closely at these different dimensions.

PRECOLONIAL TRADE AND THE BIRTH OF KISWAHILI

The language itself goes back at least to the 16th Century and possibly to the 13th. G. S. P. Freeman-Grenville has argued that Kiswahili was probably the ordinary tongue of Kilwa and the rest of the East African coast by the 13th Century.[1] But the bulk of the evidence would seem to demonstrate that the language remained overwhelmingly a coastal phenomenon until two hundred years ago. The beginnings of trade into the interior by the coastal inhabitants have been traced to the last quarter of the 18th Century. It was not until Seyyid aid bin Sultan established full residence in Zanzibar in 1832, and consolidated the el-Bussaid sultanate on the islands, that trade with the interior of the continent developed more substantially. The momentum of this trade was also a momentum of linguistic spread.[2]

There were obstacles to internal trade which in turn served as obstacles to the further spread of Kiswahili. In some parts of Eastern Africa militantly protective communities acquired the reputation of ruthless hostility to foreigners, and were thus able to keep away many an enterprising merchant from the coast. The Masai in both Kenya and Tanganyika acquired this martial reputation, and therefore served as a hindrance to both the expansion of trade and the spread of Kiswahili, especially in Kenya.

Sometimes it was periodic warfare between particular groups that discouraged commercial activity and large-scale economic contacts.

A third factor concerned economic anthropology per se. There were communities in East Africa that were not interested in economic exchange or any kind of entrepreneurship. Resistance to entrepreneurial activities was sometimes primordial, derived substantially from ancestral beliefs and values. There were communities in East Africa that relied on herding their own cattle, and augmenting them through raids rather than trade. There were other communities that were minimally based on subsistance, cultivating their own ground, without feeling the impulse for surplus and exchange. Even the Kikuyu, who showed quite early considerable signs of entrepreneurial skills in their relations with their neighbors before colonization, were for quite a while hostile or uncooperative in their relations with traders from afar. Coastal merchants found Kikuyland inhospitable for either trade bases, marketing, recruitment of porters, or replenishment of supplies. The Kamba, on the other hand, were actively trading far from their own homes in the same period, and for a while appeared to be far more entrepreneurial than the Kikuyu, and among the most enterprising of all the Bantu communities of this part of the continent.

As the 19th Century unfolded, trade expanded. Settlements inhabited by large numbers of people drawn from different linguistic groups increased, and the need for a lingua franca also arose.

> By the eighteen-sixties traders, principally from Pangani, had penetrated the Lake regions from the south and by the eighteen-seventies they had reached Mount Elgon. A route from Taveta to Ngong was also developed. In the last decades of the century, as trade increased, a number of centres of influence were established at Mumia's and at Kitoto's, for example, but . . . these were never comparable in size or in importance to the major settlements in the south.

The slave trade, especially in the second half of the 18th Century and much of the 19th Century, also played a part in the dissemination of Kiswahili. In this part of the continent the Arabs were particularly active in the slave trade, and had their own African agents in different parts of the region. As the slave trade was regarded simply as an additional area of economic activity, it ought to be seen as part of the total impact of economic considerations on the spread of Kiswahili. Those who used Kiswahili for purposes of trade and commerce ranged from the Kamba to the Mijikenda, from the Nyamwezi to newly arrived immigrants from the Persian Gulf. All these are instances of economic spontaneity in relation to linguistic spread. These were the days when the language could claim no special hold on the imagination of educators.

An orthography based on the Arabic script had already come into being among the Arabs and the Mijikenda of the coast. Kiswahili poetry goes back several centuries, and had previously used this orthography. But while many studied these poems as works of art in Eastern Africa, and others as media of religious instruction, actual preoccupation with the teaching of the language as such was still something awaiting fulfillment in the future.

The poets and religious instructors in the mosques played an important role in enriching the language, but at this stage it was still preeminently the merchants and traders who spread the language. The dissemination of the language entailed to some extent dilution as the distance grew between its place of origin and its new locale of economic function. The Swahili culture remained overwhelmingly a phenomenon of the coastal areas, but the Kiswahili language found more purely technical functions in the marketplace. The spread of Kiswahili at this stage must therefore be seen as a phenomenon almost entirely independent of schools and other sttructures of training and education.

CHURCH AND STATE IN LINGUISTIC SPREAD

The entry of Kiswahili into the mainstream of formal education in East Africa on any significant scale did not come until European countries colonized this region, and missionaries infiltrated African societies. The great debate then got under way about media of instruction for Africans, the comparative merits of Kiswahili as against what were called "vernacular languages," and the comparative merits of Kiswahili as against the English language. The debates which began at the beginning of the century are continuing to the present day. The great competition on one side was between English and Kiswahili as lingua franca; and on the other side, it was between Kiswahili and more localized indigenous African languages.

This debate, especially when it touched upon the fundamental issues of educational policy, became quite often an issue between church and state in a colonial situation. It is to the ramification of this grand dialogue, half religious and half political, that we now turn.

A rather simplistic but nevertheless suggestive distinction needs to be made in this regard. This is the distinction between training the mind of the colonized African on the one hand, and converting his soul on the other. Colonial policy makers in the administrative field at their most enlightened viewed education as a medium for the training of the African mind; but the Christian missionaries viewed education as a method of winning the African soul. In reality, there was a good deal of overlap between these two concepts, and in practice, they were rarely sharply differentiated. But it is still true to say that the missionaries in those early days were especially concerned about "spiritual transformation," the elimination of "heathen tendencies," and the spread of gospel itself. The secular colonial policy makers, on the other hand, were beginning to be interested in producing some levels of indigenous manpower for some of the practical tasks of the here and now. The settler policy makers were also interested in legitimizing colonial rule itself to the outside world, by providing education as an instrument of modernization, rather than as an aid for spiritualization.[3]

Kiswahili became involved in this debate between the soul and the mind, between the spiritually oriented missionary activist and the modernizing colonial administrator.

Because Kiswahili developed within an Islamic culture, and borrowed many Arabic words, the language initially carried considerable Islamic associations. Many of the individual loanwords from Arabic were inevitably influenced by these prior associations. And many terms connected with religious experience, ranging from the concept of the hereafter to the idea of praying, carried overtones or undertones derived ultimately from Islamic practice and thought.

In the earliest days of European colonization and evangelism, this association of Kiswahili with Islam was not held against Kiswahili by the Christian missionaries. On the contrary, quite a number felt that since both Islam and Christianity were monotheistic religions drawn from the same Middle Eastern ancestry, and sharing a considerable number of spiritual concepts and values, Kiswahili would serve well for the conversion of indigenous Africans to Christianity precisely because Kiswahili could already cope with the conceptual universe of Islam. By contrast, "vernacular languages" like Luganda or Luo were too saturated with associations and connotations .drawn from an indigenous religious experience much further moved from Christianity than Islam was. The utilization of "vernacular languages" for Christian proselytism carried the risk of conceptual distortion greater than that posed by Islam. In the words of Bishop E. Steere: "Neither there is any way by which we can make ourselves so readily intelligible or by which the Gospel can be preached as soon or so well than by means of the language of Zanzibar."[4]

Bishop Steere, the Reverend Krapf, and Father Sacleux are among the missionaries who not only championed the use of Kiswahili for the Christian gospel but also made substantial contributions toward the systematic study of the language.[5] In Uganda, Bishop A. Mackay records for November 1878:

> Fortunately Swahili is widely understood, and I am pretty much at home in that tongue, while I have many portions of the Old and New Testament in Swahili. I am thus able to read frequently to the king and the whole court [of Buganda] the word of God.[6]

There was also a feeling of using Kiswahili as at least a transitional medium for the gospel, linking European Christian vocabulary with African vernaculars." O'Flaherty records translating tales and suchlike, and teaching many Baganda catechumens the skill and art of translating from Kiswahili into Luganda. Mackay also refers to two services on Sunday at Kaitaba's Buzongora on the Nyanza—one service in Kiswahili and the other in Luganda. Other Christian missionaries also record their use of both Kiswahili and Luganda for devotional purposes. This was certainly the great transitional period, using Kiswahili as a linguistic medium which would gradually modify and influence the religious vocabulary of "vernacular languages" and bridge the conceptual gap between European theological language and the indigenous spiritual universe in Africa.[7]

For a brief while Christianity came to be identified partly with a knowledge of Kiswahili and the ability to read in that language. But as this identification began to get underway, a new swing of opinion was also becoming discernible. Certainly in Uganda, a movement to replace Kiswahili altogether with Luganda became quite strong. The old Swahiliphile views of Mackay were coming under increasing challenge, and the ancient association of Kiswahili with Islam was now regarded as ipso facto dysfunctional to Christianity. In the words of Bishop Tucker in Uganda:

> Mackay ... was very desirous of hastening the time when one language should dominate Central Africa, and that language, he hoped and believed, would be Swahili.... That there should be one language for Central Africa is a consummation devoutly to be wished, but God forbid that it should be Swahili. English? Yes! But Swahili never. The one means the Bible and Protestant Christianity,—the other Mohammedanism ..., sensuality, moral and physical degradation and ruin.... [Swahili is too closely related to Mohammedanism] to be welcome in any mission field in Central Africa.[8]

In fact, Mackay's support for the English language was hedged with a number of reservations, and these reservations were widely shared by other missionaries. As far as the missionaries were concerned, Kiswahili was deficient for spiritual purposes as compared with the "vernaculars." On the other hand, as far as colonial administrators were concerned, Kiswahili was suspect when compared with the English language, rather than with "vernaculars."

Among the missionaries, the so-called "Livingstonian principle" began to hold sway. This was the principle that in the final analysis each African community could be consolidated in its Christianity by the efforts of its own indigenous members and by using the conceptual tools of its own indigenous cultures. Kiswahili became suspect precisely because it had developed into a lingua franca. A lingua franca was "unfitted to reach the innermost thoughts of those undergoing the conversion to Christianity." There was also the argument that a child should in any case be educated initially in its own language—"one of the chief means of preserving whatever is good in native customs, ideas, and ideals, and therefore preserving ... self-respect." And underlying both the educational and the religious factor as perceived by missionaries was the question of how best to handle the business of winning souls.[9]

Westermann's educational theories exerted a considerable influence at this time. He advanced the following thesis:

> Mental life has evolved in each people in an individual shape and proper mode of expression; in this sense we speak of the soul of a people and the most immediate, the most adequate exponent of the soul of a people is its language. By taking away a people's language we cripple or destroy its soul and kill its mental individuality.... Any educational work which does not take into consideration the inseparable unity between African language and African thinking is based on false principle and must lead to the alienation of the individual from his own self, his past, his traditions, and his people.[10]

For a while longer there were still administrators willing to put up strong fight in defense of Kiswahili. From the state's point of view, there were indeed significant advantages from a lingua franca. Administration could be facilitated, regulations would be available in fewer languages, and district officers and commissioners could be moved to different parts of the country without having to learn the local "vernacular" in each case.

In Tanganyika, that is what the Germans, after some hesitation, proceeded to do. They promoted Kiswahili on a vigorous scale because it afforded considerable administrative convenience. The impact of the period of German rule in Tanganyika upon the fortunes of the language in that country was considerable. The fact that education in the German colonies was much more controlled by the state and less dominated by the missionaries than education in the British colonies in those days was itself a factor facilitating the spread of Kiswahili in German-ruled Tanganyika. The position of missionaries there in favor of "vernacular" languages, though humored to some extent, did not prevail. There were times when the missionaries even resolved not to accept subsidies from the German administration for education unless they were assured that education would be given in the "vernacular." But on balance, administrative convenience prevailed over spiritual comfort.

> In areas controlled by Britain ... the policy of leaving the control of education to the missionary orders was more marked than was the case in French colonial territories, for example, or more relevantly, in Tanganyika during the period of German occupation. Indeed, the relative success of the German government in establishing government schools at which future members of the administrative service were educated in Swahili, according to a consistent policy, facilitated the spread of Swahili in Tanganyika as the language of administration and as the lingua franca. [11]

But in British East Africa also there were, for a while, strong administrative voices championing the administrative virtues of a lingua franca like Kiswahili. Particularly noteworthy was Governor W.F. Gowers of Uganda, who submitted an incisive memorandum to the Secretary of State for the Colonies, saying:

> Kiswahili should be adopted as the *Lingua Franca* throughout a considerable portion of this Protectorate for the purposes of native education in elementary schools, and on the lines adopted in Tanganyika.... Kiswahili is the only vernacular language in East Africa which can prove in the long run anything but an educational cul-de-sac, in Uganda, as in Kenya and Tanganyika....

Governor Gowers compared the arguments for Luganda, Kiswahili, and English as educational and administrative media and concluded that in the Bantu-speaking districts of Uganda proper "Kiswahili should be introduced as an extra subject in lieu of English."

In the same memorandum he had earlier argued against the suggestion that English should be utilized as the lingua franca and against the contention that English could as easily be learned by non-Bantu tribes as could a Bantu language. Gowers feared "the dissemination of a barbarous jargon of English," and asserted that "for mutual comprehension between Europeans and Africans ... inter-communication should be in an African vernacular, even if it be not the local tribal dialect (i.e., Kiswahili) than in so-called English."[12]

A year later, in 1928, the colonial Report included reference to measures which had been adopted to introduce Kiswahili "as the dominant language for educational and administrative purposes throughout a considerable area of the Protectorate." The Annual Report of the education department for 1929 also confirmed the vigor with which the new policy was being implemented.

But champions of Kiswahili underestimated the opposition which would soon be released. Kabaka Sir Daudi Chwa, hereditary guardian of the cultural heritage of the Baganda, inevitably felt bound to oppose the introduction of Kiswahili as the official native language of Buganda. The Baganda's opposition, in alliance with the missionaries and their belief in "ultimate conversion through the vernacular," began to organize against the Swahili policies. In spite of the establishment in 1930 of an Interterritorial (Swahili) Language Committee, the Ugandan bishops, both Protestant and Roman Catholic, submitted a long and weighty memorandum to the Colonial Secretary in London through the Governor of Uganda. The burden of the memorandum was to demolish the arguments for Kiswahili as the official native language, and put a strong case for Luganda.

The education department included in its 1931 Annual Report a rebuttal of the bishop's memorandum. Controversy grew. Then a Joint Committee on Closer Union in East Africa was set up, and evidence was taken on language matters, as well as other things.

By a curious destiny, the Baganda were suspicious of Kiswahili partly because they were suspicious of the white settlers of Kenya. The very arguments by administrators in favor of Kiswahili as a lingua franca created in the minds of many Baganda the fear of being incorporated more fully into an East African protectorate encompassing Kenya as well as Uganda. The Baganda began to feel that swahilization of their country would be part of the political process of its Kenyanization. And the power of Kenya resided in the hands of the settlers. When the Baganda gave evidence to the Joint Committee on Closer Union in East Africa, their opposition to Kiswahili formed part of their opposition to closer union in the region. In fact, the only people who gave evidence in London to the Joint Committee were Luganda speakers. The views of the country were not sought on an ethnically representative basis.

It was out of the Joint Committee's report and verdict that Uganda's language policy evolved. Luganda had, at the formal level of utilization for administrative and educational purposes, won against Kiswahili. The Baganda themselves were used extensively as administrators in areas other than their own, and their language was often utilized as a medium of instruction not only in Buganda but in some of the other Bantu languages for a while.

But in terms of broader policy making, the missionaries generally had succeeded in making the "vernacular languages" in both Kenya and Uganda the medium of elementary education except at the Coast. Those administrators in favor of a lingua franca had lost that round.

On the other hand, both the missionaries and the administrators agreed after a while on the importance of using the English language at the higher levels of education and promoting it. The administrators now saw in the English language a more effective medium of "training the African mind" than Kiswahili, just as the missionaries had found "vernacular languages" better instruments of "cultivating the African soul" than Kiswahili. It looked as if Kiswahili was progressively losing both to the more localized languages of the regions and to the English language. The educational system seemed to be bypassing Kiswahili, except along the Coast of Kenya, and sharing instead "local vernaculars" and the imported metropolitan language itself.

The administration's enthusiasm for Kiswahili as a lingua franca waned further when the growth of national consciousness and anticolonialism in East Africa began to benefit from the availability of a grass-roots transethnic language like Kiswahili. Political consciousness was now regarded as a dangerous "postwar epidemic" extending from the Gold Coast to Uganda and Kenya. Educational policy makers in the region moved more decisively against "overpromoting Swahili." In the words of a Ugandan scholar, Tarsis B. Kabwegyere:

> In the light of ... the African awakening in the post-war period, it is not unreasonable to assert that the stopping of Kiswahili was a strategy to minimise intra-African contact. In addition, intensive anglicisation followed and East African peoples remained separated from each other by a language barrier. ... What this shows is that whatever interaction was officially encouraged remained at the top official level and not at the level of the African populations. That the existence of one common language at the level of the masses would have hastened the overthrowal of colonial domination is obvious. The withdrawal of official support for a common African language was meant to keep the post-war "epidemic" from spreading. [13]

Kabwegyere's observations bring us back decisively to the whole problem of national integration. It is to these processes that we now turn.

KISWAHILI AND ECONOMIC INTEGRATION

As Kiswahili was given the political cold shoulder both in up-country Kenya and in Uganda, the language spread in these areas in spite of the educational and language policies which were adopted. A major process involved concerned the role of the language as an economic medium. This is when the language became necessary in the fields of employment, trade, and the whole process of urbanization in contemporary East Africa.

Class formation in the region touched upon this whole competition between Kiswahili and the English language as national media. The English language in the region was still a medium to be acquired at school. The prestige of the imperial language converted it into a resource which was relevant for class formation. As East Africa approached independence, and both colonial policy makers and missionary paternalists sought to facilitate the emergence of an educated elite, the balance of influence and power was beginning to shift significantly in the direction of those who had acquired the cultural symbols and educational skills derived from the imported metropolitan civilization.

Opportunities for the educated and the semieducated were disproportionately located in the urban areas. The relationship between the English language and urbanization was therefore different from the relationship between Kiswahili and urbanization. Rural boys who had been educated enough to speak and write English well moved to the cities in order to capitalize on their new skills. It might even be argued that these boys joined the migration to the urban centers because they were already equipped with the potentially profitable English language.

On the other hand, rural boys who were not so well educated and wanted to go to the cities to look for employment as porters or domestic servants proceeded to acquire some competence in Kiswahili in order to facilitate their own individual urbanization. To some extent this was a reversal of cause and effect. The educated went to the cities because they had already acquired the English language; the less educated acquired Kiswahili because they wanted to move to the cities. The acquisition of European linguistic skills provided motivation for further migration to the urban areas; whereas in the case of the less educated it was the prior desire of moving to the cities which provided the motive for studying Kiswahili in the first place.

This is, of course, an oversimplification of a set of phenomena which were and continue to be sociologically complex. But the distinction being made is still defensible if we think of the educated class as *rural misfits* forced by their very qualifications at times to migrate to the cities; whereas the less educated with a smattering of Kiswahili begin by being *urban misfits*, and improve their Kiswahili as part of the process of adjustment.

The educated are deemed to be rural misfits sometimes by their own families. Many parents go to considerable trouble and sacrifice to get their children through school. Fees have to be paid, books acquired, and in some cases uniforms have to be also purchased. Rural families otherwise deeply deprived nevertheless put their trust in the future, and proceed to make sacrifices for their children's education. The last thing such parents would welcome when the day of graduation comes would be to see their sons still on their own little plot of land, seeking to earn a living in the rural areas in ancestral ways, instead of exploring wider opportunities beyond the green fields. By the time the youngster has been through school, and articulated that ultimate difference of the command of the English language, both orally and in writing, his family's expectations are in the direction of office work in the urban areas, or at any rate something which could not have been done but for the sacrifices of putting a child through school. It is in this sense that the educated in African villages become to some extent rural misfits, and are therefore under sociological pressure to seek white-collar respectability far from home.[14]

But the less educated too sometimes feel the pressure of seeking to improve their lot in the urban areas. Sometimes it might be because there are too many sons to have adequate land for cultivation together in the rural areas; or sometimes because there are too many women who would be otherwise underemployed unless the men go to the cities to earn and supplement the income of the extended family. Many an African husband works in a town, while his wife cultivates their land in the villages. The movement toward those urban centers increased the need for a lingua franca among the diverse groups. Kiswahili, even in parts of East Africa where it was completely ignored by the educational system, found its own momentum of spreading partly under the impact of these processes of urbanization.

Although no adequate comparative work has been done, it seems probable that East African cities by the 1970s are more multilingual, given their relatively small sizes, than West African cities. There are large urban centers in West Africa that are overwhelmingly unilingual. They constitute the points of demographic congregation for ethnic communities that are themselves large, sometimes numbering several million.

But East Africa has, on the one hand, fewer and smaller urban centers and, on the other hand, smaller ethnic communities. The few towns and cities, once communications improve enough, begin to draw from a larger range of linguistic groups than would be the case in, say, the old Eastern Nigeria or Western Nigeria.

In the case of some of the East African cities, communications with the rural areas are still so modest and rudimentary as to retard the full realization of linguistic diversity. But as these communications improve, the tendency will be toward greater multiethnic diversity in East African cities than in comparable urban areas on the west coast of the continent. It may already be true that, once we allow for the difference in size, there is greater ethnic and linguistic diversity in Jinja than in Ibadan, in Mombasa than in Accra. All these are approximations which have not as yet been computed nor have any comparative studies been adequately undertaken. But the combination of smaller linguistic groups in East Africa and fewer towns and cities would seem to indicate a *trend* toward greater linguistic diversity in East African towns than in West African ones.

If such trends are correct, the case for a transethnic medium in East African cities is proportionately stronger. Part of the triumph of Kiswahili in East Africa lies precisely in the fact that the great majority of East African tribes and communities are so small. Only the Baganda, the Kikuyu, and the Luo top the 2 million mark in population, whereas language groups in West Africa are in some cases in terms of 10 or 20 million people. West Africa has therefore been less successful than East Africa in evolving an adequate lingua franca, apart from the English language.

Hausa is to some extent a lingua franca in West Africa, but it suffers from the handicap of being the native language of a group already large enough and powerful enough to be feared by others. The acceptability of Hausa as a lingua franca is therefore retarded precisely because those who speak it as a first language are already so numerous, and in any case because there are rival groups almost comparable in size and with languages and cultures of their own rich enough to be regarded as the true equals of Hausa.

In East Africa the smallness of the group that speaks Kiswahili as a mother tongue improves the chances of the language being accepted by others. In Kenya only about 60,000 people speak Kiswahili as a first language in a population of up to 12 million. This smallness of the number of native speakers, and the smallness of the great majority of other linguistic groups in the country, have interacted especially toward giving Kiswahili an expanding role in the life of the nation.[15]

In Uganda, the privileges of the Baganda during the colonial period, and the fact that they were the largest group in the country, contributed to the spread of Luganda beyond the immediate confines of the kingdom. In spite of this factor, in spite of the increasing indifference of colonial and educational policy makers toward Kiswahili, and in spite of the continuing inertia with regard to language policy during the Obote years of independence, Kiswahili spread fairly widely in Uganda, under the impetus of urbanization and migrant labor. The two latter phenomena of urbanization and migrant labor, though closely related, were not identical. Urbanization included deruralization, the severance of ties among some sectors of the urban populations from their ancestral rural roots. Migrant labor, on the other hand, could at times be merely a case of the rural-urban continuum, a process by which husbands labored in towns while wives cultivated the land, a process by which some maintained continuing spiritual and economic communion with their villagers. Kiswahili received a new lease on life, in the face of the hostilities of the missionaries and the Baganda, as a result of these twin processes of the growth of towns and cities and the mobility of the working force.

The political economy of Kiswahili in Uganda has resulted in its being disproportionately a language of men rather than women. Kiswahili and Luganda competed in the great marketplace of human communication. Fifty-two percent of Uganda men are able to hold a conversation in Kiswahili, but only eighteen percent of the women. Indeed, there are more Ugandan men who can conduct a conversation in Kiswahili than Ugandan men who are competent in Luganda. And yet the percentage of Ugandans who can conduct a conversation in Luganda is higher than that of Kiswahili speakers mainly because Luganda speakers include a high proportion of female native speakers of the language. In general, many more men than women learn a second language, in any case. In the case of both Kiswahili and English in Uganda the number of male speakers of each language is well over twice the number of female speakers. But in the case of Luganda, the number of male speakers, though considerably more than that of female speakers, is nevertheless significantly less than double. This is because of the three languages, only Luganda has large numbers of native female speakers.[16]

The growth of trade unionism in East Africa added a new and important organizational role for Kiswahili independently of educational policy. The wage sector of each East African economy was expanding, and the workers after World War II began to experiment with collective bargaining. In Uganda a significant proportion of the work force came from Kenya, and trade unionism in Uganda was, for a while, partially led and controlled by Kenyan immigrants. The importance of Kiswahili was enhanced in a situation where the labor force was not only multiethnic but also international. So closely associated with workers and the beginnings of proletarian organization was Kiswahili in Uganda that the social prestige of the language among the more aristocratic Baganda declined even further. The language was deemed to be one for "lower classes" of society, and a language of the migrant proletarian. The social prestige which Kiswahili enjoyed in Tanzania, with all the associations of a complex culture and political society, was conspicuously absent in Uganda. Many of those who did speak the language did not speak it well. The Kiswahili of Uganda was indeed basically a language for the workers, functionally specific and nonversatile, and for those reasons more limited in scope. Nevertheless, the need for the language as a medium of organizing the workers in these early stages of the growth of trade unionism must be counted as one of the major aspects of the political economy of Kiswahili.

These new functions of Kiswahili in East African society were integrative at the horizontal level. We define horizontal integration simply in terms of social communication and interaction across geographical and ethnic divisions of the society as a whole. We define vertical integration as a process of interaction between different strata of the society, especially between the elite and masses. To the extent that Kiswahili served as the main language of trade unionism and organized labor, and facilitated social communication between wrokers and peasants from different geographical areas and ethnic groups, the language was performing horizontally integrative functions. To the extent to which these functions were expanding the wage sector of the economy, facilitating the circulation of money across the country as a whole, promoting a consciousness of a national economy, and defining the boundaries of the national marketplace of goods and labor, Kiswahili was involved in the critical process of economic integration within each of the East African countries.

In Kenya, even the shift of the capital from Mombasa to Nairobi later enhanced Kiswahili's potential as a mechanism for horizontal economic integration. At first the decision to transfer the capital seemed to be a blow against the spread of Kiswahili. After all, if Mombasa was no longer the hub of national life in the country, the impact of Mombasa's language on the rest of the society seemed to be minimal.

> By the beginning of the century . . . the administrative focus of the East African Protectorate had moved away from the coastal area, Nairobi replacing Mombasa as the headquarters of the Uganda railway in July 1899. In 1907, the capital of the Protectorate was moved from Mombasa to Nairobi and there is no doubt this transfer diminished the influence on Kenya's development of the coastal Swahili culture that became so important in Tanzania's history.[17]

While it may be true that the spread of the Kiswahili *culture* was adversely affected by the shift from Mombasa to Nairobi, it is by no means certain that the spread of the Kiswahili *language* suffered with this transfer. On the contrary, it is arguable that the relative centrality of Nairobi increased the spread of the lingua franca on a national level. What happened to many non-Baganda workers in Kampala did not happen to many non-Kikuyu workers in Nairobi. Because the Baganda under the colonial administration had been a privileged group, and were allowed to retain considerable influence and prestige, their language in turn commanded derivative prestige, and many of the workers who came into the capital of Uganda felt they had to learn Luganda. Indeed, Kiganda culture favored the linguistic and cultural assimilation of newcomers. In one or two generations many workers who were descended from non-Baganda became, to all intents and purposes, native Luganda speakers and were absorbed into the body politic of Buganda.

The Kikuyu in colonial Kenya, on the other hand, though comparable to the Baganda in size and proximity to the capital, were not a privileged group. On the contrary, they were often the most humiliated and exploited of all groups because of their nearness to the white settlers of Kenya. The Kikuyu also performed some of the most menial tasks even in towns very far from their own areas. These tasks ranged from sweeping the streets of Kisumu to emptying latrine buckets in Mombasa.

For the non-Kikuyu workers pouring into Nairobi there was relatively little incentive to perfect their familiarity with the Kikuyu language. Many non-Kikuyu workers did indeed learn some Kikuyu, but not for reasons of improving their social status in Nairobi or enhancing their chances of a good job. Kiswahili in Nairobi had an easier time in the competition with the Kikuyu language than it had in the competition with Luganda in Kampala. By the time of independence, very few Kikuyu politicians addressing public audiences in Nairobi regarded it as sensible to use the Kikuyu language. This was in marked contrast to Baganda politicians addressing public meetings in Kampala, who normally used Luganda in preference to both Kiswahili and English.

Mombasa itself continued to be a Swahili metropolis, continuing to grow in size and attracting an expanding noncoastal population. Though second in size to Nairobi by the time of independence, Mombasa was nevertheless large enough to be bigger than either the capital of Tanzania or Uganda. Nairobi was linguistically pluralistic, with a widespread use of the Kikuyu language and the English language. But on balance, Kiswahili had been gaining ground at least as the lingua franca for horizontal integration, and increasingly as a medium also for vertical integration in select areas of social change.

What remains remarkable is the extent to which these new functions of the language in Kenya as a whole evolved in spite of the relative indifference of educational policy makers, and quite often in spite of their actual hostility to Kiswahili. What all this reveals once again is how economic necessity for a particular language in a given sociological situation could generate the spontaneous spread of the language, notwithstanding the formal educational system. The marketplace as an arena of linguistic spread can certainly be decisively independent of the classroom.

KISWAHILI AND POLITICAL INTEGRATION

But when a language is needed for vertical integration, especially in the sense of facilitating social communication between the rulers and ruled, the educational system becomes once again a favored medium for dissemination. In Tanganyika under German rule Kiswahili had among its earliest functions that of vertical integration. The Germans had opted for the language as a medium of potential administrative convenience, and proceeded in the training of second- and third-level indigenous administrators. The bureaucratic infrastructure was modified to suit this linguistic policy. A certain cultural and linguistic intolerance characterized the implementation of the swahilization of Tanganyika under the Germans, but the policy was substantially effective nevertheless and has had long-term consequences for independent Tanzania. Certainly the swahilization of mainland Tanzania would have been far less complete today without the purposeful exercise in vertical integration pursued by German policy makers before World War I.

In Kenya and Uganda for at least the first quarter of this century, there was enough interest in using Kiswahili as a medium of communication between the rulers and ruled to give the language some role in the educational system.

In many schools it at least had the status of one of the subjects taught. In some schools, it was even used as a medium of instruction at the lower levels.

Administrators coming from England were also often required, in those days, to learn the language.

Article 19 of the Regulations of the Employment of Officers, dated Aug. 1, 1903, made Kiswahili an obligatory language. Officers appointed after that date were expected to have a fair knowledge of Kiswahili within their first year of arrival in the Uganda Protectorate, and their promotion depended in part on this linguistic skill. Certain financial incentives and bonuses were paid to administrative officers on passing the lower and higher standard examinations in Kiswahili. In Buganda the regulation was altered in 1914, replacing Kiswahili with Luganda, but Kiswahili retained for a while a residual administrative role in the face of mounting disparagement by Luganda speakers and Christian missionaries. As the language ceased to be regarded as indispensable for vertical integration between the rulers and ruled, its role in the educational system also shrank.

It was not until the eve of independence that there was once again a sense of need for the language, for purposes of vertical integration. The Uganda People's Congress especially, as a party with a nationwide perspective, and led primarily by non-Luganda speakers, showed an early awareness of the need for a grass-roots' language of politics. At their Annual Conference on attainment of independence the U.P.C. passed a resolution urging that Kiswahili should be taught in Uganda schools. And yet, partly because the first government was a coalition between the U.P.C. and Kabaka Yekka, there was considerable caution with regard to the implementation of this recommendation. Milton Obote's government dragged its feet, initially for reasons of amity with its Luganda-speaking partners in the first government after independence, and later for reasons more difficult to comprehend.

To a question from H. M. Luande in Parliament asking for the inclusion of Kiswahili as a language which an applicant for citizenship might offer in order to qualify, the Permanent Secretary to the Office of the Prime Minister, Alex Ojera, replied:

> Apart from the English language, which is provided in the Constitution as the official language, the only language so far prescribed under Section 22 of the Uganda Citizenship Order Number 63 of 1962 are mother tongues spoken by the peoples of Uganda. Swahili though spoken widely in East Africa and elsewhere is not a mother tongue in Uganda. Government does not intend prescribing Swahili as a language qualification for citizenship until such time as

Swahili is understood and used more extensively than it is today by the peoples of Uganda.

Mr. Luande moved a supplementary question, reminding the Minister of the resolution of the Annual Conference of the U.P.C. concerning the teaching of Kiswahili in Uganda schools. All that Mr. Ojera would say was:

> The question of teaching Swahili in schools is not within my portfolio but belongs to my Friend, the Minister of Education. Whatever the U.P.C. has passed will always be taken very seriously by the U.P.C./Kabaka Yekka Government.[18]

Dr. J. Luyimbazi-Zake, who came to control the Ministry of Education until the overthrow of Obote's regime in January 1971, was later to dismiss Kiswahili as being as foreign to Uganda as Gujerati. Dr. Zake was himself a native speaker of Luganda, though he was also fluent in Kiswahili. He was a member of the Uganda People's Congress, and constituted, it would seem, one of the factors which led to the linguistic drift of the Obote years in Uganda, in spite of that resolution by the Annual Conference of the U.P.C. to move toward giving Kiswahili full status in the Ugandan educational system.

The man who had answered Mr. Luande's questions in Parliament in 1963, Alex Ojera, later became Minister of Information under Obote. He and President Obote said privately to one of the authors of this chapter in 1969 that the Uganda government was on the verge of introducing Kiswahili at least on the radio. Six languages were confirmed as broadcasting languages in Uganda after independence. In February 1963, A. Lobidra asked the following question in Parliament:

> As most of the people in Uganda do understand some sort of Swahili and in view of the fact that Uganda cannot afford giving every tribe a programme on Radio Uganda, would the Government examine the possibility of including up-country Swahili for Local News Broadcasts?

The Minister of Information, Broadcasting and Tourism, A. A. Nekyon, did not agree that most people in Uganda understood some sort of Kiswahili.

> We have already commenced broadcasts in six languages and I am quite convinced that Swahili is not one of the basic languages which is understood widely in the country. . . . We are already broadcasting in so many languages that I do not think this is a really sound reason for adding to that number.[19]

By the time Mr. Ojera and Dr. Obote were suggesting privately in 1969 that Kiswahili would be introduced on Radio Uganda, the recognized broadcasting languages were already fourteen. The majority of these were understood by far fewer people in the country than Kiswahili was.

1969 was also the year of *The Common Man's Charter* in Uganda, and the Obote strategy of the "Move to the Left." A new sensitivity to the needs of the grass-roots' level of politics emerged under the impact of the move to the left. The national service scheme in Uganda envisaged the teaching of Kiswahili, among other tasks. And Obote's electoral reforms would in addition have provided a further case for the rapid introduction of Kiswahili into the country's political system. Document No. 5 of the Move to the Left envisaged a situation whereby each member of Parliament would stand in four constituencies, one in the north, one in the south, one in the west, and one in the east of the country. That meant that each parliamentary candidate would need to woo three-quarters of his electoral support from outside his own linguistic area. He would need to campaign among peasants who did not understand his language, and were equally ignorant of English. He would need a new grass-roots medium for this nationwide electioneering. A Muganda campaigning in Lango could not make much progress with his native Luganda. Each parliamentary candidate would therefore either have to learn three African languages in addition to his own if he was to communicate effectively in all his four constituencies, or the nation as a whole would have to push systematically one lingua franca for the conduct of politics at the grass-roots' level. The most serious candidate for such a role in the Ugandan situation seemed to be Kiswahili. The English language might have continued to be important for communication among parliamentarians themselves once they were elected, and were engaged in deliberations in Parliament, but Kiswahili would have been the connecting link between these parliamentarians on one side and the linguistically diverse constituents which each had to reach. The Ugandan Parliament under such a scheme would, after a while, have had to become bilingual, with simultaneous translation between English and Kiswahili, very much as the colonial legislature of Tanganyika on the eve of independence was before Parliament in independent Tanzania moved the whole way toward Kiswahili.

Under Document No. 5 by A. Milton Obote, Kiswahili for Uganda seemed destined for a new and critical role in vertical integration. By the time Obote gave his first address as Chancellor of the newly autonomous Makerere University, Kampala, he was in a position to enunciate new directions in linguistic education in the years which would follow. At long last Governor Gowers' dream about the promotion of Kiswahili in the Ugandan educational system seemed to be on the verge of fulfillment. And those delegates who had attended that historic Annual Conference of the Uganda People's Congress in 1962, and joined in voting the resolution for the introduction of Kiswahili into Ugandan schools, might have sensed at long last the nearness of implementation. The dictates of vertical integration, as the elite sought to reach the masses, had once again proved to have more direct educational consequences than the processes of horizontal integration in the marketplace.

But the Obote regime did not last long enough to fulfill its long-delayed linguistic promises. On Jan. 25, 1971, voices on Radio Uganda—ill at ease with the

English language—announced a military take-over. A new phase in the history of Kiswahili in Uganda seemed to have started.

KISWAHILI AND CULTURAL NATIONALISM

By a strange destiny, the soldiers had in fact been the residual official users of Kiswahili in Uganda. The language had, to all intents and purposes, become the language of command in the police and the armed forces. By the time of independence many Ugandan soldiers and policemen had developed a special possessiveness about Kiswahili. The psychological reasons for the popularity of Kiswahili among the soldiers are complex, and certainly include a resentment of Luganda speakers who had been politically privileged for so long during the colonial period. The armed forces and the police had been recruiting overwhelmingly from non-Ganda areas, partly because these professions under the Baganda had declined in prestige as a result of the other advantages that the Baganda enjoyed, and partly because Britain as the imperial power preferred to recruit from some of the so-called "martial tribes" in the north of the country.

By 1966, when Buganda was defeated in a military confrontation with the central government, and the Baganda were for a while humiliated, it was not uncommon for soldiers from other communities to test some of their captives linguistically in order to determine their competence in Kiswahili. More often than not, the Kiswahili tests as applied to local "suspects" arrested by the armed forces were simply intended to humiliate Luganda speakers even further. But even after making allowances for the deep emotions and tensions which the Buganda question had created in the Uganda population, there is no doubt that Kiswahili acquired a special status of loyalty among the soldiers of Uganda.

Underlying the soldiers' response was the whole phenomenon of cultural nationalism at all its four levels. These levels are ethnic (in the sense of tribal identification), racial (in the sense of identification with the heritage of black people), territorial (in the sense of identification either with the new territorial state or with a large entity within the African continent), and fourth, class (in the sense of identifying with the less educated, or the peasants, or the workers, or the common man).

The preference of the Uganda soldiers for Kiswahili as against Luganda was partly a case of ethnic cultural nationalism, partially inverted. The social prestige of Luganda, and the political influence of the Baganda during the colonial period, had resulted in a certain degree of cultural defensiveness on the part of the remaining communities. To the extent that the armed forces had recruited disproportionately from these communities, Kiswahili became a symbol of asserting their own cultural autonomy in opposition to the Baganda. This was a curious response, since Kiswahili was in fact not the mother tongue of any of the groups involved. The adoption of Kiswahili for purposes of asserting parity with the Baganda was therefore a partially inverted case of ethnic nationalism among the soldiers. They loved Kiswahili partly because it was not Luganda. They identified with it partly because it was opposed by the Baganda. The linguistic possessiveness of the Ugandan soldiers with regard to Kiswahili was therefore very much connected with one of the most central issues in Uganda's political history—the status of Buganda in national affairs.

But for as long as the educational policy of Uganda was not decided by the soldiers, and for as long as the soldiers had no say in determining the languages used for broadcasting, this semi-inverted linguistic possessiveness in the armed forces did not result in concrete policies.

Another level of cultural nationalism aroused by Kiswahili is the racial one. This, of course, goes beyond Ugandan soldiers. It encompasses the whole movement to resurrect aspects of the cultural heritage of black people in different parts of the world, and forge a new status of dignity in global cultural arrangements. Kiswahili commands this kind of symbolic attachment not only among black Africans, but also among sections of black Americans. The language has been taught in vastly differing parts of the black world, and has been regarded as a major medium for the black cultural renaissance.

In Tanzania, the language has also been promoted in part for these reasons of cultural self-reliance and self-development. One governmental area after another has been pronounced as an area in which only Kiswahili is to be used. There has definitely been a decline in the use of the English language in Tanzania, and the beginnings of a decline in general competence in that language. Law courts have increasingly used Kiswahili, and specialist committees have been appointed to work out and develop an adequate legal vocabulary. Talks in scientific education on the radio have moved in the direction of disseminating scientific knowledge through Kiswahili. The National Assembly has become unilingual, using only Kiswahili, and many ministries are changing in a similar direction. President Julius Nyerere himself has set an impressive example of competence and versatility in that language, ranging from dazzling oratory to the tough self-imposed assignments of translating Shakespeare's *Julius Caesar* and *Merchant of Venice*.

When Kiswahili is indeed recognized as an important expression of cultural nationalism in the racial sense, there are speedy educational consequences. Certainly the rise of the black attachment to Kiswahili in the United States soon resulted in the provision of classes in one Black Studies program after another, including programs below university level. And as the militancy of black cultural nationalism in the United States declines in the 1970s, the presence of Kiswahili in the educational system of black America will also decline. In other words, in a situation like that of black America, there is an easy correlation between cultural nationalism in the racial domain on one side, and the introduction of a cultural symbol like Kiswahili into schools on the other.

Further, there is cultural nationalism at the territorial level, in the sense of either consolidating the identity of the particular country or in the sense of identifying with one's neighbors in a given geographical region. Again, Tanzania has utilized Kiswahili not only as an expression of the blackness of the Tanzanian people but also as an expression of their being Tanzanian. Kiswahili in this case becomes part of Tanzania's patriotism proper, and is called upon to serve functions which would give Tanzania's national identity true expression and fulfillment.

In a situation of territorial cultural nationalism, a symbol like Kiswahili once again receives ready educational translation. The schools rise to the occasion, minimally teaching it as one of the subjects at school, maximally adopting it as a medium of instruction throughout the educational system. In Tanzania, the educational system prior to the university has been progressively swahilized. English still plays a considerable role in Tanzania's education, but there is little doubt about its decline since independence.

The rising role of Kiswahili in Tanzania has inevitably resulted in a declining role for expatriate teachers. The utilization of technical assistance in the educational system of an African country usually presupposes the continuing acceptance by that country of a major metropolitan language. To the extent that Kenya, for example, uses the English language in much of its education, or to the extent to which Senegal uses the French language, the capacity of Kenya and Senegal to absorb technical assistance in the educational system from Britain or France respectively is augmented. The utilization of the American Peace Corps in schools in Africa inevitably depended on the ability of the host countries to utilize people trained either to teach in English, or in the case of those Americans who found their way to French-speaking Africa, equipped with a special competence in the French language.

In contrast, as Tanzania has continued to swahilize its educational system, it has increased its own burden of producing its own teachers. Linguistic self-reliance implies educational self-reliance. The swahilization of the educational system reduces not only the role of British and American teachers, but also of Swedish, Hungarian, and other European teachers who could more easily be expected to teach in English among Tanzanian children than to teach in Kiswahili.

There are cases of a few expatriate teachers arriving in Tanzania equipped to participate in Kiswahili in the educational system. These include Chinese teachers for physical training. But, on the whole, the era of foreign technical assistance in the educational system of Tanzania is coming to an end. Territorial cultural nationalism has been mobilized to serve the purposes of the Arusha Declaration as an assertion of self-reliance.

Territorial cultural nationalism, with regard to Kiswahili, sometimes goes beyond the immediate country concerned. This is when Kiswahili becomes the most important cultural symbol of pan-East Africanism. The desire by East Africans to find areas of solidarity sometimes seeks stimulation from race, sometimes from the consequences of history which created shared institutions linking Kenya, Uganda, and Tanzania, and sometimes from culture. Kiswahili has particularly strong credentials in this last domain of cultural solidarity. When, at long last, Uganda under military rule adopted Kiswahili as the national language,

General Amin emphasized the value of the language from a pan-African point of view. Speaking to the nation, President Idi Amin said:

> On the advice of the entire people of Uganda, it has been decided that the National Language shall be Kiswahili. As you all know, Kiswahili is the *lingua franca* of East and Central Africa, and it is a unifying factor in our quest for total unity in Africa.[20]

Some Ugandans have been aware of the potentialities of Kiswahili not only for communication among Kenya, Uganda, and Tanzania, but also for communication with countries like Zaire and Rwanda, whose own official language is French. The adoption by different African countries of either French or English, depending on their own colonizer, has often created great barriers in communication. Among at least some sections of the population of Eastern Africa, this imperial cleavage created by the dichotomy between English and French has been mitigated by the availability of Kiswahili. General Idi Amin himself, though he speaks not a single word of French, has over the years enjoyed many a conversation with Zairean dignitaries in Kiswahili.

But, by the time Uganda adopted Kiswahili as a national language, the country was already short of teachers in other fields as a result of Amin's expulsion of the Asians and his fluctuating harassment of the British. The adoption of Kiswahili by Uganda as a national language in October 1973 required that the language be speedily introduced into schools, and after a while made to bear much of the educational system. But the exodus of Asian and other expatriate teachers made the Ministry of Education circumspect about any linguistic experiment at the time. Further, the fact that relations between Uganda and Tanzania had been uneasy since Amin's military coup, and a number of Tanzanians had been killed in Uganda over the period, made it very difficult for Uganda to recruit Tanzanian teachers to teach Kiswahili in Ugandan schools. The capacity of Uganda to recruit from Kenya had also become circumscribed by the security situation in Uganda. On balance, therefore, the adoption of Kiswahili as a national language of Uganda, though necessarily carrying educational implications, did not immediately have educational consequences. General Idi Amin saw the necessity of at least a temporary continuation of the previous linguistic policies in education. As he said in his address to the nation:

> It must be emphasized that English shall for the time being remain the official language until Kiswahili is developed to a degree that warrants national usage. Other foreign languages shall continue to be taught in our schools. Vernacular languages shall continue to be developed.[21]

What the military take-over has for the time being fulfilled is indeed the utilization of Kiswahili on the radio and television in Uganda, and the beginnings of a more respectful atmosphere for the language even among the linguistically proud Baganda.

As for cultural nationalism in relation to class, Kiswahili is clearly much more of a language of the common man than English. Certainly its appeal to some like General Idi Amin, himself only semieducated and drawn from the womb of the countryside, was partly connected with the proletarian associations of the status of Kiswahili in Uganda.

In Tanzania, the fact that the language was widespread and spoken by many more people in the country than English increased its utility as a medium for socialistic egalitarianism. The recruitment of party officials, the appointment of administrators, the election of parliamentarians, and the appointment of ministers no longer require in Tanzania a competence in the English language. Political and elite recruitment in Tanzania has therefore been substantially democratized precisely because Kiswahili has permitted the utilization of a larger pool of talent than might have been available if the English language had remained a sine qua non of political office.

The educational implications of the class factor in cultural nationalism are less straightforward than in either territorial or racial nationalism. The fact that Kiswahili was a language of the masses can have no impact on the educational system unless either the policy makers are egalitarian or socialistic or the policy makers are themselves semieducated and immediately drawn from less privileged strata of society.

In Tanzania, we have a president who is very highly educated himself, Julius Nyerere, but who is strongly, almost fanatically, egalitarian. In this kind of situation, the argument that Kiswahili is a language of the masses would itself be an important consideration for giving the language extra status in the educational system.

In Uganda, on the other hand, the President is someone of far more modest educational qualifications. Idi Amin is more nearly a peasant than Julius Nyerere, but Julius Nyerere is more egalitarian than Idi Amin. In the Ugandan case, the man at the top would not necessarily favor Kiswahili for the purpose of creating an egalitarian society; but he might favor Kiswahili for the purpose of changing the distribution of power in his society and giving greater advantage to those who were once despised. This position, though superficially egalitarian, might be perfectly compatible with simply turning the previous class structure upside down, so that the privileged of yesterday become the underprivileged of today and vice versa. Amin's policies are not precisely that, but they are in the direction of status reversal rather than egalitarianism. Nyerere's position, on the other hand, is more clearly egalitarian. Both positions carry great potentialities for the promotion of Kiswahili in those two countries as a language with a greater role in the affairs of the nation, and a clear position in the schools. Tanzania has managed to implement those policies; Uganda has at best only just started. The future of Kiswahili in the two countries should provide fascinating comparative insights into the interaction between language, ethnicity, race, territorial affinity, and social stratification.

CONCLUSION

We have seen in this economic and sociological history of Kiswahili the relationship between different media of linguistic spread and responses in the educational system. In the 20th Century, at any rate, the early phases of the spread of Kiswahili included a tense debate between church and state, especially since the missionaries controlled a substantial part of the educational structure of the colonies. The missionaries among themselves came to argue about the relative merits of Kiswahili as opposed to "vernacular languages" for the purposes of education and the conversion of the African soul. The colonial administrators argued among themselves on the merits of Kiswahili as against the English language for the promotion of administrative convenience and the training of the African mind. The administrators and the missionaries in turn engaged in dialogue on matters which at times seemed no more than little debates about exotic tongues, but matters which nevertheless resulted in long-term sociological and economic consequences for East Africa.

We have also sought to demonstrate that only certain forms of linguistic spread resulted in educational decisions. The role of Kiswahili as an economic medium in the marketplace, ranging from its utilization for trade purposes before colonialism to its adoption as a language of labor unionism after colonialism, all had relatively little impact on the chances of the language in formal education. To some extent, both in Uganda and in the hinterland of Kenya outside the Coast, Kiswahili later came to spread in spite of educational decision makers rather than because of them.

But where a language is needed for vertical integration, facilitating communication between the rulers and the ruled, educational implications become more immediate. Along the Coast of Kenya, and in much of Tanzania, considerations of vertical integration gave Kiswahili an early role in the educational system of those areas.[22]

After independence, vertical integration in Uganda became a new issue, and steps have started rather hesitantly, going back to the Obote years and partially implemented under General Amin, in the direction of a greater recognition for Kiswahili as a language for political integration.

On July 4, 1974, the Governing Council of the Kenya African National Union unanimously also resolved to make Kiswahili the official and national language of Kenya, with immediate effect. President Kenyatta then decreed that the National Assembly should switch to Kiswahili, on an experimental basis, until the clause of the Constitution which made English the legislative language was changed and until the Mansard recording facilities were modified, and other technical problems of transition solved.[23]

The Kenya government was at last formally recognizing Kiswahili as a potentially vital medium for vertical, as well as horizontal, integration. The fact that the adoption of Kiswahili as official language was done on the eve of a general election raised questions about the likely composition of the next parliament. Would there be members fluent in Kiswahili but without any competence in the English language? Would other candidates previously eligible on the strength of their English be now disqualified because they lacked Kiswahili? Would the composition of the National Assembly be significantly altered by this dramatic change in the linguistic qualifications of parliamentary candidates?

In the Kenyan situation there was a case for a transitional bilingual legislature, using both English and Kiswahili at least until the elections of 1979. Members could speak either English or Kiswahili as they wished. The possibility of installing facilities for simultaneous translation could also have been considered for this five-year period before a final decision was made.

The case for such a bilingual transition in the Kenyan situation lay precisely in the educational lag regarding the language. Kiswahili was demoted even further in the educational system following the declaration of the Mau Mau state of emergency in 1952. This was done in order to reduce even more political contacts between Africans across tribal lines. This twenty-year educational lag was harmful to the quality of the language spoken upcountry, and could in turn adversely affect the quality of debating in the National Assembly from 1974 onward.

But even the adverse effect on legislative debating would perhaps be worth it if it provided further momentum for the rapid introduction of Kiswahili in schools on an extended scale from the first year of elementary education. Opponents of Kiswahili were apt to invoke the excuse of shortage of teachers of Kiswahili before any attempts to find out what teachers might be available were in fact undertaken. There might be many more teachers of Kiswahili in both Kenya and Tanzania than might at first appear possible. Nor would such a movement of language teachers between Kenya and Tanzania be hampered by the sort of problems of security affecting aspects of Uganda's life.

But whatever the final outcome of the fluctuating policies of the Kenya government regarding Kiswahili, the status of the language in the educational system is now in the process of being raised. Once again considerations of political integration are revealing their influence on educational policy making. Bilingual education in Kenya is still in a state of flux, and the government has not yet grappled with the varied implications of such a switch in language policy. But a new phase in the history of Kiswahili in Kenya might well have started.

As Kiswahili is called upon to serve new roles, it has to augment its vocabulary! Much of the new political vocabulary has borrowed either from Bantu sources (like *Bunge* for parliament) or from the traditional foreign source of Arabic (like *Raisi* for president). But the English language is also becoming a major source of loanwords, especially in Kenya, Tanzania, and Uganda.

The impact of the *French* language on Kiswahili might need to be examined in Burundi, Zaire, and Rwanda. Rwanda and Burundi—to the extent to which they are linguistically homogeneous—need Kiswahili less for either vertical or horizontal integration. Kinyarwanda serves both roles well, supported by the French language in some matters. But in Zaire Kiswahili has been important already in horizontal integration across ethnic groups. President Mobutu Sese Seko's policy of "African authenticy" may move before long toward a fundamental reexamination of the language policy of the country. One possibility in Zaire would be the official adoption of two or three African languages and giving them recognition as *national* languages, while retaining French for the time being as the official language. The choice of three African languages promoted as national Zairean languages is almost bound to include Kiswahili, as well as Lingala. Zaire's policy makers on the language front might proceed to study Switzerland and India as countries which adopted more than two languages to cope with cultural pluralism and cultural nationalism in their own national situations.

General Mobutu's promotion of African authenticity is itself profoundly inspired and conditioned by cultural nationalism at both the racial level of black pride and the territorial level of Zairean self-realization. The impact of the "authenticity" drive on educational policies in Zaire—though still inconclusive—is already manifest.

At the ethnic and class levels cultural nationalism has a rather unsure effect on educational policy makers. But where cultural nationalism becomes necessary for territorial or racial identification, its translation into concrete educational policies can be speedy and wide-ranging. In relation to Kiswahili, these have ranged already from its role in black studies in the United States to its propagation as a legal language in Tanzania.

The church, for the time being, seems to have declined as a major factor in the fortunes of Kiswahili. New gods now command African loyalties, in addition to those that came with the church. These new gods include the quest for greater cultural dignity, the pursuit of racial fulfillment, the forging of territorial identities, the revision of class and status in societies, and the construction of a new Eastern African civilization.

NOTES

1. G.S.P. Freeman-Grenville, *The Medieval History of the Coast of Tanganyika.* London: O.U.P., 1962, p. 204.

2. J. Lamphear, "The Kamba and the Northern Mrima Coast," in R. Gray, and D. Birmingham (eds.) *Pre-Colonial African Trade.* London: O.U.P., 1970, p. 97; O.F. Raum, "German East Africa, 1892-1940," in V. Harlow and E. Chilver (eds.) *History of East Africa,* vol. ii. Oxford: Clarendon Press, 1965, p. 168; G.S.P. Freeman-Grenville, "The Coast, 1498-1840," In R. Oliver and G. Matthew (eds.) *History of East Africa,* vol. i. Oxford: Clarendon Press, 1963, p. 168.

3. T.P. Gorman, "The Development of Language Policy in Kenya with Particular Reference to the Education System" in W.H. Whiteley (ed.) *Language in Kenya.* Nairobi: O.U.P., 1974, p. 388. Marie D. Kiewiet Hemphill, "The British Sphere, 1884-94," in R. Oliver and G. Matthew, *op. cit.,* p. 420.

4. E. Steere, Preface, *A Handbook of the Swahili Language as Spoken at Zanzibar.* Sheldon Press, 1870.

5. Consult W.H. Whiteley, *The Rise of a Swahili National Language.* London: Methuen, 1969, pp. 15-17, 53ff.

6. *Mackay of Uganda.* 1898, 8th ed., p. 103.

7. Consult Theodeve Walker's entries for January 1891 and March 1892; G.L. Pilkington for Jan. 4, 1891, as recorded in E.F. Hartford's *Pilkington of Uganda,* 1899.

8. Mackay, *Eighteen Years in Uganda and East Africa,* vol. 2. 1908, p. 215.

9. Consult T.J. Jones, *Education in East Africa.* London, undated; W.H. Whiteley, *The Rise of a Swahili National Language, op. cit.,* p. 55; and *African Education: A Study of Educational Policy and Practice in British Tropical Africa.* London: Crown Agents, 1953, p. 80. I am indebted to T.P. Gorman for bibliographical guidance on these issues.

10. Cited by Gorman, *op. cit.,* footnote 47, p. 436.

11. Gorman, *op. cit.,* p. 392.

12. W.F. Gowers, Memorandum, "Development of Kiswahili as an Educational and Administrative Language in the Uganda Protectorate," Nov. 25, 1927.

13. Kabwegyere, *The Politics of State Formation: The Nature and Effects of Colonialism in Uganda.* Nairobi: East African Literature Bureau, 1974, pp. 218-219.

14. When he was still President of Uganda, A. Milton Obote showed a keen awareness of these sociological pressures. Consult his lecture "Policy Proposals for Uganda's Educational Needs," given to the Educational Association of Uganda, *Mawazo,* vol. 2, no. 2, December 1969.

15. "There are over thirty distinct languages and dialect clusters spoken in Kenya. Approximately sixty-six percent of the population speak languages belonging to the Bantu branch of the Niger-Congo family.... Nearly thirty-one percent of the population speak Nilotic and paranilotic language while three percent speak Cushitic languages.... According to initial figures derived from the *Kenya Population Census* (1969), eight African languages were spoken as first languages by over five hundred thousand people, including four languages spoken by over 1,000,000 people, these being Kikuyu, Luo, Kamba and Luyia.... The census does not provide data about the number of speakers of Swahili as a first language but I have given reasons elsewhere for estimating that Swahili is spoken as a first language in Kenya by not less than 60,000 persons." Gorman, *op. cit.,* p. 385. See also T.P. Gorman, "Language Policy in Kenya," a paper given at the Second Eastern African Conference on Language and Linguistics, Nairobi, June 10, 1970.

16. Fifty-two percent of the men of Uganda can hold a conversation in Kiswahili, fifty-one percent in Luganda, and twenty-eight percent in the English language. Eighteen percent of the women of Uganda can conduct a conversation in Kiswahili, twenty-eight percent in Luganda, and thirteen percent in the English language. For both men and women the percentage for competence in Kiswahili is thirty-five percent, in Luganda thirty-nine percent, and in the English language twenty-one percent. Consult Peter Ladefoged, Ruth Glick, and Clive Criper, *Language in Uganda.* London and Nairobi: O.U.P., 1972, pp. 24-25.

17. Gorman, "The Development of Language Policy in Kenya with Particular Reference to the Education System," *op. cit.,* p. 389.

18. *Uganda: Parliamentary Debates,* Hansard, second series, vols. 6-8, National Assembly

Official Report, first session, 1962-1963; third meeting, Feb. 4-26, 1963, Ministry of Education no. 401, Tuesday, Feb. 5, 1963.

19. Hansard, *op. cit.,* Ministry of Information, Broadcasting and Tourism, no. 503, Tuesday, Feb. 12, 1963.

20. Voice of Uganda, Oct. 10, 1973.

21. *Ibid.*

22. Consult for background A.I. Salim, *Swahili-Speaking Peoples of Kenya's Coast, 1895-1965.* Nairobi: East African Publishing House, 1973.

23. *The Standard* (Nairobi) and *The Daily Nation* (Nairobi), July 5 and 6, 1974.

XV

The Implementation

of Bilingual/Bicultural Education Programs

in the United States

George M. Blanco

Dr. George Blanco of the University of Texas at Austin wishes to express his appreciation to the Center for Applied Linguistics of Arlington, Virginia, whose grant from the Carnegie Corporation of New York City made possible both the writing of this paper and the provision of a forum for its discussion through a series of conferences on various perspectives of bilingual education, including those of linguistics, education, the social sciences, and the law. Reprinted by permission. Copyright © Center for Applied Linguistics, 1977.

A SOCIETY IN TRANSITION

> America is God's Crucible, the Great Melting Pot where all the races of Europe are melting and re-forming! Here you stand, good folk, think I, when I see them at Ellis Island, here you stand in your fifty groups, with your fifty languages and histories, and your fifty blood hatreds and rivalries. But you won't be long like that, brothers, for these are the fires of God you've come to—these are the fires of God—Germans, Frenchmen, Irishmen and Englishmen, Jews and Russians— into the Crucible with you all! God is making the American . . .

So proclaims Israel Zangwill in his early 20th Century play, *The Melting Pot* (1909, p. 37). The striving for oneness and equality has been a powerful motivating factor in the founding and evolution of the United States of America. *E pluribus unum* is a motto recited by many generations of schoolchildren in testimony of the belief that this country derives its strength and character from its multinational roots. These roots, as in a living plant, support and provide nourishment for the exposed branches, leaves, and flowers. Yet the roots themselves remain hidden. The "one out of many" motto has conveyed the idea that immigrants are expected to conform to one lifestyle and to one language if they are to succeed and reap the full benefits offered by this country. In 1972, the United States Congress passed the Ethnic Heritage Studies Act, which challenged this time-honored concept of sameness by recognizing "the heterogeneous composition of the Nation and the fact that in a multiethnic society a greater understanding of the contributions of one's heritage and those of one's fellow citizens can contribute to a more harmonious, patriotic and committed populace...." (P.L. 92-318, Sec. 901.)

What caused this apparent about-face in the thinking of America? Would this type of philosophy not undermine the very tenets on which the country had been founded? Were we not all expected to be Americans with the same language and culture? This change in attitude was a slow evolutionary process that came to maturity during the 1960s, a period of great unrest for this country, a period in which many traditional values were being questioned. The very idea of what it meant to be an American was being examined.

Out of this decade of turbulence came a concern for the individual and for the identity of that individual. Such concern, making itself felt on various fronts—social, economic, political, educational, linguistic—forced us as a nation to reexamine our comfortable attitude of superiority toward the world. An ever-increasing materialism, spurred on by a booming economy, had contributed greatly to the development of a national mentality that measured personal success largely by economic worth and potential. As the United States became involved in an undeclared war in Vietnam, large segments of society rose up in protest, not only against the war itself, but also against many of the fundamental institutions which Americans had been brought up to respect and value. The youth and the civil rights movements and the resulting riots were cause for alarm, not because of their overt destructiveness, but because they were indicative of the underlying anger brought on by discrimination against many of our citizens.

Suddenly America was no longer the crucible popularized by Israel Zangwill and even earlier by Crèvecoeur (1925) in the 18th Century. This country had always believed in its ability to assimilate the huddled masses into one society where everyone was equal. Now it seemed that certain dissonant elements of society were bent on destroying the great American philosophy of oneness. The Black-White dichotomy, with its inherent prejudices, had been with us since the days of slavery, but the United States was torn apart during the 1960s by antiwar groups and race riots which further fed the fires of discord. The anger and hostility of these groups went much deeper than the discrimination which was evident.

Herman (1974) states that the Black movement shifted emphasis from an integrationist policy to one based on Black identity and pride. She goes on to say that it was this attitudinal change, plus the declining purchasing power of blue collar workers, which made a college education for their children difficult, if not impossible, and which forced white ethnic groups to begin challenging the American dream. These groups had been taught that Americans should all be the same culturally and linguistically and were disappointed when this philosophy did not pay off. Whole segments of society turned their attention inward toward their role, their identity, and what this country could do for them. Some of the younger generation "dropped out" and searched for a simple existence in isolated communes to find themselves. Ethnic groups began to surface, and ethnic recognition was largely the response to this quest for identity. Mexican

Americans, Puerto Ricans, Native Americans, Portuguese Americans, Asian Americans, and a host of other groups let it be known that they wanted their national origins acknowledged and respected. For many individuals this recognition included acknowledgment of the validity of lifestyles and languages other than those of the mainstream society. Although America was far from unanimously giving wholehearted support to the notion that its citizens were not all alike, the country finally began to realize during this period the extent of its multicultural personality.

The concept of the United States as a multicultural nation may have begun with attention on the Black-White problem, but it soon encompassed non-Black ethnic identity and finally proceeded to include other dimensions and subcultures. The sixties also saw the emergence of the youth movement and culture. The women's movement began to make its grievances known. The sexual revolution had an impact on all strata of society, and even the gay community became visible and demanded equal rights. Young unmarried couples lived together openly and coed college dormitories came into their own as a result of student demands. This seeking of recognition of the individual as a human being, whether it was on the basis of race, sex, ethnicity, or language, had a definite influence on American education.

EDUCATIONAL RESPONSE

Curriculum Changes

The response to the awareness of the United States as a pluralistic society resulted in the implementation of multicultural educational programs. Blacks insisted that their role and contribution be incorporated into the curriculum. Black Studies soon became a common component of the curriculum in many high schools and colleges. It was not long before other groups, in their own search for identity, demanded a place in the curriculum. The 1974 Yearbook of the Association for Supervision and Curriculum Development states emphatically that "The school should help our nation become an 'open society' in which a variety of cultures, value systems, and life styles not only coexist but are nurtured. . . . Individual and group differences would be prized, not merely accepted or grudgingly tolerated, and every person would have equal access to what they want from and can give to the society" (Della-Dora and House 1974, pp. 3-4). This statement documents how far we have come in our educational philosophy from the melting pot mentality of the turn of the century.

A number of programs geared to meet the needs of different groups have sprung up under the auspices of multicultural education. James A. Banks (1975) as a proponent of ethnic studies has made a series of significant suggestions for including in the curriculum such groups as Native Americans, European Americans, Afro-Americans, Mexican Americans, Asian Americans, Puerto Rican Americans, Cuban Americans, and Native Hawaiians. This salutary climate for cultural diversity has made possible the initiation and expansion of bilingual education programs.

The awareness of our being a pluralistic society, however, also had its roots in the appalling failure of the educational system to meet the needs of the linguistically and culturally different groups. For example, the Report of the NEA—Tucson Survey on the Teaching of Spanish to the Spanish-speaking, *The Invisible Minority* (National Education Association, 1966), had a far-reaching influence on subsequent legislation for children of limited English-speaking ability (LESA). This report brought to the public eye the tremendous disparity between the educational achievement of Mexican Americans and that of the general student population. According to a study done in California in 1960, more than half of the Spanish-surnamed males and nearly half of the Spanish-surnamed females 14 years of age and over had not gone beyond the eighth grade. In contrast only 27.9% of the males and 25% of the females over the age of 14 in the total population had not gone beyond the eighth grade. The study also revealed that over 72% of the males in the total population and 75% of the females had gone through at least one or more years of high school. By contrast, only 48.5% of the Spanish-surnamed males and 52% of the females had achieved this educational level. Of the total population, 23.4% of the males and 19.4% of the females had completed one or more years of college. Yet only 8.8% of the Spanish-surnamed males and 6.2% of the females had reached this level of education.

The study also reported that the Spanish-surnamed population of the Southwest did not fare economically as well as the general population in 1960 (p. 6):

	General population	Spanish-surnamed population
Families with income under $1000	4.9%	8.8%
Families with income under $3000	21.0%	34.8%
Families with income of $10,000 or more	17.6%	6%

The cycle of poverty, plus the low esteem in which minority groups were held, contributed directly to these distressing statistics. It was these social, economic, and educational conditions which added support to the subsequent legislation and education reform which would promote educational programs meeting the needs of LESA children. However, the gradual acceptance of the United States as a multicultural country provided the necessary climate in which to begin the revolutionary bilingual education movement.

Legislation and Court Decision

In 1965, the United States Congress passed the Elementary and Secondary Education Act, P.L. 89-10. In 1968, Title VII of this law, which became known as the "Bilingual Education Act," appropriated funds for the operation of programs designed to serve the needs of "children of limited English-speaking ability."

In 1974, P.L. 93-380 was signed into law, extending and amending the Elementary and Secondary Education Act of 1965 by providing funds not only for local bilingual education programs but also for auxiliary and supplementary community activities, adult education programs, preschool programs preparatory and supplementary to bilingual education programs, teacher training programs, and planning and technical assistance. Section 723 provided for training of personnel such as teachers, administrators, paraprofessionals, teacher aides, parents, and counselors; for encouraging reform, innovation, and improvement of graduate education; and for recruitment and training of graduate students through fellowships. This federal support of bilingual education, especially in the appropriation of funds, generated a significant amount of legislation concerning bilingual education at the state level. According to a study by Geffert et al. (1975), this is the situation in the states:

12 states require the use of English for instruction.

14 states make no provision for bilingual education.

16 states have permissive bilingual education statutes.

6 states have permissive and mandatory statutes.

2 states have mandatory statutes or regulations.

Figures 1 and 2 show a breakdown by state and jurisdiction of bilingual education legislation.

In January 1974, the Supreme Court of the United States in its landmark decision, *Lau v. Nichols*, declared that "The failure of the San Francisco school system to provide English language instruction to approximately 1800 students of Chinese ancestry who do not speak English denies them a meaningful opportunity

Figure 1.   Legislation Affecting Bilingual Education in the Fifty States

	Type of statute				
	Prohibitory				
State	*P/NP*	*P*	*No provision*	*Permissive*	*Mandatory*
Alabama	X[1]				
Alaska					X
Arizona				X	
Arkansas	X				
California				X	
Colorado				X	
Connecticut				X	
Delaware		X			
Florida				X	
Georgia			X		
Hawaii			X		

Figure 1 (continued)

State	Prohibitory P/NP	Prohibitory P	No provision	Permissive	Mandatory
Idaho		X			
Illinois				X	X
Indiana			X		
Iowa	X				
Kansas				X	
Kentucky			X		
Louisiana		X			
Maine				X	
Maryland				X	
Massachusetts				X	X
Michigan				X	X
Minnesota				X	
Mississippi			X		
Missouri			X		
Montana	X²				
Nebraska	X				
Nevada			X		
New Hampshire				X	
New Jersey				X	X
New Mexico				X	
New York				X	
North Carolina	X				
North Dakota			X		
Ohio			X		
Oklahoma		X			
Oregon				X	
Pennsylvania					X³
Rhode Island				X	X
South Carolina			X		
South Dakota				X	
Tennessee			X		
Texas				X	X
Utah				X	
Vermont			X		
Virginia			X		
Washington				X	
West Virginia	X				
Wisconsin		X			
Wyoming			X		

From Geffert et al. 1975, p. 122.

[1]Prohibitory in only the first six grades.

[2]Prohibitory in only the first through the eighth grades or until 16 years of age.

[3]Regulation, not statute.

Figure 2.   Legislation Affecting Bilingual Education in Non-State American-Flag Jurisdictions

| | Prohibitory | | | | |
Jurisdiction	P/NP	P	No provision	Permissive	Mandatory
Guam				X	
Panama Canal Zone	X				
Puerto Rico					X[1]
Samoa				X	
Trust Territories			X		
Virgin Islands				X	
Washington, D.C.			X		

From Geffert et al. 1975, p. 123.

[1] Puerto Rico requires the use of Spanish as the language of instruction in the classroom.

Terms used in Figures 1 and 2:

Prohibitory: The jurisdiction has a provision which requires that instruction be exclusively in English.

P/NP: Refers to both public and nonpublic schools.

P: Refers to public schools only.

No provision: The jurisdiction has no provisions specifying any language of instruction.

Permissive: The jurisdiction has a provision which expressly or implicitly permits the use of a language of instruction other than English.

Mandatory: The jurisdiction has a provision which identifies circumstances under which a local school district must provide instructional programs employing a language other than English.

to participate in the public education program and thus violates Section 601 of the Civil Rights Act of 1964, which bans discrimination based 'on the grounds of race, color, or national origin,' in 'any program or activity receiving federal financial assistance.' " (Supreme Court of the United States, U.S. Court of Appeals, Jan. 21, 1974.)

In the summer of 1975, the Office for Civil Rights of the Department of Health, Education, and Welfare issued a document entitled "Task Force Findings Specifying Remedies Available for Eliminating Past Educational Practices Ruled Unlawful under *Lau v. Nichols.*" This document is to be used to determine compliance by schools and outlines procedures systematically to identify linguistically different students and to specify the language characteristics of these students to determine the achievement characteristics of the students and to provide an instructional program that addresses these characteristics. The curriculum which federal legislation and court decisions have delineated is compensatory education (González 1975, Vázquez 1975).

The bilingual education model which the federal government supports regards the learning of English as its primary goal and the use of the non-English language only as a necessary and dispensable vehicle. Furthermore, federal bilingual legislation addresses the students of limited English-speaking ability and makes only a cursory statement about participation by English-dominant or English monolingual children. The wording of the Act states that it will "provide financial assistance to local educational agencies and to State educational agencies . . . to demonstrate effective ways of providing, for children of limited English-speaking ability, instruction designed to enable them, while using their native language, to achieve competence in the English language." (P.L. 93-380, Aug. 21, 1974.)

HEW recently issued a memorandum which stated that bilingual education was only one remedy to meet the *Lau v. Nichols* mandate (Office for Civil Rights, Apr. 8, 1976). The press was quick to pick up on this memo and gave it publicity by stating, "The Health, Education and Welfare Department, seeking to clear up a growing U.S. education issue, has quietly affirmed that it is not necessary for school districts to provide bilingual education to children whose primary language is not English" (*The Washington Post,* Apr. 19, 1976, p. A1). Yet a task force commissioned by the Office for Civil Rights had previously placed emphasis on bilingual education as a means of providing children of limited English-speaking ability with a substantive educational program. What the consequences of the memo will be, only time will tell. This much is clear, however: the issuance of the memo underscores the federal stance regarding the compensatory nature of bilingual education.

NATURE OF BILINGUAL/BICULTURAL EDUCATION PROGRAMS

Goals of Bilingual Education

There is much evidence in the literature to show that the goals of bilingual education are compatible with the goals of general education. While one can argue about the role of education, educational philosophers (Dewey 1966) believe not only that the school must meet the needs of the individual but also that education must be based on the intensive activities and needs of the person to be educated. Thorndike and Gates (1966) indicate that the "ultimate aim of education for man is to secure the fullest satisfaction of human wants" (p. 24). Along these same lines the National Council for the Social Studies in its preliminary position statement, *Ethnic Studies Curriculum Guidelines* (in press), proposes a change within our educational system to respect, rather than reduce, ethnic diversity in American life. The Council insists that this proposed change is in keeping with such national ideals as freedom, equality, justice, and human dignity. Addressing the concept of diversity, Castañeda, Herold, and Ramírez (1975) propose a new philosophy of education which they call cultural democracy. Cultural democracy "stresses the rights of every American child to remain identified with his own home and community socialization experiences" (p. 10). They go on to say that bilingual education embodies this philosophy by emphasizing the maintenance of the child's first language for instructional purposes while learning a second language. If the educational system purports to uphold our national ideals and to transmit the culture of our society, it is duty-bound to provide equality and human dignity to its students by recognizing their linguistic and cultural strengths, whether they happen to be Anglo, Mexican American, Puerto Rican American, Black or Asian American.

A commonly accepted definition of bilingual education in this country is the one set forth by the U.S. Office of Education (1971, p. 1):

> [Bilingual education is] . . . the use of two languages, one of which is English, as mediums of instruction for the same pupil population in a well-organized program which encompasses all or part of the curriculum and includes the study of the history and culture associated with the mother tongue. A complete program develops and maintains the children's self-esteem and a legitimate pride in both cultures.

Although English is a necessary component of bilingual education, the teaching of English as a second language (ESL) by itself does not constitute a bilingual program. ESL means the field of teaching English to speakers of other languages (Alatis 1976). The professional organization, Teachers of English to Speakers of Other Languages (TESOL), identifies three educational approaches utilized to teach students of limited English-speaking ability in the United States (TESOL 1976):

1. Bilingual instruction including an English as a second language component.

2. Monolingual instruction including an English as a second language component.

3. Monolingual instruction without an English as a second language component.

Of the three approaches, TESOL recommends the first as the preferred model. In some cases the second model may be necessary, but "Under no circumstances does the third, monolingual instruction without an English as a second language component, provide equal educational opportunities to students of limited English proficiency, and it is categorically rejected as an alternative instructional model for their education" (p. 3). This third model was used almost exclusively prior to the passage of the Bilingual Education Act.

The consensus of writers in the field of bilingual education reveals that the primary thrust of bilingual education lies within the cognitive and affective domains, rather than the linguistic realm. That is, the main purpose of bilingual education is not to teach language per se but rather to provide students with the opportunity to acquire knowledge and skills through the language they know best while at the same time adding English to their linguistic repertoire. While it is obvious that the linguistic dimension is basic and necessary to the concept of bilingual education, it is felt that the primary goal of bilingual education is to allow children of limited English-speaking ability to participate successfully in the educational process (Andersson and Boyer 1970, Saville and Troike 1971, von Maltitz 1975). Such authorities address the importance of language in bilingual education, and they are convinced, along with other writers (UNESCO 1955), not only that the native language (as opposed to another language) is the best language for instructional purposes, but also that its use in school can only enhance the child's self-image and esteem for his own culture. Thus, as a result of participating in a bilingual education program, the child should acquire competence in two languages. These writers are firm supporters of maintenance, rather than transitional bilingual education programs to develop fully biliterate individuals, that is, individuals who are capable not only of understanding and speaking, but also of reading and writing two languages on a wide variety of topics.

The cultural goals of bilingual education call for a recognition of the child's home culture and its inclusion as part of the instructional program. Language and culture are inextricably interwoven, and language is the most identifiable and basic exponent of a culture. Besides language the bilingual program often incorporates other cultural elements of the children's home culture, whether it is music, cuisine, or folklore. One of the most inclusive statements concerning the role of culture in the bilingual program (or, in their words, "multicultural program") is that made by Castañeda, Herold, and Ramírez (1975, p. 11):

> A truly comprehensive multicultural program would include these curricular objectives (language, holidays, historical figures, and traditions), but would be addressed as well to those features of a child's socialization experiences which have shaped his preferred or dominant learning style. In other words, the basis for a child's learning about his own and other cultures must encompass the language, heritage, values, thinking and motivational frameworks with which the child is initially familiar. . . . His language, heritage, values, and modes of cognition and motivation can subsequently serve as a basis for exploring and developing selective loyalties to alternative expressions of thought, values, and life styles. There, the child would learn to function completely and effectively in, as well as to contribute to development of more than one cultural world.

This statement underscores the necessity of including elements of the child's home culture in the curriculum. Nelson Brooks in his speech, "Parameters of Culture" (1972), outlines 25 elements of "deep" culture with emphasis on the personal; topics range from language to religion and duties. Although there is an increasing number of programs and curriculum materials which include these elements as an integral part of bilingual education, the truth of the matter is that not enough is known about specific cultures to have a serious impact on teacher training and on school programs. A few individuals have come forth to meet these needs, however, and they are discussed later in the section on materials.

The cognitive, linguistic, and cultural goals of bilingual education are interrelated and are, in turn, closely linked to the affective goals. The importance of self-image may, in the final analysis, be the single most important outcome of bilingual education (von Maltitz 1975, p. 63):

> The concepts and practices involved in bilingual-bicultural education projects have as a major goal leading students to believe in themselves, in their basic worth as human beings, and in their native capacities. One important factor in

reinforcing these pupils' self-condidence is having the language they speak acknowledged and respected; another is having as teachers, and models whom they can emulate, persons who use that language and stem from the same cultural community as their pupils.

Speaking to the issue of the education of Mexican American children, Cárdenas and Cárdenas (1972) propose a theory of incompatibilities which prevent minority children from successfully participating in the educational process. The writers indicate that an instructional program developed for white, Anglo Saxon, English-speaking middle-class students is not adequate for non-white, non-Anglo Saxon, non-English-speaking, or non-middle-class students. More specifically, they feel that there are five major incompatibilities:

1. Poverty—Absence of success models in the family, inadequate housing, and malnutrition are some factors that promote the development of differing concepts toward education and that influence the development of poor children.

2. Culture—The school has traditionally known little about the minority students' home culture and its traditions, values, and orientation. The result has been one that has created negative stereotypes and culturally irrelevant instructional materials.

3. Language—When the Spanish-speaking child is placed in an English-language school program, he cannot participate successfully since there is an incompatibility of language. English as a second language (ESL) programs have been inadequate by themselves because the Spanish-speaking child is deprived of cognitive and skills development until he learns to communicate in English. Further, excluding the home language creates in the child a sense of inferiority.

4. Mobility—Families in lower income brackets are very mobile in their attempt to find employment. Children in such families often find themselves attending two, three, or more different schools in the same year. The mobility is incompatible with school programs based on continuity and sequence.

5. Societal perceptions—Minority children tend to perceive themselves in a negative way. The typical instructional program is designed for children with positive self-concepts and armed with certain prerequisite knowledge and skills. Minority children often do not fit in the mold and they tend to develop a negative self-concept.

The areas of culture and language, they feel, are of utmost importance in the curriculum not solely from the point of view of cognition and the performance of pupils, but also from the perspective of how the child will feel about himself. This notion of improving the students' self-image is considered so vital that one can conclude from the foregoing that it is one of the major objectives of bilingual education today. However, this writer questions the effectiveness of such an effort in a transitional bilingual education model, which does not give equal stature to both the home language and English.

MODELS OF BILINGUAL EDUCATION PROGRAMS

Program Design

A number of writers have proposed many models of bilingual education programs according to such factors as the treatment of the language, time allotments, school subjects, pupil characteristics, goals, and staffing patterns (Stern 1963, Mackey 1972, Saville and Troike 1971, Fishman and Lovas 1970, Spolsky et al. 1974). The overwhelming compensatory nature of bilingual programs in the United States has already been mentioned. Within these limitations, though, a variety of programs has surfaced. González (1975) reports five major types of bilingual education programs in the United States today (pp. 14-16):

Type A Programs: ESL/Bilingual (Transitional). Strictly remedial/compensatory orientation.

Type B Programs: Bilingual Maintenance. Student's fluency in another language is seen as an asset to be maintained and developed.

Type C Programs: Bilingual/Bicultural (Maintenance). Similar to Type B, but it also integrates "history and culture" of the target group as an integral part of curricular content and methodology.

Type D Programs: Bilingual/Bicultural (restorationist). A strong attempt is made to restore to children the option of learning the language and culture of their ancestors which may have been lost in the process of assimilation.

Type E Programs: Culturally Pluralistic. Students are not limited to a particular target group. Rather, all students are involved in linguistically and culturally pluralistic schooling.

The U.S. Commission for Civil Rights (1975) reports visitations by its staff to four different language-group bilingual education programs: Philadelphia, Pa. (Puerto Rican); Johnstown, Colo. (Mexican American); Rock Point, Ariz. (Native American); and San Francisco, Calif. (Asian American). At Johnstown and at San Francisco there were both bilingual and monolingual classrooms at each grade level, so that children from both language groups could select their preference. The Rock Point School and the Potter Thomas School in Philadelphia include all the children enrolled in the school.

Program Scheduling

The models presented previously serve as bases for practitioners in the field for the implementation of programs. Bilingual education has already been defined in this paper as the use of two languages for all or part of the instructional program. But what, exactly, is taught in a bilingual education program? Is it primarily a language program? Is the same material taught first in one language and then repeated in the other language? To begin to answer these and other questions, the Board of Education of the City of Chicago (1974) presented a list of seven statements indicating what bilingual education is and seven statements declaring what it is not. In part the document proposes the following (p. 9):

It [bilingual education] involves the entire curriculum being taught in two languages.

It is not exclusively a language-teaching program which excludes math, science, and other curriculum areas.

In line with the above statements the U.S. Commission for Civil Rights (1975) succinctly states the general content of bilingual education programs (pp. 86-87):

The content of what students learn in a bilingual bicultural classroom is similar to what students learn in a monolingual English classroom except that it is learned through two languages and includes consideration for the cultural heritage of both groups of students. Students in a bilingual classroom, like other students, are provided instruction in language skills, science, social studies, history, music, art, and physical education.

These subjects are the same basic subjects provided children in an all-English-language program. How, then, does the bilingual dimension enter the picture? Is the school day extended? Do any of the subjects suffer from inadequate treatment? To answer these questions, curriculum writers have suggested or have come up with schedules of their own. A variety of program schedules is presented more fully by Blanco (1977). These schedules are by no means considered intrinsically ideal. Rather, they have been designed to meet the needs of school districts with certain resources and student population characteristics. These schedules show that educators who are serious about bilingual education have incorporated this dual-language teaching approach into the basic program of studies. They substantiate the suggestion made by Ulibarrí (1970) that bilingual education should be an integral part of the overall educational process and not an appendage.

An important note in the models and schedules presented here is that the teaching of English as a second language (ESL) is an important, if not an indispensable, element of the bilingual program. The 1976 ESEA Title VII Proposed Regulations, Sec. 123.02 (U.S. Office of Education) imply that ESL by itself does not constitute a bilingual education program, since it does not involve the use of two languages in a structured manner. In a recent publication from the Teachers of English to Speakers of Other Languages, *Position Paper on the Role of English as a Second Language* (1976), this professional organization states its support of dual-language instruction and affirms the important role of the learning of English as a primary goal of bilingual education in the United States.

Languages of Instruction

The overwhelming majority of bilingual education programs involve English and Spanish as languages of instruction. This comes as no surprise to anyone in view of the latest survey of languages other than English spoken in the United States (Waggoner 1976). In July 1976, there were an estimated 25,334,000 persons in the United States living in households where languages other than English are spoken. A breakdown is as follows (pp. 4-5):

Figure 3

Languages	No. of Speakers
Spanish	8.2 million
Italian	1.8 million
German	1.5 million
French	1.5 million
Chinese, Greek, Japanese, Philippine languages, Portuguese, Korean	100,000–500,000 each

The rapid growth of the Spanish-speaking population in the United States, particularly in the Southwest and in large urban centers such as New York, Chicago, Miami, and Seattle, has brought almost an automatic equating of bilingual programs with the Spanish language. According to the Dissemination and Assessment Center for Bilingual Education (1975-1976), 284 of the 406 projects funded under Title VII dealt with the Spanish language. The remainder involved 46 other specific languages, including Arabic, Chinese, Choctaw, Hebrew, Portuguese, Russian, Vietnamese, Yaqui, and Yup'ik.

This linguistic diversity underscores the pluralistic makeup of the country which has only recently come to be valued. Even though the overriding features of bilingual education today are compensatory or transitional in nature, the recognition of languages other than English can be seen as a step forward. The very fact that the large number of languages has survived within these shores clearly indicates the strong desire for belonging, for identification, and for comfort from one's own kind. The 406 Title VII bilingual programs in 1975-1976 are a far cry from the first year of funding. These figures were obtained from the DACBE *Directories of Title VII ESEA Bilingual Education Programs: 1969-76* (see Figure 4).

Figure 4. Yearly Total of Projects, Children, and Languages in Bilingual Education Projects

No. of projects	Year	No. of students	No. of languages
76	1968-69*	33,732	14
63	1969-70	22,802	14
137	1970-71	45,227	16
169	1971-72	63,324	16
216	1972-73	100,391	24
211	1973-74	128,767	30
271	1974-75	147,523	34
406	1975-76	206,452	47

*Figures obtained from files of the National Consortium for Bilingual Education.

Although federal funding through ESEA Title VII has provided the necessary impetus to further the implementation of bilingual education programs, efforts at the local and state levels should be duly recognized. Descriptive information at these levels is scarce. One praiseworthy local effort, however, is discussed under Implementing the Bilingual Program.

The state legislation mentioned earlier has, of course, increased the number of bilingual education programs other than those supported by Title VII. At the time of this writing, there is no information concerning the number and extent of such non-federally-funded programs. Nonetheless, the increase in the number of programs funded by the federal government, of students, and of languages represented again shows the support in America for a pluralistic society. This pluralism, of which bilingual education is a vivid exponent, appears to have "caught on." In 1970, the Texas Education Agency came forward with its concept of "Confluence of Texan Cultures" (1970). In developing the plan to implement the concept into curriculum planning, the Texas State Board of Education not only recognized the cultural and linguistic diversity of the state but also encouraged schools to capitalize on the language and cultural strengths which all children bring to school. The concept of pluralism is also endorsed by the Council of Chief State School Officers (1977, p. 14):

> The Council believes that the development of an understanding and acceptance
> of cultural, language, and lifestyle differences among people should be an
> integral part of the instructional program for every student.

Foreign language educators are also rallying to the support of the pluralistic concept by encouraging their teachers to emphasize the non-English languages spoken in the United States. The Northeast Conference on the Teaching of Foreign Languages devotes one entire issue of its Reports of the Working Committees (1976) to cultural pluralism and to the contributions to the United States of such linguistic groups as the French, Germans, and the Spanish-speaking. Other writers have made statements supporting a close relationship between bilingual education and the foreign language teaching field (Gaarder 1975, Blanco 1976).

Levels of Instruction

The Bilingual Education Act of 1968 as amended in 1974 does not necessarily limit its scope to the elementary school. Yet instruction in the elementary school is strongly emphasized in the wording of the Act. Section 702 uses the terms "child" and "children" nine times in identifying the target audience. The same section, however, provides financial assistance "to enable local educational agencies to develop and carry out such (bilingual) programs in elementary and secondary schools" (U.S. Congress, P.L. 93-380). Schools have seen the greatest need for bilingual education at the preschool and the elementary school levels, since this is where the greatest concentration of children of limited English-speaking ability is found. Of the 406 Title VII programs in 1975-1976, only 83 were in grades 9 to 12 (DACBE 1975-1976). Programs at these grade levels are usually reserved for students who have recently immigrated to this country and are commonly found in such urban centers as New York City, Seattle, Boston, San Francisco, and Chicago. Other secondary programs are designed for students whose command of English does not allow them to participate fully in the all-English instructional program.

Adult bilingual education programs are relatively few. Although there has not been a great deal of activity in the field of adult education, the Education Service Center, Region II in Corpus Christi, Tex. (1976) has published materials in this field. The materials consist of three volumes, and their purpose is to show schools how to build on the skills and concepts known to learners in their languages and how to make a smooth transition into the English language. The materials deal with the Mexican American and include information on the following topics:

1. Formal and informal placement procedures and instruments.
2. Structure of an adult education bilingual program.
3. Staff development.
4. Sections on Spanish phonology, vocabulary, grammatical structure.
5. Sections on science, mathematics, social studies, culture, reading and writing in Spanish and English.

Although the intent of the materials is to make a transition into English, they are not solely concerned with the teaching of English as a second language. The materials do address the teaching of subject matter in Spanish as well as in English.

IMPLEMENTING THE BILINGUAL PROGRAM

In implementing the bilingual education program, schools must consider the following areas:

1. Needs assessment—a survey to determine need, to identify students, and to identify available resources.
2. Administration—the preparation, role, and duties of the program director.
3. Classroom management—the utilization of classroom resources and the scheduling of classes for maximum effectiveness.

These three areas are developed more fully by Blanco (1977).

Debate over Methodology

It was indicated earlier in this chapter that bilingual education should be considered an integral part of general education and that there is nothing exotic or unusual about this form of education other than the use of two languages rather than just one. As far as methodology in subjects such as social studies, science, and math is concerned, the main concern of the teacher should be to use the same methods as would be used with monolingual English-speaking children. The difference, of course, is the treatment given to the two languages involved.

To illustrate this point, Sánchez (n.d.) in his paper, "Introducción a las matemáticas modernas para maestros de escuelas primarias" presents some fundamental principles of modern mathematics which can be found in any program or set of materials regardless of language. Some of the main points of his paper are as follows (translation from Spanish by the present writer, pp. 3-4):

1. Modern math seeks to develop the child's intuitive abilities.
2. Modern math makes a distinction between the properties of cardinal and ordinal numbers.
3. Emphasis is placed on a knowledge of the structure of the numbering system and of relative value.
4. The arbitrary nature of symbolism is fundamental to all the subject matter presented.
5. A great deal of geometry is included.
6. The concept of the set is treated extensively.

Sánchez goes on to mention that the use of math laboratories is gaining wide acceptability and that teacher training programs have been emphasizing the methodology involved with the new math. Gibb (1974), immediate past president of the National Council of Teachers of Mathematics, expresses concern in an editorial for the LESA child studying mathematics. She states that teachers not only should have the sensitivity to the student's needs in terms of cultural differences but would also do well to speak the student's preferred language.

Saville and Troike (1971) take an opposite stand on the teaching of mathematics in the bilingual program: "Whatever the dominant language of the child, mathematical computational skills should first be developed in English since advanced work in mathematics will probably be done in this language and later switching of these skills is difficult" (p. 26). The advisability of this recommendation is questionable, since the same might be said of other subjects in the curriculum. Furthermore, the teaching of math or any other subject in a language other than the child's dominant one goes against one of the basic tenets of education itself: "It is axiomatic that the best medium for teaching a child is in his mother tongue" (UNESCO 1955, p. 7).

Pérez (1975), in her address to the Second National Conference of EPDA Bilingual Education Project Directors, spoke to the issue of instructional methods. She encouraged the use of innovative teaching techniques and strategies, such as individualized instruction and learning centers.

While one often sees the term "bilingual methodology" and "bilingual teaching techniques" used widely, there is really no indication of its existence. What turns out to be "methodology" is, in reality, the use of two languages in the instructional program. The issue becomes one of classroom management, and as was indicated earlier, the treatment of the languages of instruction is vital to the success of the program. The ratio of time devoted to the use of the two languages and the overall goals of the program, whether maintenance or transitional, would determine to a large extent the success or failure of the bilingual program. However, it should be pointed out that, if the research findings described by Castañeda, Herold and Ramírez (1975) are valid, educators would do well to develop specialized methodologies geared to the needs of bilingual children who might have different learning styles from the mainstream children.

Moving to the linguistic aspect of the curriculum, oral language development is seen as a vital yet often neglected part of the instructional program. Oral language assessment instruments are used widely to gain insights into the children's language competence. Yet, at times children are unable to understand what they read because of a limited vocabulary (Paulston 1974). This situation occurs despite recommendations by curriculum planners to include oral language development as an integral part of the language arts program (Saville and Troike 1971, Reyes 1975). It can be argued that children are provided with oral language development as they participate in bilingual instruction in the various subject areas. By using language in a meaningful context, children can increase their command of both languages significantly.

The key word in oral language development is *participation* by the student. In many instances the teacher does the majority of speaking and the children the greater part of listening. Some second-language methodologists like Finocchiaro (1964) advocate the use of structured pattern practice. This methodology is promoted by such exponents of behavioristic psychology as Skinner (1957) and Carroll (1965), who view language learning as a process of habit formation learned by means of repetition and analogy. Correct responses are reinforced by praise or by the child's getting what he wants, and incorrect responses are extinguished in the opposite manner. The child continues to imitate the language patterns of those around him and thus learns his first language. Applied to the classroom in first- or second-language lessons, the student is asked to repeat utterances and manipulate the language through pattern drills which are designed to help him internalize the language.

The other view of language learning supported by cognitive-code psychologists such as Chomsky (1966), Brown (1973), and Ervin-Tripp (1973) holds the notion that children are born with an innate capability for language acquisition. Language is not learned by imitation, practice, and reinforcement. Rather as a child's cognitive ability develops he uses increasingly more complex utterances. This view holds that the child hypothesizes about language and that he tests his language against what he hears. In other words, he learns the rules of the language with which he is able to create and understand sentences which he has never heard. Application of this view in the classroom would require exposing the student to a maximum amount of natural language without reliance on pattern drills as in the behavioristic model.

There is controversy concerning these two views of language learning. However, in terms of second-language learning, some studies suggest that children use some of the same strategies in first- and second-language acquisition (Milon 1974, Natalicio and Natalicio 1971). In their study on second-language acquisition, Dulay and Burt (1974) show that first-language interference accounts for a minimum of syntactic errors in children learning a second language. Furthermore, the study indicated that most of the syntactic errors in the children's second-language speech were indistinguishable from those in first-language acquisition. A more recent study (Mace Matluck 1977), however, showed that the phenomenon of interference is very much a factor among children learning English as a second language.

Bilingual education teachers would do well to study the implications of both schools of thought, since the approaches associated with each seem to have merit. Although the teacher would not want to rely entirely on pattern practice and repetition, certainly some areas of difficulty can be identified for the purpose of intensive practice. Children should be given an ample opportunity to use language in a great variety of situations that require actual communication with other children and adults. Because learning to read and write is among the primary goals of education, schools often do not give oral language development its rightful place in the curriculum. Certainly the development in children of the listening and speaking skills in two languages should be a primary concern for bilingual programs, since the ability to communicate orally usually precedes introduction to the reading and writing skills.

The teaching of subject matter in the home language and English is at the very core of bilingual education. We have already quoted the UNESCO axiom stating that the best language of instruction is the child's mother tongue. This procedure applies not only to the learning of such subject matter as social studies, arithmetic, and science but also, according to some foreign language methodologists, to the learning of reading as well (Brooks 1960, Rivers 1968, Finocchiaro 1964). Such methodologists have supported the learning of the graphic skills in the second language only after the student has begun to understand and communicate in the language. The idea is that writing is a graphic representation of speech and that it must be present before the sound-symbol relationships are taught. In bilingual education it is argued that the child should learn reading in his home or dominant language, since he has a command of its phonological and grammatical systems and a sizable vocabulary. This was the premise of the study carried out by Modiano (1966) in Chiapas, Mexico. At the end of three years, the Indian children who had been taught to read in their mother tongue had higher reading comprehension than those who were taught to read in Spanish. Contradictory results were reported by Lambert and Tucker (1972), who conducted the St. Lambert Experiment in Canada. In this study monolingual English-speaking children were taught only in French in grades K and 1. English language skills were introduced in the second grade, but subject matter was presented in French through the fourth grade. This experimental group was compared to a monolingual French control group and to a monolingual French control group which had learned English as a second language and French as a second language, respectively. The results were as follows: At the end of grade 1, the experimental class was at the same level in French reading and word discrimination as the French control group. Although they had not been taught

English reading, they scored at the 50th percentile on national norms for English-speaking first grade children on tests of word knowledge and word discrimination and at the 15th percentile on reading skills. In the second grade they were reading as well as either the French or English control groups, a level they maintained through the other grades.

Paulston (1974) feels one can draw tentative conclusions from the results of this study as well as those provided by the Philippines Rizal experiment and other similar studies. She stresses the fact that learning to read involves two separate skills which are often confused in the literature. The first skill is concerned with learning the sound-symbol relationships and the second with extracting lexical, syntactic, and cultural meaning from the reading. She goes on to relate that she has seen Spanish-speaking children in the second grade read a sentence like *Mi mamá me ama* and not understand it completely because the verb *amar* was not in their vocabulary. This situation is similar to the statement made to this writer by bilingual education teachers, "They read beautifully, but they don't understand what they're reading."

In her paper, *The Use of Vernacular Languages in Education* (1975), Engle surveyed 24 studies which attempted to determine whether a child will learn to read more rapidly in a second language if he is first taught to read in his primary language. She concludes that most of the studies provided no substantial evidence as to which approach is better. Engle, however, points to weaknesses in the studies themselves; that is, the variables in the studies were often not sufficiently controlled and thus the results were significantly affected.

The issues concerning methodology in a bilingual program do not differ greatly from those found in monolingual programs. The question of language use and the incorporation of elements of the home culture into the instructional program are of prime concern and offer a point of departure from monolingual education.

Community Involvement

Nowhere is the overall school program for community or parental involvement as important as in the bilingual education program. Although the notion that education is strictly the business of the school and not of the home is a fairly widespread idea (Fernández 1973), the lack of community involvement in school matters has often been particularly acute in some facets of bilingual programs. The reasons may be attributed to the following:

1. Parents work and may be unable to participate in school affairs.

2. Parents may feel they do not have anything constructive to offer the education of their children.

3. The school may appear hostile or alien to parents with a limited command of English.

4. The feeling may exist that it is the responsibility of the school, not of the home, to educate children.

While the young child may already feel that he is entering a strange world upon coming to school, despite his participation in a bilingual program, a visible link with the home is indispensable to promote positive attitudes about the school. An informative pamphlet produced by NEA, "Get Involved in Your Child's School" (n.d.), suggests answers to questions like, "What is the parent involvement program and how does it benefit my child?" "Why do teachers need my help and do they really want me in the classroom?" "How can I help in the classroom?" Another NEA publication, "Parent-Teacher Relationships" (n.d.), advances the idea that the child does not come to the school alone once the parent is involved. Home conditions, such as family illness, economic problems, or a happy event, may affect school performance, and the teacher may thus obtain a more accurate profile of the child.

One of the most important reasons for involving parents in the bilingual program, according to Smith and Caskey (1972), is to use "the cultural values and language of ethnic groups in the community" and "then greater appreciation and understanding will promote positive feelings of self-worth and bicultural interaction" (p. 247). The reality of the school incorporating elements of the home culture in the instructional program will go far in helping minority children to develop a positive self-image. On the other side of the coin, this type of involvement provides nonminority children with opportunities to experience firsthand cultural dimensions of their fellow classmates.

There is the feeling that parents can help their children at home, too. One particular program, the Spanish Dame Bilingual Bicultural Project of San José, Calif., established a model home-tutoring component described in *Planning the Program with the Home Tutor* (1975). This particular program aims to extend the school into the home through the use of tutors and parents trained to reinforce cognitive and psychomotor skills and concepts in the affective domain. The Spanish Dame Bilingual Bicultural Project has also come forth with another booklet, published by the Dissemination Center for Bilingual Bicultural Education, *Instructional Guide for the Home Tutor* (1974), which provides the tutor with concrete ideas and information concerning teaching techniques, daily lessons, and a daily curriculum guide. These lessons, based on a language maintenance model, concentrate on such elements as language development, concept formation, perceptual development, motor skills, self-awareness, positive self-concept, health and safety, community, and cultural awareness.

Bilingual Education Materials

The need for quality instructional materials has often posed serious problems for bilingual education programs. In the late 1960s bilingual education programs relied on materials imported from outside the United States. Local schools also used teacher-made materials. Teachers frequently found foreign materials difficult to use with children in this country because of linguistic and cultural differences between the world in the books and the reality in which the children lived. In the Southwest, for example, the children's Spanish dialect contained lexical items which were not used in the imported materials. Foreign materials used words like *habichuelas* for the child's familiar *frijoles, colmado* for *tienda,* and *chiringa* for *papalote* or *huila.* While these lexical differences represented linguistic diversity in the Spanish language, they were usually rejected in the Southwest by students and teachers alike. The number of unfamiliar words in the materials often proved discouraging to the students.

During this period federal funding under Title VII, ESEA, provided the necessary resources to establish the Materials Acquisition Project (Peña 1973), which compiled the most comprehensive lists of commercial instructional materials available. The Dissemination Center for Bilingual Bicultural Education— now called the Dissemination and Assessment Center for Bilingual Education or DACBE, located in Austin, Tex., and also established through Title VII—sought to identify, edit, reproduce, and distribute locally developed materials. The Center's publication, *Cartel,* provides annotated listings of commercially and non-commercially-prepared materials.

Commercial publishers recognized a potential market in the production of bilingual education curriculum materials, particularly in Spanish, the largest language group participating in bilingual education in the United States today. In some cases materials were prepared so hurriedly that speed became more important than quality. Some Spanish-language materials were translations of English textbooks and often lacked cultural authenticity. While it is not the purpose of this chapter to identify poor commercial materials or to recommend quality commercial materials, local textbook committees, teachers, and administrators are urged to evaluate materials being considered for purchase by using such instruments as the EPIE Form A (Educational Products Information Exchange Institute 1976). Since this instrument, like any other, can only ask certain questions, the reviewer in the final analysis must possess an understanding of a variety of aspects of bilingual education and curriculum theory and practice. For example, if the reviewer has insufficient knowledge of a particular culture or language, it will be difficult to identify discrepancies in these areas.

The EPIE Institute has published two volumes which evaluate a large number of bilingual education materials, EPIE Report 73, *Selector's Guide for Bilingual Education Materials, Vol. 1, Spanish Language Arts* (1976) and EPIE Report 74, *Selector's Guide for Bilingual Education Materials, Vol. 2, Spanish "Branch" Programs* (1976). These guides should serve teachers, curriculum planners, and textbook selection committees in selecting the most appropriate Spanish-language teaching materials for their programs. González (n.d.) has edited a handbook for assisting educators in reviewing materials for cultural relevancy. Among other things the handbook provides valuable information concerning "formal" culture—art, literature, music—and "deep" culture—personal values, superstitions, behavior patterns. Through careful examination and analysis, local school personnel can determine the materials which best suit their program objectives.

The present Title VII legislation has made possible the establishment of nine materials development centers (DACBE 1976). The purpose of these centers is to "develop instructional, teacher training, and testing materials in the languages and at the grade levels of the bilingual target groups being served" (p. 145). A brief description of the centers follows (pp. 150-153).

Arizona Bilingual Materials Development Center (The University of Arizona at Tucson)
Materials: Teacher training materials
             Grades K-3
             Spanish

Asian American Bilingual Center (Berkeley Unified School District)
Materials: Social studies, language arts, math, science, fine arts
             Grades PK-3
             Cantonese, Philippino, Korean, Japanese, Lauwan

             Needs Assessment
             Grades PK-3
             Samoan

Multilingual Multicultural Materials Development Center (California State Polytechnic University)
Materials: Social studies films and filmstrips
             Grades 7, 8, 9
             Spanish

             Teacher's manuals
             Grades K-12
             Spanish

             Language assessment instruments for teachers
             Grades K-12
             Spanish

Spanish Curricula Development Center (Dade County, Florida, Public Schools)
Materials: Language arts, social studies, fine arts, Spanish, science, math (teacher's guides produced in Puerto Rican, Mexican American, Cuban, and multiethnic editions will eventually encompass Grades 1-6, Spanish)

             Health (multiethnic teacher's guides only)
             Grades 4-6
             Spanish

National Materials Development Center for French and Portuguese (New Hampshire College and University Council)
Materials: Subject areas as needed
             Grades K-6 to be reviewed
             Grades K-12 and adult

French, Acadian French, Canadian French, Haitian French, Portuguese

Native American Materials Development Center (Ramah Navajo School Board, Inc.)
  Materials: Subject areas as needed
              Grades K-3
              Native American languages

Northeast Center for Curriculum Development (New York C.S.C. No. 7)
  Materials: Social studies, language arts, fine arts
              Grades 1-9
              Spanish

              Research
              Grades K-6
              Greek, Italian, Haitian

Bilingual Materials Development Center (Fort Worth, Tex., Independent School District)
  Materials: Fine arts, Spanish and English communication skills, social studies, science, math: student materials, resource materials for teachers, teacher training materials, supportive materials and media
              Grades 6-9

              English as a second language
              Grades 7-8

              Social studies, language arts
              Grade 6
              French

Midwest Materials Development Center (Milwaukee Board of School Directors)
  Materials: Language arts, fine arts, social studies—cultural aspects emphasized
              Grades 4-6
              Spanish

As can be seen, the number of centers with responsibilities in the Spanish language reflects the proportion of Spanish-English bilingual education programs in the nation. It is significant to note, however, that other languages such as Cantonese, Portuguese, Greek, and Korean are included, since commercially prepared materials in these languages have not been forthcoming. The materials prepared by the centers, then, have played an important role in helping local schools implement bilingual programs in languages other than Spanish. Furthermore, the materials development centers have met another need: that of producing materials in languages such as Spanish and French which represent a variety of dialects. These materials have helped to provide pupils with materials in a standard dialect which closely approximates their own home dialect. The illustrations and content are usually such that the children find them culturally familiar. Rather than having the situations take place in another country, they are set in contexts recognized by the children.

Another organization in materials preparation is the Southwest Educational Development Laboratory of Austin, Tex., which has developed a series of Spanish-English bilingual education materials. These materials include bilingual oral language and reading, Spanish reading, first grade social studies in Spanish, bilingual early childhood, bilingual kindergarten, and bilingual continuous progress mathematics. These materials include teacher's manuals and teacher-training materials.

Some commercial publishers which have translated materials from English into another language have not attempted to translate the teacher's manuals. It can be argued, of course, that the concepts are the same regardless of the language in which they are expressed and that the student materials are written in the target language. On the other hand, an opposite view can be argued from both psychological and linguistic perspectives. First, the fact that the teacher's manuals are in English places the target language in an inferior position: it is not sufficiently important to warrant its use in the teacher's materials. Second, the all-English manuals encourage the teacher to use the other language only when instruction takes place, but not in other situations. From a linguistic point of view, the use of the target language in the teacher's manuals increases exposure to this language, particularly as it concerns technical and pedagogical terminology. The Spanish-English materials produced by the Spanish Curricula Development Center are praiseworthy in this respect and serve as a model for other materials. The instructions to the teacher are provided in both languages, and the teacher is thus provided with the opportunity of staying in the same language used to present the lesson itself.

Schools now have access to a variety of materials for teaching culture. Some that are being used are the following:

Bilingual Program ARRIBA. *Estudio cultural de Puerto Rico* (1973).

CANBBE Northeast Regional Adaptation Center. *Carteles puertorriqueños* (1973).

Bilingual Unit, New York State Department of Education. *Puerto Rican History, Civilization and Culture: A Mini-Documentary* (1973).

Native American Materials Development Center. *Navajo Curriculum Series* (1976).

Instructional Media Center, Alaska State-Operated Schools. *Alaskan Folktales* (1976).

Of particular interest to teachers of Puerto Rican students are such resource materials as:

Matilde Colón Sánchez. *El bilingüismo en Puerto Rico y la actitud de un grupo de jóvenes bilingües hacia el idioma vernáculo.* Monograph 87, University of Puerto Rico, December 1972.

Israel Ramos Perea. "El ajuste escolar en los estudiantes migrantes—estudio piloto," Centro de Investigaciones Pedagógicas de la Universidad de Puerto Rico, *Boletín*, Vol. II, No. 1, Sept. 1, 1970.

Eduardo Seda Bonilla. "Cultural Pluralism and the Education of Puerto Rican Youths," *Phi Betta Kappan*, Vol. LIII, No. V, January 1972, pp. 294-296.

A more extensive bibliography of such materials may be obtained from the Office of the Commonwealth of Puerto Rico (Delgado Votaw 1976). These materials can be very useful to teachers, particularly in presenting folklore, history, and customs of the groups indicated. Of interest, also, are the materials compiled by Marquevich and Spiegel (1976), which provide valuable information about the folklore of Asian Americans, Eurasian Americans, Afro Americans, Native Americans, Mexican Americans, and Puerto Rican Americans.

With the influx of Vietnamese refugees and other Asian groups to this country, materials have been developed to asssit schools in meeting the needs of these students. Of special note are the following:

Los Angeles Unified School District. *Bridging the Asian Language and Cultural Gap: A Handbook for Teachers* (1971-1974).

Vietnamese Clearinghouse of the Center for Applied Linguistics. *Hints for Dealing with Cultural Differences in School: A Handbook for Teachers Who Have Vietnamese Students in Their Classrooms* (1975).

Lien Truong, Glendale Unified School District. *Counseling for Vietnamese Students* (n.d.).

Title VII has funded two dissemination and assessment centers: DACBE in Austin, Tex., and the Assessment and Dissemination Center at Fall River, located in Fall River, Mass. The Massachusetts center edits, reproduces, and distributes materials in Asian, French, Portuguese, Greek, Italian, and Spanish languages. It should be mentioned at this point that the seven resource centers funded by Title VII assist in training school personnel in the use of bilingual materials and field test the materials from the nine materials development centers. The three components, consisting of the seven resource centers, nine materials development centers, and two dissemination and assessment centers, comprise the National Network for Bilingual Education (DACBE 1976).

Professional literature for teachers in the area of bilingual education is now coming into its own. To be sure, the manuals accompanying basic instructional materials are useful in suggesting teaching strategies for their respective textbooks. The dissemination and assessment centers have a number of good publications for professional growth, and specific titles may be obtained through their respective catalogs: DACBE, *Publications Catalog* (published biannually). As yet the Fall River Center has not developed a regular catalog of materials.

Other materials useful for professional growth or initial teacher training include the classic two-volume work by Andersson and Boyer, *Bilingual Schooling in the United States* (1970), which provides a wealth of information about bilingual education from a national and international perspective, its history in the United States, a description of specific programs and curriculum models, and a very extensive bibliography. Saville and Troike's *A Handbook of Bilingual*

Education (1971) is useful from the point of view of providing the teacher with basic linguistic information, advice on the implementation of a bilingual program, the use of materials, and community involvement. Litsinger's book, *The Challenge of Teaching Mexican American Students* (1973), may be of interest to teacher trainers preparing instructors for this particular cultural and linguistic group. It presents a historical perspective of the Mexican American, a rationale for bilingual bicultural education, and pedagogical suggestions for the teaching of subject matter in English and Spanish. The Texas Education Agency has developed a comprehensive training manual designed primarily for inservice education, *An Orientation to Bilingual Education in Texas: A Training Manual* (1976). This publication, which has been used widely in Texas, includes sections on materials utilization, parental involvement, oral language development, reading, and classroom management. *New Approaches to Bilingual Bicultural Education* (1974), produced by Systems and Evaluations in Education, has consolidated a series of previously separate documents concerning the Mexican American. The publication includes chapters on pluralistic education, Mexican American values, learning styles, strategies for teaching the Mexican American, and a self-assessment section for teachers to determine level of achievement after having read the book.

It is significant that professional journals are devoting their attention to issues in bilingual education. Noteworthy are the following: *The Bilingual Review/La revista bilingüe* is devoted exclusively to the study of bilingualism and bilingual education; *TESOL Quarterly*, which was originally designed to serve the needs of teachers of English to speakers of other languages, takes an avid interest in bilingual education; *Foreign Language Annals*, published by the American Council on the Teaching of Foreign Languages, regularly includes articles on language teaching as it relates to bilingual education; *Hispania*, the journal of the American Association of Teachers of Spanish and Portuguese, Inc., includes articles concerning the Spanish-speaking population in the United States. This is not an all-inclusive list of resources for professional growth, but it can be seen that the bilingual education teacher has numerous resources on which to draw for ideas, inspiration, and practice.

Program Evaluation

Curriculum planners (Tyler et al. 1968) distinguish between formative and summative evaluation. The first has to do with the determination of the effectiveness of the instructional program. Student progress is measured periodically to determine if the program objectives are being met. The information obtained is fed back into the program through the teachers so that interim program modifications may be made as needed. Although formal testing instruments can be used for this purpose, subjective information obtained through observation of student performance is used also. Summative evaluation is based on information provided by the formative evaluation process over an extended period of time. Its purpose is to determine the extent to which the program objectives have been met.

In the bilingual program Cohen (1975) indicates that summative evaluation should be obtained over a period of years in each language, in academic achievement, and in the attitudes of the students. Cohen also mentions that all too often program evaluators assess students with yearly standardized tests in English without regard to measuring overall—cumulative—progress in both languages over a period of years.

The U.S. Commission for Civil Rights (1975) states that in a bilingual program the purpose of outcome (summative) evaluation is to determine the extent to which the bilingual bicultural education program increased the educational progress of students in comparison with monolingual English instruction with or without ESL. Relative to bilingual programs, the present report has noted the inadequacy of standardized tests which do not use the language and culture of the target population. Without proper evaluation instruments and controls, however, it is difficult to compare progress made by students in bilingual programs with that made by students in monolingual programs. Some of the variables that would influence the results of a testing program are as follows:

The entry-level skills of the students.

The students' language dominance.

The amount of time devoted to instruction in the home language and in English.

The nature of the evaluative instruments.

The attitude of the community and school toward the bilingual program and minority students.

The availability of quality instructional materials.

The preparation of the teachers in the area of bilingual education.

Although the Dissemination Center for Bilingual Bicultural Education (1975) has compiled an extensive annotated bibliography of evaluation instruments for use in bilingual programs, the truth of the matter is that there is a tremendous scarcity of hard data regarding the effectiveness of bilingual education programs. Proponents of this educational movement point to such things as improved self-concept, gains in the affective domain (Troike 1974a), and increased school attendance. Opponents use underachievement as indicated on standardized tests as an indicator of the failure of bilingual education. The reports of the Title VII projects vary in their findings, and the data are usually not the result of rigorously controlled experiments. As a consequence strong emotions, pro and con, have played a large role in the politics of bilingual education.

Recently the United States General Accounting Office (GAO) issued an important report to the Congress concerning the state of the art in bilingual education, *Bilingual Education: An Unmet Need* (1976). The report maintains that the United States Office of Education (USOE) has made little progress in three areas (p. i):

1. Identifying effective means of providing bilingual education instruction.
2. Training bilingual education teachers.
3. Developing suitable teaching materials.

In reference to the first point, the report indicates that in 1971, USOE created a task force to determine whether or not bilingual education should change from a demonstration status to an educational service program. The committee recommended that effective strategies of bilingual education should be identified systematically. This recommendation was not carried out because of the cost such a project would entail and the inability of USOE to control the experiment in each local education agency (LEA).

Concerning point 2 in March 1974, USOE had estimated that there were between 1.8 and 2.5 million children in need of bilingual education and that between 60,000 and 83,000 bilingual teachers would be needed (GAO, p. 15). These figures were not accurate since they were based only on data from four states obtained from the 1970 census and on a study carried out by the Office for Civil Rights in 1972. Quantitatively, USOE has not been able to gather information concerning the skills and knowledge actually being provided by institutions of higher education (IHE) for future bilingual teachers. USOE has, however, specified that Title VII teachers meet the following minimum qualifications (GAO, p. 16):

Bilingual capability.
Training and experience in teaching, using the native language of the target group as a medium of instruction.
Preparation and experience in ESL.
Awareness of the students' culture.

The GAO report states that the original Title VII legislation did not provide funds for scholarships or fellowships for individuals wishing to pursue a degree in bilingual education nor did it provide direct grants to IHEs. The 1974 Title VII amendments have made this type of funding possible, and they are discussed further below.

The third point of the report indicates the shortage of quality sequential materials, particularly in languages other than Spanish. LEAs, then, have been largely responsible for developing their own materials which are usually geared toward the specific needs of a given school district, and adaptation by other LEAs has been difficult. The section of this chapter concerning materials indicates that Title VII funds are being used to develop materials in languages other than Spanish.

Longitudinal studies of student achievement are often made to measure student progress for a period of over one year. The GAO report reviewed student achievement in 16 projects and did a two-year longitudinal study. A summary of the findings follows (p. 40):

The analysis showed that 85, or 45 percent, of 191 English-dominant students and 67, or 33 percent, of 205 non-English-dominant students made normal reading progress or better. In math, 73, or 57 percent, of 129 English-dominant students and 51, or 35 percent, of 147 non-English-dominant students achieved at least normal progress. Thus, gains made by English-dominant students on the average were better than those of non-English-dominant students. Also, a comparison of the longitudinal results with the 1-year analysis shows that students generally did not achieve as a high a rate of growth over the 2-year period as they did in 1 year. OE officials said that regression of this nature is common in all compensatory or remedial educational programs.

The report goes on to state that two specific factors could have caused the foregoing results. Specifically, these factors are (p. 45):

The dominant language of the limited English-speaking children might not have been used enough for classroom instruction.

There often seemed to be too many English-speaking children in the project classrooms, thereby diluting program services for the limited English-speaking children.

While the reasons above could very well affect the survey results, the report indicates that the analyses were done "on English reading and English math tests given by the LEA as part of the regular school or Title VII testing program" (p. 34). It would seem, first of all, that this statement is contradictory to the explanations of the lower test scores by the non-English-dominant students. If all-English tests were used, how can the insufficient use of the children's native language influence scores on these tests? Second, the tests were in English, even though some of the students were not dominant in this language. This procedure goes against the rationale for bilingual education, i.e., to use the students' dominant language for instructional and evaluative purposes.

It seems that the GAO has pinpointed three particularly acute areas of weakness in bilingual education. Although funds have been appropriated to create quality programs, the movement to teach children in two languages has had to face a number of obstacles, such as those identified by the GAO. It would appear unfair to try to compare the progress made in bilingual education since 1968 with that made in monolingual education, which has a longer history, experience, and general support from the public.

On the other side of the coin, Dulay, Burt, and Zappert (1976) have recently come forth with a summary of research findings graphically presented in a poster format. According to the authors, 28 research studies and 172 evaluation reports were excluded from the poster because of serious weaknesses in research design. Thus the poster includes 66 findings from 9 research studies and 3 project evaluations. Although the number of actual studies is small, the authors conclude that:

> Contrary to widespread belief, the research conducted to date is not contradictory with regards to the effects of bilingualism and bilingual education on student performance. If one applies objective criteria for applicability and soundness of research design, most of the studies show a significant positive effect, or a nonsignificant effect, on student performance. Of the 66 findings reported here, only 1 (1%) was negative; 38 (58%) were positive, and 27 (41%) were neutral.

These positive findings are encouraging and should pave the way for more work in the area. Additionally, one can turn to other countries where bilingualism and bilingual education are a fact of life (Christian and Sharp 1972, p. 364):

> Bilingualism never seems to have impaired the intelligence of the social and intellectual elite of European countries where use of more than one major languages is an important prerequisite for social position. Only where bilingualism is associated with a high degree of literacy in any two languages is it recognized as a form of achievement rather than limitation. Educational measures almost inevitably represent this cultural value.

STAFF DEVELOPMENT

University Programs

University teacher-training programs in bilingual education and other related areas such as ethnic studies have increased dramatically since the passage of the 1968 bilingual legislation. Although little information is available in terms of faculty qualifications, experience, and courses of study, the increase in the number of programs is significant, since it points to interest in and demand for bilingual teaching personnel. Figures 5 and 6, compiled from DACBE, *Teacher Education Programs for Bilingual Education in U.S. Colleges and Universities: 1974-75, 1975-76,* show this increase, particularly in terms of baccalaureate, master's, and doctoral degree programs. For example, in 1974-1975, there were 25 undergraduate programs in bilingual education in the nation, as compared with 96 in 1975-1976; there were 43 master's programs in 1974-1975 and 69 in 1975-1976; in 1974-1975, there were 8 doctoral programs and in 1976-1976, 17. The charts also indicate other types of programs related to bilingual education, and these are somewhat difficult to compare, since the information from the sources was at times not too explicit and the various categories overlapped.

During fiscal year 1976, USOE under Title VII awarded a total of 700 fellowships for study at the master's and doctoral levels in the area of bilingual education. These fellowships were awarded to fellows enrolled in 38 universities and represent 12 different languages. These figures represent an increase over fiscal year 1975, when 480 fellowships were awarded to individuals enrolled in 30 universities. The purpose of the Title VII Bilingual Education Fellowship Program

Figure 5. Teacher Education in Bilingual Bicultural Education, 1974-1975

	Assoc. in arts, paraprofessional	Bilingual instruction	Courses in bil. ed. or 2d language certification	B.A./B.S. in bil. ed.	Masters in bil. ed.	Masters in ESL or other 2d language	Doctorate in bil. ed.	B.A./B.S. in multicultural ethnic studies, in ESL or other 2d language	Summer programs, methods, inservice	Field-based courses
Alaska	1					1		1		
Arizona				1	1					
California			3	3	4	1		2		
Colorado				2	1		1			
Conn.			2	1	3					
D.C.					1					
Hawaii								1		
Idaho			2	1						
Illinois					5		1		1	
Indiana		1				2				
Iowa				1						
Louisiana			1			1				
Maine		1	1			1				
Maryland				1	1	1	1			1
Mass.	1		13	4	5		1			
Michigan	1		1	1				1		
Nevada								1		
New Jersey				1	3	1		1		
New Mexico		1	1	1	3					
New York	1	2		2	7	2	1	5		1
Ohio		2			1					
R.I.					1				2	
Texas			4	2	5	1	2			
Utah					2					
Wisconsin	1			2	1		1			
Totals	5	7	29	25	44	12	8	12	4	2

Figure 6.   Teacher Education in Bilingual Bicultural Education, 1975-1976

	Assoc. in arts, parapro-fessional	Language courses or courses taught bilingually	Courses in bil. ed, or 2d language certification	B.A./B.S. in bil. ed.	B.A./B.S. in ESL, multi-cultural ed. or ethnic studies	Masters in bil. ed.	Masters in ESL or other 2 language	Doctorate in bil. ed.
Alaska				1				1
Arizona	4			3		1	1	1
California	18			18		17		1
Colorado				4		1		
Connecticut				3		4		
D.C.				1		1		
Florida*						2		1
Idaho			2					
Illinois			1	9		5		1
Indiana							1	
Iowa				1				
Kansas*			2			2		
Louisiana								
Maine			1					
Maryland	1			1		1	1	
Massachusetts			5	17		5	1	1
Michigan	1	2		2		2		1

Figure 6 (continued)

	Assoc. in arts, parapro-fessional	Language courses or courses taught bilingually	Courses in bil. ed. or 2d language certification	B.A./B.S. in bil. ed.	B.A./B.S. in ESL, multi-cultural ed. or ethnic studies	Masters in bil. ed.	Masters in ESL or other 2 language	Doctorate in bil. ed.
Mississippi*		1			1			
Nevada					2			
New Jersey		1		2		3	2	2
New Mexico	1	1	4	4		4		
New York	3	2	11	8		8		2
Oregon†	1			1				
Pennsylvania			2	2		2	2	1
Rhode Island			3			1		
Texas	2	1	8	15		7		3
Utah				2				
Vermont*						1		
Washington*						1		1
Wisconsin	1			1	1	1	1	1
Totals	32	8	39	95	4	69	9	17

*Not on 1974-1975 survey.
†Ohio missed in 1975-1976.

is to provide tuition, fees, and stipends to individuals enrolled in an IHE which "offers a program of study leading to a degree above the baccalaureate level in the field of training teachers for programs of bilingual education" (USOE 1976, Sec. 123.42). The thrust of the fellowship program, therefore, is not to train bilingual classroom teachers but to begin to meet the demand for teacher trainers who can staff IHEs. While programs of study vary among the participating IHEs, USOE judges programs among other factors on their capability to teach courses in a language other than English, to teach culture, to select and use evaluative instruments for measuring performance of LESA children, to involve parents and community organizations in programs of bilingual education. It is hoped that the fellowship program will help to alleviate the present shortage of teacher trainers and will assist in institutionalizing bilingual education programs in IHEs throughout the country.

A vital dimension of university programs is training for bilingual classroom teachers. Before the 1974 Title VII amendments, the majority of training activities were provided through inservice programs, utilizing at times consultants from colleges and universities. Although USOE is not a regulatory agency, it sets general standards for bilingual education teacher training programs through its funding programs. State education agency certification standards for a bilingual credential, on the other hand, vary considerably. In an attempt to provide leadership in bilingual education teacher training, the Center for Applied Linguistics (CAL) produced its *Guidelines for the Preparation and Certification of Teachers of Bilingual/Bicultural Education* (1974). The various categories are those that the writing committee felt were indispensable for the bilingual education teacher. These categories are in turn expressed or broken down into competencies which the "ideal" bilingual education teacher should demonstrate: "ideal" in that it would be a rare individual who could be expected to perform all the identified competencies. They do, however, identify important areas of the bilingual program which the teacher should strive to attain.

The emphasis of university programs has been the training of teachers and teacher trainers, and this is shown in the information provided by the 1974-1975 and 1975-1976 editions of DACBE publications on teacher education which did not identify any university programs that offered administrative degrees or other credentials in bilingual education. If this is the case, it would seem that colleges and universities should now begin expanding their programs to encompass the area of bilingual program administration. Earlier in this chapter the duties and responsibilities of the bilingual program coordinator were outlined. To ensure the growth and strengthening of bilingual education, knowledgeable and qualified bilingual education administrators, such as coordinators, principals, supervisors, and superintendents, are an absolute necessity.

Inservice Education

Title VII provides funds to LEAs to support ongoing inservice activities for teachers. LEAs may request funds to implement inservice programs through the use of consultants, or they may request funds to provide inservice training in the form of university programs, usually leading toward an advanced degree.

Locally sponsored inservice activities vary greatly in scope and topics. An ERIC search of LEA inservice programs revealed 26 topics. They are presented in Figure 7. LEAs can use them as a model to develop ongoing inservice programs for bilingual education teachers. The ERIC search did not reveal the extent to which the target languages of the programs were used in the inservice sessions. It would be safe to assume, however, that the majority of activities were carried out in English. Language development for teachers in the non-English languages of bilingual programs is an area of concern, since many teachers have had limited formal training in these languages, despite their being native speakers (Blanco 1975). One can only hope that, as bilingual education programs grow, inservice programs will use ever-increasing amounts of the target languages in the activities for teachers. The inservice programs will thus be practicing what they recommend for the children's curriculum: language development in the target language of the bilingual program.

ISSUES CRITICAL TO THE
FUTURE OF BILINGUAL EDUCATION

Attitudes toward Bilingual Education

The funding which bilingual education has received can be viewed as support for this educational movement. There is much interest in bilingual education at the present time, as indicated by the ever-increasing programs at the local, state, and federal levels, and support has also been forthcoming from other educational fields, such as mathematics and social studies. Another segment which has rallied to the aid of bilingual education is the community. Martin (1975) reports that most Amerindian groups welcome the inclusion of native languages in the curriculum, although there is still some resistance stemming from the notion that the English language and English-speaking teachers are superior. Gutiérrez (1972) also noted that parents in her New Mexico study showed a positive attitude toward bilingual education. She also underscores the importance of parental support for the success of the bilingual program. In another survey (Flores Macías 1973), parents indicated very favorable support for bilingual preschool education programs. Greene and Zirkel (1973) reported that bilingual parents were found to have a more positive attitude about bilingualism than their monolingual counterparts. Lest we paint an overly positive picture of attitudes toward the use of languages other than English in American education, it is necessary to examine some of the contrary positions.

Albert Shanker (1974) of the United Federation of Teachers made the following statement aimed at bilingual education programs (Section 4, p. 11):

> While the need for the child to feel comfortable and to be able to communicate is clear, it is also clear that what these children need is intensive instruction in

Figure 7.   Topics Presented in Inservice Programs

Topic	ED 065 212	ED 065 212 (Jefferson)	ED 065 212 (Empire Gardens)	ED 057 973	ED 065 221	ED 071 795	ED 081 549	ED 041 066	ED 064 024	ED 067 197	ED 066 983
Encounter group			X								
Human relations training	X	X						X			X
Reading Skills	X	X			X		X	X	X		X
Reading Diagnosis	X	X			X						
Oral language development											
Relate art, music, linguistics or use any of these	X				X				X		
Contrastive analysis of languages					X						X
Teaching Spanish to Spanish speakers					X						

Figure 7 (continued)

Topic							
English as a second language or second language learning						X	X
Rationale for bilingual program			XX	X	X	X	X
Evaluation design of program				X	X	X	
Information on materials	X				X	X	X
Individualized instruction				X	X		
Behavior modification/ positive reinforcement				X	X	X	
Culture		X	X	X	X	X	X
Classroom arrangement		X		X	X	X	
Teaching socialization skills		X		X			
Involving parents		X					
Interaction analysis		X			X		
Writing behavioral objectives	X	X			X		
Lesson planning				X			
Testing				X	X	X	
Cognitive and intellectual development					X	X	
Use of audio-visual equipment				X	X		X
Roles of teachers and staff					X	X	X
Community resources		X			X		X
Curriculum development		X		X	X	X	X

From McBride 1974, pp. 40-41.

> English so that they may as soon as possible function with other children in regular school programs. . . . The American taxpayer, while recognizing the existence of cultural diversity, still wants the schools to be the basis of an American melting pot.

This statement, designed to appeal to the uninformed and to educators who feel their livelihood threatened by the bilingual education movement, does not mention that the learning of English is one of the basic goals of bilingual education in the United States.

More recently, a *Long Island Press* columnist also made strong statements against the teaching of languages other than English (Cuneo 1975, p. 18):

> If the parents of these children are too lazy or too ignorant to learn the American language, they ought not to be voting citizens. . . . The emphasis, therefore, should be upon teaching their children the American language to overcome the disadvantage of their parents. The object of American schooling is to teach them to think as Americans, not to continue the customs of a different culture.

This columnist goes on to say that these [minority] children are already learning the "nasty" lesson of not having acquired the American language because "third-rate politicians are bent on acquiring the votes of their parents" (p. 18). These are only two examples of opposition to the bilingual education movement, and there are other individuals over the nation who are speaking out against it and emphasizing its failure to produce quality education. Jaramillo (1973) exhorts bilingual educators to "support and expand good bicultural programs with or without Federal funds" and "to eradicate poor programs. . . . We cannot, we must not, give these critics food for thought. We must produce excellent programs only" (p. 261). Not only must we produce excellent programs, but we must continuously inform the public of our successes through the news media, parent-teacher groups, and civic organizations. Public support is vital to the continuation of bilingual education.

Another dimension of attitudes toward bilingual education lies within the ranks of bilingual educators. A great deal of parochialism still exists within the field. Presumably, bilingual educators are striving to achieve common goals. Yet we see little effort to engage in serious educational exchange programs whereby the Southwest, for example, could benefit by hiring Puerto Ricans or the Northeast could strengthen its concept of the Hispanic world by recruiting Mexican American teachers. Although bilingual education should present a united front, the internal division even within a particular language group will eventually prove to be detrimental to the very goals toward which the profession is striving; maintenance of bilingual education for LESA and for mainstream children.

Federal Funding

The impact of Title VII funds on bilingual education in the United States has yet to make the favorable impression which the authors of the Bilingual Education

Act had hoped. The resistance previously indicated and the problems hindering more visible progress have reflected poorly on bilingual education. It is significant, however, that many of the problem areas, e.g., lack of qualified teaching personnel, quality instructional materials, and good curriculum models for program implementation, are just now being addressed by the Title VII amendments of 1974. Although teachers within the ranks of bilingual education have often become discouraged by the many obstacles, the future in terms of the three elements listed above is somewhat brighter.

The funding made available under the National Defense Education Act (NDEA) of 1958 was "seed money" designed to assist schools and colleges to upgrade and institutionalize their instructional programs. The intent of NDEA was for local and state education agencies to assume fiscal and program responsibilities eventually. The same intent is present in the Title VII legislation. There are indications that federal support for bilingual education will increase. Molina (1977) states that USOE will ask Congress for increased funding to allow for such critical areas as teacher training, research, and provisions to include mainstream students in bilingual education programs. In spite of this possibility, however, schools cannot and should not rely exclusively on federal funds for bilingual education program implementation. Programs may receive funding for a specified period of time, and funding approval may cease for one of several reasons, such as:

The "seed money" has had an impact on a local program and USOE officials feel that the money would be better utilized in another LEA.

The local program receives an unfavorable evaluation and is no longer considered a good investment of federal funds.

The appropriation of funds is usually insufficient to allow 100% approval of all LEA project proposals.

Thus, while total federal funding approved by the U.S. Congress may continue to increase, it would be unrealistic to expect total funding for every local bilingual education program in the country. LEAs, state boards of education, and state legislatures must include bilingual education funding as an integral part of their public school financial plans. The Council of Chief State School Officers has gone on record as supporting cultural pluralism (Council of Chief State School Officers 1977), and this action must be capitalized on to ensure that state boards of education incorporate bilingual education into the curriculum for general education. If the profession has established high standards for its bilingual programs and the results of the programs are widely disseminated, school boards and the public in general will be more inclined not only to accept bilingual education but also to provide funding for them, once federal monies are withdrawn.

Likewise colleges and universities will have to assume the financial responsibility for training bilingual education teachers and teacher trainers. Although the number of IHEs with bilingual bicultural programs has increased greatly with the availability of federal funds, some IHE bilingual programs predate the Title VII 1974 amendments which provided them with direct grants.

Training of Personnel

With the present state and federal efforts in teacher training, the demand for qualified bilingual personnel will be somewhat alleviated. Despite federal assistance to IHEs and the state efforts in teacher preparation, however, this writer is cautious about being overly optimistic over the training of sufficient numbers of personnel necessary to make a serious impact on bilingual education programs in the near future. Although no information is presently available concerning the national need for bilingual education teachers, the figure must be large, since Texas alone needed 5000 bilingual education teachers for 1976-1977 (Cruz-Aedo 1976).

The training of teachers and teacher aides has advanced from a purely inservice activity to one sponsored by IHEs, which may lead to a degree, certification, or both. The Title VII Fellowship Program is helping to prepare teacher trainers, and the next generation of bilingual teachers will undoubtedly be better trained than those in the past. However, IHEs are faced with one of the very same problems that many local schools are trying to cope with: the tremendous scarcity of personnel proficient in languages other than English.

To be sure, IHEs should practice what they preach and should be in a position to conduct courses either bilingually or completely in the non-English language, but university personnel with this linguistic capability is still very rare. Local schools look to the colleges and universities to train their teachers. This presumes that the IHEs have the necessary personnel themselves. They do not at this time.

IHEs with bilingual personnel training programs need that rare individual who has a pedagogical background, academic training in two languages, and usually a doctorate in hand. The only solution to the problem is genuine cooperation among the various disciplines and departments that comprise bilingual education—both in the professional field of education and in other areas, such as the humanities and science. It is also a question of the IHE administration not being too hasty in abolishing positions earmarked for bilingual personnel simply because such individuals are not readily available.

Another need for bilingual education personnel lies within the ranks of administration. This chapter has indicated the central role of various administrators to the success of the bilingual education program. IHEs must now begin to think seriously about developing training programs and certification programs for bilingual education administrators. This either should take the form of a specialist in bilingual education administration or should consist of a supporting field for any administrative credential or degree from IHEs located in states with large numbers of bilingual education programs. Indubitably, administrative support is essential to the success of bilingual education programs.

Maintenance and Transitional Bilingual Education

Federal and state legislation dictates transitional bilingual education. While advocates of bilingual education can rationalize the transitional model on the grounds that "it gets our foot in the door," one cannot but wonder about the psychological damage and educational waste occasioned by this approach. The child quickly comes to understand that phasing out his home language must mean that it is inferior or that something is wrong with it. Educationally the nation squanders a great resource by not developing languages other than English spoken natively in America. To be sure, initiating programs using a transitional or compensatory model is a beginning, but it should be just that—a beginning. We cannot stand by complacently accepting tokenism, but must demand recognition of one of our greatest educational opportunities. If bilingual education in the United States is to survive, it must move quickly into a language-maintenance model. Even more, it must cease to be a program for "disadvantaged" minorities and incorporate the mainstream society as well. The hearings held before the National Advisory Council on Bilingual Education in Austin, Tex., in January 1977 and in New Orleans, La., in April 1977 (Molina 1976, 1977) clearly underscore and endorse the need for maintenance bilingual education. Fishman (1976) strongly advocates a form of bilingual education which is even more widespread internationally than the language-maintenance model. He calls it enrichment bilingual education and points out that this is the kind of education opted for by the elites in 3000 years of recorded world history. This is the type of bilingual education needed in the United States, the type which would include all pupils—not just minorities—and thus would be an integral part of general education.

Research

One of the most important areas concerning the future of bilingual education is research. As was previously indicated, longitudinal studies on bilingual education in the United States are almost nonexistent. At present bilingual education is heavily supported by federal funding. Taxpayers look closely not only at the money spent on education in general, but also particularly at programs that they consider controversial, unnecessary, or undesirable. While we can point to the success of bilingual schooling abroad, the truth is that American taxpayers want to see successful education programs in their own schools. In the final analysis bilingual education will have to depend on local and state support if it is to become an integral part of general education. The level of future state and local financial support, however, will depend largely on the reputation of past programs. If they have been successful and the public is thereby convinced that bilingual education is not a frill or just a compensatory program for "disadvantaged" minorities but an indispensable part of the regular educational program, then the chances for continued support will be far greater.

What are the research needs in bilingual education today? What has been done? What remains to be done? In terms of needs, Troike (1974b) identified 12 research priorities in bilingual education; they include such topics as:

Sociolinguistic research on regional and social variations in the use of

Spanish and English by Spanish-speaking communities in the United States, especially in the Southwest.

Research on the effect of different instructional methods with different linguistic and cultural groups, and with different age groups.

Research on the effect of teacher attitudes on student achievement, the effect of bilingual teaching on student self-concept, and the effect of linguistically and anthropologically oriented teacher training on teacher behavior and student achievement.

Research on the effect of bilingual education programs on school-community relations, and of community attitudes on school and language achievement.

Research on problems of transfer from native language reading to reading in English.

The Multicultural/Bilingual Division of the National Institute of Education (1976) has identified four general areas in which it will support research and development (p. 7):

1. Policy studies to provide information to educational policy makers necessary for making decisions on bilingual programs.

2. Linguistics research to increase the knowledge base relative to native and second language acquisition in order to enhance the effectiveness of bilingual education for persons of limited English-speaking ability.

3. Assessment procedures to develop new methods and instruments for identifying students in need of bilingual education and for assessing the educational progress of bilingual students.

4. Teaching and curriculum development to improve the instructional processes utilized in bilingual/multicultural programs at the elementary and secondary levels.

In its continued efforts to promote quality research in the area of bilingual education, the National Institute of Education in March 1977 sponsored a conference designed "to explore strategies for coordinating and supporting the dissertation research work of the ESEA Title VII doctoral fellows" (Vázquez and Miller 1977). The conference underscored the need to promote quality research and to avoid duplication of efforts among the bilingual education doctoral students. The United States Office of Education will propose to the Congress changes in the Title VII legislation to include funds for research in bilingual education (Molina 1977).

Since research is such a crucial component of the continuation of bilingual education in the United States at this time, it would indeed be sad if this educational concept were not given a fair chance to prove its worth in most of the research now being done. Reference has already been made to the report of the United States General Accounting Office (1976) and the negative results of its findings about bilingual education. According to a recent news release from the United States Department of Health, Education and Welfare (1977), the Office of Education reported interim findings of a national evaluation of bilingual education, conducted by the American Institutes for Research (1977) which indicate that the program is producing mixed results. According to the news release, the evaluation involved 38 Spanish-English projects in 11 states in their fourth and fifth year of Title VII funding. Students in grades 6 to 7 (approximately 5300 Title VII students and some 2400 students of similar background not enrolled in the program) were tested in fall of 1975 and in spring of 1976. According to the release, major findings of the study are (p. 1):

Only one-third of the students enrolled in bilingual education classrooms were of limited English-speaking ability.

During a 5½ month period Title VII Hispanic students made smaller progress in English language proficiency than their non-program counterparts, but showed greater gains in mathematics.

86% of the Title VII project directors reported that Spanish dominant students often remain in bilingual classrooms after they are able to function in English.

The Center for Applied Linguistics (CAL) has prepared a response to the AIR study (1977) and charges that, in general, the study treats all bilingual education programs alike without regard to differences. According to CAL the major drawbacks of the AIR study are (p. 1):

Weakness of pre- and post-test design over a five month period.

Inappropriate use of gain scores to assess effects of experimental treatments.

Unreliability of teacher assessment of students' language ability.

Inappropriate use of the CTBS (California Test of Basic Skills) to assess English reading ability with limited English and monolingual Spanish speakers, possibly invalidating the results.

Lack of adequate teacher training and curriculum during the first five years of Title VII funding.

Distortion of information which defeats the intended purpose of the report, i.e., to provide information for policy makers.

Aggregation of students who have received a variety of educational treatments funded by Title VII and whose language ability ranges from monolingual English to bilingual to monolingual Spanish conceals the potential effect of bilingual education.

Other instances of poor research reported by Dulay, Burt, and Zappert (1976), were discussed earlier in this chapter. As indicated, most of the students were rejected because of inherent weaknesses in the research design, such as:

No control for subjects' socioeconomic status.

No control for initial language proficiency.

No baseline comparison data or control group.

Inadequate sample.

Excessive attrition rate.

Significant differences in teacher qualifications for control and experimental groups.

Insufficient data and/or statistics reported.

A considerable amount of research on language, bilingualism, and bilingual education has been conducted as a result of the Language Research Project of The University of Texas at Austin (Horn 1976). The research consists primarily of dissertations beginning in 1964.

To be sure, not a great deal of quality research has been conducted in the field of bilingual education. It is only fair, therefore, that findings be presented as objectively as possible and that variables be accounted for and not merely ignored as has been the case in most instances up to now. With criticisms such as those reported here, it is not possible to lend credence to the negative reports concerning bilingual education. Until serious, well-designed studies are conducted, we cannot obtain a true picture of the effects of bilingual education.

Despite the dismal state of the art in research in the area of bilingual education, Dulay, Burt, and Zappert (1976) were able to report positive findings on those studies and project evaluations that met the strict criteria which they established. They conclude that:

> We believe that the research conducted to date strongly supports the use of the child's first-learned, dominant, and/or home language as a medium of instruction in U.S. schools.

CONCLUSION

The melting pot philosophy, though still prevalent in the minds of many American citizens, is being challenged. What we have today is a legacy of the turbulent sixties: It is still a time of questioning, of search for identity—but this quest is somewhat less intense; it is less emotional and more objective. The civil rights movement led the struggle for equal rights. Though we as a nation have come a long way in this quest, much remains to be done. I have attempted to show that the United States is a culturally and linguistically pluralistic society whether mainstream society is willing to recognize it or not.

The plight of the oppressed linguistic and cultural minorities has been presented to point out the arbitrary nature of judgments toward certain groups different from the mainstream and to show that there is nothing inherently wrong with this diversity. This diversity, whether it is based on lifestyle, culture, or language, must be seen as a strength—as an affirmation that we are secure in our self-identity as citizens of this country and in the belief in the very tenets on which the nation was founded.

There is nothing within the philosophy of bilingual education that diminishes the reality that English is the official language of the United States. There is nothing in the philosophy of bilingual education to support the fear that it encourages political, linguistic, or cultural fragmentation of the nation. There is nothing to support the notion that linguistic and cultural diversity is categorically linked with political alienation. Bilingual education reaffirms all these concepts.

Viewing diversity as a strength, most bilingual education practitioners support maintenance as opposed to transitional bilingual education programs. The maintenance concept encourages the intellectual development of individuals who function in two cultures and who are fully competent in two languages: They understand, speak, read, and write English and another language. This philosophy is different from the transitional model where the individual is quickly moved into English at the expense of the other language and culture. The transitional model is contradictory to the educational philosophy of our nation, which advances the needs of individuals and the satisfaction of their human wants. To date bilingual education has been viewed as a program for "disadvantaged" students. From this point of view bilingualism is seen as a deficiency rather than a strength, as in other parts of the world where it is the uneducated person who is monolingual.

It is important for critics of bilingual education who claim that bilingual education and bilingualism are harmful to realize that there is little in terms of serious, well-designed, and carefully controlled research that upholds this viewpoint. What little good research is available indicates that in most cases bilingual education is either beneficial in terms of scholastic achievement or is neutral—in which case the individual has the added advantage of coming out of the experience as one who has been exposed to two languages. Much more serious research in bilingual education needs to be done to improve the quality of the curriculum, instructional procedures, and teaching materials for children with limited English-speaking skill. Much work also needs to be done to explore ways of including children from the mainstream society in bilingual education programs.

Only when individuals from all segments of American society are given the opportunity of participating in bilingual and multicultural experiences—regardless of socioeconomic status, color, sex, ethnic, cultural, or linguistic background—will the United States prove its mettle, its ability to recognize individual freedom. Individuality, and thereby diversity, is a source of strength and a basic human right which transcends political boundaries. In direct opposition to Israel Zangwill's call for unity through amalgamation in the melting pot, cultural and linguistic pluralism responds to Walt Whitman's (1891-1892) earlier call for unity through recognition and exaltation of the individual (p. 360):

> I swear I begin to see the meaning of these things,
> It is not the earth, it is not America who is so great,
> It is I who am great or to be great, it is You up there, or any one,
> It is to walk rapidly through civilizations, governments, theories,
> Through poems, pageants, shows, to form individuals.
>
> Underneath all, individuals,
> I swear nothing is good to me now that ignores individuals,
> The American compact is altogether with individuals,
> The only government is that which makes minute of individuals,
> The whole theory of the universe is directed unerringly to one single
>   individual—namely to You.

REFERENCES

Chapter I

Anon. 1967. "Enquête sociologique sur l'opinion publique belge concernant le problème de l'Université de Louvain et divers problèmes connexes,"Sobemap, Société belge d'economie et le mathématiques appliquées, Bruxelles.

Baetens Beardsmore, H. 1971a. "Aspects of plurilingualism amongst lower level social groups," in De Coster et al. 1971, pp. 76-91.

––– 1971b. *Le français régional de Bruxelles,* Bruxelles: Presses universitaires de Bruxelles.

Balkan, L. 1970. *Les effets du bilinguisme français-anglais sur les aptitudes intellectuelles,* Bruxelles: Aimav.

Boileau, A. 1946. "Le problème du bilinguisme et la théorie des substrats," *Revue des langues vivantes, XII*:113-125, 169-193, 213-224.

––– 1969. "Comment mesurer les effects exercés par une langue sur une autre dans la langue d'un bilingue," in Kelly, L. (ed.), *Description and measurement of bilingualism,* Toronto: University of Toronto Press, 156-164.

Bong, G., 1972. *Acquisition d'une deuxième langue et développement opératoire,* Mémoire de licence en Pédagogie, Louvain.

Bourgeois, R., et al. 1963. *Le bilinguisme en Suisse, en Belgique et au Canada,* Foundation Plisnier, Etudes et Documents, no. 5, Bruxelles.

Brecht, A. 1966. *Je parle . . . belgicain,* Editions Vie Ouvrière, Bruxelles.

Bruneau, C. 1952. "Le français en Belgique," *Vie et Language III*:99-104.

Bustamente, H. 1973. *Le bilinguisme en Belgique, Effets de la seconde langue sur la langue maternelle,* Thèse de doctorat, Louvain.

Cohen, G. 1954. "Le parler belge," *Vie et Language V*:263-270.

Debrock, M., and J. Jouret 1971a. "Eléments d'une étude contrastive des systèmes phonétiques français et néerlandais," *Revue de Phonétique Appliquée,* 19:3-30.

––– and ––– 1961b. "Système verbo-tonal de correction phonétique de néerlandophones qui apprennent le français," *Revue de Phonétique Appliquée,* 20:33-49.

Decoster, S., and Derume, E. 1962. *Retard pédagogique et situation sociale dans la région du Centre et du Borinage,* Bruxelles: Institut de sociologie.

Decoster, S., H. Leclercq, and L. Vande Velde 1968. "Etude précooe de langues vivantes autres que la langue maternelle, *Le langage et l'homme,* Bruxelles, Institu Marie Haps, pp. 99-105.

Decoster, S., H. Baetens-Beardsmore, L. Balkan, J. Fishman, P. Godaert, S. Kesavan, Y. Lebrun, M. Van Overbeke, and S. Wojowasito 1971. "Aspects sociologiques du plurilinguisme," *Actes du 1er Colloque Aimav* (Assoc. Intern. pour la recherche et la diffusion des méthodes audio-visuelles et structuro-globales), Bruxelles, Sept. 23-25, 1970, Paris: Didier.

Decroly, O. 1926. "Essai d'application du test de Ballard dans les écoles belges" *Année psychologique,* 59-93.

De Rooij, J., and J. B. Berns 1972. *Auidelijk Nederlands in het olgemeen en in het bijzonder,* Amsterdam: Elsevier.

DeVriendt, S., and M. Wambach 1966. "Correction phonétique des francophones belges qui apprennent le néerlandais," *Revue de Phonétique Appliquée,* 3:17-41.

Di Pietro, R. 1968. "Contrastive Analysis and the Theory of Deep and Surface Structure," *Monograph Series in Languages and Linguistics,* Georgetown, no. 21.

Du Ry, J. 1965. "Wallse standpunten en rêacties," *De Maand, 8,* 5:305-317.

Emma, D. 1968. "Problèmes de plurilinguisme à l'Ecole Européenne, *Le Langage et l'Homme,* October.

Fishman, J. 1971. "Bilingual and bidialected education: an attempt at a joint model for policy description," prepared for the "Conference on Child Language," Chicago.

Florquin, J. 1968. *Hier spreekt men Nederlands,* Heideland, Hasselt.

Fourquet, J. 1959. "Le système verbal du néerlandais et du français," *Bulletin de la société linguistique de Paris LIV*:xlii-xlv.

Galle, M. 1967. *Voor wie haar soms geweld aandoet,* Heideland, Hasselt.

Geerts, G. 1969a. "A.B.N.-Malaise," *Wetenschappelijke Tijdingen, 28*:132-136.

——— 1969b. *Taal of taaltje? Een bloemlezing beschouwingen over het Nederlands,* Louvain: Acco.

———, J. Van den Broeck, and A. Verdoodt 1977. "Successes and failures in Dutch spelling reform," in Fishman, J. (ed.) *Advances in the Creation and Revision of Writing Systems,* The Hague: Mouton.

Goossens, J. 1968. *Wat zijn Nederlandse dialecten?* Groningen: Wolters-Noordhoff.

Grootaers, L. 1953. "Het Nederlands substraat van het Brussels-Frans klank-systeem," *De Nieuwe Taalgids, 46*:38-41.

Hanse, J. 1964. *Maîtrise de la langue maternelle et bilinguisme scolaire,* Liège: Les Documents Wallons.

——— 1965. "Langue française, notre beau souci," *Revue générale Belge,* November.

Heeroma, K. 1964. "De volwaardigheid van het Nederlands," Syllabus van de Lodewijk de Raet Stichting, Bruxelles: Georges Debra- Studieconferenties, pp. 3-6.

Hogenraad, R. 1969. "Inciolence d'une situation bilingue-biculturelle sur la personnalité et les problèmes de formation concomitants, NATO Conference, Brussels, July, 229-238.

Hogenraad, R., and C. Mertens 1970. Les modifications de certains aspects cognitifs au cours d'une expérience de formation en situation bilingue-biculturelle, *Bulletin d'Etudes et Recherches psychologiques XIX*: 31-41.

Kirfel, B. 1967. *Studenten in Löwen. Flamen, Deutschbelgier, Wallonen,* Roth/Kr. Prüm, Selbstverlag.

Lambert, W. E. 1955. "Measurement of the linguistic dominance of bilinguals," *Journal of Abnormal and Social Psychology 50*:197-200.

Lebrun, Y., and J. Hasquin 1970. "Bilinguisme précoce et troubles du langage," *Actes du 1er Colloque AIMAV sur les aspects sociologiques du plurilinguisme,* Bruxelles, Sept. 23-25, pp. 60-74.

Leconte, N. 1971. *Etude des effets du bilinguisme,* Application d'épreuves de langue oral et écrit à des enfants de 5e primaire, Mémoire de licence en Pédagogie, Louvain.

Leys, O. 1962. "Vleurgat. Symptoom van een kontaktsituatie," *Mededelingen van de*

Vereniging voor Naamkunde te Leuven en de Comissie voor Naamkunde te Amsterdam 38:133-139.

Martinet, A. 1972. "Préface," *Bordas Encyclopédie: Sciences sociales (2): Linguistique*, Paris: Bordas.

Mounin, G. 1963. *Les problèmes théoriques de la traduction*, Paris: Gallimard.

Nelde, O. 1974. "Zum gegenwärtigen Leitungdeutsch in Ostbelgien," *Cahiers de l'Institut de Linguistique, II*, 3:113-145.

Nieuwborg, E. 1969. "Quelques remarques à propos des constituants nominaux dans la phrase néerlandaise," *ITL Review I*, 4:34-44.

Mussafia, M. 1965. "Réactions affectives et intellectives au plurilinguisme," *Revue belge de psychologie et de pédagogie*, 112:124-126.

——— 1967. "Plurilinguisme et troubles du language," *Folia Phoniatrica*, 19:63-68.

Nuijtens, E. 1962. *De tweetalige mens*, Van Gorcum, Assen.

Nuttin, J. R., Sr. 1969. "Sub-group formation, dominance, task-orientedness, and contact in heterogeneous cultural groups," NATO Conference, Brussels, July, 188-208.

Österberg, T. 1961. *Bilingualism and the First School Language*, Uppsala: Umea.

Paardekooper, P. s.d. *A.B.N.-Gids*, Antwerpen-Amsterdam: Standaard.

Pauwels, J. L. 1948. "Nederlandse opvattingen over het Nederlands in België," *Handelingen van het XXe Nederlands Filologencongres*, 25-28.

——— 1954. "In hoever geeft het Noorden de toon aan? " *Nu nog IV, II*, 4:1-9.

——— 1956. "La situation linguistique dans le nord de la Belgique," *Orbis V, I*:116-122.

——— 1965. *Verzamelde opstellen*, Van Gorcum, Assen.

——— 1967. *Les difficultés de la construction de la phrase néerlandaise*, Liège, H. Dessain.

Pietkin, N. 1904. *La germanisation de la Wallonie prusienne. Aperçu historique*, Bruxelles: Schepens.

Pollain, J. 1971. "Problèmes d'intégration des jeunes immigrés dans l'enseignement primaire et secondaire," *Revue du travail*, April-May, pp. 588 et seq.

Querinjean, E. 1954. "La structure linguistique du village de Waimes," *Bulletin de l'Institut de recherches économiques et sociales 20*, 7:683-705.

Renson, J. 1972. "Bilinguisme dialectal et culture: la situation en Belgique," *XIIIe Congrès International de Linguistique et Philologie romanes.*

Ripoche, J. 1966. "Résultats d'une enquête sur les réactions des élèves au plurilinguisme à l'Ecole Européenne de Bruxelles," *Enfance*, 1:89-98.

Skalmowski, W., and M. Van Overbeke 1969. "Computational analysis of interference phenomena on the lexical level," *ITL Review*, 5:92-103.

Soffietti, J. P. 1955. "Bilingualism and Biculturalism," *Journal of Educational Psychology 46.*

Stockwell, R. P. 1968. "Contrastive analysis and lapsed time," *Georgetown Monograph Series in Languages and Linguistics*, 21:11-26.

Styns, L. 1965. "L'apprentissage de la seconde langue à Bruxelles: une expérience vécue de bilinguisme," in Stern, H. (ed.), *Les langues étrangères dans l'enseignement primaire*, Hambourg, Institut de l'UNESCO pour l'éducation, 159-164.

Toussaint, N. 1935. *Bilinguisme et Education*, Bruxelles: Lamartin.

Valkhoff, M. 1931. *Les mots français d'origine néerlandaise*, Amersfoort: Valkhoff and Cie.

——— 1950. "Réflexes phonologiques des deux côtés de la frontière linguistique," *Bulletin du dictionnaire wallon XIX*:145-153.

Vanderick, Pol 1972. *Bilinguisme et personnalité*, Mémoire de lic. en psychologie, Louvain.

Vanhuysse, A. s.d. *Een experimenteel onderzoek te Moeskroen om de invloed na te gaan van het bilinguisme Frans-Nederlands op verbale en niet verbale intellingentie*. Bienst voor Studie en Beroeps orientering, Moeskroen.

Van Loey, A. 1954. "Les mots français et néerlandais," *Académie Royale de Belgique*, sér. 5, XXIII, XL:227-290.

——— 1958. "Les problèmes du bilinguisme en Belgique," *Etudes germaniques*, XXIII:289-302.

Van Nierop, M. 1962. *De taal waarmee wij leven*, Antwerpen-Amsterdam: Standaard.

Van Overbeke, M. 1968. "La description phonétique et phonologique d'une situation bilingue," *La linguistique 8*:93-109.

––– 1971a. "Entropie et valence de la parole bilingue," *Aspects sociologiques du plurilinguisme*, Paris, Bruxelles: Didier-Aimav.

––– 1971b. "De functie van leenwoorden en composita in tweetalige context," in Feitsma, A., and M. Van Overbeke (eds.), *Tweetaligheids problemen*, Amsterdam: North-Holland.

––– 1974. *Mécanismes de l'interférence linguistique; étude macroscopïque de la performance bilingue*, The Hague: Juana Linguarum, Series Major, Mouton.

Verdoodt, A. 1968. *Zweisprachige Nachbarn. Die deutschen Hochsprach- und Mundartgruppen in Ost-Belgien, dem Elsass, Ost-Lothringen und Luxemburg*, Préface de J. Fishman, Wien: Braumüller, Universitäts-Verlagbuchhandlung.

––– 1971. "The differential impact of immigrant French speakers on indigenous German speakers: a case study in the light of two theories," *International Migration Review 5*, 138-146. [Reprinted in Fishman, J. (ed.), *Advances in the sociology of language*, The Hague: Mouton, vol. 2, pp. 377-385.]

––– 1972. *Problèmes linguistiques des travailleurs migrants adultes et problèmes sociolinguistiques des travailleurs migrants scolarisés dans le pays d'accueil*, Strasbourg, Conseil de l'Europe, Division de l'enseignement supérieur et de la recherche.

––– 1973. *Les problèmes des groupes linguistiques en Belgique. Une introduction à la bibliographie et un guide pour la recherche*, Préface de P. de Bie, Louvain: Centre de recherches sociologiques.

––– in press a. "Educational Policies on Languages: the Case of the Children of Migrant Workers," *Fetschrift, in Honour of Prof. R. Rudnyckyj*, Winnipeg.

––– in press b. "Tweetaligheid," *Encyclopedie van de Vlaamse Beweging*, vol. 2.

Verheyen, J. E. 1928. "Le bilinguisme en Belgique, données et recherches," *Le Bilinguisme et l'Education*, Travaux de la Conférence internationale tenue au Luxembourg, April 2-5.

Vildomec, V. 1963. *Multilingualism. General Linguistics and Psychology of Speech*, Leiden: Brill.

Weinreich, U. 1953. *Languages in Contact; Findings and Problems*, New York: The Linguistic Circle of New York.

Weisshaupt, J. 1970. "Place de l'adjectif en néerlandais et en français," in E. Nieuwborg (ed.) *Mélanges offerts à J. L. Pauwels*, Louvain, pp. 109-119.

Wind, H. 1947. "De quelques curiosités syntaxiques propres au français belge," *Neophilologus XXI*:161-167.

––– 1960. "Nederlands-Franse taalcontacten," *Neophilologus XLIV*:86-94.

Yioshioka, J. 1929. "A Study of Bilingualism," *Pedagogical Seminar 36*:346-367.

Chapter II

Alberta Department of Education 1973. *Bilingual Education–The Alberta Experience*. Edmonton: The Alberta Department of Education.

AuCoin, J. R. 1973. Inverness County Municipal School Board, personal communication.

Barik, H. C. 1975. *French Comprehension Test, Level 1*. Toronto: Ontario Institute for Studies in Education.

––– 1976. *French Comprehension Test, Primer*. Toronto: Ontario Institute for Studies in Education.

––– and M. Swain 1974. English-French bilingual education in the early grades: The Elgin Study. *The Modern Language Journal 58*:392-403.

––– and ––– 1975a. Three-year evaluation of a large scale early grade French immersion program: The Ottawa Study. *Language Learning 25*:1-30.

––– and ––– 1975b. Early grade French immersion classes in a unilingual English Canadian setting: The Toronto Study. *Scientia Paedagogica Experimentalis 12*:153-177.

––– and ––– 1976a. Primary-grade French immersion in a unilingual English-Canadian setting: The Toronto study through Grade 2. *Canadian Journal of Education 1* (1):39-58.

––– and ––– 1976b. Update on French immersion: The Toronto Study through Grade 3. *Canadian Journal of Education 1* (4):33-42.

––– and ––– 1976c. English-French bilingual education in the early grades: The Elgin Study through Grade Four. *The Modern Language Journal 60*:3-17.

––– and ––– 1976d. A Canadian experiment in bilingual education at the grade eight and nine levels: The Peel Study. *Foreign Language Annals 9*:465-479.

––– and ––– 1977 in press. French immersion in Canada: The Ottawa Study through Grade Four. *ITL, A Review of Applied Linguistics 36.*

–––, –––, and V. A. Gaudino 1976. A Canadian experiment in bilingual schooling in the senior grades: The Peel Study through Grade 10. *International Review of Applied Psychology 25*:99-113.

Bereiter, C., and S. Englemann 1966. *Teaching Disadvantaged Children in the Preschool.* Englewood Cliffs, N.J.: Prentice-Hall.

Bruck, M., J. Jakimik, and G. R. Tucker 1971. Are French immersion programs suitable for working-class children? A follow-up investigation. *Word 27*:311-314.

Bruck, M., W. E. Lambert, and G. R. Tucker 1974. Bilingual schooling through the elementary grades: The St. Lambert Project at grade seven. *Language Learning 24*:183-204.

–––, –––, and ––– in press. Cognitive and attitudinal consequences of bilingual schooling: The St. Lambert Project through grade six. *International Journal of Psycholinguistics.*

––– and M. A. Rabinovitch 1974. The Effects of French Immersion Programs on Children with Language Learning Difficulties. Paper presented at the Eighth Annual Convention of Teachers of English to Speakers of Other Languages (TESOL), Denver, Colo.

––– and G. R. Tucker 1974. Social class differences in the acquisition of school language. *Merrill-Palmer Quarterly 20*:205-220.

Canada 1968. *Report of the Royal Commission on Bilingualism and Biculturalism.* Vol. 2. Ottawa: The Queen's Printer.

––– 1972. Statistics Canada. *Special Bulletin, 1971 Census of Canada. Population: Specified Mother Tongues for Census Divisions and Subdivisions.* Ottawa: Statistics Canada.

Carroll, J. B. 1975. *The Teaching of French as a Foreign Language in Eight Countries: International Studies in Evaluation V.* New York: John Wiley & Sons; Stockholm: Almqvist & Wiksell.

––– in press. *French as a Foreign Language in Seven Countries: International Studies in Evaluation V.* Stockholm: Alqvist & Wiksell.

Coleman, P. 1973. St. Boniface School Division No. 4, personal communication.

Comber, L. C., and J. P. Keeves 1973. *Science Education in Nineteen Countries: International Studies in Evaluation I.* New York: John Wiley & Sons; Stockholm: Almqvist & Wiksell.

Committee on French Language Schools in Ontario. 1968. *Report.* Toronto: Ontario Department of Education.

Currie, N. S. 1973. Sault Ste. Marie Board of Education, personal communication.

Dufour, A. 1973. *La législation récente en matière linguistique dans les provinces d'Ontario, du Manitoba et de Nouveau-Brunswick.* Etude E2. Etudes réalisées pour la Commission Gendron. Québec: L'Editeur Officiel du Québec.

Edwards, H. P., and M. C. Casserly 1971. Research and Evaluation of the French Program:

1970-71 Annual Report. Ottawa: The Ottawa Roman Catholic Separate School Board.

——— and ——— 1972. Research and Evaluation of Second Language Programs: 1971-72 Annual Report. Ottawa: The Ottawa Roman Catholic Separate School Board.

——— and ——— 1973. Evaluation of Second Language Programs in the English Schools: Annual Report 1972-73. Ottawa: The Ottawa Roman Catholic Separate School Board.

Gardner, R. C., and W. E. Lambert 1972. *Attitudes and Motivation in Second-Language Learning*. Rowley, Mass: Newbury House Publishers.

Giroux, J. W., R. H. Desjardins, and R. Babin 1974. *Programme d'Etudes—Ecole Secondaire Conféderation*. Welland: Conseil Scolaire de Niagara Sud.

Jakobovits, L. A. 1970. *Foreign Language Learning: A Psycholinguistic Analysis of the Issues*. Rowley, Mass.: Newbury House Publishers.

Lambert, W. E., and J. Macnamara 1969. Some cognitive consequences of following a first-grade curriculum in a second language. *Journal of Educational Psychology* 60:86-96.

———, and G. R. Tucker 1972. *Bilingual Education of Children*. Rowley, Mass.: Newbury House Publishers.

———, ———, and A. d'Anglejan 1973. Cognitive and attitudinal consequences of bilingual schooling: The St. Lambert Project through Grade Five. *Journal of Educational Psychology* 65:141-159.

Melikoff, O. 1972. Parents as Change Agents in Education: The St. Lambert Experiment. In Lambert, W. E., and G. R. Tucker *Bilingual Education of Children*, Appendix A. Rowley, Mass.: Newbury House Publishers.

Ministerial Commission on French Language Secondary Education 1972. *Report*. Toronto: The Queen's Printer.

Murphy, J. D. 1973. Frontenac County Board of Education, personal communication.

Papen, M. J. 1973. Saskatchewan Association of Teachers of French, personal communication.

Poulin, G. 1969. *Paroisse du Sacré-Coeur 1919-1969*. Welland: Les Artisans.

Protestant School Board of Greater Montreal 1973. Report on the Evaluation of the Grade 7 Immersion Programme, 1971-72. Student Personnel Services and Curriculum Departments.

Purves, A. C. 1973. *Literature Education in Ten Countries: International Studies in Evaluation II*. New York: John Wiley & Sons; Stockholm: Almqvist & Wiksell.

Roy, R. 1973. Winnipeg School Division No. 1, personal communication.

Royal Commission on Education in Ontario 1950. *Report*. Toronto: Baptist Johnston.

Savard, J.-G., and J. Richards 1970. *Les indices d'utilité du vocabulaire fondamental français*. Québec: Les Presses de l'Université Laval.

Sissons, C. B. 1964. *The Memoirs of C. B. Sissons*. Toronto: University of Toronto Press.

Stern, H. H. 1972. Introduction. In M. Swain (ed.), *Bilingual Schooling: Some Experience in Canada and the United States*. Toronto: The Ontario Institute for Studies in Education.

Stewart, E. E. 1973. Ontario Ministry of Education, personal communication.

Swain, M. (ed.) 1972. *Bilingual Schooling: Some Experiences in Canada and the United States*. Toronto: The Ontario Institute for Studies in Education.

——— 1974. French immersion programs across Canada: Research findings. *Canadian Modern Language Review 31*:117-129.

——— 1975. Writing Skills of Grade Three French immersion pupils. *Working Papers on Bilingualism* (Ontario Institute for Studies in Education 7:1-38.

———, and H. C. Barik 1976a. Bilingual Education for the English-Canadian: Recent developments. In A. Simoes (ed.), *The Bilingual Child: Research and Analysis of Existing Educational Themes*. New York: Academic Press, Inc., pp. 91-111.

———, and ——— 1976b. A large-scale study in French immersion: The Ottawa Study through Grade Three. *ITL, A Review of Applied Linguistics 33*:1-25.

———, and ——— 1976c. *Five Years of Primary French Immersion: Annual Reports of the*

Bilingual Education Project to the Carleton Board of Education and the Ottawa Board of Education up to 1975. Toronto: The Ontario Institute for Studies in Education.

Tucker, G. R. 1974. Methods of second-language teaching. *Canadian Modern Language Review 31*:102-107.

———, W. E. Lambert, and A. d'Anglejan 1973. French immersion programs: A Pilot investigation. *Language Sciences 25*:19-26.

Wilson, J. D., R. M. Stamp, and L.-P. Audet (eds.) 1970. *Canadian Education: A History.* Toronto: Prentice-Hall.

Wilton, F. 1974. Implications of a Second-Language Program: Coquitlam Experience. Paper presented at the Federal-Provincial Conference on Bilingualism in Education, Halifax, Nova Scotia.

Chapter IV

Abid Husain, S., K. E. Saiyidain, and J. P. Naik 1952. "Compulsory education in India," *Unesco Studies in Compulsory Education XI,* Chap. 4.

Azad, Maulana A. 1949. "Inaugural address," *Proceedings of the Educational Conference:* New Delhi: Ministry of Education, Pamphlet 5.

Barpujari, S. K. 1973. "Naga education in the nineteenth century," *Highlander (Kohima) 1*: 1, 24-30.

Burton, Richard F. 1851. *Sindh and the Races That Inhabit the Valley of the Indus with Notices of the Topology and History of the Province.* London: W. H. Allens.

Chaturvedi, M. G. 1974. *Position of Languages in School Curriculum in India.* New Delhi: National Council for Educational Research & Training.

Dakin, Julian 1968. "Language and education in India," in J. Dakin, B. Tiffen, and H. G. Widdowson, *Language in Education: The Problem in Commonwealth Africa and the Indo-Pakistan Sub-continent.* Language and Language Learning Series 20. London: Oxford University Press, pp. 1-61.

Das Gupta, Jyotirinda 1970. *Language Conflict and National Development: Group Politics and National Language Policy in India.* Berkeley: University of California.

Emeneau, Murray B. 1962. "Bilingualism and structural borrowing," *Proceedings of the American Philosophical Society 106*:5, 430-442.

Gait, E. A. 1913. *Census of India: 1911, I*—India, part I—Report Calcutta: India Government.

Gandhi, Mohandas K. 1916. "The present system of education," in M. K. Gandhi, *The Problem of Education* (collected works: 1962). Ahmedabad: Navajivan Press.

Goel, B. S., and S. K. Saini 1972. *Mother Tongue and Equality of Opportunity in Education.* New Delhi: National Council for Educational Research & Training.

Gumperz, John J., and C. M. Naim 1960. "Formal and informal standards in the Hindi regional language area," in C. A. Ferguson and J. J. Gumperz (eds.) *Linguistic Diversity in South Asia, IJAL 26*:3, 92-118.

Hartog, Philip J. 1929. *Interim Report of the Indian Statutory Commission.* London: Her Majesty's Stationery Office.

Howell, Arthur 1872. *Education in British India.* Calcutta.

India, Government of 1948. *Report of the Committee on the Medium of Instruction at the University Stage.* New Delhi: Ministry of Education, Pamphlet 57.

——— 1949. *Report of the University Education Commission.* New Delhi: Ministry of Education.

——— 1950. *The Constitution of India.* New Delhi: Ministry of Law.

——— 1953. *Secondary Education Commission Report.* New Delhi: Ministry of Education.

——— 1954. *Census of India: 1951.* New Delhi: The Registrar General, India.

——— 1956. *Report of the Official Language Commission.* New Delhi.

——— 1960. *Report of the University Grants Commission.* New Delhi.

——— 1961. *Silver Jubilee Souvenir: Ministry of Education.* New Delhi.

— — 1961. *The Unity of India.* New Delhi: Ministry of Information and Broadcasting.

— — 1965. *Report on Standards of University Education.* New Delhi: University Grants Commission.

— — 1966. *Report of the Education Commission.* New Delhi: Ministry of Education.

— — 1968. *Education in Universities in India: 1964-65.* New Delhi: Ministry of Education.

— — 1972. *Pocket Book of Population Statistics: 1971.* Census Centenary Publication, New Delhi: Registrar General & Census Commissioner.

Katre, S. M. 1959. "Towards linguistic uniformity," *Studies in Education and Culture.*

Kelkar, Ashok R. 1968. *Studies in Hindi-Urdu,* Part I. Poona: Deccan College Postgraduate & Research Institute.

Khubchandani, Lachman M. 1967. "Education policy for a multilingual society: Comments on the Education Commission's Recommendations," *Education Quarterly* (January issue): reprinted with discussion, special issue of the *Bulletin of the Deccan College Research Institute,* 1968, 27: I-II; and in L. M. Khubchandani (ed.) 1969, 32-50.

— — 1968. "Planned change in the media of instruction: Problems of switch over," *Proceedings of the Seminar on Historical Survey of Language Controversy,* Shantiniketan (New Delhi: National Institute of Education); also in *La Monda Lingvo-Problemo* (1972) 4, London-Rotterdam, 142-152.

— — 1969a. "Sindhi," in T. A. Sebeok (ed.) *Linguistics in South Asia (Current Trents in Linguistics,* Vol. 5.) The Hague: Mouton. pp. 201-234.

— — 1969b. "Language planning in multilingual communication network: A study of Indian situation," *Actes du X Congres International des Linguistes 1*:591-597.

— — 1969c. "Functional importance of Hindi and English in India," in Poddar 1969, pp. 178-189.

— — 1969d. "Media of education for a multilingual nation," in Poddar 1969, pp. 304-309.

— — 1969e. "Equipping major Indian languages for new roles," in Poddar 1969, pp. 89-98.

— — 1971. "Language education policy of British rulers in India," South Asia Seminar, University of Pennsylvania (Philadelphia).

— — 1972. "Mother tongue in multilingual societies," in A. Chandra Sekhar (ed.): *Economic and Socio-Cultural Dimensions of Regionalisation* (Census Centenary Monograph 7). New Delhi: The Registrar General India. pp. 427-450.

— — 1973a. "An overview on sociolinguistics," *Sociolinguistics Newsletter IV*:2, 3-8; also in L. M. Khubchandani (ed.): *Language and Plural Society.* Simla: Indian Institute of Advanced Study. forthcoming.

— — 1973b. "English in India: A sociolinguistic appraisal," *International Journal of Dravidian Linguistics II*:2, 199-211.

— — 1973c. "Language policy" (review of Das Gupta 1970), *Language in Society 2*:2, 239-293.

— — 1973d. "Language planning processes for pluralistic societies; Tradition-inspired or situation bound?" International Language Planning Conference, Skokloster (Sweden).

— — 1974a. "Fluidity in mother tongue identity," A. Verdoodt (ed.): Applied Sociolinguistics, Proceedings of the Copenhagen International Congress of Applied Linguistics. Heidelberg: J. G. Verlag. pp. 81-102; also in Mehrotra and Khubchandani 1975, pp. 63-79.

— — 1974b. "Language policy for a plural society," in S. Saberwal (ed.): *Towards a Cultural Policy for India.* New Delhi: Vikas Publishing House. pp. 97-111.

— — 1975a. "Distribution of contact languages in India: A study of the 1961 bilingualism returns," Indian Census Centenary Seminar (New Delhi); also in J. A. Fishman (ed.): *Advances in the Study of Societal Multilingualism.* The Hague: Mouton.

— — 1975b. "Dilemmas of language transition: Challenges to language planning in India," *Topics in Culture Learning,* Vol. 3. Honolulu: East-West Center. pp. 151-164.

— — 1975c. "Foreign language teaching: Instruction and interaction strategies," *RELC Journal 6*:1, 1-5; also in Mehrotra and Khubchandani 1975. pp. 81-87.

— — — 1975d. "Language planning," review of J. Rubin and R. Shuy (eds.): *Language Planning, Current Issues and Research 1973.* Washington: Georgetown University Press, *Sociolinguistics Newsletter VI*:2, 38-40; also in *International Journal of the Sociology of Language,* vol. 4. The Hague: Mouton. pp. 159-164.

— — — 1976a. "Language factor in census: A sociolinguistic appraisal," A. Verdoodt and Kjolseth (eds.): *Language in Sociology.* Louvain: Editions Peeters.

— — — 1976b. "Language ideology and language development: An appraisal of Indian education policy," *International Journal of the Sociology of Language.* The Hague: Mouton. forthcoming.

— — — 1976c. "English as a contact language in South Asia," *RELC Journal 7*:1.

— — — 1976d. *Language and Communication in Modern Setting: Implications of Cultural Pluralism in South Asia.* Honolulu: East-West Center. forthcoming.

— — — (ed.) 1969. *Linguistics and Language Planning in India.* Poona: Deccan College Postgraduate & Research Institute. (gen. ed. N. G. Kalekar.)

— — — (ed.) 1974. *Language and Plural Society.* Transactions of the Workshop on Social Stratification and Language Behaviour. Simla: Indian Institute of Advanced Study. forthcoming.

Kloss, Heinz 1967. "Abstand languages and Ausbau language," *Anthropological Linguistics 9*:29-41.

Le Page, R. B. 1964. *The National Language Question: Linguistics Problems of Newly Independent States.* London: Institute of Race Relations.

Mathai, S. 1959. "The future of the three language formula," *Secondary Education.*

Mehrotra, R. R., and L. M. Khubchandani 1975. *Studies in Linguistics,* Occasional Papers Series. Simla: Indian Institute of Advanced Study.

Mitra, Ashok 1964. *Census of India—1961,* Vol. I—India, part II-C (ii), Language Tables. New Delhi: The Registrar General, India.

Naik, J. P. 1963. *Selections from Educational Records of the Government of India,* Vol. II. Development of University Education, 1860-87. New Delhi: National Archives of India.

Nehru, Jawahar Lal 1948. "Inaugural address," Central Advisory Board of Education: 14th Meeting, *Silver Jubilee Souvenir* (1961). New Delhi: Ministry of Education.

Nigam, R. C. 1972. *Language Handbook on Mother Tongues in Census,* Census Centenary Monograph No. 10. New Delhi, The Registrar General, India.

Pandit, Prabodh B. 1972. *India as a Sociolinguistic Area.* Poona: Gune Memorial Lectures, Poona University.

Poddar, A. (ed.) 1969. *Language and Society in India.* Transactions, Vol. 8. Simla: Indian Institute of Advanced Study.

Richey, J. A. 1922. *Selections from Educational Records of the Government of India: 1840-59,* Part II, Bureau of Education.

Sargent, 1944. *Post War Educational Development in India. Delhi: Manager of Publications.*

Sharma, R. K. 1971. "Tribal Education in Nagaland." Proceedings of the Conference of Tribal Research Bureaus in India. Mysore: Central Institute of India Languages.

Sharp, H. 1920. *Selections from Educational Records,* Part I: 1781-1839. Bureau of Education.

Siqueira, T. N. 1960. *Modern Indian Education.* London: Oxford University Press.

Spolsky, Bernard 1971. "The limits of language education," *The Linguistic Reporter 13:*3, 1-5.

Tagore, Rabindranath 1906. "The problem of education," in R. B. Tagore: *Towards Universal Man* (Collected works: 1961). Bombay: Asia Publishing House.

UNESCO 1953. *The Use of Vernacular Languages in Education.* Monographs on Fundamental Education.

Zakir Hussain 1950. *Convention of the Cultural Unity of India.* Bombay: T. A. Parekh Endowment.

Chapter V

Andersen, Johannes 1931a. Introduction to Jackson (ed.) 1931, 1-16.

––– 1931b. "Polynesian Literature," in Jackson (ed.) 1931, 88-106.

Anderson, Graham 1957. "Ko nga Taonga o Mua hei Pupuri ma Tatou," *Te Ao Hou 20.*

Andersson, Theodore 1973. "Bilingual schooling in the United States," *Education 22.6*:15-19.

Armstrong, Alan 1967. "The Maori on T.V." *Te Ao Hou 58*:21-22.

––– 1971. "The non-person," *Te Ao Hou 70*:22-23.

Ausubel, David P. 1970. "Teaching of the Maori Language," in John Ewing and Jack Shallcrass (eds.) *Introduction to Maori Education,* 111-115, Wellington, N.Z. University Press.

Ball, D. G. 1940. "Maori Education," in ILG Sutherland (ed.) *The Maori People Today,* 269-306, Wellington, NZIIA and NZCER.

––– 1973. "If only I knew then what I know now," *Education 22.3*:9-13; also *Te Ao Hou 73*:22-27.

Barrington, J. M. 1966. "Maori scholastic achievement: A historical review of policies and provisions," *New Zealand Journal of Educational Studies 1.1*:1-14.

––– 1971. "Maori attitudes to Pakeha institutions after the wars: A note on the establishment of schools," *New Zealand Journal of Educational Studies 6.1*:24-28.

Beaglehole, T. M., and J. M. Barrington 1974. *Maori Schools in a Changing Society.* Wellington: New Zealand Council for Educational Research.

Beavis, Cindy 1975. "The Maori language: Is it alive and well?" *N.Z. Language Teacher 1.3*:23-27.

Beeby, C. E., and others 1945. *Report on Education in the Cook Islands.* Wellington: Department of Education.

Bell, Terry 1973. "The Maori language battle," *Te Maori 5.1*:42-43.

Belshaw, H., and V. C. Stace 1955. *"A programme of economic development in the Cook Islands,"* Wellington: Department of Island Territories.

Bender, Byron W. 1971a. "Micronesian Languages," in Thomas A. Sebeok (ed.) *Current Trends in Linguistics 8: Linguistics in Oceania,* 426-465. The Hague: Mouton.

––– 1971b. *Linguistic Factors in Maori Education.* Wellington: New Zealand Council for Educational Research.

Benton, Richard A. 1966. *Research into the English Language Difficulties of Maori School Children 1963-1964.* Wellington: Maori Education Foundation.

––– 1970. "What is to be done," in John Ewing and Jack Shallcrass (eds.) *Introduction to Maori Education.* 116-121, Wellington: New Zealand University Press.

––– 1973a. *Should Bilingual Schooling be Fostered in New Zealand?* Wellington: New Zealand Council for Educational Research.

––– 1973b. "Bilingual schooling for New Zealand children," *Education 22.3*:14-16.

––– 1973c. "E rua nga reo mo te kura?–bilingual preschool?" *Play Centre Journal 28.4*:8-9.

––– 1974. *He waka pakaru kino?* Wellington: *New Zealand Council for Educational Research; also Te Maori 5.3*:34-35.

––– 1975a. "Sociolinguistic survey of Maori language use," *Language Planning Newsletter 1.2*:3-4.

––– 1975b. "The role of ethnic languages in the education of New Zealanders," Address to the World Education Conference, New Zealand Educational Institute, Auckland, August 1975.

––– 1975c. "Language and the Maori child," in *Children and Language.* Wellington: Association for the Study of Childhood.

––– 1976. "The Maori language: Patterns of use in contemporary Maori society," Paper presented to First New Zealand Linguistics Conference, University of Auckland, August 1976.

Biggs, Bruce G. 1968. "The Maori Language Past and Present," in Schwimmer (ed.) 1968, 65-84.

——— 1971. "The Languages of Polynesia," in Thomas A. Sebeok (ed.) *Current Trends in Linguistics 8: Linguistics in Oceania,* 466-505, The Hague: Mouton.

Binstead, H. 1931. "Education in the Cook Islands," in Jackson 1931, 357-392.

Blass, Birgit A., Dora E. Johnson, and William W. Gage 1969. *A Provisional Survey of Materials for the Study of Neglected Languages.* Washington D.C. Center for Applied Linguistics.

Bosch, Ahi Hona 1967. "Me Pehea Tatou—What can we do?" *Te Ao Hou 60*:9-10.

Brandl, Maria 1973. "Relations of aboriginal staff in schools," *Developing Education 1.4*:28.

Christie, W. E. 1972. *Review of Education in Niue.* Niue Department of Education.

Clay, Marie M. 1970. "Language Skills: A Comparison of Maori, Samoan and Pakeha children aged five to seven years," *New Zealand Journal of Educational Studies 5.2*:153-162.

Collins, Anthony 1973. "Second language learning starts early in Samoa." *Culture and Language Learning Newsletter,* East-West Center, No. 2-3.

Consultative Committee on Aboriginal Education 1966. *Submissions to the Joint Committee of the Legislative Council and Legislative Assembly [of New South Wales] upon Aborigine Welfare, March 1966.* Sydney: Department of Adult Education. University of Sydney.

Coppell, W. G. 1973. "Education in the Cook Islands 1923-1965," *New Zealand Journal of Educational Studies 8.2*:95-111.

Currie, Sir George, and others 1962. *Report of the Commission on Education in New Zealand.* Wellington: Government Printer.

Dale, W. S. 1931. "The Maori Language—Its Place in Native Life," in Jackson (ed.) 1931, 249-260.

Department of Education, Darwin 1973a. *Report on Meeting of Bilingual Education Consultative Committee.* Darwin: Department of Education.

——— 1973b. *Progress Report on the Bilingual Education Program in Schools in the Northern Territory.* Darwin: Department of Education.

——— 1974a. *Report on Second Meeting of Bilingual Education Consultative Committee.* Darwin: Department of Education.

——— 1974b. *Second Progress Report on the Bilingual Education Program in Schools in the Northern Territory.* Darwin: Department of Education.

Dewes, Koro 1968. "Some food for thought on Waitangi day," *Te Kaunihera Maori 3.1*:3-9.

——— 1970. "The Pakeha Veto" *Te Maori 1.6*:5.

Dow, R. J. 1973. "Bilingual schooling for New Zealand children," *Education 22.4*:10-11.

Fischer, John L., and Ann M. Fischer 1966. *The Eastern Carolines.* New Haven, Conn.: Human Relations Area Files Press.

Fishman, Joshua 1968. "A Sociolinguistic Census of a Bilingual Neighborhood" in Joshua Fishman et al., *Bilingualism in the Barrio,* 260-299. Washington, D.C.: U.S. Department of Health, Education and Welfare, Office of Education, Bureau of Research.

——— 1972. "National Languages and Languages of Wider Communication," in Joshua Fishman, *Language in Sociocultural Change* (introduced by Anwar S. Dil), Stanford, Calif.: Stanford University Press.

Fitzgerald, T. K. 1970. "The first generation of Maori University graduates: A historical sketch," *New Zealand Journal of Educational Studies 5.1*:47-62.

——— 1972. "Education and identity: A reconsideration of some models of acculturation and identity," *New Zealand Journal of Educational Studies 7.1*:45-58.

Gaarder, A. Bruce 1967. "Organization of the bilingual school," *Journal of Social Issues 23.2*:110-120.

George, H. V. 1968. "Our privileged children," *Te Kaunihera Maori* Spring Issue, 3-7.

——— 1969. "Language and social equality," *Te Kaunihera Maori* Autumn Issue, 31-37.

Government White Paper on Proposed Amendments to the Maori Affairs Act 1953, The Maori Affairs Amendment Act 1967, and Other Related Acts.
––– 1973. Wellington: Government Printer.

Green, Roger 1966. "Linguistic subgrouping within Polynesia: the implications for prehistoric settlement." *Journal of Polynesian Society 75.6*:38.

Halferty, Nancy M. 1974. "Bilingual education in Truk: An experiment in cooperation," *Micronesian Reporter 12*:17-19.

Hanan, Ralph 1967. "Progress in education," *Te Kaunihera Maori 1.5*:49-51.

Hau, P. W. 1968. "Maori-Tanga," *Te Ao Hou 62*:24.

Hauraki, Veronica 1971. "Language key to cultural survival," *Te Maori 2.4*:3.

Hawthorn, H. B. 1944. *The Maori: A Study of Acculturation.* Menasha, Wis.: American Anthropological Association.

Hill, C., et al. 1971. *Report of the Committee of Enquiry into Preschool Education.* Wellington: Department of Education.

Hollyman, K. J. 1962. "The lizard and the axe: A study of the effects of European contact on the indigenous languages of Polynesia and Island Melanesia," *Journal of the Polynesian Society 71.3*:310-327.

Howard, Alan 1970. *Learning to Be Rotuman.* New York: Teachers College Press.

Jackson, Patrick M. (ed.) 1931. *Maori and Education, or the Education of Natives in New Zealand and Its Dependencies.* Wellington: Ferguson and Osborn Limited.

John, Vera P., and Vivian M. Horner 1971. *Early Childhood Bilingual Education.* New York: Modern Language Association of America.

Keen, F. G. B. 1969. "The teaching of Maori language in New Zealand schools," *Te Ao Hou 67*:48-49.

Keesing, Felix M. 1928. *The Changing Maori.* New Plymouth: Board of Maori Ethnological Research.

––– 1931. "Language Change in Relation to Native Education in Samoa." *The Mid-Pacific Magazine 44*:303-313.

––– 1937. *Education in Pacific Countries.* Shanghai: Kelly and Walsh.

Laughton, L. G. 1954. "Maoritanga," *Te Ao Hou 8.*

Lawrence, P. J., and others 1974. *Improving Learning and Teaching: Report of the Working Party on Improving Learning and Teaching.* Wellington: Educational Development Conference.

Loeffen, L. A. 1966. "Play centres and Maori education," *Te Ao Hou 55*:59.

McGrath, Patrick 1973. "An Irish Schooling," *Education 22.7*:23-24.

McGrath, W. J. 1973a. "Bilingual education in schools in Aboriginal communities in the Northern Territory," *Developing Education 1.1*:4-5.

––– 1973b. "Some aims of bilingual education in Northern Territory schools," *Developing Education 1.4*:27-28.

––– 1974. "The roles of teachers involved in bilingual education programmes," *Developing Education 1.5*:19-22.

––– 1975. "The Northern Territory bilingual program," *Educational News* (Canberra) *15*:2, 3.

Mackey, William F. 1970. "A typology of bilingual education," *Foreign Language Annuals 3*:596-608.

Mahuta, R., and others 1974. *Maori Education: A Report Prepared for the Working Party on Improving Learning and Teaching.* Wellington: Educational Development Conference.

Managreve, Mamao P. 1970. "A Critical Examination of Education in Rotuma," in Howard 1970, 177-182.

Masters, W. T. 1956. "Another point of view" (letter to Editor of Journal of the Polynesian Society) *Journal of the Polynesian Society 65.1*:12.

Ma'ia'i, Fanaafi 1956. A study of the developing pattern of education and the factors influencing development in New Zealand's Pacific dependencies. Unpublished M.A. thesis, Victoria: University of Wellington.

Mead, S. M. 1960. "Education bridge should have solid foundations on Maori side," *National Education 41*:547.

Metge, Joan 1964. *A New Maori Migration: Rural and Urban Relations in Northern New Zealand.* London: Athlone Press.

––– 1966. *The Maoris of New Zealand.* London: Routledge and Kegan Paul.

New Zealand Educational Institute 1967. *Report and Recommendations on Maori Education Presented to the 1967 Annual Meeting.* Wellington: New Zealand Educational Institute.

Ngata, Wiremu 1958. "Ko te Whakaako o te Reo Maori," *Te Ao Hou 25.*

Northwest Regional Education Laboratory 1973. *Annual Report to Members.* Portland, Ore.: Northwest Regional Education Laboratory.

O'Grady, Geoffrey, and Kenneth Hale 1974. *Recommendations Concerning Bilingual Education in the Northern Territory.* Darwin: Department of Education.

O'Grady, Geoffrey N., C. F. Voegelin, and F. M. Voegelin 1966. "Languages of the world: Indo-Pacific Fascicle Six," *Anthropological Linguistics 8.2.*

Parr, C. J. 1963. "Maori literacy 1843-1867," *Journal of the Polynesian Society 72.3*:211-234.

Parsonage, William 1953. "Maori language teaching in Maori schools," *Report of the Seventh Science Congress (Christchurch 1951),* 191-197, Royal Society of New Zealand.

––– 1956. "The education of Maoris in New Zealand," *Journal of the Polynesian Society 65.1*:5-11.

Pawley, Andrew 1966. "Polynesian languages: A subgrouping based on shared innovations in morphology," *Journal of the Polynesian Society 75*:39-64.

Piddington, Ralph 1968. "Emergent Development and Integration," in Schwimmer (ed.) 1968, 257-269.

Potatau, Hemi 1973. "In praise of Maori language," *Te Maori 5.6*:6-7.

Powell, Guy 1955. "The Maori school–A cultural dynamic," *Journal of the Polynesian Society 64.3*:259-266.

Puketapu, Ihakara Porutu 1966. "Maori language," in A. H. McIntock (ed.) *An Encyclopaedia of New Zealand 2*:463-439.

Puriri, N. P. K. 1967. "The Maori on T.V." *Te Ao Hou 58*:19-20.

Ramsay, Peter D. K. 1969. *Planning, Policy and Practice in Maori Education.* Unpublished MA Thesis, Wellington: Victoria University of Wellington.

––– 1972. "A question of control: The Administration of Maori schools," *New Zealand Journal of Educational Studies 7.2*:119-129.

Reading, Greg 1975. "Not to lose you, my language," *Education News* (Canberra) *15*:2, 3.

Reweti, P. B. 1971. "more than appeasement needed in language tuition," *Te Maori 2.4*:21.

Richards, Jack 1970. "The Language Factor in Maori Schooling," in John Ewing and Jack Shallcrass (eds.) *Introduction to Maori Education,* 122-134. Wellington: New Zealand University Press.

Rikihana, Gabrielle 1973. "Bilingual schooling for New Zealand children," *Education 22.9*:19.

Ritchie, James E. 1956. "Human problems and educational change in a Maori community," *Journal of the Polynesian Society 65.1*:13-34.

Saville, Muriel R., and Rudolph C. Troike 1971. *A Handbook of Bilingual Education.*

Royal, Turoa K. 1968. "Looking at the future," *Te Ao Hou 63*:44-47.

Rutherford, D. A. J. 1931. "Education in Western Samoa," in P. M. Jackson (ed.) 1931:311-356.

Saville, Muriel R., and Rudolph C. Troike 1971. *A Handbook of Bilingual Education.* Washington, D.C.: TESOL.

Schonell, F. J., I. G. Meddleton, and B. H. Watts 1960. *School Attainments and Home Backgrounds of Aboriginal Children.* Brisbane: University of Queensland Press.

Schutz, Albert J. 1972. *The Languages of Fiji.* Oxford: Clarendon Press.

Schwimmer, Eric 1966. "The People Who Saved Their Language," *Te Ao Hou 25.*

——— 1968. *The Maori People in the Nineteen Sixties.* Auckland: Blackwood and Janet Paul.

Sherlock, Philip, et al. 1969. *Education for Modern Fiji: Report of the 1969 Fiji Education Commission.* Suva: Fiji Education Commission.

Smyth, Patrick 1931. "The problem of educating the Maori," in Jackson (ed.) 1931, 230-248.

Sommer, Bruce A., and James Marsh 1969. "Vernacular and English: language comprehension by some North Queensland Aborigines," *Anthropological Linguistics 11*:48-57.

Sorensen, Klaus 1973. "T.V., Pakeha Institutes killing Maori, language researcher claims," *Te Maori November 1973*:8.

Spolsky, Bernard, Joanna B. Green, and John Read 1974. *A Model for the Description, Analysis, and Perhaps Evaluation of Bilingual Education.* Navajo Reading Study Progress Report 23, Albuquerque: The University of New Mexico.

Strehlow, Theodor G. H. 1971. "Australian Languages," *Encyclopaedia Britannica 2*, 811-812. Chicago: Encyclopaedia Britannica Inc.

Sutherland, I. L. G. 1935. *The Maori Situation.* Wellington: Whitcombe & Tombs.

——— 1940. "The Maori situation," in I. L. G. Sutherland (ed.) *The Maori People Today*, 399-441. Wellington: New Zealand Institute of International Affairs and New Zealand Council for Educational Research.

Taepa, Hepa 1972. "He Aha Oti i te Ingoa Maori: What's in a Maori name?" *Te Ao Hou 71*:7-17.

Thomson, Virginia, and Richard Adolff 1971. *The French Pacific Islands.* Berkeley: University of California Press.

Trifonovitch, Gregory J. 1975. "Roots of bilingual bicultural education in the Trust Territory of the Pacific Islands," Unpublished paper, East West Cultural Learning Institute, East West Centre, Honolulu.

Tryon, D. T. 1975. "Bilingual education in the Northern Territory," *Education News* (Canberra) *15*:2, 3.

UNESCO 1958. *World Survey of Education, Volume II: Primary Education.* Paris: UNESCO.

van der Schaaf, Arjen 1971. "Maori: the language of the complete New Zealander," *Te Maori 2.1*:11.

Walker, Ranginui 1972. "The Maori in contemporary society," *Te Maori 3.1*:4-5.

Watson, John E. 1967. *Horizons of Unknown Power.* Wellington: Council for Educational Research.

——— 1973. "Schooling for Minority Children," in Cole S. Brembeck and Walker H. Hill (eds.) *Cultural Challenges to Education 43-62.* Lexington, Mass.: Lexington Books.

Watts, B. H., W. J. McGrath, and J. L. Tandy 1973. *Recommendations for the Implementation and Development of a Program of Bilingual Education in Schools in Aboriginal Communities in the Northern Territory.* Canberra: Department of Education.

Wenkham, Robert, and Byron Baker 1972. *Micronesia: The Breadfruit Revolution.* Honolulu: The University Press of Hawaii.

White, Ronald V. 1971. "Language use in a South Pacific urban community," *Anthropological Linguistics 13*:361-384.

Willmot, Eric 1975. "Aboriginal education in Australia," *Education News* (Canberra) *15.1*:6-15.

Chapter VI

Aucamp, A. 1926. *Bilingual Education and Nationalism with Special Reference to South Africa.*

Barker, Sir Ernest 1927. *National Character and the Factors in Its Formation.*

Barnouw, A. J. 1934. *Language and Race Problems in South Africa.*

Bigelow, Karl W. (ed.) 1951. *Cultural Groups and Human Relations.* Columbia University.

Burger, J. F. 1944. *The Dual Medium School*. Pamphlet published by F. A. K. Cape Town.

Cape Education Department 1952. *Report on the Experiment of Using the Second Official Language as a Medium of Instruction.*

Davies, R. E. 1950. *English as Second Language in the South African University.*

――― 1954. *Bilingualism in Wales.*

Dodson, C. J. 1962. *The Bilingual Method*. Pamphlet, University of Wales.

Gaarder, A. Bruce 1967. "Organisation of a bilingual school," *Journal of Social Issues XXIII*:2.

Jones, W. R. 1966. *Bilingualism in Welsh Education.*

Kelly, L. G. (ed.) 1967. *Description and Measurement of Bilingualism*. Moncton: International Seminar.

Mackey, William F. 1967. *Bilingualism as a World Problem.*

――― 1969. *A Typology of Bilingual Education.*

McNab, Roy 1957. "The Emergence of Afrikaans as a Literary Language," *Journal of the Royal Society of Arts,* 29 March.

Macnamara, John 1967. "Effects of Instruction in a Weaker Language," *Journal of Social Issues XXIII*:2.

McRae, Kenneth D. 1964. *Switzerland, Example of Cultural Co-existence*. Canadian Institute of International Affairs.

Malherbe, E. G. 1925. *Education in South Africa, 1652-1922.*

――― 1945. *The Bilingual School.*

――― (ed.) 1937. *Educational Adaptations in a Changing Society.*

――― 1962. *Problems of School Medium in a Bilingual Country in Education,* August.

――― 1966. *Demographic and Socio-political Forces Determining the Position of English in the South African Republic,* No. 3, Publication of the English Academy of Southern Africa.

――― 1969. National Bureau for Educational and Social Research. *Research Series,* Nos. 40-43.

Nel, B. F. 1942. *Naturelle-Opvoeding en Onderwys in 'N Christelike Nasionale Stelsel.*

――― 1965-1968. *Report of the Royal Commission on Bilingualism and Biculturalism in Canada.*

――― 1961. *Report of the Commonwealth Conference on the Teaching of English as a Second Language.* Entebbe, Uganda: Government Printer.

Schmidt, C. H. 1926. *The Language Medium Question.*

Snelling, Sir Arthur 1970. *The Contribution of the British Settlers to South Africa.*

Standard Encyclopaedia of Southern Africa 1970. Articles on Afrikaans; Bilingualism, Language Medium in Schools.

Die Transvaler, Feb. 21, 1942, 1955.

UNESCO 1960. *Report on Bilingualism in Education,* International Seminar Aberysthwyth, Wales.

Welsh Department of Education 1949. *Bilingualism in the Secondary School of Wales,* Pamphlet 4.

West, Michael 1926. *Bilingualism*. India: Bureau of Education.

Chapter VII

Allworth, E. (ed.) 1967. *Central Asia—A Century of Russian Rule*. New York.

――― 1971. *Soviet Nationality Problems.* New York: Columbia University Press.

――― 1973. *The Nationality Question in Soviet Central Asia.* New York: Praeger.

Arutyunyan, I. V. 1968. *"Preliminary socio-ethnic investigation of Tatar materials," *Sovetskaya Etnografiya* 4:3-13.

––– 1969. *"Concrete sociological study of ethnic relations," *Voprosy Filosofii 12*:129-139.

––– 1973. Interaction of Cultures of USSR Peoples, paper delivered at IXth International Congress of Anthropology and Ethnological Sciences, Chicago.

Avtorkhanov, A. 1964. "Denationalization of Soviet Ethnic Minorities," *Studies in the Soviet Union II.*

Azimov, P. A., et al. 1972. **Problems of Bilingualism and Multilingualism.* Moscow.

Barber, B., and A. Inkeles (eds.) 1971. *Stability and Change.* Boston.

Barrett, R. J. 1973. Convergence and National Literature of Central Asia, in Allworth 1973.

Baskakov, N. A. 1960. *The Turkic Languages of Central Asia: Problems of Planned Culture Contact* (Trans.). Oxford.

––– 1973. The Scope of Adstrat Influences on a Language Functioning in Complicated Inter-ethnic relations, paper read at IXth Congress of Anthropology and Ethnological Sciences, Chicago.

Bennigsen, A. 1967. "The Problems of Bilingualism and Assimilation in the North Caucusus," *Central Asian Review XV*:205-211.

Bilinsky, Y. 1962. "The Soviet Education Laws of 1958-1959 and Soviet National Policy," *Soviet Studies XIV,* 2:138-157.

Bolsboya sovetskaya entsiplopediya (Great Soviet Encyclopedia). Moscow.

Busygin, E. P., and N. V. Zorin 1973. Interethnic families in the National Republics the Middle Reaches of the Volga, paper read at the IXth Congress of Anthropology and Ethnological Sciences, Chicago.

Clem, E. 1973. In Allworth, E. 1967, 34.

Danilov, A. 1972.Monogonatsional'naya shkola RSFSR-prakitcheskoe voploschenie leninskoi natsional'noi politiki, Narodnoe obrazovanie no. 12.

Davletshin, T. 1967. Analysis of Current Developments in the Soviet Union. November 21, 1967.

Desheriev, Yu D. 1958. **On the Development of the Peoples of the USSR* (Problems of the Construction of Communism in the USSR). Moscow.

––– 1959. **The Development of the Languages of the Peoples of the USSR with Recently Established Systems of Writing.* Moscow.

––– 1966. **Patterns in the Development and Interaction of Languages in Soviet Society.* Moscow.

––– 1968. Problema funkstional'nogo razvitiya yazykov i zadachi sotsiolingvistiki' in F.P. Filin (ed.) Yazyk i obshchestvo. Moscow.

––– 1973. "Social Linguistics," *Linguistics 113*:5-40.

Desheriev, Yu, and I. F. Procenko 1968. **The Development of the Languages of the USSR.* Moscow.

Desheriev, Yu, et al. 1966. **"The Development and Mutual Enrichment of the Languages of the USSR," *Kommunist XIII*:55-56.

Dunn, S. P., and E. Dunn 1973. "Soviet Regime and Native Cultures in Central Asia and Kazakhstan," *Current Anthropology VIII*:3.

Galazov, A. 1965. **"The Native and Russian Languages in Our Schools," *Narodnoe Obraz ii.*

Gantaskaya, C. A., and L. N. Terentieva 1973. The Ethnos and the Family in the USSR, paper read to the IXth Congress of Anthropology and Ethnological Sciences, Chicago.

Garunov, E. 1970. "Schools with a Multinational Composition," *Narodnoe Obraz iii.* (*Transactions in Soviet Education, XIII*:4-16.)

Groshev, I. I. 1967. **Istoricheskii opyt KPSS po osushchestuleniiu leninskoi natsional'noi politiki.* Moscow.

Gurvich, I. S. 1973. Contemporary Ethnic Processes in Siberia, paper read to IXth Congress of Anthropology and Ethnological Sciences, Chicago.

Johnson, H. M. 1971. Stability and Change in Ethnic Group Relations, in Barker and Inkeles 1971. 311-353.

Khaimov, I. 1971. **In *Komsomolets Uzbekistan,* Aug. 21.

Khanazarov, K. 1963. **Raprochement of Nations and Nationality Languages in USSR.*

Tashkent.

Kholmogorov, A. 1969. *"Assimilation and Flourishing of the Socialist Nations," Komm. Sov. Lat. (Riga).

——— 1970. *International Character of Soviet Nations; Based on Concrete Sociological Studies of the Baltic Area.* Moscow.

Kotliarov, V. F., D. S. Leshchenskii and N. K. Sokolovskii 1971. Organizatsiia i planirovanie narodnogo obrazovaniia v Belorusskoi SSR (The Organiztion and Planning of Public Education in the Belorussian SSR), "Narodnaia asveta" Publishing House, Minsk 1971.

Kozlov, V. I. 1973. Problems of Identifying Ethnic Processes, paper read to IXth Congress of Anthropology and Ethnological Sciences, Chicago.

Kulichenko, M. I. 1972. *Multinational Soviet State.* Moscow.

——— 1973. Social and Ethnic Characteristics of a Nation, paper read at IXth Congress of Anthropology and Ethnological Sciences, Chicago.

Lenin, V. I. 1929-1935. *Sochineniya* (Works). Moscow.

——— 1958. O Natsionalnom i natsionalno-kolonialnom voprose (The National and National- -Colonial Question), Moscow. (English translation.)

Lewis, E. G. 1972. *Multilingualism in the Soviet Union: Language Policy and Its Implementation.* The Hague: Mouton.

Malinovsky, N. P. 1914. Rech (periodical) 340.

Medlin, W. K., et al. 1971. *Education and Development in Central Asia.* Leiden: Brill.

Naby, E. 1973. Tadzbik and Uzbek Nationality Identity: The Non-Literary Arts, in Allworth 1973.

Nisbet, R. (ed.) 1972. *Social Change.* Oxford: Blackwell.

Pennar, J. 1969. "The Changing Nature of Soviet Education," *Bulletin of the Institute for the Study of the USSR XVI*:12.

Pennar, J., et al. 1971. *Modernization and Diversity in Soviet Education: With Special Reference to the Nationality Groups.* New York: Praeger.

Pokshishevskiy, V. V. 1971. *Urbanization and Ethnogeographic Processes, In Problemy urbanizatsii v. SSSR pp. 53-62. Moscow.

Rogachev, P. and M. Sverdlin 1963. "Sovetskij narod-novaya isturicheskaya obshchnost lyudi." *Kommunist 9*:11-20.

Rosen, B. M. 1973. An Awareness of Traditional Tadzbik Identity in Central Asia, in Allworth 1973.

Savoskul, S. S. 1971. *"Socio-ethnic Features of Rural Tatar Intellectual Life," *Sovetskaya Etnografiya 4*:3-13.

Sembaev, A. I. 1958. *Essays on the History of Soviet Kazakh Schools.* Alma Ata.

Sergeeva, G. A., and I. Smirnova 1971. *"The Question of Ethnic Self-Identification of Urban Youth," *Sovetskaya Etnografiya 4*:86-92.

Shulman, E. 1971. *A History of Jewish Education in the Soviet Union.* New York.

Silver, B. D. 1974. "The Status of National Minority Languages in Soviet Education: An Assessment of Recent Changes," *Soviet Studies 1974.*

Sovetskin, F. F. (ed.) 1958. *Nationality Schools of the RSFSR during Forty Years.* Moscow.

Stalin, J. V. 1949-1952. *Sochineniya* (Works). Moscow. (Supplementary volumes 1-3. Hoover Institute, Stanford, 1967.)

——— 1961. Collected Edition vol VII (2nd edition) English Trans. London.

Tumin, G. G., and V. A. Zelenko 1915. *Schools for the Aliens.* Petrograd.

Umurzakova, O. P. 1961. *"Problems of the Stages of the Development of the Uzbek Nation," *Obs. Nauk. Uzb. 8*:11-19.

——— 1971. 'Reconciliation of Convergence and Tradition in Socialist Nations.* Tashkent.

Ushinskiy, K. D. I. 1939. *Izbrannye Sochineniya* (Works). 2 vols. Moscow.

Williams, R. M. 1971. Change and Stability in Values and Value Systems. In Barker and Inkeles 1971:123-159.

*Items asterisked are in Russian.

Chapter VIII

Alun 1851. *Ceinion Alun (The Treasures of Alun)*; pseudonym for Blackwell, *op cit.*

Arnold, Matthew 1853. *Evidence to Royal Commission on Education.* London.

Barke, E. M. 1933. "A study of the comparative intelligence of children in certain bilingual schools in South Wales," *British Journal of Educational Psychology* 3:237-250.

Barke, E. M., and D. E. P. Williams 1938. "A further study of the comparative intelligence of certain children in bilingual schools in South Wales," *British Journal of Educational Psychology* 8:62-67.

Bebb, Ambrose 1951. "The Welsh language in schools and colleges" (In Welsh) *Y Genbinen I:29-33, 101-106.*

——— 1960. Yr Iaith Gymraeg yn yr Ysgolion a'r Colegau (The Welsh Language in Schools and Colleges), Y Genhinen I:29-33.

Blackwell, John 1851. *Ceinion Alun* (Works). In Welsh. London.

Bowstead, R. 1856. *British schools but adapted to the educational wants of Wales.* Carmarthen.

Caernarfonshire Educational Authority 1944-1960. *Four Successive Reports on the Language Survey for Caernarfonshire* (Jenny Thomas). Caernarfon.

Census of the Population of England and Wales, decennial reports from 1861, including separate report on the Welsh Language in Wales. London.

Central Advisory Council for Education (Wales) 1953. The Place of Welsh and English in the Schools of Wales (E.G. Lewis, ed.). London: Her Majesty's Stationery Office.

——— 1967. *Primary Education in Wales.* (G. Morgan, ed.). London: Her Majesty's Stationery Office.

Commission of Enquiry into the State of Education in Wales 1847. London.

Committee for the Privy Council on Education 1840-1860. Minutes. London.

Council for Wales and Monmouthshire (Aaron, R.I.) 1963. *Report on the Welsh Language.* London: Her Majesty's Stationery Office.

Cymmrodorion, The Honourable Society of 1884. *Preliminary Report on the Use of the Welsh Language in Elementary Schools in Welsh Speaking Districts.* London.

——— 1885. *Report of the Committee on the Advisability of the Introduction of Welsh into Elementary Education.* London.

Darlington, Thomas 1891. *Language and Nationality* (In Welsh). London.

Davies, Dan Isaac 1885. "The Utilization of the Welsh Language in Schools and Colleges," *Cambrian Society Transactions.*

——— 1885. "Address to the Cymmrodorion Society," *Transactions.* London.

——— 1886. The Welsh Language—1785, 1885, 1985. Denbigh.

——— 1887. Quoted in *Minutes of Evidence on Bilingual Teaching in Welsh Elementary Schools.* Royal Commission of Education. London: Her Majesty's Stationery Office.

Davies, D. J. 1882. "The advantages of teaching English through the medium of Welsh in Welsh speaking districts," *Cymmrodorion Transactions* 5:1-13.

Davies, E. 1881. *Intermediate and University Education in Wales: An Appeal to Gladstone.* London.

Denbighshire Education Authority 1950. *A Report on the Language and Culture Survey of the Schools of Denbighshire (Dodd, L1.C.P.).* Denbigh.

Derfel, R. J. 1864. *Essays and Addresses* (In Welsh). Manchester.

Dodson, C. J. 1962. *The Bilingual Method.* University College, Aberystwyth.

——— 1966. *Foreign and Second Language Learning in Primary Schools.* Aberystwyth.

Education Commission 1861. *The State of Popular Education in England* (Wales is also included). London.

Evans, Beriah G. 1889. "Welshmen and the Welsh language in relation to education" (In Welsh), *Transactions of the Liverpool National Society.*

——— 1887. *Our National Language and the Education of Our Children* (In Welsh). Traethodydd.

Fisher, H. A. L. (Minister of Education) 1920. The Welsh Language and the Welsh Heritage. Address to the Union of Welsh Societies.

Griffiths, H. R. 1845. Address on the Importance of Training Teachers in Wales. Brecon.

——— 1848. *Education in Wales*– Remarks addressed to Lewis Edwards. Brecon.

Home Office (London) 1952. *Report of the Committee on Welsh Language Publishing.* London: Her Majesty's Stationery Office.

Hughes, John 1882. *An Essay on the Ancient and Present State of the Welsh Language.* London.

Jones, Griffith 1740-1746. *Welsh Piety* (W.M. Williams, ed., 1938). London.

Jones, Kilsby 1859. *The Educational State of Wales* (2d ed.). Llanidloes.

Jones, W. R. 1959. *Bilingualism and Intelligence.* Cardiff.

——— 1960. A Critical Study of Bilingualism and Non-Verbal Intelligence. *British Journal of Educational Psychology* 30:71-76.

——— 1966. *Bilingualism in Welsh Education* (A survey of his own contributions to the study of the psychology of bilingualism, published in several journals). University of Wales Press, Cardiff.

Jones, W. R., and W. A. C. Stewart 1951. "Bilingualism and verbal intelligence," *British Journal of Psychology, Statistics Section* 4:3-8.

Jones, W. R., and others 1957. *The Educational Attainment of Bilingual Children,* Cardiff: University of Wales Press.

Lewis, Daniel 1887. *Evidence to Royal Commission 1887.* London.

Lewis, D. G. 1960. "Differences in attainment between primary schools in mixed-language areas," *British Journal of Educational Psychology* 63-70.

Lewis, E. Glyn 1968. Reading Ability in Welsh and English.

——— 1972. *Multilingualism in the Soviet Union.* The Hague: Mouton.

——— 1974a. *Factors Influencing Bilingualism in Wales and the USSR: A Comparative Study. Planet 20*: 1973.

——— 1974b. *Linguistics and Second Language Pedagogy.* The Hague: Mouton.

——— 1974c. Migration and the Decline of the Welsh Language, in Joshua A. Fishman, *Aspects of Societal Bilingualism.* The Hague: Mouton.

——— 1976. "Bilingualism and Bilingual Education in the Ancient World to the Renaissance," in Joshua A. Fishman. *Bilingual Education: An International Perspective.* Rowley, Mass.: Newbury House.

Lewis, E. Glyn (ed.) 1962. Bilingualism in Education. Report of UNESCO Seminar at Aberystwyth University College. London: Her Majesty's Stationery Office.

Lewis, Saunders 1949. *Canlyn Arthur* (In Welsh, In the Tradition of King Arthur). Cardiff.

Merionethshire Education Committee 1960. *Report on the Language Survey* (D.J. Evans, ed.). Dolgellau.

Mills, Richard 1836. *The Duty of the Welsh to Retain Their Language* (In Welsh). Llanidloes.

——— 1838. *Traethawd ar Ddyletswydd y Cymry i Goleddu eu Hiaith (The duty of Welshmen to safeguard their language).* Llanidloes.

Ministry of Education (London) 1960. *Standards of Reading 1948-1956* (G.F. Peaker). London: Her Majesty's Stationery Office.

——— 1962. *Language.* London: Her Majesty's Stationery Office.

Ministry of Education (Welsh Department) 1927. *Welsh in Education and Life– Report of the Departmental Committee.* London: Her Majesty's Stationery Office.

——— 1932. *Memorandum I– Suggestions to Teachers.* London: Her Majesty's Stationery Office.

——— 1936. *Bilingualism in Primary Schools.* London: Her Majesty's Stationery Office.

——— 1938. *Language in Secondary Schools.* London: Her Majesty's Stationery Office.

——— 1953. *The Curriculum and the Community.* London: Her Majesty's Stationery Office.

Morgan, T. J. 1966. *Geiriadurwyr y Ddeunawfed Ganrif* (In Welsh, *Lexicographers of the 18th Century*). *Llen Cumru IX*: 3-18.

Morris, E. 1887. Quoted in Minutes of Evidence on Bilingual Teaching in Welsh Elementary Schools: Royal Commission of Education. London: Her Majesty's Stationery Office.

Phillips, Sir Thomas 1849. *Wales: The Language, Society and Moral Character*. London.

Rees, Owen 1858. *The Welsh and the English Language* (In Welsh). Y Traethodyyd.

Rees, R. 1868. *A Vindication of the Educational and Moral Condition of Wales*. London.

Richards, Melville 1949. "Standard and dialect in Welsh," *Archivum Linguisticum II*:i, 46-55.

Rowlands, Daniel 1886. *Education. Y Traethodydd. 413-453.*

Royal Commission on Education in England and Wales. Reports of Commissioners of Inquiry into the State of Education in Wales 1847. (3 volumes). London: Her Majesty's Stationery Office.

— — — 1853.

— — — 1881.

— — — 1886-1887.

Saer, D. J. 1922. "An enquiry into the effects of bilingualism upon the intelligence of young children," *Journal of Experimental Pedagogy VI*232-240.

— — — 1928. Psychological Problems of Bilingualism. *Welsh Outlook 15*:131-134, 161-163.

— — — 1932. "The effect of bilingualism on intelligence, *British Journal of Educational Psychology XIV*:25-38, 266-274.

Saer, D. J., F. Smith, and J. Hughes 1924. *The Bilingual Problem*. Wrexham.

Salisbury, E. G. 1848. *Remarks on the Report of the Commissioners*. 2d ed. Bangor.

Schools Council for England and Wales 1973. Attitudes to Welsh and English—*Report of Research Project* (D. Sharp and others, ed.). London.

Smith, F. 1923. "Bilingualism and mental development," *British Journal of Psychology XIII*:271-282.

Society for the Utilization of the Welsh Language 1886. Memorial presented to the Royal Commission (1887). Llandilo.

Thirwall, E. (Bishop) 1848. Diocesan Charge of the Bishop of St. Davids. (Quoted in Philips 1849, p. 26). London.

Thomas, Alan R., and Morris Jones 1973. *Linguistic Source Book*. Bangor: University College of North Wales.

Tremenheere, Seymour 1840. *Report of the Committee of the Council on Education on the State of Elementary Education in the Mining Districts of South Wales*. London: Her Majesty's Stationery Store.

Turner, Sr Llewellyn, and reply by John Bright 1887. Letter to the North Wales Observer and reply by Hon. John Bright. December 1887.

University of Wales—Board of Celtic Studies 1950. *Termau Technegol* (Technical Terms). Cardiff.

— — — 1955. *Termau Crefft* (Craft Terms). Cardiff.

— — — 1957. *Termau Mathemateg* (Mathematic Terms). Cardiff.

— — — 1959. *Termau Hanes* (History Terms). Cardiff.

— — — 1960. *Termau Coginio* (Cookery Terms). Cardiff.

University of Wales—School of Education 1958. *Termau Egwyddorion Addysg* (Principles of Education Terms). Cardiff.

— — — 1959. *Termau Daearyddiaeth* (Geology Terms). Cardiff.

— — — 1965. *Termau Chwaraeon* (Terms for Athletics). Cardiff.

— — — 1965. *Termau Mathemateg a Ffiseg* (Terms for Physics). Cardiff.

Watkins, Arwyn 1961. *Ieithyddiaeth* (Linguistics, in Welsh). Cardiff.

Welsh Joint Education Committee 1963. *Language Survey*. Cardiff.

— — — 1964. *Cymraeg Byw* (Living Welsh, in Welsh). Cardiff.

Welsh Joint Education Committee and National Foundation for Educational Research 1969. *A Report of the 1960 National Survey* (W.R. Jones, ed). Cowbridge: Brown and Sons.

Williams, J. L. (ed.) 1961. *The Presentation of Welsh as a Second Language.* Aberystwyth.
— — — 1971. *Towards Bilingualism.*
Williams, T. Marchant 1887. Evidence to Royal Commission 1887. London.
Williams, William. n.d. Quoted in Daniel Evans, Life and World of William Williams, M.P. Llandysul.

Chapter IX

Allen, Virginia 1967. "Teaching Standard English as a Second Dialect," *Teachers College Record.* Reprinted in *Linguistic-Cultural Differences and American Education, Special Anthology Issue 7*:1, *Florida Foreign Language Reporter,* Alfred C. Aarons, Barbara Y. Gordon, and William A. Stewart, eds.
— — — 1969. "A Second Dialect is Not a Foreign Language," *Linguistics and the Teaching of Standard English to Speakers of Other Languages or Dialects,* James Alatis, ed. Washington, D.C.: Georgetown University Press.
Bailey, Beryl Loftman 1965. "A New Perspective on American Negro Dialectology," *American Speech XL*:171;77.
— — — 1970. "Some Arguments against the Use of Dialect Readers in the Teaching of Initial Reading," *Florida Foreign Language Reporter 8*:1, 2.
Baratz, Joan C. 1969a. "A Bidialectal Task for Determining Language Proficiency in Economically Disadvantaged Children," *Child Development 40*:889-901.
— — — 1969b. "Educational Considerations for Teaching Standard English to Negro Children," in *Teaching Standard English in the Inner City,* Ralph W. Fasold and Roger W. Shuy, eds. Washington, D.C.: Center for Applied Linguistics, pp. 20-36.
— — — 1971. " 'Ain't' Ain't No Error," *Florida Foreign Language Reporter 9*:39-40.
— — — 1973. "Language Abilities of Black Americans, Review of Research: 1966-1970," in Miller and Dreger, *Comparative Studies of Negroes and Whites in the United States.* New York: Basic Books.
Baratz, Joan C., and Roger W. Shuy (eds.) 1969a. *Teaching Black Children to Read.* Washington, D.C.: Center for Applied Linguistics.
Baratz, Joan C., Roger W. Shuy, and Walter Wolfram 1969b. "Sociolinguistic Factors in Speech Identification," NIMH Grant 15048, Final Report.
Baughman, E. Earl 1971. *Black Americans.* New York: Academic Press.
Beck, Robert (pseudonym Iceberg Slim) 1967. *Pimp, The Story of My Life.* Los Angeles: Holloway House.
Berdan, Robert 1973. "Have/Got in the Speech of Anglo and Black Children," Los Angeles: Southwest Regional Laboratory.
Bereiter, C. E. 1965. "Academic Instruction and Preschool Children," *Language Programs for the Disadvantaged.* Corbin and Crosby, eds. National Council of Teachers of English.
Bereiter, C. E. and Sigfried Engelmann 1966. *Teaching Disadvantaged Children in the Preschool.* Englewood Cliffs, N.J.: Prentice-Hall.
Bloomfield, Leonard 1933. *Language.* New York: Henry Holt.
Board of Education, City of Chicago 1968, 1969. *Psycholinguistics Reading Series: A Bidialectal Approach.* Chicago: Board of Education.
Brookes, George S. 1937. *Friend Anthony Benezet.* Philadelphia.
Bryden, James 1968. "An Acoustic and Social Dialect Analysis of Perceptual Variables in Listener Identification and Rating of Negro Speakers," U.S. Department of Health, Education, and Welfare.
Buck, Joyce 1968. "The Effects of Negro and White Dialectical Variants upon Attitudes of College Students," *Speech Monographs 181-86.*
Carroll, William S. 1967. "A Teaching Experiment," *TESOL Quarterly 1*:31-36.

Cazden, Courtney, Dell Hymes, and Vera John-Steiner (eds.) 1972. *Functions of Language in the Classroom.* New York: Teachers College Press.

Chomsky, A. Noam 1959. Review of B. F. Skinner, *Verbal Behavior, Language 35*:26-58.

Cohen, S. Alan 1969. *Teach Them All to Read.* New York: Random House.

Coleman, J. 1966. *Equality of Education.* Washington, D.C.: U.S. Office of Education.

Crawford, Robert H., and Samuel D. Bentley 1973. "An Inner City 'IQ' Test," *Black Language Reader,* Crawford and Bentley, eds. Glenview, Ill.: Scott, Foresman, and Company.

Crowell, Sheila C., and Ellen D. Kolba manuscript. "Using Contrastive Analysis in the Junior High School."

Crowell, Sheila C., Ellen D. Kolba, William A. Stewart, and Kenneth R. Johnson 1974. *Talkacross.* Chicago: Instructional Dynamics, Inc.

Crystal, Daisy 1972. "On Beryl L. Bailey on Negro Dialect Readers," *Florida Foreign Language Reporter 9*:44-56.

Dalby, David 1969. *Black through White: Patterns of Communication in Africa and the New World.* Bloomington, Ind.: Hans Wolff Memorial Lecture.

––– 1972. "The African Element in Black American English," in *Rappin' and Stylin' Out Communication in Urban Black America,* Thomas Kochman, ed. Urbana, Ill.: University of Illinois Press.

Deutsch, Cynthia 1964. "Auditory Discrimination and Learning: Social Factors," *Morrill-Palmer Quarterly 10*:277-296.

Dillard, J. L. 1964. "The Writings of Herskovits and the Study of the Language of the Negro in the New World," *Caribbean Studies IV*:35-42.

––– 1966. "The Urban Language Study of the Center for Applied Linguistics," *The Linguistic Reporter 8*:1.

––– 1972. *Black English: Its History and Usage in the United States.* New York: Random House.

––– 1974. "Lay My Isogloss Bundle Down: The Contribution of Black English to American Dialectology," *Linguistics 119*:5-14.

––– in press. *Perspectives on Black English.* The Hague: Mouton.

Douglass, Frederick 1855. *My Freedom and Bondage.* New York.

Education Study Center 1968. *Ollie, Friends, and Old Tales.* Washington, D.C.: Education Study Center.

Farr, Beverly P. 1972. "Oral Language Competence and Learning to Read," *Viewpoints 48*:41-49.

Fasold, Ralph W. 1969a. "Orthography in Reading Materials for Black English-Speaking Children," *Teaching Black Children to Read,* Joan C. Baratz and Roger W. Shuy, eds. Washington, D.C.: Center for Applied Linguistics.

––– 1969b. "Tense and the Form *be* in Black English," *Language 45*:763:776.

Fasold, Ralph W., and Walt Wolfram 1970. "Some Linguistic Features of Negro Dialect," in *Teaching Standard English in the Inner City,* Ralph W. Fasold and Roger W. Shuy, eds.

Feigenbaum, Irwin 1970a. "The Use of Nonstandard English in Teaching Standard: Contrast and Comparison," in *Teaching Standard English in the Inner City,* Ralph W. Fasold and Roger W. Shuy, eds.

––– 1970b. *English Now.* New York: New Century.

Ferguson, Charles A. 1959. "Diglossia," *Word 15*:325-340.

Fickett, Joan 1970. *Aspects of Morphemics, Syntax, and Semology of an Inner-City Dialect (Merican).* West Rush, N.Y.: Meadowood Publications.

––– forthcoming. "*Ain't, Not,* and *Don't* in Black English," in *Perspectives on Black English,* J.L. Dillard, ed. The Hague: Mouton.

Fishman, Joshua A. 1971. "The Sociology of Language: An Interdisciplinary Social Science Approach to Language," *Advances in the Sociology of Language,* Joshua A. Fishman, ed. The Hague: Mouton.

Fishman, Joshua A., and Erica Lueders-Salmon 1972. "What Has the Sociology of Language to Say to the Teacher," *Functions of Language in the Classroom,* Courtney Cazden, Dell Hymes, and Vera P. John-Steiner, eds.

Fox, Robert P. (ed.) 1973. *English as a Second Language and as a Second Dialect.* Urbana, Ill.: National Council of Teachers of English.

Frazier, E. Franklin 1957. *Black Bourgeoisie: The Rise of a New Middle Class.* New York.

Fries, Charles C. 1927. "The Rules of the Common School Grammars," *Publications of the Modern Language Association.* 221-237.

——— 1952. *The Structure of English: An Introduction to the Construction of English Sentences.* New York: Holt, Rinehart and Winston.

Garvin, Paul 1959. "The Standard Language Problem: Concepts and Methods," *Anthropological Linguistics 1*:28-31.

Gonzales, Ambrose 1922. *The Black Border: Gullah Stories of the Carolina Coast (with a Glossary).* Columbia, S.C.: The State Company.

Goodman, Kenneth 1969. "Dialect Barriers to Reading Comprehension," in *Teaching Black Children to Read.* Baratz and Shuy, eds.

Gross, Mary Anne 1972. *Ah, Man, You Found Me Again.* Boston: Beacon Press.

Hancock, Ian F. 1972. "A Domestic Origin for the English-Derived Pidgins and Creoles," *Florida Foreign Language Reporter 10*:7-9.

——— manuscript. "The Relationship of Black Vernacular English to the Atlantic Creoles."

Haskins, Jim, and Hugh F. Butts 1973. *The Psychology of Black Language.* New York: Barnes and Noble.

Horner, Vivian, and Joan D. Gussow 1972. "John and Mary: A Pilot Study in Linguistic Ecology," in *Functions of Language in the Classroom.* Courtney Cazden, Dell Hymes, and Vera P. John-Steiner, eds.

Horsmanden, Daniel P. 1744. *The New York Conspiracy, or A History of the Negro Plot, with the Journal of the Proceedings against the Conspirators in New York in the Years 1741-2.* New York.

Houston, Susan 1969. "A Sociolinguistic Consideration of Child Black English in Northern Florida," *Language 45*:599-607.

——— in press. "A Sociolinguistic Consideration of the Black English of Children in Northern Florida" (revised version of the above), in *Perspectives on Black English.* J.L. Dillard, ed.

Hurst, Charles 1965. *Psychological Correlates in Dialectolalia,* Cooperative Research Project 2610, Howard University. Washington, D.C.: Howard University Communication Sciences Research Center.

Jensen, Arthur R. 1969. "How Much Can We Boost IQ and Scholastic Achievement?" *Harvard Educational Review 39*:1-123.

Johnson, Dale 1972. "Linguistics and Reading: What's Happening?" *Journal of Reading 16*:133-35.

Johnson, Kenneth R. 1968. "Teaching Grammatical Structures." Los Angeles: University of Southern California.

Johnson, Kenneth R., and Herbert D. Simons 1973. *Black Children's Reading of Dialect and Standard Texts.* U.S. Department of Health, Education, and Welfare, Office of Education Project No. 1-1-096, Grant No. OEG-9-0011, Final Report.

Jones, Charles Colcock 1832. *The Religious Education of the Negroes.* Savannah, Ga.

Jones, Charles Colcock, Jr. 1888. *Negro Myths from the Georgia Coast.* Boston.

Joos, Martin 1962. *The Five Clocks, International Journal of American Linguistics 28*:2, Part V. Bloomington, Ind.

Kligman, Donna Schwab, Bruce A. Connell, and Gary B. Verna 1972. "Black English Pronunciation and Spelling Performance," *Elementary English.* 1247-1253.

Kochman, Thomas 1969. "Rapping in the Black Ghetto," *Trans-Action 6*:26-34.

——— 1972. "Black American Speech Events and a Language Program for the Classroom,"

Functions of Language in the Classroom. Courtney Cazden, Dell Hymes, and Vera P. John-Steiner, eds.

Labov, William 1969a. "Contraction, Deletion, and Inherent Variability of the English Copula," *Language 45*:715-62.

—— 1969b. "The Logic of Nonstandard English," in *Georgetown Monograph Series on Language and Linguistics*, No. 22, James Alatis, ed.

—— 1972. *Language in the Inner City: Studies in the Black English Vernacular.* Philadelphia: University of Pennsylvania Press.

Labov, William, and Paul Cohen 1968. "A Note on the Relation of Reading Failure to Peer Group Status in Urban Ghettos," *Teachers College Record.*

Labov, William, Paul Cohen, Clarence Robins, and John Lewis 1968. *A Study of the Nonstandard English of Negro and Puerto Rican Speakers in New York City.* Final Report, Cooperative Research Project 3288. Washington, D.C.: U.S. Office of Education.

Lin, San-Su 1963. "An Experiment in Changing Dialect Patterns: The Claflin Project," *College English,* 644-647.

—— 1965. *Pattern Practice in the Teaching of Standard English to Students with a Non-Standard Dialect.* New York: Teachers College Press.

Loflin, Marvin D. 1967. "A Note on the Deep Structure of English in Washington, D.C.," *Glossa 1*:1.

—— 1970. "On the Structure of the Verb in a Dialect of American Negro English," *Linguistics 59*:14-28.

—— in press. "Black American English and Syntactic Dialectology," *Perspectives on Black English.* J.L. Dillard, ed. The Hague: Mouton.

Loflin, Marvin D., Nicholas Sobin, and J. L. Dillard forthcoming. "Auxiliary Structures and Tense Adverbs in Black American English," *American Speech.*

Luelsdorff, Philp A. 1970. "A Segmental Phonology of Black English." Washington, D.C.: Georgetown University.

—— manuscript. "Black American English to Standard American English." Madison, Wis.: University of Wisconsin.

McDavid, Raven I., Jr. 1967. "Historical, Regional, and Social Variation," *Journal of English Linguistics 1.*

—— 1971. "Addendum" to reprint of McDavid and McDavid 1951, *Black White Speech Differences,* Walter Wolfram and Ralph Fasold, eds. Washington, D.C.: Center for Applied Linguistics.

McDavid, Raven I., Jr., and Virginia Glenn McDavid 1951. "The Relationship of the Speech of American Negroes to the Speech of Whites," *American Speech XXVI*:3-16.

Marwit, Samuel J., Karen L. Marwit, and John J. Boswell 1972. "Negro Children's Use of Nonstandard Grammar," *Journal of Educational Psychology 63.*

Melmed, Paul Jay 1970. *Black English Phonology: The Question of Reading Interference.* Monographs of the Language-Behavior Research Laboratory, No. 2. Berkeley: University of California.

Mitchell-Kernan, Claudia 1969. *Language Behavior in a Black Urban Community.* Working Paper No. 23, Research Laboratory. Berkeley: University of California.

Morgan, Raleigh 1959. "Structural Sketch of Saint Martin Creole," *Anthropological Linguistics I*:20-24.

—— 1960. "The Lexicon of Saint Martin Creole, *Anthropological Linguistics II*:7-29.

Morse, J. Mitchell 1973. "Reply to Elaine Chailla," *College English 35*:216.

National Assessment of Education Programs 1970-71. "Reading Assessment: Selected Exercises. Denver: Education Commission of the United States, Report 02-R-20.

National Association for the Advancement of Colored People 1971. "Which English?" *Ford Foundation Letter 2*:2.

Newton, E. S. 1962. "The Culturally Deprived Child in Our Verbal Schools," *Journal of Negro Education 31*:184-187.

Nolen, Patricia 1972. "Reading Nonstandard Dialect Materials: A Study at Grades Two and Four," *Child Development 43*:1092-1097.

O'Neill, Wayne. "The politics of bidialectalism," *College English 33*:457-460.

Österberg, Tore 1961. *Bilingualism and the First School Language—An Educational Problem Illustrated by Results from a Swedish Dialect Area*. Umea, Sweden: Västerbottens Tryckerei AB.

Politzer, Robert L. 1968. "Problems in Applying Foreign Language Teaching Methods to the Teaching of Standard English as a Second Dialect," Research and Development Memorandum No. 4. Stanford, Calif.: Stanford Center for Research and Development in Teaching.

Politzer, Robert L., and Sheila McMahon 1970. "Auditory Discrimination Performance of Pupils from English- and Spanish-Speaking Homes," Memorandum No. 67. Stanford, Calif.: Stanford Center for Research and Development in Teaching.

Politzer, Robert L., and Mary R. Hoover 1972. "The Development of Awareness of the Black Standard/Black Nonstandard Dialect Contrast," Stanford Center for Research and Development in Teaching, Memorandum No. 72.

Politzer, Robert L., and Dwight Brown manuscript. "A Production Test in Black Standard and Nonstandard Speech," revised Version of Research and Development Memorandum No. 114, Stanford Center for Research and Development in Teaching.

Read, William A. 1931. *Louisiana-French*. Baton Rouge: Louisiana State University Press.

Reed, Carol 1973. "Adapting TESL Approaches to the Teaching of Written Standard English as a Second Dialect to Speakers of American Black English Vernacular," *TESOL Quarterly 7*:289-308.

Roberts, Elsa 1969. "An Evaluation of Standardized Tests as Tools for the Measurement of Language Development." Cambridge, Mass.: Language Research Foundation.

Robinson, Jay 1973. "The Wall of Babel; or, Up against the Language Barrier," in *Varieties of Present-Day English*. New York: Macmillan. Richard W. Bailey and Jay L. Robinson, eds.

Ross, Stephen 1972. "A Syntactic Analysis of the Written Language of Selected Black Elementary School Children with Reference to Sociological Variables." Los Angeles: University of Southern California.

Rystrom, Richard 1970. "Dialect Training and Reading: A Further Look." *Reading Research Quarterly 5*:581-599.

Schaaf, E. 1971. "A Study of Black English Syntax and Reading Comprehension." Berkeley: University of California.

Schotta, Sarita 1970. "Toward Standard English through Writing: An Experiment in Prince Edward County, Virginia," *TESOL Quarterly 4*:261-276.

Serwer, Blanche L. 1969. "Linguistic Support for a Method of Teaching Beginning Reading to Black Children," *Reading Research Quarterly 4*:449-464.

Shuy, Roger W. 1970. "Teacher Training and Urban Language Problems," in *Teaching Standard English in the Inner City*, Ralph Fasold and Roger W. Shuy, eds. Washington, D.C.: Center for Applied Linguistics.

Silverman, Stuart Harold 1971. "The Effects of Peer Group Membership on Puerto Rican English." New York: Ferkauf Graduate School, Yeshiva University.

Sims, R. 1972. "A Psycholinguistic Description of Miscues Created by Selected Young Readers during Oral Reading of Texts in Black Dialect and Standard English." Detroit: Wayne State University.

Sledd, James 1973. "Response to George R. Beissel." "Response to Dr. Crew and Dr. Guth," *College English 34*:584-585, 591-593.

Smith, Holly 1973. "Standard or Nonstandard: Is There an Answer?" *Elementary English*, ERIC-RCS Report 50.

Smith, Reed 1926. *Gullah*. Columbia: University of South Carolina Press.

Smyth, J. F. D. 1775. *A Tour of the United States of America*. London.

Stewart, William A. 1962a. "Creole Languages in the Caribbean," *Study of the Role of*

Second Languages in Asia, Africa, and Latin America. F.A. Rice, ed. Washington, D.C.: Center for Applied Linguistics.

——— 1962b. "The Functional Distribution of Creole and French in Haiti," *Georgetown University Monograph Series on Languages and Linguistics 15.* Washington, D.C.: Georgetown University Press.

——— 1964. "Urban Negro Speech: Sociolinguistic Factors Affecting English Teaching," *Social Dialects and Language Learning.* Roger W. Shuy, ed. National Council of Teachers of English.

——— 1965. "Foreign Language Teaching Methods in Quasi-Foreign Language Situations," in *Non-Standard Speech and the Teaching of English.* W.A. Stewart, ed. Washington, D.C.: Center for Applied Linguistics.

——— 1967. "Sociolinguistic Factors in the History of American Negro Dialects," *Florida Foreign Language Reporter 5*:11-29.

——— 1968. "Continuity and Change in American Negro Dialects," *Florida Foreign Language Reporter 6*:3-14.

——— 1969. "On the Use of Negro Dialect in the Teaching of Reading," *Teaching Black Children to Read.* Joan C. Baratz and Roger W. Shuy, eds. Washington, D.C.: Center for Applied Linguistics.

——— 1970. "Sociopolitical Issues in the Linguistic Treatment of Negro Dialect," *Report of the Twentieth Roundtable.* Washington, D.C.: Georgetown University Press.

Tinker, Edward Larocque 1936. "Gombo: The Creole Dialect of Louisiana," New York *Herald-Tribune XIII*:29.

Troike, Rudolph C. 1970. "Receptive Competence, Productive Competence, and Performance," *Reports of the 20th Annual Roundtable Meeting on Linguistics and Language Studies, Linguistics and the Teaching of Standard English to Speakers of Other Languages and Dialects.* James Alatis, ed. Washington, D.C.: Georgetown University Press.

Tucker, G. Richard, and Wallace Lambert 1969. "White and Negro Listeners' Reactions to Various American English Dialects," *Social Forces 47*:463-468.

Turner, Lorenzo Dow 1949. *Africanisms in the Gullah Dialect.* Chicago: University of Chicago Press.

UNESCO 1953. *The Use of Vernacular Language in Education.* Paris.

Wepman, J. M. 1958. *Auditory Discrimination Test, Manual of Directions.* Chicago.

Williams, Maurice, Edith Weinstein, and Ralph C. Blackwood 1970. "An Analysis of Oral Language Compared with Reading Achievement," *Elementary English 47*:394-396.

Wise, Claude M. 1933. "Negro Dialect," *Quarterly Journal of Speech XIX*:522-528.

Wolfram, Walter 1969. *A Sociolinguistic Description of Detroit Speech.* Washington, D.C.: Center for Applied Linguistics.

——— 1971. "Black-White Speech Differences Revisited," *Viewpoints 2*:27-50.

Wolfram, Walter, and Ralph W. Fasold 1969. "Toward Reading Materials for Black English-Speaking Children," *Teaching Black Children to Read,* Joan C. Baratz and Roger W. Shuy, eds.

Wood, Barbara Sundene, and Julia Curry 1969. "Everyday Talk and School Talk of the City Black Child," *Speech Teacher 18*:181-196.

Chapter X

Aleichem, Sholem 1973. The Student Committee for Yiddish. New York, pp. 1-4.

Amol Un Haint 1940. "Long Ago and Today," collection of Essays of Mittleschule Students. Chicago: Workmen Circle.

Aron, Milton 1969. *Ideas and Ideals of the Hasidism.* New York: Citadel Press.

Bleter Far Yiddishe Dertsiyung 1962. "Pages for Yiddish Education." New York: Congress for Jewish Culture.

Buber, Martin 1960. *The Origin and Meaning of Hasidism.* New York: Harper Row.

Chanin, N. 1944. "Kultur Tetikait in un Arum Die Schulen" ("Cultural Activity in and Around Our Schools"). *Kultur un Dertsiyung.* New York: Workmen Circle, pp. 6-7.

Chanukah 1967. New York: Sholem Aleichem Folk Institute.

Chazden, H. 1949. "Die Limud Fun Literature" ("The Teaching of Literature"). *Bleter Far Yiddishe Dertsiyung.* New York: Congress for Jewish Culture.

Concert Program 1931. Bronx, New York: Workmen Circle School No. 8.

Der Masquen Ball fun der Yiddishe Folk Schule 1926. *The Masquerade Ball of the Yiddish Folk School.* Los Angeles: Farband.

Eisenberg, A. 1968. "The American Association of Jewish Education's 1967 Annual Census of Jewish Schools–Editorial Comment," *Jewish Education XXXVIII*:3.

Elbe, L. 1914. *Die Yiddishe Shprach* (The Yiddish Language). New York: Gurevitch Publishing Co.

Fishman, J. 1953. "Summary of Findings Reported in a Study of Attitudes Held by Teachers in Jewish Schools toward Children and toward Other Various Aspects of Jewish Teaching Work," *Jewish Education Survey.* New York: Jewish Education Committee.

––– 1965a. "Yiddish in America," *International Journal of American Linguistics III*:2. Indiana University Research Center.

––– 1965b. "Language Maintenance and Language Shift," *Sociologus XVI*:1. Berlin: Dunker and Humblet.

Fishman, J. et al. 1966. *Language Loyalties in the United States.* The Hague: Mouton.

"Fun Die Kinder in America–Far Die Kinder in Polien" 1940. ("From the Children in America–for the Children in Poland") *Kindertzaitung.* New York: Workmen Circle.

Garvin, Phillip 1970. *A People Apart, Hasidism in America.* New York: Dutton.

Gingold, P. 1938. "Vie Zollen Mir Batzien Tzum Bar Mitzvah Yom Tov" ("What Should Be Our Attitude toward the Bar Mitzvah Celebration"). *Yiddish Dertsiyung.* New York: Jewish National Workers' Alliance, pp. 20-23.

Glazer, N., and D.P. Moynihan 1970. *Beyond the Melting Pot.* Cambridge, Mass.: M.I.T. Press.

Goldberg, I. n.d. *Die Nave Hagaddah* (*The New Hagaddah*). New York: Service Bureau for Jewish Education.

––– 1965. *Veltlechkeit un Dertsiyung in America* (*Secularism and Education in America*). New York: Friends of Secular Education and Kinderbuch Publications.

––– 1966. *Yiddish Stories for Young People.* New York: Kinderbuch Publications.

––– 1971. "Jewish Secularism in the Year Two Thousand," *Jewish Currents.* New York: Jewish Currents, Inc.

Goodman, H. 1961, 1963. *Our People through the Middle Ages,* Vols. I and II. New York: Kinderbuch Publications.

Hagaddah n.d. Service Bureau for Jewish Education.

Hagaddah Shel Pesach n.d. (*Hagaddah of Passover*). *A New Hagaddah for Passover, Festival of Freedom.* Brookline, Mass.: I.L. Peretz Children's School of the Workmen Circle.

In Dorem Land 1943. (*In The South Land*), Work of Eight Children in the Mittleschule Class. Atlanta, Ga.: Workmen Circle.

Israel, B. 1956. *Our People in Olden Days.* New York: Kinderbuch Publishers.

Jewish Folk Songs of Social Significance 1968. New York: Education Department of the Workmen Circle.

Kalish, M. Y. 1941. "Familiness–Memories and Impressions," *Yehudah Steinberg Folk Schule Anniversary Book.* Philadelphia: Yehudah Steinberg Folk Schule.

Kaminski, P. 1963. "My Inheritance," *Fiftieth Jubilee Journal of the Sholem Aleichem Schools.* New York: Sholem Aleichem Folk Institute.

Kinder Journal 1956. New York: Matones Publishing Co.

Kinderklangen 1942. (*Children's Sounds*). Montreal, Canada: Committee of School Pupils of Jewish People's Schule.

Kindervelt Teater 1937. (*Kindervelt Theatre*). Plays and Productions in Camp Kindervelt, Highlang Mills, N.Y.

Lehrer, L. 1928. "Boiberick," *Yearbook*. New York: Scholem Aleichem Folk Institute.

——— 1940. *Yiddishkeit un Andere Problemen (Judaism and Other Problems)*. New York: Natanot Publishing Co.

——— 1956. "The Role of Yiddish in the Jewish School," *Why Yiddish for Our Children?* New York: Sholem Aleichem Folk Institute.

Lifshitz, I. I. 1969. *Unzer Buch: A Ler Buch far Yiddish,* Part I. New York: Gross Brothers Printing Company, Inc.

Lipshitz, Y. 1950. "Der Zin Fun Geshichte Limud in die Folk Schulen" ("The Value of History in the Folk Schules"). *Yiddishe Dertsiyung*. New York: Jewish National Workers' Alliance.

Lomir Kinder Zingen 1970. (*Let's Sing a Yiddish Song*). New York: Kinderbuch Publications.

Lomir Kinder Zingen 1953. (*Let Us Sing, Children*). New York: Workmen Circle.

Minimum Dergraichungen in Drei Togike Schulen 1968. (*Minimum Achievements in Three-Day Schools*). New York: Workmen Circle.

Mlotek, J. 1959. *Yiddishe Kinder (Jewish Children)*. Part A. New York: Workmen Circle.

——— 1962. "Morris Rosenfeld in der Moderne Yiddishe Schule" ("Morris Rosenfeld in the Modern Yiddish School"). *Bleter Far Yiddishe Dertsiyung*, No. 1. New York: Congress for Jewish Culture.

——— 1971. *Yiddishe Kinder (Jewish Children)*, Part A. New York: Workmen Circle.

National Census of Jewish Schools, December 1967 1967. New York: American Association of Jewish Education.

Niger, S. 1940. *In Kampf far a Nayer Yiddishe Dertziung (Struggling for a New Jewish Education)*. New York: The Education Department of the Workmen Circle.

Noskowitz, J. 1962, 1966. *Mayn Folk (My People)*, Parts I and II. New York: Workmen Circle.

Parker, Sandra 1973. *Inquiry into the Yiddish Secular Schools in the United States: A Curricular Perspective*. Doctoral Dissertation, Cambridge, Mass.: Harvard University.

Pessin, D. 1957. *History of the Jews in America*. New York: United Synagogue Commission on Jewish Education.

Poll, Solomon 1962. *The Hasidic Community of Williamsburg: A Study in the Sociology of Religion*. New York: Schocken Books.

Program fun die Arbeiter Ring Shulen 1927. (*Program of the Workmen Circle Schools*). Philadelphia: Workmen Circle.

Purim 1970. New York: Sholem Aleichem Folk Institute.

Rabinowicz, Harry M. 1960. *A Guide to Hasidism*. London.

Rosh Hashanah 1967. New York: Sholem Aleichem Folk Institute.

Rothenberg, D. 1935. "A Shmues Tvishen Tzvai Kinder, A Vaysen un a Shvartzen" ("A Discussion between Two Children, a White One and a Black One"). *Mittleschule Navos*. New York: Workmen Circle.

Rubin, Israel 1972. *Satmar: An Island in the City*. Chicago: Quadrangle Books.

Saks, H. 1964. "The Kinder Day School," *Jewish Frontier* 55-57.

Schiff, A. 1966. *The Jewish Day School in America*. New York: Jewish Education Committee Press.

——— 1967. "An Appreciation of the Jewish Day School in America," *Jewish Education XXXVII*:1, 2.

Schulman, E. 1967. "Tzvai Shprachikait in America un die Meglechkaiten far Yiddish" ("Bilingualism in America and the Possibilities for Yiddish"), *Kulture un Dertsiyung*, No. 1. New York: Workmen Circle, pp. 1-3.

——— 1971. *A History of Jewish Education in the Soviet Union*. New York: Ktav Publishing Co.

Shapiro, S., and J. Gupkin 1954. *Dos Nave Vort (The New Word)*. New York: Gingold Publishing Co.

Shmuessin mit Kinder un Yugent 1973. New York: Mercaz Leinyanei Chinuch.

Schneider, V. 1939. "Geshichte fun die Yiden in America Als Limud in Unzere Shulen" ("The History of Jews in America As a Subject in Our Schools"), *Yiddishe Dertsiyung.* New York: Jewish National Workers' Alliance, pp. 14-17.

The Suburban Jewish School 1958. New Jersey: Cooperative Enterprise of Parent Body.

The Suburban Jewish School Graduation 1970. Whippany, N.J.: Suburban Jewish School.

Tarant, D. n.d. *Mayn Yiddish Buch (My Yiddish Book).* New York: Kinderbuch Publishers.

Unzer Hagaddah Shel Pesach 1954. *(Our Hagaddah of Passover).* New York: New York School Committee, Farband.

Warsaw Ghetto Program 1967. New York: Workmen Circle Education Department.

Waxman, B. 1949. "Die Grenetzen fun Fraiheit in Dertsiyung" ("The Boundaries of Freedom in Education"), *Bleter far Yiddishe Dertsiyung.* New York: Congress for Jewish Culture, pp. 1-11.

Weingartner, Y. 1950. "Metodik fun Yiddishe Dertsiyung" ("Methodology of Yiddish Education"), *Bleter far Yiddishe Dertsiyung,* New York: Congress for Jewish Culture, pp. 1-11.

Why Yiddish for Our Children? 1956. New York: Sholem Aleichem Folk Institute.

Wiseman, S. 1927. "The Speech Method in the Modern Folk Schule," *Shul und Lerer.* New York: Teachers' Organization of the Jewish Secular Schools of the United States and Canada, pp. 22-28.

——— 1931. *Dos Vort, Literature Chrestomathia (The Word, Literature Anthology).* New York: Jewish Folk Schools of the Jewish National Workers' Alliance and Poele Zion.

——— 1938. *Dos Vort (The Word).* New York: Jewish Folk Schools of the Jewish National Workers' Alliance.

——— 1951. "Vegn Dem Limud fun Hebraiyish in Unzere Shulen" ("The Teaching of Hebrew in Our Schools"), *Bleter far Yiddishe Dertsiyung.* New York: Congress for Jewish Culture, pp. 42-50.

——— 1962. "Die Yiddishe Yom Tovim un die Yiddishe Dertsiyung" ("The Jewish Holidays and Jewish Education"), *Bleter far Yiddishe Dertsiyung.* New York: Congress for Jewish Culture.

Yefroiken, S., and H. Bass 1938. *Mayn Shprach Buch (My Language Book).* New York: Workmen Circle.

——— 1939. *Unzer Vort (Our Word).* New York: Atlantic Publishing.

——— 1947. *Dos Yiddishe Vort.* New York: Workmen Circle.

Yefroiken, S., and H. Chazden 1948. ——— 1951. "The Y.L. Peretz Schules of the Workmen Circle," *Bleter far Yiddishe Dertsiyung.* New York: Congress for Jewish Culture.

Yefroiken, S., and H. Chazden 1948. *Baym Kval (Hear the Source).* New York: Workmen Circle.

——— 1951. "The Y.L. Peretz Schules of the Workmen Circle," *Bleter far Yiddishe Dertsiyung.* New York: Congress for Jewish Culture.

Yefroiken, S., and H. Bass 1954. *Dos Lebedike Vort (The Living Word),* Reading Text for the Third Year. New York: Workmen Circle.

Yiddishen Lerer Seminar 1929. *(Yiddish Teachers' Seminar). Nave Klassen und Nave Kursen (New Classes and New Courses).* New York: Catalogue-Brochure.

Chapter XI

Beatty, Willard 1944. *Education for Action: Selected Articles from Indian Education, 1936-1943.* Washington, D.C.: Educational Division, United States Indian Service.

Division of Education, The Navajo Tribe 1974. Position Paper for the Conference on Federal Policy and Navajo Education, Apr. 2-3, 1974.

Dracon, John 1969. The Extent of Bilingualism among the Crow and the Northern Cheyenne

Indian School Populations, Grades One through Twelve, A Study, ERIC (ED 044 205).

Fishman, Joshua A. 1973. "The Third Century of Non-English Language Maintenance and Non-Anglo Ethnic Maintenance in the United States of America," *TESOL Quarterly* 7:221-233.

Fuchs, Estelle, and Robert J. Havighurst 1972. *To Live on This Earth.* Garden City, N.Y.: Doubleday.

Harris, David P. (ed.) 1970. *Report of the Evaluation of English as a Second Language Programs in Navajo Area Schools.* Washington, D.C.: TESOL.

Holland, R. Fount 1972. "School in Cherokee and English," *Elementary School Journal* 8:412-418.

Krauss, Michael 1974. Note on E.S. Rubtsova, *International Journal of American Linguistics* 40:44-46.

Lewis, E. Glyn to appear. The Dynamics of Societal Bilingualism—Bilingual Education in Wales and the Soviet Union.

National Indian Bilingual Education Conference 1973. *Proceedings* (Curriculum Bulletin 15). Washington, D.C.: United States Bureau of Indian Affairs.

Pulte, William n.d. "Cherokee: A Flourishing or Obsolescing Language?" manuscript.

Spolsky, Bernard 1970. "Navajo Language Maintenance: Six-Year-Olds in 1969," *Language Sciences 13*:19-24.

——— 1974. "Speech Communities and Schools," *TESOL Quarterly 8*:17-26.

Spolsky, Bernard, Agnes Holm, and Penny Murphy 1970. *Analytical Bibliography of Navajo Reading Materials* (Curriculum Bulletin No. 10). Washington, D.C.: United States Bureau of Indian Affairs (ED 043 413).

Spolsky, Bernard, Joanna B. Green, and John Read 1974. *A Model for the Description, Analysis, and Perhaps Evaluation of Bilingual Education, Navajo Reading Study Progress Report* 23. Albuquerque: University of New Mexico.

Spolsky, Bernard, and James Kari 1974. "Apachean Language Maintenance," *International Journal of the Sociology of Language 2*:91-100.

Wahrhaftig, Albert 1970. *Social and Economic Characteristics of the Cherokee Population of Eastern Oklahoma, Anthropological Studies,* No. 5. American Anthropological Association.

Walker, Willard 1965. "An Experiment in Programmed Cross-Cultural Education: The Import of the Cherokee Primer for the Cherokee Community and for the Behavioral Sciences."

White, John K. 1962. "On the Revival of Printing in the Cherokee Language," *Current Anthropology 3*:511-514.

Young, Robert W. 1972. *Written Navajo: A Brief History, Navajo Reading Study Progress Report* 19. Albuquerque: University of New Mexico (ED 068 229).

Young, Robert W., and William Morgan, Sr. 1943. *The Navaho Language.* Phoenix, Ariz.: Educational Division, United States Indian Service.

Chapter XII

Bickley, Verner C. 1973. "Cultural Aspects of Language Imposition in Malaysia, Singapore, and Indonesia," *Topics in Culture Learning* Vol. 1. Honolulu: East-West Center.

Chan, Leok Har 1975. "Chinese Dialects in Southeast Asia," *Working Papers in Linguistics* 7:4, 1-37.

Chang, David W. 1973. "Current status of Chinese minorities in Southeast Asia," *Asian Survey 8*:587-603.

Ch'en, Lieh-fu 1968. "Fei-lü-pin Hua ch'iao chiao yü ti hsien chie tuan chi ch'i wen t'i (Current situation and problems on Overseas Chinese education in the Philippines),"

Hua Ch'iao Wen T'i Lun Ts'ung (Collections of Articles on Overseas Chinese Problems). Taipei: Ch'iao Wu Wei Yuan Hui, pp. 357-371.

Cheng, Robert L. 1973a. "Second-Language Learners' Classification of Chinese Dialects and Related Languages," *Gengo Kenkyu* (Linguistic Society of Japan) *63*:27-43.

——— 1973b. "Language Unification in Taiwan: Present and Future," *Proceedings of International Congress of Anthropological and Ethnological Sciences.*

Cheng, Susie S. 1977. "Chinese Dialect Literature," *Journal of Chinese Language Teachers Association,* Vol. XII:55-62.

Ch'iao Wu Pao She 1957. *Ch'iao wu cheng ts'e wen chi* (Collection of Documents of Policy on Overseas Chinese Affairs). Peking: Pei-ching Jen-min Ch'u Pan She.

Ch'iao Wu Wei Yüan Hui 1963. *Chung-hua-min-kuo wu shih i nien ch'iao wu t'ung chi* (1962 Statistics on Overseas Chinese Affairs). Taipei, Taiwan.

——— 1971. Hai-wai Hua-wen Hsue-hsiao Chiao-yu Chuan-chi (Special Collection of Articles on Overseas Chinese School Education). Taipei, Taiwan.

——— 1972. *Ch'iao Sheng Hui Kuo Sheng Hsüeh Kai K'uang* (General Situation of Education for Overseas Chinese Students in Taiwan). Taipei, Taiwan.

——— 1973. *Hai Wai Hua Ch'iao Chiao Yü Chien Pao* (Brief Report of Overseas Chinese Education). Taipei, Taiwan.

China Executive Yuan Administrative Research and Evaluation Commission 1973. *A Review of Public Administration–The Republic of China, Taipei, Taiwan.*

Chinese University of Hong Kong 1970. "Chungkuo Yü Wen Chiao Hsüeh Yen T'ao Hui Pao Kao Shu" (Report of Seminar on the Teaching of Chinese in Hong Kong). Chinese University of Hong Kong, Hong Kong.

Chiu, Rosaline K.W. 1970. *Language Contact and Language Planning in China 1900-1967, A Selected Bibliography.* Quebec: Les Presses de L'Université Laval.

Chou, Fa-Kao 1970. "Ju He Chia Ch'iang Chungkuo Yü Wen Chiao Yü Ping Lun Kuo Yüeh Pi Chiao Yen Chiu Chih Chung Yao Hsing" (On How to Promote Chinese Language Education and Also on the Importance of Contrastive Studies between Mandarin and Cantonese), Chungkuo Yü Wen Chiao Hsüeh Yen T'ao Hui Pao Kao Shu (Report of Seminar on the Teaching of Chinese in Hong Kong). Hong Kong: Chinese University of Hong Kong, pp. 11-16.

Chou, Lu-ch'iao 1961. "Ch'iao hsiao chiao yü wu-shih nien (Fifty years of Overseas Chinese Education)," *Hua Ch'iao Wen T'i Lun Wen Chi* (Collection of articles on Overseas Chinese problems). Taipei: Chung-kuo Ch'iao Sheng Hsüeh Hui, pp. 74-87.

Chu, Tull 1967. *Political Attitudes of the Overseas Chinese in Japan.* Hong Kong: Union Research Institute.

Cole, Allan B. 1967. "Political Roles of Taiwanese Enterprises," *Asian Survey* 7:645-654.

DeFrancis, John 1950. *Nationalism and Language Reform in China.* Princeton, N.J.: Princeton University Press.

Engstrom, Kristina 1966. "The Chinese in the Philippines," unpublished mimeographed paper.

Enloe, Cynthia H. 1968. "Issues and Integration in Malaysia," *Pacific Affairs 41*:372-385.

Fincher, Beverly Hong 1973. "The Chinese Language in Its Social Context," *Journal of Chinese Linguistics 1*:163-169.

——— 1972. "Impressions of Language in the People's Republic of China," *China Quarterly 50.*

Fitzgerald, C.P. 1965. *The Third China.* Vancouver: University of British Columbia.

Fitzgerald, Stephen 1969. "Overseas Chinese Affairs and the Cultural Revolution," *China Quarterly 40*:103-126.

——— 1970. "China and the Overseas Chinese," *China Quarterly 44*:1-37.

——— 1972. *China and the Overseas Chinese.* London: Cambridge University Press.

Freadman, Maurice 1965. *The Chinese in Southeast Asia, A Longer View* (Occasional Paper 14). London: The Chinese Society. 24 pp.

Fried, Morton H. (ed.) 1958. *Colloquium on Overseas Chinese*. New York: Institute of Pacific Relations.

Fryer, Donald W. 1967. "The Problems of Regional Integration in Southeast Asia," *Seadag Papers on Development and Development Policy Problems 18*.

He, Chungchung 1970. "Kuanyü Chiaohsüeh Fangfa Chih Shangchüeh" (On Problems in Teaching Methods), Report of Seminar on the Teaching of Chinese in Hong Kong. Hong Kong: Chinese University of Hong Kong, pp. 57-60.

Howell, Llewellyn D., Jr. 1973. "Attitudinal Distance in Southeast Asia: Social and Political Ingredients in Integration," *Southeast Asia 2*, 4.

Huang, H.H. 1974. "On Mandarin Lexicon," *Central Daily News*, International Edition, May 15, 16, 1974.

LePage, R.B. 1964. The National Language Question—Linguistic Problems of Newly Independent State. London.

Linguistic Reporter 1974. "Bilingual-Bicultural Education—Supreme Court Rules in Lau vs. Nichols case," *The Linguistic Reporter*, March 1974, pp. 6-7.

Liu, Ts'un-jen 1970a. "Kung Yeh She Hui Ti K'o Ch'eng He Chiao Ts'ai (Teaching Materials and Curriculum in Industrial Society)," *Chungkuo Yü Wen Chiao Hsüeh Yen T'ao Hui Pao Kao Shu* (Report of Seminar on the Teaching of Chinese in Hong Kong). Hong Kong: Chinese University of Hong Kong, pp. 39-47.

——— 1970b. "Mandarin or Cantonese?" *Report of Seminar on the Teaching of Chinese in Hong Kong*. Hong Kong: Chinese University of Hong Kong, pp. 49-56.

Ma, Hung-shu, and Chen Chen-ming 1958. *Overseas Chinese Education in Hong Kong*. Taipei: Overseas Publication Service.

Ma, Meng 1970a. "Chungkuo Shu Mien Yü Ti P'ou Shih (An Analysis of Written Chinese)," *Chungkuo Yü Wen Chiao Hsüeh Yen T'ao Hui Pao Kao Shu* (Report of Seminar on the Teaching of Chinese in Hong Kong). Hong Kong: Chinese University of Hong Kong, pp. 113-125.

——— 1970b. "The Background and Future of the Promotion of Chinese-Language Education in Hong Kong," *Report of Seminar on the Teaching of Chinese in Hong Kong*. Hong Kong: Chinese University of Hong Kong, pp. 17-24.

Marina Junior High School 1973. Chinese Bilingual AB116 Project.

Milsky, Constantin 1973. "New Developments in Language Reform," *The China Quarterly* 53:98-133.

Murray, Douglas P. 1964. "Chinese Education in Southeast Asia," *The China Quarterly* 20:64-95.

Purcell, Victor W.W.S. 1960. *The Chinese in Modern Malaya*. Singapore: D. Moore.

——— 1965. *The Chinese in Southeast Asia*. London: Oxford University Press.

Puyodyana, Boonsanong 1971. *Chinese-Thai Differential Assimilation in Bangkok*. New York: Cornell University.

Pye, Lucian W. 1954. *Some Observations on the Political Behavior of Overseas Chinese*. Cambridge, Mass.: Center for International Studies, MIT.

Quek, Ah Chian 1973. "Bilingualism as a Major Objective in Education Policy in Singapore," unpublished paper at the University of Hawaii.

Roff, Margaret 1967. "The Politics of Language in Malaya," *Asian Survey* 7:316-328.

Simoniya, N.A. 1961. "Overseas Chinese in Southeast Asia—A Russian Study," *Department of Far East Studies, Cornell University, Southeast Asia Program, Data Paper No. 45*.

Tanapatchiyapong, Pagawan 1973. "The Chinese Minority in Thailand and Their Language Shift," unpublished paper at the University of Hawaii.

Ts'ai, Cho-t'ang 1970. "Chung Hsüeh Sheng Kuo-wen Ch'eng Tu Chien T'ao" (Evaluation of Secondary School Students' Competence in Chinese), *Chungkuo Yü Wen Chiao Hsüeh Yen T'ao Hui Pao Kao Shu* (Report on the Seminar on the Teaching of Chinese in Hong Kong. Hong Kong: Chinese University of Hong Kong, pp. 25-37.

Uchida, Naosaku 1960. *The Overseas Chinese, A Bibliographical Essay Based on the Resources of the Hoover Institute,* Hoover Institution on War, Revolution and Peace, Stanford University.

UNESCO 1974. UNESCO Statistical Yearbook.

——— 1953. "The Use of Vernacular Languages in Education," *Monograph on Fundamental Education,* Vol. XIII. Paris.

Van der Kroef, Justus M. 1964. "Nanyang University and the Dilemmas of Overseas Chinese Education," *The China Quarterly 20*:96-127.

Wang, Yü-te 1960. "Lexicostatistics Estimation of the Time Depth of the Five Main Chinese Dialects," *Gengo Kenkyu 38*:33-105.

Williams, Lea E. 1966. *The Future of the Overseas Chinese in Southeast Asia,* New York: McGraw-Hill, for the Council on Foreign Relations.

Wilmott, W.E. 1966. "The Chinese in Southeast Asia," *Australian Outlook 20*:3.

Wu, Shou-li 1963. Taiwan Fang-yan Wen-hsien Mu-lu (Bibliography of Studies on Dialects in Taiwan) T'ai-wan Wen-hsien No. 6. Taipei, Taiwan.

Yu, Arthur Yuh-chao 1971. "A Study of Chinese Organizations in Hawaii, with Special Reference to Assimilative Trends," *Working Papers of the East-West Center, Culture Learning Institute,* No. 3.

Chapter XIII

Aarons, B., and Stewart, W.A. (eds.) 1969. "Linguistic-cultural differences and American education," *The Florida FL Reporter,* anthology issue 1969.

Abrahams, R.D. 1970. "The advantages of black English," *Southern Conference of Language Learning,* Florida 1970.

——— 1972. "The training of the men of words in talking sweet," *Language in Society 1*:1.

Alatis, J.W. (ed.) 1969. Twentieth annual round table meeting. No. 22. Georgetown University School of Linguistics.

Alleyne, M.C. 1961. "Communication and politics in Jamaica," *Caribbean Studies 3.*

——— 1963. "Language and society in St. Lucia," *Caribbean Studies 1* (1).

Allsopp, S.R.R. 1958a. "The English language in British Guiana," *English Language Teaching 12* (2).

——— 1958b. "Pronominal forms in the dialect of English used in Georgetown (British Guiana) and its environs by people engaged in non-clerical occupations." Master's Thesis, University of London.

——— 1962. "Expression of state and action in the dialect of English used in the Georgetown area of British Guiana." Ph.D. dissertation, University of London.

——— 1965. "British Honduras—The linguistic dilemma," *Caribbean Quarterly 11* (3, 4).

——— 1972a. Some suprasegmental features of Caribbean English.

——— 1972b. The problem of acceptability in Caribbean creolized English. In Craig (ed. Ms.).

Anastasi, A., and Cordova, F.A. 1953. "Some effects of bilingualism upon the intelligence test performance of Puerto Rican children in New York City," *Journal of Educational Psychology, XLIV*:1.

Armstrong, B. 1968. "The teaching of English in Guiana," *The Guiana Teacher 2* (7).

Bailey, B.L. 1953. "Creole languages of the Caribbean area." Master's thesis, Columbia University.

——— 1962. *A Language Guide to Jamaica.* New York: Research Institute for the Study of Man.

——— 1963. "Teaching of English noun-verb concord in primary schools in Jamaica," *Caribbean Quarterly 9* (4).

––– 1964. "Some problems in the language teaching situation in Jamaica." In *Social Dialects and Language Learning,* Roger W. Shuy (ed.). Illinois: National Council of Teachers of English, 1964.

––– 1966. *Jamaican Creole Syntax. A Transformational Approach.* Cambridge University Press.

––– 1971. Jamaican creole: Can dialect boundaries be defined? In Hymes, 1971.

Bailey, C.J.N. 1969-1970. Studies in three-dimensional language theory I-IV. Working Papers in Linguistics. University of Hawaii.

––– 1970. Using data variation to confirm, rather than undermine, the validity of abstract syntactic structures. Working Papers in Linguistics, University of Hawaii.

Baratz, J.C. 1969. Teaching reading in an urban negro school system. In Baratz and Shuy, 1969.

Baratz, J. and Shuy, R.W. (eds.) 1969. *Teaching Black Children to Read.* Washington: Center for Applied Linguistics.

Bereiter et al. 1966. *Teaching Disadvantaged Children in the Pre-school.* Englewood Cliffs, N.J.: Prentice-Hall.

Bernstein, B. 1961a. "Social structure, language and learning," *Educational Research 3.*

––– 1961b. Social class and linguistic development: A theory of social learning. In Halsey, Floud, and Anderson 1961.

––– 1961c. "Aspects of language and learning in the genesis of the social process," *Journal of Child Psychology & Psychiatry 1*:313. Reprint in Hymes, *Language, Culture, and Society,* pp. 251-263. 1964.

––– 1962a. "Linguistic codes, hesitation phenomena and intelligence." *Language & Speech 5*:31-46.

––– 1962b. "Social class, linguistic codes and grammatical elements," *Language & Speech 5*:221-224.

––– 1965. A socio-linguistic approach to social learning. In *Social Science Survey.* J. Gould (ed.), London: Pelican.

––– 1966. Elaborated and restricted codes: An outline. In Lieberson 1966.

––– 1972. A critique of the concept of compensatory education. In Cazden, John, and Hymes 1972.

Berry, J. 1972. Some observations on residual tone in West Indian English. In Craig (ed. Ms.).

Bickerton, D. 1971. Guyanese Speech. Ms. University of Guyana.

––– 1971. "Inherent variability and variable rules," *Foundations of Language 7.*

––– 1972. The structure of polyectal grammars. In Shuy 1973.

––– 1973. "On the nature of a creole continuum," *Language 49* (3).

Brooks, C.E. 1964. Some approaches to teaching English as a second language. In Stewart 1964.

Bruner et al. 1956. *A Study of Thinking.* London: Chapman & Hall.

––– 1966. *Studies in Cognitive Growth.* New York: Wiley.

Bull, W.B. 1955. Review of: "The use of vernacular languages in education," *IJAL 21*:288-294.

Carrington, L.D. 1967. "St. Lucia Creole: A descriptive analysis of its phonology and morphosyntax." Ph.D. dissertation, University of the West Indies, Mona.

––– 1968. "English language learning problems in the Caribbean," *Trinidad and Tobago Modern Language Review,* No. 1.

––– 1969. "Deviations from standard English in the speech of primary school children in St. Lucia and Dominica," *IRAL VIII/*3.

––– 1970. "English language teaching in the Commonwealth Caribbean," *Commonwealth Education Liaison Committee Newsletter 2* (10).

Carrington, L.D., and C. Borely 1969. "An investigation into English language learning and teaching problems in Trinidad and Tobago." St. Augustine: UWI Institute of Education.

Carrington, L.D., C. Borely, and Knight 1972. Away Robin run: A critical description of the teaching of the language arts in the primary schools of Trinidad and Tobago. St. Augustine Trinidad: Institute of Education.
——— 1972a. Linguistic exposure of Trinidad children. St. Augustine Trinidad: Institute of Education.
Cassidy, F.G. 1961. *Jamaica Talk: Three Hundred Years of the English Language in Jamaica.* London: Macmillan.
Cassidy, F.G., and R.B. LePage 1967. *Dictionary of Jamaica English.* Cambridge University Press.
——— 1972. Jamaican creole and Twi: Some comparisons. In Craig (ed. Ms.).
Cave, G.N. 1970. "Sociolinguistic factors in Guyana language," *Language Learning 20* (2).
——— 1971. Primary School language in Guyana. Georgetown: Guyana Teachers' Association.
——— 1972. Measuring linguistic maturity: the case of the noun steam. In Craig (ed. Ms.).
Cazden, C.B., V.P. John, and D. Hymes (eds.) 1972. *Functions of Language in the Classroom.* New York: Teachers College Press.
Christie, P. 1969. "A sociolinguistic study of some Dominican creole speakers." Ph.D. dissertation, University of New York.
Corbin, R., and M. Crosby 1965. Language programs for the disadvantaged, N.C.T.E. Illinois.
Coulthard et al. 1968. "The structure of the nominal group and elaboratedness of code," *Language & Speech 11.* 2:234-250.
Craig, D.R. 1964. The written English of some 14-year-old Jamaican and English children. In Faculty of Education 1965.
——— 1966. "Teaching English to Jamaican creole speakers: A model of a multi-dialect situation," *Language Learning 16* (1-2).
——— 1966a. "Some developments in language teaching in the West Indies," *Caribbean Quarterly 12* (1).
——— 1967. "Some early indications of learning a second dialect," *Language Learning 17* (3, 4).
——— 1969. *An Experiment in Teaching English.* London: Caribbean University Press (Ginn & Co. Ltd.).
——— 1971. Education and creole English in the West Indies: Some sociolinguistic factors. In Hymes 1971.
——— To appear. *Social Class and the Use of Language: A Case Study of Jamaican Children.* Washington, D.C.: Center for Applied Linguistics.
——— 1973. Social class, language and communication in Jamaican children. In Education in the Commonwealth 6. London: Commonwealth Secretariat.
——— (Ms.). Creole languages and educational development: Papers from the conference sponsored by UNESCO and the UWI, July 1972. Jamaica: Sebat of Education, U.W.I.
——— 1974. "Developmental and social class differences in language," *Caribbean Journal of Education 1*:2. Jamaica: University of the West Indies.
——— 1974a. "Language-education research in the Commonwealth Caribbean," *Caribbean Journal of Education 1*:1. Jamaica: University of the West Indies.
——— 1975. A Creole English continuum and the theory of grammar. In Papers from the International Conference on Pidgin and Creole Languages, Hawaii University Press (to appear).
——— 1976. Bidialectal education: Creole and standard in the West Indies, *International Journal of the Sociology of Language 8.* The Hague: Mouton.
Crow, Lester D., Walter I. Murray, and Hugh H. Smythe 1966. *Educating the Culturally Disadvantaged Child: Principles and Programs.* New York: D. McKay Co.
Cuffie, D. 1964. "Problems in the teaching of English in the island of Trinidad from 1797 to the present day." Master's thesis. University of London, Institute of Education.
DeCamp, D. 1971. The study of pidgin and creole languages. In Hymes 1971.
——— 1971a. Toward a generative analysis of a post creole speech continuum. In Hymes 1971.

――― 1972. Standard English books and creole speaking children. In Craig (ed. Ms.).

Douglas, J.W.B. 1964. *The Home and the School.* London and New York: MacGibbon and Kee.

Edwards, W. 1972. "Have" and "be" in Guyanese creole. In Craig (ed. Ms.).

Eichon, D.H., and H.E. Jones 1952. Bilingualism, Chapter 2 of *Review of Educational Research,* vol. XXII, 5.

Engle, P.L. 1973. *The Use of the Vernacular Languages in Education: Revisited.* Ford Foundation.

Eysenck, H.J. 1971. *Race, Intelligence and Education.* London: Temple Smith.

Faculty of Education, University of the West Indies 1965. Language teaching, linguistics and the teaching of English in a multilingual society. Report of the Conference at University of the West Indies. April 1964.

Fasold, R.W. 1968. Isn't English the first language too? NCTE, Annual Conference, Wisconsin, 1968.

――― 1969. Orthography in reading materials for black English speaking children. In Baratz and Shuy 1969.

Fasold, R.W., and R.W. Shuy (eds.) 1970. *Teaching Standard English in the Inner City.* Washington: Center for Applied Linguistics.

Ferguson, G. 1954. "On learning and human ability," *Canadian Journal of Psychology* *8*:95-112.

――― 1959. "Diglossia," *Word 15*:325-340.

Figueroa, J. 1962. "Language teaching: Part of a general and professional problem," *English Language Teaching 16* (3).

――― 1966. "Notes on the teaching of English in the West Indies," *New World Quarterly 2* (4).

――― 1972. Some notes, together with samples of language occurring in the creole context. In Craig (ed. Ms.).

Fishman, Joshua, and John Lovas 1970. Bilingual education in a sociolinguistic perspective. *TESOL Quarterly 4*:215-222.

Fishman, J.A., and E. Lueders-Salmon 1972. What has the sociology of language to say to the teacher? On teaching the standard variety to speakers of dialectal or sociolectal varieties. In Cazden and Hymes 1972.

Floud, J., and A.H. Halsey 1957. Social class, intelligence tests and selection for secondary schools. In Halsey, Floud, and Anderson 1961. pp. 209-215.

Fraser, B. 1973. Optional rules in a grammar. In Shuy 1973.

Goodman, K.S., and C. Buck 1973. "Dialect barriers to reading comprehension revisited," *The Reading Teacher 27*:1.

Goodnow, J.J. 1968. Cultural variations in cognitive skills. In Price-Williams 1969.

Grant, D.R.B. 1964. A study of some common language and spelling errors of elementary school children in Jamaica. In Faculty of Education 1965.

Gray, C.R. 1963. "Teaching English in the West Indies," *Caribbean Quarterly 9* (1, 2).

Gumperz, J., and D. Hymes (eds.) 1972. *Directions in Sociolinguistics: The Ethnography of Communication.* New York: Holt, Rinehart and Winston.

Hall, R. 1966. *Pidgin and Creole Languages.* Ithaca: Cornell University Press.

Halsey, A.H., J. Floud, and C.A. Anderson 1961. *Education, Economy and Society.* New York: Collier-Macmillan.

Hawkins, R.R. 1969. "Social class, the nominal group and reference," *Language & Speech 12*, 2:125-135.

Hughes, A. 1966. "Non-standard English of Grenada," *Caribbean Quarterly 12* (4).

Hymes, D.H. 1961a. Linguistic aspects of cross cultural personality study. In Bert Kaplan (ed.) *Studying Personality Cross Culturally.* New York: Harper & Row.

――― 1961b. Functions of speech: An evolutionary approach. In Fred Gruber (ed.). *Anthropology and Education.* Philadelphia: University of Pennsylvania Press. P. 55.

――― 1962. The Ethnography of speaking. In Gladwin, T, and W.C. Stuyvesant (eds.).

Anthropology and Human Behaviour. Washington, D.C.: Anthropological Society of Washington.

——— 1967. "Models of the interaction of language and social setting," *Journal of Social Issues XXIII*:2.

——— (ed.) 1971. *Pidginization and Creolization of Language.* Cambridge University Press.

Jensen, A.R. et al. 1969. "Environment, heredity and intelligence," Harvard Reprint, Series 2.

John, V.P. 1962. The intellectual development of slum children. American Orthopsychiatric Association. Annual Meeting.

Jones, J.A. 1966. "English in the West Indies," *English Language Teaching 20* (2).

Klein, J. 1965. *Samples from English Cultures.* London: Routledge and Kegan Paul.

Knight, H.E., L.D. Carrington, and C.B. Borely 1972. Preliminary comments on language arts textbooks in use in the primary schools of Trinidad and Tobago. University of the West Indies. Institute of Education.

Kochman, T. 1969. Social factors in the consideration of teaching standard English. In Aarons and Stewart 1969.

——— 1972. Black American speech events and a language program for the classroom. In Cazden and Hymes 1972.

Labov, W. 1964. Stages in the acquisition of standard English. In Shuy 1964.

——— 1966. The social stratification of English in New York City. Washington, D.C.: Center for Applied Linguistics.

——— 1969. The logic of non-standard English. In Alatis 1969.

——— 1971. The notion of "system" in creole languages. In Hymes 1971.

——— 1973. Where do grammars stop? In Shuy 1973.

Labov, W. et al. 1965. A preliminary study of the structure of English used by Negro and Puerto Rican speakers in New York City. Co-operative Research Project. No. 3091. New York: Columbia University.

Labov, W., and P. Cohen 1967. Systematic relations of standard and non-standard rules in the grammar of negro speakers. Project Literacy Report, 8. Ithaca, N.Y.: Cornell University.

Lambert, W.E., and G.R. Tucker 1972. *Bilingual Education of Children: The St. Lambert Experiment.* Rowley, Mass.: Newbury House.

Lawton, D.L. 1963. "Suprasegmental phenomena in Jamaica creole." Ph.D. dissertation. Michigan State University.

——— 1965. "Some problems of teaching a creolized language to Peace Corps Members," *Language Learning 14.*

——— 1971. "Tone and Jamaican Creole." Paper read at the Annual Conference on Caribbean Linguistics. May 17-21, Mona, University of the West Indies.

Lawton, D. 1963. "Social class differences in language development," *Language & Speech 6,* 3, 120-143.

——— 1964. "Social class language differences in group discussions," *Language & Speech 7,* 3, 182.

——— 1968. *Social Class, Language and Education.* London: Routledge and Kegan Paul.

LePage, R.N. 1952. "A survey of dialects in the British Caribbean," *Caribbean Quarterly 2* (3).

——— 1955. "The language problem in the British Caribbean," *Caribbean Quarterly 4* (1).

——— 1957. "General outlines of English Creole dialects," *Orbis 6.*

——— (ed.) 1961. Proceedings of the conference on Creole Language Studies. London: Macmillan.

——— 1972. "The concept of competence in a creole English situation," *York Papers in Linguistics 3.*

LePage, R.N., and D. DeCamp 1960. *Jamaican Creole; an Historical Introduction to Jamaican Creole* (by R.B. LePage and four Jamaican creole texts by David DeCamp). London: Macmillan.

Lieberson, S. (ed.) 1966. "Explorations in sociolinguistics," *Social Enquiry 36.*

L.S.A. Bulletin 1972. Linguistic Society of America Bulletin, March.

Luria, A.R., and F.J. Judovic 1959 (translated). *Speech and the Development of Mental Processes.* London: Staples Press.

McClelland, B.C. et al. 1953. *The Achievement Motive.* New York: Appleton-Century-Croft.

——— 1958. *Talent and Society. New Perspectives in the Identification of Talent.* Princeton, N.J.: Van Nostrand.

——— 1961. *The Achieving Society.* Princeton, N.J.: Van Nostrand.

Malinowsky, B. 1923. The problem of meaning in primitive cultures. In Ogden, C., and I.A. Richards. *The Meaning of Meaning.* London: Routledge.

Nisbet, J. 1953. Family environment and intelligence. In Halsey, Floud, and Anderson 1961. Pp. 273-287.

Price-Williams, D.R. (ed.) 1969. *Cross Cultural Studies.* Penguin Modern Psychology Readings.

Reisman, Karl 1961. "The English-based creole of Antigua" (Research Notes), *Carribean Quarterly 1* (1).

——— 1965. "The isle is full of noises: A study of creole in the speech patterns of Antigua, West Indies." Ph.D. dissertation, Harvard University.

Reissman, F. 1962. *The Culturally Deprived Child.* New York: Harper & Row.

Rice, F.A. (ed.) 1962. Study of the role of second languages in Asia, Africa, and Latin America. Washington, D.C.: Center for Applied Linguistics.

Richards, J.C. 1972. "Social factors, interlanguage and language learning," *Language Learning 22*:2.

Robinson, W.P. 1965. "The elaborated code in working class language," *Language & Speech 8,* 4:243-252.

Robinson, W.P., and C.D. Creed 1968. "Perceptual and verbal discriminations of 'elaborated' and 'restricted' code users," *Language & Speech 11*:3, 182-193.

Russell, T. 1868. *The Etymology of Jamaica Grammar by a Young Gentleman.* Kingston: MacDougall & Co.

Schuchdardt, H. 1882. *Kreolische Studien,* 11 vols. Vienna.

Schumann, J.H. 1974. "The implications of interlanguage, pidginization and creolization for the study of adult second language acquisition," *TESOL Quarterly 8*:2.

Selinker, L. 1972. "Interlanguage," *IRAL 10*:3.

Shuy, R.W. 1972. Strategies for implementing sociolinguistic principles in the schools. In Craig (ed. Ms.).

——— (ed.) 1973. Proceedings of the 23rd Annual Round Table. Washington, D.C.: Georgetown University.

——— 1964. "Social dialects and language learning," NCTE, Ill.

Shuy, R.W., W.A. Wolfram, and W.K. Riley 1967. Linguistic correlates of social stratification in Detroit speech. Final Report. Co-operative Research Project 6-1347, Office of Education.

Solomon, D. 1966. "The system of predication in the speech of Trinidad: A quantitative study of decreolization." Master's thesis. Columbia University.

——— 1972. Form, content and the post-creole continuum. In Craig (ed. Ms.).

Spears, R. 1972. Pitch and intonation in Cayman English. In Craig (ed. Ms.).

Stewart, W.A. 1962. Creole languages in the Caribbean. In Rice 1962.

——— 1964. Urban Negro Speech: Sociolinguistic factors affecting English teaching. In Shuy 1964.

——— (ed.) 1964. Non-standard speech and the teaching of English. Washington, D.C.: Center for Applied Linguistics.

——— 1967. "Sociolinguistic factors in the history of American negro dialects." *The Florida FL Reporter 5,* 2.

——— 1969. Negro dialect in the teaching of reading. In Baratz and Shuy 1969.

Taylor, D. 1945. "Certain Carib morphological influences on creole," *International Journal of American Linguistics 11* (3).

––– 1952. "A note on the phoneme /r/ in Dominican creole," *Word 8* (3).

––– 1955. "Phonic Interference in Dominican Creole," *Word* 11.

––– 1961. "Some Dominican creole descendants of the French definite article." In LePage (ed.), Conference on Creole Language Studies. London: Macmillan.

––– 1963. "Remarks on the lexicon of Dominican French creole," *Romance Philology* 16.

––– 1968. "New languages for old in the West Indies." In J.A. Fishman (ed.). *Readings in the Sociology of Language*. The Hague: Mouton.

Thomas, J.J. 1869. *The Theory and Practice of Creole Grammar*. London: New Beacon Books, 1969.

Trotman, J. 1973. The teaching of English in Guyana: A linguistic approach. Faculty of Education, University of Guyana.

Tyndall, B. 1965. "Some grammatical aspects of the written work of creolese-speaking school children in British Guiana." Master's Thesis, University of Manchester.

––– 1973. Reading habit and the written expression of secondary school first formers. Faculty of Education University of Guyana.

UNESCO 1953. *The Use of Vernacular Languages in Education: Monographs on Fundamental Education*. Paris.

Van Name, A. 1870. "Contributions to Creole grammar," *Transactions of the American Philological Association*. (Boston) *1*.

Vernon, P.E. 1955. "The bearing of recent advances in psychology on educational problems," *Studies in Education 7*. University of London Institute of Education.

––– 1965a. "Environmental handicaps and intellectual development," *British Journal of Educational Psychology 35*:1-12, 117-126.

––– 1965b. "Ability factors and environmental influences," *American Psychologist 20*:723-733.

––– 1966. "Education and intellectual development among Canadian Indians and Eskimos," *Educational Review 18*:79-91.

––– 1967. Abilities and educational attainments in an East African environment. In Price-Williams 1969.

Vigotsky, L.S. 1962. *Thought and Language*. Cambridge: MIT Press.

Walters, E. 1958. "Learning to read in Jamaica." Mona, Jamaica: Department of Education, University of the West Indies.

Warner, M. 1967. "Language in Trinidad with special reference to English." Master's Thesis. University of New York, 1967.

Wilson, E. 1968. "Grammar in English teaching," *The Guiana Teacher 2* (7).

Winford, D. 1972. "A sociolinguistic description of two communities in Trinidad." Ph.D. thesis, University of York.

Wolfram, W. 1969. A sociolinguistic description of Detroit Negro speech. Washington, D.C.: Center for Applied Linguistcs.

––– 1970. "Sociolinguistic alternatives in teaching reading to non-standard speakers," *Reading Research Quarterly VI*:1, Delaware.

Chapter XV

Alatis, James E. 1976. "The Compatibility of TESOL and Bilingual Education," in James E. Alatis and Kristie Twaddell, eds. *English as a Second Language in Bilingual Education*. Washington, D.C.: Teachers of English to Speakers of Other Languages.

American Institutes for Research (AIR) 1977. *Evaluation of the Impact of ESEA Title VII Spanish/English Bilingual Education Program*. Palo Alto, Calif.: AIR.

Andersson, Theodore, and Mildred Boyer 1970. *Bilingual Schooling in the United States*, Vol. I. Austin, Tex.: Southwest Educational Development Laboratory.

Banks, James A. 1975. *Teaching Strategies for Ethnic Studies*. Boston: Allyn & Bacon, Inc.

Blanco, George M. 1975. "Language Proficiency and Linguistics," in *Second National Conference of EPDA Bilingual Education Project Directors*. Arlington, Va.: Center for Applied Linguistcs, pp. 7-22.

——— 1976. The Role of Foreign Language Educators in Bilingual Education, *Texas Conference on Coordinating Foreign Languages: A Report of the Proceedings*. Austin, Tex.: Texas Education Agency, pp. 22-29.

——— 1977. "Cross-Disciplinary Perspectives in Bilingual Education: Education Review." Arlington, Va.: Center for Applied Linguistics.

Board of Education of the City of Chicago 1974. *A Comprehensive Design for Bilingual-Bicultural Education*. Chicago: The Board of Education.

Brooks, Nelson 1960. *Language and Language Learning: Theory and Practice*. New York: Harcourt Brace & World, Inc.

——— 1972. "Parameters of Culture," based on a talk entitled "Culture vs. Civilization" delivered at the Connecticut Foreign Language Teachers Convention, New Britain, Conn., Oct. 27, 1972.

Brown, Roger 1973. "Development of the First Language in the Human Species," *American Psychologist 28,* 2 (February 1973): 97-106.

Cárdenas, Blandina, and José A. Cárdenas 1972. *The Theory of Incompatibilities: A Conceptual Framework for Responding to the Educational Needs of Mexican American Children*. San Antonio, Tex.: Intercultural Development Research Association. Originally in NEA Journal *Today's Education* (February 1972).

Carroll, John B. 1965. *Language and Thought*. Englewood Cliffs, N.J.: Prentice-Hall.

Castañeda, Alfredo, Leslie P. Herold, and Manuel Ramírez III 1975. *A New Philosophy of Education*. Austin, Tex.: Dissemination and Assessment Center for Bilingual Education.

Center for Applied Linguistics (CAL) 1974. *Guidelines for the Preparation and Certification of Teachers of Bilingual/Bicultural Education*. Arlington, Va.: CAL.

——— 1977. "Response to AIR Study *Evaluation of the Impact of ESEA Title VII Spanish/English Bilingual Education Program*." Arlington, Va.: CAL, Apr. 18, 1977.

Chomsky, Noam 1966. "Linguistic Theory," in *Language Teaching: Broader Contexts,* Northeast Conference on the Teaching of Foreign Languages. New York: MLA Materials Center, pp. 43-49.

Christian, Chester C., and John M. Sharp 1972. "Bilingualism in a Pluralistic Society," in Dale L. Lange, ed., *Foreign Language Education: A Reappraisal*. Skokie, Ill.: National Textbook Co.

Cohen, Andrew 1975. *Sociolinguistic Approach to Bilingual Education*. Rowley, Mass.: Newbury House.Publishers.

Council of Chief State School Officers 1977. *Policy Statements*. Washington, D.C.: The Council of Chief State School Officers.

Crèvecoeur, Michel Guillaume de 1925. *Letters from an American Farmer* (Reprint of 1782 ed.). New York: Albert & Charles Boni.

Cruz-Aedo, Víctor 1976. Letter on supply and demand of bilingual education teachers for the State of Texas. Austin, Tex.: Texas Education Agency, Sept. 10, 1976.

Cuneo, Ernest 1975. "Bilingual Teaching Is a Grave Error," *Long Island Press*, June 19, 1975, p. 18.

DACBE. See Dissemination and Assessment Center for Bilingual Education.

Delgado Votaw, Carmen 1976. "Bibliografía." Washington, D.C.: Office of The Commonwealth of Puerto Rico.

Della-Dora, Delmo, and James E. House (eds.) 1974. *Education for an Open Society*. Washington, D.C.: Association for Supervision and Curriculum Development.

Dewey, John 1966. "Aims in Education," in John M. Rich, ed., *Readings in the Philosophy of Education*. Belmont, Calif.: Wadsworth Publishing Co., Inc. Pp. 32-41.

Dissemination and Assessment Center for Bilingual Education (DACBE) 1969-1976. *Directories of Title VII ESEA Bilingual Education Programs: 1969-76.* Austin, Tex.: DACBE.

——— 1975. *Evaluation Instruments for Bilingual Education.* Austin, Tex.: DACBE.

——— *Publications Catalog.* Austin, Tex.: DACBE, published biannually.

——— 1975-1976. *Teacher Education Programs for Bilingual Education in U.S. Colleges and Universities.* Austin, Tex.: DACBE.

Dissemination Center for Bilingual Bicultural Education. See Dissemination and Assessment Center for Bilingual Education (DACBE).

Dulay, Heidi, and Marina K. Burt 1974. "Errors and Strategies in Child Second Language Acquisition," *TESOL Quarterly 8,* 2 (June 1974):129-136.

Dulay, Heidi, Marina Burt, and Loraine Zappert 1976. *Why Bilingual Education: A Summary of Research Findings* (Research Poster). Berkeley, Calif.: BABEL/LAU Center.

Education Service Center, Region II 1976. *Adult Education: Bilingual Handbook.* Corpus Christi, Tex.: The Education Service Center.

Educational Products Information Exchange Institute 1976. EPIE Forms A. New York: 1976. EPIE Report 73, *Selector's Guide for Educational Materials: Vol. 1, Spanish Language Arts.* New York: The Educational Products Information Exchange Institute.

——— 1976. EPIE Report 74, *Selector's Guide for Bilingual Education Materials, Vol. 2, Spanish "Branch" Programs.* New York: The Educational Products Information Exchange Institute.

Ervin-Tripp, Susan M. 1973. "Structure and Process in Language Acquisition, in A. Dil, ed., *Language Acquisition and Communicative Choice.* Stanford: Stanford University Press, pp. 204-238.

Fernández, Irene 1973. *Parental Involvement in Bilingual Education.* U.S. Educational Resources Information Center. ERIC Document ED 088 290, November.

Finocchiaro, Mary 1964. *Teaching Children Foreign Languages.* New York: McGraw-Hill Book Co.

Fishman, Joshua 1976. "Bilingual Education: An International Sociological Perspective." Keynote address delivered at the Fifth Annual International Bilingual/Bicultural Education Conference, San Antonio, Tex., Apr. 30-May 3, 1976. Tape available from Minute Tape, Culver City, Calif.

Fishman, Joshua, and John Lovas 1970. "Bilingual Education in Sociolinguistic Perspective," *TESOL Quarterly 4,* 3 (September 1970):215-222.

Flores, Macías, Reynaldo 1973. "Opinions of Chicano Community Parents on Curriculum and Language Use in Bilingual Preschool Education," *Aztlán 4,* 2 (fall 1973):315-334.

Foreign Language Annals, published by the American Council on the Teaching of Foreign Languages (ACTFL). New York: ACTFL.

Gaarder, A. Bruce 1975. "Linkages between Foreign Language Teaching and Bilingual Education," *Bulletin of the Association of Departments of Foreign Languages, 6,* 3 (March 1975):8-11.

Geffert, Hannah N., Robert J. Harper, Salvador Sarmiento, and Daniel M. Schember 1975. *The Current Status of U.S. Bilingual Education Legislation,* Bilingual Education Series: 4. Arlington, Va.: Center for Applied Linguistics.

Gibb, Glenadine 1974. "Mathematics and the Bilingual Student," *Newsletter of the National Council of Teachers of Mathematics,* December 1974, pp. 1, 4.

González, Josué M. (ed.) n.d. *Reviewing Instructional Materials for Cultural Relevancy.* San Antonio, Tex.: Curriculum Adaptation Network for Bilingual/Bicultural Education.

——— 1975. "Coming of Age in Bilingual/Bicultural Education: A Historical Perspective," *Inequality in Education 19* (February 1975:5-17.

Gutiérrez, Lorraine 1972. *Attitudes towards Bilingual Education: A Study of Parents with Children in Selected Bilingual Programs.* U.S. Educational Resources Information Center, ERIC Document ED 070 550.

Herman, Judith (ed.) 1974. *The Schools and Group Identity: Educating for a New Pluralism.* New York: Institute on Pluralism and Group Identity.

Hispania, published by The American Association of Teachers of Spanish and Portuguese. Worcester, Mass.: Holy Cross College.

Horn, Thomas D. 1976. "Information Concerning the Language Research Project," Austin, Tex.: The University of Texas at Austin, Learning Disabilities Center, August.

Lambert, Wallace E., and Richard G. Tucker 1972. *Bilingual Education of Children.* Rowley, Mass.: Newbury House.Publishers.

Litsinger, Dolores Escobar 1973. *The Challenge of Teaching Mexican American Students.* New York: American Book Co.

McBride, Christine 1974. "A Survey of ERIC Reports on Inservice Programs for Teachers in Spanish Bilingual Education Programs." Unpublished Master's Report, The University of Texas at Austin.

Mace Matluck, Betty J. 1977. "The Order of Acquisition of Certain Oral English Structures by Native-Speaking Children of Spanish, Cantonese, Tagalog, and Ilokano Learning English as a Second Language between the Ages of Five and Ten." Unpublished Ph.D. Dissertation, The University of Texas at Austin.

Mackey, William F. 1972. *Bilingual Education in a Binational School.* Rowley, Mass.: Newbury House Publishers.

Marquevich, Pat, and Shelly Spiegel 1976. *Multiethnic Studies in the Elementary School Classroom.* Rico Rivera, Calif.: Education in Motion.

Martin, Jeanette P. 1975. *A Survey of the Current Study and Teaching of North American Indian Languages in the U.S. and Canada.* CAL-ERIC/CLL Series on Languages and Linguistics, No. 17. Arlington, Va.: Center for Applied Linguistics.

Milon, John P. 1974. "The Development of Negation in English by a Second Language Learner," *TESOL Quarterly 8,* 2 (June 1974):137-143.

Modiano, Nancy 1966. "Reading Comprehension in the National Language: A Comparative Study of Bilingual and All-Spanish Approaches to Reading Instruction in Selected Indian Schools in the Highlands of Chiapas, Mexico." Unpublished Ph.D. Dissertation, New York University.

Molina, John 1976, 1977. Letters of invitation to testify before the National Council on Bilingual Education. Washington, D.C.: U.S. Office of Education.

——— 1977. "Proposed Legislative Changes and the Future of Bilingual Education." Address delivered at the Sixth Annual International Bilingual/Bicultural Education Conference, New Orleans, La.: Apr. 4-8.

Natalicio, Diana S., Luis F.S. Natalicio 1971. "A Comparative Study of English Pluralization by Native and Non-Native English Speakers," *Child Development 42,* 4 (October 1971):1302-1306.

National Council for the Social Studies. In press. *Ethnic Studies Curriculum Guidelines: Position Statement.* Washington, D.C.: The Council.

National Education Association, Department of Rural Education 1966. *The Invisible Minority: Pero no vencibles.* Washington, D.C.: NEA.

——— n.d. "Get Involved in Your Child's School." Hyattsville, Md.: American Education Week.

——— n.d. "Parent-Teacher Relationships." Hyattsville, Md.: American Education Week.

National Institute of Education 1976. *Multicultural/Bilingual Division Fiscal Year 1976 Program Plan.* Washington, D.C.: NIE.

Northeast Conference on the Teaching of Foreign Languages 1976. *Language and Culture: Heritage and Horizons,* Reports of the Working Committees. Middlebury, Vt.

Paulston, Christina Bratt 1974. *Implications of Language Learning Theory for Language Planning: Concerns in Bilingual Education,* Bilingual Education Series: 1. Arlington, Va.: Center for Applied Linguistics.

Peña, Albar 1973. *Federal Legislative Funding for Bilingual Programs.* Paper presented at the

International Multilingual-Multicultural Conference in San Diego, Calif. Sacramento, Calif.: State Department of Education.

Pérez, Carmen 1975. "Instructional Methods and Supervised Teacing," in *Second National Conference of EPDA Bilingual Education Project Directors*. Arlington, Va.: Center for Applied Linguistcs, pp. 47-64.

Reyes, Vinicio H. 1975. *Bilingual-Bicultural Education: The Chicago Experience*. Chicago: Bicultural-Bilingual Studies.

Rivers, Wilga M. 1968. *Teaching Foreign-Language Skills*. Chicago: The University of Chicago Press.

Sánchez, Willie n.d. "Introducción a las matemáticas modernas para maestros de escuelas primarias." Las Vegas, N.M.: Highlands University.

Saville, Muriel R., and Rudolph C. Troike 1971. *A Handbook of Bilingual Education*, rev. ed. Washington, D.C.: Teachers of English to Speakers of Other Languages.

Shanker, Albert 1974. "Bilingual Education: Not 'Why' But 'How'," *The New York Times*, Nov. 3, 1974, Sec. 4, p. 11.

Skinner, B.F. 1957. *Verbal Behavior*. New York: Appleton-Century-Crofts.

Smith, George W., and Owen L. Caskey 1972. *Promising School Practices for Mexican Americans*. Austin, Tex.: Southwest Educational Development Laboratory.

Spanish Dame Bilingual Bicultural Project 1974. *Instructional Guide for the Home Tutor*. Austin, Tex.: Dissemination Center for Bilingual Bicultural Education.

——— 1975. *Planning the Program with the Home Tutor*. Austin, Tex.: Dissemination Center for Bilingual Bicultural Education.

Spolsky, Bernard, Joanna B. Green, and John Read 1974. *A Model for the Description, Analysis and Perhaps Evaluation of Bilingual Education*. Navajo Reading Study Progress Report No. 23. Albuquerque, N.M.: University of New Mexico.

Stern, H.H. (ed.) 1963. *Foreign Languages in Primary Education: The Teaching of Foreign or Second Languages to Younger Children*. (Report on an International Meeting of Experts Apr. 9-14, 1962, International Studies in Education). Hamburg: UNESCO Institute for Education.

Systems and Evaluations in Education 1974. *New Approaches to Bilingual Bicultural Education*. Austin, Tex.: Dissemination Center and Assessment Center for Bilingual Education.

Teachers of English to Speakers of Other Languages (TESOL) 1976. *Position Paper on the Role of English as a Second Language in Bilingual Education*. Washington, D.C.: TESOL.

TESOL Quarterly, published by Teachers of English to Speakers of Other Languages, Georgetown University, Washington, D.C.

Texas Education Agency 1970. *A Design for Implementing in Public School Curriculum the Concept of Confluence of Texan Cultures*. Austin, Tex.

——— 1976. *An Orientation to Bilingual Education in Texas: A Training Manual*. Austin, Tex.

Thorndike, Edward L., and Arthur I. Gates 1966. "The Ultimate Aims of Education," in John M. Rich., ed., *Readings in the Philosophy of Education*. Belmont, Calif.: Wadsworth Publishing Co., Inc., pp. 22-32.

Troike, Rudolph C. 1974a. *Statement on Linguistic Concerns in Bilingual Education*. U.S. Educational Resources Information Center, ERIC Document ED 093 176, January.

——— 1974b. "Research Priorities in Bilingual Education." Arlington, Va.: Center for Applied Linguistics.

Tyler, Ralph W., Robert M. Gagné, and Michael Scriven (eds.) 1968. *Perspectives of Curriculum Evaluation*. Chicago: Rand McNally.

Ulibarrí, Horacio 1970. *Bilingual Education: A Handbook for Education*. U.S. Educational Resources Information Center, ERIC Document ED 038 078.

UNESCO 1955. *The Teaching of Modern Languages*. Problems in Education Series, Vol. X. Paris: UNESCO.

United States Commission for Civil Rights 1975. *A Better Chance to Learn: Bilingual-Bicultural Education,* Clearinghouse Publication No. 51. Washington, D.C.: Government Printing Office.

United States Congress 1964. P.L. 88-352, *Civil Rights Act.*

——— 1965. P.L. 89-10, *Elementary and Secondary Education Act.*

——— 1972. P.L. 92-318, *Ethnic Heritage Studies Act.*

——— 1974. P.S. 93-380, *Elementary and Secondary Education Act,* as amended.

United States Department of Health, Education and Welfare 1977. News release announcing interim findings of the AIR Impact Study. Washington, D.C.: HEW, Apr. 18.

United States General Accounting Office (GAO) 1976. Comptroller General. *Bilingual Education: An Unmet Need.* Report to The Congress. Washington, D.C.

United States Office for Civil Rights 1975. "Task Force Findings Specifying Remedies Available for Eliminating Past Educational Practices Ruled Unlawful under Lau v. Nichols." Washington, D.C.: Department of Health, Education and Welfare.

United States Office of Education 1971. *Programs under Bilingual Education Act: Manual for Project Applicants and Grantees, 1971,* Washington, D.C.: Government Printing Office.

——— 1976. "Bilingual Education Proposed Regulations," *Federal Register, 41,* 69, Thursday, Apr. 8.

Vázquez, José A. 1975. *National Perspective on Bilingual Education.* U.S. Educational Resources Information Center, ERIC Document ED 108 481, May 10, 1975.

Vázquez, José A., and La Mar Miller 1977. Letter of invitation sent to directors of ESEA Title VII Fellowship Programs. Washington, D.C.: National Institute of Education.

von Maltitz, Frances Willard 1975. *Living and Learning in Two Languages: Bilingual-Bicultural Education in the United States.* New York: McGraw-Hill Book Co.

Waggoner, Dorothy 1976. *Results of the Survey of Languages Supplement to the July 1975 Current Population Survey.* Paper presented at the Fifth Annual International Bilingual Bicultural Conference, San Antonio, Tex. Washington, D.C.: National Center for Education Statistics.

The Washington Post, Apr. 19, 1976, pp. A1, A24.

Whitman, Walt 1891-1892. "By Blue Ontario's Shore," *Leaves of Grass.* New York: Aventin Press, Inc., reprinted 1931.

Zangwill, Israel 1909. *The Melting Pot, Drama in Four Acts.* New York: Macmillan.